Preface

The purpose of this *Guide* is to highlight the funds that would be of most interest to investors: widely held funds with historically superior returns in their classes, low expenses, low loads and that are directly available from the fund, no intermediary required. The funds are classified into useful categories of similar funds, the way investors approach fund selection, which makes comparison of fund alternatives more efficient and effective. This will allow you to dedicate more time to evaluating the better fund opportunities.

Inside the *Guide* are the information and performance statistics you will need to make well-informed decisions on your mutual fund investments. Our goal is to provide pertinent information, organized to minimize your time spent collecting and comparing data on the increasingly large universe of mutual funds.

AAII members who would like performance figures for no-load and low-load mutual funds they own that do not appear in this *Guide* can access this information on our Web site at www.aaii.com.

Information for this *Guide* was gathered from direct contact with funds and from Standard & Poor's Micropal. As always, our objective is full, accurate, and timely disclosure of investment information.

John Bajkowski oversaw the development of the fund analysis format and supervised the data collection and verification. Jean Henrich provided copy editing and Marika Magnee designed the cover. Alyna M. Johnson served as project editor for the *Guide*.

Chicago
March 2003

John Markese, Ph.D.
President

Table of Contents

The Individual Investor's Guide to

The Top Mutual *Funds*®

The American Association of Individual Investors

22nd Edition 2003

The American Association of Individual Investors is an independent, not-for-profit corporation formed in 1978 for the purpose of assisting individuals in becoming effective managers of their own assets through programs of education, information, and research.

American Association of Individual Investors
625 North Michigan Avenue
Chicago, Illinois 60611
(312) 280-0170; (800) 428-2244
E-mail: members@aaii.com
Web site: www.aaii.com

ISBN 1-883328-17-9
ISSN: 1538-7070

Data in this guide was provided by Standard & Poor's Micropal and directly from the funds. While the material in this Guide cannot be guaranteed to be error free, it has been obtained from sources believed to be reliable.

1

How to Use This Guide

Selecting a mutual fund, while less time-consuming than investing in individual securities, does require some homework. No one should put money into an investment that is not understood. This does not require a detailed investigation of the fund's investments, but it does require an understanding of the investment objectives and strategies and the possible risks and returns of a fund.

This *Guide* is designed to provide you with that understanding. We have kept the chapters brief and to the point, so that individuals new to mutual fund investing will not be overwhelmed with unnecessary details.

Chapters 2 through 10 deal with the basics of investing in mutual funds—diversification; loads; various categories of mutual funds and what they mean; how to read a mutual fund's prospectus and annual report, as well as any other material they send you; how to evaluate the risk of a mutual fund; how to invest and redeem; common sense rules for mutual fund investors; practical answers to common questions; tie-breakers when choosing a mutual fund; and when to sell.

Chapter 11 describes how the mutual funds were chosen for inclusion in the *Guide*. Chapter 12 is a key to the terms used in the performance tables and the mutual fund data pages, and includes an explanation of how the returns were calculated and what the different risk measures mean.

Chapter 13 presents performance tables, which include the historical performance of funds along with corresponding benchmarks. While past performance is no indication of future performance, it may indicate the quality and consistency of fund management. From this section, you should pick out mutual funds that meet your investment objectives and risk tolerance. These funds can then be examined more closely in the individual mutual fund data pages that follow each performance category listing (Chapter 14).

The funds are grouped by category and listed alphabetically within each category; their ticker symbol and investment category are indicated at the top of the page after the fund's name. These pages provide 10 years of per share data, performance statistics and risk measures, portfolio information, and shareholder services provided by the fund. Use the telephone numbers and Web addresses provided to contact the funds to request a copy of the prospectus and annual report. Make sure you read the prospectus carefully before investing in any mutual fund.

At the back of the *Guide* is a list of a special category of funds, index funds. And finally, there is an index of all funds that appear in the *Guide*.

2

Investing in Mutual Funds

A mutual fund is an investment company that pools investors' money to invest in securities. An open-end mutual fund continuously issues new shares when investors want to invest in the fund, and it redeems shares when investors want to sell. A mutual fund trades directly with its shareholders, and the share price of the fund represents the market value of the securities that the fund holds.

There are several advantages that mutual funds offer individual investors. They provide:

- Professional investment management usually at a low cost, even for small accounts;
- A diversified group of securities that only a large portfolio can provide;
- Information through prospectuses and annual reports that facilitates comparisons among funds;
- Special services such as check writing, dividend reinvestment plans, telephone switching, and periodic withdrawal and investment plans;
- Account statements that make it easy to track the value of your investment and that ease the paperwork at tax time.

Successful investing takes time and effort, and it requires special knowledge and relevant, up-to-date information. Investors must spend a considerable amount of energy searching for opportunities and monitoring each investment. Professional investment management is relatively cheap with mutual funds. The typical adviser charges about 0.5% annually for managing a fund's assets. For an individual making a $10,000 investment, that comes to only $50 a year.

Of course, mutual fund investing does not preclude investing in securities on your own. One useful strategy would be to invest in mutual funds and individual securities. The mutual funds would ensure your participation in overall market moves and lend diversification to your portfolio, while the individual securities would provide you with the opportunity to apply your specific investment analysis skills.

DIVERSIFICATION

If there is one ingredient to successful investing that is universally agreed upon, it is the benefit of diversification. This is a concept that is backed by a great deal of research, market experience, and common sense. Diversification reduces risk. Risk to investors is frequently defined as volatility of return—in other words, how much an investment's return might vary over a year. Investors prefer returns that are relatively predictable, and thus less volatile. On the other hand, they want returns that are high, but higher returns are accompanied by higher risks. Diversification eliminates some of the risk without reducing potential returns.

Mutual funds, because of their size and the laws governing their operation, provide investors with diversification that might be difficult for an individual to duplicate. This is true not only for common stock funds, but also for bond funds, municipal bond funds, international bond and stock funds—in fact, for almost all mutual funds. Even the sector funds that invest only within one industry offer diversification within that industry. The degree of diversification will vary among funds, but most will provide investors with some amount of diversification.

AVOIDING EXCESSIVE CHARGES

This book focuses on no-load and low-load mutual funds. Investors should realize that:

- A load is a sales commission that goes to the seller of the fund shares;
- A load does not go to anyone responsible for managing the fund's assets and does not serve as an incentive for the fund manager to perform better;
- Funds with loads, on average, consistently underperform no-load funds when the load is taken into consideration in performance calculations;
- For every high-performing load fund, there exists a similar no-load or low-load fund that can be purchased more cheaply;
- Loads understate the real commission charged because they reduce the total amount being invested: $10,000 invested in a 6% front-end load fund results in a $600 sales charge and only a $9,400 investment in the fund;
- If the money paid for the load had been working for you, as in

a no-load fund, it would have been compounding over your holding period.

The bottom line in any investment is how it performs for you, the investor, and that performance includes consideration of all loads, fees, and expenses. There may be some load funds that will do better even if you factor in the load, but you have no way of finding that fund in advance. The only guide you have is historical performance, which is not necessarily an indication of future performance. With a heavily loaded fund, you are starting your investment with a significant loss—the load. Avoid unnecessary charges whenever possible.

SORTING OUT CHARGES

It is best to stick with no-load or low-load funds, but they are becoming more difficult to distinguish from heavily loaded funds. The use of high front-end loads has declined, and funds are now turning to other kinds of charges. Some mutual funds sold by brokerage firms, for example, have lowered their front-end loads to 5%, and others have introduced back-end loads (deferred sales charges), which are sales commissions paid when exiting the fund. In both instances, the load is often accompanied by annual charges.

On the other hand, some no-load funds have found that to compete, they must market themselves much more aggressively. To do so, they have introduced charges of their own.

The result has been the introduction of low loads, redemption fees, and annual charges. Low loads—up to 3%—are sometimes added instead of the annual charges. In addition, some funds have instituted a charge for investing or withdrawing money.

Redemption fees work like back-end loads: You pay a percentage of the value of your fund when you get out. Loads are on the amount you have invested, while redemption fees are calculated against the value of your fund assets. Some funds have sliding scale redemption fees, so that the longer you remain invested, the lower the charge when you leave. Some funds use redemption fees to discourage short-term trading, a policy that is designed to protect longer-term investors. These funds usually have redemption fees that disappear after six months.

Some funds, usually index funds, charge a fee, 1% for example, on all new money invested in the fund. This charge defrays the cost of investing the new money. In effect, the new investment pays its way rather than having the transaction costs charged to investments already in the fund.

Probably the most confusing charge is the annual charge, the 12b-1 plan. The adoption of a 12b-1 plan by a fund permits the adviser to use fund assets to pay for distribution costs, including advertising, distribution of fund literature such as prospectuses and annual reports, and sales commissions paid to brokers. Some funds use 12b-1 plans as masked load charges: They levy very high rates on the fund and use the money to pay brokers to sell the fund. Since the charge is annual and based on the value of the investment, this can result in a total cost to a long-term investor that exceeds a high up-front sales load. A fee table (see Chapter 4: Understanding Mutual Fund Statements) is required in all prospectuses to clarify the impact of a 12b-1 plan and other charges.

The fee table makes the comparison of total expenses among funds easier. Selecting a fund based solely on expenses, including loads and charges, will not give you optimal results, but avoiding funds with high expenses and unnecessary charges is important for long-term performance.

3

Mutual Fund Categories

Mutual funds come in all shapes and sizes; there are thousands of mutual funds, each with its own characteristics. Many mutual funds, however, have shared investments that generally lead to other characteristics that are similar.

These shared characteristics allow us to divide mutual funds into categories. This chapter defines the mutual fund categories we used for this book. In this guide, the individual fund data pages appear alphabetically within each category; the fund's category is indicated beneath the fund's name.

The tables on pages 26 and 71 provide average returns and risk (see Chapter 12 for definition of these terms) of funds by category, which illustrate some of the differences between these categories.

STOCK FUNDS

Portfolio managers of mutual funds that invest in common stocks can choose from the stocks of different industries, stocks at different stages of development, and even stocks of different countries and regions. Over the stock market cycles, large stocks behave differently from small stocks, domestic stocks do not move in unison with foreign or emerging market stocks, and stocks in different sectors or industries react differently to the same economic and business conditions.

For investors to make initial investment decisions on stock mutual funds and to compare and evaluate the ongoing performance of investments in stock mutual funds, grouping similar funds together into cohesive categories is a logical first step. The stock fund categories provided in this guide to facilitate your selection and monitoring of fund investments encompass domestic funds, sector funds, and international funds.

DOMESTIC STOCK FUNDS

The "cap" in large cap stands for capitalization (market share price

Fund Categories

Domestic Stock Funds
- Large-Cap Stock
- Mid-Cap Stock
- Small-Cap Stock

Sector Stock Funds
- Energy/Resources Sector Stock
- Financial/Banking Sector Stock
- Gold Sector Stock
- Health Sector Stock
- Real Estate Sector Stock
- Technology Sector Stock
- Telecommunications Sector Stock
- Utilities Sector Stock

International Stock Funds
- Global Stock
- Foreign Stock
- Regional/Country Stock
- Emerging Stock

Balanced Stock/Bond Funds
- Balanced Stock/Bond

Taxable Bond Funds
- Corporate Bond
- Corporate High-Yield Bond
- Mortgage-Backed Bond
- Government: Short-Term Bond
- Government: Intermediate-Term Bond

times number of shares of common stock outstanding).

Large-cap stocks are usually stocks of national or multinational firms with well-known products or services provided to consumers, other businesses, or governments. Most of the stocks in the Dow Jones industrial average, the S&P 500 and the Nasdaq 100 are, for example, large-cap stocks. While some large-cap stocks are more volatile than others, a well-diversified mutual fund portfolio of large-cap stocks

Government: Long-Term Bond
General Bond

Municipal Bond Funds

National Muni: Short-Term Bond
National Muni: Intermediate-Term Bond
National Muni: Long-Term Bond

State-Specific Bond Funds

Muni: Arizona Bond
Muni: California Bond
Muni: Connecticut Bond
Muni: Florida Bond
Muni: Georgia Bond
Muni: Hawaii Bond
Muni: Kentucky Bond
Muni: Massachusetts Bond
Muni: Maryland Bond
Muni: Minnesota Bond
Muni: Michigan Bond
Muni: New Jersey Bond
Muni: New York Bond
Muni: Ohio Bond
Muni: Oregon Bond
Muni: Pennsylvania Bond
Muni: Virginia Bond
Muni: Wisconsin Bond

International Bond Funds

International Bond

would perform similarly to most investors' conception of the stock market. Large-cap stocks, as a category, also tend to pay the highest cash dividends, although many large-cap stocks pay no dividends. Large-cap stock funds in summary tend to have the lowest volatility, highest dividend yield in the domestic common stock group.

Mid-cap stocks are, as their name implies, smaller than the largest domestic stocks. They are usually established firms in established industries with regional, national and sometimes international markets for their products and services. The S&P MidCap 400 index is a common benchmark for mid-cap stocks. These funds would tend to have lower dividend yields than large-cap funds and to have somewhat higher volatility.

Small-cap stocks are often emerging firms in sometimes emerging industries. But also, these small companies are established firms with local, regional and sometimes even national and international markets. The benchmark for this group is the S&P SmallCap 600. These stocks must have liquid enough trading for mutual funds to invest, and although small, are still listed on the New York Stock Exchange, the American Stock Exchange or Nasdaq. These small-cap funds tend to be more volatile than large-cap and mid-cap funds, have very low dividend yields, and often do not move in tandem with large-cap and mid-cap funds.

The large-, mid- and small-cap categories capture a fund's predominant focus and are important because these size categories do not all behave alike in a market sense. The stocks do tend to move in somewhat different cycles and have pronounced differences in risk and return over time.

One other element can be superimposed over these stock size distinctions to better understand performance and risk in different market environments: the growth or value investment management style of the fund portfolio manager.

A small-cap growth fund will act differently than a small-cap value fund and a mid-cap growth fund is more likely to correlate with a small-cap growth fund than a mid-cap value fund. Portfolio managers of growth-managed funds seek out stocks that have either experienced rapid growth in sales or earnings or are expected to have rapid growth. Often these stocks have high price-earnings ratios (price per share divided by earnings per share) and are volatile when expectations for earnings or sales growth change even slightly. Few growth stocks pay any significant dividend, and they are often concentrated in industries such as technology, health, telecommunications and software, for example.

The value style of investment management emphasizes low price to earnings, low price to sales (price per share divided by sales per share), and higher dividend yields. The trade-off relative to growth stocks is that value stocks have a lower expected growth rate in earnings and sales, but also less risk. Value stocks are often concentrated in insurance, banking, and electric and gas utilities, for example.

For purposes of diversification and risk, it pays to keep in mind the growth/value investment style mix of your stock mutual funds.

SECTOR STOCK FUNDS

Sector funds concentrate their stock holdings in just one industry or a few related industries. They are diversified within the sector, but are not broadly diversified. They are still influenced and react to industry/sector factors as well as general stock market factors. Sector funds have greater risk than diversified common stock funds. While there are a substantial number of sectors represented by mutual funds, a handful of sector designations cover most of the sector fund offerings: energy/resources, financial/banking, gold, health, real estate (real estate investment trusts, or REITs), technology, telecommunications, and utilities. As is clear from this sector category list, some sectors are of greater risk than others—technology versus utilities, for example. By definition, sector funds are a concentrated, not diversified, fund holding.

INTERNATIONAL STOCK FUNDS

International stock funds invest in stocks of foreign firms. Some funds specialize in a single country, others in regions, such as the Pacific or Europe, and others invest in multiple foreign regions. In addition, some funds—usually termed "global funds"—invest in both foreign and U.S. securities. We have four classifications by type of investment of international funds—foreign stock funds, global stock funds, regional/country stock funds and emerging markets stock funds.

International funds provide investors with added diversification. The most important factor when diversifying a portfolio is selecting investments whose returns are not highly correlated. Within the U.S., investors can diversify by selecting securities of firms in different industries. In the international realm, investors take the diversification process one step further by holding securities of firms in different countries. The more independently these foreign markets move in relation to the U.S. stock market, the greater the diversification benefit will be, and the lower the risk of the total portfolio.

In addition, international funds overcome some of the difficulties investors face in making foreign investments directly. For instance, individuals have to thoroughly understand the foreign brokerage process, be familiar with the various foreign marketplaces and their economies, be aware of currency fluctuation trends, and have access to reliable financial information in order to invest directly in foreign stocks. This can be a monumental task for the individual investor.

There are some risks unique to investing internationally. In addition to the risk inherent in investing in any security, there is an additional exchange rate risk. The return to a U.S. investor from a foreign security depends on both the security's return in its own currency and the rate at which that currency can be exchanged for U.S. dollars. Another uncertainty is political risk, which includes government restriction, taxation, or even total prohibition of the exchange of one currency into another. Of course, the more the mutual fund is diversified among various countries, the less the risk involved.

BALANCED STOCK/BOND FUNDS

In general, the portfolios of balanced funds consist of investments in common stocks and substantial investments in bonds and convertible securities. The range as a percentage of the total portfolio of stocks and bonds is usually stated in the investment objective, and the portfolio manager has the option of allocating the proportions within the range. Some asset allocation funds—funds that have a wide latitude of portfolio composition change—can also be found in the balanced category. Balanced funds are generally less volatile than all stock funds and balanced funds provide a high dividend yield.

BOND FUNDS

Bond mutual funds are attractive to investors because they provide diversification and liquidity, which is not as readily attainable in direct bond investments.

Bond funds have portfolios with a wide range of average maturities. Many funds use their names to characterize their maturity structure. Generally, short term means that the portfolio has a weighted average maturity of less than three years. Intermediate implies an average maturity of three to 10 years, and long term is over 10 years. The longer the maturity, the greater the change in fund value when interest rates change. Longer-term bond funds are riskier than shorter-term funds, and they usually offer higher yields.

TAXABLE BOND FUNDS

Bond funds are principally categorized by the types of bonds they hold. Corporate bond funds invest primarily in investment-grade corporate bonds of various maturities; however, corporate high-yield bond funds provide high income but invest generally in corporate bonds rated below investment grade, making them riskier.

Government bond funds invest in the bonds of the U.S. government and its agencies, while mortgage funds invest primarily in mortgage-backed bonds. General bond funds invest in a mix of government and agency bonds, corporate bonds, and mortgage-backed bonds.

MUNICIPAL BOND FUNDS

Tax-exempt municipal bond funds invest in bonds whose income is exempt from federal income tax. Some tax-exempt funds may invest in municipal bonds whose income is also exempt from the income tax of a specific state.

INTERNATIONAL BOND FUNDS

International bond funds allow mutual fund investors to hold a diversified portfolio of foreign corporate and government bonds. These foreign bonds often offer higher yields, but carry additional risks beyond those of domestic bonds. As with foreign common stocks, currency risk can be as significant as the potential default of foreign government bonds—a particular risk with the debt of emerging countries.

INDEX FUNDS

One other fund type deserves a special mention—the index fund. An example of an index fund is Vanguard's Index Trust 500, categorized as a large-cap stock fund. This fund is designed to match the Standard & Poor's 500 stock index and does so by investing in all 500 stocks in the S&P 500; the amounts invested in each stock are proportional to the firm's market value representation in the S&P 500. Statistics on index funds are quite useful for comparison with other funds, since indexes represent a widely followed segment of the market. Index funds are available covering most major segments of the bond and stock markets—domestic and international. Because they are unmanaged, they make no research efforts to select particular stocks or bonds, nor do they make timing decisions. They are always 100% invested. This passive management approach makes the cost of managing an index fund extremely low. Lists of index funds appear at the back of this *Guide*.

4 Understanding Mutual Fund Statements

One of the advantages of mutual fund investing is the wealth of information that mutual funds provide to fund investors and prospective investors. Taken together, the various reports provide investors with vital information concerning financial matters and how the fund is managed, both key elements in the selection process. In fact, mutual fund prospectuses, annual reports, and performance statistics are key sources of information most investors will need in the selection and monitoring process.

To new mutual fund investors, the information may seem overwhelming. However, regulations governing the industry have standardized the reports: Once you know where to look for information, the location will hold true for almost all funds.

There are basically five types of statements produced by the mutual fund: the prospectus; the statement of additional information; annual, semiannual, and quarterly reports; marketing brochures; and account statements. Actually, the second report—the statement of additional information—is part of the prospectus. However, mutual funds are allowed to simplify and streamline the prospectus, if they choose, by dividing it into two parts: a prospectus that all prospective investors must receive if requested, and the statement of additional information—which the fund must send investors if they specifically request it. Some fund families also currently offer an abbreviated profile prospectus.

THE PROSPECTUS

The prospectus is the single most important document produced by the mutual fund, and it is must-reading for investors before investing. Current shareholders must be sent new prospectuses when they are updated, at least once every 14 months.

The prospectus is generally organized into sections, and it must cover specific topics. The cover usually gives a quick synopsis of the fund: investment category, sales or redemption charges, minimum investment, retirement plans available, and address and telephone number.

THE PROSPECTUS FEE TABLE: AN EXAMPLE

The following table describes the fees and expenses that are incurred when you buy, hold or sell shares of the fund. The annual fund operating expenses provided below for the fund do not reflect the effect of any reduction of certain expenses during the period.

Shareholder Fees (paid by the investor directly)

Sales charge (load) on purchases and reinvested distributions	None
Deferred sales charge (load) on redemptions	None
Annual Fund Operating Expenses (paid from fund assets)	
Management fee	0.81%
Distribution and/or Service (12b-1) fees	None
Other Expenses	0.26%
Total annual fund operating expenses	**1.07%**

A portion of the brokerage commissions that the fund pays may be reimbursed and used to reduce the fund's expenses. In addition, through arrangements with the fund's transfer agent, credits realized as a result of uninvested cash balances are used to reduce transfer agent expenses. Including these reductions, the total fund operating expenses would have been 1.03%.

This **example** helps you compare the cost of investing in the fund with the cost of investing in other mutual funds.

Let's say, hypothetically, that the fund's annual return is 5% and that your shareholder fees and the fund's annual operating expenses are exactly as described in the fee table. This example illustrates the effect of fees and expenses, but is not meant to suggest actual or expected fees and expenses or returns, all of which may vary. For every $10,000 you invested, here's how much you would pay in total expenses if you sell all of your shares at the end of each time period indicated.

1 year	**$109**
3 years	**$340**
5 years	**$590**
10 years	**$1,306**

Source: Fidelity Capital Appreciation Fund prospectus, December 26, 2002.

SELECTED PER SHARE DATA AND RATIOS: AN EXAMPLE

	Vanguard 500 Index Fund Investor Shares Year Ended December 31,				
	2001	2000	1999	1998	1997
Net Asset Value, Beginning of Year	**$121.86**	**$135.33**	**$113.95**	**$ 90.07**	**$69.17**
Investment Operations					
Net Investment Income	1.260	1.29	1.370	1.33	1.31
Net Realized and Unrealized Gain (Loss) on Investments	(15.955)	(13.46)	22.415	24.30	21.50
Total from Investment Operations	(14.695)	(12.17)	23.785	25.63	22.81
Distributions					
Dividends from Net Investment Income	(1.275)	(1.30)	(1.410)	(1.33)	(1.32)
Distributions from Realized Capital Gains	—	—	(.995)	(.42)	(.59)
Total Distributions	(1.275)	(1.30)	(2.405)	(1.75)	(1.91)
Net Asset Value, End of Year	**$105.89**	**$121.86**	**$135.33**	**$113.95**	**$90.07**
Total Return*	**–12.02%**	**–9.06%**	**21.07%**	**28.62%**	**33.19%**
Ratios/Supplemental Data					
Net Assets, End of Year (Millions)	$73,151	$88,240	$104,652	$74,229	$49,358
Ratio of Total Expenses to Average Net Assets	0.18%	0.18%	0.18%	0.18%	0.19%
Ratio of Net Investment Income to Average Net Assets	1.14%	0.98%	1.13%	1.35%	1.66%
Turnover Rate**	4%	9%	6%	6%	5%

*Total return figures do not reflect the $10 annual account maintenance fee applied on balances under $10,000.

**Turnover rates excluding in-kind redemptions were 3%, 7%, 3%, 3%, and 3%, respectively.

Source: Vanguard U.S. Stock Index Funds prospectus, April 26, 2002.

More detailed descriptions are in the body of the prospectus.

Fee Table

All mutual fund prospectuses must include a table near the front that delineates all fees and charges to the investor (see example at top left). The table contains three sections: The first section lists shareholder fees, including all front-end and back-end loads and redemption fees; the second section lists all annual fund operating expenses, including management fees and any 12b-1 charges, as a percentage of net assets; and the third section is an illustration of the total cost of these fees and charges to an investor over time. The illustration assumes an initial investment of $10,000 and a 5% growth rate for the fund, and states the total dollar cost to an investor if shares were redeemed at the end of one year, three years, five years, and 10 years.

Selected Per Share Data and Ratios

One of the most important sections of the prospectus contains the selected per share data and ratios, which provides statistics on income and capital changes per share of the fund (see example at bottom left). The per share figures are given for the life of the fund or 10 years, whichever is less. Also included are important statistical summaries of investment activities throughout each period. These financial statements are also contained in the annual report.

The per share section summarizes the financial activity over the fund's fiscal year, which may or may not correspond to the calendar year, to arrive at the ending net asset value for the fund. The financial activity summarized includes increases in net asset value due to dividend and interest payments received and capital gains from investment activity. Decreases in net asset value are due to capital losses from investment activity, investment expenses, and payouts to fund shareholders in the form of distributions.

Potential investors may want to note the line items in this section. *Investment income* represents the dividends and interest earned by the fund during its fiscal year. *Expenses* reflect such fund costs as the management fee, legal fees, and transfer agent fees. These expenses are given in detail in the statement of operations section of the annual report.

Net investment income is investment income less expenses. This line is important for investors to note because it reflects the level and stability of net income over the time period. A high net investment income would most likely be found in funds that have income, rather than growth, as their investment category. Since net investment income must be distributed to shareholders to avoid direct taxation of the fund, a high net investment income has the potential of translating into a high tax liability for the investor.

Net realized and unrealized gain (loss) on investments is the change in the value of investments that have been sold (realized) during the year or that continue to be held (unrealized) by the fund.

Distributions to fund shareholders are also detailed. These distributions will include dividends from net investment income for the current fiscal period. Tax law requires that income earned must be distributed in the calendar year earned. Also included in distributions will be any realized net capital gains.

The last line in the per share section will be the *net asset value* at the end of the year, which reflects the value of one share of the fund. It is calculated by determining the total assets of the fund and dividing by the number of mutual fund shares outstanding. The figure will change for a variety of reasons, including changes in investment income, expenses, gains, losses, and distributions. Depending upon the source of change, a decline in net asset value may or may not be due to poor performance. For instance, a decline in net asset value may be due to a distribution of net realized gains on securities.

The financial ratios at the bottom of the per share financial data are important indicators of fund performance and strategy. The *expense ratio* relates expenses incurred by the fund to average net assets. These expenses include the investment advisory fee, legal and accounting fees, and 12b-1 charges to the fund; they do not include fund brokerage costs, loads, or redemption fees. A high expense ratio is difficult for a fund manager to overcome and detracts from your investment return. In general, common stock funds have higher expense ratios than bond funds, and smaller funds have higher expense ratios than larger funds. International funds also tend to have higher expense ratios than domestic funds. Index funds usually have the lowest expense ratios. The average expense ratio for common stock funds is 1.10%, international stock funds 1.30%, index stock funds 0.40%, and bond funds (taxable and non-taxable) about 0.70%.

The *ratio of net investment income to average net assets* is very similar to a dividend yield. This, too, should reflect the investment category of the fund. Common stock funds with income as a significant part of their investment objective, such as growth and income funds, would be expected to have the highest ratios and aggressive growth funds would normally have ratios close to 0%. Bond funds would normally have the highest ratios of all funds.

The portfolio *turnover rate* is the lower of purchases or sales divided by average net assets. It reflects how frequently securities are bought and sold by the fund. For purposes of determining the turnover rate for common stock funds, fixed-income securities with a maturity of less than a year are excluded, as are all government securities, short and long term. For bond funds, however, long-term U.S. government bonds are included.

Investors should take note of the portfolio turnover rate, because the higher the turnover, the greater the brokerage costs incurred by the fund. Brokerage costs are not reflected in the expense ratio but instead are directly reflected as a decrease in net asset value. In addition, mutual funds with high turnover rates generally have higher capital gains distributions—a potential tax liability. Small-cap growth stock funds are most likely to have high turnover rates. Some bond funds, for example, may also have very high portfolio turnover rates. A 100% portfolio turnover rate indicates that the value of the portfolio was completely turned over in a year; a 200% portfolio turnover indicates that the value of the portfolio was completely turned over twice in a year. The portfolio turnover rate for the average mutual fund is around 100% but varies with market conditions and investment category.

Investment Objective/Policy

The investment objective section of the prospectus elaborates on the brief sentence or two from the prospectus cover. In this section, the fund describes the types of investments it will make—whether it is bonds, stocks, convertible securities, options, etc.—along with some general guidelines as to the proportions these securities will represent in the fund's portfolio. The investment objective statement usually indicates whether it will be oriented toward capital gains or income. In this section, the management will also briefly discuss its approach to market timing, risk assumption, and the anticipated level of portfolio turnover. Some prospectuses may indicate any investment restrictions they have placed on the fund, such as purchasing securities on margin, selling short, concentrating in firms or industries, trading foreign securities, and lending securities; this section may also state the allowable proportions in certain investment categories. The restrictions section is usually given in more detail in the statement of additional information.

Fund Management

The fund management section names the investment adviser and gives the advisory fee schedule. Most advisers charge a management fee on a sliding scale that decreases as assets under management increase. Occasionally, some portion of the fund adviser's fees is subject to the fund's performance relative to the market.

Some prospectuses will describe the fund's officers and directors with a short biography of affiliations and relevant experience. For most funds, however, this information is provided in more detail in the statement of additional information. The fund shareholders elect the board of directors; the board of directors selects the fund adviser. The adviser is usually a firm operated by or affiliated with officers of the fund. Information on fund officers and directors is not critical to fund selection. The prospectus also names the portfolio manager of the fund. The portfolio manager is responsible for the day-to-day investment decisions of the fund and is employed by the fund adviser. Who the portfolio manager is and how long the manager has been in the position can be useful in judging historical performance.

Other Important Sections

There are several other sections in a mutual fund prospectus of which investors should be aware. They will appear under various headings, depending upon the prospectus, but they are not difficult to find.

Mutual funds that have 12b-1 plans must describe them in the prospectus. A description of these plans must be prominently and clearly placed in the prospectus, usually in a section titled "Distribution Plan." The distribution plan details the marketing aspects of the fund and how it relates to fund expenses. For instance, advertising, distribution of fund literature, and any arrangements with brokers would be included in the marketing plan; the 12b-1 plan pays for these distribution expenses. The distribution plan section specifies the maximum annual 12b-1 charge that can be made. Funds often charge less than the maximum. The actual charge to the fund of a 12b-1 plan is listed at the front of the prospectus in the fee table.

The *capital stock* section, or *fund share characteristics* section, provides shareholders with a summary of their voting rights, participation in dividends and distributions, and the number of authorized and issued shares of the fund. Often, a separate section will discuss the tax treatment that will apply to fund distributions, which may include dividends, interest, and capital gains.

The *how-to-buy-shares* section gives the minimum initial investment and any subsequent minimums; it will also list load charges or fees. In addition, information on mail, wire, and telephone purchases is provided, along with distribution reinvestment options, automatic exchange, investment and withdrawal plans, and retirement options.

The *how-to-redeem-shares* section discusses telephone, written, and wire redemption options, including automatic withdrawal plans, with a special section on signature guarantees and other documents that may be needed. Also detailed are any fees for reinvestment or redemption. Shareholder services are usually outlined here, with emphasis on exchanges among funds in a family of funds. This will include any fees for exchanging, any limits on the number of exchanges allowed, and any other exchange restrictions.

STATEMENT OF ADDITIONAL INFORMATION

This document elaborates on the prospectus. The investment objectives section is more in-depth, with a list and description of investment restrictions. The management section gives brief biographies of directors and officers, and provides the number of fund shares owned beneficially by the officers and directors named. The investment adviser section, while reiterating the major points made in the prospectus, gives all the expense items and contract provisions of the agreement between the adviser and the fund. If the fund has a 12b-1 plan, further details will likely be in the statement of additional information.

Many times, the statement of additional information will include much more information on the tax consequences of mutual fund distributions and investment. Conditions under which withholding for federal income tax will take place are also provided. The fund's financial statements are incorporated by reference to the annual report to shareholders and generally do not appear in the statement of additional information. Finally, the independent auditors give their opinion on the accuracy of the fund's financial statements.

ANNUAL, SEMIANNUAL, AND QUARTERLY REPORTS

All funds must send their shareholders audited annual and semiannual reports. Mutual funds are allowed to combine their prospectus and annual report; some do this, but many do not.

The annual report describes the fund activities over the past year and provides a listing of all investments of the fund at market value as of the end of the fiscal year. Sometimes the cost basis of each investment is also given. Looking in-depth at the individual securities held by the fund is probably not the best use of time. However, it is helpful to be aware of the overall investment categories. For instance, investors should look at the percentage invested in common stocks, bonds, convertible bonds, and any other holdings. In addition, a look at the types of common stocks held and the percentage of fund assets by industry classification gives the investor some indication of how the portfolio will fare in various market environments.

The annual report will also have a balance sheet, listing all assets and liabilities of the fund by general category. This holds little interest for investors.

The statement of operations, similar to an income statement, is of interest only in that the fund expenses are broken down. For most funds, the management fee is by far the largest expense; the expense ratio in the prospectus conveys much more useful information. The statement of changes in net assets is very close to the financial information provided in the prospectus, but the information is not on a per share basis. Per share information will, however, frequently be detailed in the annual report in a separate section. Footnotes to the financial statements elaborate on the entries, but other than any pending litigation against the fund, they are most often routine.

The quarterly or semiannual reports are current accounts of the investment portfolio and provide more timely views of the fund's investments than does the annual report.

MARKETING BROCHURES AND ADVERTISEMENTS

These will generally provide a brief description of the fund. However, the most important bit of information is the telephone number to call and request the fund prospectus and annual report, if you have not received them already.

The rules regarding mutual fund advertising have been tightened and standardized. All mutual funds that use performance figures in their ads must now include one-, five-, and 10-year total return figures. Bond funds that quote yields must use a standardized method for computing yield, and they must include total return figures as well. Finally, any applicable sales commissions must be mentioned in the advertisement.

ACCOUNT STATEMENTS

Mutual funds send out periodic account statements detailing reinvestment of dividend and capital gains distributions, new purchases or redemptions, and any other account activity such as service fees. This statement provides a running account balance by date with share accumulations, an account value to date, and a total of distributions made to date. *These statements are invaluable for tax purposes and should be saved.* The fund will also send out, in January, a Form 1099-DIV for any distributions made in the previous year and a Form 1099-B if any mutual fund shares were sold.

5

Understanding Risk

Risk tolerance refers to the level of volatility of an investment that an investor finds acceptable. The anticipated holding period of an investment is important because it should affect the investor's risk tolerance. Time is a form of diversification; longer holding periods provide greater diversification across different market environments. Investors who anticipate longer holding periods can take on more risk.

The liquidity needs of an investor similarly help define the types of funds that the investor should consider. Liquidity implies preservation of capital, and if liquidity is important, then mutual funds with smaller variations in value should be considered. A liquid mutual fund is one in which withdrawals from the fund can be made at any time with a reasonable certainty that the per share value will not have dropped sharply. Highly volatile small-cap growth funds are the least liquid, and short-term bond funds are the most liquid. The table on page 26 lists the risk characteristics for different mutual fund categories.

A LOOK AT RISK

Risk is the most difficult concept for many investors to grasp, and yet much of the mutual fund investment decision depends on an understanding of risk. There are many different ways to categorize investment risk and numerous approaches to the measurement of risk. If we can assume that the volatility of the return on your mutual fund investment is the concern you grapple with when you think of risk, the task of making decisions about risk becomes easier.

Questions about how much value a mutual fund is likely to lose in a down market or how certain it is that a fund will be worth a given amount at the end of the year are the same concerns as volatility of return. Changes in the domestic and international economies, interest rates, exchange rates, corporate profits, consumer confidence, and general expectations all combine to move markets up and down, creating volatility, or risk.

Risk Characteristics for Different Mutual Fund Categories

Stock Funds	Total Risk	Standard Deviation (%)	Beta (X)	Average Maturity (yrs)	Bull Market Return (%)	Bear Market Return (%)
Large-Cap	abv av	19.1	0.97	na	74.7	-39.1
Mid-Cap	abv av	20.4	0.84	na	82.7	-24.0
Small-Cap	high	23.8	0.82	na	95.4	-20.6
Growth Style	high	26.7	1.07	na	138.8	-53.1
Value Style	av	17.4	0.73	na	30.6	-4.7
Energy/Resources Sector	abv av	21.9	0.67	na	64.3	-3.1
Financial/Banking Sector	abv av	21.8	0.75	na	23.8	8.1
Gold Sector	high	32.9	0.19	na	16.9	64.9
Health Sector	high	28.0	0.39	na	57.5	-1.1
Real Estate Sector	blw av	12.7	0.17	na	5.8	41.3
Technology Sector	high	50.5	2.09	na	349.6	-78.7
Telecommunications Sector	high	35.0	1.46	na	220.5	-76.6
Utilities Sector	abv av	18.8	0.60	na	63.8	-49.2
Global	av	16.6	0.75	na	70.3	-38.2
Foreign	av	18.3	0.68	na	77.2	-47.2
Regional/Country	high	23.6	0.83	na	128.5	-47.0
Emerging	abv av	23.1	0.92	na	104.5	-41.9
Balanced Stock/Bond	blw av	10.9	0.53	7.8	31.8	-14.2
Bond Funds						
Corporate	low	3.5	0.00	8.5	5.3	18.1
Corporate High-Yield	blw av	9.5	0.22	6.5	6.3	-10.8
Mortgage-Backed	low	2.7	-0.02	6.7	4.3	23.7
Gov't: Short-Term	low	1.7	-0.04	2.2	5.0	21.3
Gov't: Int-Term	low	4.2	-0.09	7.5	2.9	29.2
Gov't: Long-Term	blw av	7.8	-0.17	18.7	-1.1	30.0
General	low	3.3	-0.04	7.6	4.5	21.9
National Muni: Short-Term	low	1.5	-0.01	2.0	4.5	13.0
National Muni: Int-Term	low	3.6	-0.06	7.2	2.4	21.4
National Muni: Long-Term	blw av	4.8	-0.06	16.8	0.0	23.2
International	blw av	7.2	-0.01	8.4	20.4	15.5

Total risk for a mutual fund measures variation in return from all sources. As an example, variation in return for common stocks is caused by factors unique to the firm, industry variables, and conditions affecting all stocks. Market risk refers to the variables such as interest rates, inflation, and the business cycle that affect all stocks to some degree. In well-diversified portfolios of common stock, the firm and industry risk of the various stocks in the portfolio offset each other; thus, these portfolios tend to have lower total risk, and this total risk is usually composed almost entirely of market risk. For less diversified portfolios, funds that hold very few stocks, or sector funds that concentrate investment in one industry, total risk is usually higher and is composed of firm and industry risk in addition to market risk.

Risk levels based upon total risk are given for all funds with 36 months of performance data. The five categories (high, above average, average, below average, and low) serve as a way to compare the risk inherent in common stock funds, international funds, sector funds, bond funds, or any type of mutual fund. Shorter-term bond funds would be expected to have relatively low total risk while some of the concentrated, less-diversified, small-cap stock funds would likely be ranked in the high total risk category.

The total risk measure will enable you to construct a portfolio of funds that reflects your risk tolerance and the holding period you anticipate for your portfolio. Portfolios for individuals with low risk tolerance and short holding periods should be composed predominantly of funds that are less volatile, with lower total risk. Individuals with high risk tolerances and longer holding periods can form appropriate portfolios by combining mutual funds with higher total risk.

STANDARD DEVIATION

Total risk is measured by the standard deviation statistic, a numerical measure of how much the return on a mutual fund has varied, no matter what the cause, from the historical average return of the fund. Higher standard deviations indicate higher total risk. The category risk rank measures the total risk of a fund to the median total risk for all funds in the same investment category. The rankings for category risk are high, above average, average, below average, and low. Funds ranked above average and high for category risk should produce returns above the average for the investment category.

The risk index indicates the magnitude of the standard deviation for a fund relative to the median standard deviation for funds in the category. A risk index of 1.2, for example, means that the standard deviation for a fund is 20% higher than the median standard deviation for the category.

MARKET RISK

Market risk is a part of total risk, but measures only the sensitivity of the fund to movements in the general market. This is valuable information to the individual investor, particularly when combined with use of the total risk and category risk rank measures, to judge how a mutual fund will perform in different market situations. The market risk measure used for common stock funds is beta; for bond funds, average maturity is used.

BETA

Beta is a measure of the relative volatility inherent in a mutual fund investment. This volatility is compared to some measure of the market such as Standard & Poor's index of 500 common stocks. The market's beta is always 1.0 by definition, and a money market fund's beta is always 0. If you hold a mutual fund with a beta of 1.0, it will move, on average, in tandem with the market. If the market is up 10%, the fund will be up, on average, 10%, and if the market drops 10%, the fund will drop, on average, 10%. A mutual fund with a beta of 1.5 is 50% more volatile than the market: If the market is up 10%, the fund will be up, on average, 50% more, or 15%; conversely, if the market is down 10%, the fund, on average, will be down 15%. A negative beta, a rare occurrence, implies that the mutual fund moves in the opposite direction of the market's movement.

The higher the fund's beta, the greater the volatility of the investment in the fund and the less appropriate the fund would be for shorter holding periods or to meet liquidity needs. Remember that beta is a relative measure: A low beta only implies that the fund's movement is not volatile relative to the market. Its return, however, may be quite variable, resulting in high total risk. For instance, industry-specific sector fund moves may not be related to market volatility, but changes in the industry may cause these funds' returns to fluctuate widely. For a well-diversified stock fund, beta is a very useful measure of risk, but for concentrated funds, beta only captures a portion of the variability that the fund may experience. Betas for certain sector funds, for example, can be very misleading. Sector funds often have relatively low betas, but these funds are extremely volatile. In addition, the betas of sector funds sometimes change significantly from year to year.

AVERAGE MATURITY

For all bond funds, the average maturity of the bonds in the portfolio is reported as a market risk measure, rather than beta. The volatility of a bond fund is determined by how the fund reacts primarily to changes in interest rates, although high-yield (junk) bond funds and international bond funds can be affected significantly by factors other than interest rates. When interest rates rise, bond funds fall in value, and conversely, when interest rates fall, bond mutual funds rise in value. The longer the average maturity of the bond fund, the greater will be the variation in the return on the bond fund when interest rates change. Bond mutual fund investors with less risk tolerance and shorter holding periods should seek shorter maturity funds, and longer-term bond fund investors who are more risk tolerant will find funds with longer maturities a better match.

In the case where a bond fund holds mortgage-backed securities, average maturity may not capture the potential for decline in effective maturity when interest rates fall and mortgages are refinanced. Some mortgage funds also use derivatives, highly leveraged financial instruments that derive their value from movements in specific interest rates or indexes, which further complicate an analysis of their risk. Bond funds that hold corporate bonds and municipal bonds also face changing effective maturities when interest rates decline and bond issuers call bonds before maturity.

Investing and Redeeming: A Look at Fund Services

6

Mutual fund investors are usually most concerned with building and monitoring a portfolio that will deliver the best results, given their objectives. While total return and risk are crucial, services play an important role in facilitating the investment process.

A variety of useful shareholder options exist for investing and withdrawing money, both on an individual transaction and a systematic basis. By using services like those examined in this chapter, you may be able to manage your investments in a simpler, more efficient manner. This may even lead to improved results. Since our coverage is quite comprehensive, you may not find all the services discussed offered by the mutual funds you deal with. In addition, individual procedures can vary somewhat among funds.

MAKING INVESTMENTS

The traditional way of investing in a fund is simply to place a check in the mail. But it could take up to a week—or longer—for your money to arrive and be put to work. By letting a few days elapse you risk paying more per share for a volatile fund than you had expected. Of course, if you're lucky you might pay less.

It frequently makes sense to have a better idea about the price you will pay, especially if you're going to invest a fairly large sum in a more volatile fund. By taking action prior to 4 p.m. Eastern time, it's possible to buy at the price prevailing on the day you place your order. Of course, the price you'll pay is not the only consideration—putting the money to work sooner is beneficial to fixed-income investors who are placing a large amount—say $50,000 or more—into an account and don't want to wait to begin accruing dividends.

Buying at Today's Price

There are several ways to accomplish the purchase of shares at that day's net asset value:

- Transfer from a money fund. You can park your investment in the family's money market fund, wait until you're ready to invest, call the company before 4 p.m. Eastern time and request that the funds be transferred to the portfolio of your choice. Of course, you can usually also transfer from other bond and stock funds in the group.

- Wire transfer from your bank. This is the quickest way to move money and is especially recommended for large sums. You will buy in at the day's net asset value if the wire arrives at your account prior to 4 p.m. Eastern time. Your fund company will provide the instructions that you need to convey to your bank. Banks generally charge for this service but mutual funds usually do not. (Incidentally, if you invest by wire you can redeem immediately if you need to—there is no clearing period before your funds will be released.)
- Telephone purchase. Some companies allow you to place a purchase order by phone, locking in that day's price if your order is entered before 4 p.m. Eastern time. You give your instructions to the telephone representative, then send a check or wire for the cost. The payment must reach the account in five to seven business days (depending on the requirements of the company), otherwise the order will be canceled with the investor assuming any resultant losses. Some funds will only accept wires for telephone purchases. There are special conditions that need to be satisfied when you place a telephone purchase order. These requirements, which vary by company, typically include investment minimums and maximums. Minimums may or may not be higher than the fund's usual investment minimum and could be $5,000 or $10,000. The maximum may be based on the total value of your existing accounts with the family. The details should be spelled out in the prospectus. It's best to verify the information with a shareholder representative before entering your order.
- Opening a new account by wire. A number of mutual funds allow you to establish an account by wire, provided you promptly send in a completed application and wire in the cost of your shares. If your wire arrives at your new account before 4 p.m. Eastern time you will buy at the current day's price. Again, there are minimum investment requirements and other details which vary by fund. The first step is to phone for instructions.

Systematic Investments

The best way to build up your mutual fund assets is simply to put money to work on a regular basis. Modest, ongoing investments can be relatively painless and may eventually lead to significant wealth. For example, at 10% compounded annually, $100 invested at the beginning of each month would grow to $76,566 in 20 years; continuing the investments for just five additional years yields $133,780.

Systematic investment plans offer an ideal way to benefit from dollar-cost averaging. With fixed, periodic investments, you buy more shares when prices are low and fewer when they're high. This results in a lower average cost per share than a simple average of prices on your purchase dates. Dollar-cost averaging works especially well with more volatile portfolios.

There are several ways periodic investments can be made automatically, without sending in a check.

- Direct, systematic transfers. The systematic investment program, where money is taken either from your bank account or paycheck, transfers a predetermined, fixed amount at approximately the same date each month. In order for the payments to be routed directly from your bank account, your financial institution must be an Automated Clearing House (ACH) member, which most are. If you want the investment deducted directly from your paycheck, you need your employer's consent. In addition to the ACH periodic purchase you can make individual ACH purchases in varying amounts whenever you like by phoning your fund company. You would be purchasing your shares at the next business day's price if you call prior to the market's 4 p.m. closing. If you call after 4 p.m., you would buy at the price prevailing at the close of the second business day.
- Dividend transfers. By investing periodic distributions received from one mutual fund into shares of another in the same family, you can build a position in the latter. For example, the monthly dividends from a fixed-income fund could be moved into a small-cap portfolio. Although dividends from investment income are not fixed in amount like systematic purchases, they can be sufficiently stable. It wouldn't take an enormous investment in a fixed-income fund to generate $100 monthly in dividends. Another example might be the transfer of quarterly income dividends and annual capital gains distributions from a large-cap fund into shares of a money market or short-term bond fund.

MAKING REDEMPTIONS

A variety of useful approaches are also available when you need to withdraw money from your mutual fund.

Mailing in a redemption letter is the old-fashioned way to withdraw money from a fund account. The letter must contain the necessary information—including name(s) of registered owner(s), fund name, account number and redemption amount—and be properly signed by the account owner(s). You may need a signature guarantee for your request to be processed.

There are several faster, simpler ways to redeem shares. Be sure to sign up for these additional services, if necessary.

- Requesting a check by phone. You may telephone your shareholder representative and request that a check be mailed to you or your bank. Of course, you lose interest during the mail transit time, an important consideration with larger redemptions.
- Drawing a check on a fixed-income fund. You can write a check on a money market or other fixed-income fund, perhaps on money just transferred in from another portfolio in the family. Funds generally place a minimum, commonly $100 or $500, on individual checks. If you draw your check on a fund with a fluctuating share price, it would give rise to a taxable event. Money market funds ordinarily maintain a stable $1 price, so you need not be concerned about taxable events when drawing checks on these funds.
- Wiring money from your fund. You can request your company to wire the proceeds to your bank account. This is the quickest way to make a direct transfer of money, and it is recommended for large sums. Your bank and fund will tell you about their fee policies.
- Making an ACH redemption. If you have established an Automated Clearing House linkage between your fund and bank, you can simply phone your company and request that the balance be transferred to your bank. However, it could take a few days for the money to reach your account.

Systematic Withdrawal Plans

Systematic withdrawal plans are useful for retirees and others who want to receive regular monthly or quarterly checks. The payments could be sent to someone besides the account holder, such as a student in college or another dependent. A certain minimum account balance, such as $10,000, is required to establish the program. You can change your withdrawals or discontinue them at will. Most funds offer systematic withdrawal programs.

Three key variables you need to come to grips with in establishing a withdrawal plan are:

- Your fund's expected total return;
- The expected rate of inflation; and
- Your target withdrawal percentage.

For people who may be withdrawing money over a decade or longer, a conservative stock fund can lead to the best results. Stocks have generated significantly higher long-run total returns than bonds. In fact, it may be unwise to use a withdrawal plan with a fixed-income fund if you plan on making redemptions over an extended period. For longer-term bond fund investors it's better to only take the monthly dividend checks and not disturb the corpus, since doing so can significantly deplete your capital.

For example, an income-oriented stock fund is a good withdrawal plan candidate. Because your investment in an income-oriented stock fund may not yield sufficient dividends to meet your needs, you may need to dip into principal. But your capital can still grow if your withdrawal rate is not excessive.

The best way to plan your future withdrawal stream is to make some projections. You can get a good estimate of how long your capital will last under different assumptions using annual redemptions, even though you may want to redeem more frequently. The percentage of your initial capital withdrawn annually must be realistic; you don't want to deplete your nest egg too soon.

How Long Will Your Money Last?

If the rate at which you withdraw is too close to or exceeds your fund's total return (or growth rate), you will eventually deplete your capital. The table on page 36 shows approximately how long, in years, your principal will last given the return generated by your fund and your withdrawal rate. The numbers in the body of the table are conservative estimates since they assume withdrawals are made at the beginning of the year. Thus, the first annual redemption would occur immediately. When the portfolio's growth exceeds the withdrawal percentage by a sufficient amount, you could continue withdrawing for an indefinite period; asterisks appear in these instances.

Withdrawal Plans: How Long Will Your Capital Last?

Average Annual Growth[2] (%)	If the Annual Withdrawal Rate of Your Initial Capital Is[1]:											
	16%	15%	14%	13%	12%	11%	10%	9%	8%	7%	6%	5%
	The Number of Years Your Capital Will Last Is:											
1	6	6	7	7	8	9	10	11	13	15	18	22
2	6	7	7	8	9	9	11	12	14	16	19	25
3	6	7	7	8	9	10	11	13	15	18	22	29
4	7	7	8	8	9	10	12	14	16	20	26	37
5	7	7	8	9	10	11	13	15	18	23	32	62
6	7	8	8	9	10	12	14	17	21	28	49	*
7	7	8	9	10	11	13	15	19	25	40	*	*
8	8	8	9	10	12	14	17	22	33	*	*	*
9	8	9	10	11	13	16	20	28	*	*	*	*
10	8	9	10	12	14	18	25	*	*	*	*	*
11	9	10	11	13	16	22	45	*	*	*	*	*
12	9	11	12	15	19	32	*	*	*	*	*	*

[1]Assumes withdrawals are made annually at the beginning of the year.

[2]Can be expressed either as a nominal total return or real (inflation-adjusted) rate.

**Capital will last indefinitely.*

The table can help you determine the best redemption rate. For example, if you assume your fund will grow at 9% per year in nominal terms, you could withdraw 10% annually for 20 years. If you trim your withdrawal rate back to 8%, or less, your capital would last indefinitely.

What about inflation? Suppose you expect the price level to increase by 4% per year on average and want to withdraw 10% in constant dollars. This means the amount you withdraw each year would need to increase by 4%. In this more realistic case, your capital would be growing at a real, or inflation-adjusted, rate of 5% (9% – 4%). You've simply reduced your 9% nominal return by the anticipated inflation percentage.

Now look in the 5% "average annual growth" row in the table. Your nest egg would last only 13 years, when inflation is factored in, with a

10% withdrawal rate. If you want the capital to last longer you have to reduce your withdrawals. For instance, at an 8% redemption rate your capital would last 18 years; at 6% it would stretch for 32 years.

Taxes are another consideration. In addition to reducing an expected return for inflation, the careful planner can scale it back further based on an estimate of the impact of taxes on his or her results. Depending on your tax bracket and the fund you're using, your expected return after inflation and taxes could be as low as 2% to 1%, or less.

The table can also help you determine an appropriate withdrawal rate, based on how long your capital must last. Suppose your capital must last at least 20 years, during which you expect 4% inflation yearly. How much can you safely withdraw? If you estimate that your stock fund can return at least 9% annually in nominal terms (5% in real terms) you could withdraw up to 7%, in which case your principal should hold out for 23 years. It would be safer to withdraw a bit less than 7% to provide some margin for error. In fact, in a world with taxes and inflation you risk eventually depleting your capital with a withdrawal rate that exceeds 6% or so, especially if your returns don't live up to your expectations.

In addition to withdrawing a target dollar amount each year, there are other ways to establish a withdrawal plan.

Fixed-Percentage Withdrawals

The most common withdrawal plan involves redeeming a fixed dollar amount over a year, often in monthly increments. The redemptions may be increased periodically for inflation. But if your withdrawal rate is too close to or exceeds the expected annual return after inflation, you would be redeeming an increasing percentage of your remaining balance each year.

Enter the fixed-percent option. You might withdraw, say, 6% of your capital based on its value at the beginning of each year. Your annual dollar withdrawals would differ depending on the changing value of your principal. But if your withdrawal percentage is below the average total returns the mutual fund generates, your dollar redemptions would gradually trend upward as your account grows. Naturally, there would be declines following years in which your fund had negative total returns. The fixed-percentage plan could be useful if you want to preserve your capital and perhaps even see it grow, but your withdrawals may not keep pace with inflation.

Fixed-Share Redemptions

Redeeming a constant number of fund shares can be advantageous for some people. Your dollar withdrawals will fluctuate with changes in the fund's share price, but fewer shares will be sold over the years to generate a given sum of withdrawals. Conversely, with a fixed dollar withdrawal plan you sell more shares when prices are low and fewer when they are high.

The table below illustrates a fixed-share program where 2,000 shares are redeemed annually. The dollar amount withdrawn equals the net asset value multiplied by 2,000. In total, 6,000 shares are withdrawn over three years. Conversely, 6,167 shares would need to be redeemed to accommodate a $20,000 fixed yearly withdrawal. In both cases, $60,000 is redeemed over three years.

The more volatile the fund's price, the fewer shares you would have to redeem to withdraw a given sum of money. But more volatility results in greater variations in monthly withdrawals.

In any case, if you can tolerate the fluctuations you might want to consider the fixed-share withdrawal plan.

Fixed-Share Withdrawal vs. Fixed-Dollar Withdrawal

Fixed-Share Plan

Year	Price ($)	Shares (No.)	Redemption ($)
1	10	2,000	20,000
2	8	2,000	16,000
3	12	2,000	24,000
Total		6,000	60,000

Fixed-Dollar Plan

Year	Price ($)	Shares (No.)	Redemption ($)
1	10	2,000	20,000
2	8	2,500	20,000
3	12	1,667	20,000
Total		6,167	60,000

Since a number of mutual funds do not formally offer a fixed-share withdrawal option, you could simply phone in periodically and request that the shares be sold and the money transferred to your money fund or sent to you by check.

Liquidation Over a Fixed Period

You could withdraw an increasing percentage of your account balance each year in order to liquidate it within a fixed period. For example, if you want the principal paid out over a four-year period to a child attending college, you could withdraw one-fourth of the account in the first year, one-third in the second, half in the third and the remainder in the fourth.

You may be required to use this approach when making withdrawals from an IRA or other tax-qualified retirement plan. Specifically, after age 70½ you must make your withdrawals over a maximum number of years based on an IRS life expectancy table or face a penalty tax for withdrawing less than your minimum required distribution.

Important Considerations

While withdrawal plans are a useful service, they can lead to certain problems. Here are some to ponder.

- Recordkeeping for tax purposes can be a headache, especially with more frequent redemptions. Each time you make a withdrawal you're selling shares, which results in a taxable event. You need to adopt a systematic procedure for calculating gains and losses on each withdrawal.
- Volatile stock and sector stock funds are generally poor candidates for withdrawal plans. These funds can plunge as fast as they can surge. Withdrawing money when the value of your account has taken a steep decline can lead to problems if it doesn't rebound quickly.
- It's best to be conservative. Too high a withdrawal rate can deplete your capital too soon. Be sure to compare your withdrawal rate with the rate at which you expect your fund to compound, after inflation. If the former exceeds the latter by too many per centage points, your capital might not last as long as you'd like. The numbers in the table on page 36 are useful in this regard.
- Make sure you consider the impact of taxes on your investment earnings and withdrawals. Of course, the effect of taxes varies

depending upon your circumstances, and tax rates are subject to change, but the tax factor is too important to overlook.

- It's a good idea to reevaluate your situation every year or so. Do some revised numbers crunching to see if you need to make any adjustments in your withdrawals.

What Every Investor Should Know About Mutual Funds

7

In mutual fund investing there are no immutable laws to guide us, as we have in physics. But the collective experience of fund investors can be distilled into a few general rules. Some of it has empirical evidence pointing its way. Most is simply common sense that investors often set aside or forget in the heat of making an investment decision.

TOP PERFORMANCE LISTS ARE DANGEROUS

Probably the single most potentially dangerous action a mutual fund investor can take is to glance at these ubiquitous lists. Funds make the top of the lists not because they are like all the rest of the funds, but because they are decidedly different in some important way. Risk is usually the first important difference. For stock funds, holding stocks that are more volatile than the average stock, holding fewer stocks, or concentrating on only a few industries, raises risk and puts a fund in position to have a greater chance at making the top of the list.

As an example, take sector funds. You can't beat the market by holding it, which is why you can always find a sector fund of one kind or another at the top of most performance lists. Call it stock picking, or industry weighting, or both, but the net effect is increased risk, and less diversification than the overall stock market.

Picking the funds at the top of the performance lists assumes that either these same stocks or sectors will continue to do well, or that the managers can continue to deftly take high risk and move money around better than all the rest.

For domestic bond funds, making the top of the list is a result of the maturity structure of the fund's portfolio. The longest maturity bond funds will be at the top of the performance lists when interest rates are falling, and at the bottom of the lists when interest rates rise. So, investing in bond funds that are at the top of the list is a forecast of interest rates—that they will stay constant or continue in the same direction, a prediction that even professional interest rate prognosticators have been woefully unsuccessful in getting right.

However, these top/bottom lists may hold a small glimmer of value. There is some empirical evidence that stock funds at the top of the heap one period have a greater likelihood to have this superior performance in the next period, on average—"hot hands" may stay hot. Why might a fund's superior performance persist? Probably because the stocks/sectors emphasized in the portfolio continue to have positive momentum into the next period. The shorter the time periods observed, the more likely this is to be true: quarter-to-quarter performance persistance is more likely than year-to-year. But be careful, this is based on performances of top funds on average, and investors don't invest in fund averages, but instead invest in individual funds.

What is more telling, however, is that bad funds tend to continue to be bad. But again, be careful. If an entire category of funds—small stock value funds or emerging market funds, for example—do poorly, then making the bottom list is probably meaningless if your fund has a lot of peer companions. But if large stock growth funds populate the top list or simply are not to be found in numbers on the bottom list, and your large stock growth fund makes an appearance at the bottom of the pile, it isn't a good sign.

And, of course, being a knee-jerk contrarian and buying funds that make the bottom list on the theory that what falls must rise, is probably a seriously flawed approach to fund selection.

SIZE MATTERS

The amount of money invested in a fund does matter, but whether larger is better than smaller depends on the investment objective of the fund. With a large stock index fund, a U.S. government bond fund or a money market fund, the more dollars under management the better. This is because they all operate in very liquid segments of the market where large block transactions are less likely to impact prices—pushing prices up when purchasing and down when selling—and large-scale transactions might prove to be cheaper to accomplish. In addition, large amounts to manage in these funds will not interfere with their investment objective. And, since some fund expenses are fixed, spreading these expenses over more investment dollars should reduce expenses as a percentage of fund assets.

On the other hand, funds with investment objectives that cover less liquid market segments—small stocks or emerging markets—can be too large. That means that individual trades will tend to be larger, which may in turn lead to higher transaction costs tied to security pricing, a wide bid-asked spread on the stocks, and make portfolio changes harder to accomplish. The classic response of funds that focus on small stocks is to migrate investments to mid-cap and large stocks when they start to achieve a large asset base.

Actively managed stock funds, when managers are picking stocks and industries and moving money around, can be flooded with new money and find themselves unable to deploy new money expeditiously or effectively. And a flood of new money usually comes after a performance that garners widespread attention and is often difficult to replicate, particularly with the surge of new investment in the fund. An index fund, passively managed and operating in a liquid segment of the market, would not be stumped by a large, sudden inflow of cash.

How large is large? When it comes to net assets, $100 billion may be just fine for an S&P 500 index fund, but $1 billion may choke an actively managed small stock fund. And beware of funds that had extraordinary performance when they had $100 million or less, a relatively small amount in net assets. In order to invest larger amounts they may have to invest money in more stocks and industries, increasing diversification and decreasing risk, dulling performance.

FUND EXPENSES CAN BE COSTLY

Fund expenses count. And they count more for some investment categories than others. The general rule is that if you invest in a fund that has a significantly higher expense ratio than the average for its category, the long-term performance drag will be costly. Few active fund managers cover the cost of the increased expenses of active management compared to the rock-bottom cost of passively managing an index fund. And if a fund manager is saddled with a relatively high expense ratio due to a small net asset base or high management/research costs, or both, the task of providing above-average category performance is all the more difficult. Some managers, when faced with this dilemma, may boost the risk level of the fund to remain competitive.

Stock funds are more expensive to manage than bond funds, international funds are more expensive than domestic funds, and funds with large asset bases are cheaper than small funds. But if the expense ratio of a bond fund is approaching 1.00%, or a stock fund 1.50%, think twice before investing. And don't forget stock index funds often charge 0.25% or less.

LOADS ARE LOADS

Whether the sales charge, or load, is up front when you buy into the fund, at the end when you sell the fund, or is an as-you-go 12b-1 charge included in the expense ratio, it will cost you. As explained in Chapter 2, loads go to sales organizations and sales personnel; they are not used to secure better portfolio managers, better research or better anything. A load reduces your return dollar for dollar. So if you are not getting financial advice worth the load, buying a loaded fund will cost you, perhaps dearly. Load funds do not outperform on average similar objective funds with no loads, and in fact, they tend to underperform by the amount of the load. How could they, given what loads are used for? Want to invest with a hot manager in a fund that is loaded? Given the iffiness of historical performance as a predictor of future performance, find a no-load fund with a similar style, performance and risk, and save the load charge.

Don't forget that almost all fund performance data is reported without adjusting for front-end or back-end loads. However, performance data does adjust for the 12b-1 charge because it is included in the expense ratio, and fund performance net of the expense ratio is accounted for in performance statistics.

MARKET TIMING DOESN'T WORK

Wouldn't it be wonderful if either you or your fund manager could time the market? You'd make a mint, but it's only a dream. Nobody, but nobody, has consistently guessed the direction of the bond or stock market over any meaningful length of time, although many will make the claim. And remember that to be successful, timing requires two calls: When to get out, and when to get back in.

One reason beyond low expense ratios that index funds are tough to beat is that they are always 100% invested in the market—they have no cash holdings—when the market takes off. Index funds always call bull markets correctly and they never miss a rally. Yet, they always fail to call a bear market or correction. However, being right on every bull market, as well as avoiding transaction costs and minimizing taxable distributions, is tough to beat.

Since returns on stock and bond funds have been distinctly positive on average annually since we have started keeping records, being ready for bull markets is more important than avoiding bear markets.

When investing in actively managed stock funds, you should hope for superior stock and industry selection, not market timing. If your actively managed portfolio is building up a large cash balance, in excess of 10% of the portfolio, your manager is either engaging in some subtle market timing or there has been a recent rush of cash into the fund. Either case may ultimately lead to poorer performance. For bond funds, when maturities are significantly shortened or lengthened, the impetus is usually market timing driven by an interest rate forecast.

GIVE NEW MANAGERS AND FUNDS TIME TO PROVE THEMSELVES BEFORE INVESTING WITH THEM

With the thousands of funds and fund managers in the investing universe that have track records of at least three years, why invest in an untried fund or manager? While finding funds that will be top performers in their category before the fact is daunting, avoiding disastrous fund investments is within reach. But it requires something upon which to base a judgment. At least a three-year performance history that can be compared to the performance of funds with similar investment objectives and assumed risk is indispensable to evaluate a fund manager or a fund. Consistently favorable performance relative to a peer group of funds over different market environments provides no guarantees of future performance, but it is infinitely better than nothing. You would be surprised how many new funds are quietly buried and new fund managers transferred after the first few disappointing years.

8 Practical Answers to Some Common Mutual Fund Questions

While you can easily call a mutual fund company with specific questions concerning the mechanics of your account and receive a prompt direct answer, the telephone representatives are unlikely to offer an answer to a general investment question, such as: "How many different funds should I own?"

This chapter provides practical answers to commonly asked mutual fund questions. While a series of often-asked questions and answers cannot substitute for a careful and thorough study of mutual funds, the more you know about how mutual funds operate and what contributes to performance, the better prepared you will be to make decisions when investing.

PORTFOLIO MANAGEMENT

How many different mutual funds should I own?

The number of funds suitable for an individual investor will vary depending on individual circumstances—there is no universal number that applies for everyone.

However, as a useful yardstick, consider the range of funds derived from the rationale that diversification should be one of every investor's goals. Simple but broad diversification would imply these funds: a domestic stock fund, a domestic bond fund, and an international stock fund. Dividing the domestic stock portion into these funds—one specializing in small stocks, one in mid-cap stocks, and the other in large-cap stocks, brings the count up to five. Splitting the international stock portion into funds specializing in developed economies and funds specializing in developing and emerging economies makes six. If you prefer a separate European fund and Far East fund, the total is up to seven. Building diversity in your domestic bonds by adding a junk bond fund stretches the number of funds to eight. For tax purposes, the addition of a tax-exempt bond fund would make nine funds. And if we include a money market fund, the number is 10.

The benefits of diversification are difficult to achieve with commitments of less than 10% of your portfolio to any one area, which sets the upper range at not much more than 10 funds. Thus, diversification implies a range of around four to nine funds—all unique in investment objective and security coverage.

Overdiversification results in fund investments that essentially duplicate each other; this adds nothing to performance, but it will add frustration as well as cost in keeping track of and monitoring so many funds.

Should I make sure to invest in more than one fund family, for diversification?

No—it is possible to stay within a fund family and be adequately diversified. However, there is a danger in remaining doggedly within one fund family solely for convenience, and that is that you could overlook a better-managed fund elsewhere. For instance, rather than seek out the best international fund, you may choose the one offered by the fund family you are in currently because it is most convenient.

What should I do when my fund closes?

Nothing. Many funds that close their doors to new investors will allow existing shareholders to continue to invest new money, although sometimes with limits, and all closed funds allow continuation of investments for existing IRA-type accounts.

In the long run, you may be better off if your fund closes and maintains its investment style and flexibility rather than outgrowing its past success.

Should I switch out of a fund if the portfolio manager changes?

No. The change of a portfolio manager is not reason, in and of itself, to leave a fund. Instead, monitor the fund closely to make sure the new manager is continuing the old manager's style, and that any changes won't significantly affect your investment. New portfolio managers have been known to take command of a fund and sell off securities, reflecting a change in style. A significant portfolio realignment might mean greater capital gains distributions, and therefore taxes, unless you hold the fund in a tax-sheltered account. On the other hand, if the fund is an index fund or less actively managed, the portfolio manager may not be all that important. Or the new portfolio manager may continue with the old style and perform just fine.

Switch to a fund with a similar investment objective only when the performance of your fund falls off against other funds with the same investment objective, or if your existing fund changes objectives so that it no longer reflects the objective you are seeking.

If a fund closes before I have a chance to invest and a clone is available, should I invest in the clone fund?

Most funds close because the portfolio manager feels a larger fund size will hamper his investment flexibility and style. Therefore, it is unlikely that any "clone" fund will in fact be a perfect clone of the original—what would be the point of closing the first one?

Clone funds—the Roman numeral II funds—often do not have the same portfolio manager or precisely the same investment strategy as the original. Any fund should be judged independently on its own financial merits.

PORTFOLIO EXPENSES AND CHARGES

If a fund offers class A, B, C, etc., shares, which one should I buy?

Many funds that have sales charges are offering investors a choice as to how the load will be paid. The different share classes reflect these various options, and generally the choices run somewhat like this: Class A shares have a front-end load, a sales commission on the money invested that is charged when the money is invested; Class B shares have a back-end load, a sales charge levied on the value of the fund shares when they are sold, which sometimes decreases and eventually disappears; Class C shares might have no front-end or back-end load, but instead contain an annual charge against your fund's value, a 12b-1 load. Other combinations of varying levels of these three loads may also be offered as an investment option.

If you intend to be invested in the fund for a long time, opt for the front-end or back-end load option, and avoid a high (greater than 0.25%) 12b-1 charge. If you intend to be in the fund only for a few years, select the fund class that does not charge a front-end or back-end load.

Of course, the best course of action is to avoid all loads, or at least high loads.

My fund just imposed a load. Should I bail out?

If your fund imposed a load, you may be grandfathered in and allowed to invest new funds without a load. But if they do charge a load on additional money you want to invest, you are faced with a dilemma. Don't sell on the news that the fund is going to impose a load, but certainly don't commit new money if you will be charged an unreasonable load.

Should I be concerned with fund expenses? After all, it's already reflected in the fund's performance numbers.

Fund expenses, including the management fee, reduce fund performance and all quoted return numbers reflect these costs. But the reason to examine past performance is to get an indication of the portfolio manager's skill. And while the performance numbers may provide some indication of the manager's past skill, the future performance of that manager remains uncertain. The only certainty about the fund's future are the expenses, which are assessed regardless of whether a fund's performance has been relatively good or bad.

Exceptionally high expenses are nearly impossible for portfolio managers to overcome relative to similar funds with average or low expenses. The lower the expenses, the better. Funds with low total assets under management, particularly if they are not part of a large family of funds, will have high expenses relative to assets under management. In addition, newly established funds have a high expense hurdle to overcome.

Should I pay any attention to mutual fund portfolio turnover rates?

The portfolio turnover rate (given in the prospectus) is the lower of purchases or sales of assets in the fund relative to the average assets in the fund for the year. A turnover ratio of 100% indicates that the dollar value of fund purchases or sales equaled the dollar value of total fund assets during the year. This doesn't mean that every single share was changed once during the year; perhaps only a small portion of the assets was transacted intensely. A portfolio turnover ratio of 200% indicates the portfolio by value was turned over twice during the year, and so on.

Is this important? Yes. The higher the portfolio turnover, the greater the transaction costs, which can hurt the performance of the fund; while these costs are reflected in the fund's net asset value and its performance figures, they are a concern for the future performance as noted in the question above.

Equally important for taxable investors, the higher the turnover, the more likely the fund is to make capital gains distributions; and taxes must be paid on these distributions.

What is high turnover and what is low? Stock funds average around 80% portfolio turnover, and bond funds are close to 100%.

Use portfolio turnover as a tie-breaker. If you find two funds in the same category that are equally appealing, lean toward the fund with a lower portfolio turnover.

Should I deal only with the fund family or go through some of the discount brokers that offer mutual funds?

Discount brokers such as Charles Schwab and Fidelity Brokerage offer the convenience of buying different funds without going directly to each fund family and opening separate accounts. Only one brokerage account is necessary, and all mutual fund positions are consolidated in one report. Some of these transactions incur brokerage costs; others are essentially costless.

Not all funds or fund families participate, but if convenience is important and your mutual fund transaction sizes are reasonably large, these fund services offered by discount brokers may deserve a look.

9

Tie-Breakers: Key Points to Consider When It's a Close Call Between Funds

Even when you've done your research and narrowed down your choices for a particular type of fund, sometimes it's not a clear choice between the final two funds.

Flipping a coin is one approach. But a better strategy would be to zero in on a few key points that serve as tie-breakers. While no two funds are precisely alike, top-performing funds can share almost identical investment style and return profiles. This chapter reveals fund tie-breakers to consider and when they might be most important.

AFTERTAX RETURNS

Making tax avoidance your investment focus is a formula for investment disaster. But keeping your eye on aftertax returns is simply wise investing. For example, two funds have similar compound average annual five-year before-tax returns. A five-year period is probably long enough to get a picture of how the funds have performed in different market environments, but still recent enough to be relevant.

However, one fund wins on a tax-adjusted return basis for the period, producing a higher aftertax return. Why? The fund might have a lower dividend yield, defined as income divided by net asset value, or simply made less or no distributions of capital gains. With capital gains rates significantly lower than income tax rates, the tax penalty on dividend income is serious. And no capital gains distributions means no taxes, even at the lower capital gains rate. The tax-adjusted return assumes maximum tax rates, where the disparities between capital gains tax rates and income tax rates are the greatest. For investors in lower tax brackets, the tax-adjusted rate difference might not be great.

RISK

Risk is easy to ignore when funds are on the way up, but when markets fall, risk is suddenly right in your face. There are two useful quantitative measures of risk, both calculated based upon monthly fund returns for the last three years. Beta is a measure of a fund's return sensitivity to the returns of the overall stock market, and works well as a risk measure for diversified funds. The higher the beta, the higher the volatility, and therefore risk. Beta can range from very large negative numbers to very large positive numbers, theoretically, but most stock mutual fund betas cluster in the range of 0.5 to 1.5. A zero beta would imply no sensitivity to the stock market, and would more likely belong to a money market fund than a stock fund. A negative beta indicates that, on average, the fund and the market move in opposite directions—also an unlikely figure for any stock fund. The stock market's beta is by definition always 1.0; a fund with a beta of 1.5 is expected to be 50% more volatile than the market, and a fund with a beta of 0.5 would be only half as volatile. For instance, if the market rose 20%, a fund with a beta of 1.5 would be expected to be up 30% [20% + 0.50 (20%)] and if the market fell by 20%, the fund might drop 30%. When two stock funds with similar returns are considered give a nod to the one with the lower beta.

A second measure of risk is standard deviation, a barometer of volatility from any source, rather than just the stock market. Numerically, standard deviation is less intuitive than beta, but the higher the standard deviation, the greater the risk. Beta assumes a diversified portfolio so that other factors such as the risk unique to individual stocks and industries is virtually eliminated, leaving only the risk of market moves. Standard deviation works for all portfolios, diversified or not, and captures the risk from all elements.

If the two funds have similar returns, but are not well diversified, you cannot count on beta. Pick the fund with the lower standard deviation. [For more on fund risk, see Chapter 5: Understanding Risk.]

FUND SIZE

What about total assets under management by the fund? Is bigger better or is smaller better? The answer, of course, is: It depends. A U.S. government bond fund or an index fund probably can't be 'too big,' since, in general, average costs decline and size doesn't get in the way of managing the assets. On the other hand, an aggressively managed fund, particularly one concentrating in mid-cap and small-cap stocks, can lose flexibility and be less nimble when assets grow too large. A fund that is growing too fast can also pose difficulties for the manager, who may have trouble simply getting the new money invested effectively and in a timely manner. Size and rapid growth often force funds to change their investment strategies. For actively managed mid- and small-cap stock funds, give the nod to the smaller asset size fund.

EXPENSE RATIOS

Expense ratios (fund expenses per share divided by net asset value per share) are often overlooked because expenses are netted out against income, and reported returns already include the impact of expenses. So, if the return is competitive, who cares about expenses? Well, two points are important. First, expense ratios are relatively unchangeable—they are easy to forecast, whereas returns are not. Second, the higher the expense of a fund, the greater the drag that a portfolio manager must overcome in the long run in order to be consistently better than other funds in the category. Also, high expense ratios are relatively easier to overcome in fund categories that produce higher returns on average, such as stock funds, than in fixed-income fund categories where expenses have a greater effect on returns. Two municipal bond funds share the same investment objectives and almost identical performance figures, but one is hard to beat on expenses. No contest. [For more on expense ratios, see Chapter 4: Understanding Mutual Fund Statements.]

PORTFOLIO MANAGER TENURE

What better way to judge a fund manager than by the performance of the fund? But the current fund portfolio manager may not have been running the fund when the performance numbers were inked. In an uncertain world, a manager's tenure and performance record provide useful information, at least valuable enough to break a tie.

LOADS

Sales commissions, also known as loads, are probably the clearest tie-breakers. Take the case of two international European stock funds. Both have comparable performance records and even similar risk, expense ratios, size, and manager profiles. They have identical investment objectives, focusing on European stocks, and they are offered by large fund families with a long menu of services. One charges a 3.0% front-end load and a 1.0% redemption fee for all money removed in less than 90 days. Neither front- and back-end loads nor redemption fees are reflected in performance figures. And while returns going forward are always uncertain, the load is charged with perfect certainty and reduces your performance dollar-for-dollar without any beneficial effect on fund performance. Choose the no-load fund. [For more on loads, see Chapter 2: Investing in Mutual Funds.]

10

The Sell Decision: Knowing When to Walk Away

Many people hop in and out of investments all too frequently. That's due in part to the fact that mutual fund advice and information are so freely available that individuals often are persuaded to switch from their more prosaic funds to those that have been delivering more exciting short-term returns. At the opposite extreme, others take the attitude that, once bought, mutual funds can practically be held for a lifetime. That can be true in some instances, but it's often not—you really must rethink your portfolio periodically.

This chapter analyzes legitimate reasons for selling funds, as well as several reasons for staying put.

LOUSY PERFORMANCE

Continuing poor performance of a fund relative to a relevant benchmark and its peers is the number one fund-related reason for selling a mutual fund. You should focus on a fund's returns over the past one, three, and five years. Longer periods can be misleading if there have been major changes in the fund or its management.

While quarterly returns can be monitored to alert you to signs of deteriorating performance, one-year returns are the shortest relevant performance span for long-term investors to examine. However, that doesn't mean you should automatically sell if one-year returns turn up poor. Deciding how much time to give a poor performer to rebound is not easy, but you should seriously start to think about selling a fund that has lagged its benchmark and peers for the past 18 months to two years.

How do you decide on a relevant benchmark? Different benchmarks are available for different market segments and investment styles. In this *Guide*, peer and index benchmarks are provided for each investment category and investment style.

A simple way to determine which benchmark to use is to check your fund's prospectus or annual report to find out what the fund compares its performance against. Another possibility is to compare your fund's performance with an index fund that has roughly the same portfolio composition. However, you're never going to find a perfect benchmark because each fund has its own unique portfolio.

Keep the following points in mind when comparing a fund's performance with its benchmark:

- Mutual funds hold some cash, which will affect their returns relative to a fully invested index.
- Mutual funds incur expenses and trading costs, which will result in some underperformance relative to an index.
- Each fund holds its own blend of stocks and sectors, which will cause its returns to deviate from an index or benchmark.
- A mutual fund may be more or less risky than its benchmark.

A fund that trails its benchmark may be considerably less risky than another in its category that beats the yardstick. For that reason, it's often more revealing to see how a fund performed relative to its peers. You can compare a fund with several of its most similar competitors or against an average for the category.

It's always important to prune out any genuine duds. Some people tenaciously hang onto unproductive investments because they hate to admit that they made a mistake, or they may hate to deal with the tax consequences, or they are loath to expend the effort to fill out the paperwork and move to a new fund or fund family. The problem is that these individuals face a high opportunity cost by clinging to losing or mediocre funds.

OTHER REASONS TO SELL

Don't sell solely because your fund's performance has been disappointing during the past year. Rather, view a single year of underperformance as a signal to take a closer look at the fund and how it fits with your objectives. You should examine the following factors that may impact a fund's performance or its suitability for your portfolio.

- ***A management change:*** Management's ability is crucial for stock funds. But a management change by itself is not always a reason to sell. Perhaps the manager who left was not exceptional. A good replacement for a skilled manager may be waiting in the wings at a large fund company. Conversely, if a star manager leaves a fund, an equal replacement may be hard to find. So take the exit of a star manager as a warning flag, but not an automatic sell. Finally, think seriously about selling if a fund has had more than its share of management turnover, because frequent changes are not healthy and constant shifting of a portfolio creates negative tax and transaction cost consequences.

- ***Rising expenses:*** Significantly higher expenses can hurt performance. Perhaps a 12b-1 fee has been added or management fees have increased. A money market fund may have lifted a fee waiver, causing its yield to drop significantly relative to other similar money market funds. An increase in costs is particularly hard on bond and money market funds because they earn lower gross returns than stock funds.

- ***A surge in assets:*** Performance could falter if a small-stock or micro-cap fund is flooded with investor money. And the fund could experience style drift if it is forced to start investing in bigger companies. Conversely, a surge in assets may be no problem for many other types of funds, particularly for high-grade bond and money market funds or index funds that could benefit from economies of scale.

- ***Shrinking assets:*** Watch out if a fund is rapidly losing assets because investors are jumping ship for some reason. Sizable redemptions can force management to dump good stocks to raise cash. If gains are realized, the fund could make an unusually high capital gains distribution, saddling those who hold shares in taxable accounts with a potentially large tax bill.

- ***A strategy change:*** Funds change strategies in various ways. A new portfolio manager might decide to fully hedge currency risk for a foreign stock fund that previously did not hedge. An active trader might take the helm of a fund that was noted for low turnover. Or a small-cap value fund might become a mid-cap growth fund. A strategy change will not necessarily hurt a fund's performance, but it might not help a laggard either. If the new strategy does not mesh with your objectives, it may be time to move on.

Even if your funds have compared favorably to their benchmarks and peers, there can be other, compelling reasons to sell. Conversely, you may not want to walk away from a laggard just yet. That's because personal factors often dominate in the decision-making process.

TAX CONSIDERATIONS

If selling seems warranted by the performance numbers and other factors, you also need to weigh any potential tax liability you would incur by taking a large gain. On the plus side, the tax consequences may be less painful with long-term capital gains taxed at lower rates. In addition, the long-term capital gains holding period is 12 months. Nevertheless, if you would be in for a hefty tax bill it may make sense to give a lazy performer more time. This obviously is not a concern if your fund is held in an individual retirement account or other tax-advantaged plan.

On the other hand, tax considerations may argue for a sale. Do you have a paper loss in a taxable account? Perhaps you hold a fund that has done poorly because it invests in a stock-market sector, country, or region that has experienced major problems. You might expect an eventual rebound, but in the meantime you could lock in your loss to offset other gains, thereby reducing your tax bill, and then reinvest in a peer fund that has better performance.

DUMPING EXCESS BAGGAGE

Individuals who own too many funds might consider paring their holdings down to a manageable number, perhaps to as few as five or six. Money-losing investments should be pruned along with unsuitable ones. Check for redundancy in your fund portfolio: Funds with different names may in fact share the same objectives and investing style. Your performance likely will improve, and your financial life will be a lot simpler. Plus, it will be much easier to track your asset allocation.

People often make purchases that they regret later. These could include a narrowly focused fund that makes you uncomfortable due to its risk, or any gimmicky fund that really doesn't add to your portfolio. A broad-based asset allocation fund is unnecessary if you've allocated your assets properly in the first place.

Suppose you hold a fund invested in an asset class that has done poorly even though the manager has fared better than the benchmark. In this case, you need to decide whether you still want that asset class. This is often a difficult call. It depends on factors such as your age, time horizon, and investment outlook.

Generally, mutual funds are viewed as safe because you won't lose as much as you could with an individual stock. But narrowly focused funds such as sector funds can be dicey. If you have allocated too much to a focused fund that's on the skids, think about reducing or eliminating that position before the loss becomes unmanageable. If a volatile fund plunges 50%, it must rebound 100% just to recoup its loss. Consider selling when a speculative fund has fallen 15% to 20% below your cost. Even if you have a relatively minor position, you still may want to walk away.

ALLOCATION CHANGES

Other reasons to sell may arise in your periodic asset allocation review, which should be done at least annually. This entails checking your allocations to large-cap stocks, small-cap stocks, foreign equities, bonds, money market funds, and any subcategories. Recognize that your stock funds could plunge anywhere from 20% to more than 40% within a few months during a bear market. You might want to check and see how your funds and similar ones did during down periods to get a feel for what could happen during a bear market. If you feel uncomfortable with a decline of that magnitude you should rethink your asset allocation.

However, if selling would result in large capital gains, you may wish to consider the following alternatives:

- Sell stock funds held in tax-deferred retirement plans to restore your risk balance.
- Make a more gradual change in your asset allocation by investing any new money in the underweighted categories or reinvesting distributions from your overweighted funds into your underweighted holdings. This second alternative is particularly desirable if you feel there is a good chance your overweighted funds will continue to advance and you wish to make a more modest reallocation for the time being.

STAYING THE COURSE

It's generally unwise to make a big shift from stocks to cash because you fear a bear market. Trimming your stock allocation back a moderate amount—say, from 80% to 65% of your assets—can make sense if you are uncomfortable with the risk level of your fund portfolio, but drastically reducing it because you fear a plunge is basically market timing. The stock market will fluctuate, but you can't pinpoint when it will tumble or shoot up. If you have allocated your assets properly and have sufficient emergency money, you shouldn't need to worry.

Finally, don't panic and sell just after a big plunge. You could lock in a loss and miss any rebound. Panic-selling rarely makes sense because investors tend to overreact to recent bad news, hammering prices to unrealistic lows. But even if a bear market is long and painful, it's important to remember that stocks have a bullish bias and gain a lot more in the bullish phases than they lose on the downside—that's why the long-term trend of the market is up.

Of course, this assumes you have sufficient liquid assets in money market and short-term bond funds to meet emergencies and planned big-ticket expenditures over the next several years. The following is a good rule to keep in mind: Don't have money invested in stock funds that you will need within the next five years. By following the five-year rule, you greatly reduce the risk of having to sell shares after a market tumble.

11

Which Funds Were Included

The funds that appear in *The Individual Investor's Guide to the Top Mutual Funds* were selected from the universe of funds. Following are the various screens we used to arrive at the final selection.

HISTORICAL RECORD

Only those funds with three full years of data are included in the *Guide* so that there is a performance record of significant length and all performance measures can be calculated.

SIZE

Funds must appear on the National Association of Securities Dealers mutual fund list found in most major newspapers and are required to have at least $50 million in assets to qualify for inclusion in the *Guide*.

LOADS

The decision as to what constitutes a significant load is difficult, but we took this approach in the *Guide*:

All funds with front-end loads, back-end loads, or redemption fees of 3% or less are included if the fund does not also have a 12b-1 charge. Funds with redemption fees that disappear after six months that also have 12b-1 charges appear in this *Guide*.

Funds with 12b-1 plans and no front- or back-end loads are included in the *Guide*; we note, however, if the fund has a 12b-1 plan and what the annual charge is. Investors should carefully assess these plans individually.

Funds that impose a load that exceeds 3% or increase an existing load above 3% are dropped from the *Guide*.

EXPENSES

Funds with significantly higher expense ratios than the average for their category are not included in this *Guide*.

PERFORMANCE

Funds that significantly underperformed the average performance of their category are not included in this *Guide*.

INTEREST AND AVAILABILITY

Only those funds of general interest to mutual fund investors and typically only those funds that are open (not closed to new investors) and available for investment by individual investors directly from the fund, without restrictions, are included in this *Guide*.

FUNDS NOT INCLUDED

AAII members who would like performance figures for no-load and low-load mutual funds they own that do not appear in this *Guide* can access this information on our Web site at www.aaii.com.

12

A Key to Terms and Statistics

Most of the information used in the mutual fund data pages and performance tables is provided by Standard & Poor's Micropal, but some may come from mutual fund reports (the prospectus and annual and quarterly reports) and solicitation of information directly from the fund. Any data source has the potential for error, however, and before investing in any mutual fund, the prospectus for the fund should be read and the annual report examined.

When *na* appears in the performance tables or on the mutual fund page, it indicates that the number was not available or does not apply in that particular instance. For example, the 10-year annual return figure would not be available for funds that have been operating less than 10 years. We do not compile the bull and bear ratings for funds not operating during the entire bull or bear market period. Dashes (—) are used generally during years when the fund was not in operation or did not have a complete calendar year of operations. All numbers are truncated rather than rounded when necessary, unless noted otherwise in the following descriptions.

The following provides an explanation of the terms we have used in the performance tables and mutual fund data pages. The explanations are listed in the order in which the data and information appear on the mutual fund pages.

Fund Name: The funds are presented alphabetically by fund name within each category.

Ticker: The ticker symbol for each fund is given in parentheses for those investors who may want to access data with their computer or touch-tone phone. The ticker is four letters and is usually followed by an "X," indicating that this is a mutual fund. For example, the Liberty Acorn fund ticker symbol is ACRNX.

Investment Category: The fund's investment category is indicated at the top of the page below the fund's ticker symbol. After evaluating the information and statistics, we classified all mutual funds in exclusive categories by investment type. [For more complete definitions of the mutual fund investment categories used in the *Guide*, see Chapter 3: Mutual Fund Categories.]

Fund Telephone Number(s) and Internet Address: The management company telephone number and Internet address (if applicable) that investors can call or access to have specific questions answered or to obtain a copy of the prospectus.

Fund Inception Date: The day the fund was made available to the public for purchase.

Performance

Return (%): Return percentages for the periods below.

3yr Annual: Assuming an investment on January 1, 2000, the annual total return if held through December 31, 2002.

5yr Annual: Assuming an investment on January 1, 1998, the annual total return if held through December 31, 2002.

10yr Annual: Assuming an investment on January 1, 1993, the annual total return if held through December 31, 2002.

Bull: This return reflects the fund's performance in the most recent bull market, starting September 1, 1998, and continuing through March 31, 2000.

Bear: This return reflects the fund's performance in the most recent bear market, from April 1, 2000, through September 30, 2002.

Differ From Category (+/–): The difference between the return for the fund and the average return for all funds in the same category for the *3yr Annual*, *5yr Annual*, *10yr Annual*, *Bull*, and *Bear* periods. When the difference from category is negative, the fund underperformed the average fund in its investment category for the period by the percent indicated. The rankings, with possibilities of high, above average, average, below average, and low, are relative to all other funds within the same investment category. A rank of high, for example, would indicate that the return is in the highest 20% for that time period of all funds in the investment category. (Note: State-specific muni fund averages are only calculated against other muni funds from the same state.)

Standard Deviation: A measure of total risk, expressed as an annual return, that indicates the degree of variation in return experienced relative to the average return for a fund as measured over the last three years. The higher the standard deviation, the greater the total risk of the fund. Standard deviation of any fund can be compared to any other fund. Possibilities are high, above average, average, below average, and low.

Category Risk Index: A numerical measure of relative category risk, the risk index is a ratio of the total risk of the fund to the average total risk of funds in the category as measured over the last three years. Ratios above 1.0 indicate higher than average risk and ratios below 1.0 indicate lower than average risk for the category. The possibilities are high, above average, average, below average, and low.

Beta: A risk measure that relates the fund's volatility of returns to the market. The higher the beta of a fund, the higher the market risk of the fund. The figure is based on monthly returns for 36 months. A beta of 1.0 indicates that the fund's returns will on average be as volatile as the market and move in the same direction; a beta higher than 1.0 indicates that if the market rises or falls, the fund will rise or fall respectively but to a greater degree; a beta of less than 1.0 indicates that if the market rises or falls, the fund will rise or fall to a lesser degree. The S&P 500 index always has a beta of 1.0 because it is the measure we selected to represent the overall stock market. Beta is a meaningful figure of risk only for well-diversified common stock portfolios. For sector funds and other concentrated portfolios, beta is less useful than total risk as a measure of risk. Beta was not calculated for bond funds since they do not react in the same way to the factors that affect the stock market. For bond funds, the average maturity of the bond portfolio is more indicative of market risk, so it is used in place of beta.

Avg Mat: For bond funds, average maturity in years is an indication of market risk. When interest rates rise, bond prices fall, and when interest rates fall, bond prices rise. The longer the average maturity of the bonds held in the portfolio, the greater the fund's sensitivity to interest rate changes will be, and thus, the greater the risk. The refinancing of mortgages and the calling of outstanding bonds can affect average maturity when interest rates decline. An *na* indicates that the mutual fund did not provide an average maturity figure.

Return (%): This is a total return figure, expressed as a percentage. All distributions were assumed to have been reinvested. Rate of return is calculated on the basis of the calendar year. Return figures do not take into account front-end and back-end loads, redemption fees, or one-time or annual account charges, if any. The 12b-1 charge, as part of the expense ratio, is reflected in the return figure.

Differ from Category (+/–): The difference between the return for the fund and average return for all funds in the same investment category for the time period.

Return, Tax-Adjusted (%): Annual return after adjusting for the maximum federal income tax, currently 38.6% on income and short-term capital gains distributions and 20% on long-term capital gains distributions.

Per Share Data

Dividends, Net Income ($): Per share income distributions for the calendar year. The timing of net income distributions can be found in the prospectus.

Distrib'ns, Cap Gains ($): Per share distributions for the calendar year from realized capital gains after netting out realized losses. The timing of capital gains distributions can be found in the prospectus.

Net Asset Value ($): Calendar year-end net asset value is the sum of all securities held, based on their market value, divided by the number of mutual fund shares outstanding.

Expense Ratio (%): The sum of administrative fees plus adviser management fees and 12b-1 fees divided by the average net asset value of the fund, stated as a percentage. Brokerage costs incurred by the fund are not included in the expense ratio but are instead reflected directly in net asset value. Front-end loads, back-end loads, redemption fees, and account activity charges are not included in this ratio.

Yield (%): The per share annual income distribution made by the fund divided by the sum of the year-ending net asset value plus any capital gains distributions made during the year. This ratio is similar to a dividend yield and would be higher for income-oriented funds and lower for growth-oriented funds. The figure only reflects income; it is not total return. For some funds the yield may be distorted if the fund reports short-term capital gains as income.

Portfolio Turnover (%): A measure of the trading activity of the fund, which is computed by dividing the lesser of purchases or sales for the year by the monthly average value of the securities owned by the fund during the year. Securities with maturities of less than one year are excluded from the calculation. The result is expressed as a percentage, with 100% implying a complete turnover within one year.

Total Assets (Millions $): Aggregate fund value in millions of dollars at the end of the calendar year.

Portfolio

Portfolio Manager: The name of the portfolio manager(s) and the year when the senior manager(s) began managing the fund are noted, providing additional information useful in evaluating past performance. (Senior managers are listed first.) Funds managed by a committee are so noted. For some funds, a recent change in the portfolio manager(s) may indicate that the long-term annual performance figures and other performance classifications are less meaningful.

Investment Style: For domestic stock funds investment style can be categorized by the size of firms the fund invests in as measured by market capitalization and the investment approach employed by the fund, either growth or value or both. The investment style attributed to the fund indicates that the historical performance of the fund most closely follows the style(s) checked (listed below). More than one size may be checked, indicating a mixture of size, and growth/value may be checked, indicating a blend of growth and value investment approaches. Style is *only* calculated for domestic stock funds.

Style Categories: Large Cap, Mid Cap, Small Cap, Growth, Value, Grth/Val ('Cap' denotes capitalization, which is market price per share for a firm's stock times the number of common stock shares outstanding).

Portfolio: The portfolio composition classifies investments by type and gives the percentage of the total portfolio invested in each. Due to rounding of the percentages and the practice of leverage (borrowing) to buy securities, the portfolio total percentage may not equal 100.0%.

Shareholder Information

Minimum Investment and Minimum IRA Investment:

The minimum initial and subsequent investments, by mail, in the fund are detailed. Minimum investment by telephone or by wire may be different. Often, funds will have a lower minimum IRA investment; this is also indicated.

Maximum Fees:

Load: The maximum load is given, if any, and whether the load is front-end or back-end is indicated.

12b-1: If a fund has a 12b-1 plan, the percentage that the fund charges is given.

Other: Redemption fees are given along with the time period, if appropriate.

Services:

IRA: Notes whether the fund offers an individual retirement account option.

Keogh: Notes whether the fund offers a Keogh account option.

Telephone Exchange: Indicates whether telephone exchanges with other funds in the family are permitted.

Check in the prospectus to determine whether the fund allows for an automatic exchange between funds in the family; whether the fund allows for automatic investments through an investor's checking account; and whether the fund allows the automatic and systematic withdrawal of money from the fund. All funds have automatic reinvestment of distributions options.

Fund Performance Rankings and Information 13

When choosing among mutual funds, most investors start with performance statistics: How well have the various mutual funds performed in the past? If past performance alone could perfectly predict future performance, selection would be easy.

What past performance can tell you is how well the fund's management has handled different market environments, how consistent the fund has been, and how well the fund has done relative to its risk level, relative to other similar funds, and relative to the market.

We present performance statistics in several different forms. First, we provide an overall picture, with the average performance of each mutual fund category for the last five years, along with benchmarks for large, mid-cap and small company domestic stocks; international stocks; bonds; and Treasury bills. The top 20 and bottom 20 mutual fund performers for the last year are given as a recent reference of performance. The list changes each year and reflects the cyclical nature of financial markets and the changing success of individual mutual fund managers. Lists of the top 50 mutual funds ranked by annual return over the last 10 years, five years, and three years are given for a long-term perspective on investment trends of performance.

Since the performance of a fund must be judged relative to similar funds, we have also classified the funds by investment category and ranked them according to their total return performance for the last year. These performance lists appear in Chapter 14 at the start of each category section. To make the comparison easier, we have also provided other data. The funds' annual returns for the last three years, five years, and 10 years give a longer-term perspective on the performance of the fund; category and total risk ranks are also given to judge performance. (To maintain ranking accuracy, funds are sorted by more decimal points of return than those published in the *Guide*.)

Key to Fund Categories Used in Performance Tables

Stk-LC	Large-Cap Stock
Stk-MC	Mid-Cap Stock
Stk-SC	Small-Cap Stock
Sec-E	Energy/Resources Sector Stock
Sec-F	Financial/Banking Sector Stock
Sec-G	Gold Sector Stock
Sec-H	Health Sector Stock
Sec-R	Real Estate Sector Stock
Sec-T	Technology Sector Stock
Sec-TC	Telecommunications Sector Stock
Sec-U	Utilities Sector Stock
IntS-Glb	Global Stock
IntS-F	Foreign Stock
IntS-R/C	Regional/Country Stock
IntS-E	Emerging Stock
Bal	Balanced Stock/Bond
B-Corp	Corporate Bond
B-CHY	Corporate High-Yield Bond
B-MB	Mortgage-Backed Bond
B-GvST	Government: Short-Term Bond
B-GvIT	Government: Intermediate-Term Bond
B-GvLT	Government: Long-Term Bond
B-Gen	General Bond
B-MNST	National Muni: Short-Term Bond
B-MNIT	National Muni: Intermediate-Term Bond
B-MNLT	National Muni: Long-Term Bond
B-MS-AZ	Muni: Arizona Bond
B-MS-CA	Muni: California Bond
B-MS-CT	Muni: Connecticut Bond
B-MS-FL	Muni: Florida Bond
B-MS-GA	Muni: Georgia Bond
B-MS-HI	Muni: Hawaii Bond
B-MS-KY	Muni: Kentucky Bond
B-MS-MA	Muni: Massachusetts Bond
B-MS-MD	Muni: Maryland Bond
B-MS-MI	Muni: Michigan Bond
B-MS-MN	Muni: Minnesota Bond
B-MS-NJ	Muni: New Jersey Bond
B-MS-NY	Muni: New York Bond
B-MS-OH	Muni: Ohio Bond
B-MS-OR	Muni: Oregon Bond
B-MS-PA	Muni: Pennsylvania Bond
B-MS-VA	Muni: Virginia Bond
B-MS-WI	Muni: Wisconsin Bond
IntB	International Bond

Total Risk and Return Performances for Different Mutual Fund Categories

Stock Funds	Annual Return (%) 2002	2001	2000	1999	1998	5yr	Total Return (%) Bull	Bear	Std Dev (%)	Total Risk
Large-Cap	-22.1	-12.8	-5.2	25.4	24.4	-0.9	74.7	-39.1	19.1	abv av
Mid-Cap	-18.0	-5.9	5.8	29.7	10.0	1.7	82.7	-24.0	20.4	abv av
Small-Cap	-20.5	2.4	4.2	37.0	0.7	1.2	95.4	-20.6	23.8	high
Growth Style	-27.0	-18.9	-9.9	53.7	21.3	-1.5	138.8	-53.1	26.7	high
Value Style	-14.3	5.6	12.3	7.4	6.7	2.6	30.6	-4.7	17.4	av
Energy/Resources Sector	-4.7	-10.8	39.4	29.0	-18.9	3.2	64.3	-3.1	21.9	abv av
Financial/Banking Sector	-10.0	-5.1	34.9	-0.7	8.6	4.0	23.8	8.1	21.8	abv av
Gold Sector	65.5	19.2	-21.3	1.7	-15.5	5.4	16.9	64.9	32.9	high
Health Sector	-23.8	-11.1	44.9	9.5	29.1	5.5	57.5	-1.1	28.0	high
Real Estate Sector	5.5	9.5	24.2	1.4	-18.5	3.2	5.8	41.3	12.7	blw av
Technology Sector	-43.5	-30.7	-24.5	122.4	50.4	-1.1	349.6	-78.7	50.5	high
Telecomm Sector	-35.4	-31.7	-28.6	95.8	37.9	-4.2	220.5	-76.6	35.0	high
Utilities Sector	-25.2	-20.5	0.2	16.8	28.7	-2.6	63.8	-49.2	18.8	abv av
Global	-16.7	-15.1	-9.2	40.6	11.1	-0.8	70.3	-38.2	16.6	av
Foreign	-15.9	-20.6	-15.9	51.7	13.4	-1.1	77.2	-47.2	18.3	av
Regional/Country	-12.4	-12.3	-23.8	76.7	1.6	-1.5	128.5	-47.0	23.6	high
Emerging	-6.4	-3.4	-28.9	66.4	-25.0	-4.4	104.5	-41.9	23.1	abv av
Balanced Stock/Bond	-8.7	-2.2	2.2	10.7	13.7	2.5	31.8	-14.2	10.9	blw av
Bond Funds										
Corporate	5.1	7.1	8.5	1.0	6.1	5.5	5.3	18.1	3.5	low
Corporate High-Yield	-1.2	1.1	-7.1	5.6	1.8	-0.1	6.3	-10.8	9.5	blw av
Mortgage-Backed	7.6	7.3	9.8	1.0	6.4	6.4	4.3	23.7	2.7	low
Gov't: Short-Term	6.3	7.4	8.1	1.9	6.4	6.0	5.0	21.3	1.7	low
Gov't: Int-Term	11.0	6.9	12.8	-1.7	8.8	7.4	2.9	29.2	4.2	low
Gov't: Long-Term	15.8	2.1	21.1	-9.1	11.9	7.5	-1.1	30.0	7.8	blw av
General	7.2	7.4	9.5	0.3	7.1	6.2	4.5	21.9	3.3	low
Nat'l Muni: Short-Term	4.1	4.6	5.0	2.0	4.6	4.1	4.5	13.0	1.5	low
Nat'l Muni: Int-Term	8.3	4.9	8.8	-1.1	5.7	5.2	2.4	21.4	3.6	low
Nat'l Muni: Long-Term	8.9	4.0	11.8	-4.4	5.7	5.0	0.0	23.2	4.8	blw av
International Bond	13.3	4.7	5.5	5.0	2.4	5.5	20.4	15.5	7.2	blw av
Index Comparisons										
Dow Jones Ind'l Avg	-15.0	-5.4	-4.6	27.2	18.1	2.8	48.6	-27.2	19.1	abv av
S&P 500	-22.0	-11.8	-9.0	21.0	28.5	-0.5	59.7	-43.7	18.8	abv av
S&P MidCap 400	-14.5	-0.5	17.4	14.7	19.1	6.4	81.1	-16.2	20.4	abv av
Russell 2000*	-20.4	2.4	-3.0	21.2	-2.5	-1.3	62.8	-30.4	24.7	high
MSCI EAFE**	-15.6	-21.2	-13.9	27.2	20.3	-2.6	48.9	-46.2	16.2	av
MSCI Europe	-18.0	-19.6	-8.1	16.2	28.9	-1.9	32.8	-45.5	18.4	av
MSCI Far East	-10.8	-28.2	-26.9	62.6	2.5	-4.8	105.6	-50.9	17.6	av
Lehman Brothers Bond Indexes										
Corporate	10.5	10.4	9.3	-1.9	8.5	7.2	3.2	27.6	4.1	low
High-Yield	-1.4	5.2	-5.8	2.3	1.8	0.3	2.5	-6.2	10.4	blw av
Government	11.4	7.2	13.2	-2.2	9.8	7.7	3.6	30.0	4.3	low
Mortgage-Backed	8.7	8.2	11.1	1.8	6.9	7.3	5.3	27.3	2.6	low
Municipal	9.6	5.1	11.6	-2.0	6.4	6.0	2.6	25.0	4.1	low
Treasury Bills	1.7	4.4	6.1	4.8	5.2	4.4	8.0	10.8	0.5	low

** Index of small company stocks* *** Europe, Australia, Far East Index*

The Top 20 Performers: 2002

Category	Fund (Ticker)	Annual Return (%) 2002	3yr	5yr	10yr	Category Risk	Total Risk
Sec-G	US Glob Inv:Wrld Prec Mils (UNWPX)	83.4	6.8	-2.1	1.4	high	high
Sec-G	US Glob Inv:Gold Shares (USERX)	81.3	12.2	-1.5	-7.3	high	high
Sec-G	Amer Cnt Global Gold/Inv (BGEIX)	72.9	20.8	8.4	3.4	abv av	high
Sec-G	USAA Inv:Prec Metal&Min (USAGX)	67.6	23.1	15.1	6.4	av	high
Sec-G	Fidelity Sel Gold (FSAGX)	64.2	18.9	10.7	7.3	av	high
B-GvLT	Amer Cnt Target 2020/Inv (BTTTX)	36.6	21.5	9.7	12.9	high	abv av
B-GvLT	Amer Cnt Target 2025/Inv (BTTRX)	35.0	22.8	12.2	na	high	abv av
B-GvLT	Amer Cnt Target 2015/Inv (BTFTX)	27.0	19.3	10.6	12.5	high	blw av
B-GvIT	Amer Cnt Target 2010/Inv (BTTNX)	26.7	19.2	11.3	11.7	high	blw av
IntB	Amer Cnt Intl Bond/Inv (BEGBX)	23.5	6.2	4.8	6.1	abv av	blw av
IntB	T Rowe Price Intl Bd (RPIBX)	21.8	4.4	3.8	5.8	abv av	blw av
B-GvLT	Wasatch-Hoisington:US Trs (WHOSX)	16.8	13.6	8.0	8.0	abv av	blw av
B-GvLT	Vanguard LT Treas/Inv (VUSTX)	16.6	13.3	8.5	9.1	abv av	blw av
B-GvLT	T Rowe Price Treas Long (PRULX)	15.1	12.3	7.8	8.3	av	blw av
B-GvIT	Amer Cnt Target 2005/Inv (BTFIX)	14.6	14.2	11.1	10.6	high	blw av
B-Gen	Vanguard LT Bd Idx (VBLTX)	14.3	12.8	8.2	na	high	blw av
B-GvIT	Vanguard Int Tm Tsy/Inv (VFITX)	14.1	11.8	8.3	7.8	high	blw av
IntB	Fidelity New Markets Inc (FNMIX)	13.8	12.0	8.3	na	high	blw av
B-Corp	Vanguard LT Crp (VWESX)	13.2	11.5	7.2	8.4	high	blw av
B-GvIT	T Rowe Price Treas Int (PRTIX)	12.0	10.5	7.5	6.9	high	blw av

The Bottom 20 Performers: 2002

Category	Fund (Ticker)	Annual Return (%) 2002	3yr	5yr	10yr	Category Risk	Total Risk
Sec-T	Firsthand:Tech Value (TVFQX)	-56.1	-39.5	-4.4	na	high	high
Sec-T	Fidelity Sel Electronics (FSELX)	-50.5	-29.7	1.6	16.4	abv av	high
Sec-TC	Fidelity Sel Develop Comm (FSDCX)	-47.7	-38.3	-2.6	6.5	high	high
Sec-T	Fidelity Sel Computers (FDCPX)	-42.0	-33.5	0.8	12.4	blw av	high
Stk-MC	Fidelity Aggressive Grth (FDEGX)	-41.1	-39.0	-8.0	3.9	high	high
Sec-T	T Rowe Price Sci&Tech (PRSCX)	-40.5	-38.7	-8.0	5.5	av	high
Sec-H	Fidelity Sel Biotech (FBIOX)	-40.5	-16.0	6.4	7.4	high	high
Stk-SC	RS:Diversifed Growth/A (RSDGX)	-39.1	-23.1	5.6	na	high	high
Stk-LC	Rydex:OTC/Inv (RYOCX)	-38.5	-37.0	-1.3	na	high	high
Sec-T	Fidelity Sel Technology (FSPTX)	-37.7	-33.9	3.0	11.7	abv av	high
Stk-SC	SAFECO Growth Opp/Inv (SAFGX)	-36.9	-9.6	-4.5	8.2	abv av	high
Stk-SC	FTI Small Cap Equity Fund (FTSCX)	-35.4	-17.4	-0.4	na	abv av	high
Stk-LC	Gabelli Growth (GABGX)	-33.7	-23.3	-3.1	7.5	high	high
Stk-LC	Fidelity Growth Company (FDGRX)	-33.4	-22.4	1.2	8.8	high	high
Stk-SC	PBHG Strategic Small Co (PSSCX)	-33.3	-12.4	0.8	na	abv av	high
Stk-SC	PBHG Small Cap Value (PBSVX)	-31.9	-1.7	2.6	na	av	high
Stk-MC	Marshall:Mid Cap Gr/Inv (MRMSX)	-31.7	-18.4	0.2	na	abv av	high
Stk-SC	INVESCO Small Co Grth/Inv (FIEGX)	-31.3	-21.8	-0.1	7.3	high	high
Stk-MC	Strong Growth 20/Inv (SGRTX)	-30.8	-28.6	0.7	na	high	high
Stk-MC	PBHG Growth (PBHGX)	-30.3	-29.4	-7.4	5.2	high	high

The Top 50 Performers: 10 Years, 1993 – 2002

Category	Fund (Ticker)	Annual Return (%) 10yr	5yr	3yr	2002	Category Risk	Total Risk
Sec-H	Vanguard Health Care (VGHCX)	18.6	14.7	9.7	-11.3	low	blw av
Sec-T	Fidelity Sel Electronics (FSELX)	16.4	1.6	-29.7	-50.5	abv av	high
Sec-F	Fidelity Sel Brokerage (FSLBX)	16.4	5.8	-1.2	-17.2	high	high
Sec-T	Fidelity Sel Software (FSCSX)	15.8	9.8	-17.1	-23.3	av	high
Stk-LC	Mairs & Power Growth (MPGFX)	15.4	7.8	7.5	-7.7	low	av
Stk-LC	Clipper Fund (CFIMX)	15.1	10.8	12.7	-5.5	low	av
Stk-LC	Excelsior Val & Restrctg (UMBIX)	14.9	4.1	-7.8	-23.3	abv av	abv av
Sec-E	Fidelity Sel Energy Serv (FSESX)	14.7	0.4	5.6	-0.6	high	high
Stk-LC	Legg Mason Eq:Value/P (LMVTX)	14.4	5.0	-11.9	-18.9	abv av	abv av
Stk-SC	Fidelity Low Priced Stock (FLPSX)	14.2	8.3	12.2	-6.1	low	av
Stk-MC	Weitz Srs:Value (WVALX)	14.2	9.1	-0.2	-17.1	blw av	av
Sec-F	Fidelity Sel Financl Serv (FIDSX)	14.1	3.7	1.1	-11.3	low	abv av
Stk-LC	Dodge & Cox Stock (DODGX)	14.1	7.5	4.3	-10.5	blw av	av
Stk-LC	Longleaf Partners Fund (LLPFX)	14.1	7.3	6.8	-8.3	blw av	av
Sec-H	Fidelity Sel Health Care (FSPHX)	13.6	5.4	-1.6	-18.0	blw av	av
Sec-F	Fidelity Sel Banking (FSRBX)	13.5	2.0	3.2	-7.7	av	abv av
Stk-LC	Vanguard PRIMECAP (VPMCX)	13.3	3.8	-11.9	-24.5	high	high
B-GvLT	Amer Cnt Target 2020/Inv (BTTTX)	12.9	9.7	21.5	36.6	high	abv av
Stk-MC	T Rowe Price Md Cp Gr (RPMGX)	12.8	4.8	-5.7	-21.2	abv av	abv av
Stk-MC	Vontobel US Value (VUSVX)	12.5	6.0	10.8	-2.0	blw av	av
B-GvLT	Amer Cnt Target 2015/Inv (BTFTX)	12.5	10.6	19.3	27.0	high	blw av
Stk-SC	Liberty Acorn Fund/Z (ACRNX)	12.4	7.4	0.4	-13.3	blw av	abv av
Sec-T	Fidelity Sel Computers (FDCPX)	12.4	0.8	-33.5	-42.0	blw av	high
Stk-MC	Muhlenkamp Fund (MUHLX)	12.2	4.7	3.1	-19.9	abv av	high
Stk-MC	CA Inv:S&P Mid Cap Index (SPMIX)	11.9	6.9	0.9	-14.2	av	abv av
Bal	Dodge & Cox Balanced (DODBX)	11.9	8.0	7.1	-2.9	av	blw av
Bal	T Rowe Price Cap Apprec (PRWCX)	11.8	8.9	10.6	0.5	av	blw av
Stk-SC	Heartland Grp:Value Fund (HRTVX)	11.7	5.2	5.3	-11.4	blw av	av
Sec-E	Vanguard Energy (VGENX)	11.7	4.9	9.7	-0.6	abv av	abv av
Sec-T	Fidelity Sel Technology (FSPTX)	11.7	3.0	-33.9	-37.7	abv av	high
B-GvIT	Amer Cnt Target 2010/Inv (BTTNX)	11.7	11.3	19.2	26.7	high	blw av
Stk-MC	Ariel Fund (ARGFX)	11.6	7.6	11.7	-5.1	blw av	av
Stk-SC	Royce:Micro-Cap/Inv (RYOTX)	11.6	6.4	7.5	-13.4	av	abv av
Stk-LC	Fidelity Contrafund (FCNTX)	11.5	3.9	-9.7	-9.6	low	blw av
Stk-SC	Third Avenue Value (TAVFX)	11.5	4.3	1.7	-15.1	low	av
Stk-MC	Ariel Appreciation Fund (CAAPX)	11.5	7.3	7.3	-10.3	blw av	av
Stk-SC	T Rowe Price Sm Cp Stk (OTCFX)	11.3	3.3	2.2	-14.2	blw av	abv av
Stk-MC	Dreyfus Index:Midcap Idx (PESPX)	11.3	5.8	-0.6	-15.0	av	abv av
Stk-LC	Oakmark Fund/I (OAKMX)	11.3	1.0	4.2	-14.4	av	abv av
Stk-SC	Gabelli Sm Cp Grth (GABSX)	11.1	4.7	3.3	-5.3	low	av
Stk-LC	Selected American Shares (SLASX)	11.0	2.4	-6.9	-17.0	low	av
Stk-SC	Royce:Premier (RYPRX)	11.0	7.1	5.7	-7.7	low	av
Stk-LC	Janus Growth & Income (JAGIX)	11.0	3.9	-15.8	-21.5	blw av	av
Stk-MC	Fidelity Value (FDVLX)	11.0	3.6	3.2	-9.2	av	abv av
Stk-SC	Value Line Spcl Situation (VALSX)	11.0	6.4	-13.3	-15.1	abv av	high
Stk-MC	Legg Mason Eq:Special/P (LMASX)	11.0	6.5	-6.3	-8.7	abv av	high
Stk-LC	T Rowe Price Eq Inc (PRFDX)	10.9	2.5	0.0	-13.0	blw av	av
Bal	Janus Balanced (JABAX)	10.7	7.0	-4.6	-6.5	blw av	blw av
Stk-MC	Sound Shore Fund (SSHFX)	10.7	0.9	0.2	-15.4	blw av	av
Sec-R	Cohen & Steers Realty Shs (CSRSX)	10.7	2.9	11.2	2.7	abv av	blw av

The Top 50 Performers: 5 Years, 1998 – 2002

Category	Fund (Ticker)	Annual Return (%) 5yr	10yr	3yr	2002	Category Risk	Total Risk
IntS-R/C	Matthews Korea (MAKOX)	28.9	na	-4.4	8.1	high	high
Sec-G	USAA Inv:Prec Metal&Min (USAGX)	15.1	6.4	23.1	67.6	av	high
Stk-MC	Vanguard Capital Opp/Inv (VHCOX)	14.9	na	-8.4	-27.9	abv av	high
Sec-H	Vanguard Health Care (VGHCX)	14.7	18.6	9.7	-11.3	low	blw av
B-GvLT	Amer Cnt Target 2025/Inv (BTTRX)	12.2	na	22.8	35.0	high	abv av
IntS-R/C	Fidelity Japan Smaller Co (FJSCX)	12.1	na	-26.2	0.9	abv av	high
B-GvIT	Amer Cnt Target 2010/Inv (BTTNX)	11.3	11.7	19.2	26.7	high	blw av
B-GvIT	Amer Cnt Target 2005/Inv (BTFIX)	11.1	10.6	14.2	14.6	high	blw av
Stk-MC	PBHG Mid Cap Value (PBMCX)	11.1	na	2.9	-19.7	av	abv av
Bal	Oakmark Eqty & Income/I (OAKBX)	10.9	na	11.4	-2.1	blw av	blw av
Stk-LC	Clipper Fund (CFIMX)	10.8	15.1	12.7	-5.5	low	av
Sec-G	Fidelity Sel Gold (FSAGX)	10.7	7.3	18.9	64.2	av	high
B-GvLT	Amer Cnt Target 2015/Inv (BTFTX)	10.6	12.5	19.3	27.0	high	blw av
Stk-MC	Hennessy Crnst Grth (HFCGX)	9.9	na	4.0	-4.7	av	abv av
Sec-T	Fidelity Sel Software (FSCSX)	9.8	15.8	-17.1	-23.3	av	high
B-GvLT	Amer Cnt Target 2020/Inv (BTTTX)	9.7	12.9	21.5	36.6	high	abv av
Stk-MC	Weitz Partners Value Fund (WPVLX)	9.4	na	-0.1	-16.9	blw av	av
Stk-MC	Weitz Srs:Value (WVALX)	9.1	14.2	-0.2	-17.1	blw av	av
Bal	T Rowe Price Cap Apprec (PRWCX)	8.9	11.8	10.6	0.5	av	blw av
B-GvLT	Vanguard LT Treas/Inv (VUSTX)	8.5	9.1	13.3	16.6	abv av	blw av
Sec-G	Amer Cnt Global Gold/Inv (BGEIX)	8.4	3.4	20.8	72.9	abv av	high
Stk-SC	Fidelity Low Priced Stock (FLPSX)	8.3	14.2	12.2	-6.1	low	av
B-GvIT	Vanguard Int Tm Tsy/Inv (VFITX)	8.3	7.8	11.8	14.1	high	blw av
IntB	Fidelity New Markets Inc (FNMIX)	8.3	na	12.0	13.8	high	blw av
B-Gen	Vanguard LT Bd Idx (VBLTX)	8.2	na	12.8	14.3	high	blw av
Bal	Dodge & Cox Balanced (DODBX)	8.0	11.9	7.1	-2.9	av	blw av
IntS-F	Wm Blair:Intl Grth/N (WBIGX)	8.0	9.7	-12.3	-15.1	av	av
B-GvLT	Wasatch-Hoisington:US Trs (WHOSX)	8.0	8.0	13.6	16.8	abv av	blw av
B-Gen	Harbor Bond/Inst (HABDX)	7.9	8.0	10.3	10.6	abv av	low
Stk-LC	Mairs & Power Growth (MPGFX)	7.8	15.4	7.5	-7.7	low	av
B-GvLT	T Rowe Price Treas Long (PRULX)	7.8	8.3	12.3	15.1	av	blw av
B-Gen	Fremont:Bond (FBDFX)	7.8	na	10.3	9.4	high	low
IntS-F	Artisan International (ARTIX)	7.8	na	-15.1	-18.8	high	abv av
B-Gen	Vanguard Int Tm Bd (VBIIX)	7.8	na	10.9	10.8	high	blw av
B-Gen	Dodge & Cox Income (DODIX)	7.7	7.9	10.5	10.7	blw av	low
Stk-MC	Amer Cnt Eqty Income/Inv (TWEIX)	7.7	na	8.8	-4.9	low	blw av
Stk-MC	Ariel Fund (ARGFX)	7.6	11.6	11.7	-5.1	blw av	av
Stk-LC	Fidelity Export & Multi (FEXPX)	7.6	na	-5.9	-18.6	av	abv av
Stk-LC	Dodge & Cox Stock (DODGX)	7.5	14.1	4.3	-10.5	blw av	av
B-GvIT	Fidelity Spart Govt Inc (SPGVX)	7.5	6.9	10.3	11.5	av	low
B-GvIT	T Rowe Price Treas Int (PRTIX)	7.5	6.9	10.5	12.0	high	blw av
Stk-SC	Liberty Acorn Fund/Z (ACRNX)	7.4	12.4	0.4	-13.3	blw av	abv av
IntB	Payden Glbl Fixed Inc/R (PYGFX)	7.4	7.9	8.9	7.8	blw av	low
Stk-SC	Royce:Total Return (RYTRX)	7.4	na	10.4	-1.6	low	blw av
Stk-LC	Longleaf Partners Fund (LLPFX)	7.3	14.1	6.8	-8.3	blw av	av
Stk-MC	Ariel Appreciation Fund (CAAPX)	7.3	11.5	7.3	-10.3	blw av	av
B-Gen	Fidelity Spart Inv Grade (FSIBX)	7.3	7.6	9.7	9.5	av	low
B-MB	Strong Government Sec/Inv (STVSX)	7.3	7.6	10.0	10.1	high	low
B-Corp	Vanguard Int Tm Crp (VFICX)	7.3	na	10.1	10.2	abv av	low
B-Corp	Vanguard LT Crp (VWESX)	7.2	8.4	11.5	13.2	high	blw av

The Top 50 Performers: 3 Years, 2000 – 2002

Category	Fund (Ticker)	Annual Return (%) 3yr	5yr	10yr	2002	Category Risk	Total Risk
Sec-G	USAA Inv:Prec Metal&Min (USAGX)	23.1	15.1	6.4	67.6	av	high
B-GvLT	Amer Cnt Target 2025/Inv (BTTRX)	22.8	12.2	na	35.0	high	abv av
B-GvLT	Amer Cnt Target 2020/Inv (BTTTX)	21.5	9.7	12.9	36.6	high	abv av
Sec-G	Amer Cnt Global Gold/Inv (BGEIX)	20.8	8.4	3.4	72.9	abv av	high
B-GvLT	Amer Cnt Target 2015/Inv (BTFTX)	19.3	10.6	12.5	27.0	high	blw av
B-GvIT	Amer Cnt Target 2010/Inv (BTTNX)	19.2	11.3	11.7	26.7	high	blw av
Sec-G	Fidelity Sel Gold (FSAGX)	18.9	10.7	7.3	64.2	av	high
Sec-R	Stratton Monthly Div REIT (STMDX)	16.2	5.4	6.7	6.4	low	blw av
Sec-R	Fidelity Real Est Inv (FRESX)	15.0	4.1	9.9	5.7	blw av	blw av
Stk-LC	Yacktman Fund (YACKX)	14.7	4.7	9.5	11.4	blw av	av
B-GvIT	Amer Cnt Target 2005/Inv (BTFIX)	14.2	11.1	10.6	14.6	high	blw av
Sec-R	Vanguard REIT Idx (VGSIX)	13.7	3.4	na	3.7	av	blw av
B-GvLT	Wasatch-Hoisington:US Trs (WHOSX)	13.6	8.0	8.0	16.8	abv av	blw av
B-GvLT	Vanguard LT Treas/Inv (VUSTX)	13.3	8.5	9.1	16.6	abv av	blw av
Sec-H	Fidelity Sel Med Dlvry (FSHCX)	12.9	-0.9	7.8	-12.1	av	abv av
B-Gen	Vanguard LT Bd Idx (VBLTX)	12.8	8.2	na	14.3	high	blw av
Stk-LC	Clipper Fund (CFIMX)	12.7	10.8	15.1	-5.5	low	av
B-GvLT	T Rowe Price Treas Long (PRULX)	12.3	7.8	8.3	15.1	av	blw av
Stk-SC	Fidelity Low Priced Stock (FLPSX)	12.2	8.3	14.2	-6.1	low	av
Sec-G	US Glob Inv:Gold Shares (USERX)	12.2	-1.5	-7.3	81.3	high	high
IntB	Fidelity New Markets Inc (FNMIX)	12.0	8.3	na	13.8	high	blw av
Stk-SC	Babson Enterprise Fund (BABEX)	12.0	2.9	9.9	-3.4	blw av	av
Sec-R	CGM Realty Fund (CGMRX)	12.0	2.6	na	3.5	high	av
B-GvIT	Vanguard Int Tm Tsy/Inv (VFITX)	11.8	8.3	7.8	14.1	high	blw av
Stk-MC	Ariel Fund (ARGFX)	11.7	7.6	11.6	-5.1	blw av	av
Stk-MC	Delafield Fund (DEFIX)	11.7	5.9	na	-7.4	av	abv av
B-Corp	Vanguard LT Crp (VWESX)	11.5	7.2	8.4	13.2	high	blw av
Bal	Oakmark Eqty & Income/I (OAKBX)	11.4	10.9	na	-2.1	blw av	blw av
IntB	T Rowe Price Emg Mkt Bd (PREMX)	11.3	5.4	na	9.5	high	blw av
Sec-R	Cohen & Steers Realty Shs (CSRSX)	11.2	2.9	10.7	2.7	abv av	blw av
B-Gen	Vanguard Int Tm Bd (VBIIX)	10.9	7.8	na	10.8	high	blw av
Stk-MC	Vontobel US Value (VUSVX)	10.8	6.0	12.5	-2.0	blw av	av
Bal	T Rowe Price Cap Apprec (PRWCX)	10.6	8.9	11.8	0.5	av	blw av
B-Gen	Dodge & Cox Income (DODIX)	10.5	7.7	7.9	10.7	blw av	low
B-GvIT	T Rowe Price Treas Int (PRTIX)	10.5	7.5	6.9	12.0	high	blw av
Stk-SC	Royce:Total Return (RYTRX)	10.4	7.4	na	-1.6	low	blw av
B-Gen	Harbor Bond/Inst (HABDX)	10.3	7.9	8.0	10.6	abv av	low
B-Gen	Fremont:Bond (FBDFX)	10.3	7.8	na	9.4	high	low
B-GvIT	Fidelity Spart Govt Inc (SPGVX)	10.3	7.5	6.9	11.5	av	low
B-GvLT	Dreyfus US Treasury Long (DRGBX)	10.3	6.4	7.3	11.4	av	blw av
B-Corp	Vanguard Int Tm Crp (VFICX)	10.1	7.3	na	10.2	abv av	low
B-MB	Strong Government Sec/Inv (STVSX)	10.0	7.3	7.6	10.1	high	low
B-GvIT	Fidelity Government Inc (FGOVX)	10.0	7.1	7.0	10.9	av	low
B-GvIT	Amer Cnt Govt Bond/Inv (CPTNX)	9.9	7.2	6.7	10.5	abv av	blw av
B-GvLT	INVESCO US Govt Secur/Inv (FBDGX)	9.8	6.7	7.4	9.7	blw av	blw av
Bal	USAA Mutual:Income (USAIX)	9.8	6.7	7.2	8.6	low	low
Sec-H	Vanguard Health Care (VGHCX)	9.7	14.7	18.6	-11.3	low	blw av
B-Gen	Fidelity Spart Inv Grade (FSIBX)	9.7	7.3	7.6	9.5	av	low
B-MNLT	SAFECO Muni Bond/Inv (SFCOX)	9.7	5.7	6.5	10.3	high	blw av
Sec-E	Vanguard Energy (VGENX)	9.7	4.9	11.7	-0.6	abv av	abv av

14

Individual Fund Listings

DOMESTIC STOCK FUNDS

Large-Cap Stock Funds
Category Performance Ranked by 2002 Returns

Category	Fund (Ticker)	Annual Return (%) 2002	3yr	5yr	10yr	Category Risk	Total Risk
Stk-LC	Yacktman Fund (YACKX)	11.4	14.7	4.7	9.5	blw av	av
Stk-LC	Fidelity Fifty (FFTYX)	0.3	-5.6	7.1	na	abv av	abv av
Stk-LC	Gateway Tr:Gateway Fd (GATEX)	-4.8	-0.7	4.4	6.8	low	blw av
Stk-LC	Clipper Fund (CFIMX)	-5.5	12.7	10.8	15.1	low	av
Stk-LC	Mairs & Power Growth (MPGFX)	-7.7	7.5	7.8	15.4	low	av
Stk-LC	Longleaf Partners Fund (LLPFX)	-8.3	6.8	7.3	14.1	blw av	av
Stk-LC	Fidelity Contrafund (FCNTX)	-9.6	-9.7	3.9	11.5	low	blw av
Stk-LC	Dodge & Cox Stock (DODGX)	-10.5	4.3	7.5	14.1	blw av	av
Stk-LC	T Rowe Price Eq Inc (PRFDX)	-13.0	0.0	2.5	10.9	blw av	av
Stk-LC	Babson Value Fund (BVALX)	-14.4	-3.3	-0.6	9.5	blw av	av
Stk-LC	Oakmark Fund/I (OAKMX)	-14.4	4.2	1.0	11.3	av	abv av
Stk-LC	Fidelity Equity Income II (FEQTX)	-15.4	-5.5	1.6	9.7	blw av	av
Stk-LC	Vanguard Equity Income (VEIPX)	-15.6	-2.1	1.8	10.0	low	av
Stk-LC	Fidelity Independence (FDFFX)	-15.8	-14.5	4.4	9.2	high	high
Stk-LC	Marsico Focus (MFOCX)	-16.6	-18.4	4.9	na	abv av	abv av
Stk-LC	Vanguard Windsor II/Inv (VWNFX)	-16.8	-2.0	0.5	10.1	blw av	av
Stk-LC	Selected American Shares (SLASX)	-17.0	-6.9	2.4	11.0	low	av
Stk-LC	Dreyfus Appreciation (DGAGX)	-17.1	-9.0	1.6	9.6	low	av
Stk-LC	Fidelity Equity Income (FEQIX)	-17.1	-5.1	0.5	10.0	blw av	av
Stk-LC	Fidelity Freedom 2030 (FFFEX)	-17.3	-11.4	1.6	na	low	av
Stk-LC	Fidelity Grth & Inc (FGRIX)	-18.0	-10.0	0.6	10.3	low	blw av
Stk-LC	Janus Core Equity (JAEIX)	-18.0	-12.5	5.3	na	low	av
Stk-LC	Fidelity Disciplined Eqty (FDEQX)	-18.5	-12.3	0.1	8.8	low	av
Stk-LC	Fidelity Export & Multi (FEXPX)	-18.6	-5.9	7.6	na	av	abv av
Stk-LC	Legg Mason Eq:Value/P (LMVTX)	-18.9	-11.9	5.0	14.4	abv av	abv av
Stk-LC	Masters Select Equity (MSEFX)	-19.0	-6.6	3.4	na	abv av	abv av
Stk-LC	Amer Cnt Income & Gr/Inv (BIGRX)	-19.3	-12.8	0.0	9.6	blw av	av
Stk-LC	Fidelity Dividend Growth (FDGFX)	-20.4	-4.9	4.9	na	av	abv av
Stk-LC	T Rowe Price Spect Gr (PRSGX)	-20.8	-9.9	0.1	8.5	av	abv av
Stk-LC	Vanguard Tot Stk Idx/Inv (VTSMX)	-20.9	-14.3	-0.8	8.6	av	abv av
Stk-LC	Fidelity Spart Total Mkt (FSTMX)	-20.9	-14.3	-0.8	na	av	abv av

Category	Fund (Ticker)	Annual Return (%) 2002	3yr	5yr	10yr	Category Risk	Total Risk
Stk-LC	Vanguard Value Idx/Inv (VIVAX)	-20.9	-9.5	-0.9	9.2	av	abv av
Stk-LC	Schwab Inv 1000 Fd/I (SNXFX)	-21.1	-14.0	-0.4	8.8	blw av	av
Stk-LC	Fidelity Capital Apprec (FDCAX)	-21.2	-15.8	0.3	9.1	high	high
Stk-LC	Janus Growth & Income (JAGIX)	-21.5	-15.8	3.9	11.0	blw av	av
Stk-LC	Vanguard Gr&In/Inv (VQNPX)	-21.9	-14.2	-0.2	9.7	blw av	av
Stk-LC	Vanguard Tx Mg Gr&Inc (VTGIX)	-21.9	-14.4	-0.5	na	blw av	av
Stk-LC	Vanguard 500 Idx/Inv (VFINX)	-22.1	-14.5	-0.6	9.2	av	av
Stk-LC	Fidelity Spart 500 Index (FSMKX)	-22.1	-14.6	-0.7	9.0	av	abv av
Stk-LC	Fidelity Fund (FFIDX)	-22.2	-14.9	0.0	9.8	abv av	abv av
Stk-LC	Vanguard Windsor/Inv (VWNDX)	-22.2	-1.6	1.3	9.8	abv av	abv av
Stk-LC	Amer Cnt Select/Inv (TWCIX)	-22.7	-16.7	-0.8	6.5	low	av
Stk-LC	T Rowe Price Gr Stock (PRGFX)	-22.9	-11.3	1.6	9.8	abv av	abv av
Stk-LC	Amer Cnt Ultra/Inv (TWCUX)	-23.1	-19.2	0.0	8.5	abv av	abv av
Stk-LC	Excelsior Val & Restrctg (UMBIX)	-23.3	-7.8	4.1	14.9	abv av	abv av
Stk-LC	Vanguard Tx Mg Cp Apr (VMCAX)	-23.4	-16.4	-0.1	na	abv av	abv av
Stk-LC	Vanguard Morgan Gr/Inv (VMRGX)	-23.5	-16.6	-1.0	8.1	abv av	abv av
Stk-LC	Fidelity Magellan (FMAGX)	-23.6	-15.1	0.2	9.1	av	abv av
Stk-LC	Vanguard Gr Idx/Inv (VIGRX)	-23.6	-19.7	-1.0	8.6	abv av	abv av
Stk-LC	T Rowe Price Gr & Inc (PRGIX)	-23.8	-6.7	-1.5	7.8	av	abv av
Stk-LC	TIAA-CREF Growth & Income (TIGIX)	-23.8	-15.1	-0.1	na	av	abv av
Stk-LC	T Rowe Price Bl Chp Gr (TRBCX)	-24.2	-14.1	-0.4	na	abv av	abv av
Stk-LC	PBHG Large Cap Value (PLCVX)	-24.4	-2.6	6.6	na	av	abv av
Stk-LC	Vanguard PRIMECAP (VPMCX)	-24.5	-11.9	3.8	13.3	high	high
Stk-LC	Fidelity Blue Chip Growth (FBGRX)	-25.3	-17.6	-1.3	9.1	abv av	abv av
Stk-LC	Amer Cnt Growth/Inv (TWCGX)	-26.1	-19.9	-1.2	5.5	abv av	abv av
Stk-LC	Janus Fund (JANSX)	-27.5	-23.0	-1.4	6.8	high	high
Stk-LC	Fidelity Growth Company (FDGRX)	-33.4	-22.4	1.2	8.8	high	high
Stk-LC	Gabelli Growth (GABGX)	-33.7	-23.3	-3.1	7.5	high	high
Stk-LC	Rydex:OTC/Inv (RYOCX)	-38.5	-37.0	-1.3	na	high	high
Large-Cap Stock Average		**-22.1**	**-13.8**	**-0.9**	**7.9**	—	**abv av**

Note: AAII members who would like performance figures for no-load and low-load mutual funds they own that do not appear in this Guide can access this information on our Web site at www.aaii.com.

Amer Cnt Growth/Inv (TWCGX)

800-345-2021, 816-531-5575
www.americancentury.com

Large-Cap Stock

PERFORMANCE — fund inception date: 10/31/58

	3yr Annual	5yr Annual	10yr Annual	Bull	Bear
Return (%)	-19.9	-1.2	5.5	93.3	-56.4
Differ From Category (+/-)	-6.1 blw av	-0.3 av	-2.4 low	18.6 high	-17.3 low

Standard Deviation	Category Risk Index	Beta
21.7%—abv av	1.13—abv av	1.04

	2002	2001	2000	1999	1998	1997	1996	1995	1994	1993
Return (%)	-26.1	-18.6	-14.7	34.6	36.1	29.2	15.0	20.3	-1.4	3.7
Differ From Category (+/-)	-4.0	-5.8	-9.5	9.2	11.7	2.1	-5.6	-12.6	-1.5	-9.0
Return, Tax-Adjusted (%)	-26.1	-18.6	-16.9	31.6	31.7	25.4	14.3	15.6	-5.5	0.4

PER SHARE DATA

	2002	2001	2000	1999	1998	1997	1996	1995	1994	1993
Dividends, Net Income ($)	0.00	0.00	0.00	0.00	0.00	0.00	0.18	0.06	0.05	0.05
Distrib'ns, Cap Gain ($)	0.00	0.00	3.57	4.13	5.22	4.16	0.24	3.05	3.22	2.76
Net Asset Value ($)	14.42	19.52	24.00	32.28	27.16	24.01	21.88	19.39	18.74	22.40
Expense Ratio (%)	1.00	1.00	1.00	1.00	1.00	1.00	1.00	1.00	1.00	1.00
Yield (%)	0.00	0.00	0.00	0.00	0.00	0.00	0.81	0.26	0.22	0.19
Portfolio Turnover (%)	135	114	102	92	126	75	122	141	100	94
Total Assets (Millions $)	4,115	6,273	8,376	9,630	7,092	5,168	4,667	4,849	4,158	4,552

PORTFOLIO (as of 9/30/02)

Portfolio Manager: G Woodhams/ E Prescott - 1998

Investment Style

✔ Large Cap	✔ Growth
Mid Cap	Value
Small Cap	Grth/Val

Portfolio

0.0% cash	0.0% corp bonds
91.4% stocks	0.0% gov't bonds
0.0% preferred	0.0% muni bonds
0.0% conv't bds/wrnts	8.6% other

SHAREHOLDER INFORMATION

Minimum Investment
Initial: $2,500 — Subsequent: $50

Minimum IRA Investment
Initial: $1,000 — Subsequent: $50

Maximum Fees
Load: none — 12b-1: none
Other: none

Services
✔ IRA
✔ Keogh
✔ Telephone Exchange

Amer Cnt Income & Gr/Inv (BIGRX)

800-345-2021, 816-531-5575
www.americancentury.com

Large-Cap Stock

PERFORMANCE

fund inception date: 12/17/90

	3yr Annual	5yr Annual	10yr Annual	Bull	Bear
Return (%)	-12.8	0.0	9.6	53.6	-39.3
Differ From Category (+/-)	1.0 abv av	0.9 abv av	1.7 high	-21.1 blw av	-0.2 abv av

Standard Deviation	Category Risk Index	Beta
18.3%—av	0.96—blw av	0.96

	2002	2001	2000	1999	1998	1997	1996	1995	1994	1993
Return (%)	-19.3	-8.3	-10.5	17.9	27.6	34.4	24.1	36.8	-0.5	11.3
Differ From Category (+/-)	2.8	4.5	-5.3	-7.5	3.2	7.3	3.5	3.9	-0.6	-1.4
Return, Tax-Adjusted (%)	-19.8	-8.7	-10.8	17.4	26.0	31.4	20.9	34.1	-2.8	9.7

PER SHARE DATA

	2002	2001	2000	1999	1998	1997	1996	1995	1994	1993
Dividends, Net Income ($)	0.32	0.30	0.28	0.33	0.35	0.38	0.43	0.42	0.42	0.42
Distrib'ns, Cap Gain ($)	0.00	0.00	0.00	0.06	1.29	2.29	1.43	0.75	0.65	0.18
Net Asset Value ($)	21.74	27.35	30.19	34.05	29.25	24.30	20.16	17.81	13.92	15.08
Expense Ratio (%)	na	0.68	0.67	0.68	0.69	0.65	0.62	0.70	0.73	0.75
Yield (%)	1.47	1.09	0.92	0.96	1.14	1.42	1.99	2.26	2.88	2.75
Portfolio Turnover (%)	na	61	64	58	86	102	92	69	67	31
Total Assets (Millions $)	3,344	4,474	5,417	6,346	4,284	1,790	715	372	224	229

PORTFOLIO (as of 9/30/02)

Portfolio Manager: Team Managed - 1990

Investment Style

✔ Large Cap	Growth
Mid Cap	Value
Small Cap	✔ Grth/Val

Portfolio

0.0% cash	0.0% corp bonds
99.6% stocks	0.0% gov't bonds
0.4% pref/conv't pref	0.0% muni bonds
0.0% conv't bds/wrnts	0.0% other

SHAREHOLDER INFORMATION

Minimum Investment
Initial: $2,500 Subsequent: $50

Minimum IRA Investment
Initial: $1,000 Subsequent: $50

Maximum Fees
Load: none 12b-1: none
Other: none

Services
✔ IRA
✔ Keogh
✔ Telephone Exchange

Amer Cnt Select/Inv (TWCIX)

800-345-2021, 816-531-5575
www.americancentury.com

Large-Cap Stock

PERFORMANCE — fund inception date: 10/31/58

	3yr Annual	5yr Annual	10yr Annual	Bull	Bear
Return (%)	-16.7	-0.8	6.5	70.8	-48.0
Differ From Category (+/-)	-2.9 blw av	0.1 av	-1.4 blw av	-3.9 abv av	-8.9 blw av

Standard Deviation	Category Risk Index	Beta
16.8%—av	0.87—low	0.87

	2002	2001	2000	1999	1998	1997	1996	1995	1994	1993
Return (%)	-22.7	-18.1	-8.7	22.2	35.6	27.9	19.2	22.6	-8.0	14.6
Differ From Category (+/-)	-0.6	-5.3	-3.5	-3.2	11.2	0.8	-1.4	-10.3	-8.1	1.9
Return, Tax-Adjusted (%)	-22.8	-18.2	-9.8	20.0	30.8	24.4	15.9	18.3	-10.3	10.9

PER SHARE DATA

	2002	2001	2000	1999	1998	1997	1996	1995	1994	1993
Dividends, Net Income ($)	0.07	0.06	0.00	0.00	0.16	0.19	0.32	0.26	0.28	0.43
Distrib'ns, Cap Gain ($)	0.00	0.00	2.79	5.09	9.78	6.35	3.68	4.65	2.87	4.46
Net Asset Value ($)	28.50	37.00	45.29	52.68	47.39	42.59	38.53	35.62	33.10	39.46
Expense Ratio (%)	1.00	1.00	1.00	1.00	1.00	1.00	1.00	1.00	1.00	1.00
Yield (%)	0.24	0.16	0.00	0.00	0.27	0.38	0.75	0.64	0.77	0.97
Portfolio Turnover (%)	168	98	67	130	165	94	105	61	126	82
Total Assets (Millions $)	3,657	4,972	6,474	7,674	6,498	5,019	4,060	3,982	3,995	4,939

PORTFOLIO (as of 9/30/02)

Portfolio Manager: Reynolds/Sykora - 1998

Investment Style

✔ Large Cap — Growth
Mid Cap — Value
Small Cap — ✔ Grth/Val

Portfolio

0.0%	cash	0.0%	corp bonds
95.6%	stocks	0.0%	gov't bonds
0.0%	preferred	0.0%	muni bonds
0.0%	conv't bds/wrnts	4.5%	other

SHAREHOLDER INFORMATION

Minimum Investment
Initial: $2,500 — Subsequent: $50

Minimum IRA Investment
Initial: $1,000 — Subsequent: $50

Maximum Fees
Load: none — 12b-1: none
Other: none

Services
✔ IRA
✔ Keogh
✔ Telephone Exchange

Amer Cnt Ultra/Inv

800-345-2021, 816-531-5575
www.americancentury.com

(TWCUX)

Large-Cap Stock

PERFORMANCE — fund inception date: 11/2/81

	3yr Annual	5yr Annual	10yr Annual	Bull	Bear
Return (%)	-19.2	0.0	8.5	100.0	-52.6
Differ From Category (+/-)	-5.4 blw av	0.9 abv av	0.6 av	25.3 high	-13.5 blw av

Standard Deviation	Category Risk Index	Beta
21.8%—abv av	1.14—abv av	1.06

	2002	2001	2000	1999	1998	1997	1996	1995	1994	1993
Return (%)	-23.1	-14.6	-19.9	41.4	34.5	23.1	13.8	37.6	-3.6	21.8
Differ From Category (+/-)	-1.0	-1.8	-14.7	16.0	10.1	-4.0	-6.8	4.7	-3.7	9.1
Return, Tax-Adjusted (%)	-23.2	-14.6	-21.8	40.6	32.2	18.0	12.0	35.8	-4.4	21.8

PER SHARE DATA

	2002	2001	2000	1999	1998	1997	1996	1995	1994	1993
Dividends, Net Income ($)	0.06	0.00	0.00	0.00	0.00	0.01	0.00	0.00	0.00	0.00
Distrib'ns, Cap Gain ($)	0.00	0.00	4.40	1.37	3.12	7.07	1.68	1.29	0.64	0.00
Net Asset Value ($)	21.18	27.64	32.37	45.78	33.41	27.30	28.09	26.11	19.95	21.39
Expense Ratio (%)	0.99	0.98	0.99	1.00	1.00	1.00	1.00	1.00	1.00	1.00
Yield (%)	0.28	0.00	0.00	0.00	0.00	0.02	0.00	0.00	0.00	0.00
Portfolio Turnover (%)	92	86	62	42	128	107	87	87	78	53
Total Assets (Millions $)	19,209	26,911	33,786	43,192	30,076	22,455	18,418	14,551	9,850	8,362

PORTFOLIO (as of 9/30/02)

Portfolio Manager: Stowers/Wimberly/Slome - 1998

Investment Style

✔ Large Cap	✔ Growth
✔ Mid Cap	Value
Small Cap	Grth/Val

Portfolio

1.7%	cash	0.4%	corp bonds
97.9%	stocks	0.0%	gov't bonds
0.0%	preferred	0.0%	muni bonds
0.0%	conv't bds/wrnts	0.0%	other

SHAREHOLDER INFORMATION

Minimum Investment
Initial: $2,500 Subsequent: $50

Minimum IRA Investment
Initial: $1,000 Subsequent: $50

Maximum Fees
Load: none 12b-1: none
Other: none

Services
✔ IRA
✔ Keogh
✔ Telephone Exchange

Babson Value Fund

800-422-2766, 816-751-5900
www.babsonfunds.com

(BVALX)

Large-Cap Stock

PERFORMANCE

fund inception date: 12/21/84

	3yr Annual	5yr Annual	10yr Annual	Bull	Bear
Return (%)	-3.3	-0.6	9.5	13.7	-4.0
Differ From Category (+/-)	10.5 high	0.3 av	1.6 abv av	-61.0 low	35.1 high

Standard Deviation	Category Risk Index	Beta
17.1%—av	0.90—blw av	0.61

	2002	2001	2000	1999	1998	1997	1996	1995	1994	1993
Return (%)	-14.4	-3.1	9.0	1.0	6.0	26.5	22.7	31.7	2.5	22.8
Differ From Category (+/-)	7.7	9.7	14.2	-24.4	-18.4	-0.6	2.1	-1.2	2.4	10.1
Return, Tax-Adjusted (%)	-14.8	-4.0	7.1	-0.2	4.6	25.2	21.5	30.4	1.1	20.6

PER SHARE DATA

	2002	2001	2000	1999	1998	1997	1996	1995	1994	1993
Dividends, Net Income ($)	0.46	0.73	0.91	0.69	0.57	0.50	0.49	0.56	0.47	0.53
Distrib'ns, Cap Gain ($)	0.00	0.67	2.35	1.40	1.97	1.46	0.60	0.34	0.60	0.91
Net Asset Value ($)	35.27	41.70	44.55	44.25	45.88	45.71	37.74	31.68	24.78	25.22
Expense Ratio (%)	0.96	0.96	0.96	0.96	0.98	0.97	0.96	0.98	0.99	1.00
Yield (%)	1.30	1.72	1.94	1.51	1.19	1.05	1.27	1.74	1.85	2.02
Portfolio Turnover (%)	25	27	18	13	42	17	11	6	14	26
Total Assets (Millions $)	358	432	515	823	1,453	1,421	783	308	121	45

PORTFOLIO (as of 11/30/02)

Portfolio Manager: Anthony Maramarco - 1999

Investment Style

✔ Large Cap	Growth
✔ Mid Cap	✔ Value
Small Cap	Grth/Val

Portfolio

0.0%	cash	0.0%	corp bonds
100.0%	stocks	0.0%	gov't bonds
0.0%	preferred	0.0%	muni bonds
0.0%	conv't bds/wrnts	0.0%	other

SHAREHOLDER INFORMATION

Minimum Investment
Initial: $1,000 Subsequent: $100

Minimum IRA Investment
Initial: $250 Subsequent: $100

Maximum Fees
Load: none 12b-1: none
Other: none

Services
✔ IRA
✔ Keogh
✔ Telephone Exchange

Clipper Fund
(CFIMX)
Large-Cap Stock

800-776-5033, 310-247-3940
www.clipperfund.com

PERFORMANCE **fund inception date: 2/29/84**

	3yr Annual	5yr Annual	10yr Annual	Bull	Bear
Return (%)	12.7	10.8	15.1	13.0	35.7
Differ From Category (+/-)	26.5 high	11.7 high	7.2 high	-61.7 low	74.8 high

Standard Deviation	Category Risk Index	Beta
15.6%—av	0.81—low	0.49

	2002	2001	2000	1999	1998	1997	1996	1995	1994	1993
Return (%)	-5.5	10.2	37.4	-2.0	19.2	30.4	19.4	45.2	-2.4	11.1
Differ From Category (+/-)	16.6	23.0	42.6	-27.4	-5.2	3.3	-1.2	12.3	-2.5	-1.6
Return, Tax-Adjusted (%)	-6.5	9.0	33.7	-4.8	15.0	26.7	16.9	41.3	-4.1	6.9

PER SHARE DATA

	2002	2001	2000	1999	1998	1997	1996	1995	1994	1993
Dividends, Net Income ($)	1.07	1.07	1.87	2.24	1.63	1.35	0.83	0.75	0.70	0.75
Distrib'ns, Cap Gain ($)	2.11	2.74	8.38	6.15	12.86	9.83	4.27	5.42	2.00	6.72
Net Asset Value ($)	75.73	83.53	79.25	65.28	75.37	76.86	67.57	60.74	46.09	50.02
Expense Ratio (%)	na	1.08	1.09	1.10	1.06	1.08	1.08	1.12	1.11	1.11
Yield (%)	1.37	1.24	2.13	3.13	1.84	1.55	1.15	1.13	1.45	1.32
Portfolio Turnover (%)	na	23	46	63	65	31	24	37	45	64
Total Assets (Millions $)	5,016	2,685	1,366	960	1,234	824	542	403	247	271

PORTFOLIO (as of 9/30/02)

Portfolio Manager: Team Managed - 1984

Investment Style

✔ Large Cap Growth
✔ Mid Cap ✔ Value
Small Cap Grth/Val

Portfolio

0.5%	cash	3.3%	corp bonds
86.8%	stocks	8.1%	gov't bonds
0.0%	preferred	0.0%	muni bonds
0.0%	conv't bds/wrnts	1.4%	other

SHAREHOLDER INFORMATION

Minimum Investment
Initial: $5,000 Subsequent: $1,000

Minimum IRA Investment
Initial: $2,000 Subsequent: $200

Maximum Fees
Load: none 12b-1: none
Other: none

Services
✔ IRA
Keogh
✔ Telephone Exchange

Dodge & Cox Stock (DODGX)

800-621-3979, 415-981-1710
www.dodgeandcox.com

Large-Cap Stock

PERFORMANCE

fund inception date: 1/4/65

	3yr Annual	5yr Annual	10yr Annual	Bull	Bear
Return (%)	4.3	7.5	14.1	42.7	4.9
Differ From Category (+/-)	18.1 high	8.4 high	6.2 high	-32.0 blw av	44.0 high

Standard Deviation	Category Risk Index	Beta
17.3%—av	0.91—blw av	0.71

	2002	2001	2000	1999	1998	1997	1996	1995	1994	1993
Return (%)	-10.5	9.3	16.3	20.2	5.3	28.4	22.2	33.3	5.1	18.3
Differ From Category (+/-)	11.6	22.1	21.5	-5.2	-19.1	1.3	1.6	0.4	5.0	5.6
Return, Tax-Adjusted (%)	-11.2	7.9	12.1	18.1	3.1	26.1	20.8	31.0	3.8	15.8

PER SHARE DATA

	2002	2001	2000	1999	1998	1997	1996	1995	1994	1993
Dividends, Net Income ($)	1.51	1.73	2.09	1.48	1.56	1.49	1.29	1.46	1.15	1.05
Distrib'ns, Cap Gain ($)	0.42	3.20	17.10	6.70	7.42	6.09	1.68	2.46	0.89	2.84
Net Asset Value ($)	88.05	100.51	96.67	100.52	90.70	94.57	79.81	67.83	53.94	53.23
Expense Ratio (%)	na	0.54	0.54	0.55	0.57	0.57	0.59	0.61	0.61	0.62
Yield (%)	1.70	1.66	1.83	1.38	1.58	1.48	1.58	2.07	2.09	1.87
Portfolio Turnover (%)	na	10	32	18	19	19	10	13	7	15
Total Assets (Millions $)	13,859	9,395	5,728	4,624	4,400	4,087	2,252	1,227	543	435

PORTFOLIO (as of 9/30/02)

Portfolio Manager: Team Managed - 1965

Investment Style

✔ Large Cap	Growth
✔ Mid Cap	✔ Value
Small Cap	Grth/Val

Portfolio

3.4%	cash	1.1%	corp bonds
93.5%	stocks	0.0%	gov't bonds
2.1%	pref/conv't pref	0.0%	muni bonds
0.0%	conv't bds/wrnts	0.0%	other

SHAREHOLDER INFORMATION

Minimum Investment
Initial: $2,500 Subsequent: $100

Minimum IRA Investment
Initial: $1,000 Subsequent: $100

Maximum Fees
Load: none 12b-1: none
Other: none

Services
✔ IRA
✔ Keogh
✔ Telephone Exchange

Dreyfus Appreciation (DGAGX)

800-645-6561, 516-794-5452
www.dreyfus.com

Large-Cap Stock

PERFORMANCE — fund inception date: 1/18/84

	3yr Annual	5yr Annual	10yr Annual	Bull	Bear
Return (%)	-9.0	1.6	9.6	40.0	-29.6
Differ From Category (+/-)	4.8 abv av	2.5 abv av	1.7 abv av	-34.7 blw av	9.5 abv av

Standard Deviation	Category Risk Index	Beta
14.8%—av	0.77—low	0.71

	2002	2001	2000	1999	1998	1997	1996	1995	1994	1993
Return (%)	-17.1	-10.7	1.8	9.9	30.8	27.8	25.6	37.8	3.6	0.7
Differ From Category (+/-)	5.0	2.1	7.0	-15.5	6.4	0.7	5.0	4.9	3.5	-12.0
Return, Tax-Adjusted (%)	-17.4	-11.0	0.1	9.5	30.5	27.3	25.1	36.9	2.8	-0.1

PER SHARE DATA

	2002	2001	2000	1999	1998	1997	1996	1995	1994	1993
Dividends, Net Income ($)	0.29	0.30	0.28	0.23	0.22	0.26	0.25	0.33	0.27	0.26
Distrib'ns, Cap Gain ($)	0.01	0.00	3.22	0.30	0.07	0.06	0.00	0.02	0.00	0.06
Net Asset Value ($)	31.20	38.02	42.94	45.73	42.07	32.38	25.58	20.55	15.17	14.92
Expense Ratio (%)	na	0.91	0.88	0.88	0.89	0.87	0.91	0.92	0.96	1.07
Yield (%)	0.92	0.78	0.60	0.49	0.52	0.80	0.97	1.60	1.77	1.73
Portfolio Turnover (%)	na	5	4	11	1	1	4	4	6	9
Total Assets (Millions $)	3,274	3,427	3,853	4,750	4,168	1,978	876	460	233	237

PORTFOLIO (as of 9/30/02)

Portfolio Manager: Fayez Sarofim - 1990

Investment Style

✔ Large Cap	Growth
Mid Cap	Value
Small Cap	✔ Grth/Val

Portfolio

5.5%	cash	0.0%	corp bonds
93.4%	stocks	0.0%	gov't bonds
1.1%	pref/conv't pref	0.0%	muni bonds
0.0%	conv't bds/wrnts	0.0%	other

SHAREHOLDER INFORMATION

Minimum Investment
Initial: $2,500 Subsequent: $100

Minimum IRA Investment
Initial: $750 Subsequent: $1

Maximum Fees
Load: none 12b-1: none
Other: none

Services
✔ IRA
✔ Keogh
✔ Telephone Exchange

Excelsior Val & Restrctg (UMBIX)

800-446-1012, 617-483-7297
www.excelsiorfunds.com

Large-Cap Stock

PERFORMANCE

fund inception date: 12/31/92

	3yr Annual	5yr Annual	10yr Annual	Bull	Bear
Return (%)	-7.8	4.1	14.9	86.8	-30.7
Differ From Category (+/-)	6.0 abv av	5.0 high	7.0 high	12.1 abv av	8.4 abv av

Standard Deviation	Category Risk Index	Beta
21.1%—abv av	1.10—abv av	1.02

	2002	2001	2000	1999	1998	1997	1996	1995	1994	1993
Return (%)	-23.3	-4.9	7.2	41.9	10.3	32.4	25.0	38.8	2.4	39.9
Differ From Category (+/-)	-1.2	7.9	12.4	16.5	-14.1	5.3	4.4	5.9	2.3	27.2
Return, Tax-Adjusted (%)	-23.5	-5.0	6.5	41.8	10.0	32.0	23.6	37.7	1.9	39.4

PER SHARE DATA

	2002	2001	2000	1999	1998	1997	1996	1995	1994	1993
Dividends, Net Income ($)	0.13	0.08	0.59	0.08	0.11	0.09	0.12	0.09	0.06	0.07
Distrib'ns, Cap Gain ($)	0.00	0.00	0.00	0.00	0.13	0.09	0.47	0.23	0.09	0.01
Net Asset Value ($)	24.46	32.06	33.82	32.14	22.71	20.82	15.87	13.20	9.76	9.69
Expense Ratio (%)	0.94	0.95	0.90	0.93	0.89	0.91	0.91	0.98	0.99	0.99
Yield (%)	0.53	0.24	1.74	0.24	0.48	0.43	0.73	0.67	0.60	0.72
Portfolio Turnover (%)	8	15	20	43	30	62	56	82	75	9
Total Assets (Millions $)	1,816	2,221	1,730	964	597	230	111	57	25	7

PORTFOLIO (as of 9/30/02)

Portfolio Manager: David Williams - 1992

Investment Style

✔ Large Cap   Growth
✔ Mid Cap   ✔ Value
Small Cap   Grth/Val

Portfolio

-0.6%	cash	0.0%	corp bonds
100.6%	stocks	0.0%	gov't bonds
0.0%	pref/conv't pref	0.0%	muni bonds
0.0%	conv't bds/wrnts	0.0%	other

SHAREHOLDER INFORMATION

Minimum Investment
Initial: $500   Subsequent: $50

Minimum IRA Investment
Initial: $250   Subsequent: $50

Maximum Fees
Load: none   12b-1: none
Other: none

Services
✔ IRA
✔ Keogh
✔ Telephone Exchange

Fidelity Blue Chip Growth (FBGRX)

800-544-8544, 800-522-7297
www.fidelity.com

Large-Cap Stock

PERFORMANCE — fund inception date: 12/31/87

	3yr Annual	5yr Annual	10yr Annual	Bull	Bear
Return (%)	-17.6	-1.3	9.1	74.3	-50.6
Differ From Category (+/-)	-3.8 blw av	-0.4 blw av	1.2 abv av	-0.4 abv av	-11.5 blw av

Standard Deviation	Category Risk Index	Beta
20.9%—abv av	1.09—abv av	1.05

	2002	2001	2000	1999	1998	1997	1996	1995	1994	1993
Return (%)	-25.3	-16.5	-10.5	24.2	34.7	27.0	15.3	28.3	9.8	24.5
Differ From Category (+/-)	-3.2	-3.7	-5.3	-1.2	10.3	-0.1	-5.3	-4.6	9.7	11.8
Return, Tax-Adjusted (%)	-25.4	-16.5	-11.3	23.3	33.6	25.6	12.9	25.5	9.1	19.4

PER SHARE DATA

	2002	2001	2000	1999	1998	1997	1996	1995	1994	1993
Dividends, Net Income ($)	0.13	0.06	0.00	0.14	0.10	0.26	0.28	0.12	0.00	0.01
Distrib'ns, Cap Gain ($)	0.00	0.00	2.52	2.07	2.06	1.75	2.25	2.47	0.58	4.12
Net Asset Value ($)	31.94	42.94	51.53	60.11	50.39	39.46	32.69	30.77	25.95	24.17
Expense Ratio (%)	0.74	0.87	0.88	0.70	0.70	0.78	0.95	1.02	1.22	1.25
Yield (%)	0.40	0.13	0.00	0.22	0.19	0.63	0.80	0.36	0.00	0.03
Portfolio Turnover (%)	33	46	40	38	49	51	206	182	271	319
Total Assets (Millions $)	16,682	21,958	26,646	27,876	19,904	13,428	9,569	7,801	3,287	1,094

PORTFOLIO (as of 7/31/02)

Portfolio Manager: John McDowell - 1996

Investment Style

✔ Large Cap	✔ Growth
Mid Cap	Value
Small Cap	Grth/Val

Portfolio

0.0%	cash	0.0%	corp bonds
98.0%	stocks	0.0%	gov't bonds
0.0%	preferred	0.0%	muni bonds
0.0%	conv't bds/wrnts	2.0%	other

SHAREHOLDER INFORMATION

Minimum Investment
Initial: $2,500 — Subsequent: $250

Minimum IRA Investment
Initial: $500 — Subsequent: $250

Maximum Fees
Load: none — 12b-1: none
Other: none

Services
✔ IRA
✔ Keogh
✔ Telephone Exchange

Fidelity Capital Apprec (FDCAX)

800-544-8544, 800-522-7297
www.fidelity.com

Large-Cap Stock

PERFORMANCE

fund inception date: 11/26/86

	3yr Annual	5yr Annual	10yr Annual	Bull	Bear
Return (%)	-15.8	0.3	9.1	107.7	-49.1
Differ From Category (+/-)	-2.0 blw av	1.2 abv av	1.2 abv av	33.0 high	-10.0 blw av

Standard Deviation	Category Risk Index	Beta
25.9%—high	1.36—high	1.18

	2002	2001	2000	1999	1998	1997	1996	1995	1994	1993
Return (%)	-21.2	-7.5	-18.1	45.8	16.9	26.5	15.1	18.7	2.5	33.4
Differ From Category (+/-)	.0.9	5.3	-12.9	20.4	-7.5	-0.6	-5.5	-14.2	2.4	20.7
Return, Tax-Adjusted (%)	-21.2	-7.5	-19.7	43.4	16.2	23.1	12.2	15.8	-1.0	30.9

PER SHARE DATA

	2002	2001	2000	1999	1998	1997	1996	1995	1994	1993
Dividends, Net Income ($)	0.00	0.00	0.15	0.57	0.10	0.08	0.12	0.40	0.17	0.10
Distrib'ns, Cap Gain ($)	0.00	0.00	2.13	1.49	0.45	2.85	1.54	1.00	1.85	1.06
Net Asset Value ($)	16.18	20.55	22.23	29.87	22.07	19.38	17.64	16.78	15.31	16.92
Expense Ratio (%)	1.03	0.91	0.83	0.65	0.67	0.66	0.80	1.07	1.17	0.86
Yield (%)	0.00	0.00	0.61	1.81	0.44	0.35	0.62	2.24	0.99	0.55
Portfolio Turnover (%)	80	120	85	78	121	176	205	93	124	120
Total Assets (Millions $)	1,795	2,311	2,707	3,686	2,602	2,109	1,642	1,669	1,623	1,428

PORTFOLIO (as of 10/31/02)

Portfolio Manager: Harry Lange - 1996

Investment Style

✔ Large Cap	✔ Growth
✔ Mid Cap	Value
Small Cap	Grth/Val

Portfolio

1.1%	cash	0.0%	corp bonds
97.4%	stocks	0.0%	gov't bonds
0.0%	preferred	0.0%	muni bonds
0.0%	conv't bds/wrnts	1.5%	other

SHAREHOLDER INFORMATION

Minimum Investment
Initial: $2,500 Subsequent: $250

Minimum IRA Investment
Initial: $500 Subsequent: $250

Maximum Fees
Load: none 12b-1: none
Other: none

Services
✔ IRA
✔ Keogh
✔ Telephone Exchange

Fidelity Contrafund (FCNTX)

800-544-8544, 800-522-7297
www.fidelity.com

Large-Cap Stock

PERFORMANCE

fund inception date: 5/17/67

	3yr Annual	5yr Annual	10yr Annual	Bull	Bear
Return (%)	-9.7	3.9	11.5	73.2	-31.0
Differ From Category (+/-)	4.1 abv av	4.8 high	3.6 high	-1.5 abv av	8.1 abv av

Standard Deviation	Category Risk Index	Beta
12.6%—blw av	0.65—low	0.50

	2002	2001	2000	1999	1998	1997	1996	1995	1994	1993
Return (%)	-9.6	-12.5	-6.8	25.0	31.5	22.9	21.9	36.2	-1.1	21.4
Differ From Category (+/-)	12.5	0.3	-1.6	-0.4	7.1	-4.2	1.3	3.3	-1.2	8.7
Return, Tax-Adjusted (%)	-9.6	-12.7	-9.2	21.2	29.4	20.4	19.0	33.2	-1.3	18.8

PER SHARE DATA

	2002	2001	2000	1999	1998	1997	1996	1995	1994	1993
Dividends, Net Income ($)	0.05	0.22	0.24	0.28	0.30	0.35	0.38	0.09	0.00	0.18
Distrib'ns, Cap Gain ($)	0.00	0.00	6.62	10.22	4.22	4.56	3.45	3.13	0.22	2.25
Net Asset Value ($)	38.60	42.77	49.18	60.02	56.81	46.63	42.15	38.02	30.28	30.84
Expense Ratio (%)	na	0.91	0.84	0.65	0.65	0.67	0.79	0.97	1.03	1.06
Yield (%)	0.12	0.51	0.43	0.39	0.49	0.68	0.83	0.21	0.00	0.54
Portfolio Turnover (%)	na	141	166	177	197	144	159	210	235	255
Total Assets (Millions $)	27,695	32,320	40,284	46,927	38,821	30,808	23,797	14,831	8,682	6,193

PORTFOLIO (as of 6/30/02)

Portfolio Manager: William Danoff - 1990

Investment Style

✔ Large Cap	✔ Growth
✔ Mid Cap	Value
Small Cap	Grth/Val

Portfolio

8.8% cash	0.3% corp bonds
90.7% stocks	0.0% gov't bonds
0.0% preferred	0.0% muni bonds
0.2% conv't bds/wrnts	0.0% other

SHAREHOLDER INFORMATION

Minimum Investment
Initial: $2,500 Subsequent: $250

Minimum IRA Investment
Initial: $500 Subsequent: $250

Maximum Fees
Load: 3.00% front 12b-1: none
Other: none

Services
✔ IRA
✔ Keogh
✔ Telephone Exchange

Fidelity Disciplined Eqty (FDEQX)

800-544-8544, 800-522-7297
www.fidelity.com

Large-Cap Stock

PERFORMANCE

fund inception date: 12/28/88

	3yr Annual	5yr Annual	10yr Annual	Bull	Bear
Return (%)	-12.3	0.1	8.8	62.7	-38.0
Differ From Category (+/-)	1.5 abv av	1.0 abv av	0.9 av	-12.0 av	1.1 abv av

Standard Deviation	Category Risk Index	Beta
16.5%—av	0.86—low	0.84

	2002	2001	2000	1999	1998	1997	1996	1995	1994	1993
Return (%)	-18.5	-14.2	-3.4	22.4	21.8	33.3	15.1	29.0	3.0	13.9
Differ From Category (+/-)	3.6	-1.4	1.8	-3.0	-2.6	6.2	-5.5	-3.9	2.9	1.2
Return, Tax-Adjusted (%)	-18.6	-14.3	-5.9	18.7	20.1	29.9	12.6	24.9	1.7	11.7

PER SHARE DATA

	2002	2001	2000	1999	1998	1997	1996	1995	1994	1993
Dividends, Net Income ($)	0.03	0.05	0.16	0.27	0.22	0.25	0.23	0.30	0.25	0.21
Distrib'ns, Cap Gain ($)	0.00	0.00	3.57	4.90	1.82	3.30	1.49	2.23	0.52	1.04
Net Asset Value ($)	17.97	22.10	25.82	30.51	29.32	25.86	22.04	20.64	17.94	18.18
Expense Ratio (%)	1.00	0.84	0.79	0.62	0.64	0.69	0.81	0.92	1.05	1.09
Yield (%)	0.16	0.22	0.54	0.76	0.70	0.85	0.97	1.31	1.35	1.09
Portfolio Turnover (%)	68	101	118	113	125	127	297	222	143	279
Total Assets (Millions $)	2,752	2,991	3,393	3,613	3,145	2,557	2,099	2,145	1,160	795

PORTFOLIO (as of 10/31/02)

Portfolio Manager: Steven Snider - 2000

Investment Style

✔ Large Cap   Growth
✔ Mid Cap   Value
Small Cap   ✔ Grth/Val

Portfolio

0.1%	cash	0.4%	corp bonds
94.6%	stocks	0.0%	gov't bonds
0.0%	preferred	0.0%	muni bonds
0.0%	conv't bds/wrnts	4.9%	other

SHAREHOLDER INFORMATION

Minimum Investment
Initial: $2,500   Subsequent: $250

Minimum IRA Investment
Initial: $500   Subsequent: $250

Maximum Fees
Load: none   12b-1: none
Other: none

Services
✔ IRA
✔ Keogh
✔ Telephone Exchange

Fidelity Dividend Growth (FDGFX)

800-544-8544, 800-522-7297
www.fidelity.com

Large-Cap Stock

PERFORMANCE — fund inception date: 4/28/93

	3yr Annual	5yr Annual	10yr Annual	Bull	Bear
Return (%)	-4.9	4.9	na	43.3	-23.4
Differ From Category (+/-)	8.9 high	5.8 high	na	-31.4 blw av	15.7 high

Standard Deviation	Category Risk Index	Beta
19.8%—abv av	1.03—av	1.00

	2002	2001	2000	1999	1998	1997	1996	1995	1994	1993
Return (%)	-20.4	-3.7	12.2	8.8	35.8	27.8	30.1	37.5	4.2	—
Differ From Category (+/-)	1.7	9.1	17.4	-16.6	11.4	0.7	9.5	4.6	4.1	—
Return, Tax-Adjusted (%)	-20.7	-4.1	10.3	7.1	33.7	25.3	29.2	34.8	3.6	—

PER SHARE DATA

	2002	2001	2000	1999	1998	1997	1996	1995	1994	1993
Dividends, Net Income ($)	0.22	0.15	0.18	0.14	0.13	0.15	0.09	0.09	0.01	—
Distrib'ns, Cap Gain ($)	0.00	0.33	2.40	2.14	2.19	2.19	0.37	1.07	0.24	—
Net Asset Value ($)	22.32	28.33	29.96	28.99	28.73	23.27	20.09	15.84	12.37	—
Expense Ratio (%)	0.95	0.94	0.77	0.84	0.86	0.92	0.99	1.19	1.40	—
Yield (%)	0.98	0.52	0.55	0.44	0.42	0.58	0.43	0.53	0.07	—
Portfolio Turnover (%)	81	88	86	104	109	141	129	162	291	—
Total Assets (Millions $)	13,479	15,210	11,781	12,623	10,368	4,480	2,345	528	102	—

PORTFOLIO (as of 7/31/02)

Portfolio Manager: Charles Mangum - 1997

Investment Style

✔ Large Cap	Growth
Mid Cap	✔ Value
Small Cap	Grth/Val

Portfolio

0.0%	cash	2.1%	corp bonds
92.4%	stocks	0.1%	gov't bonds
0.0%	pref/conv't pref	0.0%	muni bonds
0.7%	conv't bds/wrnts	4.7%	other

SHAREHOLDER INFORMATION

Minimum Investment
Initial: $2,500 — Subsequent: $250

Minimum IRA Investment
Initial: $500 — Subsequent: $250

Maximum Fees
Load: none — 12b-1: none
Other: none

Services
✔ IRA
✔ Keogh
✔ Telephone Exchange

Fidelity Equity Income

800-544-8544, 800-522-7297
www.fidelity.com

(FEQIX)

Large-Cap Stock

PERFORMANCE

fund inception date: 5/16/66

	3yr Annual	5yr Annual	10yr Annual	Bull	Bear
Return (%)	-5.1	0.5	10.0	28.5	-20.0
Differ From Category (+/-)	8.7 high	1.4 abv av	2.1 high	-46.2 low	19.1 high

Standard Deviation	Category Risk Index	Beta
17.8%—av	0.93—blw av	0.81

	2002	2001	2000	1999	1998	1997	1996	1995	1994	1993
Return (%)	-17.1	-5.0	8.5	7.1	12.5	29.9	21.0	31.8	0.2	21.3
Differ From Category (+/-)	5.0	7.8	13.7	-18.3	-11.9	2.8	0.4	-1.1	0.1	8.6
Return, Tax-Adjusted (%)	-17.7	-6.0	6.6	4.7	10.9	28.1	18.6	29.3	-2.8	19.6

PER SHARE DATA

	2002	2001	2000	1999	1998	1997	1996	1995	1994	1993
Dividends, Net Income ($)	0.68	0.76	0.87	0.80	0.85	0.96	1.02	0.96	0.98	1.15
Distrib'ns, Cap Gain ($)	0.14	1.18	3.32	5.14	2.39	2.04	1.84	1.36	2.22	0.12
Net Asset Value ($)	39.67	48.77	53.43	53.48	55.55	52.41	42.83	37.93	30.70	33.84
Expense Ratio (%)	0.67	0.67	0.67	0.67	0.65	0.66	0.67	0.69	0.66	0.67
Yield (%)	1.70	1.52	1.53	1.36	1.46	1.76	2.28	2.44	2.97	3.38
Portfolio Turnover (%)	23	25	26	30	23	30	39	50	70	84
Total Assets (Millions $)	17,733	21,831	22,352	22,828	23,707	21,177	14,258	10,492	7,412	6,641

PORTFOLIO (as of 7/31/02)

Portfolio Manager: Stephen Petersen - 1993

Investment Style

✔ Large Cap	Growth
Mid Cap	✔ Value
Small Cap	Grth/Val

Portfolio

0.0%	cash	1.8%	corp bonds
94.8%	stocks	0.1%	gov't bonds
2.0%	pref/conv't pref	0.0%	muni bonds
0.1%	conv't bds/wrnts	1.3%	other

SHAREHOLDER INFORMATION

Minimum Investment
Initial: $2,500 Subsequent: $250

Minimum IRA Investment
Initial: $500 Subsequent: $250

Maximum Fees
Load: none 12b-1: none
Other: none

Services
✔ IRA
✔ Keogh
✔ Telephone Exchange

Fidelity Equity Income II (FEQTX)

800-544-8544, 800-522-7297
www.fidelity.com

Large-Cap Stock

PERFORMANCE — fund inception date: 8/21/90

	3yr Annual	5yr Annual	10yr Annual	Bull	Bear
Return (%)	-5.5	1.6	9.7	30.4	-23.1
Differ From Category (+/-)	8.3 high	2.5 abv av	1.8 high	-44.3 low	16.0 high

Standard Deviation	Category Risk Index	Beta
17.6%—av	0.92—blw av	0.84

	2002	2001	2000	1999	1998	1997	1996	1995	1994	1993
Return (%)	-15.4	-7.1	7.4	4.3	22.9	27.1	18.7	26.3	3.1	18.8
Differ From Category (+/-)	6.7	5.7	12.6	-21.1	-1.5	0.0	-1.9	-6.6	3.0	6.1
Return, Tax-Adjusted (%)	-16.0	-8.3	3.2	1.5	20.5	24.2	16.3	24.6	0.9	16.5

PER SHARE DATA

	2002	2001	2000	1999	1998	1997	1996	1995	1994	1993
Dividends, Net Income ($)	0.24	0.33	0.42	0.36	0.33	0.43	0.51	0.37	0.39	0.45
Distrib'ns, Cap Gain ($)	0.21	0.79	4.98	3.50	2.65	2.63	1.14	0.55	0.88	0.73
Net Asset Value ($)	17.39	21.03	23.86	27.37	30.01	27.01	23.75	21.43	17.72	18.41
Expense Ratio (%)	na	0.62	0.63	0.66	0.66	0.68	0.72	0.78	0.81	0.88
Yield (%)	1.36	1.51	1.45	1.16	1.01	1.45	2.04	1.68	2.09	2.35
Portfolio Turnover (%)	na	136	151	71	62	77	46	51	75	55
Total Assets (Millions $)	9,400	12,211	13,914	17,579	19,453	16,977	15,238	11,977	7,697	5,021

PORTFOLIO (as of 5/31/02)

Portfolio Manager: Stephen Dufour - 2000

Investment Style

✔ Large Cap	Growth
Mid Cap	✔ Value
Small Cap	Grth/Val

Portfolio

0.1%	cash	2.7%	corp bonds
91.6%	stocks	0.1%	gov't bonds
2.8%	pref/conv't pref	0.0%	muni bonds
0.6%	conv't bds/wrnts	2.2%	other

SHAREHOLDER INFORMATION

Minimum Investment
Initial: $2,500 — Subsequent: $250

Minimum IRA Investment
Initial: $500 — Subsequent: $250

Maximum Fees
Load: none — 12b-1: none
Other: none

Services
✔ IRA
✔ Keogh
✔ Telephone Exchange

Fidelity Export & Multinatl (FEXPX)

800-522-7297
www.fidelity.com

Large-Cap Stock

PERFORMANCE — fund inception date: 10/4/94

	3yr Annual	5yr Annual	10yr Annual	Bull	Bear
Return (%)	-5.9	7.6	na	88.7	-28.7
Differ From Category (+/-)	7.9 high	8.5 high	na	14.0 abv av	10.4 abv av

Standard Deviation	Category Risk Index	Beta
19.4%—abv av	1.01—av	0.90

	2002	2001	2000	1999	1998	1997	1996	1995	1994	1993
Return (%)	-18.6	0.7	1.4	41.8	22.4	23.6	38.6	32.2	—	—
Differ From Category (+/-)	3.5	13.5	6.6	16.4	-2.0	-3.5	18.0	-0.7	—	—
Return, Tax-Adjusted (%)	-18.7	0.6	-3.5	36.9	21.5	19.1	36.7	29.9	—	—

PER SHARE DATA

	2002	2001	2000	1999	1998	1997	1996	1995	1994	1993
Dividends, Net Income ($)	0.05	0.03	0.10	0.05	0.00	0.00	0.00	0.00	—	—
Distrib'ns, Cap Gain ($)	0.00	0.00	5.21	4.80	0.77	3.79	0.86	0.84	—	—
Net Asset Value ($)	13.75	16.97	16.88	21.97	19.88	17.02	16.75	12.72	—	—
Expense Ratio (%)	0.78	0.81	0.86	0.86	0.93	0.98	1.03	1.22	—	—
Yield (%)	0.36	0.17	0.45	0.18	0.00	0.00	0.00	0.00	—	—
Portfolio Turnover (%)	228	170	380	265	281	429	313	245	—	—
Total Assets (Millions $)	674	672	494	514	411	465	397	382	—	—

PORTFOLIO (as of 8/31/02)

Portfolio Manager: Tim Cohen - 2002

Investment Style

✔ Large Cap ✔ Growth
✔ Mid Cap Value
Small Cap Grth/Val

Portfolio

0.0%	cash	0.0%	corp bonds
98.7%	stocks	0.4%	gov't bonds
0.0%	preferred	0.0%	muni bonds
0.0%	conv't bds/wrnts	0.9%	other

SHAREHOLDER INFORMATION

Minimum Investment
Initial: $2,500 Subsequent: $250

Minimum IRA Investment
Initial: $500 Subsequent: $250

Maximum Fees
Load: 0.75% redemption 12b-1: none
Other: redemption fee applies for 1 month

Services
✔ IRA
✔ Keogh
✔ Telephone Exchange

Fidelity Fifty (FFTYX)

800-544-8544, 800-522-7297
www.fidelity.com

Large-Cap Stock

PERFORMANCE — fund inception date: 9/20/93

	3yr Annual	5yr Annual	10yr Annual	Bull	Bear
Return (%)	-5.6	7.1	na	98.6	-27.2
Differ From Category (+/-)	8.2 high	8.0 high	na	23.9 high	11.9 abv av

Standard Deviation	Category Risk Index	Beta
20.3%—abv av	1.06—abv av	0.57

	2002	2001	2000	1999	1998	1997	1996	1995	1994	1993
Return (%)	0.3	-12.4	-4.5	45.7	15.5	23.0	15.9	32.1	3.9	—
Differ From Category (+/-)	22.4	0.4	0.7	20.3	-8.9	-4.1	-4.7	-0.8	3.8	—
Return, Tax-Adjusted (%)	0.0	-12.6	-7.5	43.9	14.6	20.0	13.8	28.4	3.6	—

PER SHARE DATA

	2002	2001	2000	1999	1998	1997	1996	1995	1994	1993
Dividends, Net Income ($)	0.13	0.08	0.25	0.03	0.02	0.05	0.09	0.13	0.02	—
Distrib'ns, Cap Gain ($)	0.00	0.00	2.90	1.43	0.67	2.00	0.83	1.24	0.10	—
Net Asset Value ($)	16.04	16.12	18.50	22.81	16.86	15.22	14.04	12.97	10.88	—
Expense Ratio (%)	1.09	0.90	0.88	0.79	0.77	0.84	0.99	1.19	1.58	—
Yield (%)	0.81	0.49	1.16	0.12	0.11	0.29	0.60	0.91	0.18	—
Portfolio Turnover (%)	50	158	295	316	121	131	152	180	320	—
Total Assets (Millions $)	717	424	453	609	178	174	147	155	60	—

PORTFOLIO (as of 6/30/02)

Portfolio Manager: Fergus Shiel - 2002

Investment Style

✔ Large Cap	Growth
Mid Cap	Value
Small Cap	✔ Grth/Val

Portfolio

21.7% cash	0.0% corp bonds
78.3% stocks	0.0% gov't bonds
0.0% preferred	0.0% muni bonds
0.0% conv't bds/wrnts	0.0% other

SHAREHOLDER INFORMATION

Minimum Investment
Initial: $2,500 — Subsequent: $250

Minimum IRA Investment
Initial: $500 — Subsequent: $250

Maximum Fees
Load: 0.75% redemption — 12b-1: none
Other: redemption fee applies for 1 month

Services
✔ IRA
✔ Keogh
✔ Telephone Exchange

Fidelity Freedom 2030

800-544-8544, 801-534-1910
www.fidelity.com

(FFFEX)

Large-Cap Stock

PERFORMANCE — fund inception date: 10/17/96

	3yr Annual	5yr Annual	10yr Annual	Bull	Bear
Return (%)	-11.4	1.6	na	69.4	-38.6
Differ From Category (+/-)	2.4 abv av	2.5 high	na	-5.3 av	0.5 abv av

Standard Deviation	Category Risk Index	Beta
16.3%—av	0.85—low	0.79

	2002	2001	2000	1999	1998	1997	1996	1995	1994	1993
Return (%)	-17.3	-11.6	-5.0	28.4	22.1	21.3	—	—	—	—
Differ From Category (+/-)	.4.8	1.2	0.2	3.0	-2.3	-5.8	—	—	—	—
Return, Tax-Adjusted (%)	-17.8	-12.8	-6.6	26.5	20.5	19.9	—	—	—	—

PER SHARE DATA

	2002	2001	2000	1999	1998	1997	1996	1995	1994	1993
Dividends, Net Income ($)	0.15	0.20	0.34	0.41	0.24	0.31	—	—	—	—
Distrib'ns, Cap Gain ($)	0.00	0.53	0.71	0.48	0.48	0.12	—	—	—	—
Net Asset Value ($)	10.24	12.56	15.00	16.88	13.89	11.99	—	—	—	—
Expense Ratio (%)	0.07	0.06	0.08	0.07	0.08	0.08	—	—	—	—
Yield (%)	1.46	1.52	2.16	2.36	1.67	2.55	—	—	—	—
Portfolio Turnover (%)	5	37	26	16	34	19	—	—	—	—
Total Assets (Millions $)	2,090	1,708	1,273	787	282	57	—	—	—	—

PORTFOLIO (as of 12/31/02)

Portfolio Manager: Ren Cheng - 1996

Investment Style

✔ Large Cap	✔ Growth
✔ Mid Cap	Value
Small Cap	Grth/Val

Portfolio

0.0% cash	0.0% corp bonds
0.0% stocks	0.0% gov't bonds
0.0% preferred	0.0% muni bonds
0.0% conv't bds/wrnts	100.0% other

SHAREHOLDER INFORMATION

Minimum Investment
Initial: $2,500 — Subsequent: $250

Minimum IRA Investment
Initial: $500 — Subsequent: $250

Maximum Fees
Load: none — 12b-1: none
Other: none

Services
✔ IRA
✔ Keogh
✔ Telephone Exchange

Fidelity Fund
(FFIDX)

800-544-8544, 800-522-7297
www.fidelity.com

Large-Cap Stock

PERFORMANCE — fund inception date: 4/30/30

	3yr Annual	5yr Annual	10yr Annual	Bull	Bear
Return (%)	-14.9	0.0	9.8	65.8	-44.7
Differ From Category (+/-)	-1.1 av	0.9 abv av	1.9 high	-8.9 av	-5.6 av

Standard Deviation	Category Risk Index	Beta
20.1%—abv av	1.05—abv av	0.99

	2002	2001	2000	1999	1998	1997	1996	1995	1994	1993
Return (%)	-22.2	-11.2	-10.9	24.2	31.0	32.0	19.8	32.8	2.5	18.3
Differ From Category (+/-)	-0.1	1.6	-5.7	-1.2	6.6	4.9	-0.8	-0.1	2.4	5.6
Return, Tax-Adjusted (%)	-22.5	-11.5	-13.6	22.7	29.4	29.6	16.9	29.8	0.5	13.6

PER SHARE DATA

	2002	2001	2000	1999	1998	1997	1996	1995	1994	1993
Dividends, Net Income ($)	0.21	0.21	0.23	0.29	0.30	0.32	0.37	0.42	0.33	0.44
Distrib'ns, Cap Gain ($)	0.00	0.00	5.20	2.21	1.81	2.35	1.82	1.40	0.94	2.55
Net Asset Value ($)	22.26	28.88	32.77	42.61	36.69	29.81	24.70	22.61	18.48	19.27
Expense Ratio (%)	0.53	0.51	0.56	0.55	0.56	0.59	0.60	0.64	0.65	0.66
Yield (%)	0.94	0.72	0.60	0.64	0.77	0.99	1.39	1.74	1.69	2.01
Portfolio Turnover (%)	155	217	113	71	65	107	150	157	207	261
Total Assets (Millions $)	8,695	12,452	15,082	16,114	10,563	6,529	4,450	3,213	1,886	1,546

PORTFOLIO (as of 6/30/02)

Portfolio Manager: John Avery - 2002

Investment Style

✔ Large Cap	✔ Growth
✔ Mid Cap	Value
Small Cap	Grth/Val

Portfolio

0.0% cash	0.0% corp bonds
97.0% stocks	0.0% gov't bonds
0.0% pref/conv't pref	0.0% muni bonds
0.0% conv't bds/wrnts	3.0% other

SHAREHOLDER INFORMATION

Minimum Investment
Initial: $2,500 — Subsequent: $250

Minimum IRA Investment
Initial: $500 — Subsequent: $250

Maximum Fees
Load: none — 12b-1: none
Other: none

Services
- ✔ IRA
- ✔ Keogh
- ✔ Telephone Exchange

Fidelity Growth Company (FDGRX)

800-544-8544, 800-522-7297
www.fidelity.com

Large-Cap Stock

PERFORMANCE

fund inception date: 1/17/83

	3yr Annual	5yr Annual	10yr Annual	Bull	Bear
Return (%)	-22.4	1.2	8.8	184.7	-64.9
Differ From Category (+/-)	-8.6 low	2.1 abv av	0.9 abv av	110.0 high	-25.8 low

Standard Deviation	Category Risk Index	Beta
34.2%—high	1.79—high	1.18

	2002	2001	2000	1999	1998	1997	1996	1995	1994	1993
Return (%)	-33.4	-25.3	-6.3	79.4	27.2	18.9	16.8	39.6	-2.2	16.1
Differ From Category (+/-)	-11.3	-12.5	-1.1	54.0	2.8	-8.2	-3.8	6.7	-2.3	3.4
Return, Tax-Adjusted (%)	-33.4	-25.3	-8.1	76.9	25.4	16.5	15.3	37.8	-3.4	13.0

PER SHARE DATA

	2002	2001	2000	1999	1998	1997	1996	1995	1994	1993
Dividends, Net Income ($)	0.00	0.00	0.00	0.00	0.09	0.22	0.28	0.16	0.22	0.07
Distrib'ns, Cap Gain ($)	0.00	0.16	7.50	6.29	3.73	4.35	1.60	1.57	0.92	2.92
Net Asset Value ($)	35.42	53.22	71.43	84.30	51.02	43.32	40.46	36.29	27.26	29.06
Expense Ratio (%)	na	0.95	0.85	0.74	0.65	0.71	0.85	0.94	1.05	1.07
Yield (%)	0.00	0.00	0.00	0.00	0.16	0.46	0.66	0.42	0.78	0.21
Portfolio Turnover (%)	na	93	69	86	76	93	78	119	135	159
Total Assets (Millions $)	14,797	22,741	30,397	24,337	11,440	10,509	9,272	6,278	2,993	2,542

PORTFOLIO (as of 6/30/02)

Portfolio Manager: Steven Wymer - 1997

Investment Style

✔ Large Cap	✔ Growth
✔ Mid Cap	Value
✔ Small Cap	Grth/Val

Portfolio

0.3% cash	0.0% corp bonds
99.7% stocks	0.0% gov't bonds
0.0% preferred	0.0% muni bonds
0.0% conv't bds/wrnts	0.0% other

SHAREHOLDER INFORMATION

Minimum Investment
Initial: $2,500 Subsequent: $250

Minimum IRA Investment
Initial: $500 Subsequent: $250

Maximum Fees
Load: none 12b-1: none
Other: none

Services
✔ IRA
✔ Keogh
✔ Telephone Exchange

Fidelity Grth & Inc (FGRIX)

800-544-8544, 800-522-7297
www.fidelity.com

Large-Cap Stock

PERFORMANCE — fund inception date: 12/30/85

	3yr Annual	5yr Annual	10yr Annual	Bull	Bear
Return (%)	-10.0	0.6	10.3	42.9	-31.4
Differ From Category (+/-)	3.8 abv av	1.5 abv av	2.4 high	-31.8 blw av	7.7 abv av

Standard Deviation	Category Risk Index	Beta
13.8%—blw av	0.72—low	0.70

	2002	2001	2000	1999	1998	1997	1996	1995	1994	1993
Return (%)	-18.0	-9.3	-1.9	10.4	28.3	30.1	20.0	35.3	2.2	19.5
Differ From Category (+/-)	4.1	3.5	3.3	-15.0	3.9	3.0	-0.6	2.4	2.1	6.8
Return, Tax-Adjusted (%)	-18.4	-9.8	-3.9	8.8	26.8	28.7	18.2	33.2	-0.1	17.4

PER SHARE DATA

	2002	2001	2000	1999	1998	1997	1996	1995	1994	1993
Dividends, Net Income ($)	0.34	0.39	0.37	0.39	0.39	0.43	0.46	0.48	0.40	0.52
Distrib'ns, Cap Gain ($)	0.00	0.38	3.91	2.90	2.16	1.36	1.12	0.90	1.24	0.77
Net Asset Value ($)	30.31	37.38	42.10	47.16	45.84	38.10	30.73	27.05	21.09	22.22
Expense Ratio (%)	0.68	0.66	0.67	0.66	0.68	0.71	0.74	0.77	0.82	0.83
Yield (%)	1.12	1.03	0.80	0.77	0.81	1.08	1.44	1.71	1.79	2.26
Portfolio Turnover (%)	36	46	41	35	32	38	41	67	92	87
Total Assets (Millions $)	26,268	34,255	39,963	48,528	48,639	36,656	23,896	14,818	9,344	7,684

PORTFOLIO (as of 7/31/02)

Portfolio Manager: Steven Kaye - 1993

Investment Style

✔ Large Cap	Growth
Mid Cap	Value
Small Cap	✔ Grth/Val

Portfolio

0.0%	cash	1.1%	corp bonds
89.6%	stocks	0.1%	gov't bonds
2.4%	pref/conv't pref	0.0%	muni bonds
0.0%	conv't bds/wrnts	6.9%	other

SHAREHOLDER INFORMATION

Minimum Investment
Initial: $2,500 — Subsequent: $250

Minimum IRA Investment
Initial: $500 — Subsequent: $250

Maximum Fees
Load: none — 12b-1: none
Other: none

Services
✔ IRA
✔ Keogh
✔ Telephone Exchange

Fidelity Independence (FDFFX)

800-544-8544, 800-522-7297
www.fidelity.com

Large-Cap Stock

PERFORMANCE — fund inception date: 3/24/83

	3yr Annual	5yr Annual	10yr Annual	Bull	Bear
Return (%)	-14.5	4.4	9.2	129.9	-52.0
Differ From Category (+/-)	-0.7 av	5.3 high	1.3 abv av	55.2 high	-12.9 blw av

Standard Deviation	Category Risk Index	Beta
33.5%—high	1.75—high	1.16

	2002	2001	2000	1999	1998	1997	1996	1995	1994	1993
Return (%)	-15.8	-27.2	1.7	47.0	35.8	18.5	8.3	24.2	0.0	22.1
Differ From Category (+/-)	6.3	-14.4	6.9	21.6	11.4	-8.6	-12.3	-8.7	-0.1	9.4
Return, Tax-Adjusted (%)	-16.3	-27.6	-1.7	43.3	32.9	14.3	4.4	20.6	-3.1	18.8

PER SHARE DATA

	2002	2001	2000	1999	1998	1997	1996	1995	1994	1993
Dividends, Net Income ($)	0.21	0.20	0.08	0.05	0.14	0.13	0.26	0.35	0.22	0.14
Distrib'ns, Cap Gain ($)	0.00	0.06	4.19	3.66	2.13	3.41	2.15	1.58	1.68	1.75
Net Asset Value ($)	13.07	15.77	22.01	25.85	20.51	16.85	17.29	18.19	16.24	18.14
Expense Ratio (%)	na	0.92	0.85	0.58	0.62	0.64	0.70	1.03	1.07	1.05
Yield (%)	1.60	1.26	0.30	0.16	0.61	0.64	1.33	1.77	1.22	0.70
Portfolio Turnover (%)	na	187	249	310	266	205	230	54	72	101
Total Assets (Millions $)	4,239	5,485	8,474	7,268	4,946	3,932	4,045	4,071	3,184	2,848

PORTFOLIO (as of 6/30/02)

Portfolio Manager: Fergus Shiel - 1996

Investment Style

✔ Large Cap	✔ Growth
✔ Mid Cap	Value
✔ Small Cap	Grth/Val

Portfolio

5.6%	cash	0.0%	corp bonds
94.4%	stocks	0.0%	gov't bonds
0.0%	preferred	0.0%	muni bonds
0.0%	conv't bds/wrnts	0.0%	other

SHAREHOLDER INFORMATION

Minimum Investment
Initial: $2,500 — Subsequent: $250

Minimum IRA Investment
Initial: $500 — Subsequent: $250

Maximum Fees
Load: none — 12b-1: none
Other: none

Services
✔ IRA
✔ Keogh
✔ Telephone Exchange

Fidelity Magellan (FMAGX)

800-544-8544, 800-522-7297
www.fidelity.com

Large-Cap Stock

this fund is closed to new investors

PERFORMANCE

fund inception date: 5/2/63

	3yr Annual	5yr Annual	10yr Annual	Bull	Bear
Return (%)	-15.1	0.2	9.1	75.4	-45.7
Differ From Category (+/-)	-1.3 av	1.1 abv av	1.2 abv av	0.7 abv av	-6.6 blw av

Standard Deviation	Category Risk Index	Beta
19.3%—abv av	1.01—av	1.01

	2002	2001	2000	1999	1998	1997	1996	1995	1994	1993
Return (%)	-23.6	-11.6	-9.2	24.0	33.6	26.5	11.6	36.8	-1.8	24.6
Differ From Category (+/-)	-1.5	1.2	-4.0	-1.4	9.2	-0.6	-9.0	3.9	-1.9	11.9
Return, Tax-Adjusted (%)	-23.8	-11.9	-10.0	21.9	32.2	24.6	6.9	34.5	-2.9	21.2

PER SHARE DATA

	2002	2001	2000	1999	1998	1997	1996	1995	1994	1993
Dividends, Net Income ($)	0.64	0.46	0.27	0.73	0.67	1.25	1.10	0.59	0.13	0.75
Distrib'ns, Cap Gain ($)	0.00	0.80	4.69	11.39	5.15	5.21	12.85	4.69	2.64	6.50
Net Asset Value ($)	78.96	104.22	119.30	136.63	120.82	95.27	80.65	85.98	66.80	70.85
Expense Ratio (%)	0.88	0.88	0.74	0.60	0.61	0.64	0.92	0.96	0.99	1.00
Yield (%)	0.81	0.43	0.21	0.49	0.53	1.24	1.17	0.65	0.18	0.96
Portfolio Turnover (%)	15	24	28	37	34	67	155	120	132	155
Total Assets (Millions $)	56,750	79,515	93,066	105,938	83,552	63,766	53,988	53,702	36,441	31,705

PORTFOLIO (as of 9/30/02)

Portfolio Manager: Robert Stansky - 1996

Investment Style

✔ Large Cap	Growth
Mid Cap	Value
Small Cap	✔ Grth/Val

Portfolio

0.0%	cash	0.1%	corp bonds
95.2%	stocks	0.0%	gov't bonds
0.0%	preferred	0.0%	muni bonds
0.0%	conv't bds/wrnts	4.7%	other

SHAREHOLDER INFORMATION

Minimum Investment
Initial: $2,500 Subsequent: $250

Minimum IRA Investment
Initial: $500 Subsequent: $250

Maximum Fees
Load: 3.00% front 12b-1: none
Other: none

Services
✔ IRA
✔ Keogh
✔ Telephone Exchange

Fidelity Spart 500 Index (FSMKX)

800-544-8544, 801-534-1910
www.fidelity.com

Large-Cap Stock

PERFORMANCE — fund inception date: 3/6/90

	3yr Annual	5yr Annual	10yr Annual	Bull	Bear
Return (%)	-14.6	-0.7	9.0	59.3	-43.8
Differ From Category (+/-)	-0.8 av	0.2 av	1.1 abv av	-15.4 av	-4.7 av

Standard Deviation	Category Risk Index	Beta
18.8%—abv av	0.98—av	1.00

	2002	2001	2000	1999	1998	1997	1996	1995	1994	1993
Return (%)	-22.1	-12.0	-9.1	20.6	28.4	33.0	22.5	36.9	1.0	9.6
Differ From Category (+/-)	.0.0	0.8	-3.9	-4.8	4.0	5.9	1.9	4.0	0.9	-3.1
Return, Tax-Adjusted (%)	-22.6	-12.4	-9.5	19.9	27.5	31.8	21.1	35.5	0.1	8.5

PER SHARE DATA

	2002	2001	2000	1999	1998	1997	1996	1995	1994	1993
Dividends, Net Income ($)	0.99	0.96	0.97	1.19	0.79	0.97	0.91	0.96	0.80	0.80
Distrib'ns, Cap Gain ($)	0.00	0.00	0.00	0.70	1.68	1.38	1.05	0.37	0.00	0.18
Net Asset Value ($)	60.47	78.89	90.76	100.89	85.29	68.50	53.42	45.32	34.15	34.60
Expense Ratio (%)	0.19	0.19	0.19	0.19	0.19	0.44	0.45	0.45	0.45	0.44
Yield (%)	1.63	1.21	1.06	1.17	0.90	1.38	1.67	2.10	2.34	2.30
Portfolio Turnover (%)	4	5	8	4	6	6	5	2	3	0
Total Assets (Millions $)	6,787	8,602	9,572	10,437	7,149	3,869	1,597	689	306	299

PORTFOLIO (as of 10/31/02)

Portfolio Manager: Jennifer Farrelly - 1994

Investment Style

✔ Large Cap	Growth
Mid Cap	Value
Small Cap	✔ Grth/Val

Portfolio

0.9%	cash	0.1%	corp bonds
98.1%	stocks	0.0%	gov't bonds
0.0%	preferred	0.0%	muni bonds
0.0%	conv't bds/wrnts	0.9%	other

SHAREHOLDER INFORMATION

Minimum Investment
Initial: $10,000 Subsequent: $1,000

Minimum IRA Investment
Initial: $500 Subsequent: $250

Maximum Fees
Load: 0.50% redemption 12b-1: none
Other: redemption fee applies for 3 months

Services
✔ IRA
✔ Keogh
✔ Telephone Exchange

Fidelity Spart Total Mkt

800-544-8544, 801-534-1910
www.fidelity.com

(FSTMX)

Large-Cap Stock

PERFORMANCE **fund inception date: 11/5/97**

	3yr Annual	5yr Annual	10yr Annual	Bull	Bear
Return (%)	-14.3	-0.8	na	66.7	-43.9
Differ From Category (+/-)	-0.5 av	0.1 av	na	-8.0 av	-4.8 av

Standard Deviation	Category Risk Index	Beta
19.1%—abv av	0.99—av	0.98

	2002	2001	2000	1999	1998	1997	1996	1995	1994	1993
Return (%)	-20.9	-10.7	-10.9	23.2	24.0	—	—	—	—	—
Differ From Category (+/-)	1.2	2.1	-5.7	-2.2	-0.4	—	—	—	—	—
Return, Tax-Adjusted (%)	-21.3	-11.1	-11.3	22.7	23.4	—	—	—	—	—

PER SHARE DATA

	2002	2001	2000	1999	1998	1997	1996	1995	1994	1993
Dividends, Net Income ($)	0.32	0.32	0.30	0.29	0.23	—	—	—	—	—
Distrib'ns, Cap Gain ($)	0.00	0.00	0.18	0.19	0.28	—	—	—	—	—
Net Asset Value ($)	23.05	29.56	33.50	38.13	31.36	—	—	—	—	—
Expense Ratio (%)	0.25	0.25	0.25	0.27	0.25	—	—	—	—	—
Yield (%)	1.38	1.08	0.89	0.75	0.72	—	—	—	—	—
Portfolio Turnover (%)	7	16	11	4	7	—	—	—	—	—
Total Assets (Millions $)	1,033	1,102	1,028	755	166	—	—	—	—	—

PORTFOLIO (as of 8/31/02)

Portfolio Manager: Team Managed - 1997

Investment Style

✔ Large Cap	Growth
✔ Mid Cap	Value
Small Cap	✔ Grth/Val

Portfolio

1.6% cash	0.1% corp bonds
96.4% stocks	0.0% gov't bonds
0.0% pref/conv't pref	0.0% muni bonds
0.0% conv't bds/wrnts	1.9% other

SHAREHOLDER INFORMATION

Minimum Investment
Initial: $15,000 Subsequent: $1,000

Minimum IRA Investment
Initial: $15,000 Subsequent: $1

Maximum Fees
Load: 0.50% redemption 12b-1: none
Other: redemption fee applies for 3 months

Services
✔ IRA
✔ Keogh
✔ Telephone Exchange

Gabelli Growth
(GABGX)

800-422-3554
www.gabelli.com

Large-Cap Stock

PERFORMANCE — fund inception date: 4/10/87

	3yr Annual	5yr Annual	10yr Annual	Bull	Bear
Return (%)	-23.3	-3.1	7.5	118.1	-60.4
Differ From Category (+/-)	-9.5 low	-2.2 blw av	-0.4 av	43.4 high	-21.3 low

Standard Deviation	Category Risk Index	Beta
26.2%—high	1.37—high	1.31

	2002	2001	2000	1999	1998	1997	1996	1995	1994	1993
Return (%)	-33.7	-24.0	-10.5	46.2	29.7	42.6	19.4	32.7	-3.3	11.2
Differ From Category (+/-)	-11.6	-11.2	-5.3	20.8	5.3	15.5	-1.2	-0.2	-3.4	-1.5
Return, Tax-Adjusted (%)	-33.7	-24.0	-12.2	43.3	28.5	37.8	16.5	27.0	-6.7	10.2

PER SHARE DATA

	2002	2001	2000	1999	1998	1997	1996	1995	1994	1993
Dividends, Net Income ($)	0.00	0.00	0.00	0.00	0.00	0.00	0.02	0.05	0.08	0.09
Distrib'ns, Cap Gain ($)	0.00	0.00	3.84	5.16	1.74	5.78	2.30	3.90	2.70	0.67
Net Asset Value ($)	18.99	28.68	37.79	46.51	35.40	28.63	24.14	22.16	19.68	23.26
Expense Ratio (%)	na	1.40	1.38	1.37	1.41	1.43	1.43	1.41	1.36	1.41
Yield (%)	0.00	0.00	0.00	0.00	0.00	0.00	0.07	0.19	0.35	0.37
Portfolio Turnover (%)	na	26	55	52	40	83	88	140	40	80
Total Assets (Millions $)	1,680	2,957	3,835	3,155	1,864	951	623	526	426	695

PORTFOLIO (as of 11/30/02)

Portfolio Manager: Howard Ward - 1995

Investment Style

✔ Large Cap ✔ Growth
Mid Cap Value
Small Cap Grth/Val

Portfolio

0.2%	cash	0.0%	corp bonds
99.8%	stocks	0.0%	gov't bonds
0.0%	preferred	0.0%	muni bonds
0.0%	conv't bds/wrnts	0.0%	other

SHAREHOLDER INFORMATION

Minimum Investment
Initial: $1,000 Subsequent: $1

Minimum IRA Investment
Initial: $250 Subsequent: $1

Maximum Fees
Load: none 12b-1: 0.25%
Other: none

Services
✔ IRA
Keogh
✔ Telephone Exchange

Gateway Tr:Gateway Fd (GATEX)

800-354-6339
www.gatewayfund.com

Large-Cap Stock

PERFORMANCE — fund inception date: 12/7/77

	3yr Annual	5yr Annual	10yr Annual	Bull	Bear
Return (%)	-0.7	4.4	6.8	28.7	-13.5
Differ From Category (+/-)	13.1 high	5.3 high	-1.1 blw av	-46.0 low	25.6 high

Standard Deviation	Category Risk Index	Beta
9.5%—blw av	0.49—low	0.46

	2002	2001	2000	1999	1998	1997	1996	1995	1994	1993
Return (%)	-4.8	-3.5	6.6	12.9	12.2	12.3	10.5	11.0	5.5	7.4
Differ From Category (+/-)	17.3	9.3	11.8	-12.5	-12.2	-14.8	-10.1	-21.9	5.4	-5.3
Return, Tax-Adjusted (%)	-5.1	-3.7	4.6	12.8	11.9	10.1	10.0	10.3	3.1	5.7

PER SHARE DATA

	2002	2001	2000	1999	1998	1997	1996	1995	1994	1993
Dividends, Net Income ($)	0.15	0.10	0.07	0.07	0.12	0.17	0.20	0.26	0.27	0.29
Distrib'ns, Cap Gain ($)	0.00	0.02	2.23	0.00	0.01	1.72	0.00	0.00	0.97	0.51
Net Asset Value ($)	20.76	21.98	22.92	23.67	21.02	18.85	18.48	16.91	15.48	15.85
Expense Ratio (%)	na	0.97	0.98	0.98	0.99	1.07	1.14	1.22	1.21	1.11
Yield (%)	0.72	0.45	0.27	0.29	0.57	0.82	1.08	1.53	1.64	1.77
Portfolio Turnover (%)	na	18	22	11	12	82	17	0	4	17
Total Assets (Millions $)	1,118	1,287	1,491	922	464	254	194	176	164	207

PORTFOLIO (as of 9/30/02)

Portfolio Manager: J Patrick Rogers - 1994

Investment Style

✔ Large Cap	Growth
Mid Cap	Value
Small Cap	✔ Grth/Val

Portfolio

0.0% cash	0.1% corp bonds
100.1% stocks	0.0% gov't bonds
0.0% preferred	0.0% muni bonds
0.0% conv't bds/wrnts	-0.2% other

SHAREHOLDER INFORMATION

Minimum Investment
Initial: $1,000 — Subsequent: $100

Minimum IRA Investment
Initial: $500 — Subsequent: $100

Maximum Fees
Load: none — 12b-1: 0.36%
Other: none

Services
✔ IRA
✔ Keogh
✔ Telephone Exchange

Janus Core Equity (JAEIX)

800-525-0020, 303-333-3863
www.janus.com

Large-Cap Stock

PERFORMANCE — fund inception date: 6/28/96

	3yr Annual	5yr Annual	10yr Annual	Bull	Bear
Return (%)	-12.5	5.3	na	100.8	-39.1
Differ From Category (+/-)	1.3 abv av	6.2 high	na	26.1 high	0.0 abv av

Standard Deviation	Category Risk Index	Beta
15.4%—av	0.80—low	0.75

	2002	2001	2000	1999	1998	1997	1996	1995	1994	1993
Return (%)	-18.0	-12.1	-7.1	38.5	40.0	31.0	—	—	—	—
Differ From Category (+/-)	4.1	0.7	-1.9	13.1	15.6	3.9	—	—	—	—
Return, Tax-Adjusted (%)	-18.2	-12.4	-9.4	37.6	39.6	29.2	—	—	—	—

PER SHARE DATA

	2002	2001	2000	1999	1998	1997	1996	1995	1994	1993
Dividends, Net Income ($)	0.11	0.15	0.16	0.15	0.05	0.06	—	—	—	—
Distrib'ns, Cap Gain ($)	0.00	0.00	2.53	0.57	0.17	0.88	—	—	—	—
Net Asset Value ($)	14.63	17.98	20.63	25.14	18.72	13.54	—	—	—	—
Expense Ratio (%)	na	0.93	0.93	1.01	1.18	1.45	—	—	—	—
Yield (%)	0.75	0.83	0.69	0.58	0.26	0.41	—	—	—	—
Portfolio Turnover (%)	na	115	116	81	101	180	—	—	—	—
Total Assets (Millions $)	733	816	963	948	349	88	—	—	—	—

PORTFOLIO (as of 10/31/02)

Portfolio Manager: Karen Reidy - 1999

Investment Style

✔ Large Cap	✔ Growth
✔ Mid Cap	Value
Small Cap	Grth/Val

Portfolio

7.1%	cash	0.9%	corp bonds
89.9%	stocks	0.0%	gov't bonds
2.2%	pref/conv't pref	0.0%	muni bonds
0.0%	conv't bds/wrnts	0.0%	other

SHAREHOLDER INFORMATION

Minimum Investment
Initial: $2,500 — Subsequent: $100

Minimum IRA Investment
Initial: $500 — Subsequent: $100

Maximum Fees
Load: none — 12b-1: none
Other: none

Services
✔ IRA
✔ Keogh
✔ Telephone Exchange

Janus Fund
(JANSX)

800-525-0020, 303-333-3863
www.janus.com

Large-Cap Stock

PERFORMANCE — fund inception date: 2/5/70

	3yr Annual	5yr Annual	10yr Annual	Bull	Bear
Return (%)	-23.0	-1.4	6.8	123.3	-59.5
Differ From Category (+/-)	-9.2 low	-0.5 blw av	-1.1 blw av	48.6 high	-20.4 low

Standard Deviation	Category Risk Index	Beta
25.1%—high	1.31—high	1.19

	2002	2001	2000	1999	1998	1997	1996	1995	1994	1993
Return (%)	-27.5	-26.1	-14.9	47.1	38.8	22.7	19.6	29.4	-1.1	10.9
Differ From Category (+/-)	-5.4	-13.3	-9.7	21.7	14.4	-4.4	-1.0	-3.5	-1.2	-1.8
Return, Tax-Adjusted (%)	-27.5	-26.1	-16.9	44.0	38.1	18.4	15.7	27.0	-1.7	8.7

PER SHARE DATA

	2002	2001	2000	1999	1998	1997	1996	1995	1994	1993
Dividends, Net Income ($)	0.00	0.00	0.00	0.00	0.00	0.23	0.20	0.77	0.00	0.38
Distrib'ns, Cap Gain ($)	0.00	0.00	4.39	5.21	0.90	4.74	2.91	0.49	0.38	0.94
Net Asset Value ($)	17.82	24.60	33.29	44.05	33.65	24.90	24.45	23.04	18.78	19.39
Expense Ratio (%)	na	0.83	0.84	0.84	0.86	0.86	0.85	0.87	0.91	0.92
Yield (%)	0.00	0.00	0.00	0.00	0.00	0.77	0.73	3.27	0.00	1.86
Portfolio Turnover (%)	na	51	65	63	70	132	104	118	139	127
Total Assets (Millions $)	17,001	25,621	39,174	42,330	25,490	19,200	15,890	12,466	9,400	9,199

PORTFOLIO (as of 10/31/02)

Portfolio Manager: Blaine Rollins - 2000

Investment Style

✔ Large Cap ✔ Growth
Mid Cap Value
Small Cap Grth/Val

Portfolio

0.5%	cash	0.0%	corp bonds
99.6%	stocks	0.0%	gov't bonds
0.0%	preferred	0.0%	muni bonds
0.0%	conv't bds/wrnts	0.0%	other

SHAREHOLDER INFORMATION

Minimum Investment
Initial: $2,500 Subsequent: $100

Minimum IRA Investment
Initial: $500 Subsequent: $100

Maximum Fees
Load: none 12b-1: none
Other: none

Services
✔ IRA
✔ Keogh
✔ Telephone Exchange

Janus Growth & Income (JAGIX)

800-525-0020, 303-333-3863
www.janus.com

Large-Cap Stock

PERFORMANCE — fund inception date: 5/15/91

	3yr Annual	5yr Annual	10yr Annual	Bull	Bear
Return (%)	-15.8	3.9	11.0	114.7	-48.0
Differ From Category (+/-)	-2.0 blw av	4.8 high	3.1 high	40.0 high	-8.9 blw av

Standard Deviation	Category Risk Index	Beta
17.7%—av	0.93—blw av	0.83

	2002	2001	2000	1999	1998	1997	1996	1995	1994	1993
Return (%)	-21.5	-14.3	-11.4	51.1	34.8	34.6	26.0	36.3	-4.8	6.6
Differ From Category (+/-)	.0.6	-1.5	-6.2	25.7	10.4	7.5	5.4	3.4	-4.9	-6.1
Return, Tax-Adjusted (%)	-21.8	-14.6	-12.4	49.7	32.9	32.0	22.6	31.7	-5.1	5.5

PER SHARE DATA

	2002	2001	2000	1999	1998	1997	1996	1995	1994	1993
Dividends, Net Income ($)	0.19	0.30	0.23	0.09	0.07	0.07	0.11	0.07	0.09	0.16
Distrib'ns, Cap Gain ($)	0.00	0.00	1.61	1.83	2.01	2.37	1.86	2.16	0.00	0.33
Net Asset Value ($)	23.34	29.97	35.35	41.94	29.10	23.15	19.05	16.67	13.88	14.69
Expense Ratio (%)	na	0.86	0.88	0.90	0.94	0.96	1.03	1.19	1.22	1.28
Yield (%)	0.81	1.00	0.62	0.20	0.22	0.27	0.52	0.37	0.64	1.06
Portfolio Turnover (%)	na	59	41	43	95	127	153	195	123	138
Total Assets (Millions $)	5,575	7,147	8,349	7,492	3,504	2,004	1,100	632	456	513

PORTFOLIO (as of 10/31/02)

Portfolio Manager: David Corkins - 1997

Investment Style

✔ Large Cap	✔ Growth
Mid Cap	Value
Small Cap	Grth/Val

Portfolio

12.9%	cash	3.0%	corp bonds
76.8%	stocks	5.7%	gov't bonds
1.5%	pref/conv't pref	0.0%	muni bonds
0.1%	conv't bds/wrnts	0.0%	other

SHAREHOLDER INFORMATION

Minimum Investment
Initial: $2,500 Subsequent: $100

Minimum IRA Investment
Initial: $500 Subsequent: $100

Maximum Fees
Load: none 12b-1: none
Other: none

Services
✔ IRA
✔ Keogh
✔ Telephone Exchange

Legg Mason Eq:Value/P (LMVTX)

800-822-5544, 410-539-0000
www.leggmason.com

Large-Cap Stock

PERFORMANCE — fund inception date: 4/16/82

	3yr Annual	5yr Annual	10yr Annual	Bull	Bear
Return (%)	-11.9	5.0	14.4	83.9	-39.7
Differ From Category (+/-)	1.9 abv av	5.9 high	6.5 high	9.2 abv av	-0.6 abv av

Standard Deviation	Category Risk Index	Beta
23.1%—abv av	1.21—abv av	1.14

	2002	2001	2000	1999	1998	1997	1996	1995	1994	1993
Return (%)	-18.9	-9.2	-7.1	26.7	48.0	37.0	38.4	40.7	1.3	11.2
Differ From Category (+/-)	3.2	3.6	-1.9	1.3	23.6	9.9	17.8	7.8	1.2	-1.5
Return, Tax-Adjusted (%)	-18.9	-9.3	-10.9	25.9	47.3	35.6	36.4	38.5	1.1	10.4

PER SHARE DATA

	2002	2001	2000	1999	1998	1997	1996	1995	1994	1993
Dividends, Net Income ($)	0.00	0.00	0.00	0.00	0.00	0.03	0.16	0.17	0.05	0.23
Distrib'ns, Cap Gain ($)	0.00	0.26	14.47	2.46	1.40	2.32	1.53	1.24	0.04	0.15
Net Asset Value ($)	40.59	50.06	55.44	75.27	61.58	42.74	32.99	25.19	19.04	18.87
Expense Ratio (%)	1.68	1.68	1.68	1.69	1.73	1.77	1.82	1.81	1.82	1.86
Yield (%)	0.00	0.00	0.00	0.00	0.00	0.06	0.46	0.64	0.26	1.20
Portfolio Turnover (%)	24	27	19	19	12	10	20	20	25	21
Total Assets (Millions $)	7,853	9,788	10,596	12,540	7,507	3,683	1,978	1,340	967	914

PORTFOLIO (as of 9/30/02)

Portfolio Manager: Bill Miller/Nancy Dennin - 2001

Investment Style

✔ Large Cap	Growth
Mid Cap	Value
Small Cap	✔ Grth/Val

Portfolio

0.9% cash	0.0% corp bonds
99.1% stocks	0.0% gov't bonds
0.0% preferred	0.0% muni bonds
0.0% conv't bds/wrnts	0.0% other

SHAREHOLDER INFORMATION

Minimum Investment
Initial: $1,000 — Subsequent: $100

Minimum IRA Investment
Initial: $1,000 — Subsequent: $100

Maximum Fees
Load: none — 12b-1: 0.95%
Other: none

Services
✔ IRA
✔ Keogh
✔ Telephone Exchange

Longleaf Partners Fund

800-445-9469, 901-818-5100
www.longleafpartners.com

(LLPFX)

Large-Cap Stock

PERFORMANCE — fund inception date: 3/24/87

	3yr Annual	5yr Annual	10yr Annual	Bull	Bear
Return (%)	6.8	7.3	14.1	11.0	21.2
Differ From Category (+/-)	20.6 high	8.2 high	6.2 high	-63.7 low	60.3 high

Standard Deviation	Category Risk Index	Beta
17.6%—av	0.92—blw av	0.61

	2002	2001	2000	1999	1998	1997	1996	1995	1994	1993
Return (%)	-8.3	10.3	20.6	2.1	14.2	28.2	21.0	27.4	8.9	22.2
Differ From Category (+/-)	13.8	23.1	25.8	-23.3	-10.2	1.1	0.4	-5.5	8.8	9.5
Return, Tax-Adjusted (%)	-8.5	9.7	18.6	-1.8	10.1	25.1	17.1	26.1	6.6	20.1

PER SHARE DATA

	2002	2001	2000	1999	1998	1997	1996	1995	1994	1993
Dividends, Net Income ($)	0.08	0.19	0.15	0.28	0.24	0.21	0.38	0.24	0.16	0.09
Distrib'ns, Cap Gain ($)	0.13	0.32	1.71	4.23	4.81	3.11	2.38	0.44	1.13	0.95
Net Asset Value ($)	22.24	24.51	22.71	20.49	24.39	25.98	22.85	21.15	17.13	16.92
Expense Ratio (%)	na	0.94	0.93	0.92	0.93	0.94	0.95	1.06	1.17	1.26
Yield (%)	0.35	0.76	0.61	1.13	0.82	0.72	1.50	1.11	0.87	0.50
Portfolio Turnover (%)	na	18	20	50	43	38	33	12	27	19
Total Assets (Millions $)	4,973	4,509	3,756	3,630	3,687	2,605	2,300	1,876	753	397

PORTFOLIO (as of 9/30/02)

Portfolio Manager: Hawkins/Cates/Buford - 1987

Investment Style

✔ Large Cap	Growth
✔ Mid Cap	✔ Value
Small Cap	Grth/Val

Portfolio

2.4%	cash	0.0%	corp bonds
92.8%	stocks	0.0%	gov't bonds
0.0%	preferred	0.0%	muni bonds
6.1%	conv't bds/wrnts	-1.3%	other

SHAREHOLDER INFORMATION

Minimum Investment
Initial: $10,000 — Subsequent: $1

Minimum IRA Investment
Initial: $10,000 — Subsequent: $1

Maximum Fees
Load: none — 12b-1: none
Other: none

Services
✔ IRA
✔ Keogh
✔ Telephone Exchange

Mairs & Power Growth

800-304-7404, 651-222-8478

(MPGFX)

Large-Cap Stock

PERFORMANCE — fund inception date: 11/7/58

	3yr Annual	5yr Annual	10yr Annual	Bull	Bear
Return (%)	7.5	7.8	15.4	33.0	14.5
Differ From Category (+/-)	21.3 high	8.7 high	7.5 high	-41.7 low	53.6 high

Standard Deviation	Category Risk Index	Beta
15.2%—av	0.79—low	0.56

	2002	2001	2000	1999	1998	1997	1996	1995	1994	1993
Return (%)	-7.7	6.4	26.4	7.1	9.3	28.6	26.4	49.3	5.6	12.8
Differ From Category (+/-)	14.4	19.2	31.6	-18.3	-15.1	1.5	5.8	16.4	5.5	0.1
Return, Tax-Adjusted (%)	-8.3	5.8	23.9	5.5	8.7	27.6	25.2	47.7	4.2	11.4

PER SHARE DATA

	2002	2001	2000	1999	1998	1997	1996	1995	1994	1993
Dividends, Net Income ($)	0.66	0.51	0.55	0.46	0.36	0.39	0.35	0.28	0.35	0.21
Distrib'ns, Cap Gain ($)	0.24	2.00	4.82	2.74	0.68	0.95	0.69	0.75	0.49	0.61
Net Asset Value ($)	49.26	54.36	53.41	46.45	46.34	43.33	34.74	28.32	19.68	19.42
Expense Ratio (%)	na	0.76	0.78	0.79	0.82	0.84	0.89	0.99	0.99	0.98
Yield (%)	1.33	0.90	0.93	0.94	0.76	0.88	1.00	0.96	1.61	1.07
Portfolio Turnover (%)	na	8	15	5	2	5	3	4	5	4
Total Assets (Millions $)	770	676	581	546	580	412	150	70	41	39

PORTFOLIO (as of 9/30/02)

Portfolio Manager: George Mairs/William Frels - 1980

Investment Style

✔ Large Cap	Growth
✔ Mid Cap	✔ Value
Small Cap	Grth/Val

Portfolio

0.0%	cash	0.0%	corp bonds
100.0%	stocks	0.0%	gov't bonds
0.0%	preferred	0.0%	muni bonds
0.0%	conv't bds/wrnts	0.0%	other

SHAREHOLDER INFORMATION

Minimum Investment
Initial: $2,500 — Subsequent: $100

Minimum IRA Investment
Initial: $1,000 — Subsequent: $100

Maximum Fees
Load: none — 12b-1: none
Other: none

Services
✔ IRA
Keogh
Telephone Exchange

Marsico Focus
(MFOCX)

888-860-8686
www.marsico.com

Large-Cap Stock

PERFORMANCE fund inception date: 12/31/97

	3yr Annual	5yr Annual	10yr Annual	Bull	Bear
Return (%)	-18.4	4.9	na	104.0	-44.2
Differ From Category (+/-)	-4.6 blw av	5.8 high	na	29.3 high	-5.1 av

Standard Deviation	Category Risk Index	Beta
21.9%—abv av	1.15—abv av	0.76

	2002	2001	2000	1999	1998	1997	1996	1995	1994	1993
Return (%)	-16.6	-20.8	-17.9	55.2	51.3	—	—	—	—	—
Differ From Category (+/-)	5.5	-8.0	-12.7	29.8	26.9	—	—	—	—	—
Return, Tax-Adjusted (%)	-16.6	-20.9	-19.6	55.1	51.3	—	—	—	—	—

PER SHARE DATA

	2002	2001	2000	1999	1998	1997	1996	1995	1994	1993
Dividends, Net Income ($)	0.00	0.00	0.00	0.00	0.00	—	—	—	—	—
Distrib'ns, Cap Gain ($)	0.00	0.04	1.96	0.03	0.00	—	—	—	—	—
Net Asset Value ($)	11.33	13.60	17.23	23.45	15.13	—	—	—	—	—
Expense Ratio (%)	na	1.30	1.27	1.31	1.56	—	—	—	—	—
Yield (%)	0.00	0.00	0.00	0.00	0.00	—	—	—	—	—
Portfolio Turnover (%)	na	127	176	173	170	—	—	—	—	—
Total Assets (Millions $)	1,430	1,400	2,325	3,256	1,204	—	—	—	—	—

PORTFOLIO (as of 10/31/02)

Portfolio Manager: Thomas Marsico - 1997

Investment Style

✔ Large Cap ✔ Growth
✔ Mid Cap Value
✔ Small Cap Grth/Val

Portfolio

3.3%	cash	0.0%	corp bonds
94.8%	stocks	0.0%	gov't bonds
2.0%	pref/conv't pref	0.0%	muni bonds
0.0%	conv't bds/wrnts	0.0%	other

SHAREHOLDER INFORMATION

Minimum Investment
Initial: $2,500 Subsequent: $100

Minimum IRA Investment
Initial: $1,000 Subsequent: $100

Maximum Fees
Load: none 12b-1: 0.25%
Other: none

Services
✔ IRA
✔ Keogh
✔ Telephone Exchange

Masters Select Equity

800-656-8864
www.mastersselect.com

(MSEFX)

Large-Cap Stock

PERFORMANCE — fund inception date: 12/31/96

	3yr Annual	5yr Annual	10yr Annual	Bull	Bear
Return (%)	-6.6	3.4	na	69.7	-29.1
Differ From Category (+/-)	7.2 high	4.3 high	na	-5.0 abv av	10.0 abv av

Standard Deviation	Category Risk Index	Beta
19.9%—abv av	1.04—abv av	0.98

	2002	2001	2000	1999	1998	1997	1996	1995	1994	1993
Return (%)	-19.0	-2.5	3.1	26.4	14.8	29.1	—	—	—	—
Differ From Category (+/-)	3.1	10.3	8.3	1.0	-9.6	2.0	—	—	—	—
Return, Tax-Adjusted (%)	-19.0	-2.7	-1.8	18.5	14.7	24.8	—	—	—	—

PER SHARE DATA

	2002	2001	2000	1999	1998	1997	1996	1995	1994	1993
Dividends, Net Income ($)	0.00	0.05	1.76	2.69	0.03	1.08	—	—	—	—
Distrib'ns, Cap Gain ($)	0.00	0.00	0.00	0.00	0.00	0.00	—	—	—	—
Net Asset Value ($)	10.19	12.59	12.98	14.38	13.57	11.84	—	—	—	—
Expense Ratio (%)	na	1.26	1.24	1.26	1.38	1.47	—	—	—	—
Yield (%)	0.00	0.39	13.55	18.70	0.22	9.12	—	—	—	—
Portfolio Turnover (%)	na	95	129	116	135	145	—	—	—	—
Total Assets (Millions $)	457	508	468	448	405	296	—	—	—	—

PORTFOLIO (as of 6/30/02)

Portfolio Manager: Team Managed - 1996

Investment Style

✔ Large Cap	Growth
✔ Mid Cap	Value
Small Cap	✔ Grth/Val

Portfolio

6.3% cash	0.6% corp bonds
93.2% stocks	0.0% gov't bonds
0.0% preferred	0.0% muni bonds
0.0% conv't bds/wrnts	0.0% other

SHAREHOLDER INFORMATION

Minimum Investment
Initial: $5,000 Subsequent: $250

Minimum IRA Investment
Initial: $1,000 Subsequent: $250

Maximum Fees
Load: 2.00% redemption 12b-1: none
Other: redemption fee applies for 6 months

Services
✔ IRA
✔ Keogh
✔ Telephone Exchange

Oakmark Fund/I
(OAKMX)

800-625-6275, 312-621-0600
www.oakmark.com

Large-Cap Stock

PERFORMANCE — fund inception date: 8/5/91

	3yr Annual	5yr Annual	10yr Annual	Bull	Bear
Return (%)	4.2	1.0	11.3	-4.9	15.6
Differ From Category (+/-)	18.0 high	1.9 abv av	3.4 high	-79.6 low	54.7 high

Standard Deviation	Category Risk Index	Beta
19.6%—abv av	1.02—av	0.77

	2002	2001	2000	1999	1998	1997	1996	1995	1994	1993
Return (%)	-14.4	18.2	11.7	-10.4	3.7	32.5	16.2	34.4	3.3	30.5
Differ From Category (+/-)	7.7	31.0	16.9	-35.8	-20.7	5.4	-4.4	1.5	3.2	17.8
Return, Tax-Adjusted (%)	-14.5	17.9	11.1	-13.3	0.5	30.8	14.0	32.9	1.2	28.9

PER SHARE DATA

	2002	2001	2000	1999	1998	1997	1996	1995	1994	1993
Dividends, Net Income ($)	0.11	0.19	0.38	0.26	0.44	0.39	0.34	0.28	0.23	0.23
Distrib'ns, Cap Gain ($)	0.00	0.00	0.00	4.73	5.63	1.97	1.86	0.84	1.46	0.77
Net Asset Value ($)	30.08	35.27	29.99	27.20	35.82	40.41	32.35	29.75	22.97	23.93
Expense Ratio (%)	1.17	1.15	1.21	1.11	1.08	1.08	1.18	1.17	1.22	1.32
Yield (%)	0.36	0.53	1.26	0.81	1.06	0.92	0.99	0.91	0.94	0.93
Portfolio Turnover (%)	44	57	50	13	43	17	23	18	29	18
Total Assets (Millions $)	3,924	3,644	2,205	3,368	7,320	7,301	4,194	3,301	1,626	1,214

PORTFOLIO (as of 9/30/02)

Portfolio Manager: William Nygren/Kevin Grant - 2000

Investment Style

✔ Large Cap	Growth
✔ Mid Cap	✔ Value
Small Cap	Grth/Val

Portfolio

6.5% cash	0.0% corp bonds
93.5% stocks	0.0% gov't bonds
0.0% preferred	0.0% muni bonds
0.0% conv't bds/wrnts	0.0% other

SHAREHOLDER INFORMATION

Minimum Investment
Initial: $1,000 — Subsequent: $100

Minimum IRA Investment
Initial: $1,000 — Subsequent: $100

Maximum Fees
Load: none — 12b-1: none
Other: none

Services
- ✔ IRA
- ✔ Keogh
- ✔ Telephone Exchange

PBHG Large Cap Value

800-433-0051, 610-647-4100
www.pbhgfunds.com

(PLCVX)

Large-Cap Stock

PERFORMANCE **fund inception date: 12/31/96**

	3yr Annual	5yr Annual	10yr Annual	Bull	Bear
Return (%)	-2.6	6.6	na	57.3	-18.0
Differ From Category (+/-)	11.2 high	7.5 high	na	-17.4 blw av	21.1 high

Standard Deviation	Category Risk Index	Beta
19.4%—abv av	1.01—av	0.81

	2002	2001	2000	1999	1998	1997	1996	1995	1994	1993
Return (%)	-24.4	-1.4	23.9	11.0	34.7	25.5	—	—	—	—
Differ From Category (+/-)	-2.3	11.4	29.1	-14.4	10.3	-1.6	—	—	—	—
Return, Tax-Adjusted (%)	-24.8	-1.5	22.9	5.4	31.6	23.5	—	—	—	—

PER SHARE DATA

	2002	2001	2000	1999	1998	1997	1996	1995	1994	1993
Dividends, Net Income ($)	0.15	0.02	0.08	0.08	0.09	0.06	—	—	—	—
Distrib'ns, Cap Gain ($)	0.00	0.00	0.40	3.69	1.59	0.89	—	—	—	—
Net Asset Value ($)	10.17	13.66	13.88	11.61	13.82	11.59	—	—	—	—
Expense Ratio (%)	1.14	1.16	1.11	1.01	1.17	1.50	—	—	—	—
Yield (%)	1.47	0.14	0.56	0.52	0.58	0.48	—	—	—	—
Portfolio Turnover (%)	948	1,184	1,018	568	403	na	—	—	—	—
Total Assets (Millions $)	329	563	143	32	94	70	—	—	—	—

PORTFOLIO (as of 9/30/02)

Portfolio Manager: Ray McCaffrey - 1999

Investment Style

✔ Large Cap Growth
Mid Cap ✔ Value
Small Cap Grth/Val

Portfolio

7.9%	cash	0.0%	corp bonds
91.5%	stocks	0.0%	gov't bonds
0.0%	preferred	0.0%	muni bonds
0.0%	conv't bds/wrnts	0.6%	other

SHAREHOLDER INFORMATION

Minimum Investment
Initial: $2,500 Subsequent: $1

Minimum IRA Investment
Initial: $2,000 Subsequent: $1

Maximum Fees
Load: none 12b-1: none
Other: none

Services
✔ IRA
✔ Keogh
✔ Telephone Exchange

Rydex:OTC/Inv (RYOCX)

800-820-0888, 301-296-5406
www.rydexfunds.com

Large-Cap Stock

PERFORMANCE — fund inception date: 2/14/94

	3yr Annual	5yr Annual	10yr Annual	Bull	Bear
Return (%)	-37.0	-1.3	na	279.1	-82.0
Differ From Category (+/-)	-23.2 low	-0.4 blw av	na	204.4 high	-42.9 low

Standard Deviation	Category Risk Index	Beta
44.7%—high	2.34—high	1.95

	2002	2001	2000	1999	1998	1997	1996	1995	1994	1993
Return (%)	-38.5	-34.6	-37.9	100.6	86.4	21.8	43.4	44.2	—	—
Differ From Category (+/-)	-16.4	-21.8	-32.7	75.2	62.0	-5.3	22.8	11.3	—	—
Return, Tax-Adjusted (%)	-38.5	-34.6	-37.9	100.4	86.2	21.7	43.3	41.7	—	—

PER SHARE DATA

	2002	2001	2000	1999	1998	1997	1996	1995	1994	1993
Dividends, Net Income ($)	0.00	0.00	0.00	0.00	0.00	0.00	0.04	0.07	—	—
Distrib'ns, Cap Gain ($)	0.00	0.00	0.17	0.15	0.09	0.03	0.00	0.24	—	—
Net Asset Value ($)	6.79	11.05	16.91	27.45	13.78	7.45	6.14	4.29	—	—
Expense Ratio (%)	1.08	1.16	1.15	1.15	1.13	1.27	1.33	1.41	—	—
Yield (%)	0.00	0.00	0.00	0.00	0.00	0.00	0.21	0.51	—	—
Portfolio Turnover (%)	109	228	385	773	971	1,140	2,578	2,241	—	—
Total Assets (Millions $)	442	926	1,742	3,010	1,109	206	174	30	—	—

PORTFOLIO (as of 9/30/02)

Portfolio Manager: Michael Byrum/Team Managed - 1997

Investment Style

✔ Large Cap	✔ Growth
✔ Mid Cap	Value
✔ Small Cap	Grth/Val

Portfolio

0.9% cash	0.3% corp bonds
98.8% stocks	0.0% gov't bonds
0.0% preferred	0.0% muni bonds
0.0% conv't bds/wrnts	0.0% other

SHAREHOLDER INFORMATION

Minimum Investment
Initial: $25,000 — Subsequent: $1

Minimum IRA Investment
Initial: $25,000 — Subsequent: $1

Maximum Fees
Load: none — 12b-1: none
Other: none

Services
✔ IRA
✔ Keogh
✔ Telephone Exchange

Schwab Inv 1000 Fd/I

800-435-4000, 800-266-5623
www.schwab.com

(SNXFX)

Large-Cap Stock

PERFORMANCE — fund inception date: 4/2/91

	3yr Annual	5yr Annual	10yr Annual	Bull	Bear
Return (%)	-14.0	-0.4	8.8	62.6	-43.1
Differ From Category (+/-)	-0.2 av	0.5 av	0.9 abv av	-12.1 av	-4.0 av

Standard Deviation	Category Risk Index	Beta
18.7%—av	0.98—blw av	0.98

	2002	2001	2000	1999	1998	1997	1996	1995	1994	1993
Return (%)	-21.1	-12.2	-8.2	21.0	27.1	31.9	21.5	36.6	-0.1	9.6
Differ From Category (+/-)	1.0	0.6	-3.0	-4.4	2.7	4.8	0.9	3.7	-0.2	-3.1
Return, Tax-Adjusted (%)	-21.5	-12.5	-8.4	20.7	26.7	31.4	20.9	35.9	-0.9	8.8

PER SHARE DATA

	2002	2001	2000	1999	1998	1997	1996	1995	1994	1993
Dividends, Net Income ($)	0.32	0.27	0.23	0.25	0.25	0.26	0.25	0.23	0.26	0.25
Distrib'ns, Cap Gain ($)	0.00	0.00	0.00	0.00	0.00	0.00	0.00	0.00	0.00	0.00
Net Asset Value ($)	24.86	31.95	36.73	40.28	33.51	26.56	20.34	16.94	12.57	12.85
Expense Ratio (%)	na	0.46	0.46	0.46	0.46	0.46	0.49	0.54	0.51	0.45
Yield (%)	1.28	0.84	0.62	0.62	0.74	0.97	1.22	1.35	2.06	1.94
Portfolio Turnover (%)	na	8	9	3	2	0	2	2	3	1
Total Assets (Millions $)	3,190	4,163	4,730	5,311	4,184	2,823	1,908	1,063	553	529

PORTFOLIO (as of 9/30/02)

Portfolio Manager: Geri Hom - 1995

Investment Style

✔ Large Cap	Growth
Mid Cap	Value
Small Cap	✔ Grth/Val

Portfolio

-0.1% cash	0.1% corp bonds
99.9% stocks	0.0% gov't bonds
0.0% preferred	0.0% muni bonds
0.0% conv't bds/wrnts	0.1% other

SHAREHOLDER INFORMATION

Minimum Investment
Initial: $2,500 Subsequent: $500

Minimum IRA Investment
Initial: $500 Subsequent: $100

Maximum Fees
Load: 0.75% redemption 12b-1: none
Other: redemption fee applies for 6 months

Services
✔ IRA
✔ Keogh
✔ Telephone Exchange

Selected American Shares (SLASX)

800-279-0279, 800-243-1575
www.selectedfunds.com

Large-Cap Stock

PERFORMANCE

fund inception date: 2/28/33

	3yr Annual	5yr Annual	10yr Annual	Bull	Bear
Return (%)	-6.9	2.4	11.0	67.6	-30.9
Differ From Category (+/-)	6.9 abv av	3.3 high	3.1 high	-7.1 av	8.2 abv av

Standard Deviation	Category Risk Index	Beta
16.2%—av	0.85—low	0.80

	2002	2001	2000	1999	1998	1997	1996	1995	1994	1993
Return (%)	-17.0	-11.1	9.3	20.3	16.2	37.2	30.7	38.0	-3.2	5.4
Differ From Category (+/-)	5.1	1.7	14.5	-5.1	-8.2	10.1	10.1	5.1	-3.3	-7.3
Return, Tax-Adjusted (%)	-17.2	-11.4	7.2	19.2	15.8	34.9	28.2	37.0	-5.4	-0.5

PER SHARE DATA

	2002	2001	2000	1999	1998	1997	1996	1995	1994	1993
Dividends, Net Income ($)	0.20	0.14	0.13	0.15	0.15	0.20	0.18	0.22	0.22	0.26
Distrib'ns, Cap Gain ($)	0.00	0.24	3.46	1.44	0.26	2.02	1.30	0.15	0.82	3.22
Net Asset Value ($)	25.51	30.99	35.33	35.80	31.16	27.18	21.53	17.68	13.09	14.60
Expense Ratio (%)	na	0.92	0.92	0.93	0.94	0.96	1.03	1.16	1.26	1.01
Yield (%)	0.78	0.44	0.33	0.40	0.47	0.68	0.78	1.23	1.58	1.45
Portfolio Turnover (%)	na	22	22	21	20	26	29	27	23	79
Total Assets (Millions $)	4,569	5,562	5,703	3,703	2,905	2,218	1,378	924	502	451

PORTFOLIO (as of 8/31/02)

Portfolio Manager: Christopher Davis/Ken Feinberg - 1997

Investment Style

✔ Large Cap	Growth
Mid Cap	✔ Value
Small Cap	Grth/Val

Portfolio

6.4% cash	0.6% corp bonds
92.8% stocks	0.1% gov't bonds
0.0% preferred	0.0% muni bonds
0.1% conv't bds/wrnts	0.0% other

SHAREHOLDER INFORMATION

Minimum Investment
Initial: $1,000 Subsequent: $25

Minimum IRA Investment
Initial: $250 Subsequent: $25

Maximum Fees
Load: none 12b-1: 0.25%
Other: none

Services
✔ IRA
✔ Keogh
✔ Telephone Exchange

T Rowe Price Bl Chp Gr (TRBCX)

800-638-5660, 410-345-2000
www.troweprice.com

Large-Cap Stock

PERFORMANCE

fund inception date: 6/30/93

	3yr Annual	5yr Annual	10yr Annual	Bull	Bear
Return (%)	-14.1	-0.4	na	68.6	-44.8
Differ From Category (+/-)	-0.3 av	0.5 av	na	-6.1 av	-5.7 av

Standard Deviation	Category Risk Index	Beta
20.8%—abv av	1.09—abv av	1.07

	2002	2001	2000	1999	1998	1997	1996	1995	1994	1993
Return (%)	-24.2	-14.4	-2.5	19.9	28.8	27.5	27.7	37.8	0.8	—
Differ From Category (+/-)	-2.1	-1.6	2.7	-5.5	4.4	0.4	7.1	4.9	0.7	—
Return, Tax-Adjusted (%)	-24.2	-14.4	-3.4	19.6	28.3	27.2	27.2	37.1	0.1	—

PER SHARE DATA

	2002	2001	2000	1999	1998	1997	1996	1995	1994	1993
Dividends, Net Income ($)	0.00	0.00	0.00	0.03	0.11	0.12	0.14	0.15	0.11	—
Distrib'ns, Cap Gain ($)	0.00	0.00	1.62	0.33	0.39	0.01	0.08	0.08	0.11	—
Net Asset Value ($)	21.95	28.97	33.85	36.34	30.60	24.17	19.06	15.09	11.11	—
Expense Ratio (%)	na	0.96	0.91	0.91	0.91	0.95	1.12	1.25	1.25	—
Yield (%)	0.00	0.00	0.00	0.08	0.35	0.49	0.73	0.98	0.98	—
Portfolio Turnover (%)	na	48	50	41	35	23	26	43	75	—
Total Assets (Millions $)	4,868	6,242	7,113	6,708	4,330	2,344	539	146	38	—

PORTFOLIO (as of 9/30/02)

Portfolio Manager: Team Managed - 1996

Investment Style

✔ Large Cap	Growth
Mid Cap	Value
Small Cap	✔ Grth/Val

Portfolio

0.0% cash	0.0% corp bonds
100.0% stocks	0.0% gov't bonds
0.0% preferred	0.0% muni bonds
0.0% conv't bds/wrnts	0.0% other

SHAREHOLDER INFORMATION

Minimum Investment
Initial: $2,500 Subsequent: $100

Minimum IRA Investment
Initial: $1,000 Subsequent: $50

Maximum Fees
Load: none 12b-1: none
Other: none

Services
✔ IRA
✔ Keogh
✔ Telephone Exchange

T Rowe Price Eq Inc

800-638-5660, 410-345-2000
www.troweprice.com

(PRFDX)

Large-Cap Stock

PERFORMANCE — fund inception date: 10/31/85

	3yr Annual	5yr Annual	10yr Annual	Bull	Bear
Return (%)	0.0	2.5	10.9	17.9	-5.6
Differ From Category (+/-)	13.8 high	3.4 high	3.0 high	-56.8 low	33.5 high

Standard Deviation	Category Risk Index	Beta
16.9%—av	0.88—blw av	0.70

	2002	2001	2000	1999	1998	1997	1996	1995	1994	1993
Return (%)	-13.0	1.6	13.1	3.8	9.2	28.8	20.3	33.3	4.5	14.8
Differ From Category (+/-)	9.1	14.4	18.3	-21.6	-15.2	1.7	-0.3	0.4	4.4	2.1
Return, Tax-Adjusted (%)	-14.0	0.2	10.2	1.5	7.1	25.7	17.8	30.7	1.7	12.1

PER SHARE DATA

	2002	2001	2000	1999	1998	1997	1996	1995	1994	1993
Dividends, Net Income ($)	0.36	0.36	0.51	0.53	0.61	0.66	0.65	0.65	0.59	0.54
Distrib'ns, Cap Gain ($)	0.45	1.01	2.64	1.97	1.49	2.14	0.84	0.54	0.81	0.72
Net Asset Value ($)	19.79	23.65	24.67	24.81	26.32	26.07	22.54	20.01	15.98	16.65
Expense Ratio (%)	na	0.80	0.60	0.77	0.77	0.79	0.81	0.85	0.88	0.91
Yield (%)	1.77	1.45	1.86	1.97	2.19	2.33	2.78	3.16	3.51	3.10
Portfolio Turnover (%)	na	17	21	22	23	23	25	28	36	31
Total Assets (Millions $)	9,382	10,128	10,186	12,321	13,495	12,771	7,818	5,214	3,203	2,851

PORTFOLIO (as of 9/30/02)

Portfolio Manager: Team Managed - 1993

Investment Style

✔ Large Cap — Growth
✔ Mid Cap — ✔ Value
Small Cap — Grth/Val

Portfolio

4.6%	cash	0.0%	corp bonds
95.0%	stocks	0.0%	gov't bonds
0.5%	pref/conv't pref	0.0%	muni bonds
0.0%	conv't bds/wrnts	0.0%	other

SHAREHOLDER INFORMATION

Minimum Investment
Initial: $2,500 — Subsequent: $100

Minimum IRA Investment
Initial: $1,000 — Subsequent: $50

Maximum Fees
Load: none — 12b-1: none
Other: none

Services
✔ IRA
✔ Keogh
✔ Telephone Exchange

T Rowe Price Gr & Inc

800-638-5660, 410-345-2000
www.troweprice.com

(PRGIX)

Large-Cap Stock

PERFORMANCE

fund inception date: 12/21/82

	3yr Annual	5yr Annual	10yr Annual	Bull	Bear
Return (%)	-6.7	-1.5	7.8	22.7	-25.3
Differ From Category (+/-)	7.1 abv av	-0.6 blw av	-0.1 av	-52.0 low	13.8 high

Standard Deviation	Category Risk Index	Beta
18.8%—abv av	0.98—av	0.94

	2002	2001	2000	1999	1998	1997	1996	1995	1994	1993
Return (%)	-23.8	-2.1	8.9	3.7	9.9	23.5	25.6	30.9	-0.1	12.9
Differ From Category (+/-)	-1.7	10.7	14.1	-21.7	-14.5	-3.6	5.0	-2.0	-0.2	0.2
Return, Tax-Adjusted (%)	-24.2	-3.2	6.9	1.2	7.5	21.7	23.2	28.3	-2.0	10.8

PER SHARE DATA

	2002	2001	2000	1999	1998	1997	1996	1995	1994	1993
Dividends, Net Income ($)	0.16	0.26	0.34	0.51	0.53	0.56	0.51	0.59	0.49	0.47
Distrib'ns, Cap Gain ($)	0.15	0.78	1.83	2.25	2.13	0.97	0.90	0.60	0.42	0.48
Net Asset Value ($)	17.11	22.82	24.44	24.44	26.25	26.36	22.63	19.18	15.63	16.57
Expense Ratio (%)	na	0.81	0.77	0.77	0.77	0.78	0.82	0.81	0.81	0.83
Yield (%)	0.92	1.10	1.29	1.91	1.86	2.04	2.16	2.98	3.05	2.75
Portfolio Turnover (%)	na	66	80	20	21	15	13	26	25	22
Total Assets (Millions $)	1,782	2,394	2,989	3,439	3,563	3,446	2,488	1,748	1,228	1,167

PORTFOLIO (as of 9/30/02)

Portfolio Manager: R Sharps/Team
Managed - 2002

Investment Style

✔ Large Cap	Growth
Mid Cap	✔ Value
Small Cap	Grth/Val

Portfolio

2.4%	cash	0.3%	corp bonds
96.5%	stocks	0.0%	gov't bonds
0.7%	pref/conv't pref	0.0%	muni bonds
0.0%	conv't bds/wrnts	0.0%	other

SHAREHOLDER INFORMATION

Minimum Investment
Initial: $2,500 Subsequent: $100

Minimum IRA Investment
Initial: $1,000 Subsequent: $50

Maximum Fees
Load: none 12b-1: none
Other: none

Services
✔ IRA
✔ Keogh
✔ Telephone Exchange

T Rowe Price Gr Stock

800-638-5660, 410-345-2000
www.troweprice.com

(PRGFX)

Large-Cap Stock

PERFORMANCE

fund inception date: 4/11/50

	3yr Annual	5yr Annual	10yr Annual	Bull	Bear
Return (%)	-11.3	1.6	9.8	72.8	-40.7
Differ From Category (+/-)	2.5 abv av	2.5 high	1.9 high	-1.9 abv av	-1.6 av

Standard Deviation	Category Risk Index	Beta
20.9%—abv av	1.09—abv av	1.06

	2002	2001	2000	1999	1998	1997	1996	1995	1994	1993
Return (%)	-22.9	-9.7	0.2	22.1	27.4	26.5	21.7	30.9	0.8	15.5
Differ From Category (+/-)	-0.8	3.1	5.4	-3.3	3.0	-0.6	1.1	-2.0	0.7	2.8
Return, Tax-Adjusted (%)	-23.0	-10.0	-3.7	18.6	24.1	23.2	18.9	29.0	-1.8	13.7

PER SHARE DATA

	2002	2001	2000	1999	1998	1997	1996	1995	1994	1993
Dividends, Net Income ($)	0.04	0.08	0.07	0.10	0.25	0.20	0.19	0.23	0.18	0.14
Distrib'ns, Cap Gain ($)	0.00	0.27	6.28	5.42	4.27	3.87	2.06	0.97	1.66	0.99
Net Asset Value ($)	18.58	24.18	27.20	33.27	32.07	28.99	26.18	23.35	18.75	20.42
Expense Ratio (%)	na	0.77	0.73	0.74	0.74	0.75	0.77	0.80	0.81	0.82
Yield (%)	0.21	0.32	0.20	0.25	0.68	0.60	0.67	0.94	0.88	0.65
Portfolio Turnover (%)	na	64	74	56	55	40	49	44	54	35
Total Assets (Millions $)	3,941	4,684	5,428	5,672	5,041	3,988	3,430	2,761	2,067	1,975

PORTFOLIO (as of 9/30/02)

Portfolio Manager: Team Managed - 1997

Investment Style

✔ Large Cap	✔ Growth
Mid Cap	Value
Small Cap	Grth/Val

Portfolio

3.1% cash	0.0% corp bonds
96.9% stocks	0.0% gov't bonds
0.0% preferred	0.0% muni bonds
0.0% conv't bds/wrnts	0.0% other

SHAREHOLDER INFORMATION

Minimum Investment
Initial: $2,500 Subsequent: $100

Minimum IRA Investment
Initial: $1,000 Subsequent: $50

Maximum Fees
Load: none 12b-1: none
Other: none

Services
✔ IRA
✔ Keogh
✔ Telephone Exchange

T Rowe Price Spect Gr (PRSGX)

800-638-5660, 410-345-2000
www.troweprice.com

Large-Cap Stock

PERFORMANCE — fund inception date: 6/29/90

	3yr Annual	5yr Annual	10yr Annual	Bull	Bear
Return (%)	-9.9	0.1	8.5	57.4	-34.9
Differ From Category (+/-)	3.9 abv av	1.0 abv av	0.6 av	-17.3 blw av	4.2 abv av

Standard Deviation	Category Risk Index	Beta
19.3%—abv av	1.01—av	0.94

	2002	2001	2000	1999	1998	1997	1996	1995	1994	1993
Return (%)	-20.8	-7.6	-0.1	21.1	13.6	17.3	20.5	29.9	1.3	20.9
Differ From Category (+/-)	1.3	5.2	5.1	-4.3	-10.8	-9.8	-0.1	-3.0	1.2	8.2
Return, Tax-Adjusted (%)	-20.8	-8.4	-2.5	18.4	11.4	14.7	18.0	27.2	-1.0	18.4

PER SHARE DATA

	2002	2001	2000	1999	1998	1997	1996	1995	1994	1993
Dividends, Net Income ($)	0.00	0.16	0.12	0.17	0.18	0.20	0.20	0.21	0.17	0.16
Distrib'ns, Cap Gain ($)	0.00	0.28	1.85	1.91	1.37	1.60	0.93	0.76	0.73	0.72
Net Asset Value ($)	11.13	14.07	15.72	17.71	16.45	15.93	15.13	13.49	11.13	11.87
Expense Ratio (%)	na	0.87	0.83	na	na	na	na	na	na	na
Yield (%)	0.00	1.11	0.68	0.86	1.01	1.14	1.24	1.47	1.43	1.27
Portfolio Turnover (%)	na	6	11	20	18	20	2	8	20	7
Total Assets (Millions $)	1,840	2,373	2,888	3,030	2,768	2,605	2,104	1,358	879	584

PORTFOLIO (as of 12/31/02)

Portfolio Manager: E Notzon/Team
Managed - 1998

Investment Style

✔ Large Cap	✔ Growth
✔ Mid Cap	Value
Small Cap	Grth/Val

Portfolio

0.0% cash	0.0% corp bonds
0.0% stocks	0.0% gov't bonds
0.0% preferred	0.0% muni bonds
0.0% conv't bds/wrnts	100.0% other

SHAREHOLDER INFORMATION

Minimum Investment
Initial: $2,500 — Subsequent: $100

Minimum IRA Investment
Initial: $1,000 — Subsequent: $50

Maximum Fees
Load: none — 12b-1: none
Other: none

Services
✔ IRA
✔ Keogh
✔ Telephone Exchange

TIAA-CREF Growth & Income (TIGIX)

800-223-1200, 212-490-9000
www.tiaa-cref.org

Large-Cap Stock

PERFORMANCE — fund inception date: 9/2/97

	3yr Annual	5yr Annual	10yr Annual	Bull	Bear
Return (%)	-15.1	-0.1	na	67.6	-45.3
Differ From Category (+/-)	-1.3 av	0.8 abv av	na	-7.1 av	-6.2 av

Standard Deviation	Category Risk Index	Beta
18.9%—abv av	0.99—av	1.00

	2002	2001	2000	1999	1998	1997	1996	1995	1994	1993
Return (%)	-23.8	-13.3	-7.3	24.4	30.5	—	—	—	—	—
Differ From Category (+/-)	-1.7	-0.5	-2.1	-1.0	6.1	—	—	—	—	—
Return, Tax-Adjusted (%)	-24.1	-13.6	-8.4	23.3	30.1	—	—	—	—	—

PER SHARE DATA

	2002	2001	2000	1999	1998	1997	1996	1995	1994	1993
Dividends, Net Income ($)	0.10	0.10	0.11	0.11	0.10	—	—	—	—	—
Distrib'ns, Cap Gain ($)	0.00	0.00	0.61	0.53	0.02	—	—	—	—	—
Net Asset Value ($)	9.09	12.07	14.05	15.93	13.33	—	—	—	—	—
Expense Ratio (%)	na	0.43	0.43	0.43	0.43	—	—	—	—	—
Yield (%)	1.10	0.82	0.75	0.66	0.74	—	—	—	—	—
Portfolio Turnover (%)	na	70	21	39	71	—	—	—	—	—
Total Assets (Millions $)	530	637	664	541	na	—	—	—	—	—

PORTFOLIO (as of 9/30/02)

Portfolio Manager: Team Managed - 1997

Investment Style

✔ Large Cap	Growth
Mid Cap	Value
Small Cap	✔ Grth/Val

Portfolio

0.1% cash	0.0% corp bonds
99.9% stocks	0.0% gov't bonds
0.0% preferred	0.0% muni bonds
0.0% conv't bds/wrnts	0.0% other

SHAREHOLDER INFORMATION

Minimum Investment
Initial: $1,500 — Subsequent: $50

Minimum IRA Investment
Initial: $500 — Subsequent: $50

Maximum Fees
Load: none — 12b-1: none
Other: none

Services
✔ IRA
Keogh
✔ Telephone Exchange

Vanguard 500 Idx/Inv (VFINX)

800-662-7447, 610-436-5152
www.vanguard.com

Large-Cap Stock

PERFORMANCE — fund inception date: 8/31/76

	3yr Annual	5yr Annual	10yr Annual	Bull	Bear
Return (%)	-14.5	-0.6	9.2	59.9	-43.7
Differ From Category (+/-)	-0.7 av	0.3 av	1.3 abv av	-14.8 av	-4.6 av

Standard Deviation	Category Risk Index	Beta
18.8%—av	0.98—av	0.99

	2002	2001	2000	1999	1998	1997	1996	1995	1994	1993
Return (%)	-22.1	-12.0	-9.0	21.0	28.6	33.2	22.8	37.4	1.1	9.8
Differ From Category (+/-)	0.0	0.8	-3.8	-4.4	4.2	6.1	2.2	4.5	1.0	-2.9
Return, Tax-Adjusted (%)	-22.6	-12.4	-9.4	20.3	27.9	32.3	21.8	36.2	-0.1	8.7

PER SHARE DATA

	2002	2001	2000	1999	1998	1997	1996	1995	1994	1993
Dividends, Net Income ($)	1.36	1.27	1.30	1.41	1.33	1.32	1.28	1.22	1.17	1.13
Distrib'ns, Cap Gain ($)	0.00	0.00	0.00	0.99	0.42	0.59	0.25	0.13	0.20	0.03
Net Asset Value ($)	81.15	105.89	121.86	135.33	113.95	90.07	69.16	57.60	42.97	43.83
Expense Ratio (%)	na	0.18	0.18	0.18	0.18	0.19	0.20	0.20	0.19	0.19
Yield (%)	1.67	1.19	1.06	1.03	1.16	1.45	1.84	2.11	2.71	2.57
Portfolio Turnover (%)	na	4	9	6	6	5	5	4	6	6
Total Assets (Millions $)	59,672	73,150	88,240	104,652	74,228	49,357	30,331	17,371	9,356	8,272

PORTFOLIO (as of 9/30/02)

Portfolio Manager: George Sauter - 1987

Investment Style

✔ Large Cap	Growth
Mid Cap	Value
Small Cap	✔ Grth/Val

Portfolio

0.0% cash	0.0% corp bonds
100.0% stocks	0.0% gov't bonds
0.0% preferred	0.0% muni bonds
0.0% conv't bds/wrnts	0.0% other

SHAREHOLDER INFORMATION

Minimum Investment
Initial: $3,000 Subsequent: $100

Minimum IRA Investment
Initial: $1,000 Subsequent: $100

Maximum Fees
Load: none 12b-1: none
Other: none

Services
✔ IRA
✔ Keogh
✔ Telephone Exchange

Vanguard Equity Income (VEIPX)

800-662-7447, 610-436-5152
www.vanguard.com

Large-Cap Stock

PERFORMANCE — fund inception date: 3/21/88

	3yr Annual	5yr Annual	10yr Annual	Bull	Bear
Return (%)	-2.1	1.8	10.0	19.1	-12.4
Differ From Category (+/-)	11.7 high	2.7 high	2.1 high	-55.6 low	26.7 high

Standard Deviation	Category Risk Index	Beta
15.8%—av	0.83—low	0.65

	2002	2001	2000	1999	1998	1997	1996	1995	1994	1993
Return (%)	-15.6	-2.3	13.5	-0.1	17.3	31.1	17.3	37.3	-1.5	14.6
Differ From Category (+/-)	6.5	10.5	18.7	-25.5	-7.1	4.0	-3.3	4.4	-1.6	1.9
Return, Tax-Adjusted (%)	-16.4	-3.6	11.5	-1.8	15.4	28.7	14.8	35.1	-3.4	11.6

PER SHARE DATA

	2002	2001	2000	1999	1998	1997	1996	1995	1994	1993
Dividends, Net Income ($)	0.48	0.51	0.61	0.65	0.64	0.67	0.64	0.60	0.58	0.61
Distrib'ns, Cap Gain ($)	0.00	0.60	1.14	0.87	0.83	0.89	0.58	0.17	0.09	0.52
Net Asset Value ($)	18.70	22.71	24.44	23.17	24.73	22.39	18.32	16.69	12.77	13.66
Expense Ratio (%)	0.47	0.47	0.43	0.41	0.39	0.45	0.42	0.47	0.43	0.40
Yield (%)	2.56	2.18	2.38	2.70	2.50	2.87	3.38	3.55	4.51	4.30
Portfolio Turnover (%)	21	31	36	18	23	22	21	31	18	15
Total Assets (Millions $)	1,996	2,249	2,561	2,874	2,938	2,099	1,424	1,102	869	1,067

PORTFOLIO (as of 9/30/02)

Portfolio Manager: Team Managed - 1988

Investment Style

✔ Large Cap	Growth
Mid Cap	✔ Value
Small Cap	Grth/Val

Portfolio

2.5%	cash	0.4%	corp bonds
97.1%	stocks	0.0%	gov't bonds
0.0%	preferred	0.0%	muni bonds
0.0%	conv't bds/wrnts	0.0%	other

SHAREHOLDER INFORMATION

Minimum Investment
Initial: $3,000 Subsequent: $100

Minimum IRA Investment
Initial: $1,000 Subsequent: $100

Maximum Fees
Load: none 12b-1: none
Other: none

Services
✔ IRA
✔ Keogh
✔ Telephone Exchange

Vanguard Gr Idx/Inv (VIGRX)

800-662-7447, 610-436-5152
www.vanguard.com

Large-Cap Stock

PERFORMANCE — fund inception date: 11/2/92

	3yr Annual	5yr Annual	10yr Annual	Bull	Bear
Return (%)	-19.7	-1.0	8.6	78.1	-53.5
Differ From Category (+/-)	-5.9 blw av	-0.1 av	0.7 av	3.4 abv av	-14.4 blw av

Standard Deviation	Category Risk Index	Beta
21.4%—abv av	1.12—abv av	1.07

	2002	2001	2000	1999	1998	1997	1996	1995	1994	1993
Return (%)	-23.6	-12.9	-22.2	28.7	42.2	36.2	23.8	38.0	2.8	0.6
Differ From Category (+/-)	-1.5	-0.1	-17.0	3.3	17.8	9.1	3.2	5.1	2.7	-12.1
Return, Tax-Adjusted (%)	-23.9	-13.1	-22.3	27.8	41.7	35.4	22.9	37.2	2.0	-0.2

PER SHARE DATA

	2002	2001	2000	1999	1998	1997	1996	1995	1994	1993
Dividends, Net Income ($)	0.22	0.18	0.12	0.22	0.21	0.23	0.22	0.20	0.21	0.21
Distrib'ns, Cap Gain ($)	0.00	0.00	0.00	1.04	0.11	0.25	0.14	0.00	0.00	0.00
Net Asset Value ($)	19.95	26.41	30.57	39.43	31.67	22.53	16.91	13.97	10.28	10.20
Expense Ratio (%)	na	0.22	0.22	0.22	0.22	0.20	0.20	0.20	0.20	0.20
Yield (%)	1.10	0.68	0.39	0.54	0.66	1.00	1.29	1.43	2.04	2.05
Portfolio Turnover (%)	na	31	33	33	29	26	29	23	28	36
Total Assets (Millions $)	6,566	8,444	11,162	15,232	6,644	2,365	786	271	86	50

PORTFOLIO (as of 9/30/02)

Portfolio Manager: Team Managed - 1992

Investment Style

✔ Large Cap	✔ Growth
Mid Cap	Value
Small Cap	Grth/Val

Portfolio

0.0% cash	0.0% corp bonds
100.0% stocks	0.0% gov't bonds
0.0% preferred	0.0% muni bonds
0.0% conv't bds/wrnts	0.0% other

SHAREHOLDER INFORMATION

Minimum Investment
Initial: $3,000 — Subsequent: $100

Minimum IRA Investment
Initial: $1,000 — Subsequent: $100

Maximum Fees
Load: none — 12b-1: none
Other: none

Services
✔ IRA
✔ Keogh
Telephone Exchange

Vanguard Gr&In/Inv
(VQNPX)

800-662-7447, 610-436-5152
www.vanguard.com

Large-Cap Stock

PERFORMANCE — fund inception date: 12/10/86

	3yr Annual	5yr Annual	10yr Annual	Bull	Bear
Return (%)	-14.2	-0.2	9.7	60.7	-40.9
Differ From Category (+/-)	-0.4 av	0.7 abv av	1.8 high	-14.0 av	-1.8 av

Standard Deviation	Category Risk Index	Beta
18.7%—av	0.98—blw av	0.98

	2002	2001	2000	1999	1998	1997	1996	1995	1994	1993
Return (%)	-21.9	-11.1	-8.9	26.0	23.9	35.5	23.0	35.9	-0.6	13.8
Differ From Category (+/-)	0.2	1.7	-3.7	0.6	-0.5	8.4	2.4	3.0	-0.7	1.1
Return, Tax-Adjusted (%)	-22.3	-11.5	-10.1	24.7	22.4	31.9	19.7	33.5	-2.2	9.9

PER SHARE DATA

	2002	2001	2000	1999	1998	1997	1996	1995	1994	1993
Dividends, Net Income ($)	0.28	0.30	0.35	0.33	0.33	0.42	0.40	0.42	0.39	0.39
Distrib'ns, Cap Gain ($)	0.00	0.00	1.47	1.28	1.28	3.18	1.82	0.74	0.40	1.69
Net Asset Value ($)	21.75	28.20	32.06	37.08	30.76	26.19	22.23	19.95	15.56	16.45
Expense Ratio (%)	0.45	0.40	0.38	0.37	0.36	0.36	0.38	0.50	0.48	0.50
Yield (%)	1.28	1.06	1.04	0.86	1.02	1.43	1.66	2.02	2.44	2.14
Portfolio Turnover (%)	70	41	65	54	47	66	75	78	71	85
Total Assets (Millions $)	4,870	6,924	8,967	8,816	5,160	2,141	1,285	909	596	530

PORTFOLIO (as of 9/30/02)

Portfolio Manager: John Cone - 1986

Investment Style

✔ Large Cap	Growth
Mid Cap	Value
Small Cap	✔ Grth/Val

Portfolio

0.1%	cash	0.0%	corp bonds
99.9%	stocks	0.0%	gov't bonds
0.0%	preferred	0.0%	muni bonds
0.0%	conv't bds/wrnts	0.0%	other

SHAREHOLDER INFORMATION

Minimum Investment
Initial: $3,000 — Subsequent: $100

Minimum IRA Investment
Initial: $1,000 — Subsequent: $100

Maximum Fees
Load: none — 12b-1: none
Other: none

Services
✔ IRA
✔ Keogh
Telephone Exchange

Vanguard Morgan Gr/Inv (VMRGX)

800-662-7447, 610-436-5152
www.vanguard.com

Large-Cap Stock

PERFORMANCE

fund inception date: 12/31/68

	3yr Annual	5yr Annual	10yr Annual	Bull	Bear
Return (%)	-16.6	-1.0	8.1	91.1	-49.3
Differ From Category (+/-)	-2.8 blw av	-0.1 av	0.2 av	16.4 abv av	-10.2 blw av

Standard Deviation	Category Risk Index	Beta
22.8%—abv av	1.19—abv av	1.13

	2002	2001	2000	1999	1998	1997	1996	1995	1994	1993
Return (%)	-23.5	-13.6	-12.5	34.1	22.2	30.8	23.3	35.9	-1.6	7.3
Differ From Category (+/-)	-1.4	-0.8	-7.3	8.7	-2.2	3.7	2.7	3.0	-1.7	-5.4
Return, Tax-Adjusted (%)	-23.6	-13.8	-15.3	30.7	20.2	27.2	19.9	32.5	-2.8	3.7

PER SHARE DATA

	2002	2001	2000	1999	1998	1997	1996	1995	1994	1993
Dividends, Net Income ($)	0.04	0.07	0.15	0.15	0.18	0.16	0.14	0.15	0.14	0.18
Distrib'ns, Cap Gain ($)	0.00	0.05	2.95	3.08	1.43	2.52	1.53	1.16	0.31	1.35
Net Asset Value ($)	11.15	14.63	17.08	22.92	19.72	17.54	15.63	14.09	11.36	12.01
Expense Ratio (%)	na	0.40	0.40	0.42	0.44	0.48	0.51	0.47	0.50	0.49
Yield (%)	0.35	0.47	0.74	0.57	0.85	0.79	0.81	0.98	1.19	1.34
Portfolio Turnover (%)	na	53	94	65	81	76	73	72	84	72
Total Assets (Millions $)	2,738	3,492	4,660	5,066	3,555	2,795	2,053	1,471	1,074	1,135

PORTFOLIO (as of 9/30/02)

Portfolio Manager: Team Managed - 1990

Investment Style

✔ Large Cap ✔ Growth
✔ Mid Cap Value
Small Cap Grth/Val

Portfolio

1.7% cash	0.0% corp bonds
98.3% stocks	0.0% gov't bonds
0.0% preferred	0.0% muni bonds
0.0% conv't bds/wrnts	0.0% other

SHAREHOLDER INFORMATION

Minimum Investment
Initial: $3,000 Subsequent: $100

Minimum IRA Investment
Initial: $1,000 Subsequent: $100

Maximum Fees
Load: none 12b-1: none
Other: none

Services
✔ IRA
✔ Keogh
✔ Telephone Exchange

Vanguard PRIMECAP (VPMCX)

800-662-7447, 610-436-5152
www.vanguard.com

Large-Cap Stock

PERFORMANCE

fund inception date: 11/1/84

	3yr Annual	5yr Annual	10yr Annual	Bull	Bear
Return (%)	-11.9	3.8	13.3	128.5	-47.6
Differ From Category (+/-)	1.9 abv av	4.7 high	5.4 high	53.8 high	-8.5 blw av

Standard Deviation	Category Risk Index	Beta
24.1%—high	1.26—high	1.06

	2002	2001	2000	1999	1998	1997	1996	1995	1994	1993
Return (%)	-24.5	-13.3	4.4	41.3	25.4	36.8	18.3	35.4	11.4	18.0
Differ From Category (+/-)	-2.4	-0.5	9.6	15.9	1.0	9.7	-2.3	2.5	11.3	5.3
Return, Tax-Adjusted (%)	-24.7	-13.7	2.8	39.1	24.3	35.7	17.2	34.1	10.5	16.8

PER SHARE DATA

	2002	2001	2000	1999	1998	1997	1996	1995	1994	1993
Dividends, Net Income ($)	0.21	0.28	0.49	0.27	0.35	0.20	0.20	0.22	0.19	0.07
Distrib'ns, Cap Gain ($)	0.00	0.52	4.05	4.65	1.52	1.30	0.73	0.59	0.34	0.59
Net Asset Value ($)	38.66	51.52	60.38	62.07	47.66	39.57	30.08	26.23	19.98	18.42
Expense Ratio (%)	0.49	0.50	0.48	0.51	0.51	0.51	0.59	0.60	0.64	0.67
Yield (%)	0.54	0.53	0.76	0.40	0.71	0.48	0.64	0.82	0.93	0.36
Portfolio Turnover (%)	11	7	11	19	13	13	10	4	8	16
Total Assets (Millions $)	14,053	18,096	21,762	17,911	11,209	8,186	4,203	3,236	1,533	790

PORTFOLIO (as of 9/30/02)

Portfolio Manager: Team Managed - 1984

Investment Style

✔ Large Cap	✔ Growth
✔ Mid Cap	Value
Small Cap	Grth/Val

Portfolio

6.6%	cash	0.0%	corp bonds
93.4%	stocks	0.0%	gov't bonds
0.0%	preferred	0.0%	muni bonds
0.0%	conv't bds/wrnts	0.0%	other

SHAREHOLDER INFORMATION

Minimum Investment
Initial: $3,000 Subsequent: $100

Minimum IRA Investment
Initial: $1,000 Subsequent: $100

Maximum Fees
Load: none 12b-1: none
Other: none

Services
✔ IRA
✔ Keogh
✔ Telephone Exchange

Vanguard Tot Stk Idx/Inv (VTSMX)

800-662-7447, 610-436-5152
www.vanguard.com

Large-Cap Stock

PERFORMANCE

fund inception date: 4/27/92

	3yr Annual	5yr Annual	10yr Annual	Bull	Bear
Return (%)	-14.3	-0.8	8.6	66.6	-43.7
Differ From Category (+/-)	-0.5 av	0.1 av	0.7 av	-8.1 av	-4.6 av

Standard Deviation	Category Risk Index	Beta
19.0%—abv av	0.99—av	0.97

	2002	2001	2000	1999	1998	1997	1996	1995	1994	1993
Return (%)	-20.9	-10.9	-10.5	23.8	23.2	30.9	20.9	35.7	-0.1	10.6
Differ From Category (+/-)	1.2	1.9	-5.3	-1.6	-1.2	3.8	0.3	2.8	-0.2	-2.1
Return, Tax-Adjusted (%)	-21.3	-11.3	-11.0	23.1	22.5	29.9	19.9	34.5	-1.1	9.6

PER SHARE DATA

	2002	2001	2000	1999	1998	1997	1996	1995	1994	1993
Dividends, Net Income ($)	0.29	0.29	0.33	0.33	0.32	0.32	0.29	0.28	0.27	0.26
Distrib'ns, Cap Gain ($)	0.00	0.00	0.14	0.32	0.12	0.27	0.11	0.09	0.03	0.03
Net Asset Value ($)	20.07	25.74	29.26	33.22	27.42	22.64	17.77	15.04	11.37	11.69
Expense Ratio (%)	na	0.20	0.20	0.20	0.20	0.20	0.22	0.20	0.20	0.20
Yield (%)	1.44	1.12	1.12	0.98	1.16	1.39	1.62	1.85	2.36	2.21
Portfolio Turnover (%)	na	7	7	3	3	2	3	2	2	1
Total Assets (Millions $)	14,916	15,781	16,855	18,133	9,307	5,092	3,530	1,570	785	512

PORTFOLIO (as of 9/30/02)

Portfolio Manager: George Sauter - 1992

Investment Style

✔ Large Cap　　Growth
✔ Mid Cap　　Value
Small Cap　　✔ Grth/Val

Portfolio

0.3% cash　　0.0% corp bonds
99.7% stocks　　0.0% gov't bonds
0.0% preferred　　0.0% muni bonds
0.0% conv't bds/wrnts　　0.0% other

SHAREHOLDER INFORMATION

Minimum Investment
Initial: $3,000　　Subsequent: $100

Minimum IRA Investment
Initial: $1,000　　Subsequent: $100

Maximum Fees
Load: none　　12b-1: none
Other: none

Services
✔ IRA
✔ Keogh
Telephone Exchange

Vanguard Tx Mg Cp Apr (VMCAX)

800-662-7447, 610-436-5152
www.vanguard.com

Large-Cap Stock

PERFORMANCE

fund inception date: 9/6/94

	3yr Annual	5yr Annual	10yr Annual	Bull	Bear
Return (%)	-16.4	-0.1	na	93.2	-50.2
Differ From Category (+/-)	-2.6 blw av	0.8 abv av	na	18.5 abv av	-11.1 blw av

Standard Deviation	Category Risk Index	Beta
21.6%—abv av	1.13—abv av	1.11

	2002	2001	2000	1999	1998	1997	1996	1995	1994	1993
Return (%)	-23.4	-15.3	-10.1	33.5	27.9	27.2	20.9	34.3	—	—
Differ From Category (+/-)	-1.3	-2.5	-4.9	8.1	3.5	0.1	0.3	1.4	—	—
Return, Tax-Adjusted (%)	-23.7	-15.5	-10.2	33.3	27.6	26.9	20.6	33.9	—	—

PER SHARE DATA

	2002	2001	2000	1999	1998	1997	1996	1995	1994	1993
Dividends, Net Income ($)	0.20	0.17	0.11	0.12	0.13	0.12	0.11	0.09	—	—
Distrib'ns, Cap Gain ($)	0.00	0.00	0.00	0.00	0.00	0.00	0.00	0.00	—	—
Net Asset Value ($)	19.49	25.73	30.59	34.17	25.68	20.18	15.95	13.28	—	—
Expense Ratio (%)	na	0.18	0.19	0.19	0.19	0.17	0.20	0.20	—	—
Yield (%)	1.02	0.66	0.35	0.35	0.50	0.59	0.68	0.67	—	—
Portfolio Turnover (%)	na	13	17	12	5	4	12	7	—	—
Total Assets (Millions $)	1,244	1,677	2,643	2,378	1,478	892	517	254	—	—

PORTFOLIO (as of 9/30/02)

Portfolio Manager: Team Managed/George Sauter - 1994

Investment Style

✔ Large Cap	Growth
Mid Cap	Value
Small Cap	✔ Grth/Val

Portfolio

0.1%	cash	0.0%	corp bonds
99.9%	stocks	0.0%	gov't bonds
0.0%	preferred	0.0%	muni bonds
0.0%	conv't bds/wrnts	0.0%	other

SHAREHOLDER INFORMATION

Minimum Investment
Initial: $10,000 Subsequent: $100

Minimum IRA Investment
Initial: $10,000 Subsequent: $100

Maximum Fees
Load: 2.00% redemption 12b-1: none
Other: redemption fee applies for 12 months

Services
✔ IRA
Keogh
✔ Telephone Exchange

Vanguard Tx Mg Gr&Inc (VTGIX)

800-662-7447, 610-436-5152
www.vanguard.com

Large-Cap Stock

PERFORMANCE

fund inception date: 9/6/94

	3yr Annual	5yr Annual	10yr Annual	Bull	Bear
Return (%)	-14.4	-0.5	na	59.8	-43.5
Differ From Category (+/-)	-0.6 av	0.4 av	na	-14.9 av	-4.4 av

Standard Deviation	Category Risk Index	Beta
18.7%—av	0.98—blw av	0.99

	2002	2001	2000	1999	1998	1997	1996	1995	1994	1993
Return (%)	-21.9	-11.9	-9.0	21.1	28.6	33.3	23.0	37.5	—	—
Differ From Category (+/-)	0.2	0.9	-3.8	-4.3	4.2	6.2	2.4	4.6	—	—
Return, Tax-Adjusted (%)	-22.4	-12.3	-9.4	20.6	28.1	32.6	22.2	36.5	—	—

PER SHARE DATA

	2002	2001	2000	1999	1998	1997	1996	1995	1994	1993
Dividends, Net Income ($)	0.32	0.29	0.29	0.31	0.29	0.28	0.28	0.25	—	—
Distrib'ns, Cap Gain ($)	0.00	0.00	0.00	0.00	0.00	0.00	0.00	0.00	—	—
Net Asset Value ($)	19.15	24.93	28.66	31.81	26.55	20.88	15.89	13.16	—	—
Expense Ratio (%)	na	0.18	0.19	0.19	0.19	0.17	0.20	0.20	—	—
Yield (%)	1.67	1.16	1.01	0.97	1.09	1.34	1.76	1.89	—	—
Portfolio Turnover (%)	na	5	5	4	4	2	7	6	—	—
Total Assets (Millions $)	1,174	1,606	2,319	2,240	1,352	579	234	98	—	—

PORTFOLIO (as of 9/30/02)

Portfolio Manager: Team Managed/George Sauter - 1994

Investment Style

✔ Large Cap	Growth
Mid Cap	Value
Small Cap	✔ Grth/Val

Portfolio

0.0%	cash	0.0%	corp bonds
100.0%	stocks	0.0%	gov't bonds
0.0%	preferred	0.0%	muni bonds
0.0%	conv't bds/wrnts	0.0%	other

SHAREHOLDER INFORMATION

Minimum Investment
Initial: $10,000 Subsequent: $100

Minimum IRA Investment
Initial: $10,000 Subsequent: $100

Maximum Fees
Load: 2.00% redemption 12b-1: none
Other: redemption fee applies for 12 months

Services
✔ IRA
Keogh
✔ Telephone Exchange

Vanguard Value Idx/Inv

800-662-7447, 610-436-5152
www.vanguard.com

(VIVAX)

Large-Cap Stock

PERFORMANCE — fund inception date: 11/2/92

	3yr Annual	5yr Annual	10yr Annual	Bull	Bear
Return (%)	-9.5	-0.9	9.2	40.5	-32.8
Differ From Category (+/-)	4.3 abv av	0.0 av	1.3 abv av	-34.2 blw av	6.3 abv av

Standard Deviation	Category Risk Index	Beta
19.1%—abv av	0.99—av	0.92

	2002	2001	2000	1999	1998	1997	1996	1995	1994	1993
Return (%)	-20.9	-11.8	6.0	12.5	14.6	29.7	21.7	37.0	-0.6	18.2
Differ From Category (+/-)	1.2	1.0	11.2	-12.9	-9.8	2.6	1.1	4.1	-0.7	5.5
Return, Tax-Adjusted (%)	-21.5	-13.2	4.5	10.1	13.0	28.0	19.6	35.6	-2.3	16.6

PER SHARE DATA

	2002	2001	2000	1999	1998	1997	1996	1995	1994	1993
Dividends, Net Income ($)	0.31	0.31	0.35	0.36	0.36	0.37	0.38	0.40	0.38	0.38
Distrib'ns, Cap Gain ($)	0.00	0.97	0.98	1.95	0.99	0.75	0.57	0.00	0.16	0.06
Net Asset Value ($)	14.65	18.90	22.87	22.89	22.51	20.85	17.02	14.80	11.12	11.73
Expense Ratio (%)	na	0.22	0.22	0.22	0.22	0.20	0.20	0.20	0.20	0.20
Yield (%)	2.11	1.56	1.46	1.44	1.53	1.71	2.16	2.70	3.36	3.22
Portfolio Turnover (%)	na	38	37	41	33	26	29	26	32	30
Total Assets (Millions $)	2,353	3,017	3,449	3,377	2,420	1,795	1,015	496	296	190

PORTFOLIO (as of 9/30/02)

Portfolio Manager: Team Managed - 1992

Investment Style

✔ Large Cap	Growth
Mid Cap	✔ Value
Small Cap	Grth/Val

Portfolio

0.0% cash	0.0% corp bonds
100.0% stocks	0.0% gov't bonds
0.0% preferred	0.0% muni bonds
0.0% conv't bds/wrnts	0.0% other

SHAREHOLDER INFORMATION

Minimum Investment
Initial: $3,000 — Subsequent: $100

Minimum IRA Investment
Initial: $1,000 — Subsequent: $100

Maximum Fees
Load: none — 12b-1: none
Other: none

Services
✔ IRA
✔ Keogh
Telephone Exchange

Vanguard Windsor II/Inv (VWNFX)

800-662-7447, 610-436-5152
www.vanguard.com

Large-Cap Stock

PERFORMANCE

fund inception date: 6/24/85

	3yr Annual	5yr Annual	10yr Annual	Bull	Bear
Return (%)	-2.0	0.5	10.1	14.6	-11.1
Differ From Category (+/-)	11.8 high	1.4 abv av	2.2 high	-60.1 low	28.0 high

Standard Deviation	Category Risk Index	Beta
17.4%—av	0.91—blw av	0.69

	2002	2001	2000	1999	1998	1997	1996	1995	1994	1993
Return (%)	-16.8	-3.3	16.8	-5.8	16.3	32.3	24.1	38.8	-1.1	13.6
Differ From Category (+/-)	5.3	9.5	22.0	-31.2	-8.1	5.2	3.5	5.9	-1.2	0.9
Return, Tax-Adjusted (%)	-17.6	-4.2	14.8	-8.4	13.5	29.4	21.3	36.1	-3.2	11.5

PER SHARE DATA

	2002	2001	2000	1999	1998	1997	1996	1995	1994	1993
Dividends, Net Income ($)	0.51	0.54	0.61	0.68	0.64	0.66	0.63	0.58	0.55	0.51
Distrib'ns, Cap Gain ($)	0.00	0.15	1.24	2.50	2.67	2.19	1.16	0.69	0.47	0.50
Net Asset Value ($)	20.80	25.59	27.20	24.97	29.85	28.62	23.83	20.66	15.82	17.04
Expense Ratio (%)	na	0.40	0.37	0.37	0.41	0.37	0.39	0.42	0.39	0.39
Yield (%)	2.45	2.09	2.14	2.47	1.96	2.14	2.52	2.71	3.37	2.90
Portfolio Turnover (%)	na	33	26	26	31	30	32	25	24	26
Total Assets (Millions $)	18,493	22,428	25,082	26,901	31,538	24,376	15,700	11,012	7,958	7,616

PORTFOLIO (as of 9/30/02)

Portfolio Manager: Team Managed - 1985

Investment Style

✔ Large Cap	Growth
✔ Mid Cap	✔ Value
Small Cap	Grth/Val

Portfolio

2.5%	cash	0.0%	corp bonds
97.5%	stocks	0.0%	gov't bonds
0.0%	preferred	0.0%	muni bonds
0.0%	conv't bds/wrnts	0.0%	other

SHAREHOLDER INFORMATION

Minimum Investment
Initial: $3,000 — Subsequent: $100

Minimum IRA Investment
Initial: $1,000 — Subsequent: $100

Maximum Fees
Load: none — 12b-1: none
Other: none

Services
✔ IRA
✔ Keogh
✔ Telephone Exchange

Vanguard Windsor/Inv (VWNDX)

800-662-7447, 610-436-5152
www.vanguard.com

Large-Cap Stock

PERFORMANCE — fund inception date: 10/23/58

	3yr Annual	5yr Annual	10yr Annual	Bull	Bear
Return (%)	-1.6	1.3	9.8	34.2	-14.1
Differ From Category (+/-)	12.2 high	2.2 abv av	1.9 high	-40.5 blw av	25.0 high

Standard Deviation	Category Risk Index	Beta
20.6%—abv av	1.08—abv av	0.94

	2002	2001	2000	1999	1998	1997	1996	1995	1994	1993
Return (%)	-22.2	5.7	15.8	11.5	0.8	21.9	26.3	30.1	-0.1	19.3
Differ From Category (+/-)	-0.1	18.5	21.0	-13.9	-23.6	-5.2	5.7	-2.8	-0.2	6.6
Return, Tax-Adjusted (%)	-22.6	4.8	12.7	8.4	-1.2	17.7	22.6	25.6	-3.1	16.2

PER SHARE DATA

	2002	2001	2000	1999	1998	1997	1996	1995	1994	1993
Dividends, Net Income ($)	0.17	0.19	0.27	0.27	0.25	0.32	0.41	0.46	0.44	0.37
Distrib'ns, Cap Gain ($)	0.00	0.31	1.85	1.90	1.23	2.88	1.33	1.38	0.86	0.89
Net Asset Value ($)	12.00	15.64	15.29	15.17	15.57	16.98	16.59	14.53	12.59	13.91
Expense Ratio (%)	na	0.41	0.31	0.28	0.27	0.27	0.31	0.43	0.45	0.40
Yield (%)	1.41	1.19	1.57	1.58	1.48	1.61	2.28	2.89	3.27	2.50
Portfolio Turnover (%)	na	33	41	56	48	61	34	21	34	25
Total Assets (Millions $)	11,738	16,026	16,614	16,699	18,187	20,914	16,738	13,646	10,672	10,610

PORTFOLIO (as of 9/30/02)

Portfolio Manager: Freeman/Fedak/Pisarkiewicz - 1996

Investment Style

✔ Large Cap　Growth
Mid Cap　✔ Value
Small Cap　Grth/Val

Portfolio

2.0%	cash	0.0%	corp bonds
98.0%	stocks	0.0%	gov't bonds
0.0%	preferred	0.0%	muni bonds
0.0%	conv't bds/wrnts	0.0%	other

SHAREHOLDER INFORMATION

Minimum Investment
Initial: $3,000　Subsequent: $100

Minimum IRA Investment
Initial: $1,000　Subsequent: $100

Maximum Fees
Load: none　12b-1: none
Other: none

Services
✔ IRA
✔ Keogh
✔ Telephone Exchange

Yacktman Fund
(YACKX)

800-525-8258, 312-201-9480
www.yacktman.com

Large-Cap Stock

PERFORMANCE

fund inception date: 7/2/92

	3yr Annual	5yr Annual	10yr Annual	Bull	Bear
Return (%)	14.7	4.7	9.5	-9.2	45.7
Differ From Category (+/-)	28.5 high	5.6 high	1.6 abv av	-83.9 low	84.8 high

Standard Deviation	Category Risk Index	Beta
17.2%—av	0.90—blw av	0.67

	2002	2001	2000	1999	1998	1997	1996	1995	1994	1993
Return (%)	11.4	19.4	13.4	-16.9	0.6	18.2	26.0	30.4	8.7	-6.5
Differ From Category (+/-)	33.5	32.2	18.6	-42.3	-23.8	-8.9	5.4	-2.5	8.6	-19.2
Return, Tax-Adjusted (%)	11.0	18.2	11.4	-17.5	-3.2	15.3	21.4	27.4	7.4	-7.0

PER SHARE DATA

	2002	2001	2000	1999	1998	1997	1996	1995	1994	1993
Dividends, Net Income ($)	0.10	0.05	0.06	0.09	0.13	0.22	0.23	0.22	0.21	0.14
Distrib'ns, Cap Gain ($)	0.00	0.49	0.81	0.15	2.37	1.50	1.64	0.77	0.12	0.00
Net Asset Value ($)	12.33	11.16	9.80	9.40	11.61	14.05	13.34	12.09	10.05	9.56
Expense Ratio (%)	na	1.17	1.23	0.71	1.14	0.86	0.90	0.89	1.07	1.18
Yield (%)	0.81	0.42	0.56	0.94	0.92	1.41	1.53	1.71	2.06	1.46
Portfolio Turnover (%)	na	43	19	4	14	69	58	55	49	61
Total Assets (Millions $)	421	112	70	109	307	1,082	755	566	295	143

PORTFOLIO (as of 11/30/02)

Portfolio Manager: Donald Yacktman - 1992

Investment Style

✔ Large Cap	Growth
Mid Cap	✔ Value
Small Cap	Grth/Val

Portfolio

24.1% cash	6.4% corp bonds
68.3% stocks	0.0% gov't bonds
0.4% pref/conv't pref	0.0% muni bonds
0.8% conv't bds/wrnts	0.0% other

SHAREHOLDER INFORMATION

Minimum Investment
Initial: $2,500 Subsequent: $100

Minimum IRA Investment
Initial: $500 Subsequent: $100

Maximum Fees
Load: none 12b-1: none
Other: none

Services
✔ IRA
✔ Keogh
✔ Telephone Exchange

Mid-Cap Stock Funds

Category Performance Ranked by 2002 Returns

Category	Fund (Ticker)	Annual Return (%) 2002	3yr	5yr	10yr	Category Risk	Total Risk
Stk-MC	Vontobel US Value (VUSVX)	-2.0	10.8	6.0	12.5	blw av	av
Stk-MC	Hennessy Crnst Grth (HFCGX)	-4.7	4.0	9.9	na	av	abv av
Stk-MC	Fenimore Value Fd (FAMVX)	-4.8	9.2	5.6	10.0	low	av
Stk-MC	Amer Cnt Eqty Income/Inv (TWEIX)	-4.9	8.8	7.7	na	low	blw av
Stk-MC	Ariel Fund (ARGFX)	-5.1	11.7	7.6	11.6	blw av	av
Stk-MC	Merger Fund (MERFX)	-5.6	4.2	6.9	9.4	low	blw av
Stk-MC	T Rowe Price Mid-Cp Val (TRMCX)	-7.3	9.1	6.4	na	blw av	av
Stk-MC	Delafield Fund (DEFIX)	-7.4	11.7	5.9	na	av	abv av
Stk-MC	Legg Mason Eq:Special/P (LMASX)	-8.7	-6.3	6.5	11.0	abv av	high
Stk-MC	Fidelity Value (FDVLX)	-9.2	3.2	3.6	11.0	av	abv av
Stk-MC	Vanguard Selected Value (VASVX)	-9.7	6.8	0.8	na	av	abv av
Stk-MC	Ariel Appreciation Fund (CAAPX)	-10.3	7.3	7.3	11.5	blw av	av
Stk-MC	Homestead Fds Value (HOVLX)	-11.5	0.6	1.3	10.0	blw av	av
Stk-MC	Marshall:Mid Cap Val/Inv (MRVEX)	-11.5	8.1	7.1	na	blw av	abv av
Stk-MC	Strong Discovery (STDIX)	-12.1	-1.6	1.4	6.4	av	abv av
Stk-MC	Amer Cnt Value/Inv (TWVLX)	-12.6	5.2	3.9	na	blw av	av
Stk-MC	Vanguard Strategic Eqty (VSEQX)	-13.1	-0.5	3.3	na	blw av	av
Stk-MC	Brandywine Blue Fund (BLUEX)	-13.4	-10.6	1.0	10.3	blw av	av
Stk-MC	CA Inv:S&P Mid Cap Index (SPMIX)	-14.2	0.9	6.9	11.9	av	abv av
Stk-MC	Tweedy Browne Amcn Value (TWEBX)	-14.9	-0.9	1.6	na	low	blw av
Stk-MC	Dreyfus Index:Midcap Idx (PESPX)	-15.0	-0.6	5.8	11.3	av	abv av
Stk-MC	Sound Shore Fund (SSHFX)	-15.4	0.2	0.9	10.7	blw av	av
Stk-MC	Amer Cnt Heritage/Inv (TWHIX)	-15.9	-9.7	2.0	8.1	abv av	abv av
Stk-MC	T Rowe Price Value (TRVLX)	-16.5	-0.6	2.7	na	av	abv av
Stk-MC	Weitz Partners Value Fund (WPVLX)	-16.9	-0.1	9.4	na	blw av	av
Stk-MC	Weitz Srs:Value (WVALX)	-17.1	-0.2	9.1	14.2	blw av	av
Stk-MC	Wayne Hummer Growth (WHGRX)	-17.6	-9.5	3.7	8.4	blw av	av
Stk-MC	Selected Special Shares (SLSSX)	-17.6	-11.3	0.2	7.0	av	abv av
Stk-MC	Meridian Growth Fund (MERDX)	-17.8	6.5	7.1	10.0	av	abv av
Stk-MC	Westcore:MIDCO Growth (WTMGX)	-17.9	-15.3	1.2	7.8	high	high
Stk-MC	PBHG Mid Cap Value (PBMCX)	-19.7	2.9	11.1	na	av	abv av
Stk-MC	Baron Asset Fund (BARAX)	-19.9	-10.2	-2.6	9.8	abv av	high
Stk-MC	Muhlenkamp Fund (MUHLX)	-19.9	3.1	4.7	12.2	abv av	high
Stk-MC	Nicholas II (NCTWX)	-20.3	-8.9	-3.5	6.5	av	abv av
Stk-MC	Amer Cnt Vista/Inv (TWCVX)	-20.9	-17.2	1.2	5.3	high	high
Stk-MC	T Rowe Price Md Cp Gr (RPMGX)	-21.2	-5.7	4.8	12.8	abv av	abv av
Stk-MC	Brandywine Fund (BRWIX)	-21.7	-12.6	0.3	8.9	blw av	av
Stk-MC	Vanguard Div Growth/Inv (VDIGX)	-23.1	-9.7	-2.7	4.9	low	av
Stk-MC	Fidelity OTC (FOCPX)	-23.2	-24.7	0.6	7.4	high	high
Stk-MC	Oak Value (OAKVX)	-24.3	-3.8	0.4	na	av	abv av
Stk-MC	Columbia Special/Z (CLSPX)	-24.5	-12.0	1.5	8.2	abv av	high
Stk-MC	Strong Growth/Inv (SGROX)	-25.2	-23.6	-0.2	na	high	high
Stk-MC	Strong Opportunity/Inv (SOPFX)	-26.9	-8.9	3.0	10.2	av	abv av
Stk-MC	Fidelity Mid Cap Stock (FMCSX)	-27.5	-5.8	6.0	na	abv av	high
Stk-MC	Vanguard Capital Opp/Inv (VHCOX)	-27.9	-8.4	14.9	na	abv av	high

Category	Fund (Ticker)	Annual Return (%) 2002	3yr	5yr	10yr	Category Risk	Total Risk
Stk-MC	Janus Enterprise (JAENX)	-28.2	-33.1	-2.3	5.8	high	high
Stk-MC	PBHG Growth (PBHGX)	-30.3	-29.4	-7.4	5.2	high	high
Stk-MC	Strong Growth 20/Inv (SGRTX)	-30.8	-28.6	0.7	na	high	high
Stk-MC	Marshall:Mid Cap Gr/Inv (MRMSX)	-31.7	-18.4	0.2	na	abv av	high
Stk-MC	Fidelity Aggressive Grth (FDEGX)	-41.1	-39.0	-8.0	3.9	high	high
Mid-Cap Stock Average		**-18.0**	**-6.8**	**1.7**	**8.8**	**—**	**abv av**

Note: AAII members who would like performance figures for no-load and low-load mutual funds they own that do not appear in this Guide can access this information on our Web site at www.aaii.com.

Amer Cnt Eqty Income/Inv (TWEIX)

800-345-2021, 816-531-5575
www.americancentury.com

Mid-Cap Stock

PERFORMANCE — fund inception date: 8/1/94

	3yr Annual	5yr Annual	10yr Annual	Bull	Bear
Return (%)	8.8	7.7	na	18.2	20.6
Differ From Category (+/-)	15.6 high	6.0 high	na	-64.5 low	44.6 high

Standard Deviation	Category Risk Index	Beta
13.1%—blw av	0.64—low	0.54

	2002	2001	2000	1999	1998	1997	1996	1995	1994	1993
Return (%)	-4.9	11.3	21.9	-0.1	12.9	28.2	23.3	29.6	—	—
Differ From Category (+/-)	13.1	17.2	16.1	-29.8	2.9	5.6	3.5	-1.5	—	—
Return, Tax-Adjusted (%)	-6.0	10.1	20.6	-3.0	8.7	22.9	19.4	25.5	—	—

PER SHARE DATA

	2002	2001	2000	1999	1998	1997	1996	1995	1994	1993
Dividends, Net Income ($)	0.15	0.17	0.17	0.21	0.21	0.25	0.18	0.19	—	—
Distrib'ns, Cap Gain ($)	0.09	0.04	0.00	0.47	0.96	1.16	0.54	0.45	—	—
Net Asset Value ($)	6.53	7.14	6.62	5.60	6.31	6.66	6.34	5.76	—	—
Expense Ratio (%)	1.00	1.00	1.00	1.00	1.00	1.00	0.98	1.00	—	—
Yield (%)	2.26	2.36	2.56	3.45	2.88	3.19	2.61	3.05	—	—
Portfolio Turnover (%)	139	169	141	180	158	159	170	na	—	—
Total Assets (Millions $)	1,208	831	384	327	326	297	187	96	—	—

PORTFOLIO (as of 9/30/02)

Portfolio Manager: P Davidson/ S Moore - 1998

Investment Style

✔ Large Cap	Growth
✔ Mid Cap	✔ Value
Small Cap	Grth/Val

Portfolio

0.0%	cash	12.5%	corp bonds
68.9%	stocks	0.0%	gov't bonds
11.7%	pref/conv't pref	0.0%	muni bonds
1.4%	conv't bds/wrnts	5.6%	other

SHAREHOLDER INFORMATION

Minimum Investment
Initial: $2,500 — Subsequent: $50

Minimum IRA Investment
Initial: $1,000 — Subsequent: $50

Maximum Fees
Load: none — 12b-1: none
Other: none

Services
✔ IRA
✔ Keogh
✔ Telephone Exchange

Amer Cnt Heritage/Inv (TWHIX)

800-345-2021, 816-531-5575
www.americancentury.com

Mid-Cap Stock

PERFORMANCE — fund inception date: 11/10/87

	3yr Annual	5yr Annual	10yr Annual	Bull	Bear
Return (%)	-9.7	2.0	8.1	121.1	-38.8
Differ From Category (+/-)	-2.9 blw av	0.3 av	-0.7 blw av	38.4 abv av	-14.8 blw av

Standard Deviation	Category Risk Index	Beta
23.2%—abv av	1.14—abv av	0.75

	2002	2001	2000	1999	1998	1997	1996	1995	1994	1993
Return (%)	-15.9	-25.5	17.3	51.2	-0.1	19.3	15.3	26.6	-6.3	20.4
Differ From Category (+/-)	2.1	-19.6	11.5	21.5	-10.1	-3.3	-4.5	-4.5	-6.1	3.8
Return, Tax-Adjusted (%)	-15.9	-25.5	12.6	48.5	-0.2	14.6	13.2	24.6	-7.9	18.6

PER SHARE DATA

	2002	2001	2000	1999	1998	1997	1996	1995	1994	1993
Dividends, Net Income ($)	0.00	0.00	0.00	0.04	0.02	0.07	0.09	0.04	0.03	0.06
Distrib'ns, Cap Gain ($)	0.00	0.00	3.64	1.48	0.00	2.70	0.70	0.61	0.54	0.50
Net Asset Value ($)	9.10	10.83	14.55	15.64	11.46	11.50	12.07	11.17	9.35	10.61
Expense Ratio (%)	1.00	1.00	1.00	1.00	1.00	1.00	0.99	1.00	1.00	1.00
Yield (%)	0.00	0.00	0.00	0.23	0.17	0.49	0.70	0.33	0.30	0.54
Portfolio Turnover (%)	128	152	119	134	148	69	122	121	136	116
Total Assets (Millions $)	1,044	1,280	1,860	1,349	1,070	1,277	1,125	1,026	851	724

PORTFOLIO (as of 9/30/02)

Portfolio Manager: L Peterson/K Stalzer - 1998

Investment Style

Large Cap	✔ Growth
✔ Mid Cap	Value
✔ Small Cap	Grth/Val

Portfolio

3.1%	cash	0.0%	corp bonds
96.9%	stocks	0.0%	gov't bonds
0.0%	preferred	0.0%	muni bonds
0.0%	conv't bds/wrnts	0.0%	other

SHAREHOLDER INFORMATION

Minimum Investment
Initial: $2,500 Subsequent: $50

Minimum IRA Investment
Initial: $1,000 Subsequent: $50

Maximum Fees
Load: none 12b-1: none
Other: none

Services
✔ IRA
✔ Keogh
✔ Telephone Exchange

Amer Cnt Value/Inv (TWVLX)

800-345-2021, 816-531-5575
www.americancentury.com

Mid-Cap Stock

PERFORMANCE

fund inception date: 9/1/93

	3yr Annual	5yr Annual	10yr Annual	Bull	Bear
Return (%)	5.2	3.9	na	14.3	9.9
Differ From Category (+/-)	12.0 high	2.2 abv av	na	-68.4 low	33.9 high

Standard Deviation	Category Risk Index	Beta
18.2%—av	0.89—blw av	0.73

	2002	2001	2000	1999	1998	1997	1996	1995	1994	1993
Return (%)	-12.6	12.8	18.2	-0.7	4.9	26.0	24.2	32.7	3.9	—
Differ From Category (+/-)	5.4	18.7	12.4	-30.4	-5.1	3.4	4.4	1.6	4.1	—
Return, Tax-Adjusted (%)	-13.2	12.0	17.5	-2.7	1.1	21.6	20.6	28.9	1.5	—

PER SHARE DATA

	2002	2001	2000	1999	1998	1997	1996	1995	1994	1993
Dividends, Net Income ($)	0.06	0.08	0.09	0.08	0.08	0.11	0.11	0.13	0.12	—
Distrib'ns, Cap Gain ($)	0.10	0.10	0.00	0.41	1.14	1.20	0.60	0.47	0.27	—
Net Asset Value ($)	5.95	7.00	6.38	5.49	6.05	6.95	6.59	5.90	4.92	—
Expense Ratio (%)	1.00	1.00	1.00	1.00	1.00	1.00	0.97	1.00	1.00	—
Yield (%)	0.99	1.12	1.41	1.35	1.11	1.34	1.52	2.04	2.31	—
Portfolio Turnover (%)	151	150	115	130	130	111	145	94	79	—
Total Assets (Millions $)	1,767	1,928	1,516	1,605	2,082	2,461	1,548	652	153	—

PORTFOLIO (as of 9/30/02)

Portfolio Manager: Scott Moore/Phillip Davidson - 1998

Investment Style

✔ Large Cap	Growth
✔ Mid Cap	✔ Value
Small Cap	Grth/Val

Portfolio

6.2% cash	0.0% corp bonds
88.0% stocks	0.0% gov't bonds
0.0% preferred	0.0% muni bonds
0.0% conv't bds/wrnts	5.8% other

SHAREHOLDER INFORMATION

Minimum Investment
Initial: $2,500 Subsequent: $50

Minimum IRA Investment
Initial: $1,000 Subsequent: $50

Maximum Fees
Load: none 12b-1: none
Other: none

Services
✔ IRA
✔ Keogh
✔ Telephone Exchange

Amer Cnt Vista/Inv (TWCVX)

800-345-2021, 816-531-5575
www.americancentury.com

Mid-Cap Stock

PERFORMANCE — fund inception date: 11/25/83

	3yr Annual	5yr Annual	10yr Annual	Bull	Bear
Return (%)	-17.2	1.2	5.3	216.3	-51.1
Differ From Category (+/-)	-10.4 blw av	-0.5 blw av	-3.5 blw av	133.6 high	-27.1 blw av

Standard Deviation	Category Risk Index	Beta
31.3%—high	1.53—high	0.57

	2002	2001	2000	1999	1998	1997	1996	1995	1994	1993
Return (%)	-20.9	-27.5	-0.9	119.1	-14.2	-8.6	7.5	46.1	4.6	5.4
Differ From Category (+/-)	-2.9	-21.6	-6.7	89.4	-24.2	-31.2	-12.3	15.0	4.8	-11.2
Return, Tax-Adjusted (%)	-20.9	-27.5	-6.6	117.3	-14.2	-9.7	5.2	43.4	4.5	1.3

PER SHARE DATA

	2002	2001	2000	1999	1998	1997	1996	1995	1994	1993
Dividends, Net Income ($)	0.00	0.00	0.00	0.00	0.00	0.00	0.00	0.00	0.00	0.00
Distrib'ns, Cap Gain ($)	0.00	0.00	6.32	0.94	0.00	0.80	1.18	1.02	0.02	1.67
Net Asset Value ($)	8.78	11.10	15.33	22.21	10.65	12.42	14.51	14.60	10.72	10.27
Expense Ratio (%)	1.00	1.00	1.00	1.00	1.00	1.00	0.99	1.00	1.00	1.00
Yield (%)	0.00	0.00	0.00	0.00	0.00	0.00	0.00	0.00	0.00	0.00
Portfolio Turnover (%)	293	290	135	187	229	96	91	89	111	133
Total Assets (Millions $)	982	1,251	2,080	1,799	954	1,669	2,236	1,774	820	795

PORTFOLIO (as of 9/30/02)

Portfolio Manager: Glenn Fogle/David Rose - 1993

Investment Style

Large Cap	✔ Growth
✔ Mid Cap	Value
✔ Small Cap	Grth/Val

Portfolio

4.9%	cash	0.7%	corp bonds
94.4%	stocks	0.0%	gov't bonds
0.0%	preferred	0.0%	muni bonds
0.0%	conv't bds/wrnts	0.0%	other

SHAREHOLDER INFORMATION

Minimum Investment
Initial: $2,500 — Subsequent: $50

Minimum IRA Investment
Initial: $1,000 — Subsequent: $50

Maximum Fees
Load: none — 12b-1: none
Other: none

Services
✔ IRA
Keogh
✔ Telephone Exchange

Ariel Appreciation Fund (CAAPX)

800-292-7435, 312-726-0140
www.arielfunds.com

Mid-Cap Stock

PERFORMANCE — fund inception date: 1/15/90

	3yr Annual	5yr Annual	10yr Annual	Bull	Bear
Return (%)	7.3	7.3	11.5	19.2	22.0
Differ From Category (+/-)	14.1 high	5.6 high	2.7 abv av	-63.5 low	46.0 high

Standard Deviation	Category Risk Index	Beta
18.4%—av	0.90—blw av	0.70

	2002	2001	2000	1999	1998	1997	1996	1995	1994	1993
Return (%)	-10.3	16.2	18.8	-3.7	19.5	37.9	23.7	24.1	-8.3	7.9
Differ From Category (+/-)	7.7	22.1	13.0	-33.4	9.5	15.3	3.9	-7.0	-8.1	-8.7
Return, Tax-Adjusted (%)	-10.4	15.7	16.1	-5.5	17.3	35.4	21.8	21.2	-10.1	7.4

PER SHARE DATA

	2002	2001	2000	1999	1998	1997	1996	1995	1994	1993
Dividends, Net Income ($)	0.00	0.06	0.11	0.04	0.03	0.06	0.07	0.19	0.06	0.05
Distrib'ns, Cap Gain ($)	0.12	0.70	3.95	3.15	3.45	3.06	1.36	1.76	1.39	0.34
Net Asset Value ($)	33.06	37.02	32.53	30.97	35.69	32.82	26.07	22.24	19.51	22.89
Expense Ratio (%)	na	1.26	1.31	1.26	1.26	1.33	1.36	1.36	1.35	1.37
Yield (%)	0.00	0.15	0.30	0.11	0.07	0.16	0.25	0.79	0.28	0.21
Portfolio Turnover (%)	na	28	31	24	20	19	26	18	12	56
Total Assets (Millions $)	1,512	771	339	334	283	204	146	139	128	219

PORTFOLIO (as of 9/30/02)

Portfolio Manager: John Rogers - 2002

Investment Style

✔ Large Cap	Growth
✔ Mid Cap	✔ Value
Small Cap	Grth/Val

Portfolio

2.6% cash	0.0% corp bonds
97.4% stocks	0.0% gov't bonds
0.0% preferred	0.0% muni bonds
0.0% conv't bds/wrnts	0.0% other

SHAREHOLDER INFORMATION

Minimum Investment
Initial: $1,000 Subsequent: $50

Minimum IRA Investment
Initial: $250 Subsequent: $50

Maximum Fees
Load: none 12b-1: 0.25%
Other: none

Services
✔ IRA
✔ Keogh
✔ Telephone Exchange

Ariel Fund
(ARGFX)
Mid-Cap Stock

800-292-7435, 312-726-0140
www.arielfunds.com

PERFORMANCE — fund inception date: 9/29/86

	3yr Annual	5yr Annual	10yr Annual	Bull	Bear
Return (%)	11.7	7.6	11.6	12.0	43.1
Differ From Category (+/-)	18.5 high	5.9 high	2.8 high	-70.7 low	67.1 high

Standard Deviation	Category Risk Index	Beta
17.5%—av	0.85—blw av	0.51

	2002	2001	2000	1999	1998	1997	1996	1995	1994	1993
Return (%)	-5.1	14.2	28.7	-5.7	9.8	36.4	23.5	18.5	-4.2	8.7
Differ From Category (+/-)	12.9	20.1	22.9	-35.4	-0.2	13.8	3.7	-12.6	-4.0	-7.9
Return, Tax-Adjusted (%)	-5.4	13.8	24.7	-8.8	7.9	34.0	21.7	13.5	-6.1	6.7

PER SHARE DATA

	2002	2001	2000	1999	1998	1997	1996	1995	1994	1993
Dividends, Net Income ($)	0.00	0.11	0.24	0.07	0.08	0.14	0.00	0.43	0.23	0.29
Distrib'ns, Cap Gain ($)	0.52	0.53	5.75	6.04	3.71	3.57	1.78	4.18	1.70	1.73
Net Asset Value ($)	35.24	37.72	33.61	31.11	39.96	39.88	31.96	27.32	26.98	30.19
Expense Ratio (%)	na	1.19	1.24	1.25	1.21	1.25	1.31	1.37	1.25	1.16
Yield (%)	0.00	0.28	0.60	0.18	0.18	0.32	0.00	1.36	0.80	0.90
Portfolio Turnover (%)	na	24	48	38	22	20	17	16	9	13
Total Assets (Millions $)	1,190	619	285	205	201	174	120	120	130	225

PORTFOLIO (as of 9/30/02)

Portfolio Manager: John Rogers - 1986

Investment Style

✔ Large Cap   Growth
✔ Mid Cap   ✔ Value
Small Cap   Grth/Val

Portfolio

10.0%	cash	0.0%	corp bonds
90.0%	stocks	0.0%	gov't bonds
0.0%	preferred	0.0%	muni bonds
0.0%	conv't bds/wrnts	0.0%	other

SHAREHOLDER INFORMATION

Minimum Investment
Initial: $1,000   Subsequent: $50

Minimum IRA Investment
Initial: $250   Subsequent: $50

Maximum Fees
Load: none   12b-1: 0.25%
Other: none

Services
✔ IRA
✔ Keogh
✔ Telephone Exchange

Baron Asset Fund
(BARAX)

800-992-2766, 212-583-2100
www.baronfunds.com

Mid-Cap Stock

PERFORMANCE — fund inception date: 6/12/87

	3yr Annual	5yr Annual	10yr Annual	Bull	Bear
Return (%)	-10.2	-2.6	9.8	70.2	-34.3
Differ From Category (+/-)	-3.4 blw av	-4.3 low	1.0 av	-12.5 av	-10.3 blw av

Standard Deviation	Category Risk Index	Beta
24.2%—high	1.19—abv av	0.97

	2002	2001	2000	1999	1998	1997	1996	1995	1994	1993
Return (%)	-19.9	-10.1	0.3	16.2	4.2	33.8	21.9	35.2	7.4	23.4
Differ From Category (+/-)	-1.9	-4.2	-5.5	-13.5	-5.8	11.2	2.1	4.1	7.6	6.8
Return, Tax-Adjusted (%)	-20.4	-11.6	-1.3	16.2	4.2	33.8	21.9	35.2	6.5	22.2

PER SHARE DATA

	2002	2001	2000	1999	1998	1997	1996	1995	1994	1993
Dividends, Net Income ($)	0.00	0.00	0.00	0.00	0.04	0.00	0.00	0.00	0.00	0.00
Distrib'ns, Cap Gain ($)	1.17	4.06	4.61	0.00	0.00	0.00	0.03	0.03	0.65	0.77
Net Asset Value ($)	34.42	44.46	54.39	58.77	50.54	48.51	36.23	29.74	22.01	21.11
Expense Ratio (%)	na	1.36	1.36	1.31	1.32	1.30	1.40	1.50	1.60	1.80
Yield (%)	0.00	0.00	0.00	0.00	0.07	0.00	0.00	0.00	0.00	0.00
Portfolio Turnover (%)	na	4	2	15	23	13	19	41	55	108
Total Assets (Millions $)	3,150	2,394	4,257	6,146	5,672	3,793	1,326	353	87	64

PORTFOLIO (as of 9/30/02)

Portfolio Manager: Ronald Baron - 1987

Investment Style

	Large Cap		Growth
✔	Mid Cap		Value
	Small Cap	✔	Grth/Val

Portfolio

0.0%	cash	0.0%	corp bonds
100.0%	stocks	0.0%	gov't bonds
0.0%	preferred	0.0%	muni bonds
0.0%	conv't bds/wrnts	0.0%	other

SHAREHOLDER INFORMATION

Minimum Investment
Initial: $2,000 — Subsequent: na

Minimum IRA Investment
Initial: $2,000 — Subsequent: $0

Maximum Fees
Load: none — 12b-1: 0.25%
Other: none

Services
✔ IRA
Keogh
✔ Telephone Exchange

Brandywine Blue Fund

800-656-3017, 302-656-6200
www.brandywine.com

(BLUEX)

Mid-Cap Stock

PERFORMANCE

fund inception date: 1/10/91

	3yr Annual	5yr Annual	10yr Annual	Bull	Bear
Return (%)	-10.6	1.0	10.3	124.8	-39.5
Differ From Category (+/-)	-3.8 blw av	-0.7 blw av	1.5 abv av	42.1 abv av	-15.5 blw av

Standard Deviation	Category Risk Index	Beta
17.3%—av	0.84—blw av	0.53

	2002	2001	2000	1999	1998	1997	1996	1995	1994	1993
Return (%)	-13.4	-22.8	6.8	49.3	-0.9	19.2	23.2	32.3	2.3	27.2
Differ From Category (+/-)	4.6	-16.9	1.0	19.6	-10.9	-3.4	3.4	1.2	2.5	10.6
Return, Tax-Adjusted (%)	-13.4	-22.8	0.9	47.6	-1.3	15.4	23.2	30.5	2.1	22.9

PER SHARE DATA

	2002	2001	2000	1999	1998	1997	1996	1995	1994	1993
Dividends, Net Income ($)	0.00	0.00	0.00	0.00	0.20	0.00	0.00	0.00	0.00	0.00
Distrib'ns, Cap Gain ($)	0.00	0.00	10.70	2.17	0.13	5.08	0.00	1.10	0.10	2.33
Net Asset Value ($)	18.41	21.28	27.57	36.24	25.91	26.58	26.47	21.48	17.05	16.77
Expense Ratio (%)	1.13	1.09	1.07	1.08	1.06	1.08	1.13	1.31	1.80	2.00
Yield (%)	0.00	0.00	0.00	0.00	0.76	0.00	0.00	0.00	0.00	0.00
Portfolio Turnover (%)	311	244	245	228	299	202	196	174	220	144
Total Assets (Millions $)	242	257	387	398	356	589	383	190	32	8

PORTFOLIO (as of 9/30/02)

Portfolio Manager: Team Managed - 1991

Investment Style

Large Cap	✔ Growth
✔ Mid Cap	Value
✔ Small Cap	Grth/Val

Portfolio

3.2% cash	0.0% corp bonds
96.8% stocks	0.0% gov't bonds
0.0% preferred	0.0% muni bonds
0.0% conv't bds/wrnts	0.0% other

SHAREHOLDER INFORMATION

Minimum Investment
Initial: $25,000 Subsequent: $1,000

Minimum IRA Investment
Initial: $1 Subsequent: $1

Maximum Fees
Load: none 12b-1: none
Other: none

Services
✔ IRA
✔ Keogh
✔ Telephone Exchange

Brandywine Fund (BRWIX)

800-656-3017, 302-656-6200
www.brandywine.com

Mid-Cap Stock

PERFORMANCE

fund inception date: 12/30/85

	3yr Annual	5yr Annual	10yr Annual	Bull	Bear
Return (%)	-12.6	0.3	8.9	132.6	-41.1
Differ From Category (+/-)	-5.8 blw av	-1.4 blw av	0.1 av	49.9 abv av	-17.1 blw av

Standard Deviation	Category Risk Index	Beta
18.4%—av	0.90—blw av	0.57

	2002	2001	2000	1999	1998	1997	1996	1995	1994	1993
Return (%)	-21.7	-20.5	7.0	53.5	-0.6	12.0	24.9	35.7	0.0	22.5
Differ From Category (+/-)	-3.7	-14.6	1.2	23.8	-10.6	-10.6	5.1	4.6	0.2	5.9
Return, Tax-Adjusted (%)	-21.7	-20.5	-0.5	51.4	-1.0	7.8	23.6	31.1	-1.6	19.0

PER SHARE DATA

	2002	2001	2000	1999	1998	1997	1996	1995	1994	1993
Dividends, Net Income ($)	0.00	0.00	0.00	0.00	0.26	0.00	0.00	0.00	0.00	0.00
Distrib'ns, Cap Gain ($)	0.00	0.00	16.10	3.12	0.07	7.02	1.34	3.84	1.45	2.87
Net Asset Value ($)	18.28	23.35	29.39	42.88	30.28	30.89	33.69	28.08	23.50	24.97
Expense Ratio (%)	1.08	1.06	1.04	1.05	1.04	1.04	1.06	1.07	1.10	1.10
Yield (%)	0.00	0.00	0.00	0.00	0.85	0.00	0.00	0.00	0.00	0.00
Portfolio Turnover (%)	273	284	244	208	263	192	202	193	190	150
Total Assets (Millions $)	3,164	4,265	5,771	5,514	4,890	8,414	6,546	4,210	2,299	1,527

PORTFOLIO (as of 9/30/02)

Portfolio Manager: Team Managed - 1985

Investment Style

Large Cap	✔ Growth
✔ Mid Cap	Value
✔ Small Cap	Grth/Val

Portfolio

3.5% cash	0.6% corp bonds
95.8% stocks	0.0% gov't bonds
0.0% preferred	0.0% muni bonds
0.0% conv't bds/wrnts	0.0% other

SHAREHOLDER INFORMATION

Minimum Investment

Initial: $25,000 — Subsequent: $1,000

Minimum IRA Investment

Initial: na — Subsequent: na

Maximum Fees

Load: none — 12b-1: none

Other: none

Services

IRA

Keogh

✔ Telephone Exchange

CA Inv:S&P Mid Cap Index (SPMIX)

800-225-8778, 415-398-2727
www.caltrust.com

Mid-Cap Stock

PERFORMANCE — fund inception date: 4/20/92

	3yr Annual	5yr Annual	10yr Annual	Bull	Bear
Return (%)	0.9	6.9	11.9	81.7	-14.5
Differ From Category (+/-)	7.7 abv av	5.2 high	3.1 high	-1.0 abv av	9.5 av

Standard Deviation	Category Risk Index	Beta
20.1%—abv av	0.99—av	0.93

	2002	2001	2000	1999	1998	1997	1996	1995	1994	1993
Return (%)	-14.2	0.3	19.4	14.7	18.4	31.8	18.8	30.5	-3.9	12.8
Differ From Category (+/-)	3.8	6.2	13.6	-15.0	8.4	9.2	-1.0	-0.6	-3.7	-3.8
Return, Tax-Adjusted (%)	-14.4	-0.1	15.5	10.0	15.2	29.3	16.6	27.8	-5.7	11.4

PER SHARE DATA

	2002	2001	2000	1999	1998	1997	1996	1995	1994	1993
Dividends, Net Income ($)	0.10	0.15	0.20	0.18	0.21	0.23	0.22	0.26	0.23	0.23
Distrib'ns, Cap Gain ($)	0.00	0.05	2.89	4.01	2.50	1.39	0.73	0.68	0.44	0.24
Net Asset Value ($)	14.14	16.60	16.77	16.83	18.55	18.22	15.11	13.53	11.10	12.27
Expense Ratio (%)	na	0.40	0.40	0.40	0.40	0.40	0.40	0.40	0.40	0.17
Yield (%)	0.70	0.90	1.01	0.86	0.99	1.17	1.38	1.82	1.99	1.83
Portfolio Turnover (%)	na	39	46	42	19	18	18	12	15	8
Total Assets (Millions $)	96	89	73	62	56	49	37	27	20	19

PORTFOLIO (as of 9/30/02)

Portfolio Manager: Roderick Baldwin - 1992

Investment Style

Large Cap	Growth
✔ Mid Cap	Value
Small Cap	✔ Grth/Val

Portfolio

7.2% cash	0.3% corp bonds
85.1% stocks	0.0% gov't bonds
0.0% preferred	0.0% muni bonds
0.0% conv't bds/wrnts	7.4% other

SHAREHOLDER INFORMATION

Minimum Investment
Initial: $5,000 Subsequent: $250

Minimum IRA Investment
Initial: $500 Subsequent: $250

Maximum Fees
Load: none 12b-1: none
Other: none

Services
✔ IRA
✔ Keogh
✔ Telephone Exchange

Columbia Special/Z (CLSPX)

800-426-3750, 800-345-6611
www.columbiafunds.com

Mid-Cap Stock

PERFORMANCE — fund inception date: 8/13/85

	3yr Annual	5yr Annual	10yr Annual	Bull	Bear
Return (%)	-12.0	1.5	8.2	130.9	-47.3
Differ From Category (+/-)	-5.2 blw av	-0.2 av	-0.6 blw av	48.2 abv av	-23.3 blw av

Standard Deviation	Category Risk Index	Beta
28.9%—high	1.41—abv av	0.86

	2002	2001	2000	1999	1998	1997	1996	1995	1994	1993
Return (%)	-24.5	-20.9	13.9	36.3	16.3	12.8	13.0	29.5	2.2	21.6
Differ From Category (+/-)	-6.5	-15.0	8.1	6.6	6.3	-9.8	-6.8	-1.6	2.4	5.0
Return, Tax-Adjusted (%)	-24.5	-21.6	8.4	34.4	16.3	10.7	7.3	25.4	0.4	16.6

PER SHARE DATA

	2002	2001	2000	1999	1998	1997	1996	1995	1994	1993
Dividends, Net Income ($)	0.00	0.00	0.00	0.00	0.00	0.00	0.00	0.02	0.07	0.01
Distrib'ns, Cap Gain ($)	0.00	0.93	8.29	2.27	0.00	2.10	4.38	2.71	1.19	3.32
Net Asset Value ($)	14.79	19.60	25.99	29.90	23.60	20.30	19.85	21.44	18.69	19.51
Expense Ratio (%)	na	1.08	0.99	1.09	1.03	0.98	0.94	1.00	1.05	1.12
Yield (%)	0.00	0.00	0.00	0.00	0.00	0.00	0.00	0.08	0.35	0.04
Portfolio Turnover (%)	na	186	169	135	135	166	150	237	178	154
Total Assets (Millions $)	600	786	1,095	918	969	1,249	1,585	1,384	889	772

PORTFOLIO (as of 9/30/02)

Portfolio Manager: Richard Johnson - 1998

Investment Style

Large Cap	✔ Growth
✔ Mid Cap	Value
✔ Small Cap	Grth/Val

Portfolio

10.8% cash	0.0% corp bonds
89.2% stocks	0.0% gov't bonds
0.0% preferred	0.0% muni bonds
0.0% conv't bds/wrnts	0.0% other

SHAREHOLDER INFORMATION

Minimum Investment
Initial: $2,000 — Subsequent: $100

Minimum IRA Investment
Initial: $2,000 — Subsequent: $100

Maximum Fees
Load: none — 12b-1: none
Other: none

Services
✔ IRA
✔ Keogh
✔ Telephone Exchange

Delafield Fund
(DEFIX)

800-221-3079, 212-830-5271
www.delafieldfund.com

Mid-Cap Stock

PERFORMANCE — fund inception date: 11/19/93

	3yr Annual	5yr Annual	10yr Annual	Bull	Bear
Return (%)	11.7	5.9	na	21.9	29.1
Differ From Category (+/-)	18.5 high	4.2 abv av	na	-60.8 low	53.1 high

Standard Deviation	Category Risk Index	Beta
21.0%—abv av	1.03—av	0.83

	2002	2001	2000	1999	1998	1997	1996	1995	1994	1993
Return (%)	-7.4	32.1	13.9	8.3	-11.4	19.6	26.3	27.3	5.5	—
Differ From Category (+/-)	10.6	38.0	8.1	-21.4	-21.4	-3.0	6.5	-3.8	5.7	—
Return, Tax-Adjusted (%)	-7.4	30.5	13.5	8.0	-11.7	17.5	21.6	24.4	4.6	—

PER SHARE DATA

	2002	2001	2000	1999	1998	1997	1996	1995	1994	1993
Dividends, Net Income ($)	0.00	0.05	0.07	0.08	0.12	0.20	0.15	0.14	0.10	—
Distrib'ns, Cap Gain ($)	0.00	1.12	0.15	0.00	0.00	1.03	1.83	0.89	0.16	—
Net Asset Value ($)	18.23	19.70	15.80	14.07	13.06	14.88	13.49	12.26	10.47	—
Expense Ratio (%)	na	1.25	1.28	1.25	1.24	1.29	1.29	1.65	1.78	—
Yield (%)	0.00	0.24	0.43	0.56	0.91	1.25	0.97	1.06	0.94	—
Portfolio Turnover (%)	na	98	99	105	81	55	75	70	42	—
Total Assets (Millions $)	152	199	98	85	103	146	61	45	10	—

PORTFOLIO (as of 9/30/02)

Portfolio Manager: D Delafield/
V Sellecchia - 1993

Investment Style

✔ Large Cap   Growth
✔ Mid Cap   ✔ Value
Small Cap   Grth/Val

Portfolio

7.3%	cash	0.0%	corp bonds
92.7%	stocks	0.0%	gov't bonds
0.0%	preferred	0.0%	muni bonds
0.0%	conv't bds/wrnts	0.0%	other

SHAREHOLDER INFORMATION

Minimum Investment
Initial: $5,000   Subsequent: $1

Minimum IRA Investment
Initial: $250   Subsequent: $1

Maximum Fees
Load: 2.00% redemption   12b-1: none
Other: redemption fee applies for 3 months

Services
✔ IRA
✔ Keogh
✔ Telephone Exchange

Dreyfus Index:Midcap Idx

800-645-6561, 516-794-5452
www.dreyfus.com

(PESPX)

Mid-Cap Stock

PERFORMANCE — fund inception date: 6/19/91

	3yr Annual	5yr Annual	10yr Annual	Bull	Bear
Return (%)	-0.6	5.8	11.3	79.1	-17.3
Differ From Category (+/-)	6.2 abv av	4.1 abv av	2.5 abv av	-3.6 av	6.7 av

Standard Deviation	Category Risk Index	Beta
20.5%—abv av	1.00—av	0.94

	2002	2001	2000	1999	1998	1997	1996	1995	1994	1993
Return (%)	-15.0	-1.0	16.7	14.0	18.4	31.5	18.5	30.3	-3.9	13.5
Differ From Category (+/-)	3.0	4.9	10.9	-15.7	8.4	8.9	-1.3	-0.8	-3.7	-3.1
Return, Tax-Adjusted (%)	-15.5	-1.8	13.2	9.9	13.2	29.2	16.5	28.0	-5.8	11.8

PER SHARE DATA

	2002	2001	2000	1999	1998	1997	1996	1995	1994	1993
Dividends, Net Income ($)	0.11	0.15	0.21	0.20	0.31	0.23	0.27	0.30	0.28	0.27
Distrib'ns, Cap Gain ($)	0.31	0.57	3.38	4.46	6.02	1.98	0.99	0.87	0.75	0.55
Net Asset Value ($)	17.47	21.06	22.03	21.94	23.58	25.64	21.24	19.00	15.48	17.19
Expense Ratio (%)	na	0.50	0.50	0.50	0.50	0.50	0.50	0.50	0.40	0.09
Yield (%)	0.61	0.69	0.82	0.75	1.04	0.83	1.21	1.50	1.72	1.52
Portfolio Turnover (%)	na	28	45	50	67	20	14	20	19	16
Total Assets (Millions $)	751	633	492	322	272	257	184	128	74	74

PORTFOLIO (as of 9/30/02)

Portfolio Manager: Team Managed - 1995

Investment Style

Large Cap	Growth
✔ Mid Cap	Value
Small Cap	✔ Grth/Val

Portfolio

6.4% cash	0.3% corp bonds
93.3% stocks	0.0% gov't bonds
0.0% preferred	0.0% muni bonds
0.0% conv't bds/wrnts	0.0% other

SHAREHOLDER INFORMATION

Minimum Investment
Initial: $2,500 — Subsequent: $100

Minimum IRA Investment
Initial: $750 — Subsequent: $1

Maximum Fees
Load: 1.00% redemption — 12b-1: none
Other: redemption fee applies for 6 months

Services
- ✔ IRA
- ✔ Keogh
- ✔ Telephone Exchange

Fenimore Value Fd
(FAMVX)
Mid-Cap Stock

800-932-3271, 518-234-7462
www.famfunds.com

PERFORMANCE — fund inception date: 1/2/87

	3yr Annual	5yr Annual	10yr Annual	Bull	Bear
Return (%)	9.2	5.6	10.0	9.4	28.2
Differ From Category (+/-)	16.0 high	3.9 abv av	1.2 av	-73.3 low	52.2 high

Standard Deviation	Category Risk Index	Beta
15.0%—av	0.74—low	0.49

	2002	2001	2000	1999	1998	1997	1996	1995	1994	1993
Return (%)	-4.8	15.0	19.2	-4.8	6.1	39.0	11.2	19.7	6.8	0.2
Differ From Category (+/-)	13.2	20.9	13.4	-34.5	-3.9	16.4	-8.6	-11.4	7.0	-16.4
Return, Tax-Adjusted (%)	-5.3	14.0	16.2	-5.8	4.1	38.1	10.2	18.8	5.7	0.0

PER SHARE DATA

	2002	2001	2000	1999	1998	1997	1996	1995	1994	1993
Dividends, Net Income ($)	0.15	0.17	0.36	0.29	0.20	0.07	0.17	0.20	0.12	0.09
Distrib'ns, Cap Gain ($)	0.55	1.29	4.02	1.09	3.24	1.05	0.62	0.39	0.62	0.04
Net Asset Value ($)	33.69	36.17	32.70	31.35	34.44	35.76	26.53	24.58	21.04	20.40
Expense Ratio (%)	na	1.21	1.26	1.23	1.19	1.24	1.27	1.37	1.39	1.39
Yield (%)	0.43	0.45	0.98	0.89	0.53	0.19	0.62	0.80	0.55	0.44
Portfolio Turnover (%)	na	10	9	16	16	9	12	3	2	5
Total Assets (Millions $)	483	501	367	373	376	331	253	266	210	220

PORTFOLIO (as of 9/30/02)

Portfolio Manager: Thomas Putnam/John Fox - 1987

Investment Style

Large Cap	Growth
✔ Mid Cap	✔ Value
Small Cap	Grth/Val

Portfolio

14.6%	cash	0.0%	corp bonds
85.4%	stocks	0.0%	gov't bonds
0.0%	preferred	0.0%	muni bonds
0.0%	conv't bds/wrnts	0.0%	other

SHAREHOLDER INFORMATION

Minimum Investment
Initial: $500 — Subsequent: $50

Minimum IRA Investment
Initial: $100 — Subsequent: $50

Maximum Fees
Load: none — 12b-1: none
Other: none

Services
✔ IRA
✔ Keogh
Telephone Exchange

Fidelity Aggressive Grth (FDEGX)

800-544-8544, 800-522-7297
www.fidelity.com

Mid-Cap Stock

PERFORMANCE — fund inception date: 12/28/90

	3yr Annual	5yr Annual	10yr Annual	Bull	Bear
Return (%)	-39.0	-8.0	3.9	229.7	-83.6
Differ From Category (+/-)	-32.2 low	-9.7 low	-4.9 low	147.0 high	-59.6 low

Standard Deviation	Category Risk Index	Beta
44.0%—high	2.15—high	1.79

	2002	2001	2000	1999	1998	1997	1996	1995	1994	1993
Return (%)	-41.1	-47.2	-27.1	103.5	42.9	19.4	15.7	35.9	-0.1	19.8
Differ From Category (+/-)	-23.1	-41.3	-32.9	73.8	32.9	-3.2	-4.1	4.8	0.1	3.2
Return, Tax-Adjusted (%)	-41.1	-47.2	-29.6	101.0	41.1	14.6	14.9	34.6	-0.6	14.1

PER SHARE DATA

	2002	2001	2000	1999	1998	1997	1996	1995	1994	1993
Dividends, Net Income ($)	0.00	0.00	0.00	0.00	0.00	0.00	0.00	0.00	0.00	0.00
Distrib'ns, Cap Gain ($)	0.00	0.09	7.58	3.92	2.08	6.00	0.60	0.80	0.31	3.57
Net Asset Value ($)	11.19	19.02	36.17	59.63	31.69	23.75	25.19	22.32	16.99	17.33
Expense Ratio (%)	na	0.92	0.89	0.97	1.08	1.09	1.09	1.10	1.02	1.19
Yield (%)	0.00	0.00	0.00	0.00	0.00	0.00	0.00	0.00	0.00	0.00
Portfolio Turnover (%)	na	118	176	186	199	212	105	97	180	332
Total Assets (Millions $)	4,131	7,410	15,220	15,199	2,897	1,981	1,854	1,249	635	652

PORTFOLIO (as of 6/30/02)

Portfolio Manager: Rajiv Kaul - 2002

Investment Style

✔ Large Cap	✔ Growth
✔ Mid Cap	Value
✔ Small Cap	Grth/Val

Portfolio

2.2%	cash	0.0%	corp bonds
97.7%	stocks	0.0%	gov't bonds
0.0%	preferred	0.0%	muni bonds
0.1%	conv't bds/wrnts	0.0%	other

SHAREHOLDER INFORMATION

Minimum Investment
Initial: $2,500 Subsequent: $250

Minimum IRA Investment
Initial: $500 Subsequent: $250

Maximum Fees
Load: 1.50% redemption 12b-1: none
Other: redemption fee applies for 3 months

Services
✔ IRA
✔ Keogh
✔ Telephone Exchange

Fidelity Mid Cap Stock (FMCSX)

800-544-8544, 800-522-7297
www.fidelity.com

Mid-Cap Stock

PERFORMANCE

fund inception date: 3/29/94

	3yr Annual	5yr Annual	10yr Annual	Bull	Bear
Return (%)	-5.8	6.0	na	123.2	-37.4
Differ From Category (+/-)	1.0 av	4.3 abv av	na	40.5 abv av	-13.4 blw av

Standard Deviation	Category Risk Index	Beta
28.3%—high	1.38—abv av	0.75

	2002	2001	2000	1999	1998	1997	1996	1995	1994	1993
Return (%)	-27.5	-12.8	32.0	39.8	15.1	27.0	18.1	33.9	—	—
Differ From Category (+/-)	-9.5	-6.9	26.2	10.1	5.1	4.4	-1.7	2.8	—	—
Return, Tax-Adjusted (%)	-27.7	-13.0	29.5	36.9	13.6	24.6	15.4	31.7	—	—

PER SHARE DATA

	2002	2001	2000	1999	1998	1997	1996	1995	1994	1993
Dividends, Net Income ($)	0.09	0.16	0.10	0.01	0.00	0.01	0.03	0.06	—	—
Distrib'ns, Cap Gain ($)	0.00	0.00	2.50	2.59	1.28	1.77	1.26	0.74	—	—
Net Asset Value ($)	16.26	22.57	26.06	21.87	17.88	16.69	14.64	13.50	—	—
Expense Ratio (%)	0.87	0.84	0.86	0.74	0.86	0.96	1.00	1.63	—	—
Yield (%)	0.55	0.70	0.35	0.04	0.00	0.05	0.18	0.42	—	—
Portfolio Turnover (%)	200	218	205	121	132	155	179	190	—	—
Total Assets (Millions $)	5,131	6,546	7,011	2,286	1,784	1,763	1,695	1,150	—	—

PORTFOLIO (as of 10/31/02)

Portfolio Manager: Beso Sikharulidze - 2001

Investment Style

Large Cap	✔ Growth
✔ Mid Cap	Value
✔ Small Cap	Grth/Val

Portfolio

2.6%	cash	7.2%	corp bonds
80.5%	stocks	0.0%	gov't bonds
1.1%	pref/conv't pref	0.0%	muni bonds
4.1%	conv't bds/wrnts	4.5%	other

SHAREHOLDER INFORMATION

Minimum Investment
Initial: $2,500 Subsequent: $250

Minimum IRA Investment
Initial: $500 Subsequent: $250

Maximum Fees
Load: 0.75% redemption 12b-1: none
Other: redemption fee applies for 1 month

Services
- ✔ IRA
- ✔ Keogh
- ✔ Telephone Exchange

Fidelity OTC
(FOCPX)

800-544-8544, 800-522-7297
www.fidelity.com

Mid-Cap Stock

PERFORMANCE

fund inception date: 12/31/84

	3yr Annual	5yr Annual	10yr Annual	Bull	Bear
Return (%)	-24.7	0.6	7.4	194.7	-66.2
Differ From Category (+/-)	-17.9 low	-1.1 blw av	-1.4 blw av	112.0 high	-42.2 low

Standard Deviation	Category Risk Index	Beta
37.7%—high	1.84—high	1.46

	2002	2001	2000	1999	1998	1997	1996	1995	1994	1993
Return (%)	-23.2	-24.0	-26.8	72.5	40.3	9.9	23.7	38.2	-2.6	8.3
Differ From Category (+/-)	-5.2	-18.1	-32.6	42.8	30.3	-12.7	3.9	7.1	-2.4	-8.3
Return, Tax-Adjusted (%)	-23.2	-24.0	-30.5	70.0	38.9	8.4	19.6	36.0	-2.9	4.4

PER SHARE DATA

	2002	2001	2000	1999	1998	1997	1996	1995	1994	1993
Dividends, Net Income ($)	0.00	0.00	0.00	0.00	0.00	0.00	0.08	0.02	0.21	0.10
Distrib'ns, Cap Gain ($)	0.00	0.00	12.66	5.51	2.38	2.52	4.32	1.80	0.00	3.42
Net Asset Value ($)	23.91	31.17	41.05	67.97	43.63	33.45	32.71	30.33	23.27	24.14
Expense Ratio (%)	1.09	0.94	0.76	0.74	0.75	0.84	0.82	0.81	0.88	1.08
Yield (%)	0.00	0.00	0.00	0.00	0.00	0.00	0.21	0.06	0.90	0.36
Portfolio Turnover (%)	120	219	196	117	125	147	133	62	222	213
Total Assets (Millions $)	5,974	8,069	10,979	11,705	5,476	3,858	3,387	2,350	1,381	1,343

PORTFOLIO (as of 7/31/02)

Portfolio Manager: Jason Weiner - 2000

Investment Style

Large Cap	✔ Growth
✔ Mid Cap	Value
✔ Small Cap	Grth/Val

Portfolio

0.0%	cash	0.0%	corp bonds
88.0%	stocks	0.0%	gov't bonds
0.0%	preferred	0.0%	muni bonds
0.0%	conv't bds/wrnts	12.0%	other

SHAREHOLDER INFORMATION

Minimum Investment
Initial: $2,500 — Subsequent: $250

Minimum IRA Investment
Initial: $500 — Subsequent: $250

Maximum Fees
Load: none — 12b-1: none
Other: none

Services
✔ IRA
✔ Keogh
✔ Telephone Exchange

Fidelity Value
(FDVLX)
Mid-Cap Stock

800-544-8544, 800-522-7297
www.fidelity.com

PERFORMANCE — fund inception date: 12/1/78

	3yr Annual	5yr Annual	10yr Annual	Bull	Bear
Return (%)	3.2	3.6	11.0	18.6	7.0
Differ From Category (+/-)	10.0 high	1.9 abv av	2.2 abv av	-64.1 low	31.0 high

Standard Deviation	Category Risk Index	Beta
19.3%—abv av	0.94—av	0.72

	2002	2001	2000	1999	1998	1997	1996	1995	1994	1993
Return (%)	-9.2	12.2	8.1	8.5	0.1	21.0	16.8	27.1	7.6	22.9
Differ From Category (+/-)	8.8	18.1	2.3	-21.2	-9.9	-1.6	-3.0	-4.0	7.8	6.3
Return, Tax-Adjusted (%)	-9.5	11.8	7.2	5.5	-2.9	17.5	13.0	25.4	5.8	20.3

PER SHARE DATA

	2002	2001	2000	1999	1998	1997	1996	1995	1994	1993
Dividends, Net Income ($)	0.36	0.51	0.95	0.73	0.55	0.48	0.53	0.48	0.17	0.34
Distrib'ns, Cap Gain ($)	0.00	0.00	0.00	5.62	7.15	7.95	5.92	1.73	2.28	2.80
Net Asset Value ($)	46.39	51.51	46.35	43.81	46.35	54.04	51.54	49.64	40.81	40.23
Expense Ratio (%)	0.95	0.77	0.48	0.54	0.61	0.66	0.88	1.01	1.08	1.11
Yield (%)	0.77	0.99	2.04	1.47	1.02	0.77	0.92	0.93	0.39	0.79
Portfolio Turnover (%)	42	49	48	50	36	56	112	113	112	117
Total Assets (Millions $)	5,092	5,237	3,522	4,383	5,522	7,913	7,080	5,745	3,720	1,716

PORTFOLIO (as of 10/31/02)

Portfolio Manager: Richard Fentin - 1996

Investment Style

✔ Large Cap	Growth
✔ Mid Cap	✔ Value
Small Cap	Grth/Val

Portfolio

0.0% cash	0.6% corp bonds
94.4% stocks	0.0% gov't bonds
2.3% pref/conv't pref	0.0% muni bonds
0.0% conv't bds/wrnts	2.7% other

SHAREHOLDER INFORMATION

Minimum Investment
Initial: $2,500 — Subsequent: $250

Minimum IRA Investment
Initial: $500 — Subsequent: $250

Maximum Fees
Load: none — 12b-1: none
Other: none

Services
✔ IRA
✔ Keogh
✔ Telephone Exchange

Hennessy Crnst Grth (HFCGX)

800-966-4354, 415-899-1555
www.hennessy-funds.com

Mid-Cap Stock

PERFORMANCE

fund inception date: 11/1/96

	3yr Annual	5yr Annual	10yr Annual	Bull	Bear
Return (%)	4.0	9.9	na	97.0	0.3
Differ From Category (+/-)	10.8 high	8.2 high	na	14.3 abv av	24.3 abv av

Standard Deviation	Category Risk Index	Beta
21.0%—abv av	1.03—av	0.79

	2002	2001	2000	1999	1998	1997	1996	1995	1994	1993
Return (%)	-4.7	12.1	5.3	37.7	3.6	31.3	—	—	—	—
Differ From Category (+/-)	13.3	18.0	-0.5	8.0	-6.4	8.7	—	—	—	—
Return, Tax-Adjusted (%)	-5.4	10.6	-3.2	37.7	3.6	24.3	—	—	—	—

PER SHARE DATA

	2002	2001	2000	1999	1998	1997	1996	1995	1994	1993
Dividends, Net Income ($)	0.00	0.00	3.50	0.00	0.00	1.78	—	—	—	—
Distrib'ns, Cap Gain ($)	0.48	1.03	0.00	0.00	0.00	0.00	—	—	—	—
Net Asset Value ($)	13.27	14.41	13.85	16.32	11.85	11.43	—	—	—	—
Expense Ratio (%)	1.10	1.11	1.18	1.15	1.16	1.56	—	—	—	—
Yield (%)	0.00	0.00	25.27	0.00	0.00	15.57	—	—	—	—
Portfolio Turnover (%)	70	103	95	125	119	na	—	—	—	—
Total Assets (Millions $)	461	167	156	157	116	54	—	—	—	—

PORTFOLIO (as of 9/30/02)

Portfolio Manager: Edward Hennessy - 1996

Investment Style

✔ Large Cap	Growth
✔ Mid Cap	Value
Small Cap	✔ Grth/Val

Portfolio

3.8% cash	0.0% corp bonds
96.2% stocks	0.0% gov't bonds
0.0% preferred	0.0% muni bonds
0.0% conv't bds/wrnts	0.0% other

SHAREHOLDER INFORMATION

Minimum Investment
Initial: $2,500 Subsequent: $1

Minimum IRA Investment
Initial: $250 Subsequent: $1

Maximum Fees
Load: 1.50% redemption 12b-1: none
Other: redemption fee applies for 3 months

Services
✔ IRA
✔ Keogh
✔ Telephone Exchange

Homestead Fds Value (HOVLX)

800-258-3030, 703-907-6026
www.nreca.org/homestead

Mid-Cap Stock

PERFORMANCE — fund inception date: 11/19/90

	3yr Annual	5yr Annual	10yr Annual	Bull	Bear
Return (%)	0.6	1.3	10.0	11.3	-3.3
Differ From Category (+/-)	7.4 abv av	-0.4 av	1.2 av	-71.4 low	20.7 abv av

Standard Deviation	Category Risk Index	Beta
17.5%—av	0.85—blw av	0.69

	2002	2001	2000	1999	1998	1997	1996	1995	1994	1993
Return (%)	-11.5	5.2	9.6	-3.2	8.3	26.6	17.9	33.7	2.4	18.8
Differ From Category (+/-)	.6.5	11.1	3.8	-32.9	-1.7	4.0	-1.9	2.6	2.6	2.2
Return, Tax-Adjusted (%)	-12.0	4.1	8.9	-5.1	7.1	25.2	16.5	31.6	1.4	17.9

PER SHARE DATA

	2002	2001	2000	1999	1998	1997	1996	1995	1994	1993
Dividends, Net Income ($)	0.32	0.16	0.38	0.41	0.39	0.36	0.38	0.40	0.28	0.22
Distrib'ns, Cap Gain ($)	0.00	1.04	0.00	1.73	0.72	0.71	0.35	0.52	0.11	0.07
Net Asset Value ($)	22.24	25.50	25.38	23.53	26.50	25.50	20.99	18.44	14.50	14.54
Expense Ratio (%)	na	0.85	0.85	0.74	0.72	0.79	0.73	0.97	1.15	1.25
Yield (%)	1.43	0.60	1.49	1.62	1.43	1.37	1.78	2.10	1.91	1.50
Portfolio Turnover (%)	na	19	18	17	10	6	5	10	4	2
Total Assets (Millions $)	303	320	335	375	434	366	232	141	90	52

PORTFOLIO (as of 6/30/00)

Portfolio Manager: Morris/Teach/Ashton - 2002

Investment Style

✔ Large Cap	Growth
✔ Mid Cap	✔ Value
Small Cap	Grth/Val

Portfolio

1.7%	cash	0.0%	corp bonds
98.0%	stocks	0.0%	gov't bonds
0.3%	pref/conv't pref	0.0%	muni bonds
0.0%	conv't bds/wrnts	0.0%	other

SHAREHOLDER INFORMATION

Minimum Investment
Initial: $500 Subsequent: $1

Minimum IRA Investment
Initial: $200 Subsequent: $1

Maximum Fees
Load: none 12b-1: none
Other: none

Services
✔ IRA
Keogh
✔ Telephone Exchange

Janus Enterprise
(JAENX)

800-525-0020, 303-333-3863
www.janus.com

Mid-Cap Stock

PERFORMANCE — fund inception date: 9/1/92

	3yr Annual	5yr Annual	10yr Annual	Bull	Bear
Return (%)	-33.1	-2.3	5.8	264.8	-73.8
Differ From Category (+/-)	-26.3 low	-4.0 blw av	-3.0 blw av	182.1 high	-49.8 low

Standard Deviation	Category Risk Index	Beta
36.4%—high	1.78—high	1.11

	2002	2001	2000	1999	1998	1997	1996	1995	1994	1993
Return (%)	-28.2	-39.9	-30.5	121.8	33.7	10.8	11.6	27.2	8.9	15.6
Differ From Category (+/-)	-10.2	-34.0	-36.3	92.1	23.7	-11.8	-8.2	-3.9	9.1	-1.0
Return, Tax-Adjusted (%)	-28.2	-39.9	-30.5	120.0	30.9	9.5	10.3	24.2	7.5	14.8

PER SHARE DATA

	2002	2001	2000	1999	1998	1997	1996	1995	1994	1993
Dividends, Net Income ($)	0.00	0.00	0.00	0.00	0.00	0.00	0.00	1.63	0.51	0.01
Distrib'ns, Cap Gain ($)	0.00	0.00	0.00	3.32	4.30	1.96	1.27	0.16	0.37	0.54
Net Asset Value ($)	22.95	32.00	53.27	76.67	36.22	30.48	29.34	27.44	22.98	21.92
Expense Ratio (%)	na	0.90	0.88	0.95	1.06	1.04	1.12	1.26	1.25	1.36
Yield (%)	0.00	0.00	0.00	0.00	0.00	0.00	0.00	5.90	2.18	0.04
Portfolio Turnover (%)	na	85	80	98	134	111	93	194	193	201
Total Assets (Millions $)	1,727	3,209	6,267	4,434	728	573	721	498	354	258

PORTFOLIO (as of 10/31/02)

Portfolio Manager: Jonathan Coleman - 2002

Investment Style

Large Cap	✔ Growth
✔ Mid Cap	Value
✔ Small Cap	Grth/Val

Portfolio

14.4%	cash	0.1%	corp bonds
85.5%	stocks	0.0%	gov't bonds
0.0%	preferred	0.0%	muni bonds
0.0%	conv't bds/wrnts	0.0%	other

SHAREHOLDER INFORMATION

Minimum Investment
Initial: $2,500 — Subsequent: $100

Minimum IRA Investment
Initial: $500 — Subsequent: $100

Maximum Fees
Load: none — 12b-1: none
Other: none

Services
✔ IRA
✔ Keogh
✔ Telephone Exchange

Legg Mason Eq:Special/P (LMASX)

800-822-5544, 410-539-0000
www.leggmason.com

Mid-Cap Stock

PERFORMANCE — fund inception date: 12/30/85

	3yr Annual	5yr Annual	10yr Annual	Bull	Bear
Return (%)	-6.3	6.5	11.0	108.0	-27.8
Differ From Category (+/-)	0.5 av	4.8 high	2.2 abv av	25.3 abv av	-3.8 av

Standard Deviation	Category Risk Index	Beta
27.0%—high	1.32—abv av	1.17

	2002	2001	2000	1999	1998	1997	1996	1995	1994	1993
Return (%)	-8.7	2.2	-12.0	35.5	23.3	22.1	28.6	22.5	-13.0	24.1
Differ From Category (+/-)	9.3	8.1	-17.8	5.8	13.3	-0.5	8.8	-8.6	-12.8	7.5
Return, Tax-Adjusted (%)	-9.4	1.6	-12.8	31.1	21.7	21.0	26.9	21.8	-13.3	23.8

PER SHARE DATA

	2002	2001	2000	1999	1998	1997	1996	1995	1994	1993
Dividends, Net Income ($)	0.00	0.00	0.00	0.00	0.00	0.00	0.00	0.03	0.00	0.03
Distrib'ns, Cap Gain ($)	1.20	1.00	1.51	8.04	2.65	1.49	1.41	0.44	0.23	0.14
Net Asset Value ($)	29.63	33.73	33.94	40.15	36.70	32.27	27.83	22.81	19.03	22.14
Expense Ratio (%)	1.79	1.79	1.80	1.84	1.86	1.92	1.96	1.93	1.94	2.00
Yield (%)	0.00	0.00	0.00	0.00	0.00	0.00	0.00	0.12	0.00	0.13
Portfolio Turnover (%)	37	36	29	47	29	29	36	27	16	32
Total Assets (Millions $)	2,170	2,241	2,281	2,587	1,730	1,366	964	713	605	510

PORTFOLIO (as of 9/30/02)

Portfolio Manager: Lisa Rapuano - 2001

Investment Style

Large Cap	✔ Growth
✔ Mid Cap	Value
✔ Small Cap	Grth/Val

Portfolio

0.7%	cash	7.3%	corp bonds
92.0%	stocks	0.0%	gov't bonds
0.0%	preferred	0.0%	muni bonds
0.0%	conv't bds/wrnts	0.0%	other

SHAREHOLDER INFORMATION

Minimum Investment
Initial: $1,000 Subsequent: $100

Minimum IRA Investment
Initial: $1,000 Subsequent: $100

Maximum Fees
Load: none 12b-1: 1.00%
Other: none

Services
✔ IRA
✔ Keogh
✔ Telephone Exchange

Marshall:Mid Cap Gr/Inv (MRMSX)

800-236-3863, 412-288-1900
www.marshallfunds.com

Mid-Cap Stock

PERFORMANCE — fund inception date: 9/30/93

	3yr Annual	5yr Annual	10yr Annual	Bull	Bear
Return (%)	-18.4	0.2	na	170.7	-58.6
Differ From Category (+/-)	-11.6 blw av	-1.5 blw av	na	88.0 high	-34.6 blw av

Standard Deviation	Category Risk Index	Beta
29.5%—high	1.44—abv av	1.06

	2002	2001	2000	1999	1998	1997	1996	1995	1994	1993
Return (%)	-31.7	-10.5	-11.1	61.1	15.7	22.7	20.6	33.7	-5.6	—
Differ From Category (+/-)	-13.7	-4.6	-16.9	31.4	5.7	0.1	0.8	2.6	-5.4	—
Return, Tax-Adjusted (%)	-31.7	-10.5	-15.4	58.9	14.5	19.9	17.7	31.0	-5.6	—

PER SHARE DATA

	2002	2001	2000	1999	1998	1997	1996	1995	1994	1993
Dividends, Net Income ($)	0.00	0.00	0.00	0.00	0.00	0.00	0.00	0.00	0.00	—
Distrib'ns, Cap Gain ($)	0.00	0.03	4.97	1.69	0.81	1.81	1.21	0.91	0.00	—
Net Asset Value ($)	9.48	13.89	15.57	23.06	15.50	14.21	13.10	11.84	9.55	—
Expense Ratio (%)	1.24	1.19	1.18	1.21	1.23	1.24	1.01	1.01	1.01	—
Yield (%)	0.00	0.00	0.00	0.00	0.00	0.00	0.00	0.00	0.00	—
Portfolio Turnover (%)	167	118	108	173	167	211	189	157	113	—
Total Assets (Millions $)	213	319	401	423	262	216	161	108	69	—

PORTFOLIO (as of 9/30/02)

Portfolio Manager: Michael Groblewski - 1999

Investment Style

Large Cap	✔ Growth
✔ Mid Cap	Value
✔ Small Cap	Grth/Val

Portfolio

11.9% cash	0.0% corp bonds
88.2% stocks	0.0% gov't bonds
0.0% preferred	0.0% muni bonds
0.0% conv't bds/wrnts	0.0% other

SHAREHOLDER INFORMATION

Minimum Investment
Initial: $1,000 — Subsequent: $50

Minimum IRA Investment
Initial: $1,000 — Subsequent: $50

Maximum Fees
Load: none — 12b-1: none
Other: none

Services
✔ IRA
Keogh
✔ Telephone Exchange

Marshall:Mid Cap Val/Inv

800-236-3863, 412-288-1900
www.marshallfunds.com

(MRVEX)

Mid-Cap Stock

PERFORMANCE fund inception date: 9/30/93

	3yr Annual	5yr Annual	10yr Annual	Bull	Bear
Return (%)	8.1	7.1	na	21.4	20.5
Differ From Category (+/-)	14.9 high	5.4 high	na	-61.3 low	44.5 high

Standard Deviation	Category Risk Index	Beta
19.2%—abv av	0.94—blw av	0.78

	2002	2001	2000	1999	1998	1997	1996	1995	1994	1993
Return (%)	-11.5	22.1	17.2	6.1	5.1	23.3	13.9	25.3	2.0	—
Differ From Category (+/-)	.6.5	28.0	11.4	-23.6	-4.9	0.7	-5.9	-5.8	2.2	—
Return, Tax-Adjusted (%)	-11.5	19.0	15.5	3.3	3.0	19.4	8.7	22.0	1.1	—

PER SHARE DATA

	2002	2001	2000	1999	1998	1997	1996	1995	1994	1993
Dividends, Net Income ($)	0.00	0.01	0.07	0.08	0.14	0.12	0.18	0.21	0.15	—
Distrib'ns, Cap Gain ($)	0.00	1.68	0.69	1.37	0.93	1.94	1.88	0.87	0.11	—
Net Asset Value ($)	10.52	11.91	11.16	10.22	11.08	11.57	11.09	11.59	10.13	—
Expense Ratio (%)	1.26	1.30	1.33	1.25	1.25	1.23	0.98	0.96	1.00	—
Yield (%)	0.00	0.07	0.59	0.69	1.16	0.88	1.38	1.68	1.46	—
Portfolio Turnover (%)	44	104	94	90	59	55	67	78	39	—
Total Assets (Millions $)	204	189	115	116	144	184	175	204	195	—

PORTFOLIO (as of 9/30/02)

Portfolio Manager: Matthew Fahey - 1997

Investment Style

Large Cap	Growth
✔ Mid Cap	✔ Value
Small Cap	Grth/Val

Portfolio

6.3%	cash	0.0%	corp bonds
93.7%	stocks	0.0%	gov't bonds
0.0%	preferred	0.0%	muni bonds
0.0%	conv't bds/wrnts	0.0%	other

SHAREHOLDER INFORMATION

Minimum Investment
Initial: $1,000 Subsequent: $50

Minimum IRA Investment
Initial: $1,000 Subsequent: $50

Maximum Fees
Load: none 12b-1: none
Other: none

Services
✔ IRA
✔ Keogh
✔ Telephone Exchange

Merger Fund

800-343-8959, 914-741-5600

(MERFX)

Mid-Cap Stock

PERFORMANCE — fund inception date: 1/31/89

	3yr Annual	5yr Annual	10yr Annual	Bull	Bear
Return (%)	4.2	6.9	9.4	31.1	4.0
Differ From Category (+/-)	11.0 high	5.2 high	0.6 av	-51.6 blw av	28.0 high

Standard Deviation	Category Risk Index	Beta
6.6%—blw av	0.32—low	0.15

	2002	2001	2000	1999	1998	1997	1996	1995	1994	1993
Return (%)	-5.6	2.0	17.5	17.3	5.3	11.6	9.9	14.1	7.1	17.6
Differ From Category (+/-)	12.4	7.9	11.7	-12.4	-4.7	-11.0	-9.9	-17.0	7.3	1.0
Return, Tax-Adjusted (%)	-6.1	0.4	14.9	15.4	3.1	9.3	6.9	12.1	5.6	15.0

PER SHARE DATA

	2002	2001	2000	1999	1998	1997	1996	1995	1994	1993
Dividends, Net Income ($)	0.20	0.20	0.13	0.07	0.22	0.02	0.18	0.07	0.00	0.00
Distrib'ns, Cap Gain ($)	0.00	0.85	1.64	1.14	1.09	1.57	1.23	0.82	0.70	1.09
Net Asset Value ($)	13.73	14.77	15.52	14.72	13.58	14.15	14.11	14.13	13.17	12.96
Expense Ratio (%)	1.38	1.34	1.34	1.38	1.33	1.36	1.36	1.39	1.58	2.19
Yield (%)	1.45	1.28	0.75	0.44	1.49	0.12	1.17	0.46	0.00	0.00
Portfolio Turnover (%)	258	383	419	386	355	271	405	418	390	186
Total Assets (Millions $)	896	980	1,041	635	346	435	473	245	171	27

PORTFOLIO (as of 9/30/02)

Portfolio Manager: Fred Green/Bonnie Smith - 1989

Investment Style

Large Cap	Growth
✔ Mid Cap	Value
Small Cap	✔ Grth/Val

Portfolio

28.2%	cash	21.1%	corp bonds
55.3%	stocks	3.0%	gov't bonds
0.0%	preferred	0.0%	muni bonds
5.2%	conv't bds/wrnts	-12.9%	other

SHAREHOLDER INFORMATION

Minimum Investment

Initial: $2,000 — Subsequent: $1

Minimum IRA Investment

Initial: $2,000 — Subsequent: $1

Maximum Fees

Load: none — 12b-1: 0.20%

Other: none

Services

✔ IRA

✔ Keogh

Telephone Exchange

Meridian Growth Fund

800-446-6662, 415-461-6237

(MERDX)

Mid-Cap Stock

PERFORMANCE **fund inception date: 8/2/84**

	3yr Annual	5yr Annual	10yr Annual	Bull	Bear
Return (%)	6.5	7.1	10.0	56.2	3.0
Differ From Category (+/-)	13.3 high	5.4 high	1.2 av	-26.5 av	27.0 high

Standard Deviation	Category Risk Index	Beta
20.5%—abv av	1.00—av	0.87

	2002	2001	2000	1999	1998	1997	1996	1995	1994	1993
Return (%)	-17.8	14.7	28.2	13.3	3.0	19.2	11.1	22.4	0.5	13.0
Differ From Category (+/-)	0.2	20.6	22.4	-16.4	-7.0	-3.4	-8.7	-8.7	0.7	-3.6
Return, Tax-Adjusted (%)	-18.3	12.7	22.9	11.6	-1.4	15.6	8.0	21.3	-0.5	12.4

PER SHARE DATA

	2002	2001	2000	1999	1998	1997	1996	1995	1994	1993
Dividends, Net Income ($)	0.05	0.00	2.43	0.15	0.14	0.31	0.36	0.30	0.17	0.02
Distrib'ns, Cap Gain ($)	0.60	2.83	1.85	1.78	6.50	4.81	2.75	0.53	0.70	0.43
Net Asset Value ($)	22.98	28.79	28.06	25.40	24.29	30.73	30.08	29.90	25.12	25.87
Expense Ratio (%)	1.02	1.04	1.09	1.01	0.95	0.96	0.96	1.06	1.22	1.47
Yield (%)	0.21	0.00	8.12	0.55	0.45	0.87	1.09	0.98	0.65	0.07
Portfolio Turnover (%)	26	43	28	51	38	37	34	29	43	61
Total Assets (Millions $)	317	208	152	138	230	332	377	395	256	160

PORTFOLIO (as of 11/30/02)

Portfolio Manager: Richard Aster - 1984

Investment Style

Large Cap	Growth
✔ Mid Cap	✔ Value
Small Cap	Grth/Val

Portfolio

4.7%	cash	2.9%	corp bonds
92.4%	stocks	0.0%	gov't bonds
0.0%	preferred	0.0%	muni bonds
0.0%	conv't bds/wrnts	0.0%	other

SHAREHOLDER INFORMATION

Minimum Investment
Initial: $1,000 Subsequent: $50

Minimum IRA Investment
Initial: $1,000 Subsequent: $50

Maximum Fees
Load: none 12b-1: none
Other: none

Services
✔ IRA
✔ Keogh
✔ Telephone Exchange

Muhlenkamp Fund (MUHLX)

800-860-3863, 724-935-5520
www.muhlenkamp.com

Mid-Cap Stock

PERFORMANCE — fund inception date: 11/18/88

	3yr Annual	5yr Annual	10yr Annual	Bull	Bear
Return (%)	3.1	4.7	12.2	44.6	-9.8
Differ From Category (+/-)	9.9 abv av	3.0 abv av	3.4 high	-38.1 av	14.2 abv av

Standard Deviation	Category Risk Index	Beta
26.3%—high	1.29—abv av	1.12

	2002	2001	2000	1999	1998	1997	1996	1995	1994	1993
Return (%)	-19.9	9.3	25.3	11.3	3.2	32.8	29.9	32.9	-7.1	18.1
Differ From Category (+/-)	-1.9	15.2	19.5	-18.4	-6.8	10.2	10.1	1.8	-6.9	1.5
Return, Tax-Adjusted (%)	-19.9	9.3	24.2	10.9	3.1	32.8	29.7	32.2	-7.7	17.9

PER SHARE DATA

	2002	2001	2000	1999	1998	1997	1996	1995	1994	1993
Dividends, Net Income ($)	0.00	0.00	0.00	0.00	0.07	0.01	0.11	0.20	0.09	0.09
Distrib'ns, Cap Gain ($)	0.00	0.00	2.33	0.80	0.00	0.00	0.00	0.11	0.25	0.00
Net Asset Value ($)	42.89	53.56	48.98	41.11	37.65	36.55	27.52	21.26	16.23	17.86
Expense Ratio (%)	na	1.17	1.28	1.35	1.32	1.33	1.55	1.40	1.57	1.30
Yield (%)	0.00	0.00	0.00	0.00	0.18	0.02	0.39	0.93	0.54	0.50
Portfolio Turnover (%)	na	11	32	14	27	13	16	22	25	14
Total Assets (Millions $)	642	538	266	176	195	125	41	23	16	12

PORTFOLIO (as of 9/30/02)

Portfolio Manager: Ronald Muhlenkamp - 1988

Investment Style

Large Cap	Growth
✔ Mid Cap	Value
✔ Small Cap	✔ Grth/Val

Portfolio

1.7%	cash	0.0%	corp bonds
99.7%	stocks	0.0%	gov't bonds
0.0%	preferred	0.0%	muni bonds
0.0%	conv't bds/wrnts	-1.4%	other

SHAREHOLDER INFORMATION

Minimum Investment
Initial: $1,500 — Subsequent: $50

Minimum IRA Investment
Initial: $1 — Subsequent: $1

Maximum Fees
Load: none — 12b-1: none
Other: none

Services
✔ IRA
✔ Keogh
Telephone Exchange

Nicholas II
(NCTWX)
Mid-Cap Stock

800-227-5987, 414-272-6133
www.nicholasfunds.com

PERFORMANCE **fund inception date: 10/17/83**

	3yr Annual	5yr Annual	10yr Annual	Bull	Bear
Return (%)	-8.9	-3.5	6.5	22.7	-26.7
Differ From Category (+/-)	-2.1 av	-5.2 low	-2.3 blw av	-60.0 blw av	-2.7 av

Standard Deviation	Category Risk Index	Beta
20.5%—abv av	1.00—av	0.99

	2002	2001	2000	1999	1998	1997	1996	1995	1994	1993
Return (%)	-20.3	-3.1	-2.0	1.1	9.2	37.0	19.3	28.5	1.0	6.4
Differ From Category (+/-)	-2.3	2.8	-7.8	-28.6	-0.8	14.4	-0.5	-2.6	1.2	-10.2
Return, Tax-Adjusted (%)	-20.3	-3.6	-9.3	0.8	6.9	33.5	16.1	25.3	-1.4	4.5

PER SHARE DATA

	2002	2001	2000	1999	1998	1997	1996	1995	1994	1993
Dividends, Net Income ($)	0.00	0.00	0.00	0.01	0.13	0.06	0.22	0.27	0.31	0.27
Distrib'ns, Cap Gain ($)	0.00	0.57	13.12	0.47	4.00	5.24	3.02	2.40	1.79	1.40
Net Asset Value ($)	16.01	20.09	21.34	35.96	36.03	36.94	30.99	28.73	24.46	26.32
Expense Ratio (%)	na	0.62	0.62	0.61	0.59	0.61	0.62	0.66	0.67	0.67
Yield (%)	0.00	0.00	0.00	0.02	0.32	0.14	0.64	0.86	1.18	0.97
Portfolio Turnover (%)	na	49	65	21	20	30	24	19	17	27
Total Assets (Millions $)	445	577	690	940	1,109	1,024	784	693	603	703

PORTFOLIO (as of 9/30/02)

Portfolio Manager: David Nicholas - 1993

Investment Style

✔ Large Cap	Growth
✔ Mid Cap	Value
Small Cap	✔ Grth/Val

Portfolio

5.4%	cash	0.0%	corp bonds
93.6%	stocks	0.0%	gov't bonds
1.0%	pref/conv't pref	0.0%	muni bonds
0.0%	conv't bds/wrnts	0.0%	other

SHAREHOLDER INFORMATION

Minimum Investment
Initial: $500 Subsequent: $100

Minimum IRA Investment
Initial: $500 Subsequent: $100

Maximum Fees
Load: none 12b-1: none
Other: none

Services
✔ IRA
✔ Keogh
✔ Telephone Exchange

Oak Value
(OAKVX)

Mid-Cap Stock

800-622-2474, 919-419-1900
www.oakvaluefund.com

PERFORMANCE — fund inception date: 1/11/93

	3yr Annual	5yr Annual	10yr Annual	Bull	Bear
Return (%)	-3.8	0.4	na	15.0	-11.2
Differ From Category (+/-)	3.0 av	-1.3 blw av	na	-67.7 low	12.8 av

Standard Deviation	Category Risk Index	Beta
20.1%—abv av	0.99—av	0.84

	2002	2001	2000	1999	1998	1997	1996	1995	1994	1993
Return (%)	-24.3	-0.4	18.1	-3.1	18.9	37.7	28.9	28.8	-1.5	—
Differ From Category (+/-)	-6.3	5.5	12.3	-32.8	8.9	15.1	9.1	-2.3	-1.3	—
Return, Tax-Adjusted (%)	-24.7	-0.6	17.6	-3.9	18.6	36.8	27.6	28.5	-3.4	—

PER SHARE DATA

	2002	2001	2000	1999	1998	1997	1996	1995	1994	1993
Dividends, Net Income ($)	0.00	0.00	0.02	0.07	0.09	0.00	0.00	0.00	0.00	—
Distrib'ns, Cap Gain ($)	0.52	0.27	0.54	0.90	0.19	0.81	0.63	0.09	0.81	—
Net Asset Value ($)	21.55	29.08	29.49	25.52	27.29	23.19	17.49	14.06	10.99	—
Expense Ratio (%)	1.23	1.22	1.13	1.10	1.22	1.59	1.90	1.89	1.89	—
Yield (%)	0.00	0.00	0.06	0.26	0.32	0.00	0.00	0.00	0.00	—
Portfolio Turnover (%)	63	52	22	38	15	22	58	103	91	—
Total Assets (Millions $)	243	320	329	394	562	139	31	13	7	—

PORTFOLIO (as of 9/30/02)

Portfolio Manager: David Carr/George Brumley - 1993

Investment Style

✔ Large Cap	Growth
✔ Mid Cap	✔ Value
Small Cap	Grth/Val

Portfolio

0.0%	cash	0.0%	corp bonds
96.1%	stocks	0.0%	gov't bonds
0.0%	preferred	0.0%	muni bonds
0.0%	conv't bds/wrnts	4.0%	other

SHAREHOLDER INFORMATION

Minimum Investment
Initial: $2,500 Subsequent: $100

Minimum IRA Investment
Initial: $1,000 Subsequent: $100

Maximum Fees
Load: none 12b-1: none
Other: none

Services
✔ IRA
✔ Keogh
✔ Telephone Exchange

PBHG Growth

(PBHGX)

Mid-Cap Stock

800-433-0051, 610-647-4100
www.pbhgfunds.com

PERFORMANCE fund inception date: 12/19/85

	3yr Annual	5yr Annual	10yr Annual	Bull	Bear
Return (%)	-29.4	-7.4	5.2	227.5	-71.5
Differ From Category (+/-)	-22.6 low	-9.1 low	-3.6 low	144.8 high	-47.5 low

Standard Deviation	Category Risk Index	Beta
42.1%—high	2.06—high	1.25

	2002	2001	2000	1999	1998	1997	1996	1995	1994	1993
Return (%)	-30.3	-34.5	-22.9	92.4	0.5	-3.3	9.8	50.3	4.7	46.7
Differ From Category (+/-)	-12.3	-28.6	-28.7	62.7	-9.5	-25.9	-10.0	19.2	4.9	30.1
Return, Tax-Adjusted (%)	-30.3	-34.5	-25.5	91.2	0.5	-3.3	9.8	50.3	4.7	46.2

PER SHARE DATA

	2002	2001	2000	1999	1998	1997	1996	1995	1994	1993
Dividends, Net Income ($)	0.00	0.00	0.00	0.00	0.00	0.00	0.00	0.00	0.00	0.00
Distrib'ns, Cap Gain ($)	0.00	0.00	6.26	1.59	0.00	0.00	0.00	0.00	0.01	0.19
Net Asset Value ($)	14.18	20.36	31.10	47.38	25.54	25.39	26.27	23.92	15.91	15.20
Expense Ratio (%)	1.32	1.25	1.23	1.32	1.26	1.25	1.48	1.50	1.55	2.39
Yield (%)	0.00	0.00	0.00	0.00	0.00	0.00	0.00	0.00	0.00	0.00
Portfolio Turnover (%)	171	104	107	80	94	64	45	118	94	209
Total Assets (Millions $)	1,322	2,273	4,249	4,370	3,939	5,464	5,931	2,028	745	121

PORTFOLIO (as of 9/30/02)

Portfolio Manager: Gary Pilgrim - 1985

Investment Style

Large Cap	✔ Growth
✔ Mid Cap	Value
✔ Small Cap	Grth/Val

Portfolio

10.0%	cash	0.5%	corp bonds
88.3%	stocks	0.0%	gov't bonds
0.0%	preferred	0.0%	muni bonds
0.0%	conv't bds/wrnts	1.2%	other

SHAREHOLDER INFORMATION

Minimum Investment
Initial: $2,500 Subsequent: $1

Minimum IRA Investment
Initial: $2,000 Subsequent: $1

Maximum Fees
Load: none 12b-1: none
Other: none

Services
- ✔ IRA
- ✔ Keogh
- ✔ Telephone Exchange

PBHG Mid Cap Value (PBMCX)

800-433-0051, 610-647-4100
www.pbhgfunds.com

Mid-Cap Stock

PERFORMANCE — fund inception date: 4/30/97

	3yr Annual	5yr Annual	10yr Annual	Bull	Bear
Return (%)	2.9	11.1	na	94.3	-10.3
Differ From Category (+/-)	9.7 abv av	9.4 high	na	11.6 abv av	13.7 abv av

Standard Deviation	Category Risk Index	Beta
21.6%—abv av	1.05—av	0.98

	2002	2001	2000	1999	1998	1997	1996	1995	1994	1993
Return (%)	-19.7	7.7	26.1	21.7	27.8	—	—	—	—	—
Differ From Category (+/-)	-1.7	13.6	20.3	-8.0	17.8	—	—	—	—	—
Return, Tax-Adjusted (%)	-19.7	7.7	25.0	13.7	26.1	—	—	—	—	—

PER SHARE DATA

	2002	2001	2000	1999	1998	1997	1996	1995	1994	1993
Dividends, Net Income ($)	0.00	0.00	0.03	0.00	0.00	—	—	—	—	—
Distrib'ns, Cap Gain ($)	0.00	0.00	0.64	6.27	1.13	—	—	—	—	—
Net Asset Value ($)	12.77	15.92	14.77	12.26	15.64	—	—	—	—	—
Expense Ratio (%)	1.31	1.35	1.44	1.33	1.47	—	—	—	—	—
Yield (%)	0.00	0.00	0.19	0.00	0.00	—	—	—	—	—
Portfolio Turnover (%)	237	248	742	732	399	—	—	—	—	—
Total Assets (Millions $)	329	464	157	34	112	—	—	—	—	—

PORTFOLIO (as of 9/30/02)

Portfolio Manager: Jerome Heppelmann - 1999

Investment Style

Large Cap	Growth
✔ Mid Cap	✔ Value
Small Cap	Grth/Val

Portfolio

3.8%	cash	0.0%	corp bonds
96.2%	stocks	0.0%	gov't bonds
0.0%	preferred	0.0%	muni bonds
0.0%	conv't bds/wrnts	0.0%	other

SHAREHOLDER INFORMATION

Minimum Investment
Initial: $2,500 — Subsequent: $1

Minimum IRA Investment
Initial: $2,000 — Subsequent: $1

Maximum Fees
Load: none — 12b-1: none
Other: none

Services
✔ IRA
✔ Keogh
✔ Telephone Exchange

Selected Special Shares

800-279-0279, 800-243-1575
www.selectedfunds.com

(SLSSX)

Mid-Cap Stock

PERFORMANCE

fund inception date: 5/1/39

	3yr Annual	5yr Annual	10yr Annual	Bull	Bear
Return (%)	-11.3	0.2	7.0	70.0	-41.7
Differ From Category (+/-)	-4.5 blw av	-1.5 blw av	-1.8 blw av	-12.7 av	-17.7 blw av

Standard Deviation	Category Risk Index	Beta
21.2%—abv av	1.04—av	1.01

	2002	2001	2000	1999	1998	1997	1996	1995	1994	1993
Return (%)	-17.6	-14.4	-1.0	16.8	24.5	26.9	11.8	34.2	-2.5	4.4
Differ From Category (+/-)	0.4	-8.5	-6.8	-12.9	14.5	4.3	-8.0	3.1	-2.3	-12.2
Return, Tax-Adjusted (%)	-17.7	-16.2	-3.8	15.5	22.5	25.8	8.7	30.3	-3.8	2.7

PER SHARE DATA

	2002	2001	2000	1999	1998	1997	1996	1995	1994	1993
Dividends, Net Income ($)	0.00	0.00	0.00	0.00	0.00	0.00	0.00	0.00	0.00	0.00
Distrib'ns, Cap Gain ($)	0.04	1.21	2.24	0.97	1.32	0.62	1.18	1.26	0.93	0.65
Net Asset Value ($)	8.61	10.50	13.68	16.17	14.76	13.03	10.89	10.80	9.02	10.20
Expense Ratio (%)	na	1.15	1.15	1.17	1.25	1.28	1.33	1.56	1.41	1.24
Yield (%)	0.00	0.00	0.00	0.00	0.00	0.00	0.00	0.00	0.00	0.00
Portfolio Turnover (%)	na	117	35	44	41	51	98	127	99	100
Total Assets (Millions $)	64	73	96	106	93	74	62	59	45	53

PORTFOLIO (as of 8/31/02)

Portfolio Manager: Elizabeth Bramwell - 1997

Investment Style

✔ Large Cap ✔ Growth
✔ Mid Cap Value
Small Cap Grth/Val

Portfolio

4.2%	cash	0.9%	corp bonds
95.0%	stocks	0.0%	gov't bonds
0.0%	preferred	0.0%	muni bonds
0.0%	conv't bds/wrnts	0.0%	other

SHAREHOLDER INFORMATION

Minimum Investment

Initial: $1,000 Subsequent: $25

Minimum IRA Investment

Initial: $250 Subsequent: $25

Maximum Fees

Load: none 12b-1: 0.25%
Other: none

Services

✔ IRA
✔ Keogh
✔ Telephone Exchange

Sound Shore Fund (SSHFX)

800-551-1980, 800-754-8758
www.soundshorefund.com

Mid-Cap Stock

PERFORMANCE — fund inception date: 5/3/85

	3yr Annual	5yr Annual	10yr Annual	Bull	Bear
Return (%)	0.2	0.9	10.7	25.4	-12.3
Differ From Category (+/-)	7.0 abv av	-0.8 blw av	1.9 abv av	-57.3 blw av	11.7 av

Standard Deviation	Category Risk Index	Beta
17.4%—av	0.85—blw av	0.66

	2002	2001	2000	1999	1998	1997	1996	1995	1994	1993
Return (%)	-15.4	-0.7	20.1	0.0	3.9	36.4	33.2	29.8	0.2	11.9
Differ From Category (+/-)	2.6	5.2	14.3	-29.7	-6.1	13.8	13.4	-1.3	0.4	-4.7
Return, Tax-Adjusted (%)	-15.5	-2.5	18.8	-0.2	3.8	35.4	29.3	26.2	-1.8	8.9

PER SHARE DATA

	2002	2001	2000	1999	1998	1997	1996	1995	1994	1993
Dividends, Net Income ($)	0.05	0.10	0.14	0.16	0.08	0.12	0.12	0.21	0.21	0.14
Distrib'ns, Cap Gain ($)	0.00	2.76	1.56	0.00	0.00	0.88	2.35	1.67	0.86	1.54
Net Asset Value ($)	25.81	30.58	33.70	29.47	29.62	28.57	21.71	18.16	15.46	16.50
Expense Ratio (%)	na	0.98	0.98	0.98	0.99	1.08	1.15	1.17	1.22	1.27
Yield (%)	0.19	0.29	0.39	0.54	0.27	0.40	0.49	1.05	1.28	0.77
Portfolio Turnover (%)	na	104	98	41	44	53	69	53	75	90
Total Assets (Millions $)	758	1,051	1,051	1,183	1,964	1,303	131	67	56	58

PORTFOLIO (as of 11/30/02)

Portfolio Manager: Harry Burn - 1985

Investment Style

✔ Large Cap	Growth
✔ Mid Cap	✔ Value
Small Cap	Grth/Val

Portfolio

5.9% cash	0.0% corp bonds
94.1% stocks	0.0% gov't bonds
0.0% preferred	0.0% muni bonds
0.0% conv't bds/wrnts	0.0% other

SHAREHOLDER INFORMATION

Minimum Investment
Initial: $10,000 — Subsequent: na

Minimum IRA Investment
Initial: $2,000 — Subsequent: $0

Maximum Fees
Load: none — 12b-1: none
Other: none

Services
✔ IRA
✔ Keogh
✔ Telephone Exchange

Strong Discovery (STDIX)

800-368-3863, 414-359-1400
www.strong-funds.com

Mid-Cap Stock

PERFORMANCE — fund inception date: 12/31/87

	3yr Annual	5yr Annual	10yr Annual	Bull	Bear
Return (%)	-1.6	1.4	6.4	46.0	-18.8
Differ From Category (+/-)	5.2 av	-0.3 av	-2.4 blw av	-36.7 av	5.2 av

Standard Deviation	Category Risk Index	Beta
20.2%—abv av	0.99—av	0.75

	2002	2001	2000	1999	1998	1997	1996	1995	1994	1993
Return (%)	-12.1	4.1	3.9	5.2	7.0	10.8	1.4	34.8	-5.6	22.2
Differ From Category (+/-)	.5.9	10.0	-1.9	-24.5	-3.0	-11.8	-18.4	3.7	-5.4	5.6
Return, Tax-Adjusted (%)	-12.6	3.8	0.8	5.0	6.7	8.2	-1.8	30.9	-8.2	19.3

PER SHARE DATA

	2002	2001	2000	1999	1998	1997	1996	1995	1994	1993
Dividends, Net Income ($)	0.00	0.00	0.03	0.00	0.00	0.00	1.11	0.10	0.69	0.49
Distrib'ns, Cap Gain ($)	0.44	0.22	2.77	0.21	0.24	2.29	0.59	2.04	0.68	0.92
Net Asset Value ($)	14.42	16.84	16.39	18.64	17.95	17.00	17.45	18.96	15.67	18.05
Expense Ratio (%)	na	1.50	1.50	1.40	1.30	1.40	1.40	1.46	1.50	1.50
Yield (%)	0.00	0.00	0.15	0.00	0.00	0.00	6.15	0.47	4.22	2.58
Portfolio Turnover (%)	na	502	481	214	186	169	792	516	408	668
Total Assets (Millions $)	143	158	165	187	321	383	513	599	388	301

PORTFOLIO (as of 9/30/02)

Portfolio Manager: Thomas Pence/Nicholas Truitt - 2001

Investment Style

Large Cap	✔ Growth
✔ Mid Cap	Value
✔ Small Cap	Grth/Val

Portfolio

5.3%	cash	0.0%	corp bonds
78.8%	stocks	0.0%	gov't bonds
8.7%	pref/conv't pref	0.0%	muni bonds
0.0%	conv't bds/wrnts	7.2%	other

SHAREHOLDER INFORMATION

Minimum Investment
Initial: $2,500 Subsequent: $100

Minimum IRA Investment
Initial: $250 Subsequent: $50

Maximum Fees
Load: none 12b-1: none
Other: none

Services
✔ IRA
✔ Keogh
✔ Telephone Exchange

Strong Growth 20/Inv (SGRTX)

800-368-3863, 414-359-1400
www.strong-funds.com

Mid-Cap Stock

PERFORMANCE — fund inception date: 6/30/97

	3yr Annual	5yr Annual	10yr Annual	Bull	Bear
Return (%)	-28.6	0.7	na	249.2	-69.5
Differ From Category (+/-)	-21.8 low	-1.0 blw av	na	166.5 high	-45.5 low

Standard Deviation	Category Risk Index	Beta
30.7%—high	1.50—high	0.95

	2002	2001	2000	1999	1998	1997	1996	1995	1994	1993
Return (%)	-30.8	-41.3	-10.3	109.4	36.5	—	—	—	—	—
Differ From Category (+/-)	-12.8	-35.4	-16.1	79.7	26.5	—	—	—	—	—
Return, Tax-Adjusted (%)	-30.8	-41.3	-11.8	107.7	36.5	—	—	—	—	—

PER SHARE DATA

	2002	2001	2000	1999	1998	1997	1996	1995	1994	1993
Dividends, Net Income ($)	0.00	0.00	0.00	0.00	0.00	—	—	—	—	—
Distrib'ns, Cap Gain ($)	0.00	0.00	2.34	1.32	0.00	—	—	—	—	—
Net Asset Value ($)	10.19	14.74	25.13	30.63	15.44	—	—	—	—	—
Expense Ratio (%)	na	1.50	1.30	1.40	1.50	—	—	—	—	—
Yield (%)	0.00	0.00	0.00	0.00	0.00	—	—	—	—	—
Portfolio Turnover (%)	na	659	521	432	541	—	—	—	—	—
Total Assets (Millions $)	208	361	765	466	71	—	—	—	—	—

PORTFOLIO (as of 9/30/02)

Portfolio Manager: Ronald Ognar - 1997

Investment Style

Large Cap	✔ Growth
✔ Mid Cap	Value
✔ Small Cap	Grth/Val

Portfolio

8.6%	cash	0.0%	corp bonds
88.4%	stocks	0.0%	gov't bonds
2.9%	pref/conv't pref	0.0%	muni bonds
0.0%	conv't bds/wrnts	0.0%	other

SHAREHOLDER INFORMATION

Minimum Investment
Initial: $2,500 — Subsequent: $100

Minimum IRA Investment
Initial: $250 — Subsequent: $50

Maximum Fees
Load: none — 12b-1: none
Other: none

Services
✔ IRA
✔ Keogh
✔ Telephone Exchange

Strong Growth/Inv (SGROX)

800-368-3863, 414-359-1400
www.strong-funds.com

Mid-Cap Stock

PERFORMANCE — fund inception date: 12/31/93

	3yr Annual	5yr Annual	10yr Annual	Bull	Bear
Return (%)	-23.6	-0.2	na	176.8	-63.8
Differ From Category (+/-)	-16.8 low	-1.9 blw av	na	94.1 high	-39.8 low

Standard Deviation	Category Risk Index	Beta
30.5%—high	1.50—high	0.90

	2002	2001	2000	1999	1998	1997	1996	1995	1994	1993
Return (%)	-25.2	-34.3	-9.2	75.0	26.9	19.0	19.5	41.0	17.2	—
Differ From Category (+/-)	-7.2	-28.4	-15.0	45.3	16.9	-3.6	-0.3	9.9	17.4	—
Return, Tax-Adjusted (%)	-25.2	-34.4	-12.1	71.1	26.9	15.2	18.6	39.8	16.8	—

PER SHARE DATA

	2002	2001	2000	1999	1998	1997	1996	1995	1994	1993
Dividends, Net Income ($)	0.00	0.00	0.00	0.00	0.00	0.00	0.02	0.02	0.10	—
Distrib'ns, Cap Gain ($)	0.00	0.06	5.23	4.48	0.00	3.51	0.45	0.45	0.00	—
Net Asset Value ($)	13.21	17.68	27.05	35.66	23.25	18.31	18.50	15.88	11.61	—
Expense Ratio (%)	na	1.40	1.20	1.20	1.30	1.30	1.30	1.50	1.60	—
Yield (%)	0.00	0.00	0.00	0.00	0.00	0.00	0.10	0.12	0.86	—
Portfolio Turnover (%)	na	400	366	324	249	295	294	321	386	—
Total Assets (Millions $)	1,387	2,021	3,411	3,353	1,834	1,597	1,308	642	106	—

PORTFOLIO (as of 9/30/02)

Portfolio Manager: Ronald Ognar - 1993

Investment Style

Large Cap	✔ Growth
✔ Mid Cap	Value
✔ Small Cap	Grth/Val

Portfolio

6.0%	cash	0.4%	corp bonds
93.3%	stocks	0.0%	gov't bonds
0.4%	pref/conv't pref	0.0%	muni bonds
0.0%	conv't bds/wrnts	0.0%	other

SHAREHOLDER INFORMATION

Minimum Investment
Initial: $2,500 Subsequent: $100

Minimum IRA Investment
Initial: $250 Subsequent: $50

Maximum Fees
Load: none 12b-1: none
Other: none

Services
✔ IRA
✔ Keogh
✔ Telephone Exchange

Strong Opportunity/Inv

800-368-3863, 414-359-1400
www.strong-funds.com

(SOPFX)

Mid-Cap Stock

PERFORMANCE **fund inception date: 12/31/85**

	3yr Annual	5yr Annual	10yr Annual	Bull	Bear
Return (%)	-8.9	3.0	10.2	80.6	-35.8
Differ From Category (+/-)	-2.1 blw av	1.3 av	1.4 abv av	-2.1 av	-11.8 blw av

Standard Deviation	Category Risk Index	Beta
21.9%—abv av	1.07—av	1.06

	2002	2001	2000	1999	1998	1997	1996	1995	1994	1993
Return (%)	-26.9	-4.8	8.5	33.3	15.4	23.4	18.1	27.2	3.1	19.3
Differ From Category (+/-)	-8.9	1.1	2.7	3.6	5.4	0.8	-1.7	-3.9	3.3	2.7
Return, Tax-Adjusted (%)	-26.9	-5.3	5.8	29.9	13.0	20.0	14.6	25.2	1.6	17.9

PER SHARE DATA

	2002	2001	2000	1999	1998	1997	1996	1995	1994	1993
Dividends, Net Income ($)	0.00	0.07	0.16	0.08	0.05	0.10	0.25	0.21	0.13	0.06
Distrib'ns, Cap Gain ($)	0.00	0.95	5.64	6.34	4.47	5.75	3.82	1.62	1.27	1.17
Net Asset Value ($)	28.70	39.29	42.35	44.69	38.62	37.41	35.26	33.35	27.71	28.23
Expense Ratio (%)	na	1.30	1.20	1.20	1.20	1.30	1.30	1.40	1.40	1.40
Yield (%)	0.00	0.17	0.33	0.15	0.11	0.23	0.63	0.60	0.44	0.20
Portfolio Turnover (%)	na	88	87	81	86	93	103	92	59	109
Total Assets (Millions $)	2,758	3,664	3,337	2,537	2,037	1,924	1,769	1,327	805	443

PORTFOLIO (as of 9/30/02)

Portfolio Manager: R Weiss/A Miletti - 2001

Investment Style

✔ Large Cap Growth
✔ Mid Cap ✔ Value
Small Cap Grth/Val

Portfolio

9.1%	cash	0.0%	corp bonds
87.0%	stocks	0.0%	gov't bonds
0.6%	pref/conv't pref	0.0%	muni bonds
0.0%	conv't bds/wrnts	3.2%	other

SHAREHOLDER INFORMATION

Minimum Investment
Initial: $2,500 Subsequent: $100

Minimum IRA Investment
Initial: $1,000 Subsequent: $100

Maximum Fees
Load: none 12b-1: none
Other: none

Services
✔ IRA
✔ Keogh
✔ Telephone Exchange

T Rowe Price Md Cp Gr (RPMGX)

800-638-5660, 410-345-2000
www.troweprice.com

Mid-Cap Stock

PERFORMANCE

fund inception date: 6/30/92

	3yr Annual	5yr Annual	10yr Annual	Bull	Bear
Return (%)	-5.7	4.8	12.8	83.5	-29.7
Differ From Category (+/-)	1.1 av	3.1 abv av	4.0 high	0.8 abv av	-5.7 av

Standard Deviation	Category Risk Index	Beta
22.9%—abv av	1.12—abv av	1.09

	2002	2001	2000	1999	1998	1997	1996	1995	1994	1993
Return (%)	-21.2	-0.9	7.4	23.7	21.9	18.3	24.8	40.9	0.2	26.2
Differ From Category (+/-)	-3.2	5.0	1.6	-6.0	11.9	-4.3	5.0	9.8	0.4	9.6
Return, Tax-Adjusted (%)	-21.2	-0.9	5.8	22.6	21.4	18.1	23.8	39.4	-0.5	25.5

PER SHARE DATA

	2002	2001	2000	1999	1998	1997	1996	1995	1994	1993
Dividends, Net Income ($)	0.00	0.00	0.00	0.00	0.00	0.00	0.00	0.00	0.00	0.00
Distrib'ns, Cap Gain ($)	0.00	0.00	3.27	1.88	0.73	0.30	0.69	0.79	0.37	0.30
Net Asset Value ($)	31.04	39.40	39.79	40.13	34.08	28.60	24.43	20.13	14.85	15.18
Expense Ratio (%)	na	0.85	0.86	0.87	0.91	0.95	1.04	1.25	1.25	1.25
Yield (%)	0.00	0.00	0.00	0.00	0.00	0.00	0.00	0.00	0.00	0.00
Portfolio Turnover (%)	na	53	54	53	47	42	38	83	48	62
Total Assets (Millions $)	5,974	6,739	6,588	5,243	3,310	1,838	1,021	263	100	65

PORTFOLIO (as of 9/30/02)

Portfolio Manager: Team Managed - 1992

Investment Style

Large Cap	✔ Growth
✔ Mid Cap	Value
Small Cap	Grth/Val

Portfolio

6.7%	cash	0.9%	corp bonds
92.4%	stocks	0.0%	gov't bonds
0.0%	preferred	0.0%	muni bonds
0.0%	conv't bds/wrnts	0.0%	other

SHAREHOLDER INFORMATION

Minimum Investment
Initial: $2,500 Subsequent: $100

Minimum IRA Investment
Initial: $1,000 Subsequent: $50

Maximum Fees
Load: none 12b-1: none
Other: none

Services
✔ IRA
✔ Keogh
✔ Telephone Exchange

T Rowe Price Mid-Cp Val (TRMCX)

800-638-5660, 410-345-2000
www.troweprice.com

Mid-Cap Stock

PERFORMANCE

fund inception date: 6/28/96

	3yr Annual	5yr Annual	10yr Annual	Bull	Bear
Return (%)	9.1	6.4	na	26.5	15.2
Differ From Category (+/-)	15.9 high	4.7 high	na	-56.2 blw av	39.2 high

Standard Deviation	Category Risk Index	Beta
17.4%—av	0.85—blw av	0.77

	2002	2001	2000	1999	1998	1997	1996	1995	1994	1993
Return (%)	-7.3	14.3	22.7	3.5	1.3	27.1	—	—	—	—
Differ From Category (+/-)	10.7	20.2	16.9	-26.2	-8.7	4.5	—	—	—	—
Return, Tax-Adjusted (%)	-7.7	12.3	21.4	2.1	-0.3	26.6	—	—	—	—

PER SHARE DATA

	2002	2001	2000	1999	1998	1997	1996	1995	1994	1993
Dividends, Net Income ($)	0.12	0.13	0.17	0.23	0.19	0.08	—	—	—	—
Distrib'ns, Cap Gain ($)	0.07	1.31	0.56	0.51	0.76	0.14	—	—	—	—
Net Asset Value ($)	15.00	16.40	15.64	13.37	13.66	14.47	—	—	—	—
Expense Ratio (%)	na	0.98	0.99	1.04	1.08	1.25	—	—	—	—
Yield (%)	0.79	0.73	1.04	1.65	1.31	0.54	—	—	—	—
Portfolio Turnover (%)	na	58	31	27	32	16	—	—	—	—
Total Assets (Millions $)	1,010	502	282	211	221	217	—	—	—	—

PORTFOLIO (as of 9/30/02)

Portfolio Manager: Team Managed - 2000

Investment Style

Large Cap	Growth
✔ Mid Cap	✔ Value
Small Cap	Grth/Val

Portfolio

3.9%	cash	0.8%	corp bonds
95.4%	stocks	0.0%	gov't bonds
0.0%	preferred	0.0%	muni bonds
0.0%	conv't bds/wrnts	0.0%	other

SHAREHOLDER INFORMATION

Minimum Investment
Initial: $2,500 Subsequent: $100

Minimum IRA Investment
Initial: $1,000 Subsequent: $50

Maximum Fees
Load: none 12b-1: none
Other: none

Services
✔ IRA
✔ Keogh
✔ Telephone Exchange

T Rowe Price Value (TRVLX)

800-638-5660, 410-345-2000
www.troweprice.com

Mid-Cap Stock

PERFORMANCE — fund inception date: 9/30/94

	3yr Annual	5yr Annual	10yr Annual	Bull	Bear
Return (%)	-0.6	2.7	na	31.7	-11.0
Differ From Category (+/-)	6.2 av	1.0 av	na	-51.0 blw av	13.0 abv av

Standard Deviation	Category Risk Index	Beta
20.2%—abv av	0.99—av	0.90

	2002	2001	2000	1999	1998	1997	1996	1995	1994	1993
Return (%)	-16.5	1.6	15.7	9.1	6.8	29.2	28.5	39.8	—	—
Differ From Category (+/-)	1.5	7.5	9.9	-20.6	-3.2	6.6	8.7	8.7	—	—
Return, Tax-Adjusted (%)	-16.8	0.8	14.2	6.2	5.3	26.4	25.8	36.6	—	—

PER SHARE DATA

	2002	2001	2000	1999	1998	1997	1996	1995	1994	1993
Dividends, Net Income ($)	0.15	0.17	0.23	0.21	0.20	0.21	0.26	0.26	—	—
Distrib'ns, Cap Gain ($)	0.04	0.40	0.84	2.20	0.96	1.83	0.91	0.82	—	—
Net Asset Value ($)	15.56	18.88	19.15	17.50	18.31	18.24	15.76	13.21	—	—
Expense Ratio (%)	na	0.94	1.10	0.92	0.98	1.05	1.10	1.10	—	—
Yield (%)	0.96	0.88	1.15	1.06	1.03	1.04	1.55	1.85	—	—
Portfolio Turnover (%)	na	42	68	68	72	67	68	90	—	—
Total Assets (Millions $)	1,199	1,321	989	851	774	546	197	46	—	—

PORTFOLIO (as of 9/30/02)

Portfolio Manager: B Rogers/Team
Managed - 1994

Investment Style

✔ Large Cap — Growth
✔ Mid Cap — ✔ Value
Small Cap — Grth/Val

Portfolio

2.5%	cash	0.0%	corp bonds
97.5%	stocks	0.0%	gov't bonds
0.0%	pref/conv't pref	0.0%	muni bonds
0.0%	conv't bds/wrnts	0.0%	other

SHAREHOLDER INFORMATION

Minimum Investment
Initial: $2,500 — Subsequent: $100

Minimum IRA Investment
Initial: $1,000 — Subsequent: $50

Maximum Fees
Load: none — 12b-1: none
Other: none

Services
✔ IRA
✔ Keogh
✔ Telephone Exchange

Tweedy Browne Amcn Value (TWEBX)

800-432-4789, 212-916-0600
www.tweedy.com

Mid-Cap Stock

PERFORMANCE — fund inception date: 12/8/93

	3yr Annual	5yr Annual	10yr Annual	Bull	Bear
Return (%)	-0.9	1.6	na	16.0	-6.0
Differ From Category (+/-)	5.9 av	-0.1 av	na	-66.7 low	18.0 abv av

Standard Deviation	Category Risk Index	Beta
13.5%—blw av	0.66—low	0.48

	2002	2001	2000	1999	1998	1997	1996	1995	1994	1993
Return (%)	-14.9	0.0	14.4	2.0	9.5	38.8	22.4	36.2	-0.5	—
Differ From Category (+/-)	3.1	5.9	8.6	-27.7	-0.5	16.2	2.6	5.1	-0.3	—
Return, Tax-Adjusted (%)	-15.4	-0.9	13.3	1.1	9.0	37.8	21.0	35.7	-0.8	—

PER SHARE DATA

	2002	2001	2000	1999	1998	1997	1996	1995	1994	1993
Dividends, Net Income ($)	0.10	0.08	0.10	0.27	0.14	0.16	0.17	0.10	0.06	—
Distrib'ns, Cap Gain ($)	0.37	0.89	1.07	0.53	0.25	0.43	0.41	0.02	0.00	—
Net Asset Value ($)	19.45	23.42	24.42	22.37	22.74	21.11	15.64	13.25	9.82	—
Expense Ratio (%)	1.36	1.36	1.37	1.39	1.39	1.39	1.39	1.74	2.26	—
Yield (%)	0.50	0.32	0.39	1.17	0.60	0.74	1.05	0.75	0.61	—
Portfolio Turnover (%)	6	10	19	16	6	16	9	4	0	—
Total Assets (Millions $)	740	936	955	1,025	1,160	721	277	168	35	—

PORTFOLIO (as of 11/30/02)

Portfolio Manager: C Browne/W Browne/ J Spears - 1993

Investment Style

✔ Large Cap	Growth
✔ Mid Cap	✔ Value
Small Cap	Grth/Val

Portfolio

7.1%	cash	0.0%	corp bonds
93.8%	stocks	0.0%	gov't bonds
0.0%	preferred	0.0%	muni bonds
0.0%	conv't bds/wrnts	-0.8%	other

SHAREHOLDER INFORMATION

Minimum Investment
Initial: $2,500 — Subsequent: $200

Minimum IRA Investment
Initial: $500 — Subsequent: $200

Maximum Fees
Load: none — 12b-1: none
Other: none

Services
✔ IRA
Keogh
✔ Telephone Exchange

Vanguard Capital Opp/Inv (VHCOX)

800-662-7447, 610-436-5152
www.vanguard.com

Mid-Cap Stock

PERFORMANCE

fund inception date: 8/14/95

	3yr Annual	5yr Annual	10yr Annual	Bull	Bear
Return (%)	-8.4	14.9	na	260.7	-48.0
Differ From Category (+/-)	-1.6 av	13.2 high	na	178.0 high	-24.0 blw av

Standard Deviation	Category Risk Index	Beta
28.2%—high	1.38—abv av	1.15

	2002	2001	2000	1999	1998	1997	1996	1995	1994	1993
Return (%)	-27.9	-9.6	18.0	97.7	31.9	-7.9	13.4	—	—	—
Differ From Category (+/-)	-9.9	-3.7	12.2	68.0	21.9	-30.5	-6.4	—	—	—
Return, Tax-Adjusted (%)	-27.9	-9.7	16.1	96.6	30.1	-8.1	13.4	—	—	—

PER SHARE DATA

	2002	2001	2000	1999	1998	1997	1996	1995	1994	1993
Dividends, Net Income ($)	0.01	0.07	0.16	0.03	0.01	0.04	0.00	—	—	—
Distrib'ns, Cap Gain ($)	0.00	0.00	1.92	0.59	0.89	0.00	0.00	—	—	—
Net Asset Value ($)	17.00	23.62	26.22	24.02	12.49	10.20	11.13	—	—	—
Expense Ratio (%)	na	0.60	0.62	0.75	0.94	0.49	0.50	—	—	—
Yield (%)	0.05	0.29	0.56	0.12	0.07	0.39	0.00	—	—	—
Portfolio Turnover (%)	na	20	15	22	103	195	128	—	—	—
Total Assets (Millions $)	3,578	4,845	5,056	2,366	206	63	117	—	—	—

PORTFOLIO (as of 9/30/02)

Portfolio Manager: Schow/Koloktrones/Fried - 1998

Investment Style

Large Cap	✔ Growth
✔ Mid Cap	Value
✔ Small Cap	Grth/Val

Portfolio

7.4%	cash	0.0%	corp bonds
92.6%	stocks	0.0%	gov't bonds
0.0%	preferred	0.0%	muni bonds
0.0%	conv't bds/wrnts	0.0%	other

SHAREHOLDER INFORMATION

Minimum Investment
Initial: $25,000 Subsequent: $100

Minimum IRA Investment
Initial: $25,000 Subsequent: $100

Maximum Fees
Load: 1.00% redemption 12b-1: none
Other: redemption fee applies for 60 months

Services
✔ IRA
✔ Keogh
✔ Telephone Exchange

Vanguard Div Growth/Inv (VDIGX)

800-662-7447, 610-436-5152
www.vanguard.com

Mid-Cap Stock

PERFORMANCE

fund inception date: 5/15/92

	3yr Annual	5yr Annual	10yr Annual	Bull	Bear
Return (%)	-9.7	-2.7	4.9	23.7	-32.0
Differ From Category (+/-)	-2.9 blw av	-4.4 low	-3.9 low	-59.0 blw av	-8.0 av

Standard Deviation	Category Risk Index	Beta
16.6%—av	0.81—low	0.48

	2002	2001	2000	1999	1998	1997	1996	1995	1994	1993
Return (%)	-23.1	-19.4	18.7	-2.9	21.8	25.0	5.2	34.0	-8.5	15.0
Differ From Category (+/-)	-5.1	-13.5	12.9	-32.6	11.8	2.4	-14.6	2.9	-8.3	-1.6
Return, Tax-Adjusted (%)	-24.3	-20.8	16.2	-5.6	18.9	22.7	3.4	31.8	-10.8	12.0

PER SHARE DATA

	2002	2001	2000	1999	1998	1997	1996	1995	1994	1993
Dividends, Net Income ($)	0.38	0.37	0.53	0.51	0.59	0.60	0.56	0.56	0.59	0.56
Distrib'ns, Cap Gain ($)	0.00	0.41	0.73	1.20	1.01	0.26	0.02	0.00	0.12	0.40
Net Asset Value ($)	8.79	11.88	15.66	14.33	16.54	14.98	12.74	12.68	9.94	11.63
Expense Ratio (%)	0.34	0.37	0.40	0.38	0.44	0.40	0.44	0.50	0.42	0.45
Yield (%)	4.32	3.01	3.23	3.28	3.36	3.93	4.38	4.41	5.86	4.65
Portfolio Turnover (%)	24	48	47	55	41	38	35	35	46	20
Total Assets (Millions $)	586	705	954	840	951	684	658	757	560	774

PORTFOLIO (as of 9/30/02)

Portfolio Manager: Minerva Butler/Earl McEvoy - 1996

Investment Style

Large Cap	Growth
✔ Mid Cap	✔ Value
Small Cap	Grth/Val

Portfolio

3.3% cash	0.0% corp bonds
96.7% stocks	0.0% gov't bonds
0.0% preferred	0.0% muni bonds
0.0% conv't bds/wrnts	0.0% other

SHAREHOLDER INFORMATION

Minimum Investment
Initial: $3,000 Subsequent: $100

Minimum IRA Investment
Initial: $1,000 Subsequent: $100

Maximum Fees
Load: none 12b-1: none
Other: none

Services
✔ IRA
✔ Keogh
✔ Telephone Exchange

Vanguard Selected Value (VASVX)

800-662-7447, 610-436-5152
www.vanguard.com

Mid-Cap Stock

PERFORMANCE

fund inception date: 2/15/96

	3yr Annual	5yr Annual	10yr Annual	Bull	Bear
Return (%)	6.8	0.8	na	17.3	14.5
Differ From Category (+/-)	13.6 high	-0.9 blw av	na	-65.4 low	38.5 high

Standard Deviation	Category Risk Index	Beta
20.1%—abv av	0.98—av	0.74

	2002	2001	2000	1999	1998	1997	1996	1995	1994	1993
Return (%)	-9.7	15.0	17.3	-2.7	-11.7	17.3	—	—	—	—
Differ From Category (+/-)	8.3	20.9	11.5	-32.4	-21.7	-5.3	—	—	—	—
Return, Tax-Adjusted (%)	-10.4	14.4	16.3	-3.3	-12.5	16.3	—	—	—	—

PER SHARE DATA

	2002	2001	2000	1999	1998	1997	1996	1995	1994	1993
Dividends, Net Income ($)	0.24	0.17	0.24	0.16	0.08	0.05	—	—	—	—
Distrib'ns, Cap Gain ($)	0.00	0.00	0.00	0.00	0.33	0.46	—	—	—	—
Net Asset Value ($)	11.46	12.97	11.42	9.94	10.39	12.28	—	—	—	—
Expense Ratio (%)	na	0.70	0.63	0.73	0.47	0.32	—	—	—	—
Yield (%)	2.09	1.31	2.10	1.60	0.74	0.39	—	—	—	—
Portfolio Turnover (%)	na	67	40	102	47	32	—	—	—	—
Total Assets (Millions $)	1,117	994	196	186	148	191	—	—	—	—

PORTFOLIO (as of 9/30/02)

Portfolio Manager: James Barrow/Mark Giambrone - 1999

Investment Style

✔ Large Cap	Growth
✔ Mid Cap	✔ Value
Small Cap	Grth/Val

Portfolio

1.3%	cash	0.0%	corp bonds
98.7%	stocks	0.0%	gov't bonds
0.0%	preferred	0.0%	muni bonds
0.0%	conv't bds/wrnts	0.0%	other

SHAREHOLDER INFORMATION

Minimum Investment
Initial: $25,000 Subsequent: $100

Minimum IRA Investment
Initial: $25,000 Subsequent: $100

Maximum Fees
Load: 1.00% redemption 12b-1: none
Other: redemption fee applies for 60 months

Services
✔ IRA
✔ Keogh
✔ Telephone Exchange

Vanguard Strategic Eqty (VSEQX)

800-662-7447, 610-436-5152
www.vanguard.com

Mid-Cap Stock

PERFORMANCE

fund inception date: 8/14/95

	3yr Annual	5yr Annual	10yr Annual	Bull	Bear
Return (%)	-0.5	3.3	na	54.0	-8.5
Differ From Category (+/-)	6.3 abv av	1.6 abv av	na	-28.7 av	15.5 abv av

Standard Deviation	Category Risk Index	Beta
16.7%—av	0.82—blw av	0.77

	2002	2001	2000	1999	1998	1997	1996	1995	1994	1993
Return (%)	-13.1	5.4	7.4	19.3	0.5	26.1	25.1	—	—	—
Differ From Category (+/-)	.4.9	11.3	1.6	-10.4	-9.5	3.5	5.3	—	—	—
Return, Tax-Adjusted (%)	-13.4	5.0	3.3	18.4	0.1	23.9	22.6	—	—	—

PER SHARE DATA

	2002	2001	2000	1999	1998	1997	1996	1995	1994	1993
Dividends, Net Income ($)	0.13	0.14	0.21	0.16	0.15	0.14	0.18	—	—	—
Distrib'ns, Cap Gain ($)	0.00	0.00	3.03	0.37	0.00	1.08	0.71	—	—	—
Net Asset Value ($)	13.10	15.23	14.58	16.76	14.52	14.60	12.57	—	—	—
Expense Ratio (%)	na	0.54	0.49	0.46	0.43	0.40	0.38	—	—	—
Yield (%)	0.99	0.91	1.19	0.93	1.03	0.89	1.35	—	—	—
Portfolio Turnover (%)	na	82	83	51	71	85	106	—	—	—
Total Assets (Millions $)	932	879	744	625	534	474	153	—	—	—

PORTFOLIO (as of 9/30/02)

Portfolio Manager: George Sauter - 1995

Investment Style

Large Cap	Growth
✔ Mid Cap	Value
Small Cap	✔ Grth/Val

Portfolio

0.1% cash	0.0% corp bonds
99.9% stocks	0.0% gov't bonds
0.0% preferred	0.0% muni bonds
0.0% conv't bds/wrnts	0.0% other

SHAREHOLDER INFORMATION

Minimum Investment
Initial: $3,000 Subsequent: $100

Minimum IRA Investment
Initial: $1,000 Subsequent: $100

Maximum Fees
Load: none 12b-1: none
Other: none

Services
✔ IRA
✔ Keogh
✔ Telephone Exchange

Vontobel US Value (VUSVX)

800-527-9500
www.vontobelfunds.com

Mid-Cap Stock

PERFORMANCE

fund inception date: 3/30/90

	3yr Annual	5yr Annual	10yr Annual	Bull	Bear
Return (%)	10.8	6.0	12.5	-1.8	35.9
Differ From Category (+/-)	17.6 high	4.3 abv av	3.7 high	-84.5 low	59.9 high

Standard Deviation	Category Risk Index	Beta
18.0%—av	0.88—blw av	0.36

	2002	2001	2000	1999	1998	1997	1996	1995	1994	1993
Return (%)	-2.0	2.9	35.1	-14.0	14.7	34.3	21.2	40.3	0.0	6.0
Differ From Category (+/-)	16.0	8.8	29.3	-43.7	4.7	11.7	1.4	9.2	0.2	-10.6
Return, Tax-Adjusted (%)	-2.8	2.9	35.1	-14.3	12.0	31.3	16.2	37.1	-5.5	5.7

PER SHARE DATA

	2002	2001	2000	1999	1998	1997	1996	1995	1994	1993
Dividends, Net Income ($)	0.00	0.02	0.00	0.11	0.16	0.10	0.21	0.04	0.25	0.08
Distrib'ns, Cap Gain ($)	0.79	0.00	0.00	0.00	1.90	1.88	2.08	1.11	2.14	0.00
Net Asset Value ($)	18.64	19.84	19.29	14.27	16.73	16.51	13.78	13.25	10.26	12.64
Expense Ratio (%)	na	1.75	1.75	1.87	1.45	1.58	1.43	1.46	1.62	1.82
Yield (%)	0.00	0.10	0.00	0.77	0.85	0.54	1.32	0.27	2.01	0.63
Portfolio Turnover (%)	na	66	103	67	123	89	108	95	98	137
Total Assets (Millions $)	121	86	136	71	200	201	69	54	30	34

PORTFOLIO (as of 9/30/02)

Portfolio Manager: Edwin Walczak - 1990

Investment Style

✔ Large Cap   Growth
✔ Mid Cap   ✔ Value
Small Cap   Grth/Val

Portfolio

0.0% cash	0.0% corp bonds
100.0% stocks	0.0% gov't bonds
0.0% preferred	0.0% muni bonds
0.0% conv't bds/wrnts	0.0% other

SHAREHOLDER INFORMATION

Minimum Investment
Initial: $1,000   Subsequent: $50

Minimum IRA Investment
Initial: $1,000   Subsequent: $50

Maximum Fees
Load: 2.00% redemption   12b-1: none
Other: redemption fee applies for 3 months

Services
✔ IRA
✔ Keogh
✔ Telephone Exchange

Wayne Hummer Growth (WHGRX)

800-621-4477, 312-431-1700
www.whummer.com

Mid-Cap Stock

PERFORMANCE — fund inception date: 12/30/83

	3yr Annual	5yr Annual	10yr Annual	Bull	Bear
Return (%)	-9.5	3.7	8.4	80.4	-30.5
Differ From Category (+/-)	-2.7 blw av	2.0 abv av	-0.4 blw av	-2.3 av	-6.5 av

Standard Deviation	Category Risk Index	Beta
17.3%—av	0.84—blw av	0.82

	2002	2001	2000	1999	1998	1997	1996	1995	1994	1993
Return (%)	-17.6	-6.7	-3.7	38.1	17.5	30.2	11.8	24.8	-0.9	3.5
Differ From Category (+/-)	0.4	-0.8	-9.5	8.4	7.5	7.6	-8.0	-6.3	-0.7	-13.1
Return, Tax-Adjusted (%)	-17.8	-7.1	-5.5	35.9	16.4	28.1	10.3	23.6	-1.7	2.9

PER SHARE DATA

	2002	2001	2000	1999	1998	1997	1996	1995	1994	1993
Dividends, Net Income ($)	0.01	0.06	0.02	0.07	0.16	0.22	0.29	0.31	0.30	0.31
Distrib'ns, Cap Gain ($)	0.32	0.74	4.17	3.99	1.51	2.49	1.00	0.48	0.21	0.03
Net Asset Value ($)	29.85	36.56	40.09	45.97	36.81	32.80	27.50	25.81	21.34	22.06
Expense Ratio (%)	0.89	0.91	0.95	0.94	0.96	0.99	1.06	1.07	1.07	1.12
Yield (%)	0.03	0.16	0.04	0.14	0.41	0.62	1.01	1.17	1.39	1.40
Portfolio Turnover (%)	5	9	10	12	7	9	6	3	2	1
Total Assets (Millions $)	125	156	170	183	143	128	104	100	87	98

PORTFOLIO (as of 9/30/02)

Portfolio Manager: Thomas Rowland - 1987

Investment Style

✔ Large Cap	Growth
✔ Mid Cap	Value
Small Cap	✔ Grth/Val

Portfolio

6.4% cash	0.0% corp bonds
93.6% stocks	0.0% gov't bonds
0.0% preferred	0.0% muni bonds
0.0% conv't bds/wrnts	0.0% other

SHAREHOLDER INFORMATION

Minimum Investment
Initial: $1,000 — Subsequent: $500

Minimum IRA Investment
Initial: $500 — Subsequent: $200

Maximum Fees
Load: 2.00% front — 12b-1: none
Other: none

Services
- ✔ IRA
- ✔ Keogh
- ✔ Telephone Exchange

Weitz Partners Value Fund (WPVLX)

800-232-4161, 402-391-1980
www.weitzfunds.com

Mid-Cap Stock

PERFORMANCE — fund inception date: 1/3/94

	3yr Annual	5yr Annual	10yr Annual	Bull	Bear
Return (%)	-0.1	9.4	na	39.3	-8.5
Differ From Category (+/-)	6.7 abv av	7.7 high	na	-43.4 blw av	15.5 abv av

Standard Deviation	Category Risk Index	Beta
17.0%—av	0.83—blw av	0.67

	2002	2001	2000	1999	1998	1997	1996	1995	1994	1993
Return (%)	-16.9	-0.8	21.0	22.0	29.1	40.6	19.0	38.6	—	—
Differ From Category (+/-)	1.1	5.1	15.2	-7.7	19.1	18.0	-0.8	7.5	—	—
Return, Tax-Adjusted (%)	-17.1	-1.4	18.1	20.5	26.5	39.7	16.6	34.6	—	—

PER SHARE DATA

	2002	2001	2000	1999	1998	1997	1996	1995	1994	1993
Dividends, Net Income ($)	0.05	0.20	0.50	0.04	0.16	0.00	0.05	0.23	—	—
Distrib'ns, Cap Gain ($)	0.12	0.26	1.88	1.23	1.66	0.53	0.79	0.84	—	—
Net Asset Value ($)	17.15	20.87	21.51	20.02	17.68	15.45	11.52	10.39	—	—
Expense Ratio (%)	1.08	1.13	1.19	1.24	1.25	1.24	1.23	1.27	—	—
Yield (%)	0.28	0.94	2.13	0.18	0.82	0.00	0.40	2.04	—	—
Portfolio Turnover (%)	10	29	5	29	36	30	37	51	—	—
Total Assets (Millions $)	2,424	2,970	1,936	1,143	292	133	94	73	—	—

PORTFOLIO (as of 9/30/02)

Portfolio Manager: Wallace Weitz - 1994

Investment Style

✔ Large Cap	Growth
✔ Mid Cap	✔ Value
Small Cap	Grth/Val

Portfolio

15.9%	cash	0.4%	corp bonds
78.7%	stocks	4.9%	gov't bonds
0.0%	preferred	0.0%	muni bonds
0.0%	conv't bds/wrnts	0.1%	other

SHAREHOLDER INFORMATION

Minimum Investment
Initial: $250,000 Subsequent: $5,000

Minimum IRA Investment
Initial: $250,000 Subsequent: $5,000

Maximum Fees
Load: none 12b-1: none
Other: none

Services
✔ IRA
Keogh
✔ Telephone Exchange

Weitz Srs:Value
(WVALX)

800-232-4161, 402-391-1980
www.weitzfunds.com

Mid-Cap Stock

PERFORMANCE **fund inception date: 5/9/86**

	3yr Annual	5yr Annual	10yr Annual	Bull	Bear
Return (%)	-0.2	9.1	14.2	33.2	-7.7
Differ From Category (+/-)	6.6 abv av	7.4 high	5.4 high	-49.5 blw av	16.3 abv av

Standard Deviation	Category Risk Index	Beta
17.5%—av	0.85—blw av	0.68

	2002	2001	2000	1999	1998	1997	1996	1995	1994	1993
Return (%)	-17.1	0.2	19.6	20.9	28.9	38.9	16.6	38.3	-8.8	20.0
Differ From Category (+/-)	.0.9	6.1	13.8	-8.8	18.9	16.3	-3.2	7.2	-8.6	3.4
Return, Tax-Adjusted (%)	-17.5	-0.6	16.9	19.2	26.2	35.8	15.2	35.1	-10.3	18.8

PER SHARE DATA

	2002	2001	2000	1999	1998	1997	1996	1995	1994	1993
Dividends, Net Income ($)	0.19	0.36	0.48	0.36	0.17	0.31	0.12	0.41	0.02	0.02
Distrib'ns, Cap Gain ($)	0.31	0.67	3.42	1.67	3.01	2.60	0.73	1.08	0.86	0.59
Net Asset Value ($)	27.92	34.29	35.22	33.08	29.07	25.15	20.59	18.38	14.43	16.80
Expense Ratio (%)	1.06	1.13	1.19	1.26	1.27	1.29	1.35	1.42	1.41	1.35
Yield (%)	0.67	1.02	1.24	1.03	0.52	1.11	0.56	2.10	0.13	0.11
Portfolio Turnover (%)	13	36	31	36	39	39	40	28	23	23
Total Assets (Millions $)	3,364	4,390	3,307	2,679	1,196	365	260	149	107	106

PORTFOLIO (as of 9/30/02)

Portfolio Manager: Wallace Weitz - 1986

Investment Style

✔ Large Cap	Growth
✔ Mid Cap	✔ Value
Small Cap	Grth/Val

Portfolio

10.2%	cash	0.6%	corp bonds
85.3%	stocks	3.7%	gov't bonds
0.1%	pref/conv't pref	0.0%	muni bonds
0.1%	conv't bds/wrnts	0.0%	other

SHAREHOLDER INFORMATION

Minimum Investment
Initial: $25,000 Subsequent: $1

Minimum IRA Investment
Initial: $25,000 Subsequent: $1

Maximum Fees
Load: none 12b-1: none
Other: none

Services
✔ IRA
✔ Keogh
✔ Telephone Exchange

Westcore:MIDCO Growth (WTMGX)

800-392-2673, 303-623-2577
www.westcore.com

Mid-Cap Stock

PERFORMANCE — fund inception date: 8/1/86

	3yr Annual	5yr Annual	10yr Annual	Bull	Bear
Return (%)	-15.3	1.2	7.8	146.7	-49.4
Differ From Category (+/-)	-8.5 blw av	-0.5 blw av	-1.0 blw av	64.0 high	-25.4 blw av

Standard Deviation	Category Risk Index	Beta
31.5%—high	1.54—high	0.99

	2002	2001	2000	1999	1998	1997	1996	1995	1994	1993
Return (%)	-17.9	-10.4	-17.5	59.3	10.4	14.8	16.9	27.4	-1.0	17.4
Differ From Category (+/-)	0.1	-4.5	-23.3	29.6	0.4	-7.8	-2.9	-3.7	-0.8	0.8
Return, Tax-Adjusted (%)	-17.9	-10.4	-27.4	49.9	7.9	11.6	12.6	26.1	-1.9	15.5

PER SHARE DATA

	2002	2001	2000	1999	1998	1997	1996	1995	1994	1993
Dividends, Net Income ($)	0.00	0.00	0.00	0.00	0.00	0.00	0.00	0.00	0.00	0.00
Distrib'ns, Cap Gain ($)	0.00	0.00	9.96	8.84	2.50	3.24	3.01	0.71	0.52	1.03
Net Asset Value ($)	4.71	5.74	6.41	20.06	18.92	19.66	20.06	19.76	16.08	16.79
Expense Ratio (%)	1.15	1.15	1.15	1.15	1.13	1.14	1.08	0.94	0.84	0.83
Yield (%)	0.00	0.00	0.00	0.00	0.00	0.00	0.00	0.00	0.00	0.00
Portfolio Turnover (%)	67	190	117	116	75	60	62	50	52	56
Total Assets (Millions $)	89	119	175	300	491	602	569	547	362	279

PORTFOLIO (as of 11/30/02)

Portfolio Manager: Todger Anderson - 1986

Investment Style

Large Cap	✔ Growth
✔ Mid Cap	Value
✔ Small Cap	Grth/Val

Portfolio

12.3% cash	0.0% corp bonds
87.7% stocks	0.0% gov't bonds
0.0% preferred	0.0% muni bonds
0.0% conv't bds/wrnts	0.0% other

SHAREHOLDER INFORMATION

Minimum Investment

Initial: $2,500 — Subsequent: $100

Minimum IRA Investment

Initial: $1,000 — Subsequent: $100

Maximum Fees

Load: 2.00% redemption — 12b-1: none

Other: redemption fee applies for 3 months

Services

✔ IRA
✔ Keogh
✔ Telephone Exchange

Small-Cap Stock Funds
Category Performance Ranked by 2002 Returns

Category	Fund (Ticker)	Annual Return (%) 2002	3yr	5yr	10yr	Category Risk	Total Risk
Stk-SC	Royce:Total Return (RYTRX)	-1.6	10.4	7.4	na	low	blw av
Stk-SC	Eclipse Funds Sm Cap Val (EEQFX)	-3.3	0.0	1.2	9.3	low	av
Stk-SC	Babson Enterprise Fund (BABEX)	-3.4	12.0	2.9	9.9	blw av	av
Stk-SC	Heartland Grp:Value Plus (HRVIX)	-3.7	5.7	1.4	na	blw av	av
Stk-SC	Gabelli Sm Cp Grth (GABSX)	-5.3	3.3	4.7	11.1	low	av
Stk-SC	Victory:Small Co Opp/G (GOGFX)	-5.5	1.1	-1.0	7.4	blw av	av
Stk-SC	Fidelity Low Priced Stock (FLPSX)	-6.1	12.2	8.3	14.2	low	av
Stk-SC	Northern Small Cap Value (NOSGX)	-6.2	2.5	2.5	na	av	abv av
Stk-SC	Skyline:Special Equities (SKSEX)	-7.2	9.4	1.0	9.9	blw av	abv av
Stk-SC	Royce:Premier (RYPRX)	-7.7	5.7	7.1	11.0	low	av
Stk-SC	Neuberger Fasciano (NBFSX)	-8.6	-1.0	2.0	9.5	low	av
Stk-SC	Royce:PA Mutual/Inv (PENNX)	-9.2	8.3	7.0	10.0	low	av
Stk-SC	Baron Small Cap (BSCFX)	-9.6	-7.8	6.4	na	av	abv av
Stk-SC	Babson Enterprise Fund II (BAETX)	-9.9	2.5	1.8	9.4	blw av	av
Stk-SC	Third Avenue Small Cap (TASCX)	-10.8	6.3	5.4	na	blw av	av
Stk-SC	Heartland Grp:Value Fund (HRTVX)	-11.4	5.3	5.2	11.7	blw av	av
Stk-SC	LKCM Small Cap Equity (LKSCX)	-11.7	1.8	2.9	na	low	av
Stk-SC	Babson Shadow Stock (SHSTX)	-12.2	6.2	4.3	10.0	low	av
Stk-SC	Baron Growth Fund (BGRFX)	-12.2	-1.9	6.4	na	blw av	abv av
Stk-SC	Oakmark Small Cap Fund/I (OAKSX)	-13.0	4.6	-1.7	na	blw av	abv av
Stk-SC	Liberty Acorn Fund/Z (ACRNX)	-13.3	0.4	7.4	12.4	blw av	abv av
Stk-SC	Royce:Micro-Cap/Inv (RYOTX)	-13.4	7.5	6.4	11.6	av	abv av
Stk-SC	T Rowe Price Sm Cp Stk (OTCFX)	-14.2	2.2	3.3	11.3	blw av	abv av
Stk-SC	Third Avenue Value (TAVFX)	-15.1	1.7	4.3	11.5	low	av
Stk-SC	Value Line Spcl Situation (VALSX)	-15.1	-13.3	6.4	11.0	abv av	high
Stk-SC	Monetta Fund (MONTX)	-15.2	-17.4	-4.9	1.8	high	high
Stk-SC	Kalmar Gr-w-Val Small Cap (KGSCX)	-16.5	-1.1	-1.1	na	av	high
Stk-SC	Lazard Sm Cap/Open (LZCOX)	-17.8	3.7	1.1	na	blw av	abv av
Stk-SC	Vanguard Ext Mkt Idx/Inv (VEXMX)	-18.0	-14.3	-1.4	7.6	abv av	high
Stk-SC	Excelsior Small Cap Fd/A (UMLCX)	-19.3	-6.6	-1.5	5.3	abv av	high
Stk-SC	Vanguard Sm Cp Idx/Inv (NAESX)	-20.0	-7.0	-0.7	7.9	av	high
Stk-SC	Fidelity Small Cap Ind (FDSCX)	-20.8	-3.8	-1.2	na	blw av	abv av
Stk-SC	Amer Cnt Giftrust/Inv (TWGTX)	-21.3	-24.8	-7.1	4.0	high	high
Stk-SC	Schwab Cap Tr Sm Cp Ix/I (SWSMX)	-22.4	-7.2	-0.9	na	av	abv av
Stk-SC	Oberweis:Emerging Growth (OBEGX)	-24.2	-12.0	0.1	5.4	high	high
Stk-SC	Vanguard Explorer (VEXPX)	-24.5	-6.0	3.3	8.4	abv av	high
Stk-SC	Schwab Sm Cp MarketMstrs (SWOSX)	-25.9	-13.1	-1.8	na	av	high
Stk-SC	WPG Tudor (TUDRX)	-26.1	-15.7	-5.3	3.7	abv av	high
Stk-SC	Sit Small Cap Growth (SSMGX)	-26.2	-17.4	3.6	na	abv av	high
Stk-SC	T Rowe Price New Horizons (PRNHX)	-26.6	-11.2	-0.2	9.1	abv av	high
Stk-SC	T Rowe Price Dvsfd Sm Cap (PRDSX)	-27.4	-15.6	-4.5	na	abv av	high
Stk-SC	Artisan Small Cap Fund (ARTSX)	-28.6	-7.5	-4.8	na	abv av	high
Stk-SC	Marshall:Sm Cap Gr/Inv (MRSCX)	-28.7	-14.5	-2.7	na	high	high
Stk-SC	Cr Suisse Emg Grth/Cmn (CUEGX)	-30.1	-22.6	-7.0	4.6	abv av	high

Category	Fund (Ticker)	Annual Return (%) 2002	3yr	5yr	10yr	Category Risk	Total Risk
Stk-SC	INVESCO Small Co Grth/Inv (FIEGX)	-31.3	-21.8	-0.1	7.3	high	high
Stk-SC	PBHG Small Cap Value (PBSVX)	-31.9	-1.7	2.6	na	av	high
Stk-SC	PBHG Strategic Small Co (PSSCX)	-33.3	-12.4	0.8	na	abv av	high
Stk-SC	FTI Small Cap Equity Fund (FTSCX)	-35.4	-17.4	-0.4	na	abv av	high
Stk-SC	SAFECO Growth Opp/Inv (SAFGX)	-36.9	-9.6	-4.5	8.2	abv av	high
Stk-SC	RS:Diversifed Growth/A (RSDGX)	-39.1	-23.1	5.6	na	high	high
Small-Cap Stock Average		**-20.5**	**-5.7**	**1.2**	**8.7**	**—**	**high**

Note: AAII members who would like performance figures for no-load and low-load mutual funds they own that do not appear in this Guide can access this information on our Web site at www.aaii.com.

Amer Cnt Giftrust/Inv (TWGTX)

800-345-2021, 816-531-5575
www.americancentury.com

Small-Cap Stock

PERFORMANCE — fund inception date: 11/25/83

	3yr Annual	5yr Annual	10yr Annual	Bull	Bear
Return (%)	-24.8	-7.1	4.0	191.2	-66.2
Differ From Category (+/-)	-19.1 low	-8.3 low	-4.7 low	95.8 high	-45.6 low

Standard Deviation	Category Risk Index	Beta
40.7%—high	1.71—high	1.15

	2002	2001	2000	1999	1998	1997	1996	1995	1994	1993
Return (%)	-21.3	-35.4	-16.4	87.2	-13.0	-1.2	5.7	38.3	13.5	31.4
Differ From Category (+/-)	-0.8	-37.8	-20.6	50.2	-13.7	-23.6	-14.9	8.0	13.6	15.3
Return, Tax-Adjusted (%)	-21.3	-35.4	-20.9	87.2	-13.0	-1.8	4.8	35.2	11.8	27.8

PER SHARE DATA

	2002	2001	2000	1999	1998	1997	1996	1995	1994	1993
Dividends, Net Income ($)	0.00	0.00	0.00	0.00	0.00	0.00	0.00	0.00	0.00	0.00
Distrib'ns, Cap Gain ($)	0.00	0.00	8.57	0.00	0.00	0.75	0.78	2.09	1.08	1.91
Net Asset Value ($)	11.84	15.06	23.32	37.92	20.25	23.30	24.39	23.81	18.77	17.53
Expense Ratio (%)	1.00	1.00	1.00	1.00	1.00	1.00	0.98	0.98	1.00	1.00
Yield (%)	0.00	0.00	0.00	0.00	0.00	0.00	0.00	0.00	0.00	0.00
Portfolio Turnover (%)	140	196	92	117	147	118	121	105	115	143
Total Assets (Millions $)	789	948	1,520	1,777	920	986	874	603	274	164

PORTFOLIO (as of 9/30/02)

Portfolio Manager: Linda Peterson - 2001

Investment Style

Large Cap	✔ Growth
Mid Cap	Value
✔ Small Cap	Grth/Val

Portfolio

0.0%	cash	0.0%	corp bonds
93.8%	stocks	0.0%	gov't bonds
0.0%	preferred	0.0%	muni bonds
0.0%	conv't bds/wrnts	6.2%	other

SHAREHOLDER INFORMATION

Minimum Investment
Initial: $2,500 — Subsequent: $50

Minimum IRA Investment
Initial: na — Subsequent: na

Maximum Fees
Load: none — 12b-1: none
Other: none

Services
- IRA
- Keogh
- ✔ Telephone Exchange

Artisan Small Cap Fund (ARTSX)

800-344-1770, 414-390-6100
www.artisanfunds.com

Small-Cap Stock

PERFORMANCE — fund inception date: 3/28/95

	3yr Annual	5yr Annual	10yr Annual	Bull	Bear
Return (%)	-7.5	-4.8	na	49.8	-36.0
Differ From Category (+/-)	-1.8 av	-6.0 low	na	-45.6 av	-15.4 blw av

Standard Deviation	Category Risk Index	Beta
27.6%—high	1.16—abv av	1.10

	2002	2001	2000	1999	1998	1997	1996	1995	1994	1993
Return (%)	-28.6	12.2	-1.4	19.1	-17.0	22.6	11.8	—	—	—
Differ From Category (+/-)	-8.1	9.8	-5.6	-17.9	-17.7	0.2	-8.8	—	—	—
Return, Tax-Adjusted (%)	-28.7	12.1	-2.4	19.1	-17.7	18.8	9.5	—	—	—

PER SHARE DATA

	2002	2001	2000	1999	1998	1997	1996	1995	1994	1993
Dividends, Net Income ($)	0.00	0.00	0.00	0.00	0.00	0.00	0.00	—	—	—
Distrib'ns, Cap Gain ($)	0.06	0.05	0.66	0.00	0.51	2.57	1.07	—	—	—
Net Asset Value ($)	9.88	13.94	12.48	13.30	11.16	14.15	13.64	—	—	—
Expense Ratio (%)	1.31	1.34	1.35	1.37	1.33	1.41	1.52	—	—	—
Yield (%)	0.00	0.00	0.00	0.00	0.00	0.00	0.00	—	—	—
Portfolio Turnover (%)	140	147	193	155	134	87	105	—	—	—
Total Assets (Millions $)	105	154	139	175	201	291	295	—	—	—

PORTFOLIO (as of 9/30/02)

Portfolio Manager: C Ziegler/ M Carlson - 1995

Investment Style

Large Cap	Growth
✔ Mid Cap	Value
✔ Small Cap	✔ Grth/Val

Portfolio

0.0%	cash	0.6%	corp bonds
99.4%	stocks	0.0%	gov't bonds
0.0%	preferred	0.0%	muni bonds
0.0%	conv't bds/wrnts	0.0%	other

SHAREHOLDER INFORMATION

Minimum Investment
Initial: $1,000 — Subsequent: $50

Minimum IRA Investment
Initial: $1,000 — Subsequent: $50

Maximum Fees
Load: none — 12b-1: none
Other: none

Services
✔ IRA
✔ Keogh
✔ Telephone Exchange

Babson Enterprise Fund (BABEX)

800-422-2766, 816-751-5900
www.babsonfunds.com

Small-Cap Stock

PERFORMANCE — fund inception date: 12/2/83

	3yr Annual	5yr Annual	10yr Annual	Bull	Bear
Return (%)	12.0	2.9	9.9	10.4	19.4
Differ From Category (+/-)	17.7 high	1.7 abv av	1.2 av	-85.0 low	40.0 high

Standard Deviation	Category Risk Index	Beta
17.8%—av	0.75—blw av	0.46

	2002	2001	2000	1999	1998	1997	1996	1995	1994	1993
Return (%)	-3.4	29.4	12.4	-7.2	-11.3	32.4	21.2	16.4	2.4	16.2
Differ From Category (+/-)	17.1	27.0	8.2	-44.2	-12.0	10.0	0.6	-13.9	2.5	0.1
Return, Tax-Adjusted (%)	-3.4	28.7	10.5	-8.7	-14.0	29.3	16.4	12.7	-0.6	14.0

PER SHARE DATA

	2002	2001	2000	1999	1998	1997	1996	1995	1994	1993
Dividends, Net Income ($)	0.00	0.05	0.04	0.01	0.05	0.05	0.00	0.11	0.03	0.05
Distrib'ns, Cap Gain ($)	0.00	0.30	1.07	1.05	2.47	2.42	2.66	1.84	1.69	1.10
Net Asset Value ($)	15.23	15.77	12.47	12.11	14.26	19.03	16.31	15.66	15.15	16.51
Expense Ratio (%)	1.08	1.15	1.14	1.11	1.09	1.08	1.08	1.09	1.08	1.09
Yield (%)	0.00	0.31	0.29	0.07	0.29	0.23	0.00	0.62	0.17	0.28
Portfolio Turnover (%)	93	55	32	12	22	22	24	13	15	17
Total Assets (Millions $)	186	130	103	116	176	217	191	201	190	220

PORTFOLIO (as of 11/30/02)

Portfolio Manager: Lance James/Lorene Heebner - 1999

Investment Style

Large Cap	Growth
Mid Cap	✔ Value
✔ Small Cap	Grth/Val

Portfolio

0.0%	cash	0.0%	corp bonds
100.0%	stocks	0.0%	gov't bonds
0.0%	preferred	0.0%	muni bonds
0.0%	conv't bds/wrnts	0.0%	other

SHAREHOLDER INFORMATION

Minimum Investment
Initial: $1,000 Subsequent: $100

Minimum IRA Investment
Initial: $250 Subsequent: $100

Maximum Fees
Load: none 12b-1: none
Other: none

Services
✔ IRA
✔ Keogh
✔ Telephone Exchange

Babson Enterprise Fund II (BAETX)

800-422-2766, 816-751-5900
www.babsonfunds.com

Small-Cap Stock

PERFORMANCE — fund inception date: 8/5/91

	3yr Annual	5yr Annual	10yr Annual	Bull	Bear
Return (%)	2.5	1.8	9.4	31.5	0.0
Differ From Category (+/-)	8.2 abv av	0.6 av	0.7 av	-63.9 blw av	20.6 abv av

Standard Deviation	Category Risk Index	Beta
17.9%—av	0.75—blw av	0.73

	2002	2001	2000	1999	1998	1997	1996	1995	1994	1993
Return (%)	-9.9	2.7	16.6	6.1	-4.3	33.2	27.6	19.8	-7.3	19.7
Differ From Category (+/-)	10.6	0.3	12.4	-30.9	-5.0	10.8	7.0	-10.5	-7.2	3.6
Return, Tax-Adjusted (%)	-10.4	1.4	15.1	5.6	-5.2	31.1	22.8	18.0	-7.5	19.1

PER SHARE DATA

	2002	2001	2000	1999	1998	1997	1996	1995	1994	1993
Dividends, Net Income ($)	0.00	0.01	0.02	0.01	0.05	0.04	0.11	0.05	0.02	0.00
Distrib'ns, Cap Gain ($)	0.60	1.65	1.74	0.49	1.07	2.05	2.98	0.94	0.08	0.32
Net Asset Value ($)	21.68	24.64	25.62	23.59	22.72	24.99	20.37	18.40	16.19	17.60
Expense Ratio (%)	1.30	1.30	1.27	1.23	1.22	1.28	1.38	1.45	1.50	1.60
Yield (%)	0.00	0.03	0.07	0.04	0.21	0.14	0.47	0.25	0.12	0.00
Portfolio Turnover (%)	37	41	23	14	25	21	30	15	9	18
Total Assets (Millions $)	50	54	55	63	82	87	48	40	36	30

PORTFOLIO (as of 11/30/02)

Portfolio Manager: Lance James - 1991

Investment Style

Large Cap	Growth
✔ Mid Cap	✔ Value
✔ Small Cap	Grth/Val

Portfolio

0.0%	cash	0.0%	corp bonds
100.0%	stocks	0.0%	gov't bonds
0.0%	preferred	0.0%	muni bonds
0.0%	conv't bds/wrnts	0.0%	other

SHAREHOLDER INFORMATION

Minimum Investment
Initial: $1,000 — Subsequent: $100

Minimum IRA Investment
Initial: $250 — Subsequent: $100

Maximum Fees
Load: none — 12b-1: none
Other: none

Services
✔ IRA
✔ Keogh
✔ Telephone Exchange

Babson Shadow Stock

800-422-2766, 816-751-5900
www.babsonfunds.com

(SHSTX)

Small-Cap Stock

PERFORMANCE

fund inception date: 9/10/87

	3yr Annual	5yr Annual	10yr Annual	Bull	Bear
Return (%)	6.2	4.3	10.0	26.4	6.3
Differ From Category (+/-)	11.9 high	3.1 abv av	1.3 abv av	-69.0 blw av	26.9 abv av

Standard Deviation	Category Risk Index	Beta
16.9%—av	0.71—low	0.51

	2002	2001	2000	1999	1998	1997	1996	1995	1994	1993
Return (%)	-12.2	22.6	11.3	4.6	-1.4	27.6	21.3	23.6	-4.0	15.2
Differ From Category (+/-)	8.3	20.2	7.1	-32.4	-2.1	5.2	0.7	-6.7	-3.9	-0.9
Return, Tax-Adjusted (%)	-12.3	21.9	8.7	2.9	-2.9	23.7	17.5	21.0	-9.3	12.4

PER SHARE DATA

	2002	2001	2000	1999	1998	1997	1996	1995	1994	1993
Dividends, Net Income ($)	0.02	0.09	0.08	0.34	0.06	0.13	0.08	0.10	0.11	0.09
Distrib'ns, Cap Gain ($)	0.00	0.22	1.32	0.31	0.83	1.99	1.35	0.75	2.14	1.02
Net Asset Value ($)	11.86	13.54	11.31	11.46	11.60	12.70	11.70	10.89	9.52	12.32
Expense Ratio (%)	1.03	1.03	1.07	1.10	1.16	1.13	1.14	1.13	1.28	1.25
Yield (%)	0.16	0.65	0.63	2.88	0.48	0.88	0.61	0.85	0.94	0.67
Portfolio Turnover (%)	34	29	18	21	43	0	25	19	43	15
Total Assets (Millions $)	83	65	41	40	50	49	39	38	33	37

PORTFOLIO (as of 11/30/02)

Portfolio Manager: Anthony Maramarco - 1999

Investment Style

Large Cap	Growth
Mid Cap	✔ Value
✔ Small Cap	Grth/Val

Portfolio

0.0%	cash	0.4%	corp bonds
94.7%	stocks	0.0%	gov't bonds
0.0%	preferred	0.0%	muni bonds
0.0%	conv't bds/wrnts	4.9%	other

SHAREHOLDER INFORMATION

Minimum Investment
Initial: $1,000 Subsequent: $100

Minimum IRA Investment
Initial: $250 Subsequent: $100

Maximum Fees
Load: none 12b-1: none
Other: none

Services
✔ IRA
✔ Keogh
✔ Telephone Exchange

Baron Growth Fund (BGRFX)

800-992-2766, 212-583-2100
www.baronfunds.com

Small-Cap Stock

PERFORMANCE — fund inception date: 1/3/95

	3yr Annual	5yr Annual	10yr Annual	Bull	Bear
Return (%)	-1.9	6.4	na	94.6	-6.7
Differ From Category (+/-)	3.8 av	5.2 high	na	-0.8 abv av	13.9 av

Standard Deviation	Category Risk Index	Beta
20.5%—abv av	0.86—blw av	0.81

	2002	2001	2000	1999	1998	1997	1996	1995	1994	1993
Return (%)	-12.2	12.6	-4.5	44.7	0.1	31.0	27.7	—	—	—
Differ From Category (+/-)	8.3	10.2	-8.7	7.7	-0.6	8.6	7.1	—	—	—
Return, Tax-Adjusted (%)	-12.2	11.5	-6.4	43.2	0.0	30.9	27.2	—	—	—

PER SHARE DATA

	2002	2001	2000	1999	1998	1997	1996	1995	1994	1993
Dividends, Net Income ($)	0.00	0.00	0.00	0.00	0.03	0.01	0.09	—	—	—
Distrib'ns, Cap Gain ($)	0.00	1.63	3.19	1.88	0.00	0.05	0.16	—	—	—
Net Asset Value ($)	26.90	30.67	28.82	33.68	24.87	24.88	19.04	—	—	—
Expense Ratio (%)	na	1.36	1.36	1.40	1.43	1.40	1.50	—	—	—
Yield (%)	0.00	0.00	0.00	0.00	0.12	0.04	0.46	—	—	—
Portfolio Turnover (%)	na	34	39	53	40	25	40	—	—	—
Total Assets (Millions $)	941	720	500	620	343	415	243	—	—	—

PORTFOLIO (as of 9/30/02)

Portfolio Manager: Ronald Baron - 1995

Investment Style

Large Cap	Growth
✔ Mid Cap	✔ Value
✔ Small Cap	Grth/Val

Portfolio

12.2%	cash	0.0%	corp bonds
87.8%	stocks	0.0%	gov't bonds
0.0%	preferred	0.0%	muni bonds
0.0%	conv't bds/wrnts	0.0%	other

SHAREHOLDER INFORMATION

Minimum Investment
Initial: $2,000 — Subsequent: na

Minimum IRA Investment
Initial: $2,000 — Subsequent: $0

Maximum Fees
Load: none — 12b-1: 0.25%
Other: none

Services
✔ IRA
Keogh
✔ Telephone Exchange

Baron Small Cap (BSCFX)

800-992-2766, 212-583-2100
www.baronfunds.com

Small-Cap Stock

PERFORMANCE — fund inception date: 10/1/97

	3yr Annual	5yr Annual	10yr Annual	Bull	Bear
Return (%)	-7.8	6.4	na	109.6	-20.9
Differ From Category (+/-)	-2.1 av	5.2 high	na	14.2 abv av	-0.3 av

Standard Deviation	Category Risk Index	Beta
23.3%—abv av	0.97—av	0.82

	2002	2001	2000	1999	1998	1997	1996	1995	1994	1993
Return (%)	-9.6	5.1	-17.5	70.7	2.2	—	—	—	—	—
Differ From Category (+/-)	10.9	2.7	-21.7	33.7	1.5	—	—	—	—	—
Return, Tax-Adjusted (%)	-10.1	5.1	-17.9	70.7	2.2	—	—	—	—	—

PER SHARE DATA

	2002	2001	2000	1999	1998	1997	1996	1995	1994	1993
Dividends, Net Income ($)	0.00	0.00	0.00	0.00	0.00	—	—	—	—	—
Distrib'ns, Cap Gain ($)	0.38	0.00	0.37	0.00	0.00	—	—	—	—	—
Net Asset Value ($)	13.37	15.21	14.46	18.00	10.54	—	—	—	—	—
Expense Ratio (%)	na	1.35	1.33	1.34	1.39	—	—	—	—	—
Yield (%)	0.00	0.00	0.00	0.00	0.00	—	—	—	—	—
Portfolio Turnover (%)	na	55	53	42	59	—	—	—	—	—
Total Assets (Millions $)	800	708	746	1,088	470	—	—	—	—	—

PORTFOLIO (as of 9/30/02)

Portfolio Manager: Cliff Greenberg - 1997

Investment Style

Large Cap	Growth
Mid Cap	✔ Value
✔ Small Cap	Grth/Val

Portfolio

7.2%	cash	0.0%	corp bonds
92.8%	stocks	0.0%	gov't bonds
0.0%	preferred	0.0%	muni bonds
0.0%	conv't bds/wrnts	0.0%	other

SHAREHOLDER INFORMATION

Minimum Investment
Initial: $2,000 Subsequent: na

Minimum IRA Investment
Initial: $2,000 Subsequent: $0

Maximum Fees
Load: none 12b-1: 0.25%
Other: none

Services
✔ IRA
✔ Keogh
✔ Telephone Exchange

Cr Suisse Emg Grth/Cmn (CUEGX)

800-927-2874, 212-878-0600
www.creditsuissefunds.com

Small-Cap Stock

PERFORMANCE — fund inception date: 1/22/88

	3yr Annual	5yr Annual	10yr Annual	Bull	Bear
Return (%)	-22.6	-7.0	4.6	105.3	-61.2
Differ From Category (+/-)	-16.9 low	-8.2 low	-4.1 low	9.9 abv av	-40.6 low

Standard Deviation	Category Risk Index	Beta
31.3%—high	1.31—abv av	1.15

	2002	2001	2000	1999	1998	1997	1996	1995	1994	1993
Return (%)	-30.1	-24.8	-12.0	41.8	5.8	21.2	9.8	46.2	-1.4	18.1
Differ From Category (+/-)	-9.6	-27.2	-16.2	4.8	5.1	-1.2	-10.8	15.9	-1.3	2.0
Return, Tax-Adjusted (%)	-30.1	-24.8	-15.4	38.7	5.8	19.8	9.7	44.0	-1.4	16.2

PER SHARE DATA

	2002	2001	2000	1999	1998	1997	1996	1995	1994	1993
Dividends, Net Income ($)	0.00	0.00	0.00	0.00	0.00	0.00	0.00	0.00	0.00	0.00
Distrib'ns, Cap Gain ($)	0.00	0.00	8.48	6.23	0.00	2.38	0.06	1.75	0.00	1.35
Net Asset Value ($)	18.85	26.99	35.90	49.86	39.97	37.77	33.22	30.30	21.99	22.31
Expense Ratio (%)	na	1.28	1.19	1.23	1.22	1.22	1.27	1.25	1.22	1.23
Yield (%)	0.00	0.00	0.00	0.00	0.00	0.00	0.00	0.00	0.00	0.00
Portfolio Turnover (%)	na	177	190	154	91	87	65	97	60	68
Total Assets (Millions $)	376	884	1,785	2,017	1,777	1,577	1,151	557	222	183

PORTFOLIO (as of 11/30/02)

Portfolio Manager: E Dater/S Oh/ R Harris - 2000

Investment Style

Large Cap	✔ Growth
Mid Cap	Value
✔ Small Cap	Grth/Val

Portfolio

5.7%	cash	2.4%	corp bonds
91.9%	stocks	0.0%	gov't bonds
0.0%	preferred	0.0%	muni bonds
0.0%	conv't bds/wrnts	0.0%	other

SHAREHOLDER INFORMATION

Minimum Investment
Initial: $2,500 Subsequent: $1

Minimum IRA Investment
Initial: $500 Subsequent: $1

Maximum Fees
Load: none 12b-1: none
Other: none

Services
✔ IRA
Keogh
✔ Telephone Exchange

Eclipse Funds Sm Cap Val (EEQFX)

866-232-5477, 201-331-2000
www.towneley.com

Small-Cap Stock

PERFORMANCE — fund inception date: 1/12/87

	3yr Annual	5yr Annual	10yr Annual	Bull	Bear
Return (%)	0.0	1.2	9.3	20.7	1.9
Differ From Category (+/-)	5.7 av	0.0 av	0.6 av	-74.7 low	22.5 abv av

Standard Deviation	Category Risk Index	Beta
16.7%—av	0.70—low	0.58

	2002	2001	2000	1999	1998	1997	1996	1995	1994	1993
Return (%)	-3.3	13.9	-9.5	3.0	3.3	33.3	29.8	19.6	-4.7	17.0
Differ From Category (+/-)	17.2	11.5	-13.7	-34.0	2.6	10.9	9.2	-10.7	-4.6	0.9
Return, Tax-Adjusted (%)	-3.7	13.5	-9.5	2.1	-0.5	27.9	21.2	18.1	-6.6	12.5

PER SHARE DATA

	2002	2001	2000	1999	1998	1997	1996	1995	1994	1993
Dividends, Net Income ($)	0.13	0.10	0.00	0.00	0.00	0.00	0.13	0.06	0.02	0.07
Distrib'ns, Cap Gain ($)	0.00	0.00	0.00	0.51	2.67	3.65	3.98	0.51	0.86	2.02
Net Asset Value ($)	11.49	12.02	10.64	11.76	11.93	14.19	13.47	13.56	11.82	13.35
Expense Ratio (%)	na	1.15	1.21	1.18	1.14	1.14	1.15	1.14	1.12	1.12
Yield (%)	1.13	0.83	0.00	0.00	0.00	0.00	0.74	0.42	0.15	0.45
Portfolio Turnover (%)	na	77	104	56	73	55	82	74	92	101
Total Assets (Millions $)	111	115	159	250	199	192	170	174	195	197

PORTFOLIO (as of 9/30/02)

Portfolio Manager: Wesley McCain/Kathy O'Connor - 1987

Investment Style

Large Cap	Growth
Mid Cap	✔ Value
✔ Small Cap	Grth/Val

Portfolio

10.0% cash	0.0% corp bonds
86.8% stocks	0.0% gov't bonds
0.0% preferred	0.0% muni bonds
0.0% conv't bds/wrnts	3.2% other

SHAREHOLDER INFORMATION

Minimum Investment
Initial: $1,000 Subsequent: $100

Minimum IRA Investment
Initial: $1,000 Subsequent: $100

Maximum Fees
Load: none 12b-1: none
Other: none

Services
✔ IRA
Keogh
✔ Telephone Exchange

Excelsior Small Cap Fd/A (UMLCX)

800-446-1012, 617-483-7297
www.excelsiorfunds.com

Small-Cap Stock

PERFORMANCE — fund inception date: 12/31/92

	3yr Annual	5yr Annual	10yr Annual	Bull	Bear
Return (%)	-6.6	-1.5	5.3	104.5	-36.4
Differ From Category (+/-)	-0.9 av	-2.7 blw av	-3.4 low	9.1 abv av	-15.8 blw av

Standard Deviation	Category Risk Index	Beta
29.9%—high	1.26—abv av	0.89

	2002	2001	2000	1999	1998	1997	1996	1995	1994	1993
Return (%)	-19.3	1.9	-1.0	29.7	-12.3	14.2	-2.2	21.3	5.2	27.9
Differ From Category (+/-)	1.2	-0.5	-5.2	-7.3	-13.0	-8.2	-22.8	-9.0	5.3	11.8
Return, Tax-Adjusted (%)	-19.3	1.8	-2.7	29.7	-12.5	14.2	-3.5	19.6	4.6	27.5

PER SHARE DATA

	2002	2001	2000	1999	1998	1997	1996	1995	1994	1993
Dividends, Net Income ($)	0.00	0.03	0.06	0.00	0.00	0.00	0.00	0.00	0.00	0.00
Distrib'ns, Cap Gain ($)	0.00	0.00	0.91	0.00	0.11	0.00	0.49	0.56	0.17	0.09
Net Asset Value ($)	9.32	11.56	11.38	12.53	9.66	11.17	9.78	10.47	9.14	8.86
Expense Ratio (%)	0.84	0.89	0.92	0.94	0.94	0.94	0.90	0.96	0.95	0.99
Yield (%)	0.00	0.25	0.48	0.00	0.00	0.00	0.00	0.00	0.00	0.00
Portfolio Turnover (%)	144	132	134	115	73	55	38	42	20	4
Total Assets (Millions $)	187	119	96	63	46	65	70	73	41	15

PORTFOLIO (as of 9/30/02)

Portfolio Manager: T Pettee/M Doyle/ T Herget - 1998

Investment Style

Large Cap	✔ Growth
Mid Cap	Value
✔ Small Cap	Grth/Val

Portfolio

1.9% cash	0.0% corp bonds
98.1% stocks	0.0% gov't bonds
0.0% preferred	0.0% muni bonds
0.0% conv't bds/wrnts	0.0% other

SHAREHOLDER INFORMATION

Minimum Investment
Initial: $500 Subsequent: $50

Minimum IRA Investment
Initial: $250 Subsequent: $50

Maximum Fees
Load: none 12b-1: none
Other: none

Services
✔ IRA
✔ Keogh
✔ Telephone Exchange

Fidelity Low Priced Stock (FLPSX)

800-544-8544, 800-522-7297
www.fidelity.com

Small-Cap Stock

PERFORMANCE fund inception date: 12/27/89

	3yr Annual	5yr Annual	10yr Annual	Bull	Bear
Return (%)	12.2	8.3	14.2	27.2	27.6
Differ From Category (+/-)	17.9 high	7.1 high	5.5 high	-68.2 blw av	48.2 high

Standard Deviation	Category Risk Index	Beta
14.5%—av	0.61—low	0.60

	2002	2001	2000	1999	1998	1997	1996	1995	1994	1993
Return (%)	-6.1	26.7	18.8	5.0	0.5	26.7	26.8	24.8	4.8	20.2
Differ From Category (+/-)	14.4	24.3	14.6	-32.0	-0.2	4.3	6.2	-5.5	4.9	4.1
Return, Tax-Adjusted (%)	-6.5	25.1	15.5	3.7	-1.4	24.7	23.8	22.1	1.3	17.0

PER SHARE DATA

	2002	2001	2000	1999	1998	1997	1996	1995	1994	1993
Dividends, Net Income ($)	0.03	0.16	0.16	0.15	0.20	0.28	0.24	0.23	0.09	0.16
Distrib'ns, Cap Gain ($)	0.54	1.54	3.43	1.19	1.94	1.58	1.66	1.24	2.05	1.62
Net Asset Value ($)	25.17	27.42	23.12	22.64	22.85	25.13	21.35	18.50	16.00	17.30
Expense Ratio (%)	0.97	1.00	0.81	1.08	0.95	1.01	1.04	1.11	1.13	1.12
Yield (%)	0.11	0.55	0.60	0.62	0.80	1.04	1.04	1.16	0.49	0.84
Portfolio Turnover (%)	26	44	15	24	47	45	79	65	54	47
Total Assets (Millions $)	15,104	12,428	6,833	6,646	9,194	10,691	5,664	3,349	2,354	2,060

PORTFOLIO (as of 7/31/02)

Portfolio Manager: Joel Tillinghast - 1989

Investment Style

Large Cap	Growth
✔ Mid Cap	✔ Value
✔ Small Cap	Grth/Val

Portfolio

0.0%	cash	0.3%	corp bonds
84.7%	stocks	0.0%	gov't bonds
0.0%	pref/conv't pref	0.0%	muni bonds
0.1%	conv't bds/wrnts	14.8%	other

SHAREHOLDER INFORMATION

Minimum Investment
Initial: $2,500 Subsequent: $250

Minimum IRA Investment
Initial: $500 Subsequent: $250

Maximum Fees
Load: 3.00% front 12b-1: none
Other: 1.5% redemption fee for 3 months

Services
✔ IRA
✔ Keogh
✔ Telephone Exchange

Fidelity Small Cap Ind (FDSCX)

800-544-8544, 800-522-7297
www.fidelity.com

Small-Cap Stock

PERFORMANCE

fund inception date: 6/28/93

	3yr Annual	5yr Annual	10yr Annual	Bull	Bear
Return (%)	-3.8	-1.2	na	51.0	-17.2
Differ From Category (+/-)	1.9 av	-2.4 blw av	na	-44.4 av	3.4 av

Standard Deviation	Category Risk Index	Beta
19.8%—abv av	0.83—blw av	0.56

	2002	2001	2000	1999	1998	1997	1996	1995	1994	1993
Return (%)	-20.8	6.2	5.7	14.1	-7.3	27.2	13.6	26.6	-3.3	—
Differ From Category (+/-)	-0.3	3.8	1.5	-22.9	-8.0	4.8	-7.0	-3.7	-3.2	—
Return, Tax-Adjusted (%)	-20.8	5.7	4.7	13.8	-8.2	25.1	12.4	24.2	-3.3	—

PER SHARE DATA

	2002	2001	2000	1999	1998	1997	1996	1995	1994	1993
Dividends, Net Income ($)	0.00	0.00	0.03	0.09	0.03	0.13	0.01	0.08	0.01	—
Distrib'ns, Cap Gain ($)	0.00	0.44	0.74	0.00	0.62	1.14	0.51	0.77	0.00	—
Net Asset Value ($)	13.30	16.80	16.23	16.09	14.19	15.93	13.56	12.39	10.45	—
Expense Ratio (%)	0.91	0.74	0.88	0.85	0.97	0.90	0.99	0.97	1.20	—
Yield (%)	0.00	0.00	0.17	0.55	0.20	0.76	0.07	0.60	0.09	—
Portfolio Turnover (%)	290	450	122	96	88	176	192	182	210	—
Total Assets (Millions $)	841	958	688	612	747	824	538	438	664	—

PORTFOLIO (as of 10/31/02)

Portfolio Manager: James Harmon - 2001

Investment Style

Large Cap	✔ Growth
Mid Cap	Value
✔ Small Cap	Grth/Val

Portfolio

0.3% cash	0.0% corp bonds
94.1% stocks	0.0% gov't bonds
0.0% preferred	0.0% muni bonds
0.0% conv't bds/wrnts	5.6% other

SHAREHOLDER INFORMATION

Minimum Investment
Initial: $2,500 Subsequent: $250

Minimum IRA Investment
Initial: $500 Subsequent: $250

Maximum Fees
Load: 1.50% redemption 12b-1: none
Other: redemption fee applies for 3 months

Services
✔ IRA
✔ Keogh
✔ Telephone Exchange

FTI Small Cap Equity Fund (FTSCX)

800-342-5236
www.ftifunds.com

Small-Cap Stock

PERFORMANCE

fund inception date: 12/22/95

	3yr Annual	5yr Annual	10yr Annual	Bull	Bear
Return (%)	-17.4	-0.4	na	161.6	-51.5
Differ From Category (+/-)	-11.7 low	-1.6 blw av	na	66.2 high	-30.9 blw av

Standard Deviation	Category Risk Index	Beta
28.3%—high	1.19—abv av	0.89

	2002	2001	2000	1999	1998	1997	1996	1995	1994	1993
Return (%)	-35.4	-15.5	3.0	69.3	3.0	17.7	23.4	—	—	—
Differ From Category (+/-)	-14.9	-17.9	-1.2	32.3	2.3	-4.7	2.8	—	—	—
Return, Tax-Adjusted (%)	-35.4	-17.0	3.0	66.7	3.0	17.1	23.4	—	—	—

PER SHARE DATA

	2002	2001	2000	1999	1998	1997	1996	1995	1994	1993
Dividends, Net Income ($)	0.00	0.00	0.00	0.00	0.00	0.00	0.00	—	—	—
Distrib'ns, Cap Gain ($)	0.00	1.70	0.00	1.90	0.00	0.34	0.00	—	—	—
Net Asset Value ($)	11.55	17.89	23.32	22.63	14.60	14.17	12.34	—	—	—
Expense Ratio (%)	na	1.30	1.27	1.44	1.50	1.50	na	—	—	—
Yield (%)	0.00	0.00	0.00	0.00	0.00	0.00	0.00	—	—	—
Portfolio Turnover (%)	na	112	90	130	158	111	na	—	—	—
Total Assets (Millions $)	54	98	116	86	52	42	20	—	—	—

PORTFOLIO (as of 9/30/02)

Portfolio Manager: Karen Fang - 2000

Investment Style

Large Cap	✔ Growth
Mid Cap	Value
✔ Small Cap	Grth/Val

Portfolio

3.6%	cash	0.8%	corp bonds
95.7%	stocks	0.0%	gov't bonds
0.0%	preferred	0.0%	muni bonds
0.0%	conv't bds/wrnts	0.0%	other

SHAREHOLDER INFORMATION

Minimum Investment
Initial: $1,000 Subsequent: $100

Minimum IRA Investment
Initial: $1 Subsequent: $1

Maximum Fees
Load: none 12b-1: none
Other: none

Services
✔ IRA
✔ Keogh
✔ Telephone Exchange

Gabelli Sm Cp Grth (GABSX)

800-422-3554
www.gabelli.com

Small-Cap Stock

PERFORMANCE — fund inception date: 10/22/91

	3yr Annual	5yr Annual	10yr Annual	Bull	Bear
Return (%)	3.3	4.7	11.1	36.5	-0.4
Differ From Category (+/-)	9.0 abv av	3.5 abv av	2.4 abv av	-58.9 blw av	20.2 abv av

Standard Deviation	Category Risk Index	Beta
16.5%—av	0.69—low	0.67

	2002	2001	2000	1999	1998	1997	1996	1995	1994	1993
Return (%)	-5.3	4.6	11.3	14.2	0.0	36.4	11.8	25.1	-2.8	22.7
Differ From Category (+/-)	15.2	2.2	7.1	-22.8	-0.7	14.0	-8.8	-5.2	-2.7	6.6
Return, Tax-Adjusted (%)	-5.6	4.2	6.8	11.9	-0.5	32.4	8.5	22.7	-4.5	21.9

PER SHARE DATA

	2002	2001	2000	1999	1998	1997	1996	1995	1994	1993
Dividends, Net Income ($)	0.00	0.01	0.05	0.00	0.00	0.00	0.00	0.00	0.00	0.00
Distrib'ns, Cap Gain ($)	0.25	0.34	4.72	2.46	0.53	3.66	2.16	1.34	1.03	0.42
Net Asset Value ($)	17.93	19.21	18.71	21.43	21.01	21.58	18.53	18.50	15.85	17.38
Expense Ratio (%)	1.45	1.45	1.49	1.56	1.44	1.62	1.58	1.54	1.54	1.64
Yield (%)	0.00	0.05	0.21	0.00	0.00	0.00	0.00	0.00	0.00	0.00
Portfolio Turnover (%)	10	17	47	24	20	14	11	17	18	13
Total Assets (Millions $)	453	440	374	338	321	292	216	228	196	214

PORTFOLIO (as of 11/30/02)

Portfolio Manager: Mario Gabelli - 1991

Investment Style

Large Cap	Growth
✔ Mid Cap	✔ Value
✔ Small Cap	Grth/Val

Portfolio

8.8% cash	0.3% corp bonds
88.8% stocks	0.0% gov't bonds
2.0% pref/conv't pref	0.0% muni bonds
0.0% conv't bds/wrnts	0.1% other

SHAREHOLDER INFORMATION

Minimum Investment
Initial: $1,000 — Subsequent: $1

Minimum IRA Investment
Initial: $250 — Subsequent: $1

Maximum Fees
Load: none — 12b-1: 0.25%
Other: none

Services
✔ IRA
Keogh
✔ Telephone Exchange

Heartland Grp:Value Fund (HRTVX)

800-432-7856, 414-289-7000
www.heartlandfunds.com

Small-Cap Stock

PERFORMANCE — fund inception date: 12/28/84

	3yr Annual	5yr Annual	10yr Annual	Bull	Bear
Return (%)	5.3	5.2	11.7	34.0	10.9
Differ From Category (+/-)	11.0 abv av	4.0 abv av	3.0 high	-61.1 blw av	31.5 high

Standard Deviation	Category Risk Index	Beta
18.7%—av	0.78—blw av	0.68

	2002	2001	2000	1999	1998	1997	1996	1995	1994	1993
Return (%)	-11.4	29.4	2.0	25.0	-11.4	23.1	20.9	29.8	1.7	18.7
Differ From Category (+/-)	.9.1	27.0	-2.2	-12.0	-12.1	0.7	0.3	-0.5	1.8	2.6
Return, Tax-Adjusted (%)	-12.2	26.2	-0.2	24.9	-11.8	19.8	18.7	27.8	0.6	17.3

PER SHARE DATA

	2002	2001	2000	1999	1998	1997	1996	1995	1994	1993
Dividends, Net Income ($)	0.00	0.00	0.00	0.00	0.05	0.17	0.06	0.13	0.00	0.00
Distrib'ns, Cap Gain ($)	1.53	5.19	4.03	0.09	0.63	4.86	2.07	1.39	0.87	1.02
Net Asset Value ($)	31.46	37.25	32.98	36.50	29.29	33.87	31.65	27.95	22.72	23.22
Expense Ratio (%)	na	1.29	1.22	1.34	1.15	1.12	1.23	1.12	1.39	1.51
Yield (%)	0.00	0.00	0.00	0.00	0.16	0.43	0.17	0.44	0.00	0.00
Portfolio Turnover (%)	na	56	48	23	36	55	31	25	35	51
Total Assets (Millions $)	967	1,093	895	1,195	1,545	2,126	1,627	1,190	338	186

PORTFOLIO (as of 9/30/02)

Portfolio Manager: William Nasgovitz/Eric Miller - 1984

Investment Style

Large Cap	Growth
Mid Cap	✔ Value
✔ Small Cap	Grth/Val

Portfolio

4.8%	cash	0.0%	corp bonds
95.2%	stocks	0.0%	gov't bonds
0.0%	preferred	0.0%	muni bonds
0.0%	conv't bds/wrnts	0.0%	other

SHAREHOLDER INFORMATION

Minimum Investment
Initial: $5,000 Subsequent: $100

Minimum IRA Investment
Initial: $500 Subsequent: $100

Maximum Fees
Load: none 12b-1: 0.25%
Other: none

Services
✔ IRA
✔ Keogh
✔ Telephone Exchange

Heartland Grp:Value Plus (HRVIX)

800-432-7856, 414-289-7000
www.heartlandfunds.com

Small-Cap Stock

PERFORMANCE — fund inception date: 10/26/93

	3yr Annual	5yr Annual	10yr Annual	Bull	Bear
Return (%)	5.7	1.4	na	19.4	-2.4
Differ From Category (+/-)	11.4 abv av	0.2 av	na	-76.0 low	18.2 abv av

Standard Deviation	Category Risk Index	Beta
18.1%—av	0.76—blw av	0.60

	2002	2001	2000	1999	1998	1997	1996	1995	1994	1993
Return (%)	-3.7	34.7	-8.8	1.6	-10.7	30.6	33.7	24.3	-4.9	—
Differ From Category (+/-)	16.8	32.3	-13.0	-35.4	-11.4	8.2	13.1	-6.0	-4.8	—
Return, Tax-Adjusted (%)	-4.0	34.1	-9.6	0.3	-12.2	27.4	30.4	21.9	-6.5	—

PER SHARE DATA

	2002	2001	2000	1999	1998	1997	1996	1995	1994	1993
Dividends, Net Income ($)	0.12	0.17	0.29	0.43	0.59	0.47	0.38	0.40	0.41	—
Distrib'ns, Cap Gain ($)	0.00	0.00	0.00	0.00	0.02	1.26	0.76	0.25	0.00	—
Net Asset Value ($)	15.39	16.12	12.11	13.57	13.80	16.13	13.73	11.17	9.53	—
Expense Ratio (%)	na	1.48	1.36	1.39	1.21	1.12	1.45	1.54	1.80	—
Yield (%)	0.77	1.05	2.39	3.16	4.26	2.70	2.62	3.50	4.30	—
Portfolio Turnover (%)	na	80	121	82	64	74	73	150	127	—
Total Assets (Millions $)	54	60	44	87	174	336	66	19	9	—

PORTFOLIO (as of 9/30/02)

Portfolio Manager: W Nasgovitz/ R Hathaway - 1993

Investment Style

Large Cap	Growth
✔ Mid Cap	✔ Value
✔ Small Cap	Grth/Val

Portfolio

7.7%	cash	0.0%	corp bonds
92.4%	stocks	0.0%	gov't bonds
0.0%	preferred	0.0%	muni bonds
0.0%	conv't bds/wrnts	0.0%	other

SHAREHOLDER INFORMATION

Minimum Investment
Initial: $1,000 — Subsequent: $100

Minimum IRA Investment
Initial: $500 — Subsequent: $100

Maximum Fees
Load: none — 12b-1: 0.25%
Other: none

Services
✔ IRA
✔ Keogh
✔ Telephone Exchange

INVESCO Small Co Grth/Inv (FIEGX)

800-525-8085
www.invesco.com

Small-Cap Stock

PERFORMANCE — fund inception date: 1/2/92

	3yr Annual	5yr Annual	10yr Annual	Bull	Bear
Return (%)	-21.8	-0.1	7.3	188.6	-59.8
Differ From Category (+/-)	-16.1 low	-1.3 blw av	-1.4 blw av	93.2 high	-39.2 low

Standard Deviation	Category Risk Index	Beta
36.5%—high	1.53—high	1.23

	2002	2001	2000	1999	1998	1997	1996	1995	1994	1993
Return (%)	-31.3	-20.9	-12.1	81.6	14.8	18.3	11.6	30.0	-3.7	23.3
Differ From Category (+/-)	-10.8	-23.3	-16.3	44.6	14.1	-4.1	-9.0	-0.3	-3.6	7.2
Return, Tax-Adjusted (%)	-31.3	-20.9	-13.1	78.2	12.7	12.8	10.3	29.3	-9.4	23.3

PER SHARE DATA

	2002	2001	2000	1999	1998	1997	1996	1995	1994	1993
Dividends, Net Income ($)	0.00	0.00	0.00	0.00	0.00	0.00	0.00	0.04	0.00	0.00
Distrib'ns, Cap Gain ($)	0.00	0.00	0.92	1.98	1.17	3.42	0.53	0.17	2.48	0.00
Net Asset Value ($)	8.33	12.14	15.35	18.62	11.58	11.21	12.52	11.69	9.17	12.11
Expense Ratio (%)	1.45	1.29	1.20	1.50	1.48	1.52	1.48	1.49	1.37	1.54
Yield (%)	0.00	0.00	0.00	0.00	0.00	0.00	0.00	0.33	0.00	0.00
Portfolio Turnover (%)	99	112	186	41	158	216	221	228	196	153
Total Assets (Millions $)	768	1,234	1,599	846	316	313	267	212	179	223

PORTFOLIO (as of 9/30/02)

Portfolio Manager: Stacie Cowell - 1996

Investment Style

Large Cap	✔ Growth
Mid Cap	Value
✔ Small Cap	Grth/Val

Portfolio

12.6%	cash	0.6%	corp bonds
86.0%	stocks	0.0%	gov't bonds
0.7%	pref/conv't pref	0.0%	muni bonds
0.0%	conv't bds/wrnts	0.0%	other

SHAREHOLDER INFORMATION

Minimum Investment
Initial: $1,000 — Subsequent: $50

Minimum IRA Investment
Initial: $250 — Subsequent: $50

Maximum Fees
Load: none — 12b-1: 0.25%
Other: none

Services
✔ IRA
✔ Keogh
✔ Telephone Exchange

Kalmar Gr-w-Val Small Cap (KGSCX)

800-282-2319, 302-658-7575
www.kalmarinvestments.com

Small-Cap Stock

PERFORMANCE — fund inception date: 4/11/97

	3yr Annual	5yr Annual	10yr Annual	Bull	Bear
Return (%)	-1.1	-1.1	na	46.8	-20.4
Differ From Category (+/-)	4.6 av	-2.3 blw av	na	-48.6 av	0.2 av

Standard Deviation	Category Risk Index	Beta
24.5%—high	1.03—av	1.01

	2002	2001	2000	1999	1998	1997	1996	1995	1994	1993
Return (%)	-16.5	0.0	15.7	6.0	-7.6	—	—	—	—	—
Differ From Category (+/-)	4.0	-2.4	11.5	-31.0	-8.3	—	—	—	—	—
Return, Tax-Adjusted (%)	-16.5	0.0	11.8	6.0	-7.6	—	—	—	—	—

PER SHARE DATA

	2002	2001	2000	1999	1998	1997	1996	1995	1994	1993
Dividends, Net Income ($)	0.00	0.00	0.00	0.00	0.00	—	—	—	—	—
Distrib'ns, Cap Gain ($)	0.00	0.00	2.58	0.00	0.00	—	—	—	—	—
Net Asset Value ($)	10.81	12.95	12.95	13.41	12.65	—	—	—	—	—
Expense Ratio (%)	na	1.23	1.22	1.25	1.24	—	—	—	—	—
Yield (%)	0.00	0.00	0.00	0.00	0.00	—	—	—	—	—
Portfolio Turnover (%)	na	46	63	52	27	—	—	—	—	—
Total Assets (Millions $)	170	208	214	195	237	—	—	—	—	—

PORTFOLIO (as of 11/30/02)

Portfolio Manager: Team Managed - 1997

Investment Style

Large Cap	Growth
✔ Mid Cap	Value
✔ Small Cap	✔ Grth/Val

Portfolio

3.9% cash	0.0% corp bonds
96.1% stocks	0.0% gov't bonds
0.0% preferred	0.0% muni bonds
0.0% conv't bds/wrnts	0.0% other

SHAREHOLDER INFORMATION

Minimum Investment
Initial: $10,000 — Subsequent: $1,000

Minimum IRA Investment
Initial: $1,000 — Subsequent: $1

Maximum Fees
Load: none — 12b-1: none
Other: none

Services
✔ IRA
Keogh
Telephone Exchange

Lazard Sm Cap/Open

800-823-6300, 212-632-6000
www.lazardfunds.com

(LZCOX)

Small-Cap Stock

PERFORMANCE — fund inception date: 1/30/97

	3yr Annual	5yr Annual	10yr Annual	Bull	Bear
Return (%)	3.7	1.1	na	30.8	2.4
Differ From Category (+/-)	9.4 abv av	-0.1 av	na	-64.6 blw av	23.0 abv av

Standard Deviation	Category Risk Index	Beta
18.9%—abv av	0.79—blw av	0.81

	2002	2001	2000	1999	1998	1997	1996	1995	1994	1993
Return (%)	-17.8	17.6	15.5	1.4	-6.6	—	—	—	—	—
Differ From Category (+/-)	.2.7	15.2	11.3	-35.6	-7.3	—	—	—	—	—
Return, Tax-Adjusted (%)	-18.4	13.8	14.2	0.1	-8.2	—	—	—	—	—

PER SHARE DATA

	2002	2001	2000	1999	1998	1997	1996	1995	1994	1993
Dividends, Net Income ($)	0.00	0.02	0.15	0.07	0.31	—	—	—	—	—
Distrib'ns, Cap Gain ($)	0.51	3.41	0.80	0.97	0.96	—	—	—	—	—
Net Asset Value ($)	14.03	17.67	18.04	16.51	17.35	—	—	—	—	—
Expense Ratio (%)	na	1.13	1.12	1.09	1.09	—	—	—	—	—
Yield (%)	0.00	0.09	0.79	0.40	1.69	—	—	—	—	—
Portfolio Turnover (%)	na	78	67	50	46	—	—	—	—	—
Total Assets (Millions $)	43	70	68	85	93	—	—	—	—	—

PORTFOLIO (as of 10/31/02)

Portfolio Manager: Gullquist/Mullin - 1997

Investment Style

Large Cap	Growth
✔ Mid Cap	✔ Value
✔ Small Cap	Grth/Val

Portfolio

2.8%	cash	0.0%	corp bonds
97.2%	stocks	0.0%	gov't bonds
0.0%	preferred	0.0%	muni bonds
0.0%	conv't bds/wrnts	0.0%	other

SHAREHOLDER INFORMATION

Minimum Investment
Initial: $10,000 Subsequent: $1

Minimum IRA Investment
Initial: $10,000 Subsequent: $1

Maximum Fees
Load: 1.00% redemption 12b-1: 0.25%
Other: redemption fee applies for 1 month

Services
✔ IRA
✔ Keogh
✔ Telephone Exchange

Liberty Acorn Fund/Z

800-426-3750, 800-345-6611
www.wanger.com

(ACRNX)

Small-Cap Stock

PERFORMANCE **fund inception date: 6/10/70**

	3yr Annual	5yr Annual	10yr Annual	Bull	Bear
Return (%)	0.4	7.4	12.4	64.8	-6.1
Differ From Category (+/-)	6.1 abv av	6.2 high	3.7 high	-30.6 av	14.5 abv av

Standard Deviation	Category Risk Index	Beta
19.4%—abv av	0.81—blw av	0.70

	2002	2001	2000	1999	1998	1997	1996	1995	1994	1993
Return (%)	-13.3	6.1	10.0	33.3	6.0	24.9	22.5	20.8	-7.4	32.3
Differ From Category (+/-)	7.2	3.7	5.8	-3.7	5.3	2.5	1.9	-9.5	-7.3	16.2
Return, Tax-Adjusted (%)	-13.3	5.6	6.7	28.9	4.7	22.3	19.2	18.0	-8.8	32.0

PER SHARE DATA

	2002	2001	2000	1999	1998	1997	1996	1995	1994	1993
Dividends, Net Income ($)	0.00	0.04	0.11	0.09	0.03	0.16	0.11	0.09	0.11	0.06
Distrib'ns, Cap Gain ($)	0.00	0.35	2.86	3.54	1.06	1.61	1.47	1.08	0.56	0.59
Net Asset Value ($)	15.50	17.88	17.21	18.53	16.85	16.99	15.04	13.60	12.24	13.95
Expense Ratio (%)	na	0.82	0.83	0.85	0.84	0.56	0.57	0.57	0.62	0.65
Yield (%)	0.00	0.21	0.54	0.40	0.16	0.86	0.66	0.61	0.85	0.41
Portfolio Turnover (%)	na	20	29	34	24	32	33	29	18	20
Total Assets (Millions $)	4,123	4,222	3,986	3,920	3,584	3,687	2,853	2,399	1,982	2,034

PORTFOLIO (as of 9/30/02)

Portfolio Manager: Ralph Wanger/Charles McQuaid - 1970

Investment Style

Large Cap	Growth
✔ Mid Cap	Value
✔ Small Cap	✔ Grth/Val

Portfolio

7.4%	cash	0.2%	corp bonds
92.4%	stocks	0.0%	gov't bonds
0.0%	pref/conv't pref	0.0%	muni bonds
0.0%	conv't bds/wrnts	0.0%	other

SHAREHOLDER INFORMATION

Minimum Investment
Initial: $100,000 Subsequent: $1

Minimum IRA Investment
Initial: $1 Subsequent: $1

Maximum Fees
Load: none 12b-1: none
Other: none

Services
✔ IRA
✔ Keogh
✔ Telephone Exchange

LKCM Small Cap Equity (LKSCX)

800-688-5526, 617-557-8785
www.lkcm.com

Small-Cap Stock

PERFORMANCE

fund inception date: 7/14/94

	3yr Annual	5yr Annual	10yr Annual	Bull	Bear
Return (%)	1.8	2.9	na	46.0	-1.9
Differ From Category (+/-)	7.5 abv av	1.7 abv av	na	-49.4 av	18.7 abv av

Standard Deviation	Category Risk Index	Beta
15.7%—av	0.66—low	0.47

	2002	2001	2000	1999	1998	1997	1996	1995	1994	1993
Return (%)	-11.7	7.5	11.3	16.7	-6.2	22.1	25.5	33.2	—	—
Differ From Category (+/-)	8.8	5.1	7.1	-20.3	-6.9	-0.3	4.9	2.9	—	—
Return, Tax-Adjusted (%)	-11.7	6.3	7.8	16.3	-6.4	18.8	23.5	32.7	—	—

PER SHARE DATA

	2002	2001	2000	1999	1998	1997	1996	1995	1994	1993
Dividends, Net Income ($)	0.00	0.07	0.04	0.02	0.06	0.07	0.06	0.14	—	—
Distrib'ns, Cap Gain ($)	0.00	0.91	3.09	0.25	0.04	2.55	0.87	0.00	—	—
Net Asset Value ($)	15.24	17.29	17.00	18.08	15.72	16.89	16.20	13.84	—	—
Expense Ratio (%)	na	0.92	0.93	0.90	0.91	0.95	1.00	1.00	—	—
Yield (%)	0.00	0.38	0.19	0.10	0.38	0.36	0.35	1.01	—	—
Portfolio Turnover (%)	na	62	79	48	35	34	66	na	—	—
Total Assets (Millions $)	213	220	211	230	246	255	199	122	—	—

PORTFOLIO (as of 9/30/02)

Portfolio Manager: J King - 1994

Investment Style

Large Cap	Growth
Mid Cap	Value
✔ Small Cap	✔ Grth/Val

Portfolio

16.6% cash	0.0% corp bonds
82.8% stocks	0.0% gov't bonds
0.0% preferred	0.0% muni bonds
0.7% conv't bds/wrnts	0.0% other

SHAREHOLDER INFORMATION

Minimum Investment
Initial: $10,000 Subsequent: $1,000

Minimum IRA Investment
Initial: $10,000 Subsequent: $1,000

Maximum Fees
Load: none 12b-1: none
Other: none

Services
✔ IRA
✔ Keogh
✔ Telephone Exchange

Marshall:Sm Cap Gr/Inv

800-236-3863, 412-288-1900
www.marshallfunds.com

(MRSCX)

Small-Cap Stock

PERFORMANCE — fund inception date: 9/4/96

	3yr Annual	5yr Annual	10yr Annual	Bull	Bear
Return (%)	-14.5	-2.7	na	112.6	-52.4
Differ From Category (+/-)	-8.8 blw av	-3.9 low	na	17.2 abv av	-31.8 blw av

Standard Deviation	Category Risk Index	Beta
37.3%—high	1.57—high	1.27

	2002	2001	2000	1999	1998	1997	1996	1995	1994	1993
Return (%)	-28.7	8.9	-19.6	34.7	3.4	23.1	—	—	—	—
Differ From Category (+/-)	-8.2	6.5	-23.8	-2.3	2.7	0.7	—	—	—	—
Return, Tax-Adjusted (%)	-28.7	8.0	-21.5	34.1	3.4	22.2	—	—	—	—

PER SHARE DATA

	2002	2001	2000	1999	1998	1997	1996	1995	1994	1993
Dividends, Net Income ($)	0.00	0.00	0.00	0.00	0.00	0.00	—	—	—	—
Distrib'ns, Cap Gain ($)	0.00	0.58	1.62	0.41	0.02	0.48	—	—	—	—
Net Asset Value ($)	9.08	12.75	12.25	17.27	13.16	12.75	—	—	—	—
Expense Ratio (%)	1.63	1.58	1.59	1.59	1.60	1.80	—	—	—	—
Yield (%)	0.00	0.00	0.00	0.00	0.00	0.00	—	—	—	—
Portfolio Turnover (%)	292	287	105	219	139	na	—	—	—	—
Total Assets (Millions $)	82	112	114	143	111	70	—	—	—	—

PORTFOLIO (as of 9/30/02)

Portfolio Manager: Sean McLeod - 2000

Investment Style

Large Cap	✔ Growth
Mid Cap	Value
✔ Small Cap	Grth/Val

Portfolio

4.2% cash	5.9% corp bonds
89.9% stocks	0.0% gov't bonds
0.0% preferred	0.0% muni bonds
0.0% conv't bds/wrnts	0.0% other

SHAREHOLDER INFORMATION

Minimum Investment
Initial: $1,000 — Subsequent: $50

Minimum IRA Investment
Initial: $1,000 — Subsequent: $50

Maximum Fees
Load: none — 12b-1: none
Other: none

Services
✔ IRA
Keogh
✔ Telephone Exchange

Monetta Fund (MONTX)

800-666-3882, 630-462-9800
www.monetta.com

Small-Cap Stock

PERFORMANCE

fund inception date: 5/6/86

	3yr Annual	5yr Annual	10yr Annual	Bull	Bear
Return (%)	-17.4	-4.9	1.8	128.6	-53.0
Differ From Category (+/-)	-11.7 low	-6.1 low	-6.9 low	33.2 abv av	-32.4 blw av

Standard Deviation	Category Risk Index	Beta
36.6%—high	1.54—high	0.94

	2002	2001	2000	1999	1998	1997	1996	1995	1994	1993
Return (%)	-15.2	-21.0	-15.9	51.8	-9.0	26.1	1.6	28.0	-6.2	0.4
Differ From Category (+/-)	.5.3	-23.4	-20.1	14.8	-9.7	3.7	-19.0	-2.3	-6.1	-15.7
Return, Tax-Adjusted (%)	-15.2	-21.0	-22.1	51.8	-9.8	22.6	1.6	22.1	-6.4	-0.5

PER SHARE DATA

	2002	2001	2000	1999	1998	1997	1996	1995	1994	1993
Dividends, Net Income ($)	0.00	0.00	0.09	0.00	0.00	0.00	0.00	0.02	0.05	0.00
Distrib'ns, Cap Gain ($)	0.00	0.00	6.90	0.00	0.65	2.75	0.00	3.00	0.00	0.53
Net Asset Value ($)	7.88	9.30	11.78	22.71	14.96	17.27	15.84	15.59	14.52	15.54
Expense Ratio (%)	na	1.49	1.32	1.45	1.36	1.48	1.38	1.40	1.35	1.38
Yield (%)	0.00	0.00	0.48	0.00	0.00	0.00	0.00	0.10	0.34	0.00
Portfolio Turnover (%)	na	470	353	210	107	97	204	148	191	227
Total Assets (Millions $)	56	74	103	135	124	163	211	362	364	524

PORTFOLIO (as of 11/30/02)

Portfolio Manager: Team Managed - 1986

Investment Style

Large Cap	✔ Growth
Mid Cap	Value
✔ Small Cap	Grth/Val

Portfolio

32.1%	cash	0.0%	corp bonds
67.9%	stocks	0.0%	gov't bonds
0.0%	preferred	0.0%	muni bonds
0.0%	conv't bds/wrnts	0.0%	other

SHAREHOLDER INFORMATION

Minimum Investment
Initial: $250   Subsequent: $1

Minimum IRA Investment
Initial: $50   Subsequent: $25

Maximum Fees
Load: none   12b-1: none
Other: none

Services
✔ IRA
✔ Keogh
✔ Telephone Exchange

Neuberger Fasciano (NBFSX)

800-366-6264, 212-476-8800
www.fascianofunds.com

Small-Cap Stock

PERFORMANCE

fund inception date: 11/10/88

	3yr Annual	5yr Annual	10yr Annual	Bull	Bear
Return (%)	-1.0	2.0	9.5	15.3	0.3
Differ From Category (+/-)	4.7 av	0.8 av	0.8 av	-80.1 low	20.9 abv av

Standard Deviation	Category Risk Index	Beta
17.2%—av	0.72—low	0.65

	2002	2001	2000	1999	1998	1997	1996	1995	1994	1993
Return (%)	-8.6	4.4	1.7	6.1	7.1	21.5	26.5	31.1	3.6	8.0
Differ From Category (+/-)	11.9	2.0	-2.5	-30.9	6.4	-0.9	5.9	0.8	3.7	-8.1
Return, Tax-Adjusted (%)	-8.6	3.7	1.3	5.6	6.2	20.4	25.7	28.9	1.8	6.4

PER SHARE DATA

	2002	2001	2000	1999	1998	1997	1996	1995	1994	1993
Dividends, Net Income ($)	0.00	0.00	0.29	0.39	0.03	0.00	0.00	0.00	0.00	0.00
Distrib'ns, Cap Gain ($)	0.00	1.08	0.00	0.00	1.25	1.49	0.59	1.34	1.14	1.00
Net Asset Value ($)	30.44	33.33	32.98	32.72	31.19	30.31	26.20	21.18	17.18	17.68
Expense Ratio (%)	1.36	1.58	1.20	1.20	1.30	1.40	1.50	1.70	1.70	1.70
Yield (%)	0.00	0.00	0.87	1.19	0.09	0.00	0.00	0.00	0.00	0.00
Portfolio Turnover (%)	24	4	29	19	49	41	45	37	99	43
Total Assets (Millions $)	220	198	236	398	233	55	33	24	17	17

PORTFOLIO (as of 9/30/02)

Portfolio Manager: Michael Fasciano - 2001

Investment Style

Large Cap	Growth
✔ Mid Cap	✔ Value
✔ Small Cap	Grth/Val

Portfolio

13.7% cash	0.0% corp bonds
86.3% stocks	0.0% gov't bonds
0.0% preferred	0.0% muni bonds
0.0% conv't bds/wrnts	0.0% other

SHAREHOLDER INFORMATION

Minimum Investment
Initial: $1,000 Subsequent: $100

Minimum IRA Investment
Initial: $250 Subsequent: $100

Maximum Fees
Load: none 12b-1: none
Other: none

Services
✔ IRA
✔ Keogh
✔ Telephone Exchange

Northern Small Cap Value (NOSGX)

800-595-9111
www.northernfunds.com

Small-Cap Stock

PERFORMANCE — fund inception date: 4/4/94

	3yr Annual	5yr Annual	10yr Annual	Bull	Bear
Return (%)	2.5	2.5	na	35.3	0.0
Differ From Category (+/-)	8.2 abv av	1.3 av	na	-60.1 blw av	20.6 abv av

Standard Deviation	Category Risk Index	Beta
22.6%—abv av	0.95—av	0.68

	2002	2001	2000	1999	1998	1997	1996	1995	1994	1993
Return (%)	-6.2	5.8	8.4	12.1	-5.9	29.8	18.9	22.5	—	—
Differ From Category (+/-)	14.3	3.4	4.2	-24.9	-6.6	7.4	-1.7	-7.8	—	—
Return, Tax-Adjusted (%)	-6.4	4.8	1.6	10.1	-6.6	28.6	17.0	20.3	—	—

PER SHARE DATA

	2002	2001	2000	1999	1998	1997	1996	1995	1994	1993
Dividends, Net Income ($)	0.04	0.01	0.05	0.11	0.01	0.03	0.05	0.06	—	—
Distrib'ns, Cap Gain ($)	0.00	0.50	4.66	1.13	0.53	0.68	0.65	0.66	—	—
Net Asset Value ($)	9.54	10.22	10.15	14.10	13.78	15.26	12.33	10.97	—	—
Expense Ratio (%)	1.00	1.00	1.00	1.00	1.00	1.00	1.00	1.00	—	—
Yield (%)	0.41	0.09	0.33	0.72	0.06	0.18	0.38	0.51	—	—
Portfolio Turnover (%)	77	16	18	18	18	18	47	82	—	—
Total Assets (Millions $)	275	247	154	239	314	336	193	142	—	—

PORTFOLIO (as of 9/30/02)

Portfolio Manager: Robert Bergson - 2001

Investment Style

Large Cap	Growth
Mid Cap	Value
✔ Small Cap	✔ Grth/Val

Portfolio

0.0% cash	0.0% corp bonds
99.4% stocks	0.0% gov't bonds
0.0% preferred	0.0% muni bonds
0.0% conv't bds/wrnts	0.6% other

SHAREHOLDER INFORMATION

Minimum Investment
Initial: $2,500 Subsequent: $50

Minimum IRA Investment
Initial: $500 Subsequent: $50

Maximum Fees
Load: none 12b-1: none
Other: none

Services
✔ IRA
✔ Keogh
✔ Telephone Exchange

Oakmark Small Cap Fund/I (OAKSX)

800-625-6275, 312-621-0600
www.oakmark.com

Small-Cap Stock

PERFORMANCE — fund inception date: 11/1/95

	3yr Annual	5yr Annual	10yr Annual	Bull	Bear
Return (%)	4.6	-1.7	na	6.8	9.2
Differ From Category (+/-)	10.3 abv av	-2.9 blw av	na	-88.6 low	29.8 high

Standard Deviation	Category Risk Index	Beta
19.9%—abv av	0.83—blw av	0.77

	2002	2001	2000	1999	1998	1997	1996	1995	1994	1993
Return (%)	-13.0	26.2	4.3	-7.9	-13.1	40.5	39.7	—	—	—
Differ From Category (+/-)	.7.5	23.8	0.1	-44.9	-13.8	18.1	19.1	—	—	—
Return, Tax-Adjusted (%)	-13.0	26.2	3.5	-7.9	-15.3	39.3	39.7	—	—	—

PER SHARE DATA

	2002	2001	2000	1999	1998	1997	1996	1995	1994	1993
Dividends, Net Income ($)	0.00	0.00	0.00	0.00	0.00	0.00	0.00	—	—	—
Distrib'ns, Cap Gain ($)	0.00	0.00	0.51	0.00	2.10	0.84	0.00	—	—	—
Net Asset Value ($)	15.03	17.29	13.69	13.60	14.77	19.42	14.44	—	—	—
Expense Ratio (%)	1.33	1.27	1.50	1.48	1.45	1.37	1.61	—	—	—
Yield (%)	0.00	0.00	0.00	0.00	0.00	0.00	0.00	—	—	—
Portfolio Turnover (%)	22	47	28	68	34	26	23	—	—	—
Total Assets (Millions $)	386	329	207	336	703	1,492	360	—	—	—

PORTFOLIO (as of 9/30/02)

Portfolio Manager: James Benson/Clyde McGregor - 1999

Investment Style

Large Cap	Growth
✔ Mid Cap	✔ Value
✔ Small Cap	Grth/Val

Portfolio

3.3% cash	0.0% corp bonds
96.7% stocks	0.0% gov't bonds
0.0% preferred	0.0% muni bonds
0.0% conv't bds/wrnts	0.0% other

SHAREHOLDER INFORMATION

Minimum Investment
Initial: $1,000 Subsequent: $100

Minimum IRA Investment
Initial: $1,000 Subsequent: $100

Maximum Fees
Load: 2.00% redemption 12b-1: none
Other: redemption fee applies for 3 months

Services
✔ IRA
✔ Keogh
✔ Telephone Exchange

Oberweis:Emerging Growth (OBEGX)

800-323-6166, 630-801-6000
www.oberweisfunds.com

Small-Cap Stock

PERFORMANCE

fund inception date: 1/7/87

	3yr Annual	5yr Annual	10yr Annual	Bull	Bear
Return (%)	-12.0	0.1	5.4	183.0	-53.7
Differ From Category (+/-)	-6.3 blw av	-1.1 av	-3.3 blw av	87.6 high	-33.1 low

Standard Deviation	Category Risk Index	Beta
38.3%—high	1.61—high	1.36

	2002	2001	2000	1999	1998	1997	1996	1995	1994	1993
Return (%)	-24.2	0.4	-10.6	53.1	-3.1	-8.5	22.4	42.5	-3.5	9.7
Differ From Category (+/-)	-3.7	-2.0	-14.8	16.1	-3.8	-30.9	1.8	12.2	-3.4	-6.4
Return, Tax-Adjusted (%)	-24.2	0.4	-17.9	53.1	-4.0	-11.3	19.9	40.6	-3.5	8.7

PER SHARE DATA

	2002	2001	2000	1999	1998	1997	1996	1995	1994	1993
Dividends, Net Income ($)	0.00	0.00	0.00	0.00	0.00	0.00	0.00	0.00	0.00	0.00
Distrib'ns, Cap Gain ($)	0.00	0.00	13.10	0.00	1.15	4.64	2.64	1.42	0.00	0.74
Net Asset Value ($)	16.13	21.29	21.19	36.15	23.60	25.71	32.86	29.09	21.41	22.19
Expense Ratio (%)	na	1.65	1.42	1.59	1.55	1.44	1.48	1.75	1.78	1.80
Yield (%)	0.00	0.00	0.00	0.00	0.00	0.00	0.00	0.00	0.00	0.00
Portfolio Turnover (%)	na	66	73	63	49	75	64	79	66	70
Total Assets (Millions $)	61	80	83	105	93	140	185	134	90	101

PORTFOLIO (as of 10/31/02)

Portfolio Manager: James Oberweis - 1987

Investment Style

Large Cap	✔ Growth
Mid Cap	Value
✔ Small Cap	Grth/Val

Portfolio

1.5%	cash	0.0%	corp bonds
98.6%	stocks	0.0%	gov't bonds
0.0%	preferred	0.0%	muni bonds
0.0%	conv't bds/wrnts	-0.1%	other

SHAREHOLDER INFORMATION

Minimum Investment
Initial: $1,000 Subsequent: $100

Minimum IRA Investment
Initial: $500 Subsequent: $100

Maximum Fees
Load: none 12b-1: 0.25%
Other: none

Services
✔ IRA
✔ Keogh
✔ Telephone Exchange

PBHG Small Cap Value (PBSVX)

800-433-0051, 610-647-4100
www.pbhgfunds.com

Small-Cap Stock

PERFORMANCE

fund inception date: 4/30/97

	3yr Annual	5yr Annual	10yr Annual	Bull	Bear
Return (%)	-1.7	2.6	na	84.0	-22.9
Differ From Category (+/-)	4.0 av	1.4 av	na	-11.4 av	-2.3 av

Standard Deviation	Category Risk Index	Beta
26.1%—high	1.10—av	1.01

	2002	2001	2000	1999	1998	1997	1996	1995	1994	1993
Return (%)	-31.9	4.9	32.8	18.6	1.1	—	—	—	—	—
Differ From Category (+/-)	-11.4	2.5	28.6	-18.4	0.4	—	—	—	—	—
Return, Tax-Adjusted (%)	-31.9	4.9	31.7	18.6	-0.1	—	—	—	—	—

PER SHARE DATA

	2002	2001	2000	1999	1998	1997	1996	1995	1994	1993
Dividends, Net Income ($)	0.00	0.00	0.00	0.00	0.00	—	—	—	—	—
Distrib'ns, Cap Gain ($)	0.00	0.00	0.82	0.00	0.84	—	—	—	—	—
Net Asset Value ($)	14.04	20.64	19.67	15.47	13.04	—	—	—	—	—
Expense Ratio (%)	1.48	1.49	1.50	1.48	1.49	—	—	—	—	—
Yield (%)	0.00	0.00	0.00	0.00	0.00	—	—	—	—	—
Portfolio Turnover (%)	145	177	352	273	263	—	—	—	—	—
Total Assets (Millions $)	135	305	241	70	104	—	—	—	—	—

PORTFOLIO (as of 9/30/02)

Portfolio Manager: Jerome Heppelmann - 1999

Investment Style

Large Cap	Growth
✔ Mid Cap	Value
✔ Small Cap	✔ Grth/Val

Portfolio

1.5%	cash	0.0%	corp bonds
98.5%	stocks	0.0%	gov't bonds
0.0%	preferred	0.0%	muni bonds
0.0%	conv't bds/wrnts	0.0%	other

SHAREHOLDER INFORMATION

Minimum Investment
Initial: $2,500 Subsequent: $1

Minimum IRA Investment
Initial: $2,000 Subsequent: $1

Maximum Fees
Load: none 12b-1: none
Other: none

Services
✔ IRA
✔ Keogh
✔ Telephone Exchange

PBHG Strategic Small Co (PSSCX)

800-433-0051, 610-647-4100
www.pbhgfunds.com

Small-Cap Stock

PERFORMANCE

fund inception date: 12/31/96

	3yr Annual	5yr Annual	10yr Annual	Bull	Bear
Return (%)	-12.4	0.8	na	150.1	-46.4
Differ From Category (+/-)	-6.7 blw av	-0.4 av	na	54.7 high	-25.8 blw av

Standard Deviation	Category Risk Index	Beta
36.0%—high	1.51—abv av	1.20

	2002	2001	2000	1999	1998	1997	1996	1995	1994	1993
Return (%)	-33.3	-9.9	11.8	51.7	2.1	25.6	—	—	—	—
Differ From Category (+/-)	-12.8	-12.3	7.6	14.7	1.4	3.2	—	—	—	—
Return, Tax-Adjusted (%)	-33.3	-9.9	8.5	49.5	1.3	23.9	—	—	—	—

PER SHARE DATA

	2002	2001	2000	1999	1998	1997	1996	1995	1994	1993
Dividends, Net Income ($)	0.00	0.00	0.00	0.00	0.00	0.00	—	—	—	—
Distrib'ns, Cap Gain ($)	0.00	0.00	2.59	1.24	0.46	0.87	—	—	—	—
Net Asset Value ($)	9.15	13.72	15.24	15.91	11.41	11.67	—	—	—	—
Expense Ratio (%)	1.49	1.50	1.50	1.50	1.45	1.50	—	—	—	—
Yield (%)	0.00	0.00	0.00	0.00	0.00	0.00	—	—	—	—
Portfolio Turnover (%)	119	143	240	140	215	na	—	—	—	—
Total Assets (Millions $)	66	102	85	59	69	117	—	—	—	—

PORTFOLIO (as of 9/30/02)

Portfolio Manager: J Smith/J Heppelmann - 1999

Investment Style

Large Cap	✔ Growth
Mid Cap	Value
✔ Small Cap	Grth/Val

Portfolio

9.0%	cash	0.0%	corp bonds
91.0%	stocks	0.0%	gov't bonds
0.0%	preferred	0.0%	muni bonds
0.0%	conv't bds/wrnts	0.0%	other

SHAREHOLDER INFORMATION

Minimum Investment
Initial: $5,000 Subsequent: $1

Minimum IRA Investment
Initial: $2,000 Subsequent: $1

Maximum Fees
Load: none 12b-1: none
Other: none

Services
✔ IRA
✔ Keogh
✔ Telephone Exchange

Royce:Micro-Cap/Inv (RYOTX)

800-221-4268, 212-486-1445
www.roycefunds.com

Small-Cap Stock

PERFORMANCE — fund inception date: 12/31/91

	3yr Annual	5yr Annual	10yr Annual	Bull	Bear
Return (%)	7.5	6.4	11.6	47.7	2.5
Differ From Category (+/-)	13.2 high	5.2 high	2.9 high	-47.7 av	23.1 abv av

Standard Deviation	Category Risk Index	Beta
21.3%—abv av	0.89—av	0.76

	2002	2001	2000	1999	1998	1997	1996	1995	1994	1993
Return (%)	-13.4	23.1	16.7	13.6	-3.3	24.6	15.5	19.0	3.5	23.6
Differ From Category (+/-)	.7.1	20.7	12.5	-23.4	-4.0	2.2	-5.1	-11.3	3.6	7.5
Return, Tax-Adjusted (%)	-13.6	22.7	14.0	13.1	-4.4	22.8	13.4	18.2	2.5	20.0

PER SHARE DATA

	2002	2001	2000	1999	1998	1997	1996	1995	1994	1993
Dividends, Net Income ($)	0.00	0.00	0.00	0.00	0.00	0.00	0.00	0.00	0.00	0.00
Distrib'ns, Cap Gain ($)	0.10	0.18	1.28	0.20	0.50	0.75	0.54	0.18	0.22	0.74
Net Asset Value ($)	10.16	11.85	9.78	9.50	8.55	9.40	8.14	7.53	6.48	6.47
Expense Ratio (%)	na	1.75	1.49	1.35	1.49	1.50	1.79	1.94	1.99	1.99
Yield (%)	0.00	0.00	0.00	0.00	0.00	0.00	0.00	0.00	0.00	0.00
Portfolio Turnover (%)	na	30	74	102	56	38	70	25	54	116
Total Assets (Millions $)	267	202	139	111	165	199	141	97	26	10

PORTFOLIO (as of 11/30/02)

Portfolio Manager: W. Whitney George - 1991

Investment Style

Large Cap	Growth
Mid Cap	✔ Value
✔ Small Cap	Grth/Val

Portfolio

7.2% cash	0.0% corp bonds
92.8% stocks	0.0% gov't bonds
0.0% preferred	0.0% muni bonds
0.0% conv't bds/wrnts	0.0% other

SHAREHOLDER INFORMATION

Minimum Investment
Initial: $2,000 — Subsequent: $50

Minimum IRA Investment
Initial: $500 — Subsequent: $50

Maximum Fees
Load: 1.00% redemption — 12b-1: none
Other: redemption fee applies for 12 months

Services
- ✔ IRA
- ✔ Keogh
- ✔ Telephone Exchange

Royce:PA Mutual/Inv

800-221-4268, 212-486-1445
www.roycefunds.com

(PENNX)

Small-Cap Stock

PERFORMANCE

fund inception date: 10/3/68

	3yr Annual	5yr Annual	10yr Annual	Bull	Bear
Return (%)	8.3	7.0	10.0	25.0	16.6
Differ From Category (+/-)	14.0 high	5.8 high	1.3 abv av	-70.4 blw av	37.2 high

Standard Deviation	Category Risk Index	Beta
17.2%—av	0.72—low	0.63

	2002	2001	2000	1999	1998	1997	1996	1995	1994	1993
Return (%)	-9.2	18.3	18.3	5.9	4.1	24.9	12.8	18.7	-0.7	11.2
Differ From Category (+/-)	11.3	15.9	14.1	-31.1	3.4	2.5	-7.8	-11.6	-0.6	-4.9
Return, Tax-Adjusted (%)	-9.5	16.1	13.7	4.5	2.0	21.8	7.0	14.4	-3.7	9.0

PER SHARE DATA

	2002	2001	2000	1999	1998	1997	1996	1995	1994	1993
Dividends, Net Income ($)	0.00	0.02	0.05	0.04	0.05	0.06	0.11	0.11	0.11	0.11
Distrib'ns, Cap Gain ($)	0.12	0.70	1.59	0.45	0.71	0.99	1.44	0.97	0.73	0.48
Net Asset Value ($)	6.59	7.39	6.88	7.28	7.35	7.82	7.11	7.71	7.41	8.31
Expense Ratio (%)	na	0.99	1.03	1.04	1.01	1.05	0.99	0.97	0.98	0.98
Yield (%)	0.00	0.24	0.59	0.51	0.62	0.68	1.28	1.26	1.35	1.25
Portfolio Turnover (%)	na	39	45	21	29	18	29	10	17	24
Total Assets (Millions $)	473	444	369	371	466	507	456	637	771	1,022

PORTFOLIO (as of 11/30/02)

Portfolio Manager: Charles Royce - 1968

Investment Style

Large Cap	Growth
✔ Mid Cap	✔ Value
✔ Small Cap	Grth/Val

Portfolio

8.7%	cash	0.2%	corp bonds
91.1%	stocks	0.0%	gov't bonds
0.0%	preferred	0.0%	muni bonds
0.0%	conv't bds/wrnts	0.0%	other

SHAREHOLDER INFORMATION

Minimum Investment

Initial: $2,000 Subsequent: $50

Minimum IRA Investment

Initial: $500 Subsequent: $50

Maximum Fees

Load: 1.00% redemption 12b-1: none

Other: redemption fee applies for 12 months

Services

✔ IRA

✔ Keogh

✔ Telephone Exchange

Royce:Premier (RYPRX)

800-221-4268, 212-486-1445
www.roycefunds.com

Small-Cap Stock

PERFORMANCE — fund inception date: 12/31/91

	3yr Annual	5yr Annual	10yr Annual	Bull	Bear
Return (%)	5.7	7.1	11.0	36.1	7.6
Differ From Category (+/-)	11.4 abv av	5.9 high	2.3 abv av	-59.3 blw av	28.2 abv av

Standard Deviation	Category Risk Index	Beta
17.3%—av	0.72—low	0.69

	2002	2001	2000	1999	1998	1997	1996	1995	1994	1993
Return (%)	-7.7	9.6	17.1	11.4	6.7	18.4	18.1	17.8	3.2	19.0
Differ From Category (+/-)	12.8	7.2	12.9	-25.6	6.0	-4.0	-2.5	-12.5	3.3	2.9
Return, Tax-Adjusted (%)	-8.3	9.1	14.3	10.1	6.3	16.8	15.6	15.4	2.5	18.1

PER SHARE DATA

	2002	2001	2000	1999	1998	1997	1996	1995	1994	1993
Dividends, Net Income ($)	0.00	0.00	0.03	0.01	0.05	0.08	0.10	0.09	0.05	0.02
Distrib'ns, Cap Gain ($)	0.34	0.23	1.27	0.58	0.09	0.46	0.49	0.41	0.09	0.14
Net Asset Value ($)	9.39	10.54	9.83	9.56	9.14	8.70	7.81	7.12	6.48	6.41
Expense Ratio (%)	na	1.19	1.20	1.35	1.23	1.24	1.25	1.29	1.38	1.50
Yield (%)	0.00	0.00	0.27	0.09	0.54	0.87	1.20	1.19	0.76	0.30
Portfolio Turnover (%)	na	41	40	70	46	18	34	39	38	85
Total Assets (Millions $)	873	798	674	567	571	533	316	302	202	47

PORTFOLIO (as of 11/30/02)

Portfolio Manager: Charles Royce - 1991

Investment Style

Large Cap	Growth
✔ Mid Cap	✔ Value
✔ Small Cap	Grth/Val

Portfolio

7.2% cash	1.4% corp bonds
91.3% stocks	0.0% gov't bonds
0.0% preferred	0.0% muni bonds
0.0% conv't bds/wrnts	0.0% other

SHAREHOLDER INFORMATION

Minimum Investment
Initial: $2,000 Subsequent: $50

Minimum IRA Investment
Initial: $500 Subsequent: $50

Maximum Fees
Load: 1.00% redemption 12b-1: none
Other: redemption fee applies for 12 months

Services
✔ IRA
✔ Keogh
✔ Telephone Exchange

Royce:Total Return (RYTRX)

800-221-4268, 212-486-1445
www.roycefunds.com

Small-Cap Stock

PERFORMANCE — fund inception date: 12/15/93

	3yr Annual	5yr Annual	10yr Annual	Bull	Bear
Return (%)	10.4	7.4	na	16.4	26.1
Differ From Category (+/-)	16.1 high	6.2 high	na	-79.0 low	46.7 high

Standard Deviation	Category Risk Index	Beta
13.9%—blw av	0.58—low	0.52

	2002	2001	2000	1999	1998	1997	1996	1995	1994	1993
Return (%)	-1.6	14.7	19.4	1.5	4.7	23.6	25.4	26.8	5.1	—
Differ From Category (+/-)	18.9	12.3	15.2	-35.5	4.0	1.2	4.8	-3.5	5.2	—
Return, Tax-Adjusted (%)	-2.0	13.6	17.0	-0.3	3.5	22.4	20.8	22.5	4.3	—

PER SHARE DATA

	2002	2001	2000	1999	1998	1997	1996	1995	1994	1993
Dividends, Net Income ($)	0.07	0.10	0.15	0.16	0.15	0.11	0.16	0.13	0.01	—
Distrib'ns, Cap Gain ($)	0.01	0.21	0.57	0.35	0.16	0.14	0.73	0.60	0.12	—
Net Asset Value ($)	8.37	8.59	7.77	7.15	7.56	7.52	6.29	5.76	5.12	—
Expense Ratio (%)	na	1.24	1.25	1.25	1.25	1.25	1.25	1.67	1.96	—
Yield (%)	0.83	1.13	1.79	2.13	1.94	1.43	2.27	2.04	0.19	—
Portfolio Turnover (%)	na	24	24	39	66	26	111	68	88	—
Total Assets (Millions $)	1,051	511	276	249	244	120	6	2	1	—

PORTFOLIO (as of 11/30/02)

Portfolio Manager: Charles Royce - 1993

Investment Style

Large Cap	Growth
✔ Mid Cap	✔ Value
✔ Small Cap	Grth/Val

Portfolio

0.0%	cash	1.5%	corp bonds
94.8%	stocks	2.4%	gov't bonds
1.2%	pref/conv't pref	0.0%	muni bonds
0.0%	conv't bds/wrnts	0.2%	other

SHAREHOLDER INFORMATION

Minimum Investment
Initial: $2,000 Subsequent: $50

Minimum IRA Investment
Initial: $500 Subsequent: $50

Maximum Fees
Load: 1.00% redemption 12b-1: none
Other: redemption fee applies for 12 months

Services
✔ IRA
✔ Keogh
✔ Telephone Exchange

RS:Diversifed Growth/A (RSDGX)

800-766-3863, 415-591-2700
www.rsim.com

Small-Cap Stock

PERFORMANCE — fund inception date: 8/1/96

	3yr Annual	5yr Annual	10yr Annual	Bull	Bear
Return (%)	-23.1	5.6	na	329.9	-67.1
Differ From Category (+/-)	-17.4 low	4.4 abv av	na	234.5 high	-46.5 low

Standard Deviation	Category Risk Index	Beta
38.7%—high	1.63—high	1.27

	2002	2001	2000	1999	1998	1997	1996	1995	1994	1993
Return (%)	-39.1	1.8	-26.9	150.2	16.2	29.4	—	—	—	—
Differ From Category (+/-)	-18.6	-0.6	-31.1	113.2	15.5	7.0	—	—	—	—
Return, Tax-Adjusted (%)	-39.1	1.8	-27.6	143.3	15.6	26.3	—	—	—	—

PER SHARE DATA

	2002	2001	2000	1999	1998	1997	1996	1995	1994	1993
Dividends, Net Income ($)	0.00	0.00	0.00	0.00	0.00	0.00	—	—	—	—
Distrib'ns, Cap Gain ($)	0.00	0.00	1.22	5.48	0.38	1.93	—	—	—	—
Net Asset Value ($)	14.16	23.26	22.83	32.99	15.89	14.04	—	—	—	—
Expense Ratio (%)	na	1.52	1.51	1.84	1.89	1.94	—	—	—	—
Yield (%)	0.00	0.00	0.00	0.00	0.00	0.00	—	—	—	—
Portfolio Turnover (%)	na	255	383	473	403	370	—	—	—	—
Total Assets (Millions $)	572	851	523	304	69	79	—	—	—	—

PORTFOLIO (as of 9/30/02)

Portfolio Manager: John Seabern/John Wallace - 1996

Investment Style

Large Cap	✔ Growth
Mid Cap	Value
✔ Small Cap	Grth/Val

Portfolio

2.7%	cash	0.8%	corp bonds
95.2%	stocks	0.0%	gov't bonds
0.2%	pref/conv't pref	0.0%	muni bonds
0.0%	conv't bds/wrnts	1.1%	other

SHAREHOLDER INFORMATION

Minimum Investment
Initial: $5,000 Subsequent: $100

Minimum IRA Investment
Initial: $1,000 Subsequent: $1

Maximum Fees
Load: none 12b-1: 0.25%
Other: none

Services
✔ IRA
Keogh
✔ Telephone Exchange

SAFECO Growth Opp/Inv (SAFGX)

800-624-5711, 206-545-7319
www.safecofunds.com

Small-Cap Stock

PERFORMANCE

fund inception date: 1/18/68

	3yr Annual	5yr Annual	10yr Annual	Bull	Bear
Return (%)	-9.6	-4.5	8.2	40.1	-35.5
Differ From Category (+/-)	-3.9 blw av	-5.7 low	-0.5 av	-55.3 blw av	-14.9 av

Standard Deviation	Category Risk Index	Beta
29.5%—high	1.24—abv av	1.12

	2002	2001	2000	1999	1998	1997	1996	1995	1994	1993
Return (%)	-36.9	22.1	-4.2	2.6	4.3	49.9	22.9	26.1	-1.6	22.1
Differ From Category (+/-)	-16.4	19.7	-8.4	-34.4	3.6	27.5	2.3	-4.2	-1.5	6.0
Return, Tax-Adjusted (%)	-36.9	22.1	-4.2	2.6	3.6	46.4	18.3	16.9	-4.6	20.9

PER SHARE DATA

	2002	2001	2000	1999	1998	1997	1996	1995	1994	1993
Dividends, Net Income ($)	0.00	0.00	0.00	0.00	0.00	0.00	0.00	0.06	0.00	0.00
Distrib'ns, Cap Gain ($)	0.00	0.00	0.00	0.00	0.73	2.99	2.66	5.67	2.15	0.70
Net Asset Value ($)	17.19	27.25	22.30	23.30	22.70	22.45	16.97	16.20	17.55	20.06
Expense Ratio (%)	na	1.03	1.05	1.07	0.77	0.99	0.99	0.98	0.95	0.91
Yield (%)	0.00	0.00	0.00	0.00	0.00	0.00	0.00	0.27	0.00	0.00
Portfolio Turnover (%)	na	65	63	38	54	82	82	110	71	57
Total Assets (Millions $)	451	837	641	815	1,394	561	192	181	150	163

PORTFOLIO (as of 11/30/02)

Portfolio Manager: Thomas Maguire - 1989

Investment Style

Large Cap	Growth
✔ Mid Cap	Value
✔ Small Cap	✔ Grth/Val

Portfolio

0.0%	cash	0.0%	corp bonds
95.5%	stocks	0.0%	gov't bonds
0.0%	preferred	0.0%	muni bonds
0.0%	conv't bds/wrnts	4.5%	other

SHAREHOLDER INFORMATION

Minimum Investment
Initial: $2,500 Subsequent: $100

Minimum IRA Investment
Initial: $1,000 Subsequent: $100

Maximum Fees
Load: none 12b-1: none
Other: none

Services
✔ IRA
✔ Keogh
✔ Telephone Exchange

Schwab Cap Tr Sm Cp Ix/I (SWSMX)

800-435-4000, 800-266-5623
www.schwab.com

Small-Cap Stock

PERFORMANCE — fund inception date: 12/3/93

	3yr Annual	5yr Annual	10yr Annual	Bull	Bear
Return (%)	-7.2	-0.9	na	64.0	-28.2
Differ From Category (+/-)	-1.5 av	-2.1 blw av	na	-31.4 av	-7.6 av

Standard Deviation	Category Risk Index	Beta
23.5%—abv av	0.99—av	0.85

	2002	2001	2000	1999	1998	1997	1996	1995	1994	1993
Return (%)	-22.4	-0.8	3.7	24.1	-3.5	25.6	15.4	27.6	-3.0	—
Differ From Category (+/-)	-1.9	-3.2	-0.5	-12.9	-4.2	3.2	-5.2	-2.7	-2.9	—
Return, Tax-Adjusted (%)	-22.7	-1.6	1.2	24.0	-4.6	25.4	15.2	27.4	-3.2	—

PER SHARE DATA

	2002	2001	2000	1999	1998	1997	1996	1995	1994	1993
Dividends, Net Income ($)	0.14	0.08	0.08	0.03	0.05	0.06	0.06	0.06	0.05	—
Distrib'ns, Cap Gain ($)	0.00	0.58	2.30	0.00	0.86	0.00	0.00	0.00	0.00	—
Net Asset Value ($)	13.43	17.50	18.36	20.14	16.25	17.87	14.27	12.41	9.77	—
Expense Ratio (%)	na	0.49	0.49	0.49	0.49	0.52	0.59	0.68	0.67	—
Yield (%)	1.04	0.44	0.38	0.14	0.29	0.33	0.42	0.48	0.51	—
Portfolio Turnover (%)	na	49	54	41	40	23	23	24	16	—
Total Assets (Millions $)	718	930	807	551	548	427	232	138	70	—

PORTFOLIO (as of 9/30/02)

Portfolio Manager: Geri Hom - 1995

Investment Style

Large Cap	Growth
Mid Cap	Value
✔ Small Cap	✔ Grth/Val

Portfolio

0.0%	cash	0.9%	corp bonds
98.6%	stocks	0.0%	gov't bonds
0.0%	preferred	0.0%	muni bonds
0.0%	conv't bds/wrnts	0.5%	other

SHAREHOLDER INFORMATION

Minimum Investment
Initial: $2,500 Subsequent: $500

Minimum IRA Investment
Initial: $500 Subsequent: $100

Maximum Fees
Load: 0.75% redemption 12b-1: none
Other: redemption fee applies for 6 months

Services
✔ IRA
✔ Keogh
✔ Telephone Exchange

Schwab Sm Cp MarketMstrs (SWOSX)

800-435-4000, 800-266-5623
www.schwab.com

Small-Cap Stock

PERFORMANCE — fund inception date: 9/16/97

	3yr Annual	5yr Annual	10yr Annual	Bull	Bear
Return (%)	-13.1	-1.8	na	75.2	-41.5
Differ From Category (+/-)	-7.4 blw av	-3.0 blw av	na	-20.2 av	-20.9 blw av

Standard Deviation	Category Risk Index	Beta
26.8%—high	1.12—av	1.02

	2002	2001	2000	1999	1998	1997	1996	1995	1994	1993
Return (%)	-25.9	0.0	-11.3	37.8	0.6	—	—	—	—	—
Differ From Category (+/-)	-5.4	-2.4	-15.5	0.8	-0.1	—	—	—	—	—
Return, Tax-Adjusted (%)	-25.9	-0.2	-14.1	35.9	0.4	—	—	—	—	—

PER SHARE DATA

	2002	2001	2000	1999	1998	1997	1996	1995	1994	1993
Dividends, Net Income ($)	0.00	0.02	0.55	0.45	0.04	—	—	—	—	—
Distrib'ns, Cap Gain ($)	0.00	0.02	0.71	0.00	0.00	—	—	—	—	—
Net Asset Value ($)	7.43	10.03	10.09	12.80	9.62	—	—	—	—	—
Expense Ratio (%)	na	0.50	0.50	0.50	0.50	—	—	—	—	—
Yield (%)	0.00	0.19	5.09	3.51	0.41	—	—	—	—	—
Portfolio Turnover (%)	na	172	91	145	166	—	—	—	—	—
Total Assets (Millions $)	82	126	145	149	137	—	—	—	—	—

PORTFOLIO (as of 9/30/02)

Portfolio Manager: Jeffrey Mortimer - 2000

Investment Style

Large Cap	✔ Growth
Mid Cap	Value
✔ Small Cap	Grth/Val

Portfolio

6.1%	cash	0.3%	corp bonds
92.1%	stocks	0.0%	gov't bonds
0.0%	preferred	0.0%	muni bonds
0.0%	conv't bds/wrnts	1.5%	other

SHAREHOLDER INFORMATION

Minimum Investment
Initial: $2,500 — Subsequent: $500

Minimum IRA Investment
Initial: $1,000 — Subsequent: $250

Maximum Fees
Load: none — 12b-1: none
Other: none

Services
✔ IRA
✔ Keogh
✔ Telephone Exchange

Sit Small Cap Growth

800-332-5580, 612-334-5888
www.sitfunds.com

(SSMGX)

Small-Cap Stock

PERFORMANCE — fund inception date: 7/1/94

	3yr Annual	5yr Annual	10yr Annual	Bull	Bear
Return (%)	-17.4	3.6	na	244.4	-57.7
Differ From Category (+/-)	-11.7 blw av	2.4 abv av	na	149.0 high	-37.1 low

Standard Deviation	Category Risk Index	Beta
35.2%—high	1.48—abv av	1.07

	2002	2001	2000	1999	1998	1997	1996	1995	1994	1993
Return (%)	-26.2	-28.1	6.2	108.6	1.9	7.6	14.9	52.1	—	—
Differ From Category (+/-)	-5.7	-30.5	2.0	71.6	1.2	-14.8	-5.7	21.8	—	—
Return, Tax-Adjusted (%)	-26.2	-28.1	5.9	108.6	-1.3	6.9	13.5	51.7	—	—

PER SHARE DATA

	2002	2001	2000	1999	1998	1997	1996	1995	1994	1993
Dividends, Net Income ($)	0.00	0.00	0.00	0.00	0.00	0.00	0.00	0.00	—	—
Distrib'ns, Cap Gain ($)	0.00	0.03	0.58	0.00	3.08	0.67	0.80	0.14	—	—
Net Asset Value ($)	18.60	25.21	35.16	33.61	16.11	19.13	18.43	16.74	—	—
Expense Ratio (%)	1.50	1.50	1.50	1.50	1.50	1.50	1.50	1.50	—	—
Yield (%)	0.00	0.00	0.00	0.00	0.00	0.00	0.00	0.00	—	—
Portfolio Turnover (%)	65	39	39	71	79	58	69	49	—	—
Total Assets (Millions $)	164	205	264	102	47	66	57	31	—	—

PORTFOLIO (as of 11/30/02)

Portfolio Manager: E Sit/P Mitchelson/ R Sit - 1994

Investment Style

Large Cap	✔ Growth
Mid Cap	Value
✔ Small Cap	Grth/Val

Portfolio

0.0%	cash	0.0%	corp bonds
98.8%	stocks	0.0%	gov't bonds
0.0%	preferred	0.0%	muni bonds
0.0%	conv't bds/wrnts	1.2%	other

SHAREHOLDER INFORMATION

Minimum Investment
Initial: $5,000 Subsequent: $100

Minimum IRA Investment
Initial: $2,000 Subsequent: $100

Maximum Fees
Load: none 12b-1: none
Other: none

Services
✔ IRA
✔ Keogh
✔ Telephone Exchange

Skyline:Special Equities

800-828-2759

(SKSEX)

Small-Cap Stock

PERFORMANCE **fund inception date: 4/23/87**

	3yr Annual	5yr Annual	10yr Annual	Bull	Bear
Return (%)	9.4	1.0	9.9	1.8	18.9
Differ From Category (+/-)	15.1 high	-0.2 av	1.2 abv av	-93.6 low	39.5 high

Standard Deviation	Category Risk Index	Beta
19.7%—abv av	0.83—blw av	0.79

	2002	2001	2000	1999	1998	1997	1996	1995	1994	1993
Return (%)	-7.2	13.9	24.2	-13.2	-7.1	35.4	30.3	13.8	-1.1	22.8
Differ From Category (+/-)	13.3	11.5	20.0	-50.2	-7.8	13.0	9.7	-16.5	-1.0	6.7
Return, Tax-Adjusted (%)	-7.2	13.9	24.2	-14.4	-7.4	32.2	24.3	12.0	-4.1	17.7

PER SHARE DATA

	2002	2001	2000	1999	1998	1997	1996	1995	1994	1993
Dividends, Net Income ($)	0.00	0.00	0.00	0.00	0.00	0.00	0.00	0.00	0.00	0.00
Distrib'ns, Cap Gain ($)	0.00	0.00	0.00	1.23	0.32	2.89	3.61	1.00	1.93	3.14
Net Asset Value ($)	20.86	22.50	19.75	15.90	19.78	21.66	18.16	16.79	15.64	17.83
Expense Ratio (%)	na	1.49	1.51	1.48	1.47	1.48	1.51	1.51	1.49	1.48
Yield (%)	0.00	0.00	0.00	0.00	0.00	0.00	0.00	0.00	0.00	0.00
Portfolio Turnover (%)	na	93	92	81	68	62	130	71	82	104
Total Assets (Millions $)	396	373	286	222	445	466	218	175	202	227

PORTFOLIO (as of 10/31/02)

Portfolio Manager: Team Managed - 1987

Investment Style

Large Cap — Growth
✔ Mid Cap — ✔ Value
✔ Small Cap — Grth/Val

Portfolio

2.5%	cash	0.0%	corp bonds
97.5%	stocks	0.0%	gov't bonds
0.0%	preferred	0.0%	muni bonds
0.0%	conv't bds/wrnts	0.0%	other

SHAREHOLDER INFORMATION

Minimum Investment
Initial: $1,000 Subsequent: $100

Minimum IRA Investment
Initial: $1,000 Subsequent: $100

Maximum Fees
Load: none 12b-1: none
Other: none

Services
✔ IRA
✔ Keogh
✔ Telephone Exchange

T Rowe Price Dvsfd Sm Cap (PRDSX)

800-638-5660, 410-345-2000
www.troweprice.com

Small-Cap Stock

PERFORMANCE — fund inception date: 6/30/97

	3yr Annual	5yr Annual	10yr Annual	Bull	Bear
Return (%)	-15.6	-4.5	na	94.4	-50.5
Differ From Category (+/-)	-9.9 blw av	-5.7 low	na	-1.0 av	-29.9 blw av

Standard Deviation	Category Risk Index	Beta
32.4%—high	1.36—abv av	1.28

	2002	2001	2000	1999	1998	1997	1996	1995	1994	1993
Return (%)	-27.4	-9.8	-8.2	27.6	3.5	—	—	—	—	—
Differ From Category (+/-)	-6.9	-12.2	-12.4	-9.4	2.8	—	—	—	—	—
Return, Tax-Adjusted (%)	-27.4	-9.8	-8.8	27.6	3.4	—	—	—	—	—

PER SHARE DATA

	2002	2001	2000	1999	1998	1997	1996	1995	1994	1993
Dividends, Net Income ($)	0.00	0.00	0.00	0.00	0.00	—	—	—	—	—
Distrib'ns, Cap Gain ($)	0.00	0.00	0.40	0.00	0.03	—	—	—	—	—
Net Asset Value ($)	8.20	11.31	12.54	14.11	11.05	—	—	—	—	—
Expense Ratio (%)	na	1.35	1.25	1.25	1.25	—	—	—	—	—
Yield (%)	0.00	0.00	0.00	0.00	0.00	—	—	—	—	—
Portfolio Turnover (%)	na	30	66	49	40	—	—	—	—	—
Total Assets (Millions $)	54	72	85	74	70	—	—	—	—	—

PORTFOLIO (as of 9/30/02)

Portfolio Manager: P Wojcik/Team
Managed - 1997

Investment Style

Large Cap	✔ Growth
Mid Cap	Value
✔ Small Cap	Grth/Val

Portfolio

0.0% cash	0.5% corp bonds
99.5% stocks	0.0% gov't bonds
0.0% preferred	0.0% muni bonds
0.0% conv't bds/wrnts	0.0% other

SHAREHOLDER INFORMATION

Minimum Investment
Initial: $2,500 Subsequent: $100

Minimum IRA Investment
Initial: $1,000 Subsequent: $50

Maximum Fees
Load: 1.00% redemption 12b-1: none
Other: redemption fee applies for 6 months

Services
✔ IRA
✔ Keogh
✔ Telephone Exchange

T Rowe Price New Horizons (PRNHX)

800-638-5660, 410-345-2000
www.troweprice.com

Small-Cap Stock

PERFORMANCE

fund inception date: 6/3/60

	3yr Annual	5yr Annual	10yr Annual	Bull	Bear
Return (%)	-11.2	-0.2	9.1	104.9	-43.8
Differ From Category (+/-)	-5.5 blw av	-1.4 blw av	0.4 av	9.5 abv av	-23.2 blw av

Standard Deviation	Category Risk Index	Beta
33.2%—high	1.39—abv av	1.23

	2002	2001	2000	1999	1998	1997	1996	1995	1994	1993
Return (%)	-26.6	-2.8	-1.8	32.5	6.2	9.7	17.0	55.4	0.3	22.0
Differ From Category (+/-)	-6.1	-5.2	-6.0	-4.5	5.5	-12.7	-3.6	25.1	0.4	5.9
Return, Tax-Adjusted (%)	-26.6	-3.3	-4.1	29.9	5.1	9.2	14.0	50.8	-2.2	17.1

PER SHARE DATA

	2002	2001	2000	1999	1998	1997	1996	1995	1994	1993
Dividends, Net Income ($)	0.00	0.00	0.00	0.00	0.00	0.00	0.00	0.00	0.00	0.00
Distrib'ns, Cap Gain ($)	0.00	0.56	3.14	3.02	1.27	0.58	2.19	2.41	1.43	2.70
Net Asset Value ($)	16.61	22.63	23.89	27.53	23.34	23.30	21.77	20.50	14.76	16.16
Expense Ratio (%)	na	0.91	0.88	0.90	0.89	0.88	0.90	0.92	0.93	0.93
Yield (%)	0.00	0.00	0.00	0.00	0.00	0.00	0.00	0.00	0.00	0.00
Portfolio Turnover (%)	na	27	47	45	41	45	41	58	44	49
Total Assets (Millions $)	3,616	5,582	6,122	6,021	5,228	5,103	4,363	2,854	1,648	1,627

PORTFOLIO (as of 9/30/02)

Portfolio Manager: J Laporte/Team
Managed - 1988

Investment Style

Large Cap	✔ Growth
Mid Cap	Value
✔ Small Cap	Grth/Val

Portfolio

1.2%	cash	1.3%	corp bonds
97.4%	stocks	0.0%	gov't bonds
0.0%	preferred	0.0%	muni bonds
0.0%	conv't bds/wrnts	0.1%	other

SHAREHOLDER INFORMATION

Minimum Investment
Initial: $2,500 Subsequent: $100

Minimum IRA Investment
Initial: $1,000 Subsequent: $50

Maximum Fees
Load: none 12b-1: none
Other: none

Services
✔ IRA
✔ Keogh
✔ Telephone Exchange

T Rowe Price Sm Cp Stk (OTCFX)

800-638-5660, 410-345-2000
www.troweprice.com

Small-Cap Stock

PERFORMANCE — fund inception date: 6/1/56

	3yr Annual	5yr Annual	10yr Annual	Bull	Bear
Return (%)	2.2	3.3	11.3	50.1	-8.8
Differ From Category (+/-)	7.9 abv av	2.1 abv av	2.6 abv av	-45.3 av	11.8 av

Standard Deviation	Category Risk Index	Beta
20.2%—abv av	0.84—blw av	0.75

	2002	2001	2000	1999	1998	1997	1996	1995	1994	1993
Return (%)	-14.2	6.8	16.4	14.6	-3.4	28.8	21.0	33.8	0.0	18.4
Differ From Category (+/-)	6.3	4.4	12.2	-22.4	-4.1	6.4	0.4	3.5	0.1	2.3
Return, Tax-Adjusted (%)	-14.4	6.6	14.0	13.6	-4.0	27.6	18.1	29.4	-2.9	15.3

PER SHARE DATA

	2002	2001	2000	1999	1998	1997	1996	1995	1994	1993
Dividends, Net Income ($)	0.01	0.10	0.14	0.08	0.10	0.04	0.09	0.12	0.03	0.00
Distrib'ns, Cap Gain ($)	0.23	0.05	2.46	0.89	0.50	1.01	1.58	2.01	1.56	1.58
Net Asset Value ($)	21.50	25.34	23.87	22.80	20.79	22.20	18.07	16.32	13.80	15.39
Expense Ratio (%)	na	0.98	0.82	0.96	1.01	1.02	1.07	1.13	1.11	1.20
Yield (%)	0.04	0.39	0.53	0.33	0.46	0.17	0.45	0.65	0.19	0.00
Portfolio Turnover (%)	na	17	32	42	26	22	31	72	41	40
Total Assets (Millions $)	3,407	3,158	2,255	1,740	1,152	816	415	278	196	204

PORTFOLIO (as of 9/30/02)

Portfolio Manager: G McCrickard/Team
Managed - 1992

Investment Style

Large Cap	Growth
Mid Cap	Value
✔ Small Cap	✔ Grth/Val

Portfolio

7.9%	cash	0.5%	corp bonds
91.6%	stocks	0.0%	gov't bonds
0.0%	preferred	0.0%	muni bonds
0.0%	conv't bds/wrnts	0.0%	other

SHAREHOLDER INFORMATION

Minimum Investment
Initial: $2,500 — Subsequent: $100

Minimum IRA Investment
Initial: $1,000 — Subsequent: $50

Maximum Fees
Load: none — 12b-1: none
Other: none

Services
✔ IRA
✔ Keogh
✔ Telephone Exchange

Third Avenue Small Cap (TASCX)

800-443-1021, 212-888-5222
www.mjwhitman.com

Small-Cap Stock

PERFORMANCE — fund inception date: 4/1/97

	3yr Annual	5yr Annual	10yr Annual	Bull	Bear
Return (%)	6.3	5.4	na	34.7	3.2
Differ From Category (+/-)	12.0 high	4.2 abv av	na	-60.7 blw av	23.8 abv av

Standard Deviation	Category Risk Index	Beta
18.3%—av	0.77—blw av	0.71

	2002	2001	2000	1999	1998	1997	1996	1995	1994	1993
Return (%)	-10.8	15.2	17.1	11.2	-2.7	—	—	—	—	—
Differ From Category (+/-)	9.7	12.8	12.9	-25.8	-3.4	—	—	—	—	—
Return, Tax-Adjusted (%)	-11.1	14.6	15.3	10.9	-3.0	—	—	—	—	—

PER SHARE DATA

	2002	2001	2000	1999	1998	1997	1996	1995	1994	1993
Dividends, Net Income ($)	0.13	0.11	0.21	0.09	0.08	—	—	—	—	—
Distrib'ns, Cap Gain ($)	0.00	0.17	0.68	0.00	0.00	—	—	—	—	—
Net Asset Value ($)	13.56	15.37	13.59	12.40	11.23	—	—	—	—	—
Expense Ratio (%)	na	1.23	1.30	1.28	1.28	—	—	—	—	—
Yield (%)	0.95	0.70	1.47	0.72	0.71	—	—	—	—	—
Portfolio Turnover (%)	na	18	19	10	6	—	—	—	—	—
Total Assets (Millions $)	414	332	151	127	144	—	—	—	—	—

PORTFOLIO (as of 11/30/02)

Portfolio Manager: Curtis Jensen - 2001

Investment Style

Large Cap	Growth
✔ Mid Cap	Value
✔ Small Cap	✔ Grth/Val

Portfolio

2.6% cash	4.1% corp bonds
87.9% stocks	5.4% gov't bonds
0.0% preferred	0.0% muni bonds
0.0% conv't bds/wrnts	0.0% other

SHAREHOLDER INFORMATION

Minimum Investment
Initial: $1,000 Subsequent: $1,000

Minimum IRA Investment
Initial: $500 Subsequent: $200

Maximum Fees
Load: 1.00% redemption 12b-1: none
Other: redemption fee applies for 12 months

Services
✔ IRA
Keogh
✔ Telephone Exchange

Third Avenue Value (TAVFX)

800-443-1021, 212-888-5222
www.mjwhitman.com

Small-Cap Stock

PERFORMANCE — fund inception date: 10/9/90

	3yr Annual	5yr Annual	10yr Annual	Bull	Bear
Return (%)	1.7	4.3	11.5	58.9	-16.3
Differ From Category (+/-)	7.4 abv av	3.1 abv av	2.8 abv av	-36.5 av	4.3 av

Standard Deviation	Category Risk Index	Beta
16.9%—av	0.71—low	0.69

	2002	2001	2000	1999	1998	1997	1996	1995	1994	1993
Return (%)	-15.1	2.8	20.7	12.8	3.9	23.8	21.9	31.7	-1.4	23.6
Differ From Category (+/-)	5.4	0.4	16.5	-24.2	3.2	1.4	1.3	1.4	-1.3	7.5
Return, Tax-Adjusted (%)	-15.5	2.0	14.4	12.5	3.4	23.0	20.7	30.5	-2.2	22.4

PER SHARE DATA

	2002	2001	2000	1999	1998	1997	1996	1995	1994	1993
Dividends, Net Income ($)	0.39	0.61	4.68	0.00	0.40	0.41	0.57	0.40	0.24	0.26
Distrib'ns, Cap Gain ($)	0.03	0.18	2.15	0.42	0.00	0.16	0.14	0.14	0.14	0.24
Net Asset Value ($)	30.47	36.43	36.22	35.99	32.29	31.46	25.86	21.80	16.97	17.62
Expense Ratio (%)	na	1.07	1.09	1.10	1.08	1.13	1.21	1.25	1.16	1.42
Yield (%)	1.27	1.66	12.19	0.00	1.23	1.29	2.19	1.82	1.40	1.45
Portfolio Turnover (%)	na	16	30	5	24	10	14	15	5	17
Total Assets (Millions $)	2,347	2,631	1,939	1,379	1,600	1,676	644	328	180	137

PORTFOLIO (as of 11/30/02)

Portfolio Manager: Martin Whitman - 1990

Investment Style

Large Cap	Growth
✔ Mid Cap	✔ Value
✔ Small Cap	Grth/Val

Portfolio

1.5%	cash	16.2%	corp bonds
77.1%	stocks	4.0%	gov't bonds
1.1%	pref/conv't pref	0.0%	muni bonds
0.0%	conv't bds/wrnts	0.0%	other

SHAREHOLDER INFORMATION

Minimum Investment
Initial: $1,000 Subsequent: $1,000

Minimum IRA Investment
Initial: $500 Subsequent: $200

Maximum Fees
Load: none 12b-1: none
Other: none

Services
✔ IRA
Keogh
✔ Telephone Exchange

Value Line Spcl Situation (VALSX)

800-223-0818, 212-907-1500
www.valueline.com

Small-Cap Stock

PERFORMANCE — fund inception date: 5/30/56

	3yr Annual	5yr Annual	10yr Annual	Bull	Bear
Return (%)	-13.3	6.4	11.0	152.0	-41.7
Differ From Category (+/-)	-7.6 blw av	5.2 high	2.3 abv av	56.6 high	-21.1 blw av

Standard Deviation	Category Risk Index	Beta
27.1%—high	1.14—abv av	0.78

	2002	2001	2000	1999	1998	1997	1996	1995	1994	1993
Return (%)	-15.1	-17.6	-6.7	61.6	29.8	32.0	7.2	28.9	1.0	12.9
Differ From Category (+/-)	5.4	-20.0	-10.9	24.6	29.1	9.6	-13.4	-1.4	1.1	-3.2
Return, Tax-Adjusted (%)	-15.1	-18.0	-8.0	60.0	28.4	27.5	0.1	21.0	-0.6	11.6

PER SHARE DATA

	2002	2001	2000	1999	1998	1997	1996	1995	1994	1993
Dividends, Net Income ($)	0.00	0.00	0.00	0.00	0.00	0.00	0.26	0.06	0.00	0.00
Distrib'ns, Cap Gain ($)	0.00	0.43	1.71	1.39	1.04	2.98	3.75	4.49	0.96	0.74
Net Asset Value ($)	16.08	18.95	23.55	27.09	17.70	14.48	13.34	16.24	16.15	16.95
Expense Ratio (%)	na	1.14	1.01	0.89	1.02	1.08	1.08	1.10	1.10	1.06
Yield (%)	0.00	0.00	0.00	0.00	0.00	0.00	1.52	0.28	0.00	0.00
Portfolio Turnover (%)	na	88	78	85	183	240	146	10	37	39
Total Assets (Millions $)	256	261	388	419	190	116	89	98	90	91

PORTFOLIO (as of 9/30/02)

Portfolio Manager: Team Managed - 1990

Investment Style

Large Cap	✔ Growth
Mid Cap	Value
✔ Small Cap	Grth/Val

Portfolio

12.4%	cash	0.0%	corp bonds
87.3%	stocks	0.0%	gov't bonds
0.3%	pref/conv't pref	0.0%	muni bonds
0.0%	conv't bds/wrnts	0.0%	other

SHAREHOLDER INFORMATION

Minimum Investment
Initial: $1,000 — Subsequent: $100

Minimum IRA Investment
Initial: $1,000 — Subsequent: $100

Maximum Fees
Load: none — 12b-1: 0.25%
Other: none

Services
✔ IRA
✔ Keogh
✔ Telephone Exchange

Vanguard Explorer (VEXPX)

800-662-7447, 610-436-5152
www.vanguard.com

Small-Cap Stock

PERFORMANCE — fund inception date: 12/11/67

	3yr Annual	5yr Annual	10yr Annual	Bull	Bear
Return (%)	-6.0	3.3	8.4	113.3	-32.7
Differ From Category (+/-)	-0.3 av	2.1 abv av	-0.3 av	17.9 abv av	-12.1 av

Standard Deviation	Category Risk Index	Beta
28.0%—high	1.17—abv av	1.00

	2002	2001	2000	1999	1998	1997	1996	1995	1994	1993
Return (%)	-24.5	0.5	9.2	37.2	3.5	14.5	13.3	26.5	0.5	15.4
Differ From Category (+/-)	-4.0	-1.9	5.0	0.2	2.8	-7.9	-7.3	-3.8	0.6	-0.7
Return, Tax-Adjusted (%)	-24.5	0.4	5.0	34.2	3.2	12.1	11.7	23.7	-1.1	12.0

PER SHARE DATA

	2002	2001	2000	1999	1998	1997	1996	1995	1994	1993
Dividends, Net Income ($)	0.00	0.10	0.25	0.23	0.20	0.25	0.27	0.24	0.17	0.14
Distrib'ns, Cap Gain ($)	0.00	0.00	13.91	8.03	0.30	5.85	2.49	4.00	2.26	5.17
Net Asset Value ($)	45.49	60.31	60.09	68.62	56.71	55.30	53.83	49.95	42.86	45.11
Expense Ratio (%)	na	0.72	0.71	0.74	0.62	0.62	0.63	0.68	0.70	0.73
Yield (%)	0.00	0.16	0.33	0.30	0.35	0.40	0.47	0.44	0.37	0.27
Portfolio Turnover (%)	na	77	123	79	72	84	51	60	82	51
Total Assets (Millions $)	3,764	4,648	4,487	3,136	2,463	2,541	2,263	1,647	1,121	847

PORTFOLIO (as of 9/30/02)

Portfolio Manager: Team Managed - 1994

Investment Style

Large Cap	✔ Growth
Mid Cap	Value
✔ Small Cap	Grth/Val

Portfolio

4.6%	cash	0.0%	corp bonds
95.5%	stocks	0.0%	gov't bonds
0.0%	preferred	0.0%	muni bonds
0.0%	conv't bds/wrnts	0.0%	other

SHAREHOLDER INFORMATION

Minimum Investment
Initial: $3,000 — Subsequent: $100

Minimum IRA Investment
Initial: $1,000 — Subsequent: $100

Maximum Fees
Load: none — 12b-1: none
Other: none

Services
✔ IRA
✔ Keogh
✔ Telephone Exchange

Vanguard Ext Mkt Idx/Inv (VEXMX)

800-662-7447, 610-436-5152
www.vanguard.com

Small-Cap Stock

PERFORMANCE — fund inception date: 12/21/87

	3yr Annual	5yr Annual	10yr Annual	Bull	Bear
Return (%)	-14.3	-1.4	7.6	95.4	-45.8
Differ From Category (+/-)	-8.6 blw av	-2.6 blw av	-1.1 blw av	0.0 abv av	-25.2 blw av

Standard Deviation	Category Risk Index	Beta
27.2%—high	1.14—abv av	1.00

	2002	2001	2000	1999	1998	1997	1996	1995	1994	1993
Return (%)	-18.0	-9.1	-15.5	36.2	8.3	26.7	17.6	33.7	-1.7	14.4
Differ From Category (+/-)	2.5	-11.5	-19.7	-0.8	7.6	4.3	-3.0	3.4	-1.6	-1.7
Return, Tax-Adjusted (%)	-18.3	-10.0	-18.2	33.4	6.4	24.7	15.0	32.5	-2.7	13.6

PER SHARE DATA

	2002	2001	2000	1999	1998	1997	1996	1995	1994	1993
Dividends, Net Income ($)	0.18	0.21	0.26	0.31	0.37	0.36	0.34	0.30	0.28	0.23
Distrib'ns, Cap Gain ($)	0.00	0.81	4.43	3.64	2.17	1.91	1.72	0.40	0.29	0.20
Net Asset Value ($)	18.74	23.09	26.62	37.07	30.62	30.75	26.19	24.07	18.52	19.43
Expense Ratio (%)	na	0.25	0.25	0.25	0.23	0.23	0.25	0.20	0.20	0.20
Yield (%)	0.96	0.87	0.83	0.76	1.12	1.10	1.21	1.22	1.48	1.17
Portfolio Turnover (%)	na	20	33	26	27	15	22	14	19	13
Total Assets (Millions $)	2,686	3,114	3,880	4,221	2,938	2,722	2,098	1,523	967	927

PORTFOLIO (as of 9/30/02)

Portfolio Manager: George Sauter - 1987

Investment Style

Large Cap	✔ Growth
✔ Mid Cap	Value
✔ Small Cap	Grth/Val

Portfolio

0.0%	cash	0.0%	corp bonds
100.0%	stocks	0.0%	gov't bonds
0.0%	preferred	0.0%	muni bonds
0.0%	conv't bds/wrnts	0.0%	other

SHAREHOLDER INFORMATION

Minimum Investment
Initial: $3,000 — Subsequent: $100

Minimum IRA Investment
Initial: $1,000 — Subsequent: $100

Maximum Fees
Load: none — 12b-1: none
Other: none

Services
✔ IRA
✔ Keogh
Telephone Exchange

Vanguard Sm Cp Idx/Inv (NAESX)

800-662-7447, 610-436-5152
www.vanguard.com

Small-Cap Stock

PERFORMANCE — fund inception date: 10/3/60

	3yr Annual	5yr Annual	10yr Annual	Bull	Bear
Return (%)	-7.0	-0.7	7.9	64.9	-29.2
Differ From Category (+/-)	-1.3 av	-1.9 blw av	-0.8 av	-30.5 av	-8.6 av

Standard Deviation	Category Risk Index	Beta
24.8%—high	1.04—av	0.82

	2002	2001	2000	1999	1998	1997	1996	1995	1994	1993
Return (%)	-20.0	3.1	-2.6	23.1	-2.6	24.5	18.1	28.7	-0.5	18.7
Differ From Category (+/-)	0.5	0.7	-6.8	-13.9	-3.3	2.1	-2.5	-1.6	-0.4	2.6
Return, Tax-Adjusted (%)	-20.4	2.6	-5.6	20.6	-4.4	22.9	15.4	27.3	-1.7	16.6

PER SHARE DATA

	2002	2001	2000	1999	1998	1997	1996	1995	1994	1993
Dividends, Net Income ($)	0.19	0.22	0.26	0.26	0.30	0.27	0.27	0.23	0.22	0.18
Distrib'ns, Cap Gain ($)	0.00	0.00	3.02	2.08	1.55	1.11	1.44	0.45	0.37	0.82
Net Asset Value ($)	15.66	19.82	19.44	23.60	21.20	23.75	20.23	18.61	14.99	15.67
Expense Ratio (%)	na	0.27	0.27	0.25	0.24	0.23	0.25	0.25	0.17	0.18
Yield (%)	1.21	1.10	1.15	1.01	1.31	1.08	1.24	1.20	1.43	1.09
Portfolio Turnover (%)	na	39	49	42	35	29	28	28	25	26
Total Assets (Millions $)	3,141	3,545	3,576	3,553	2,768	2,652	1,713	971	606	488

PORTFOLIO (as of 9/30/02)

Portfolio Manager: Team Managed - 1989

Investment Style

Large Cap	Growth
Mid Cap	Value
✔ Small Cap	✔ Grth/Val

Portfolio

0.0%	cash	0.0%	corp bonds
100.0%	stocks	0.0%	gov't bonds
0.0%	preferred	0.0%	muni bonds
0.0%	conv't bds/wrnts	0.0%	other

SHAREHOLDER INFORMATION

Minimum Investment
Initial: $3,000 — Subsequent: $100

Minimum IRA Investment
Initial: $1,000 — Subsequent: $100

Maximum Fees
Load: none — 12b-1: none
Other: none

Services
✔ IRA
✔ Keogh
Telephone Exchange

Victory:Small Co Opp/G (GOGFX)

800-539-3863, 216-689-4655
www.victoryfunds.com

Small-Cap Stock

PERFORMANCE — fund inception date: 8/16/83

	3yr Annual	5yr Annual	10yr Annual	Bull	Bear
Return (%)	1.1	-1.0	7.4	14.2	-3.0
Differ From Category (+/-)	6.8 abv av	-2.2 blw av	-1.3 blw av	-81.2 low	17.6 abv av

Standard Deviation	Category Risk Index	Beta
18.5%—av	0.78—blw av	0.74

	2002	2001	2000	1999	1998	1997	1996	1995	1994	1993
Return (%)	-5.5	-7.2	17.9	-1.0	-7.1	31.1	19.4	26.7	-2.1	11.0
Differ From Category (+/-)	15.0	-9.6	13.7	-38.0	-7.8	8.7	-1.2	-3.6	-2.0	-5.1
Return, Tax-Adjusted (%)	-5.5	-8.7	17.6	-1.0	-8.1	27.6	16.4	25.4	-3.1	9.6

PER SHARE DATA

	2002	2001	2000	1999	1998	1997	1996	1995	1994	1993
Dividends, Net Income ($)	0.00	0.00	0.00	0.00	0.14	0.27	0.16	0.18	0.25	0.07
Distrib'ns, Cap Gain ($)	0.00	2.04	0.37	0.00	1.03	3.56	2.04	0.57	0.31	0.80
Net Asset Value ($)	21.28	22.53	26.61	22.90	23.15	26.10	23.07	21.23	17.43	18.38
Expense Ratio (%)	na	1.31	1.30	1.29	1.31	1.36	1.41	1.37	1.38	1.44
Yield (%)	0.00	0.00	0.00	0.00	0.57	0.91	0.63	0.82	1.40	0.36
Portfolio Turnover (%)	na	58	28	16	42	34	23	31	40	39
Total Assets (Millions $)	73	85	99	108	151	157	115	97	82	83

PORTFOLIO (as of 9/30/02)

Portfolio Manager: Team Managed - 1998

Investment Style

Large Cap	Growth
✔ Mid Cap	✔ Value
✔ Small Cap	Grth/Val

Portfolio

7.2%	cash	0.0%	corp bonds
92.8%	stocks	0.0%	gov't bonds
0.0%	preferred	0.0%	muni bonds
0.0%	conv't bds/wrnts	0.0%	other

SHAREHOLDER INFORMATION

Minimum Investment
Initial: $500 Subsequent: $25

Minimum IRA Investment
Initial: $100 Subsequent: $25

Maximum Fees
Load: none 12b-1: 0.50%
Other: none

Services
✔ IRA
✔ Keogh
✔ Telephone Exchange

WPG Tudor
(TUDRX)

800-223-3332, 212-908-9500
www.wpginvest.com

Small-Cap Stock

PERFORMANCE — fund inception date: 3/14/69

	3yr Annual	5yr Annual	10yr Annual	Bull	Bear
Return (%)	-15.7	-5.3	3.7	107.0	-50.6
Differ From Category (+/-)	-10.0 blw av	-6.5 low	-5.0 low	11.6 abv av	-30.0 blw av

Standard Deviation	Category Risk Index	Beta
34.1%—high	1.43—abv av	1.13

	2002	2001	2000	1999	1998	1997	1996	1995	1994	1993
Return (%)	-26.1	-14.7	-5.1	63.2	-22.0	11.1	18.8	41.1	-9.8	13.3
Differ From Category (+/-)	-5.6	-17.1	-9.3	26.2	-22.7	-11.3	-1.8	10.8	-9.7	-2.8
Return, Tax-Adjusted (%)	-26.1	-15.2	-7.7	59.8	-23.2	7.7	11.1	39.6	-11.9	8.0

PER SHARE DATA

	2002	2001	2000	1999	1998	1997	1996	1995	1994	1993
Dividends, Net Income ($)	0.00	0.00	0.00	0.00	0.00	0.00	0.00	0.00	0.00	0.00
Distrib'ns, Cap Gain ($)	0.00	0.47	3.00	2.71	1.27	3.90	7.24	1.01	1.78	4.73
Net Asset Value ($)	11.24	15.21	18.41	22.91	15.74	21.90	23.28	26.24	19.34	23.40
Expense Ratio (%)	na	1.38	1.28	1.37	1.28	1.24	1.25	1.34	1.28	1.25
Yield (%)	0.00	0.00	0.00	0.00	0.00	0.00	0.00	0.00	0.00	0.00
Portfolio Turnover (%)	na	128	84	139	144	106	105	139	109	118
Total Assets (Millions $)	51	71	94	103	86	170	182	167	143	242

PORTFOLIO (as of 11/30/02)

Portfolio Manager: Walter Prendergast - 2000

Investment Style

Large Cap	✔ Growth
Mid Cap	Value
✔ Small Cap	Grth/Val

Portfolio

4.0%	cash	1.8%	corp bonds
94.1%	stocks	0.0%	gov't bonds
0.0%	preferred	0.0%	muni bonds
0.0%	conv't bds/wrnts	0.0%	other

SHAREHOLDER INFORMATION

Minimum Investment
Initial: $2,500 Subsequent: $100

Minimum IRA Investment
Initial: $250 Subsequent: $100

Maximum Fees
Load: none 12b-1: none
Other: none

Services
✔ IRA
✔ Keogh
✔ Telephone Exchange

SECTOR STOCK FUNDS

Energy/Resources Sector Stock Funds
Category Performance Ranked by 2002 Returns

Category	Fund (Ticker)	Annual Return (%) 2002	3yr	5yr	10yr	Category Risk	Total Risk
Sec-E	Vanguard Energy (VGENX)	-0.6	9.7	4.9	11.7	abv av	abv av
Sec-E	Fidelity Sel Energy Serv (FSESX)	-0.6	5.6	0.4	14.7	high	high
Sec-E	T Rowe Price New Era (PRNEX)	-6.3	2.5	3.3	9.0	blw av	abv av
Sec-E	Fidelity Sel Natural Gas (FSNGX)	-9.5	6.1	5.7	na	abv av	high
Sec-E	Fidelity Sel Energy (FSENX)	-11.4	0.8	3.2	9.5	av	abv av
Energy/Resources Sector Average		**-4.7**	**5.1**	**3.2**	**10.5**	**—**	**abv av**

Note: AAII members who would like performance figures for no-load and low-load mutual funds they own that do not appear in this Guide can access this information on our Web site at www.aaii.com.

Fidelity Sel Energy (FSENX)

800-544-8544, 800-522-7297
www.fidelity.com

Energy/Resources Sector

PERFORMANCE — fund inception date: 7/14/81

	3yr Annual	5yr Annual	10yr Annual	Bull	Bear
Return (%)	0.8	3.2	9.5	71.6	-15.9
Differ From Category (+/-)	-4.3 blw av	0.0 av	-1.0 av	7.3 abv av	-12.8 blw av

Standard Deviation	Category Risk Index	Beta
21.9%—abv av	1.00—av	0.71

	2002	2001	2000	1999	1998	1997	1996	1995	1994	1993
Return (%)	-11.4	-11.9	31.8	34.2	-14.7	10.2	32.4	21.3	0.4	19.1
Differ From Category (+/-)	-6.7	-1.1	-7.6	5.2	4.2	-1.8	0.2	-4.0	3.1	0.0
Return, Tax-Adjusted (%)	-11.6	-12.5	29.0	33.7	-15.1	6.5	30.2	20.4	-0.7	17.9

PER SHARE DATA

	2002	2001	2000	1999	1998	1997	1996	1995	1994	1993
Dividends, Net Income ($)	0.14	0.04	0.14	0.09	0.01	0.09	0.13	0.11	0.11	0.03
Distrib'ns, Cap Gain ($)	0.00	0.69	2.97	0.29	0.41	4.09	1.31	0.36	0.51	0.57
Net Asset Value ($)	20.52	23.33	27.29	23.35	17.70	21.15	23.21	18.77	15.87	16.43
Expense Ratio (%)	1.12	1.12	1.25	1.42	1.58	1.57	1.63	1.85	1.66	1.71
Yield (%)	0.68	0.16	0.46	0.38	0.05	0.35	0.53	0.57	0.67	0.17
Portfolio Turnover (%)	119	117	124	138	115	87	97	106	157	72
Total Assets (Millions $)	197	226	272	193	122	158	239	131	96	82

PORTFOLIO (as of 8/31/02)

Portfolio Manager: John Porter - 2002

Investment Style

Large Cap	Growth
Mid Cap	Value
Small Cap	Grth/Val

Portfolio

0.0% cash	0.0% corp bonds
89.2% stocks	0.0% gov't bonds
0.0% preferred	0.0% muni bonds
0.0% conv't bds/wrnts	10.8% other

SHAREHOLDER INFORMATION

Minimum Investment
Initial: $2,500 — Subsequent: $250

Minimum IRA Investment
Initial: $500 — Subsequent: $250

Maximum Fees
Load: 3.00% front — 12b-1: none
Other: 0.75% redemption fee for 1 month

Services
✔ IRA
✔ Keogh
✔ Telephone Exchange

Fidelity Sel Energy Serv (FSESX)

800-544-8544, 800-522-7297
www.fidelity.com

Energy/Resources Sector

PERFORMANCE

fund inception date: 12/16/85

	3yr Annual	5yr Annual	10yr Annual	Bull	Bear
Return (%)	5.6	0.4	14.7	153.5	-23.0
Differ From Category (+/-)	0.5 av	-2.8 low	4.2 high	89.2 high	-19.9 low

Standard Deviation	Category Risk Index	Beta
39.7%—high	1.81—high	1.13

	2002	2001	2000	1999	1998	1997	1996	1995	1994	1993
Return (%)	-0.6	-21.0	50.3	72.1	-49.7	51.8	49.3	40.8	0.4	20.9
Differ From Category (+/-)	4.1	-10.2	10.9	43.1	-30.8	39.8	17.1	15.5	3.1	1.8
Return, Tax-Adjusted (%)	-0.6	-21.0	50.3	72.1	-50.8	50.1	47.8	39.5	-0.8	20.7

PER SHARE DATA

	2002	2001	2000	1999	1998	1997	1996	1995	1994	1993
Dividends, Net Income ($)	0.00	0.00	0.00	0.00	0.00	0.00	0.01	0.04	0.02	0.05
Distrib'ns, Cap Gain ($)	0.00	0.00	0.00	0.00	1.71	1.85	0.78	0.48	0.48	0.00
Net Asset Value ($)	29.38	29.58	37.45	24.91	14.47	30.45	21.73	15.16	11.14	11.61
Expense Ratio (%)	1.07	1.04	1.23	1.35	1.25	1.47	1.58	1.79	1.65	1.76
Yield (%)	0.00	0.00	0.00	0.00	0.00	0.00	0.04	0.25	0.17	0.43
Portfolio Turnover (%)	90	78	69	75	78	167	223	209	137	236
Total Assets (Millions $)	473	515	803	618	394	1,133	562	254	50	40

PORTFOLIO (as of 8/31/02)

Portfolio Manager: Charles Hebard - 2002

Investment Style

Large Cap — Growth
Mid Cap — Value
Small Cap — Grth/Val

Portfolio

0.0% cash	0.0% corp bonds
93.2% stocks	0.0% gov't bonds
0.0% preferred	0.0% muni bonds
0.0% conv't bds/wrnts	6.8% other

SHAREHOLDER INFORMATION

Minimum Investment
Initial: $2,500 — Subsequent: $250

Minimum IRA Investment
Initial: $500 — Subsequent: $250

Maximum Fees
Load: 3.00% front — 12b-1: none
Other: 0.75% redemption fee for 1 month

Services
✔ IRA
Keogh
✔ Telephone Exchange

Fidelity Sel Natural Gas (FSNGX)

800-544-8544, 800-522-7297
www.fidelity.com

Energy/Resources Sector

PERFORMANCE — fund inception date: 4/21/93

	3yr Annual	5yr Annual	10yr Annual	Bull	Bear
Return (%)	6.1	5.7	na	79.1	-6.4
Differ From Category (+/-)	1.0 abv av	2.5 high	na	14.8 abv av	-3.3 av

Standard Deviation	Category Risk Index	Beta
25.9%—high	1.18—abv av	0.59

	2002	2001	2000	1999	1998	1997	1996	1995	1994	1993
Return (%)	-9.5	-22.7	71.2	26.1	-12.3	-8.0	34.3	30.3	-6.8	—
Differ From Category (+/-)	-4.8	-11.9	31.8	-2.9	6.6	-20.0	2.1	5.0	-4.1	—
Return, Tax-Adjusted (%)	-9.7	-22.9	70.7	25.8	-12.6	-8.4	33.5	30.1	-6.9	—

PER SHARE DATA

	2002	2001	2000	1999	1998	1997	1996	1995	1994	1993
Dividends, Net Income ($)	0.10	0.03	0.04	0.09	0.10	0.00	0.01	0.05	0.02	—
Distrib'ns, Cap Gain ($)	0.00	0.13	0.30	0.00	0.00	0.33	0.29	0.00	0.00	—
Net Asset Value ($)	16.77	18.65	24.31	14.43	11.52	13.27	14.84	11.29	8.70	—
Expense Ratio (%)	1.13	1.10	1.39	1.52	1.82	1.70	1.67	1.66	1.93	—
Yield (%)	0.59	0.15	0.16	0.62	0.86	0.00	0.06	0.44	0.22	—
Portfolio Turnover (%)	68	94	85	107	118	283	79	177	44	—
Total Assets (Millions $)	153	197	446	52	43	69	153	85	79	—

PORTFOLIO (as of 8/31/02)

Portfolio Manager: Naved Khan - 2002

Investment Style

Large Cap	Growth
Mid Cap	Value
Small Cap	Grth/Val

Portfolio

0.0%	cash	0.0%	corp bonds
88.5%	stocks	0.0%	gov't bonds
0.9%	pref/conv't pref	0.0%	muni bonds
0.0%	conv't bds/wrnts	10.6%	other

SHAREHOLDER INFORMATION

Minimum Investment
Initial: $2,500 — Subsequent: $250

Minimum IRA Investment
Initial: $500 — Subsequent: $250

Maximum Fees
Load: 3.00% front — 12b-1: none
Other: 0.75% redemption fee for 1 month

Services
✔ IRA
Keogh
✔ Telephone Exchange

T Rowe Price New Era (PRNEX)

800-638-5660, 410-345-2000
www.troweprice.com

Energy/Resources Sector

PERFORMANCE — fund inception date: 1/20/69

	3yr Annual	5yr Annual	10yr Annual	Bull	Bear
Return (%)	2.5	3.3	9.0	44.8	-1.5
Differ From Category (+/-)	-2.6 av	0.1 av	-1.5 blw av	-19.5 blw av	1.6 abv av

Standard Deviation	Category Risk Index	Beta
20.2%—abv av	0.92—blw av	0.67

	2002	2001	2000	1999	1998	1997	1996	1995	1994	1993
Return (%)	-6.3	-4.3	20.3	21.2	-9.8	10.9	24.2	20.7	5.1	15.3
Differ From Category (+/-)	-1.6	6.5	-19.1	-7.8	9.1	-1.1	-8.0	-4.6	7.8	-3.8
Return, Tax-Adjusted (%)	-6.6	-5.3	18.4	18.8	-12.9	8.4	21.4	18.1	3.2	13.0

PER SHARE DATA

	2002	2001	2000	1999	1998	1997	1996	1995	1994	1993
Dividends, Net Income ($)	0.20	0.27	0.29	0.30	0.40	0.37	0.38	0.48	0.38	0.38
Distrib'ns, Cap Gain ($)	0.00	0.68	1.51	1.82	3.17	2.54	1.71	1.20	0.87	1.03
Net Asset Value ($)	20.63	22.24	24.30	21.80	19.78	25.95	26.06	22.65	20.15	20.35
Expense Ratio (%)	na	0.72	0.72	0.74	0.75	0.74	0.76	0.79	0.80	0.80
Yield (%)	0.96	1.17	1.12	1.27	1.74	1.29	1.36	2.01	1.80	1.77
Portfolio Turnover (%)	na	18	28	33	23	27	28	21	24	24
Total Assets (Millions $)	984	1,070	1,194	1,082	998	1,492	1,467	1,090	979	752

PORTFOLIO (as of 9/30/02)

Portfolio Manager: C Ober/Team
Managed - 1997

Investment Style

Large Cap	Growth
Mid Cap	Value
Small Cap	Grth/Val

Portfolio

2.2%	cash	0.5%	corp bonds
97.2%	stocks	0.0%	gov't bonds
0.0%	preferred	0.0%	muni bonds
0.1%	conv't bds/wrnts	0.0%	other

SHAREHOLDER INFORMATION

Minimum Investment
Initial: $2,500 — Subsequent: $100

Minimum IRA Investment
Initial: $1,000 — Subsequent: $50

Maximum Fees
Load: none — 12b-1: none
Other: none

Services
- ✔ IRA
- ✔ Keogh
- ✔ Telephone Exchange

Vanguard Energy (VGENX)

800-662-7447, 610-436-5152
www.vanguard.com

Energy/Resources Sector

PERFORMANCE

fund inception date: 5/23/84

	3yr Annual	5yr Annual	10yr Annual	Bull	Bear
Return (%)	9.7	4.9	11.7	47.4	9.2
Differ From Category (+/-)	4.6 high	1.7 abv av	1.2 high	-16.9 av	12.3 high

Standard Deviation	Category Risk Index	Beta
22.8%—abv av	1.04—abv av	0.64

	2002	2001	2000	1999	1998	1997	1996	1995	1994	1993
Return (%)	-0.6	-2.5	36.4	20.9	-20.5	14.8	33.9	25.3	-1.6	26.4
Differ From Category (+/-)	4.1	8.3	-3.0	-8.1	-1.6	2.8	1.7	0.0	1.1	7.3
Return, Tax-Adjusted (%)	-2.4	-4.2	34.5	20.1	-21.4	13.1	32.7	23.9	-2.8	22.6

PER SHARE DATA

	2002	2001	2000	1999	1998	1997	1996	1995	1994	1993
Dividends, Net Income ($)	0.36	0.40	0.36	0.35	0.35	0.32	0.24	0.28	0.24	0.29
Distrib'ns, Cap Gain ($)	1.59	1.53	1.38	0.00	0.42	1.33	0.40	0.30	0.29	1.38
Net Asset Value ($)	23.20	25.29	28.07	21.92	18.42	24.14	22.54	17.31	14.29	15.06
Expense Ratio (%)	0.39	0.41	0.48	0.41	0.38	0.39	0.51	0.30	0.17	0.21
Yield (%)	1.45	1.49	1.22	1.59	1.85	1.25	1.04	1.59	1.64	1.76
Portfolio Turnover (%)	28	24	18	22	19	15	21	13	41	37
Total Assets (Millions $)	1,268	1,281	1,351	1,018	819	1,181	847	506	445	269

PORTFOLIO (as of 9/30/02)

Portfolio Manager: Ernst Von Metzsch - 1984

Investment Style

Large Cap	Growth
Mid Cap	Value
Small Cap	Grth/Val

Portfolio

4.9%	cash	0.0%	corp bonds
95.1%	stocks	0.0%	gov't bonds
0.0%	preferred	0.0%	muni bonds
0.0%	conv't bds/wrnts	0.0%	other

SHAREHOLDER INFORMATION

Minimum Investment
Initial: $3,000 Subsequent: $100

Minimum IRA Investment
Initial: $1,000 Subsequent: $100

Maximum Fees
Load: 1.00% redemption 12b-1: none
Other: redemption fee applies for 12 months

Services
✔ IRA
✔ Keogh
✔ Telephone Exchange

Financial/Banking Sector Stock Funds
Category Performance Ranked by 2002 Returns

Category	Fund (Ticker)	Annual Return (%) 2002	3yr	5yr	10yr	Category Risk	Total Risk
Sec-F	Fidelity Sel Banking (FSRBX)	-7.7	3.2	2.0	13.5	av	abv av
Sec-F	T Rowe Price Fincl Svc (PRISX)	-10.0	5.9	6.2	na	blw av	abv av
Sec-F	Fidelity Sel Financl Serv (FIDSX)	-11.3	1.1	3.7	14.1	low	abv av
Sec-F	Century Shares Trust (CENSX)	-12.5	5.4	1.8	9.5	high	high
Sec-F	Fidelity Sel Brokerage (FSLBX)	-17.2	-1.2	5.8	16.4	high	high
Financial/Banking Sector Average		**-10.0**	**4.6**	**4.0**	**13.7**	**—**	**abv av**

Note: AAII members who would like performance figures for no-load and low-load mutual funds they own that do not appear in this Guide can access this information on our Web site at www.aaii.com.

Century Shares Trust (CENSX)

800-321-1928, 617-482-3060
www.centuryfunds.com

Financial/Banking Sector

PERFORMANCE — fund inception date: 3/21/28

	3yr Annual	5yr Annual	10yr Annual	Bull	Bear
Return (%)	5.4	1.8	9.5	5.5	12.6
Differ From Category (+/-)	0.8 abv av	-2.2 blw av	-4.2 low	-18.3 blw av	4.5 abv av

Standard Deviation	Category Risk Index	Beta
24.8%—high	1.14—high	0.63

	2002	2001	2000	1999	1998	1997	1996	1995	1994	1993
Return (%)	-12.5	-2.5	37.4	-12.3	6.9	50.1	17.0	35.2	-3.8	-0.3
Differ From Category (+/-)	-2.5	2.6	2.5	-11.6	-1.7	3.4	-13.7	-4.9	0.1	-19.0
Return, Tax-Adjusted (%)	-14.3	-4.3	34.8	-14.6	5.3	48.4	15.2	33.3	-5.6	-2.2

PER SHARE DATA

	2002	2001	2000	1999	1998	1997	1996	1995	1994	1993
Dividends, Net Income ($)	0.10	0.17	0.38	0.41	0.40	0.38	0.46	0.41	0.45	0.45
Distrib'ns, Cap Gain ($)	3.29	3.60	3.75	4.30	2.72	1.90	1.11	0.92	0.88	1.10
Net Asset Value ($)	29.93	38.12	42.97	34.32	44.66	44.66	31.30	28.07	21.77	24.04
Expense Ratio (%)	na	1.05	0.83	0.82	0.78	0.82	0.82	1.01	1.01	0.82
Yield (%)	0.30	0.40	0.81	1.06	0.84	0.81	1.41	1.41	1.98	1.78
Portfolio Turnover (%)	na	17	17	11	6	6	3	3	2	19
Total Assets (Millions $)	293	322	418	309	415	413	270	267	206	233

PORTFOLIO (as of 11/30/02)

Portfolio Manager: Allan Fulkerson/ A Thorndike - 1999

Investment Style

Large Cap	Growth
Mid Cap	Value
Small Cap	Grth/Val

Portfolio

0.0%	cash	0.0%	corp bonds
100.0%	stocks	0.0%	gov't bonds
0.0%	preferred	0.0%	muni bonds
0.0%	conv't bds/wrnts	0.0%	other

SHAREHOLDER INFORMATION

Minimum Investment
Initial: $1,000 Subsequent: $50

Minimum IRA Investment
Initial: $1,000 Subsequent: $50

Maximum Fees
Load: none 12b-1: none
Other: none

Services
✔ IRA
Keogh
✔ Telephone Exchange

Fidelity Sel Banking
(FSRBX)

800-544-8544, 800-522-7297
www.fidelity.com

Financial/Banking Sector

PERFORMANCE

fund inception date: 6/30/86

	3yr Annual	5yr Annual	10yr Annual	Bull	Bear
Return (%)	3.2	2.0	13.5	11.8	12.1
Differ From Category (+/-)	-1.4 av	-2.0 av	-0.2 av	-12.0 blw av	4.0 abv av

Standard Deviation	Category Risk Index	Beta
21.8%—abv av	1.00—av	0.70

	2002	2001	2000	1999	1998	1997	1996	1995	1994	1993
Return (%)	-7.7	0.4	18.7	-10.1	11.8	45.5	35.8	46.7	0.2	11.1
Differ From Category (+/-)	2.3	5.5	-16.2	-9.4	3.2	-1.2	5.1	6.6	4.1	-7.6
Return, Tax-Adjusted (%)	-8.1	-0.2	16.4	-13.9	10.2	44.3	33.6	44.9	-2.0	5.1

PER SHARE DATA

	2002	2001	2000	1999	1998	1997	1996	1995	1994	1993
Dividends, Net Income ($)	0.34	0.47	0.60	0.36	0.28	0.28	0.27	0.25	0.26	0.15
Distrib'ns, Cap Gain ($)	0.00	0.02	2.47	7.44	2.66	1.23	1.40	0.72	1.01	3.92
Net Asset Value ($)	30.31	33.21	33.56	31.50	42.87	41.05	29.29	22.94	16.28	17.49
Expense Ratio (%)	1.09	1.18	1.19	1.16	1.25	1.46	1.40	1.56	1.60	1.49
Yield (%)	1.12	1.41	1.66	0.92	0.61	0.66	0.87	1.05	1.50	0.70
Portfolio Turnover (%)	41	63	94	22	25	43	103	106	74	63
Total Assets (Millions $)	396	492	495	514	1,178	1,351	510	322	108	113

PORTFOLIO (as of 8/31/02)

Portfolio Manager: Peter Hirsch - 2002

Investment Style

Large Cap	Growth
Mid Cap	Value
Small Cap	Grth/Val

Portfolio

0.0% cash	0.0% corp bonds
95.0% stocks	0.0% gov't bonds
0.0% pref/conv't pref	0.0% muni bonds
0.0% conv't bds/wrnts	5.0% other

SHAREHOLDER INFORMATION

Minimum Investment
Initial: $2,500 Subsequent: $250

Minimum IRA Investment
Initial: $500 Subsequent: $250

Maximum Fees
Load: 3.00% front 12b-1: none
Other: 0.75% redemption fee for 1 month

Services
✔ IRA
Keogh
✔ Telephone Exchange

Fidelity Sel Brokerage

800-544-8544, 800-522-7297
www.fidelity.com

(FSLBX)

Financial/Banking Sector

PERFORMANCE

fund inception date: 7/29/85

	3yr Annual	5yr Annual	10yr Annual	Bull	Bear
Return (%)	-1.2	5.8	16.4	78.3	-25.1
Differ From Category (+/-)	-5.8 blw av	1.8 abv av	2.7 high	54.5 high	-33.2 low

Standard Deviation	Category Risk Index	Beta
29.2%—high	1.34—high	1.44

	2002	2001	2000	1999	1998	1997	1996	1995	1994	1993
Return (%)	-17.2	-8.9	27.9	30.6	5.6	62.3	39.6	23.5	-17.2	49.3
Differ From Category (+/-)	-7.2	-3.8	-7.0	31.3	-3.0	15.6	8.9	-16.6	-13.3	30.6
Return, Tax-Adjusted (%)	-17.4	-10.3	25.1	28.9	5.3	61.6	38.4	20.7	-17.2	46.2

PER SHARE DATA

	2002	2001	2000	1999	1998	1997	1996	1995	1994	1993
Dividends, Net Income ($)	0.23	0.12	0.00	0.05	0.01	0.09	0.06	0.04	0.00	0.01
Distrib'ns, Cap Gain ($)	0.00	3.41	6.49	3.13	0.52	0.61	0.65	1.44	0.00	1.47
Net Asset Value ($)	36.54	44.42	53.14	46.83	38.47	36.86	23.17	17.18	15.14	18.30
Expense Ratio (%)	1.11	1.08	1.28	1.24	1.33	1.94	1.61	2.54	1.77	2.21
Yield (%)	0.62	0.25	0.00	0.10	0.02	0.24	0.25	0.21	0.00	0.05
Portfolio Turnover (%)	74	105	47	59	100	16	166	139	295	111
Total Assets (Millions $)	349	462	635	468	550	647	111	26	21	94

PORTFOLIO (as of 8/31/02)

Portfolio Manager: Joshua Spencer - 2002

Investment Style

Large Cap	Growth
Mid Cap	Value
Small Cap	Grth/Val

Portfolio

0.0%	cash	0.0%	corp bonds
99.3%	stocks	0.0%	gov't bonds
0.0%	preferred	0.0%	muni bonds
0.0%	conv't bds/wrnts	0.7%	other

SHAREHOLDER INFORMATION

Minimum Investment
Initial: $2,500 Subsequent: $250

Minimum IRA Investment
Initial: $500 Subsequent: $250

Maximum Fees
Load: 3.00% front 12b-1: none
Other: 0.75% redemption fee for 1 month

Services
✔ IRA
✔ Keogh
✔ Telephone Exchange

Fidelity Sel Financl Serv (FIDSX)

800-544-8544, 800-522-7297
www.fidelity.com

Financial/Banking Sector

PERFORMANCE — fund inception date: 12/10/81

	3yr Annual	5yr Annual	10yr Annual	Bull	Bear
Return (%)	1.1	3.7	14.1	25.7	-3.0
Differ From Category (+/-)	-3.5 blw av	-0.3 abv av	0.4 av	1.9 abv av	-11.1 blw av

Standard Deviation	Category Risk Index	Beta
20.2%—abv av	0.92—low	0.79

	2002	2001	2000	1999	1998	1997	1996	1995	1994	1993
Return (%)	-11.3	-9.1	28.5	1.5	14.1	41.9	32.1	47.3	-3.6	17.5
Differ From Category (+/-)	-1.3	-4.0	-6.4	2.2	5.5	-4.8	1.4	7.2	0.3	-1.2
Return, Tax-Adjusted (%)	-11.6	-10.1	27.4	0.2	11.8	38.8	29.6	46.4	-6.4	13.1

PER SHARE DATA

	2002	2001	2000	1999	1998	1997	1996	1995	1994	1993
Dividends, Net Income ($)	0.82	1.03	0.80	0.64	0.19	0.64	0.63	0.37	0.59	0.20
Distrib'ns, Cap Gain ($)	0.00	3.64	3.45	5.09	10.81	10.51	4.56	0.91	4.13	7.32
Net Asset Value ($)	88.78	101.10	116.54	94.52	98.63	95.98	76.59	62.24	43.12	49.79
Expense Ratio (%)	1.03	1.06	1.17	1.18	1.31	1.45	1.41	1.54	1.63	1.54
Yield (%)	0.92	0.98	0.66	0.64	0.17	0.60	0.77	0.58	1.24	0.35
Portfolio Turnover (%)	127	107	57	60	84	80	125	107	93	100
Total Assets (Millions $)	425	573	647	435	597	548	337	251	94	126

PORTFOLIO (as of 8/31/02)

Portfolio Manager: Marc Wait - 2002

Investment Style

Large Cap	Growth
Mid Cap	Value
Small Cap	Grth/Val

Portfolio

0.0% cash	0.6% corp bonds
98.1% stocks	0.0% gov't bonds
0.0% preferred	0.0% muni bonds
0.0% conv't bds/wrnts	1.3% other

SHAREHOLDER INFORMATION

Minimum Investment
Initial: $2,500 — Subsequent: $250

Minimum IRA Investment
Initial: $500 — Subsequent: $250

Maximum Fees
Load: 3.00% front — 12b-1: none
Other: 0.75% redemption fee for 1 month

Services
✔ IRA
✔ Keogh
✔ Telephone Exchange

T Rowe Price Fincl Svc (PRISX)

800-638-5660, 410-345-2000
www.troweprice.com

Financial/Banking Sector

PERFORMANCE — fund inception date: 9/30/96

	3yr Annual	5yr Annual	10yr Annual	Bull	Bear
Return (%)	5.9	6.2	na	33.1	4.0
Differ From Category (+/-)	1.3 abv av	2.2 high	na	9.3 high	-4.1 av

Standard Deviation	Category Risk Index	Beta
20.7%—abv av	0.95—blw av	0.85

	2002	2001	2000	1999	1998	1997	1996	1995	1994	1993
Return (%)	-10.0	-3.1	36.7	1.7	11.5	41.4	—	—	—	—
Differ From Category (+/-)	0.0	2.0	1.8	2.4	2.9	-5.3	—	—	—	—
Return, Tax-Adjusted (%)	-10.3	-4.9	35.8	0.5	10.7	40.5	—	—	—	—

PER SHARE DATA

	2002	2001	2000	1999	1998	1997	1996	1995	1994	1993
Dividends, Net Income ($)	0.13	0.15	0.09	0.10	0.16	0.10	—	—	—	—
Distrib'ns, Cap Gain ($)	0.06	1.68	0.55	0.85	0.34	0.33	—	—	—	—
Net Asset Value ($)	16.75	18.84	21.38	16.12	16.82	15.56	—	—	—	—
Expense Ratio (%)	na	0.97	1.00	1.14	1.19	1.25	—	—	—	—
Yield (%)	0.77	0.73	0.41	0.58	0.93	0.62	—	—	—	—
Portfolio Turnover (%)	na	55	32	37	47	46	—	—	—	—
Total Assets (Millions $)	282	308	337	159	224	177	—	—	—	—

PORTFOLIO (as of 9/30/02)

Portfolio Manager: A Dopkin/Team
Managed - 2000

Investment Style

Large Cap	Growth
Mid Cap	Value
Small Cap	Grth/Val

Portfolio

7.7%	cash	0.0%	corp bonds
92.3%	stocks	0.0%	gov't bonds
0.0%	preferred	0.0%	muni bonds
0.0%	conv't bds/wrnts	0.0%	other

SHAREHOLDER INFORMATION

Minimum Investment
Initial: $2,500 — Subsequent: $100

Minimum IRA Investment
Initial: $1,000 — Subsequent: $50

Maximum Fees
Load: none — 12b-1: none
Other: none

Services
- ✔ IRA
- ✔ Keogh
- ✔ Telephone Exchange

Gold Sector Stock Funds
Category Performance Ranked by 2002 Returns

Category	Fund (Ticker)	Annual Return (%) 2002	3yr	5yr	10yr	Category Risk	Total Risk
Sec-G	US Glob Inv:Wrld Prec Mils (UNWPX)	83.4	6.8	-2.1	1.4	high	high
Sec-G	US Glob Inv:Gold Shares (USERX)	81.3	12.2	-1.5	-7.3	high	high
Sec-G	Amer Cnt Global Gold/Inv (BGEIX)	72.9	20.8	8.4	3.4	abv av	high
Sec-G	USAA Inv:Prec Metal&Min (USAGX)	67.6	23.1	15.1	6.4	av	high
Sec-G	Fidelity Sel Gold (FSAGX)	64.2	18.9	10.7	7.3	av	high
Gold Sector Average		**65.5**	**15.2**	**5.4**	**2.6**	**—**	**high**

Note: AAII members who would like performance figures for no-load and low-load mutual funds they own that do not appear in this Guide can access this information on our Web site at www.aaii.com.

Amer Cnt Global Gold/Inv (BGEIX)

800-345-2021, 816-531-5575
www.americancentury.com

Gold Sector

PERFORMANCE

fund inception date: 8/17/88

	3yr Annual	5yr Annual	10yr Annual	Bull	Bear
Return (%)	20.8	8.4	3.4	8.8	90.0
Differ From Category (+/-)	5.6 high	3.0 av	0.8 av	-8.1 av	25.1 high

Standard Deviation	Category Risk Index	Beta
34.8%—high	1.06—abv av	0.02

	2002	2001	2000	1999	1998	1997	1996	1995	1994	1993
Return (%)	72.9	34.0	-23.9	-3.1	-12.1	-41.4	-2.7	9.2	-16.7	81.2
Differ From Category (+/-)	7.4	14.8	-2.6	-4.8	3.4	4.2	-14.3	1.3	-3.6	-2.7
Return, Tax-Adjusted (%)	72.6	33.4	-24.1	-3.5	-12.4	-42.1	-4.3	9.2	-16.8	81.1

PER SHARE DATA

	2002	2001	2000	1999	1998	1997	1996	1995	1994	1993
Dividends, Net Income ($)	0.03	0.05	0.02	0.05	0.04	0.09	0.05	0.00	0.02	0.01
Distrib'ns, Cap Gain ($)	0.00	0.00	0.00	0.00	0.00	0.19	0.63	0.00	0.02	0.00
Net Asset Value ($)	9.13	5.30	4.00	5.29	5.52	6.34	11.33	12.37	11.33	13.67
Expense Ratio (%)	na	0.68	0.67	0.68	0.69	0.67	0.62	0.62	0.61	0.72
Yield (%)	0.32	0.94	0.50	0.94	0.72	1.37	0.41	0.00	0.17	0.07
Portfolio Turnover (%)	na	14	17	53	68	28	45	19	41	28
Total Assets (Millions $)	323	193	142	201	228	249	433	540	570	618

PORTFOLIO (as of 9/30/02)

Portfolio Manager: Team Managed - 1996

Investment Style

Large Cap	Growth
Mid Cap	Value
Small Cap	Grth/Val

Portfolio

0.0%	cash	0.0%	corp bonds
98.2%	stocks	0.0%	gov't bonds
0.0%	preferred	0.0%	muni bonds
0.2%	conv't bds/wrnts	1.6%	other

SHAREHOLDER INFORMATION

Minimum Investment
Initial: $2,500 Subsequent: $50

Minimum IRA Investment
Initial: $1,000 Subsequent: $50

Maximum Fees
Load: none 12b-1: none
Other: none

Services
✔ IRA
✔ Keogh
✔ Telephone Exchange

Fidelity Sel Gold (FSAGX)

800-544-8544, 800-522-7297
www.fidelity.com

Gold Sector

PERFORMANCE

fund inception date: 12/16/85

	3yr Annual	5yr Annual	10yr Annual	Bull	Bear
Return (%)	18.9	10.7	7.3	41.3	79.0
Differ From Category (+/-)	3.7 abv av	5.3 abv av	4.7 high	24.4 high	14.1 abv av

Standard Deviation	Category Risk Index	Beta
33.0%—high	1.00—av	0.15

	2002	2001	2000	1999	1998	1997	1996	1995	1994	1993
Return (%)	64.2	24.9	-18.0	8.3	-8.6	-39.3	19.9	11.2	-15.4	78.6
Differ From Category (+/-)	-1.3	5.7	3.3	6.6	6.9	6.3	8.3	3.3	-2.3	-5.3
Return, Tax-Adjusted (%)	63.3	24.2	-18.2	8.3	-8.6	-40.3	19.3	11.2	-15.4	78.6

PER SHARE DATA

	2002	2001	2000	1999	1998	1997	1996	1995	1994	1993
Dividends, Net Income ($)	0.36	0.22	0.07	0.00	0.00	0.00	0.00	0.00	0.00	0.00
Distrib'ns, Cap Gain ($)	0.00	0.00	0.00	0.00	0.00	1.29	0.50	0.00	0.00	0.00
Net Asset Value ($)	23.92	14.81	12.04	14.78	13.64	14.93	26.04	22.14	19.91	23.55
Expense Ratio (%)	1.24	1.43	1.41	1.54	1.55	1.44	1.39	1.41	1.49	1.59
Yield (%)	1.50	1.48	0.58	0.00	0.00	0.00	0.00	0.00	0.00	0.00
Portfolio Turnover (%)	49	23	71	59	89	63	56	34	39	30
Total Assets (Millions $)	696	304	240	200	201	211	354	313	314	365

PORTFOLIO (as of 8/31/02)

Portfolio Manager: Niel Marotta - 2000

Investment Style

Large Cap	Growth
Mid Cap	Value
Small Cap	Grth/Val

Portfolio

0.0% cash	0.0% corp bonds
96.7% stocks	0.0% gov't bonds
0.0% preferred	0.0% muni bonds
0.3% conv't bds/wrnts	2.9% other

SHAREHOLDER INFORMATION

Minimum Investment
Initial: $2,500 Subsequent: $250

Minimum IRA Investment
Initial: $500 Subsequent: $250

Maximum Fees
Load: 3.00% front 12b-1: none
Other: 0.75% redemption fee for 1 month

Services
✔ IRA
✔ Keogh
✔ Telephone Exchange

US Glob Inv:Gold Shares (USERX)

800-873-8637, 210-308-1234
www.us-global.com

Gold Sector

PERFORMANCE

fund inception date: 7/1/74

	3yr Annual	5yr Annual	10yr Annual	Bull	Bear
Return (%)	12.2	-1.5	-7.3	3.4	52.6
Differ From Category (+/-)	-3.0 blw av	-6.9 blw av	-9.9 low	-13.5 blw av	-12.3 blw av

Standard Deviation	Category Risk Index	Beta
42.0%—high	1.27—high	0.19

	2002	2001	2000	1999	1998	1997	1996	1995	1994	1993
Return (%)	81.3	11.1	-29.8	-2.6	-32.9	-57.3	-25.4	-26.8	-2.6	123.9
Differ From Category (+/-)	15.8	-8.1	-8.5	-4.3	-17.4	-11.7	-37.0	-34.7	10.5	40.0
Return, Tax-Adjusted (%)	81.3	11.1	-29.8	-2.6	-32.9	-57.8	-26.1	-27.4	-3.3	122.8

PER SHARE DATA

	2002	2001	2000	1999	1998	1997	1996	1995	1994	1993
Dividends, Net Income ($)	0.00	0.00	0.00	0.00	0.00	0.00	0.00	0.00	0.00	0.00
Distrib'ns, Cap Gain ($)	0.00	0.00	0.00	0.00	0.00	0.03	0.05	0.06	0.07	0.05
Net Asset Value ($)	5.26	2.90	2.61	3.72	3.82	0.57	1.40	1.94	2.73	2.88
Expense Ratio (%)	3.57	5.79	5.74	5.24	2.47	1.80	1.54	1.42	1.46	1.88
Yield (%)	0.00	0.00	0.00	0.00	0.00	0.00	0.00	0.00	0.00	0.00
Portfolio Turnover (%)	164	95	82	388	220	44	24	32	29	19
Total Assets (Millions $)	35	23	21	34	37	66	153	175	291	337

PORTFOLIO (as of 6/30/00)

Portfolio Manager: Team Managed - 1999

Investment Style

Large Cap	Growth
Mid Cap	Value
Small Cap	Grth/Val

Portfolio

3.1%	cash	0.0%	corp bonds
92.8%	stocks	0.0%	gov't bonds
0.0%	pref/conv't pref	0.0%	muni bonds
2.0%	conv't bds/wrnts	2.1%	other

SHAREHOLDER INFORMATION

Minimum Investment
Initial: $5,000 Subsequent: $50

Minimum IRA Investment
Initial: $1 Subsequent: $1

Maximum Fees
Load: 0.25% redemption 12b-1: none
Other: redemption fee applies for 1 month

Services
- ✔ IRA
- ✔ Keogh
- ✔ Telephone Exchange

US Glob Inv:Wrld Prec Mils (UNWPX)

800-873-8637, 210-308-1234
www.us-global.com

Gold Sector

PERFORMANCE — fund inception date: 12/2/85

	3yr Annual	5yr Annual	10yr Annual	Bull	Bear
Return (%)	6.8	-2.1	1.4	-4.6	26.4
Differ From Category (+/-)	-8.4 blw av	-7.5 blw av	-1.2 av	-21.5 blw av	-38.5 low

Standard Deviation	Category Risk Index	Beta
44.3%—high	1.34—high	0.19

	2002	2001	2000	1999	1998	1997	1996	1995	1994	1993
Return (%)	83.4	7.5	-38.0	-12.6	-15.7	-41.0	19.5	15.9	-16.9	89.7
Differ From Category (+/-)	17.9	-11.7	-16.7	-14.3	-0.2	4.6	7.9	8.0	-3.8	5.8
Return, Tax-Adjusted (%)	81.6	7.5	-38.1	-12.6	-15.7	-41.3	16.9	15.9	-17.0	89.7

PER SHARE DATA

	2002	2001	2000	1999	1998	1997	1996	1995	1994	1993
Dividends, Net Income ($)	0.25	0.00	0.02	0.00	0.01	0.13	1.11	0.00	0.03	0.00
Distrib'ns, Cap Gain ($)	0.00	0.00	0.00	0.00	0.00	0.00	0.00	0.00	0.00	0.00
Net Asset Value ($)	9.70	5.43	5.05	8.19	9.38	11.15	19.16	16.96	14.63	17.65
Expense Ratio (%)	2.27	2.86	2.50	2.12	1.74	1.52	1.51	1.55	1.53	2.00
Yield (%)	2.57	0.00	0.39	0.00	0.10	1.16	5.79	0.00	0.20	0.00
Portfolio Turnover (%)	104	68	93	252	43	40	25	28	19	26
Total Assets (Millions $)	90	41	41	81	108	131	225	184	182	168

PORTFOLIO (as of 6/30/00)

Portfolio Manager: Team Managed - 1999

Investment Style

Large Cap	Growth
Mid Cap	Value
Small Cap	Grth/Val

Portfolio

0.6%	cash	0.0%	corp bonds
91.6%	stocks	0.0%	gov't bonds
0.0%	pref/conv't pref	0.0%	muni bonds
5.2%	conv't bds/wrnts	2.7%	other

SHAREHOLDER INFORMATION

Minimum Investment
Initial: $5,000 Subsequent: $50

Minimum IRA Investment
Initial: $1 Subsequent: $1

Maximum Fees
Load: 0.25% redemption 12b-1: none
Other: redemption fee applies for 1 month

Services
✔ IRA
✔ Keogh
✔ Telephone Exchange

USAA Inv:Prec Metal&Min (USAGX)

800-531-8181, 210-456-7211
www.usaa.com

Gold Sector

PERFORMANCE

fund inception date: 8/15/84

	3yr Annual	5yr Annual	10yr Annual	Bull	Bear
Return (%)	23.1	15.1	6.4	38.7	95.6
Differ From Category (+/-)	7.9 high	9.7 high	3.8 abv av	21.8 high	30.7 high

Standard Deviation	Category Risk Index	Beta
32.7%—high	0.99—av	0.22

	2002	2001	2000	1999	1998	1997	1996	1995	1994	1993
Return (%)	67.6	30.9	-14.9	7.1	1.0	-38.1	0.0	4.0	-9.3	58.3
Differ From Category (+/-)	2.1	11.7	6.4	5.4	16.5	7.5	-11.6	-3.9	3.8	-25.6
Return, Tax-Adjusted (%)	65.4	30.5	-15.1	7.1	1.0	-38.1	0.0	4.0	-9.3	58.2

PER SHARE DATA

	2002	2001	2000	1999	1998	1997	1996	1995	1994	1993
Dividends, Net Income ($)	0.38	0.04	0.02	0.00	0.00	0.00	0.00	0.00	0.01	0.01
Distrib'ns, Cap Gain ($)	0.00	0.00	0.00	0.00	0.00	0.00	0.00	0.00	0.00	0.00
Net Asset Value ($)	10.62	6.58	5.06	5.98	5.58	5.52	8.93	8.93	8.59	9.49
Expense Ratio (%)	1.56	1.68	1.58	1.52	1.46	1.31	1.33	1.28	1.26	1.41
Yield (%)	3.57	0.60	0.39	0.00	0.00	0.00	0.00	0.00	0.11	0.10
Portfolio Turnover (%)	41	52	27	33	19	26	16	34	34	81
Total Assets (Millions $)	112	77	69	88	91	84	129	143	158	181

PORTFOLIO (as of 9/30/02)

Portfolio Manager: Mark Johnson - 1994

Investment Style

Large Cap	Growth
Mid Cap	Value
Small Cap	Grth/Val

Portfolio

2.0%	cash	0.0%	corp bonds
98.0%	stocks	0.0%	gov't bonds
0.0%	preferred	0.0%	muni bonds
0.0%	conv't bds/wrnts	0.0%	other

SHAREHOLDER INFORMATION

Minimum Investment
Initial: $3,000 Subsequent: $50

Minimum IRA Investment
Initial: $250 Subsequent: $50

Maximum Fees
Load: none 12b-1: none
Other: none

Services
✔ IRA
✔ Keogh
✔ Telephone Exchange

Health Sector Stock Funds
Category Performance Ranked by 2002 Returns

Category	Fund (Ticker)	Annual Return (%) 2002	3yr	5yr	10yr	Category Risk	Total Risk
Sec-H	Vanguard Health Care (VGHCX)	-11.3	9.7	14.7	18.6	low	blw av
Sec-H	Fidelity Sel Med Dlvry (FSHCX)	-12.1	12.9	-0.9	7.8	av	abv av
Sec-H	Fidelity Sel Health Care (FSPHX)	-18.0	-1.6	5.4	13.6	blw av	av
Sec-H	T Rowe Price Hlth Sci (PRHSX)	-27.7	1.1	6.4	na	high	high
Sec-H	Fidelity Sel Biotech (FBIOX)	-40.5	-16.0	6.4	7.4	high	high
Health Sector Average		**-23.8**	**-0.8**	**5.5**	**11.1**	**—**	**high**

Note: AAII members who would like performance figures for no-load and low-load mutual funds they own that do not appear in this Guide can access this information on our Web site at www.aaii.com.

Fidelity Sel Biotech (FBIOX)

800-544-8544, 800-522-7297
www.fidelity.com

Health Sector

PERFORMANCE — fund inception date: 12/16/85

	3yr Annual	5yr Annual	10yr Annual	Bull	Bear
Return (%)	-16.0	6.4	7.4	194.8	-51.8
Differ From Category (+/-)	-15.2 low	0.9 abv av	-3.7 blw av	137.3 high	-50.7 low

Standard Deviation	Category Risk Index	Beta
48.0%—high	1.71—high	0.78

	2002	2001	2000	1999	1998	1997	1996	1995	1994	1993
Return (%)	-40.5	-24.9	32.7	77.7	29.7	15.2	5.5	49.1	-18.1	0.7
Differ From Category (+/-)	-16.7	-13.8	-12.2	68.2	0.6	-7.6	-9.7	3.0	-24.8	-1.7
Return, Tax-Adjusted (%)	-40.5	-24.9	32.1	76.3	28.4	12.3	2.2	49.0	-18.1	0.7

PER SHARE DATA

	2002	2001	2000	1999	1998	1997	1996	1995	1994	1993
Dividends, Net Income ($)	0.00	0.00	0.00	0.00	0.00	0.00	0.03	0.07	0.00	0.00
Distrib'ns, Cap Gain ($)	0.00	0.00	2.11	2.82	2.09	4.71	4.06	0.00	0.00	0.00
Net Asset Value ($)	38.73	65.12	86.80	67.13	39.77	32.54	32.51	34.83	23.41	28.61
Expense Ratio (%)	1.09	1.00	1.15	1.30	1.49	1.57	1.43	1.59	1.61	1.50
Yield (%)	0.00	0.00	0.00	0.00	0.00	0.00	0.08	0.20	0.00	0.00
Portfolio Turnover (%)	96	74	72	86	162	41	67	77	51	79
Total Assets (Millions $)	1,537	3,081	4,431	1,622	704	551	635	846	396	557

PORTFOLIO (as of 8/31/02)

Portfolio Manager: Andraz Razen - 2002

Investment Style

Large Cap	Growth
Mid Cap	Value
Small Cap	Grth/Val

Portfolio

3.0%	cash	3.6%	corp bonds
73.1%	stocks	0.0%	gov't bonds
0.0%	preferred	0.0%	muni bonds
0.0%	conv't bds/wrnts	20.3%	other

SHAREHOLDER INFORMATION

Minimum Investment
Initial: $2,500 — Subsequent: $250

Minimum IRA Investment
Initial: $500 — Subsequent: $250

Maximum Fees
Load: 3.00% front — 12b-1: none
Other: 0.75% redemption fee for 1 month

Services
✔ IRA
✔ Keogh
✔ Telephone Exchange

Fidelity Sel Health Care (FSPHX)

800-544-8544, 800-522-7297
www.fidelity.com

Health Sector

PERFORMANCE

fund inception date: 7/14/81

	3yr Annual	5yr Annual	10yr Annual	Bull	Bear
Return (%)	-1.6	5.4	13.6	26.9	-11.5
Differ From Category (+/-)	-0.8 av	-0.1 av	2.5 high	-30.6 blw av	-10.4 av

Standard Deviation	Category Risk Index	Beta
15.0%—av	0.53—blw av	0.29

	2002	2001	2000	1999	1998	1997	1996	1995	1994	1993
Return (%)	-18.0	-15.0	36.6	-2.8	41.2	31.1	15.4	45.8	21.4	2.4
Differ From Category (+/-)	5.8	-3.9	-8.3	-12.3	12.1	8.3	0.2	-0.3	14.7	0.0
Return, Tax-Adjusted (%)	-18.4	-15.1	33.5	-4.0	39.9	26.7	10.6	43.5	18.5	2.4

PER SHARE DATA

	2002	2001	2000	1999	1998	1997	1996	1995	1994	1993
Dividends, Net Income ($)	0.20	0.13	0.24	0.08	0.19	0.25	0.65	0.59	0.62	0.07
Distrib'ns, Cap Gain ($)	2.42	0.19	18.63	7.85	6.17	20.73	15.95	4.92	5.74	0.00
Net Asset Value ($)	101.98	127.26	150.13	124.82	136.77	101.87	95.40	97.57	70.80	63.62
Expense Ratio (%)	0.96	0.97	1.05	1.05	1.18	1.33	1.30	1.68	1.64	1.46
Yield (%)	0.19	0.10	0.14	0.06	0.13	0.20	0.58	0.57	0.81	0.11
Portfolio Turnover (%)	135	78	70	66	79	59	54	126	96	112
Total Assets (Millions $)	1,824	2,511	3,123	2,427	3,032	1,631	1,242	1,448	796	573

PORTFOLIO (as of 8/31/02)

Portfolio Manager: Steve Calhoun - 2002

Investment Style

Large Cap Growth
Mid Cap Value
Small Cap Grth/Val

Portfolio

0.0%	cash	0.0%	corp bonds
92.5%	stocks	0.0%	gov't bonds
0.0%	preferred	0.0%	muni bonds
0.0%	conv't bds/wrnts	7.5%	other

SHAREHOLDER INFORMATION

Minimum Investment
Initial: $2,500 Subsequent: $250

Minimum IRA Investment
Initial: $500 Subsequent: $250

Maximum Fees
Load: 3.00% front 12b-1: none
Other: 0.75% redemption fee for 1 month

Services
✔ IRA
✔ Keogh
✔ Telephone Exchange

Fidelity Sel Med Dlvry

(FSHCX)

800-544-8544, 800-522-7297
www.fidelity.com

Health Sector

PERFORMANCE — fund inception date: 6/30/86

	3yr Annual	5yr Annual	10yr Annual	Bull	Bear
Return (%)	12.9	-0.9	7.8	-22.5	93.4
Differ From Category (+/-)	13.7 high	-6.4 low	-3.3 av	-80.0 low	94.5 high

Standard Deviation	Category Risk Index	Beta
20.9%—abv av	0.74—av	-0.12

	2002	2001	2000	1999	1998	1997	1996	1995	1994	1993
Return (%)	-12.1	-2.3	67.8	-29.5	-6.1	20.1	11.0	32.1	19.8	5.5
Differ From Category (+/-)	11.7	8.8	22.9	-39.0	-35.2	-2.7	-4.2	-14.0	13.1	3.1
Return, Tax-Adjusted (%)	-12.1	-2.3	67.8	-29.5	-7.1	16.1	7.4	29.7	18.4	5.5

PER SHARE DATA

	2002	2001	2000	1999	1998	1997	1996	1995	1994	1993
Dividends, Net Income ($)	0.00	0.00	0.00	0.00	0.00	0.00	0.00	0.00	0.07	0.00
Distrib'ns, Cap Gain ($)	0.00	0.00	0.00	0.00	1.34	5.23	3.45	1.91	0.88	0.00
Net Asset Value ($)	23.68	26.95	27.59	16.44	23.35	26.05	26.42	26.96	21.87	19.10
Expense Ratio (%)	1.19	1.22	1.67	1.37	1.57	1.57	1.62	1.45	1.79	1.77
Yield (%)	0.00	0.00	0.00	0.00	0.00	0.00	0.00	0.00	0.30	0.00
Portfolio Turnover (%)	106	113	154	67	109	78	132	123	164	155
Total Assets (Millions $)	133	132	310	50	146	141	182	203	247	150

PORTFOLIO (as of 8/31/02)

Portfolio Manager: Jonathan Zang - 2002

Investment Style

Large Cap	Growth
Mid Cap	Value
Small Cap	Grth/Val

Portfolio

0.0% cash	0.0% corp bonds
97.5% stocks	0.0% gov't bonds
0.0% preferred	0.0% muni bonds
0.0% conv't bds/wrnts	2.5% other

SHAREHOLDER INFORMATION

Minimum Investment
Initial: $2,500 Subsequent: $250

Minimum IRA Investment
Initial: $500 Subsequent: $250

Maximum Fees
Load: 3.00% front 12b-1: none
Other: 0.75% redemption fee for 1 month

Services
✔ IRA
Keogh
✔ Telephone Exchange

T Rowe Price Hlth Sci (PRHSX)

800-638-5660, 410-345-2000
www.troweprice.com

Health Sector

PERFORMANCE — fund inception date: 12/29/95

	3yr Annual	5yr Annual	10yr Annual	Bull	Bear
Return (%)	1.1	6.4	na	63.7	-9.9
Differ From Category (+/-)	1.9 abv av	0.9 high	na	6.2 high	-8.8 abv av

Standard Deviation	Category Risk Index	Beta
32.4%—high	1.15—high	0.56

	2002	2001	2000	1999	1998	1997	1996	1995	1994	1993
Return (%)	-27.7	-5.9	52.1	7.9	22.3	19.4	26.7	—	—	—
Differ From Category (+/-)	-3.9	5.2	7.2	-1.6	-6.8	-3.4	11.5	—	—	—
Return, Tax-Adjusted (%)	-27.7	-6.2	49.0	6.3	21.3	17.8	25.6	—	—	—

PER SHARE DATA

	2002	2001	2000	1999	1998	1997	1996	1995	1994	1993
Dividends, Net Income ($)	0.00	0.00	0.00	0.00	0.00	0.00	0.00	—	—	—
Distrib'ns, Cap Gain ($)	0.00	0.31	2.48	1.26	0.66	0.97	0.40	—	—	—
Net Asset Value ($)	14.51	20.08	21.70	15.93	16.01	13.66	12.27	—	—	—
Expense Ratio (%)	na	0.95	0.98	1.11	1.16	1.18	1.35	—	—	—
Yield (%)	0.00	0.00	0.00	0.00	0.00	0.00	0.00	—	—	—
Portfolio Turnover (%)	na	63	111	82	86	104	133	—	—	—
Total Assets (Millions $)	710	960	971	302	316	271	193	—	—	—

PORTFOLIO (as of 9/30/02)

Portfolio Manager: K Jenner/Team
Managed - 2000

Investment Style

Large Cap	Growth
Mid Cap	Value
Small Cap	Grth/Val

Portfolio

2.9%	cash	5.0%	corp bonds
92.1%	stocks	0.0%	gov't bonds
0.0%	preferred	0.0%	muni bonds
0.0%	conv't bds/wrnts	0.0%	other

SHAREHOLDER INFORMATION

Minimum Investment
Initial: $2,500 — Subsequent: $100

Minimum IRA Investment
Initial: $1,000 — Subsequent: $50

Maximum Fees
Load: none — 12b-1: none
Other: none

Services
✔ IRA
✔ Keogh
✔ Telephone Exchange

Vanguard Health Care (VGHCX)

800-662-7447, 610-436-5152
www.vanguard.com

Health Sector

PERFORMANCE — fund inception date: 5/23/84

	3yr Annual	5yr Annual	10yr Annual	Bull	Bear
Return (%)	9.7	14.7	18.6	60.2	9.3
Differ From Category (+/-)	10.5 high	9.2 high	7.5 high	2.7 abv av	10.4 high

Standard Deviation	Category Risk Index	Beta
13.7%—blw av	0.49—low	0.39

	2002	2001	2000	1999	1998	1997	1996	1995	1994	1993
Return (%)	-11.3	-7.1	60.5	7.0	40.8	28.5	21.3	45.1	9.5	11.8
Differ From Category (+/-)	12.5	4.0	15.6	-2.5	11.7	5.7	6.1	-1.0	2.8	9.4
Return, Tax-Adjusted (%)	-12.7	-8.2	56.7	5.1	39.5	27.2	20.0	43.7	7.0	9.3

PER SHARE DATA

	2002	2001	2000	1999	1998	1997	1996	1995	1994	1993
Dividends, Net Income ($)	0.95	1.03	1.07	0.97	0.84	0.78	0.74	0.57	0.57	0.76
Distrib'ns, Cap Gain ($)	6.52	5.07	15.93	7.14	3.08	2.14	1.29	1.02	2.31	1.97
Net Asset Value ($)	96.16	116.84	132.74	95.21	96.85	71.88	58.35	49.82	35.47	35.07
Expense Ratio (%)	0.31	0.34	0.41	0.36	0.40	0.38	0.46	0.40	0.19	0.22
Yield (%)	0.92	0.84	0.71	0.94	0.84	1.05	1.24	1.12	1.50	2.05
Portfolio Turnover (%)	13	21	27	11	10	7	13	25	19	15
Total Assets (Millions $)	14,114	16,241	18,466	10,420	9,268	4,466	2,661	1,473	708	609

PORTFOLIO (as of 9/30/02)

Portfolio Manager: Edward Owens - 1984

Investment Style

Large Cap	Growth
Mid Cap	Value
Small Cap	Grth/Val

Portfolio

8.2%	cash	0.0%	corp bonds
91.8%	stocks	0.0%	gov't bonds
0.0%	preferred	0.0%	muni bonds
0.0%	conv't bds/wrnts	0.0%	other

SHAREHOLDER INFORMATION

Minimum Investment
Initial: $25,000 Subsequent: $100

Minimum IRA Investment
Initial: $25,000 Subsequent: $100

Maximum Fees
Load: 1.00% redemption 12b-1: none
Other: redemption fee applies for 60 months

Services
✔ IRA
✔ Keogh
✔ Telephone Exchange

Real Estate Sector Stock Funds

Category Performance Ranked by 2002 Returns

Category	Fund (Ticker)	Annual Return (%) 2002	3yr	5yr	10yr	Category Risk	Total Risk
Sec-R	Stratton Monthly Div REIT (STMDX)	6.4	16.2	5.4	6.7	low	blw av
Sec-R	Fidelity Real Est Inv (FRESX)	5.7	15.0	4.1	9.9	blw av	blw av
Sec-R	Vanguard REIT Idx (VGSIX)	3.7	13.7	3.4	na	av	blw av
Sec-R	CGM Realty Fund (CGMRX)	3.5	12.0	2.6	na	high	av
Sec-R	Cohen & Steers Realty Shs (CSRSX)	2.7	11.2	2.9	10.7	abv av	blw av
Real Estate Sector Average		**5.5**	**12.7**	**3.2**	**9.1**	**—**	**blw av**

Note: AAII members who would like performance figures for no-load and low-load mutual funds they own that do not appear in this Guide can access this information on our Web site at www.aaii.com.

CGM Realty Fund
(CGMRX)

800-345-4048, 617-483-5000
cgmfunds.com

Real Estate Sector

PERFORMANCE — fund inception date: 5/13/94

	3yr Annual	5yr Annual	10yr Annual	Bull	Bear
Return (%)	12.0	2.6	na	9.2	39.1
Differ From Category (+/-)	-0.7 av	-0.6 blw av	na	3.4 high	-2.2 av

Standard Deviation	Category Risk Index	Beta
15.6%—av	1.22—high	0.20

	2002	2001	2000	1999	1998	1997	1996	1995	1994	1993
Return (%)	3.5	5.1	29.1	2.6	-21.1	23.3	44.0	20.5	—	—
Differ From Category (+/-)	-2.0	-4.4	4.9	1.2	-2.6	0.7	9.3	4.0	—	—
Return, Tax-Adjusted (%)	1.8	3.0	26.5	0.1	-22.8	19.4	40.6	17.6	—	—

PER SHARE DATA

	2002	2001	2000	1999	1998	1997	1996	1995	1994	1993
Dividends, Net Income ($)	0.58	0.71	0.73	0.64	0.58	0.63	0.64	0.60	—	—
Distrib'ns, Cap Gain ($)	0.00	0.00	0.00	0.16	0.16	1.59	0.40	0.14	—	—
Net Asset Value ($)	13.38	13.47	13.53	11.08	11.59	15.60	14.50	10.89	—	—
Expense Ratio (%)	na	1.00	1.02	1.06	1.04	1.00	1.00	1.00	—	—
Yield (%)	4.33	5.27	5.39	5.69	4.93	3.66	4.29	5.43	—	—
Portfolio Turnover (%)	na	131	78	49	86	128	57	85	—	—
Total Assets (Millions $)	352	383	499	371	418	489	161	47	—	—

PORTFOLIO (as of 9/30/02)

Portfolio Manager: G Kenneth Heebner - 1994

Investment Style

Large Cap	Growth
Mid Cap	Value
Small Cap	Grth/Val

Portfolio

0.5%	cash	0.0%	corp bonds
99.5%	stocks	0.0%	gov't bonds
0.0%	preferred	0.0%	muni bonds
0.0%	conv't bds/wrnts	0.0%	other

SHAREHOLDER INFORMATION

Minimum Investment
Initial: $2,500 Subsequent: $50

Minimum IRA Investment
Initial: $1,000 Subsequent: $50

Maximum Fees
Load: none 12b-1: none
Other: none

Services
✔ IRA
✔ Keogh
✔ Telephone Exchange

Cohen & Steers Realty Shs (CSRSX)

800-437-9912, 212-832-3232
www.cohenandsteers.com

Real Estate Sector

PERFORMANCE — fund inception date: 7/1/91

	3yr Annual	5yr Annual	10yr Annual	Bull	Bear
Return (%)	11.2	2.9	10.7	8.4	36.3
Differ From Category (+/-)	-1.5 blw av	-0.3 blw av	1.6 high	2.6 abv av	-5.0 blw av

Standard Deviation	Category Risk Index	Beta
13.2%—blw av	1.03—abv av	0.17

	2002	2001	2000	1999	1998	1997	1996	1995	1994	1993
Return (%)	2.7	5.7	26.6	2.6	-18.0	21.1	38.4	11.1	8.3	18.6
Differ From Category (+/-)	-2.8	-3.8	2.4	1.2	0.5	-1.5	3.7	-5.4	8.9	6.1
Return, Tax-Adjusted (%)	0.6	3.7	24.2	0.5	-20.0	18.4	35.8	8.9	6.2	15.0

PER SHARE DATA

	2002	2001	2000	1999	1998	1997	1996	1995	1994	1993
Dividends, Net Income ($)	2.38	2.27	2.24	1.98	1.88	1.88	1.88	1.83	1.66	1.51
Distrib'ns, Cap Gain ($)	0.00	0.00	0.00	0.00	1.40	2.30	0.55	0.00	0.00	1.68
Net Asset Value ($)	43.34	44.41	44.26	36.91	37.98	50.18	45.09	34.62	32.90	31.92
Expense Ratio (%)	na	1.09	1.07	1.06	1.04	1.05	1.08	1.11	1.14	1.18
Yield (%)	5.49	5.11	5.06	5.36	4.77	3.58	4.11	5.28	5.04	4.49
Portfolio Turnover (%)	na	45	33	21	30	40	33	22	39	65
Total Assets (Millions $)	1,256	1,387	1,312	1,464	1,933	3,432	2,036	793	458	155

PORTFOLIO (as of 9/30/02)

Portfolio Manager: Martin Cohen/Robert Steers - 1991

Investment Style

Large Cap	Growth
Mid Cap	Value
Small Cap	Grth/Val

Portfolio

0.0%	cash	0.0%	corp bonds
100.0%	stocks	0.0%	gov't bonds
0.0%	preferred	0.0%	muni bonds
0.0%	conv't bds/wrnts	0.0%	other

SHAREHOLDER INFORMATION

Minimum Investment
Initial: $10,000 — Subsequent: $500

Minimum IRA Investment
Initial: na — Subsequent: na

Maximum Fees
Load: none — 12b-1: none
Other: none

Services
IRA
Keogh
✔ Telephone Exchange

Fidelity Real Est Inv (FRESX)

800-544-8544, 800-522-7297
www.fidelity.com

Real Estate Sector

PERFORMANCE

fund inception date: 11/14/86

	3yr Annual	5yr Annual	10yr Annual	Bull	Bear
Return (%)	15.0	4.1	9.9	5.0	45.4
Differ From Category (+/-)	2.3 abv av	0.9 high	0.8 abv av	-0.8 av	4.1 abv av

Standard Deviation	Category Risk Index	Beta
12.3%—blw av	0.96—blw av	0.17

	2002	2001	2000	1999	1998	1997	1996	1995	1994	1993
Return (%)	5.7	9.4	31.3	-0.9	-18.6	21.3	36.2	10.9	2.0	12.5
Differ From Category (+/-)	0.2	-0.1	7.1	-2.3	-0.1	-1.3	1.5	-5.6	2.6	0.0
Return, Tax-Adjusted (%)	3.6	6.8	29.3	-2.7	-20.5	18.9	34.1	8.8	0.2	10.6

PER SHARE DATA

	2002	2001	2000	1999	1998	1997	1996	1995	1994	1993
Dividends, Net Income ($)	0.77	0.78	0.73	0.69	0.77	0.79	0.72	0.71	0.63	0.60
Distrib'ns, Cap Gain ($)	0.43	0.89	0.00	0.00	0.41	0.56	0.00	0.00	0.00	0.00
Net Asset Value ($)	18.39	18.52	18.50	14.70	15.54	20.45	18.03	13.88	13.20	13.57
Expense Ratio (%)	0.79	0.82	0.88	0.89	0.84	0.90	0.95	1.03	1.13	1.16
Yield (%)	4.09	4.01	3.94	4.69	4.82	3.76	3.99	5.11	4.77	4.42
Portfolio Turnover (%)	71	71	32	28	76	55	85	75	110	82
Total Assets (Millions $)	1,719	1,244	1,037	724	1,239	2,480	1,721	708	555	424

PORTFOLIO (as of 7/31/02)

Portfolio Manager: Steve Buller - 1998

Investment Style

Large Cap	Growth
Mid Cap	Value
Small Cap	Grth/Val

Portfolio

0.1%	cash	6.1%	corp bonds
86.0%	stocks	0.0%	gov't bonds
0.0%	preferred	0.0%	muni bonds
0.0%	conv't bds/wrnts	7.8%	other

SHAREHOLDER INFORMATION

Minimum Investment
Initial: $2,500 Subsequent: $250

Minimum IRA Investment
Initial: $500 Subsequent: $250

Maximum Fees
Load: 0.75% redemption 12b-1: none
Other: redemption fee applies for 3 months

Services
✔ IRA
✔ Keogh
✔ Telephone Exchange

Stratton Monthly Div REIT

800-634-5726, 610-941-0255

(STMDX)

Real Estate Sector

PERFORMANCE

fund inception date: 5/30/80

	3yr Annual	5yr Annual	10yr Annual	Bull	Bear
Return (%)	16.2	5.4	6.7	-1.1	56.5
Differ From Category (+/-)	3.5 high	2.2 high	-2.4 blw av	-6.9 low	15.2 high

Standard Deviation	Category Risk Index	Beta
11.9%—blw av	0.94—low	0.16

	2002	2001	2000	1999	1998	1997	1996	1995	1994	1993
Return (%)	6.4	22.9	20.1	-6.2	-11.7	18.0	8.5	23.4	-12.1	6.6
Differ From Category (+/-)	0.9	13.4	-4.1	-7.6	6.8	-4.6	-26.2	6.9	-11.5	-5.9
Return, Tax-Adjusted (%)	3.6	19.7	16.5	-9.5	-14.4	15.2	5.7	20.2	-14.7	4.0

PER SHARE DATA

	2002	2001	2000	1999	1998	1997	1996	1995	1994	1993
Dividends, Net Income ($)	1.92	1.92	1.92	2.04	2.06	1.92	1.92	1.92	1.92	1.95
Distrib'ns, Cap Gain ($)	0.00	0.00	0.00	0.00	0.00	0.00	0.00	0.00	0.00	0.00
Net Asset Value ($)	26.56	26.74	23.43	21.28	24.78	30.25	27.43	27.19	23.78	29.17
Expense Ratio (%)	na	1.09	1.20	1.09	1.02	1.02	1.02	1.08	0.99	1.10
Yield (%)	7.22	7.18	8.19	9.58	8.31	6.34	6.99	7.06	8.07	6.68
Portfolio Turnover (%)	na	71	25	13	18	42	69	39	19	35
Total Assets (Millions $)	133	89	60	59	79	101	103	128	121	176

PORTFOLIO (as of 11/30/02)

Portfolio Manager: James Stratton/James Beers - 2000

Investment Style

Large Cap	Growth
Mid Cap	Value
Small Cap	Grth/Val

Portfolio

0.0%	cash	0.0%	corp bonds
97.1%	stocks	0.0%	gov't bonds
0.0%	preferred	0.0%	muni bonds
0.0%	conv't bds/wrnts	2.9%	other

SHAREHOLDER INFORMATION

Minimum Investment

Initial: $2,000 Subsequent: $100

Minimum IRA Investment

Initial: $1 Subsequent: $1

Maximum Fees

Load: 1.50% redemption 12b-1: none

Other: redemption fee applies for 4 months

Services

✔ IRA

✔ Keogh

✔ Telephone Exchange

Vanguard REIT Idx (VGSIX)

800-662-7447, 610-436-5152
www.vanguard.com

Real Estate Sector

PERFORMANCE — fund inception date: 5/13/96

	3yr Annual	5yr Annual	10yr Annual	Bull	Bear
Return (%)	13.7	3.4	na	2.1	43.4
Differ From Category (+/-)	1.0 av	0.2 av	na	-3.7 blw av	2.1 av

Standard Deviation	Category Risk Index	Beta
12.6%—blw av	0.98—av	0.11

	2002	2001	2000	1999	1998	1997	1996	1995	1994	1993
Return (%)	3.7	12.3	26.3	-4.0	-16.3	18.7	—	—	—	—
Differ From Category (+/-)	-1.8	2.8	2.1	-5.4	2.2	-3.9	—	—	—	—
Return, Tax-Adjusted (%)	1.3	9.9	23.4	-6.6	-18.4	16.6	—	—	—	—

PER SHARE DATA

	2002	2001	2000	1999	1998	1997	1996	1995	1994	1993
Dividends, Net Income ($)	0.76	0.63	0.64	0.67	0.66	0.58	—	—	—	—
Distrib'ns, Cap Gain ($)	0.00	0.17	0.17	0.10	0.14	0.18	—	—	—	—
Net Asset Value ($)	11.84	12.13	11.56	9.85	11.08	14.16	—	—	—	—
Expense Ratio (%)	0.28	0.33	0.33	0.26	0.24	0.36	—	—	—	—
Yield (%)	6.41	5.12	5.45	6.73	5.88	4.04	—	—	—	—
Portfolio Turnover (%)	10	21	12	29	2	na	—	—	—	—
Total Assets (Millions $)	1,765	1,229	1,095	875	923	1,277	—	—	—	—

PORTFOLIO (as of 9/30/02)

Portfolio Manager: George Sauter - 1996

Investment Style

Large Cap	Growth
Mid Cap	Value
Small Cap	Grth/Val

Portfolio

2.0% cash	0.0% corp bonds
98.0% stocks	0.0% gov't bonds
0.0% preferred	0.0% muni bonds
0.0% conv't bds/wrnts	0.0% other

SHAREHOLDER INFORMATION

Minimum Investment
Initial: $3,000 Subsequent: $100

Minimum IRA Investment
Initial: $1,000 Subsequent: $100

Maximum Fees
Load: 1.00% redemption 12b-1: none
Other: redemption fee applies for 12 months

Services
✔ IRA
✔ Keogh
✔ Telephone Exchange

Technology Sector Stock Funds

Category Performance Ranked by 2002 Returns

Category	Fund (Ticker)	Annual Return (%) 2002	3yr	5yr	10yr	Category Risk	Total Risk
Sec-T	Fidelity Sel Software (FSCSX)	-23.3	-17.1	9.8	15.8	av	high
Sec-T	Fidelity Sel Technology (FSPTX)	-37.7	-33.9	3.0	11.7	abv av	high
Sec-T	T Rowe Price Sci&Tech (PRSCX)	-40.5	-38.7	-8.0	5.5	av	high
Sec-T	Fidelity Sel Computers (FDCPX)	-42.0	-33.5	0.8	12.4	blw av	high
Sec-T	Fidelity Sel Electronics (FSELX)	-50.5	-29.7	1.6	16.4	abv av	high
Sec-T	Firsthand:Tech Value (TVFQX)	-56.1	-39.5	-4.4	na	high	high
Technology Sector Average		**-43.5**	**-33.8**	**-1.1**	**11.1**	**—**	**high**

Note: AAII members who would like performance figures for no-load and low-load mutual funds they own that do not appear in this Guide can access this information on our Web site at www.aaii.com.

Fidelity Sel Computers (FDCPX)

800-544-8544, 800-522-7297
www.fidelity.com

Technology Sector

PERFORMANCE

fund inception date: 7/29/85

	3yr Annual	5yr Annual	10yr Annual	Bull	Bear
Return (%)	-33.5	0.8	12.4	274.1	-79.6
Differ From Category (+/-)	0.3 abv av	1.9 abv av	1.3 abv av	-75.5 blw av	-0.9 abv av

Standard Deviation	Category Risk Index	Beta
48.9%—high	0.97—blw av	2.08

	2002	2001	2000	1999	1998	1997	1996	1995	1994	1993
Return (%)	-42.0	-27.3	-30.3	81.1	96.3	0.1	31.6	51.8	20.4	28.8
Differ From Category (+/-)	1.5	3.4	-5.8	-41.3	45.9	-8.1	-0.4	-1.4	8.8	2.0
Return, Tax-Adjusted (%)	-42.0	-27.3	-34.5	76.7	96.3	-5.4	29.8	46.4	20.4	26.3

PER SHARE DATA

	2002	2001	2000	1999	1998	1997	1996	1995	1994	1993
Dividends, Net Income ($)	0.00	0.00	0.00	0.00	0.00	0.00	0.00	0.00	0.00	0.00
Distrib'ns, Cap Gain ($)	0.00	0.00	21.79	14.92	0.00	13.39	2.47	5.61	0.00	1.80
Net Asset Value ($)	22.04	38.03	52.33	104.51	67.71	34.48	48.68	38.99	29.33	24.35
Expense Ratio (%)	1.13	0.95	1.05	1.23	1.40	1.48	1.38	1.69	1.89	1.81
Yield (%)	0.00	0.00	0.00	0.00	0.00	0.00	0.00	0.00	0.00	0.00
Portfolio Turnover (%)	206	100	129	133	333	255	129	189	145	254
Total Assets (Millions $)	571	1,159	1,948	3,205	1,514	569	664	499	175	61

PORTFOLIO (as of 8/31/02)

Portfolio Manager: Sonu Kalra - 2002

Investment Style

Large Cap	Growth
Mid Cap	Value
Small Cap	Grth/Val

Portfolio

0.0% cash	0.0% corp bonds
88.7% stocks	0.0% gov't bonds
0.1% pref/conv't pref	0.0% muni bonds
0.0% conv't bds/wrnts	11.2% other

SHAREHOLDER INFORMATION

Minimum Investment
Initial: $2,500 Subsequent: $250

Minimum IRA Investment
Initial: $500 Subsequent: $250

Maximum Fees
Load: 3.00% front 12b-1: none
Other: 0.75% redemption fee for 1 month

Services
✔ IRA
✔ Keogh
✔ Telephone Exchange

Fidelity Sel Electronics (FSELX)

800-544-8544, 800-522-7297
www.fidelity.com

Technology Sector

PERFORMANCE — fund inception date: 7/29/85

	3yr Annual	5yr Annual	10yr Annual	Bull	Bear
Return (%)	-29.7	1.6	16.4	421.3	-78.5
Differ From Category (+/-)	4.1 high	2.7 abv av	5.3 high	71.7 abv av	0.2 abv av

Standard Deviation	Category Risk Index	Beta
56.7%—high	1.12—abv av	2.37

	2002	2001	2000	1999	1998	1997	1996	1995	1994	1993
Return (%)	-50.5	-14.7	-17.6	106.6	51.1	13.7	41.7	68.9	17.1	32.0
Differ From Category (+/-)	-7.0	16.0	6.9	-15.8	0.7	5.5	9.7	15.7	5.5	5.2
Return, Tax-Adjusted (%)	-50.5	-14.7	-21.8	103.8	51.1	8.1	41.7	60.9	17.1	26.5

PER SHARE DATA

	2002	2001	2000	1999	1998	1997	1996	1995	1994	1993
Dividends, Net Income ($)	0.00	0.00	0.00	0.00	0.00	0.00	0.00	0.00	0.00	0.00
Distrib'ns, Cap Gain ($)	0.00	0.00	18.68	6.62	0.00	10.20	0.00	5.25	0.00	2.75
Net Asset Value ($)	24.37	49.27	57.78	88.88	46.56	30.81	36.48	25.74	18.49	15.78
Expense Ratio (%)	0.97	0.87	0.98	1.15	1.18	1.33	1.22	1.71	1.67	1.69
Yield (%)	0.00	0.00	0.00	0.00	0.00	0.00	0.00	0.00	0.00	0.00
Portfolio Turnover (%)	57	100	125	160	435	341	366	205	163	293
Total Assets (Millions $)	2,214	5,106	6,350	6,781	2,722	2,301	1,565	892	156	45

PORTFOLIO (as of 8/31/02)

Portfolio Manager: Sam Peters - 2002

Investment Style

Large Cap	Growth
Mid Cap	Value
Small Cap	Grth/Val

Portfolio

0.0%	cash	0.0%	corp bonds
92.6%	stocks	0.0%	gov't bonds
0.0%	preferred	0.0%	muni bonds
0.0%	conv't bds/wrnts	7.4%	other

SHAREHOLDER INFORMATION

Minimum Investment
Initial: $2,500 — Subsequent: $250

Minimum IRA Investment
Initial: $500 — Subsequent: $250

Maximum Fees
Load: 3.00% front — 12b-1: none
Other: 0.75% redemption fee for 1 month

Services
✔ IRA
✔ Keogh
✔ Telephone Exchange

Fidelity Sel Software (FSCSX)

800-544-8544, 800-522-7297
www.fidelity.com

Technology Sector

PERFORMANCE

fund inception date: 7/29/85

	3yr Annual	5yr Annual	10yr Annual	Bull	Bear
Return (%)	-17.1	9.8	15.8	203.2	-58.8
Differ From Category (+/-)	16.7 high	10.9 high	4.7 high	-146.4 low	19.9 high

Standard Deviation	Category Risk Index	Beta
49.3%—high	0.97—av	2.07

	2002	2001	2000	1999	1998	1997	1996	1995	1994	1993
Return (%)	-23.3	-6.9	-20.1	93.1	45.7	15.0	21.7	46.2	0.3	32.7
Differ From Category (+/-)	20.2	23.8	4.4	-29.3	-4.7	6.8	-10.3	-7.0	-11.3	5.9
Return, Tax-Adjusted (%)	-23.3	-7.0	-26.6	90.8	45.0	11.7	19.1	41.5	0.0	25.8

PER SHARE DATA

	2002	2001	2000	1999	1998	1997	1996	1995	1994	1993
Dividends, Net Income ($)	0.00	0.00	0.00	0.00	0.00	0.00	0.00	0.00	0.00	0.00
Distrib'ns, Cap Gain ($)	0.00	0.24	31.32	6.33	1.32	6.61	3.31	4.60	0.33	6.48
Net Asset Value ($)	36.46	47.59	51.51	96.86	54.72	38.58	39.62	35.46	27.29	27.55
Expense Ratio (%)	1.05	0.99	1.11	1.27	1.44	1.51	1.47	1.50	1.57	1.64
Yield (%)	0.00	0.00	0.00	0.00	0.00	0.00	0.00	0.00	0.00	0.00
Portfolio Turnover (%)	325	272	59	72	145	279	183	164	376	402
Total Assets (Millions $)	647	964	1,042	1,412	656	426	401	351	211	164

PORTFOLIO (as of 8/31/02)

Portfolio Manager: Christian Zann - 2001

Investment Style

Large Cap	Growth
Mid Cap	Value
Small Cap	Grth/Val

Portfolio

2.0%	cash	0.0%	corp bonds
81.8%	stocks	0.5%	gov't bonds
0.0%	preferred	0.0%	muni bonds
0.0%	conv't bds/wrnts	15.8%	other

SHAREHOLDER INFORMATION

Minimum Investment
Initial: $2,500 Subsequent: $250

Minimum IRA Investment
Initial: $500 Subsequent: $250

Maximum Fees
Load: 3.00% front 12b-1: none
Other: 0.75% redemption fee for 1 month

Services
✔ IRA
✔ Keogh
✔ Telephone Exchange

Fidelity Sel Technology (FSPTX)

800-544-8544, 800-522-7297
www.fidelity.com

Technology Sector

PERFORMANCE — fund inception date: 7/14/81

	3yr Annual	5yr Annual	10yr Annual	Bull	Bear
Return (%)	-33.9	3.0	11.7	397.7	-80.9
Differ From Category (+/-)	-0.1 av	4.1 high	0.6 av	48.1 abv av	-2.2 abv av

Standard Deviation	Category Risk Index	Beta
51.3%—high	1.01—abv av	2.06

	2002	2001	2000	1999	1998	1997	1996	1995	1994	1993
Return (%)	-37.7	-31.6	-32.2	131.7	74.1	10.3	15.8	43.8	11.1	28.6
Differ From Category (+/-)	5.8	-0.9	-7.7	9.3	23.7	2.1	-16.2	-9.4	-0.5	1.8
Return, Tax-Adjusted (%)	-37.7	-31.6	-34.9	126.7	74.1	4.7	13.8	38.4	10.0	25.4

PER SHARE DATA

	2002	2001	2000	1999	1998	1997	1996	1995	1994	1993
Dividends, Net Income ($)	0.00	0.00	0.00	0.00	0.00	0.00	0.00	0.00	0.00	0.13
Distrib'ns, Cap Gain ($)	0.00	0.00	20.73	19.80	0.00	15.69	3.68	8.05	1.50	3.70
Net Asset Value ($)	37.70	60.60	88.72	152.39	78.86	45.28	55.68	51.31	41.36	38.73
Expense Ratio (%)	1.13	0.94	1.04	1.20	1.38	1.49	1.39	1.56	1.54	1.64
Yield (%)	0.00	0.00	0.00	0.00	0.00	0.00	0.00	0.00	0.00	0.30
Portfolio Turnover (%)	184	114	210	339	556	549	112	102	213	259
Total Assets (Millions $)	1,458	2,714	4,287	5,208	1,061	526	491	400	227	229

PORTFOLIO (as of 8/31/02)

Portfolio Manager: Sonu Kalra - 2002

Investment Style

Large Cap	Growth
Mid Cap	Value
Small Cap	Grth/Val

Portfolio

0.0%	cash	0.0%	corp bonds
88.9%	stocks	0.0%	gov't bonds
0.0%	pref/conv't pref	0.0%	muni bonds
0.0%	conv't bds/wrnts	11.1%	other

SHAREHOLDER INFORMATION

Minimum Investment
Initial: $2,500 — Subsequent: $250

Minimum IRA Investment
Initial: $500 — Subsequent: $250

Maximum Fees
Load: 3.00% front — 12b-1: none
Other: 0.75% redemption fee for 1 month

Services
- ✔ IRA
- ✔ Keogh
- ✔ Telephone Exchange

Firsthand:Tech Value

888-884-2675
www.firsthandfunds.com

(TVFQX)

Technology Sector

PERFORMANCE — fund inception date: 5/20/94

	3yr Annual	5yr Annual	10yr Annual	Bull	Bear
Return (%)	-39.5	-4.4	na	561.5	-87.1
Differ From Category (+/-)	-5.7 low	-3.3 av	na	211.9 high	-8.4 low

Standard Deviation	Category Risk Index	Beta
61.3%—high	1.21—high	2.36

	2002	2001	2000	1999	1998	1997	1996	1995	1994	1993
Return (%)	-56.1	-43.9	-9.9	190.4	23.7	6.4	60.5	61.1	—	—
Differ From Category (+/-)	-12.6	-13.2	14.6	68.0	-26.7	-1.8	28.5	7.9	—	—
Return, Tax-Adjusted (%)	-56.1	-44.0	-11.6	188.7	23.7	4.7	56.1	60.1	—	—

PER SHARE DATA

	2002	2001	2000	1999	1998	1997	1996	1995	1994	1993
Dividends, Net Income ($)	0.00	0.00	0.00	0.00	0.00	0.00	0.00	0.00	—	—
Distrib'ns, Cap Gain ($)	0.00	0.38	7.86	2.72	0.00	2.23	2.90	0.40	—	—
Net Asset Value ($)	18.09	41.25	74.33	90.52	32.24	26.06	26.66	18.44	—	—
Expense Ratio (%)	na	1.84	1.83	1.91	1.95	1.93	1.81	1.98	—	—
Yield (%)	0.00	0.00	0.00	0.00	0.00	0.00	0.00	0.00	—	—
Portfolio Turnover (%)	na	57	59	41	126	101	43	45	—	—
Total Assets (Millions $)	408	1,449	3,030	1,355	178	194	35	2	—	—

PORTFOLIO (as of 9/30/02)

Portfolio Manager: Kevin Landis - 1994

Investment Style

Large Cap	Growth
Mid Cap	Value
Small Cap	Grth/Val

Portfolio

1.2%	cash	0.0%	corp bonds
94.3%	stocks	0.0%	gov't bonds
0.0%	preferred	0.0%	muni bonds
0.0%	conv't bds/wrnts	4.5%	other

SHAREHOLDER INFORMATION

Minimum Investment
Initial: $10,000 Subsequent: $50

Minimum IRA Investment
Initial: $2,000 Subsequent: $50

Maximum Fees
Load: 2.00% redemption 12b-1: none
Other: redemption fee applies for 6 months

Services
✔ IRA
✔ Keogh
✔ Telephone Exchange

T Rowe Price Sci&Tech (PRSCX)

800-638-5660, 410-345-2000
www.troweprice.com

Technology Sector

PERFORMANCE — fund inception date: 9/30/87

	3yr Annual	5yr Annual	10yr Annual	Bull	Bear
Return (%)	-38.7	-8.0	5.5	272.6	-82.8
Differ From Category (+/-)	-4.9 blw av	-6.9 low	-5.6 blw av	-77.0 blw av	-4.1 av

Standard Deviation	Category Risk Index	Beta
50.8%—high	1.01—av	2.26

	2002	2001	2000	1999	1998	1997	1996	1995	1994	1993
Return (%)	-40.5	-41.1	-34.1	100.9	42.3	1.7	14.2	55.5	15.7	24.2
Differ From Category (+/-)	3.0	-10.4	-9.6	-21.5	-8.1	-6.5	-17.8	2.3	4.1	-2.6
Return, Tax-Adjusted (%)	-40.5	-41.1	-36.4	95.2	41.6	-0.2	10.7	49.6	15.3	20.1

PER SHARE DATA

	2002	2001	2000	1999	1998	1997	1996	1995	1994	1993
Dividends, Net Income ($)	0.00	0.00	0.00	0.00	0.00	0.00	0.00	0.00	0.00	0.00
Distrib'ns, Cap Gain ($)	0.00	0.00	7.28	10.72	0.99	2.87	3.60	4.54	0.30	2.51
Net Asset Value ($)	12.43	20.92	35.57	63.71	37.67	27.26	29.71	29.12	21.64	18.95
Expense Ratio (%)	na	1.00	1.09	0.87	0.94	0.94	0.97	1.06	1.11	1.25
Yield (%)	0.00	0.00	0.00	0.00	0.00	0.00	0.00	0.00	0.00	0.00
Portfolio Turnover (%)	na	144	134	128	109	133	125	136	113	163
Total Assets (Millions $)	3,306	5,208	8,891	12,270	4,695	3,538	3,291	2,285	915	501

PORTFOLIO (as of 9/30/02)

Portfolio Manager: M Sola/Team
Managed - 2002

Investment Style

Large Cap	Growth
Mid Cap	Value
Small Cap	Grth/Val

Portfolio

4.0%	cash	0.5%	corp bonds
94.3%	stocks	0.0%	gov't bonds
0.0%	pref/conv't pref	0.0%	muni bonds
1.2%	conv't bds/wrnts	0.0%	other

SHAREHOLDER INFORMATION

Minimum Investment
Initial: $2,500 — Subsequent: $100

Minimum IRA Investment
Initial: $1,000 — Subsequent: $50

Maximum Fees
Load: none — 12b-1: none
Other: none

Services
✔ IRA
✔ Keogh
✔ Telephone Exchange

Telecommunications Sector Stock Funds
Category Performance Ranked by 2002 Returns

		Annual Return (%)				Category	Total
Category	**Fund (Ticker)**	**2002**	**3yr**	**5yr**	**10yr**	**Risk**	**Risk**
Sec-TC	T Rowe Price Media & Tele (PRMTX)	-28.3	-20.6	5.4	na	av	high
Sec-TC	Fidelity Sel Telecomm (FSTCX)	-29.3	-31.6	-5.6	5.7	abv av	high
Sec-TC	Gabelli Glbl Telcom/AAA (GABTX)	-29.5	-24.8	0.5	na	low	high
Sec-TC	Fidelity Sel Develop Comm (FSDCX)	-47.7	-38.3	-2.6	6.5	high	high
Telecommunications Sector Average		**-35.4**	**-32.3**	**-4.2**	**6.1**	**—**	**high**

Note: AAII members who would like performance figures for no-load and low-load mutual funds they own that do not appear in this Guide can access this information on our Web site at www.aaii.com.

Fidelity Sel Develop Comm (FSDCX)

800-544-8544, 800-522-7297
www.fidelity.com

Telecommunications Sector

PERFORMANCE

fund inception date: 6/29/90

	3yr Annual	5yr Annual	10yr Annual	Bull	Bear
Return (%)	-38.3	-2.6	6.5	379.2	-84.0
Differ From Category (+/-)	-6.0 blw av	1.6 abv av	0.4 high	158.7 high	-7.4 blw av

Standard Deviation	Category Risk Index	Beta
42.9%—high	1.23—high	1.56

	2002	2001	2000	1999	1998	1997	1996	1995	1994	1993
Return (%)	-47.7	-36.1	-29.7	122.4	67.6	6.0	14.5	17.3	15.1	31.7
Differ From Category (+/-)	-12.3	-4.4	-1.1	26.6	29.7	-15.5	1.8	-4.5	14.8	1.0
Return, Tax-Adjusted (%)	-47.7	-36.1	-34.6	120.4	67.5	1.9	14.5	10.4	12.7	29.1

PER SHARE DATA

	2002	2001	2000	1999	1998	1997	1996	1995	1994	1993
Dividends, Net Income ($)	0.00	0.00	0.00	0.00	0.00	0.00	0.00	0.00	0.00	0.00
Distrib'ns, Cap Gain ($)	0.00	0.00	15.45	3.07	0.07	4.35	0.00	5.00	1.67	1.47
Net Asset Value ($)	9.87	18.90	29.59	62.88	30.08	18.00	21.26	18.56	20.24	19.24
Expense Ratio (%)	1.22	0.98	1.11	1.34	1.61	1.64	1.51	1.56	1.56	1.88
Yield (%)	0.00	0.00	0.00	0.00	0.00	0.00	0.00	0.00	0.00	0.00
Portfolio Turnover (%)	198	368	112	299	383	202	249	266	280	77
Total Assets (Millions $)	320	788	1,677	2,260	445	203	275	296	276	245

PORTFOLIO (as of 8/31/02)

Portfolio Manager: Shep Perkins - 2001

Investment Style

Large Cap	Growth
Mid Cap	Value
Small Cap	Grth/Val

Portfolio

0.0%	cash	0.0%	corp bonds
90.0%	stocks	0.0%	gov't bonds
0.0%	preferred	0.0%	muni bonds
0.0%	conv't bds/wrnts	10.0%	other

SHAREHOLDER INFORMATION

Minimum Investment
Initial: $2,500 Subsequent: $250

Minimum IRA Investment
Initial: $500 Subsequent: $250

Maximum Fees
Load: 3.00% front 12b-1: none
Other: 0.75% redemption fee for 1 month

Services
✔ IRA
✔ Keogh
✔ Telephone Exchange

Fidelity Sel Telecomm (FSTCX)

800-544-8544, 800-522-7297
www.fidelity.com

Telecommunications Sector

PERFORMANCE — fund inception date: 7/29/85

	3yr Annual	5yr Annual	10yr Annual	Bull	Bear
Return (%)	-31.6	-5.6	5.7	170.3	-80.0
Differ From Category (+/-)	0.7 av	-1.4 av	-0.4 av	-50.2 av	-3.4 av

Standard Deviation	Category Risk Index	Beta
37.2%—high	1.06—abv av	1.52

	2002	2001	2000	1999	1998	1997	1996	1995	1994	1993
Return (%)	-29.3	-27.9	-37.4	66.5	41.0	25.8	5.3	29.6	4.3	29.7
Differ From Category (+/-)	6.1	3.8	-8.8	-29.3	3.1	4.3	-7.4	7.8	4.0	-1.0
Return, Tax-Adjusted (%)	-29.3	-27.9	-39.4	63.0	39.7	22.7	1.4	27.1	2.9	25.9

PER SHARE DATA

	2002	2001	2000	1999	1998	1997	1996	1995	1994	1993
Dividends, Net Income ($)	0.03	0.02	0.00	0.00	0.00	0.00	0.27	0.39	0.53	0.20
Distrib'ns, Cap Gain ($)	0.00	0.00	9.04	10.48	2.96	6.44	5.87	2.75	1.07	4.18
Net Asset Value ($)	25.57	36.22	50.31	88.70	60.36	45.13	41.16	45.21	37.48	37.54
Expense Ratio (%)	1.20	1.02	1.09	1.25	1.51	1.54	1.52	1.55	1.53	1.74
Yield (%)	0.11	0.05	0.00	0.00	0.00	0.00	0.57	0.81	1.37	0.47
Portfolio Turnover (%)	169	322	173	150	157	175	89	107	241	115
Total Assets (Millions $)	386	558	904	1,595	810	441	437	451	363	414

PORTFOLIO (as of 8/31/02)

Portfolio Manager: Brian Younger - 2002

Investment Style

Large Cap	Growth
Mid Cap	Value
Small Cap	Grth/Val

Portfolio

0.0% cash	0.0% corp bonds
89.5% stocks	2.3% gov't bonds
0.0% preferred	0.0% muni bonds
0.0% conv't bds/wrnts	8.2% other

SHAREHOLDER INFORMATION

Minimum Investment
Initial: $2,500 — Subsequent: $250

Minimum IRA Investment
Initial: $500 — Subsequent: $250

Maximum Fees
Load: 3.00% front — 12b-1: none
Other: 0.75% redemption fee for 1 month

Services
✔ IRA
✔ Keogh
✔ Telephone Exchange

Gabelli Glbl Telcom/AAA (GABTX)

800-422-3554
www.gabelli.com

Telecommunications Sector

PERFORMANCE

fund inception date: 11/1/93

	3yr Annual	5yr Annual	10yr Annual	Bull	Bear
Return (%)	-24.8	0.5	na	140.9	-66.9
Differ From Category (+/-)	7.5 high	4.7 high	na	-79.6 blw av	9.7 high

Standard Deviation	Category Risk Index	Beta
25.4%—high	0.73—low	1.14

	2002	2001	2000	1999	1998	1997	1996	1995	1994	1993
Return (%)	-29.5	-20.7	-24.0	80.2	34.7	31.8	8.9	16.1	-3.6	—
Differ From Category (+/-)	5.9	11.0	4.6	-15.6	-3.2	10.3	-3.8	-5.7	-3.9	—
Return, Tax-Adjusted (%)	-29.5	-20.7	-26.5	76.6	32.7	29.1	6.7	15.5	-3.9	—

PER SHARE DATA

	2002	2001	2000	1999	1998	1997	1996	1995	1994	1993
Dividends, Net Income ($)	0.00	0.00	0.63	0.04	0.01	0.00	0.04	0.06	0.06	—
Distrib'ns, Cap Gain ($)	0.00	0.01	2.15	2.89	1.29	1.55	0.79	0.11	0.03	—
Net Asset Value ($)	9.83	13.96	17.63	26.95	16.62	13.32	11.28	11.12	9.73	—
Expense Ratio (%)	na	1.52	1.46	1.48	1.60	1.78	1.72	1.75	1.80	—
Yield (%)	0.00	0.00	3.18	0.13	0.05	0.00	0.33	0.53	0.61	—
Portfolio Turnover (%)	na	15	49	60	20	9	7	24	14	—
Total Assets (Millions $)	138	234	331	459	170	117	108	122	137	—

PORTFOLIO (as of 11/30/02)

Portfolio Manager: Mario Gabelli/Team
Managed - 1993

Investment Style

Large Cap	Growth
Mid Cap	Value
Small Cap	Grth/Val

Portfolio

1.4%	cash	0.0%	corp bonds
97.1%	stocks	0.0%	gov't bonds
0.2%	pref/conv't pref	0.0%	muni bonds
0.7%	conv't bds/wrnts	0.5%	other

SHAREHOLDER INFORMATION

Minimum Investment
Initial: $1,000 Subsequent: $1

Minimum IRA Investment
Initial: $250 Subsequent: $1

Maximum Fees
Load: none 12b-1: 0.25%
Other: none

Services
✔ IRA
Keogh
✔ Telephone Exchange

T Rowe Price Media & Tele (PRMTX)

800-638-5660, 410-345-2000
www.troweprice.com

Telecommunications Sector

PERFORMANCE — fund inception date: 7/28/97

	3yr Annual	5yr Annual	10yr Annual	Bull	Bear
Return (%)	-20.6	5.4	na	195.4	-61.0
Differ From Category (+/-)	11.7 high	9.6 high	na	-25.1 av	15.6 high

Standard Deviation	Category Risk Index	Beta
33.9%—high	0.97—av	1.42

	2002	2001	2000	1999	1998	1997	1996	1995	1994	1993
Return (%)	-28.3	-6.9	-25.1	93.0	35.1	—	—	—	—	—
Differ From Category (+/-)	7.1	24.8	3.5	-2.8	-2.8	—	—	—	—	—
Return, Tax-Adjusted (%)	-28.3	-6.9	-29.8	90.1	34.1	—	—	—	—	—

PER SHARE DATA

	2002	2001	2000	1999	1998	1997	1996	1995	1994	1993
Dividends, Net Income ($)	0.00	0.00	0.37	0.00	0.00	—	—	—	—	—
Distrib'ns, Cap Gain ($)	0.00	0.00	8.60	3.22	0.86	—	—	—	—	—
Net Asset Value ($)	14.43	20.15	21.65	39.99	22.54	—	—	—	—	—
Expense Ratio (%)	na	1.08	0.94	0.93	1.03	—	—	—	—	—
Yield (%)	0.00	0.00	1.22	0.00	0.00	—	—	—	—	—
Portfolio Turnover (%)	na	241	197	58	49	—	—	—	—	—
Total Assets (Millions $)	465	674	797	930	246	—	—	—	—	—

PORTFOLIO (as of 9/30/02)

Portfolio Manager: R Gensler/Team
Managed - 2000

Investment Style

Large Cap	Growth
Mid Cap	Value
Small Cap	Grth/Val

Portfolio

12.2% cash	0.0% corp bonds
87.8% stocks	0.0% gov't bonds
0.0% preferred	0.0% muni bonds
0.0% conv't bds/wrnts	0.0% other

SHAREHOLDER INFORMATION

Minimum Investment
Initial: $2,500 — Subsequent: $100

Minimum IRA Investment
Initial: $1,000 — Subsequent: $50

Maximum Fees
Load: none — 12b-1: none
Other: none

Services
✔ IRA
✔ Keogh
✔ Telephone Exchange

Utilities Sector Stock Funds
Category Performance Ranked by 2002 Returns

		Annual Return (%)				Category	Total
Category	Fund (Ticker)	2002	3yr	5yr	10yr	Risk	Risk
Sec-U	Strong Dividend Income (SDVIX)	-19.7	-3.1	1.8	na	av	av
Sec-U	Fidelity Utilities (FIUIX)	-26.6	-20.9	-4.2	5.3	high	abv av
Sec-U	Amer Cnt Utilities/Inv (BULIX)	-27.4	-15.8	-3.2	na	blw av	av
Sec-U	Fidelity Sel Utilities Gr (FSUTX)	-30.3	-22.2	-3.2	5.5	high	abv av
Utilities Sector Average		**-25.2**	**-16.1**	**-2.6**	**5.0**	**—**	**av**

Note: AAII members who would like performance figures for no-load and low-load mutual funds they own that do not appear in this Guide can access this information on our Web site at www.aaii.com.

Amer Cnt Utilities/Inv

800-345-2021, 816-531-5575
www.americancentury.com

(BULIX)

Utilities Sector

PERFORMANCE **fund inception date: 3/1/93**

	3yr Annual	5yr Annual	10yr Annual	Bull	Bear
Return (%)	-15.8	-3.2	na	48.7	-49.2
Differ From Category (+/-)	0.3 high	-0.6 abv av	na	-15.1 av	0.0 high

Standard Deviation	Category Risk Index	Beta
16.1%—av	0.85—blw av	0.60

	2002	2001	2000	1999	1998	1997	1996	1995	1994	1993
Return (%)	-27.4	-20.9	3.9	11.4	27.4	35.8	4.8	35.6	-10.0	—
Differ From Category (+/-)	-2.2	-0.4	3.7	-5.4	-1.3	6.0	-4.9	3.1	-3.0	—
Return, Tax-Adjusted (%)	-28.3	-21.6	0.5	9.4	24.0	32.9	3.2	33.7	-11.7	—

PER SHARE DATA

	2002	2001	2000	1999	1998	1997	1996	1995	1994	1993
Dividends, Net Income ($)	0.27	0.24	0.98	0.34	0.37	0.42	0.45	0.41	0.41	—
Distrib'ns, Cap Gain ($)	0.00	0.02	0.83	0.92	1.66	0.84	0.00	0.00	0.02	—
Net Asset Value ($)	8.31	11.81	15.26	16.46	15.96	14.24	11.51	11.44	8.79	—
Expense Ratio (%)	na	0.68	0.67	0.68	0.69	0.72	0.71	0.75	0.75	—
Yield (%)	3.24	2.02	6.09	1.95	2.09	2.78	3.90	3.58	4.65	—
Portfolio Turnover (%)	na	10	32	50	98	92	93	68	61	—
Total Assets (Millions $)	120	199	295	319	307	206	144	217	152	—

PORTFOLIO (as of 9/30/02)

Portfolio Manager: Team Managed - 1996

Investment Style

Large Cap	Growth
Mid Cap	Value
Small Cap	Grth/Val

Portfolio

2.2%	cash	0.0%	corp bonds
97.8%	stocks	0.0%	gov't bonds
0.0%	preferred	0.0%	muni bonds
0.0%	conv't bds/wrnts	0.0%	other

SHAREHOLDER INFORMATION

Minimum Investment
Initial: $2,500 Subsequent: $50

Minimum IRA Investment
Initial: $1,000 Subsequent: $50

Maximum Fees
Load: none 12b-1: none
Other: none

Services
✔ IRA
✔ Keogh
✔ Telephone Exchange

Fidelity Sel Utilities Gr (FSUTX)

800-544-8544, 800-522-7297
www.fidelity.com

Utilities Sector

PERFORMANCE — fund inception date: 12/10/81

	3yr Annual	5yr Annual	10yr Annual	Bull	Bear
Return (%)	-22.2	-3.2	5.5	92.0	-62.6
Differ From Category (+/-)	-6.1 blw av	-0.6 high	0.5 high	28.2 high	-13.4 blw av

Standard Deviation	Category Risk Index	Beta
21.8%—abv av	1.15—high	0.91

	2002	2001	2000	1999	1998	1997	1996	1995	1994	1993
Return (%)	-30.3	-21.8	-13.5	25.9	43.1	30.3	11.3	34.3	-7.4	12.5
Differ From Category (+/-)	-5.1	-1.3	-13.7	9.1	14.4	0.5	1.6	1.8	-0.4	-3.9
Return, Tax-Adjusted (%)	-30.8	-22.4	-16.1	22.6	39.7	26.5	8.4	33.3	-9.0	7.8

PER SHARE DATA

	2002	2001	2000	1999	1998	1997	1996	1995	1994	1993
Dividends, Net Income ($)	0.48	0.26	1.97	0.42	0.25	0.58	0.70	0.84	1.05	1.13
Distrib'ns, Cap Gain ($)	0.00	0.93	4.85	9.30	7.93	7.30	3.54	0.00	0.67	4.94
Net Asset Value ($)	26.40	38.59	50.80	66.10	60.94	48.88	43.90	43.59	33.08	37.58
Expense Ratio (%)	1.09	0.99	1.04	1.16	1.33	1.47	1.38	1.42	1.35	1.42
Yield (%)	1.81	0.65	3.53	0.55	0.36	1.03	1.47	1.92	3.11	2.65
Portfolio Turnover (%)	54	80	93	113	78	31	65	24	61	34
Total Assets (Millions $)	183	319	539	626	504	358	255	312	202	275

PORTFOLIO (as of 8/31/02)

Portfolio Manager: Shep Perkins - 2002

Investment Style

Large Cap	Growth
Mid Cap	Value
Small Cap	Grth/Val

Portfolio

0.0%	cash	0.0%	corp bonds
89.8%	stocks	0.0%	gov't bonds
0.5%	pref/conv't pref	0.0%	muni bonds
0.0%	conv't bds/wrnts	9.7%	other

SHAREHOLDER INFORMATION

Minimum Investment
Initial: $2,500 — Subsequent: $250

Minimum IRA Investment
Initial: $500 — Subsequent: $250

Maximum Fees
Load: 3.00% front — 12b-1: none
Other: 0.75% redemption fee for 1 month

Services
✔ IRA
✔ Keogh
✔ Telephone Exchange

Fidelity Utilities (FIUIX)

800-544-8544, 800-522-7297
www.fidelity.com

Utilities Sector

PERFORMANCE — fund inception date: 11/27/87

	3yr Annual	5yr Annual	10yr Annual	Bull	Bear
Return (%)	-20.9	-4.2	5.3	83.0	-61.5
Differ From Category (+/-)	-4.8 av	-1.6 av	0.3 abv av	19.2 high	-12.3 av

Standard Deviation	Category Risk Index	Beta
20.5%—abv av	1.09—high	0.85

	2002	2001	2000	1999	1998	1997	1996	1995	1994	1993
Return (%)	-26.6	-15.1	-20.4	26.7	28.5	31.5	11.4	30.6	-5.2	15.6
Differ From Category (+/-)	-1.4	5.4	-20.6	9.9	-0.2	1.7	1.7	-1.9	1.8	-0.8
Return, Tax-Adjusted (%)	-27.2	-15.5	-24.2	23.8	26.5	27.9	9.3	28.4	-8.1	13.7

PER SHARE DATA

	2002	2001	2000	1999	1998	1997	1996	1995	1994	1993
Dividends, Net Income ($)	0.20	0.16	0.09	0.18	0.35	0.44	0.48	0.54	0.54	0.52
Distrib'ns, Cap Gain ($)	0.00	0.00	4.73	3.05	1.29	2.20	0.54	0.28	0.80	0.22
Net Asset Value ($)	9.70	13.49	16.09	25.77	23.18	19.46	16.91	16.16	13.06	15.18
Expense Ratio (%)	0.89	0.78	0.80	0.85	0.85	0.81	0.77	0.87	0.86	0.87
Yield (%)	2.06	1.18	0.43	0.62	1.43	2.03	2.75	3.28	3.89	3.37
Portfolio Turnover (%)	58	126	50	55	57	56	98	98	47	73
Total Assets (Millions $)	819	1,427	2,125	2,884	2,128	1,708	1,267	1,510	1,079	1,456

PORTFOLIO (as of 7/31/02)

Portfolio Manager: Martin Zinny - 2002

Investment Style

Large Cap	Growth
Mid Cap	Value
Small Cap	Grth/Val

Portfolio

0.0%	cash	0.0%	corp bonds
95.7%	stocks	0.0%	gov't bonds
2.4%	pref/conv't pref	0.0%	muni bonds
0.0%	conv't bds/wrnts	1.9%	other

SHAREHOLDER INFORMATION

Minimum Investment
Initial: $2,500 Subsequent: $250

Minimum IRA Investment
Initial: $500 Subsequent: $250

Maximum Fees
Load: none 12b-1: none
Other: none

Services
✔ IRA
✔ Keogh
✔ Telephone Exchange

Strong Dividend Income (SDVIX)

800-368-3863, 414-359-1400
www.strong-funds.com

Utilities Sector

PERFORMANCE — fund inception date: 7/1/93

	3yr Annual	5yr Annual	10yr Annual	Bull	Bear
Return (%)	-3.1	1.8	na	24.7	-16.0
Differ From Category (+/-)	13.0 high	4.4 high	na	-39.1 blw av	33.2 high

Standard Deviation	Category Risk Index	Beta
16.9%—av	0.89—av	0.47

	2002	2001	2000	1999	1998	1997	1996	1995	1994	1993
Return (%)	-19.7	-11.1	27.3	0.5	20.3	27.5	8.3	36.9	-2.6	—
Differ From Category (+/-)	5.5	9.4	27.1	-16.3	-8.4	-2.3	-1.4	4.4	4.4	—
Return, Tax-Adjusted (%)	-20.4	-11.9	25.2	-2.5	18.5	25.1	5.5	35.5	-4.4	—

PER SHARE DATA

	2002	2001	2000	1999	1998	1997	1996	1995	1994	1993
Dividends, Net Income ($)	0.14	0.35	0.35	0.40	0.38	0.36	0.40	0.32	0.46	—
Distrib'ns, Cap Gain ($)	0.25	0.00	0.82	1.76	0.61	0.76	0.67	0.00	0.00	—
Net Asset Value ($)	11.85	15.19	17.49	14.74	16.81	14.82	12.54	12.58	9.46	—
Expense Ratio (%)	na	1.10	1.00	1.00	1.00	1.10	1.20	1.30	0.50	—
Yield (%)	1.15	2.30	1.91	2.42	2.18	2.31	3.02	2.54	4.86	—
Portfolio Turnover (%)	na	77	7	69	69	61	84	56	105	—
Total Assets (Millions $)	158	234	297	216	245	187	134	118	37	—

PORTFOLIO (as of 9/30/02)

Portfolio Manager: Reaves/Ferer/Sorenson/Luftig - 1993

Investment Style

Large Cap	Growth
Mid Cap	Value
Small Cap	Grth/Val

Portfolio

3.8% cash	0.0% corp bonds
95.0% stocks	0.0% gov't bonds
1.2% pref/conv't pref	0.0% muni bonds
0.0% conv't bds/wrnts	0.0% other

SHAREHOLDER INFORMATION

Minimum Investment
Initial: $2,500 — Subsequent: $100

Minimum IRA Investment
Initial: $250 — Subsequent: $50

Maximum Fees
Load: none — 12b-1: none
Other: none

Services
✔ IRA
✔ Keogh
✔ Telephone Exchange

INTERNATIONAL STOCK FUNDS

Global Stock Funds

Category Performance Ranked by 2002 Returns

Category	Fund (Ticker)	Annual Return (%) 2002	3yr	5yr	10yr	Category Risk	Total Risk
IntS-Glb	Vanguard Global Equity (VHGEX)	-5.6	-3.1	4.5	na	av	av
IntS-Glb	Tweedy Browne Glbl Value (TBGVX)	-12.1	-1.9	5.5	na	blw av	blw av
IntS-Glb	Fremont:Global (FMAFX)	-12.9	-9.9	-0.3	5.3	blw av	blw av
IntS-Glb	UMB Scout Worldwide (UMBWX)	-15.8	-11.7	1.2	na	av	av
IntS-Glb	Fidelity Worldwide (FWWFX)	-18.8	-11.1	-0.3	7.0	abv av	av
IntS-Glb	Janus Worldwide (JAWWX)	-26.6	-22.2	-0.5	9.1	abv av	abv av
Global Stock Average		**-16.7**	**-13.8**	**-0.8**	**5.9**	**—**	**av**

Note: AAII members who would like performance figures for no-load and low-load mutual funds they own that do not appear in this Guide can access this information on our Web site at www.aaii.com.

Fidelity Worldwide (FWWFX)

800-544-8544, 800-522-7297
www.fidelity.com

Global Stock

PERFORMANCE — fund inception date: 5/30/90

	3yr Annual	5yr Annual	10yr Annual	Bull	Bear
Return (%)	-11.1	-0.3	7.0	53.4	-35.2
Differ From Category (+/-)	2.7 abv av	0.5 abv av	1.1 high	-16.9 abv av	3.0 abv av

Standard Deviation	Category Risk Index	Beta
17.0%—av	1.02—abv av	0.81

	2002	2001	2000	1999	1998	1997	1996	1995	1994	1993
Return (%)	-18.8	-6.2	-8.0	30.7	7.1	12.0	18.7	7.1	2.9	36.5
Differ From Category (+/-)	-2.1	8.9	1.2	-9.9	-4.0	-2.5	1.0	-10.8	4.2	8.3
Return, Tax-Adjusted (%)	-18.9	-6.2	-11.1	28.6	6.3	10.2	17.4	6.6	1.3	35.7

PER SHARE DATA

	2002	2001	2000	1999	1998	1997	1996	1995	1994	1993
Dividends, Net Income ($)	0.02	0.00	0.40	0.10	0.10	0.11	0.17	0.15	0.07	0.10
Distrib'ns, Cap Gain ($)	0.00	0.00	2.25	1.52	0.44	1.16	0.38	0.00	0.66	0.15
Net Asset Value ($)	11.88	14.66	15.63	19.90	16.53	15.95	15.39	13.44	12.68	13.03
Expense Ratio (%)	1.20	1.05	1.04	1.07	1.12	1.16	1.18	1.17	1.32	1.40
Yield (%)	0.16	0.00	2.23	0.46	0.58	0.64	1.07	1.11	0.52	0.75
Portfolio Turnover (%)	120	152	235	164	100	85	49	49	69	57
Total Assets (Millions $)	642	807	928	1,125	1,013	1,145	925	654	703	339

PORTFOLIO (as of 10/31/02)

Portfolio Manager: Richard Mace - 2002

Investment Style

Large Cap	Growth
Mid Cap	Value
Small Cap	Grth/Val

Portfolio

0.8% cash	0.2% corp bonds
97.4% stocks	0.0% gov't bonds
0.0% preferred	0.0% muni bonds
0.0% conv't bds/wrnts	1.7% other

SHAREHOLDER INFORMATION

Minimum Investment
Initial: $2,500 Subsequent: $250

Minimum IRA Investment
Initial: $500 Subsequent: $250

Maximum Fees
Load: 1.00% redemption 12b-1: none
Other: redemption fee applies for 1 month

Services
✔ IRA
✔ Keogh
✔ Telephone Exchange

Fremont:Global (FMAFX)

800-548-4539, 800-565-0254
www.fremontfunds.com

Global Stock

PERFORMANCE **fund inception date: 11/18/88**

	3yr Annual	5yr Annual	10yr Annual	Bull	Bear
Return (%)	-9.9	-0.3	5.3	48.2	-33.5
Differ From Category (+/-)	3.9 abv av	0.5 av	-0.6 blw av	-22.1 av	4.7 abv av

Standard Deviation	Category Risk Index	Beta
13.0%—blw av	0.78—blw av	0.60

	2002	2001	2000	1999	1998	1997	1996	1995	1994	1993
Return (%)	-12.9	-10.2	-6.6	22.3	10.0	9.9	13.9	19.2	-4.1	19.5
Differ From Category (+/-)	3.8	4.9	2.6	-18.3	-1.1	-4.6	-3.8	1.3	-2.8	-8.7
Return, Tax-Adjusted (%)	-13.1	-10.6	-9.8	19.1	7.8	7.6	9.0	16.4	-4.8	18.3

PER SHARE DATA

	2002	2001	2000	1999	1998	1997	1996	1995	1994	1993
Dividends, Net Income ($)	0.06	0.14	0.61	0.49	0.24	0.47	0.49	0.49	0.13	0.32
Distrib'ns, Cap Gain ($)	0.00	0.00	1.22	1.30	1.04	0.60	1.80	0.57	0.13	0.07
Net Asset Value ($)	9.57	11.07	12.50	15.30	14.11	14.04	13.77	14.16	12.79	13.62
Expense Ratio (%)	na	0.93	0.90	0.86	0.85	0.85	0.87	0.89	0.95	0.99
Yield (%)	0.62	1.26	4.44	2.95	1.58	3.21	3.14	3.32	1.00	2.33
Portfolio Turnover (%)	na	173	112	113	75	48	71	70	52	40
Total Assets (Millions $)	529	631	747	772	646	661	596	502	438	214

PORTFOLIO (as of 7/31/02)

Portfolio Manager: Team Managed - 1988

Investment Style

Large Cap	Growth
Mid Cap	Value
Small Cap	Grth/Val

Portfolio

3.5%	cash	8.5%	corp bonds
63.8%	stocks	24.3%	gov't bonds
0.0%	preferred	0.0%	muni bonds
0.0%	conv't bds/wrnts	0.0%	other

SHAREHOLDER INFORMATION

Minimum Investment
Initial: $2,000 Subsequent: $100

Minimum IRA Investment
Initial: $1,000 Subsequent: $100

Maximum Fees
Load: none 12b-1: none
Other: none

Services
✔ IRA
✔ Keogh
✔ Telephone Exchange

Janus Worldwide (JAWWX)

800-525-0020, 303-333-3863
www.janus.com

Global Stock

PERFORMANCE — fund inception date: 5/15/91

	3yr Annual	5yr Annual	10yr Annual	Bull	Bear
Return (%)	-22.2	-0.5	9.1	113.8	-59.0
Differ From Category (+/-)	-8.4 blw av	0.3 av	3.2 high	43.5 high	-20.8 blw av

Standard Deviation	Category Risk Index	Beta
22.0%—abv av	1.33—abv av	0.91

	2002	2001	2000	1999	1998	1997	1996	1995	1994	1993
Return (%)	-26.6	-22.8	-16.8	64.3	25.8	20.4	26.4	21.8	3.6	28.4
Differ From Category (+/-)	-9.9	-7.7	-7.6	23.7	14.7	5.9	8.7	3.9	4.9	0.2
Return, Tax-Adjusted (%)	-26.6	-22.8	-18.7	63.7	25.6	18.6	24.2	20.1	1.6	27.3

PER SHARE DATA

	2002	2001	2000	1999	1998	1997	1996	1995	1994	1993
Dividends, Net Income ($)	0.03	0.01	0.41	0.02	0.19	0.19	0.15	0.26	0.53	0.27
Distrib'ns, Cap Gain ($)	0.00	0.00	6.50	1.28	0.00	2.59	2.04	1.06	1.00	0.37
Net Asset Value ($)	32.13	43.84	56.86	76.43	47.36	37.78	33.69	28.40	24.39	25.03
Expense Ratio (%)	na	0.85	0.86	0.88	0.90	0.95	1.01	1.24	1.12	1.32
Yield (%)	0.09	0.02	0.64	0.02	0.40	0.47	0.41	0.88	2.08	1.06
Portfolio Turnover (%)	na	78	58	68	86	79	80	142	158	124
Total Assets (Millions $)	13,793	21,678	33,144	33,802	16,322	10,567	5,046	1,975	1,542	935

PORTFOLIO (as of 10/31/02)

Portfolio Manager: Helen Hayes/Laurence Chang - 1991

Investment Style

Large Cap	Growth
Mid Cap	Value
Small Cap	Grth/Val

Portfolio

9.0% cash	0.0% corp bonds
87.8% stocks	0.0% gov't bonds
0.6% pref/conv't pref	0.0% muni bonds
0.0% conv't bds/wrnts	2.5% other

SHAREHOLDER INFORMATION

Minimum Investment
Initial: $2,500 Subsequent: $100

Minimum IRA Investment
Initial: $500 Subsequent: $100

Maximum Fees
Load: none 12b-1: none
Other: none

Services
✔ IRA
✔ Keogh
✔ Telephone Exchange

Tweedy Browne Glbl Value (TBGVX)

800-432-4789, 212-916-0600
www.tweedy.com

Global Stock

PERFORMANCE — fund inception date: 6/15/93

	3yr Annual	5yr Annual	10yr Annual	Bull	Bear
Return (%)	-1.9	5.5	na	46.0	-13.7
Differ From Category (+/-)	11.9 high	6.3 high	na	-24.3 blw av	24.5 high

Standard Deviation	Category Risk Index	Beta
11.4%—blw av	0.68—blw av	0.43

	2002	2001	2000	1999	1998	1997	1996	1995	1994	1993
Return (%)	-12.1	-4.6	12.3	25.2	10.9	22.9	20.2	10.6	4.3	—
Differ From Category (+/-)	4.6	10.5	21.5	-15.4	-0.2	8.4	2.5	-7.3	5.6	—
Return, Tax-Adjusted (%)	-12.8	-5.3	9.4	23.9	8.8	19.8	17.3	10.1	3.9	—

PER SHARE DATA

	2002	2001	2000	1999	1998	1997	1996	1995	1994	1993
Dividends, Net Income ($)	0.19	0.18	0.20	0.25	0.37	0.87	0.55	0.00	0.00	—
Distrib'ns, Cap Gain ($)	0.26	0.32	2.51	0.58	0.99	0.48	0.56	0.20	0.16	—
Net Asset Value ($)	15.81	18.53	19.98	20.21	16.82	16.39	14.45	12.95	11.88	—
Expense Ratio (%)	1.37	1.38	1.38	1.41	1.42	1.58	1.60	1.65	1.73	—
Yield (%)	1.18	0.95	0.88	1.20	2.07	5.15	3.66	0.00	0.00	—
Portfolio Turnover (%)	7	12	16	23	16	20	17	16	143	—
Total Assets (Millions $)	4,237	4,075	3,529	3,141	2,492	1,985	1,211	801	565	—

PORTFOLIO (as of 11/30/02)

Portfolio Manager: C Browne/W Browne/ J Spears - 1993

Investment Style

Large Cap	Growth
Mid Cap	Value
Small Cap	Grth/Val

Portfolio

0.0%	cash	0.0%	corp bonds
92.9%	stocks	0.0%	gov't bonds
1.2%	pref/conv't pref	0.0%	muni bonds
0.0%	conv't bds/wrnts	5.9%	other

SHAREHOLDER INFORMATION

Minimum Investment
Initial: $2,500 Subsequent: $200

Minimum IRA Investment
Initial: $500 Subsequent: $200

Maximum Fees
Load: none 12b-1: none
Other: none

Services
✔ IRA
Keogh
✔ Telephone Exchange

UMB Scout Worldwide (UMBWX)

800-996-2862, 816-860-3714
www.umb.com

Global Stock

PERFORMANCE — fund inception date: 9/14/93

	3yr Annual	5yr Annual	10yr Annual	Bull	Bear
Return (%)	-11.7	1.2	na	52.8	-36.6
Differ From Category (+/-)	2.1 av	2.0 abv av	na	-17.5 av	1.6 av

Standard Deviation	Category Risk Index	Beta
14.7%—av	0.89—av	0.66

	2002	2001	2000	1999	1998	1997	1996	1995	1994	1993
Return (%)	-15.8	-11.0	-8.1	31.4	17.9	18.3	18.3	14.6	4.2	—
Differ From Category (+/-)	0.9	4.1	1.1	-9.2	6.8	3.8	0.6	-3.3	5.5	—
Return, Tax-Adjusted (%)	-16.1	-11.4	-8.7	30.6	17.1	17.3	17.3	13.5	3.2	—

PER SHARE DATA

	2002	2001	2000	1999	1998	1997	1996	1995	1994	1993
Dividends, Net Income ($)	0.13	0.22	0.04	0.21	0.31	0.24	0.23	0.22	0.22	—
Distrib'ns, Cap Gain ($)	0.00	0.00	0.56	0.36	0.01	0.22	0.10	0.12	0.07	—
Net Asset Value ($)	15.58	18.67	21.24	23.77	18.56	16.02	13.94	12.08	10.84	—
Expense Ratio (%)	1.12	0.91	0.91	0.86	0.87	0.86	0.85	0.85	0.85	—
Yield (%)	0.83	1.17	0.18	0.87	1.66	1.47	1.63	1.80	2.01	—
Portfolio Turnover (%)	13	10	8	8	3	18	5	27	24	—
Total Assets (Millions $)	387	358	307	267	107	57	42	23	17	—

PORTFOLIO (as of 11/30/02)

Portfolio Manager: James Moffett - 1993

Investment Style

Large Cap	Growth
Mid Cap	Value
Small Cap	Grth/Val

Portfolio

15.7%	cash	1.1%	corp bonds
81.3%	stocks	0.7%	gov't bonds
0.0%	preferred	0.0%	muni bonds
0.0%	conv't bds/wrnts	1.2%	other

SHAREHOLDER INFORMATION

Minimum Investment
Initial: $1,000 — Subsequent: $100

Minimum IRA Investment
Initial: $250 — Subsequent: $100

Maximum Fees
Load: none — 12b-1: none
Other: none

Services
✔ IRA
✔ Keogh
✔ Telephone Exchange

Vanguard Global Equity (VHGEX)

800-662-7447, 610-436-5152
www.vanguard.com

Global Stock

PERFORMANCE — fund inception date: 8/14/95

	3yr Annual	5yr Annual	10yr Annual	Bull	Bear
Return (%)	-3.1	4.5	na	48.9	-15.9
Differ From Category (+/-)	10.7 high	5.3 high	na	-21.4 av	22.3 high

Standard Deviation	Category Risk Index	Beta
16.7%—av	1.00—av	0.75

	2002	2001	2000	1999	1998	1997	1996	1995	1994	1993
Return (%)	-5.6	-3.7	-0.1	25.9	9.3	6.9	15.5	—	—	—
Differ From Category (+/-)	11.1	11.4	9.1	-14.7	-1.8	-7.6	-2.2	—	—	—
Return, Tax-Adjusted (%)	-5.9	-4.8	-2.5	23.9	7.2	5.4	14.5	—	—	—

PER SHARE DATA

	2002	2001	2000	1999	1998	1997	1996	1995	1994	1993
Dividends, Net Income ($)	0.08	0.12	0.26	0.18	0.26	0.23	0.14	—	—	—
Distrib'ns, Cap Gain ($)	0.02	0.44	1.17	0.84	0.75	0.44	0.19	—	—	—
Net Asset Value ($)	10.83	11.58	12.62	14.14	12.06	11.98	11.84	—	—	—
Expense Ratio (%)	na	1.08	0.70	0.71	0.68	0.71	0.85	—	—	—
Yield (%)	0.73	0.99	1.88	1.20	2.02	1.85	1.16	—	—	—
Portfolio Turnover (%)	na	27	31	36	34	24	29	—	—	—
Total Assets (Millions $)	244	157	142	144	128	126	106	—	—	—

PORTFOLIO (as of 9/30/02)

Portfolio Manager: Jeremy Hosking - 1995

Investment Style

Large Cap	Growth
Mid Cap	Value
Small Cap	Grth/Val

Portfolio

4.4%	cash	0.0%	corp bonds
95.6%	stocks	0.0%	gov't bonds
0.0%	preferred	0.0%	muni bonds
0.0%	conv't bds/wrnts	0.0%	other

SHAREHOLDER INFORMATION

Minimum Investment
Initial: $3,000 Subsequent: $100

Minimum IRA Investment
Initial: $1,000 Subsequent: $100

Maximum Fees
Load: none 12b-1: none
Other: none

Services
✔ IRA
✔ Keogh
✔ Telephone Exchange

Foreign Stock Funds

Category Performance Ranked by 2002 Returns

		Annual Return (%)				Category	Total
Category	Fund (Ticker)	2002	3yr	5yr	10yr	Risk	Risk
IntS-F	Harbor Intl/Inst (HAINX)	-6.3	-7.9	1.3	10.1	av	av
IntS-F	Preferred Intl Value (PFIFX)	-7.6	-8.4	2.4	8.4	av	av
IntS-F	Oakmark Intl/I (OAKIX)	-8.4	-0.7	4.8	9.7	abv av	abv av
IntS-F	USAA Inv:International (USIFX)	-9.0	-12.4	-2.3	6.0	low	av
IntS-F	Fidelity Diversified Intl (FDIVX)	-9.3	-10.4	4.3	10.6	low	av
IntS-F	Fidelity Intl Grth & Inc (FIGRX)	-9.8	-13.8	1.5	6.7	blw av	av
IntS-F	Fidelity Aggressive Intl (FIVFX)	-11.0	-17.5	-0.1	na	high	abv av
IntS-F	Vanguard Intl Value (VTRIX)	-13.3	-11.6	0.0	4.7	av	av
IntS-F	Masters Select Intl (MSILX)	-14.3	-12.5	5.4	na	abv av	av
IntS-F	Harding Loevner Intl Eqty (HLMIX)	-15.0	-16.3	-0.6	na	blw av	av
IntS-F	Vanguard Tot Itl Stk Idx (VGTSX)	-15.0	-16.9	-2.9	na	blw av	av
IntS-F	Wm Blair:Intl Grth/N (WBIGX)	-15.1	-12.3	8.0	9.7	av	av
IntS-F	Schwab Intl Index/I (SWINX)	-15.6	-18.7	-3.6	na	blw av	av
IntS-F	TIAA-CREF Intl Equity (TIINX)	-15.7	-20.0	-1.0	na	abv av	abv av
IntS-F	Vanguard Intl Gr (VWIGX)	-17.7	-15.2	-2.0	6.0	blw av	av
IntS-F	T Rowe Price Intl Stk (PRITX)	-18.1	-19.1	-3.7	4.3	abv av	av
IntS-F	Schwab Intl MarketMstrs (SWOIX)	-18.3	-15.6	3.5	na	abv av	abv av
IntS-F	Artisan International (ARTIX)	-18.8	-15.1	7.8	na	high	abv av
IntS-F	Amer Cnt Intl Gr/Inv (TWIEX)	-19.2	-20.4	-0.3	7.4	abv av	av
IntS-F	Fidelity Overseas (FOSFX)	-19.4	-19.3	-3.2	5.0	av	av
Foreign Stock Average		**-15.9**	**-17.6**	**-1.1**	**5.5**	**—**	**av**

Note: AAII members who would like performance figures for no-load and low-load mutual funds they own that do not appear in this Guide can access this information on our Web site at www.aaii.com.

Amer Cnt Intl Gr/Inv (TWIEX)

800-345-2021, 816-531-5575
www.americancentury.com

Foreign Stock

PERFORMANCE — fund inception date: 5/9/91

	3yr Annual	5yr Annual	10yr Annual	Bull	Bear
Return (%)	-20.4	-0.3	7.4	84.0	-53.6
Differ From Category (+/-)	-2.8 blw av	0.8 abv av	1.9 abv av	6.8 abv av	-6.4 blw av

Standard Deviation	Category Risk Index	Beta
18.8%—av	1.02—abv av	0.57

	2002	2001	2000	1999	1998	1997	1996	1995	1994	1993
Return (%)	-19.2	-26.7	-15.0	64.4	19.0	19.7	14.4	11.8	-4.7	42.6
Differ From Category (+/-)	-3.3	-6.1	0.9	12.7	5.6	14.8	-1.4	0.8	-3.0	2.3
Return, Tax-Adjusted (%)	-19.5	-26.8	-17.3	62.9	18.6	16.3	11.1	11.8	-6.1	40.6

PER SHARE DATA

	2002	2001	2000	1999	1998	1997	1996	1995	1994	1993
Dividends, Net Income ($)	0.05	0.03	0.00	0.00	0.01	0.02	0.00	0.00	0.00	0.00
Distrib'ns, Cap Gain ($)	0.00	0.00	1.75	0.69	0.14	1.27	0.91	0.00	0.37	0.40
Net Asset Value ($)	6.38	7.97	10.93	14.97	9.58	8.19	7.96	7.78	6.96	7.70
Expense Ratio (%)	na	1.21	1.20	1.27	1.33	1.38	1.65	1.77	1.84	1.90
Yield (%)	0.78	0.37	0.00	0.00	0.10	0.21	0.00	0.00	0.00	0.00
Portfolio Turnover (%)	na	178	116	117	190	163	158	169	242	255
Total Assets (Millions $)	2,417	3,311	4,754	4,521	2,640	1,809	1,364	1,258	1,272	944

PORTFOLIO (as of 9/30/02)

Portfolio Manager: H Strabo/M Kopinski - 1994

Investment Style

Large Cap	Growth
Mid Cap	Value
Small Cap	Grth/Val

Portfolio

0.0%	cash	0.0%	corp bonds
92.8%	stocks	0.0%	gov't bonds
0.0%	preferred	0.0%	muni bonds
1.3%	conv't bds/wrnts	5.9%	other

SHAREHOLDER INFORMATION

Minimum Investment
Initial: $2,500 Subsequent: $50

Minimum IRA Investment
Initial: $1,000 Subsequent: $50

Maximum Fees
Load: none 12b-1: none
Other: none

Services
✔ IRA
✔ Keogh
✔ Telephone Exchange

Artisan International

800-344-1770, 414-390-6100
www.artisanfunds.com

(ARTIX)

Foreign Stock

PERFORMANCE — fund inception date: 12/28/95

	3yr Annual	5yr Annual	10yr Annual	Bull	Bear
Return (%)	-15.1	7.8	na	145.2	-50.2
Differ From Category (+/-)	2.5 abv av	8.9 high	na	68.0 high	-3.0 blw av

Standard Deviation	Category Risk Index	Beta
21.2%—abv av	1.16—high	0.66

	2002	2001	2000	1999	1998	1997	1996	1995	1994	1993
Return (%)	-18.8	-15.8	-10.5	81.2	32.1	3.4	34.3	—	—	—
Differ From Category (+/-)	-2.9	4.8	5.4	29.5	18.7	-1.5	18.5	—	—	—
Return, Tax-Adjusted (%)	-19.0	-15.9	-13.0	80.5	31.6	1.1	34.0	—	—	—

PER SHARE DATA

	2002	2001	2000	1999	1998	1997	1996	1995	1994	1993
Dividends, Net Income ($)	0.10	0.06	0.00	0.02	0.03	0.19	0.01	—	—	—
Distrib'ns, Cap Gain ($)	0.00	0.00	3.55	0.53	0.24	1.12	0.09	—	—	—
Net Asset Value ($)	14.79	18.36	21.90	28.50	16.12	12.46	13.32	—	—	—
Expense Ratio (%)	1.21	1.22	1.27	1.38	1.45	1.61	2.50	—	—	—
Yield (%)	0.67	0.32	0.00	0.06	0.18	1.39	0.07	—	—	—
Portfolio Turnover (%)	51	72	99	79	109	103	57	—	—	—
Total Assets (Millions $)	7,221	5,693	4,927	3,027	612	271	193	—	—	—

PORTFOLIO (as of 9/30/02)

Portfolio Manager: Mark Yockey - 1995

Investment Style

Large Cap	Growth
Mid Cap	Value
Small Cap	Grth/Val

Portfolio

0.0%	cash	0.0%	corp bonds
97.4%	stocks	0.0%	gov't bonds
0.0%	preferred	0.0%	muni bonds
0.0%	conv't bds/wrnts	2.6%	other

SHAREHOLDER INFORMATION

Minimum Investment
Initial: $1,000 Subsequent: $50

Minimum IRA Investment
Initial: $1,000 Subsequent: $50

Maximum Fees
Load: none 12b-1: none
Other: none

Services
✔ IRA
✔ Keogh
✔ Telephone Exchange

Fidelity Aggressive Intl (FIVFX)

800-544-8544, 800-522-7297
www.fidelity.com

Foreign Stock

PERFORMANCE — fund inception date: 11/1/94

	3yr Annual	5yr Annual	10yr Annual	Bull	Bear
Return (%)	-17.5	-0.1	na	83.4	-45.2
Differ From Category (+/-)	0.1 av	1.0 abv av	na	6.2 abv av	2.0 abv av

Standard Deviation	Category Risk Index	Beta
22.8%—abv av	1.24—high	0.86

	2002	2001	2000	1999	1998	1997	1996	1995	1994	1993
Return (%)	-11.0	-8.8	-30.9	58.8	11.7	7.8	9.5	13.9	—	—
Differ From Category (+/-)	4.9	11.8	-15.0	7.1	-1.7	2.9	-6.3	2.9	—	—
Return, Tax-Adjusted (%)	-11.0	-9.0	-31.6	57.2	11.5	7.1	8.6	13.0	—	—

PER SHARE DATA

	2002	2001	2000	1999	1998	1997	1996	1995	1994	1993
Dividends, Net Income ($)	0.01	0.06	0.02	0.08	0.05	0.06	0.10	0.01	—	—
Distrib'ns, Cap Gain ($)	0.00	0.00	0.70	0.90	0.00	0.28	0.22	0.30	—	—
Net Asset Value ($)	10.73	12.07	13.31	20.31	13.48	12.11	11.55	10.84	—	—
Expense Ratio (%)	1.40	1.02	1.16	1.14	1.21	1.28	1.26	1.72	—	—
Yield (%)	0.09	0.49	0.14	0.37	0.37	0.48	0.84	0.08	—	—
Portfolio Turnover (%)	188	242	344	173	137	86	71	109	—	—
Total Assets (Millions $)	305	220	346	697	435	390	267	72	—	—

PORTFOLIO (as of 10/31/02)

Portfolio Manager: Kevin McCarey - 1999

Investment Style

Large Cap	Growth
Mid Cap	Value
Small Cap	Grth/Val

Portfolio

2.5%	cash	0.0%	corp bonds
91.4%	stocks	0.0%	gov't bonds
0.0%	preferred	0.0%	muni bonds
0.0%	conv't bds/wrnts	6.1%	other

SHAREHOLDER INFORMATION

Minimum Investment
Initial: $2,500 Subsequent: $250

Minimum IRA Investment
Initial: $500 Subsequent: $250

Maximum Fees
Load: 1.00% redemption 12b-1: none
Other: redemption fee applies for 1 month

Services
✔ IRA
✔ Keogh
✔ Telephone Exchange

Fidelity Diversified Intl (FDIVX)

800-544-8544, 800-522-7297
www.fidelity.com

Foreign Stock

PERFORMANCE — fund inception date: 12/30/91

	3yr Annual	5yr Annual	10yr Annual	Bull	Bear
Return (%)	-10.4	4.3	10.6	72.4	-32.5
Differ From Category (+/-)	7.2 high	5.4 high	5.1 high	-4.8 av	14.7 high

Standard Deviation	Category Risk Index	Beta
15.4%—av	0.84—low	0.58

	2002	2001	2000	1999	1998	1997	1996	1995	1994	1993
Return (%)	-9.3	-12.9	-8.9	50.6	14.3	13.7	20.0	17.9	1.0	36.6
Differ From Category (+/-)	6.6	7.7	7.0	-1.1	0.9	8.8	4.2	6.9	2.7	-3.7
Return, Tax-Adjusted (%)	-9.6	-12.9	-10.4	49.3	13.2	12.6	18.7	16.1	0.0	36.2

PER SHARE DATA

	2002	2001	2000	1999	1998	1997	1996	1995	1994	1993
Dividends, Net Income ($)	0.13	0.01	0.55	0.25	0.23	0.19	0.15	0.22	0.03	0.01
Distrib'ns, Cap Gain ($)	0.00	0.00	0.81	0.70	0.47	0.41	0.36	0.41	0.39	0.10
Net Asset Value ($)	17.16	19.08	21.94	25.62	17.72	16.13	14.71	12.69	11.30	11.60
Expense Ratio (%)	1.19	1.16	1.12	1.18	1.19	1.23	1.27	1.10	1.25	1.47
Yield (%)	0.75	0.05	2.41	0.94	1.26	1.14	0.99	1.67	0.25	0.08
Portfolio Turnover (%)	55	86	94	73	95	81	94	111	89	56
Total Assets (Millions $)	7,135	6,378	6,579	4,908	2,156	1,536	754	340	306	238

PORTFOLIO (as of 10/31/02)

Portfolio Manager: William Bower - 2001

Investment Style

Large Cap	Growth
Mid Cap	Value
Small Cap	Grth/Val

Portfolio

0.3%	cash	3.4%	corp bonds
91.6%	stocks	0.0%	gov't bonds
0.1%	pref/conv't pref	0.0%	muni bonds
0.2%	conv't bds/wrnts	4.4%	other

SHAREHOLDER INFORMATION

Minimum Investment
Initial: $2,500 Subsequent: $250

Minimum IRA Investment
Initial: $500 Subsequent: $250

Maximum Fees
Load: 1.00% redemption 12b-1: none
Other: redemption fee applies for 1 month

Services
✔ IRA
✔ Keogh
✔ Telephone Exchange

Fidelity Intl Grth & Inc (FIGRX)

800-544-8544, 800-522-7297
www.fidelity.com

Foreign Stock

PERFORMANCE — fund inception date: 12/29/86

	3yr Annual	5yr Annual	10yr Annual	Bull	Bear
Return (%)	-13.8	1.5	6.7	79.8	-39.9
Differ From Category (+/-)	3.8 high	2.6 abv av	1.2 abv av	2.6 abv av	7.3 high

Standard Deviation	Category Risk Index	Beta
17.4%—av	0.95—blw av	0.67

	2002	2001	2000	1999	1998	1997	1996	1995	1994	1993
Return (%)	-9.8	-17.4	-14.0	53.7	9.9	7.1	12.6	12.2	-2.8	35.0
Differ From Category (+/-)	6.1	3.2	1.9	2.0	-3.5	2.2	-3.2	1.2	-1.1	-5.3
Return, Tax-Adjusted (%)	-10.0	-17.4	-16.4	51.6	9.1	5.5	11.4	10.8	-3.6	34.7

PER SHARE DATA

	2002	2001	2000	1999	1998	1997	1996	1995	1994	1993
Dividends, Net Income ($)	0.09	0.00	0.51	0.33	0.09	0.37	0.29	0.60	0.00	0.06
Distrib'ns, Cap Gain ($)	0.00	0.00	2.66	1.50	0.63	0.88	0.37	0.00	0.53	0.05
Net Asset Value ($)	16.82	18.76	22.72	30.10	20.91	19.70	19.55	17.95	16.53	17.57
Expense Ratio (%)	1.12	1.09	1.05	1.10	1.13	1.15	1.14	1.17	1.21	1.52
Yield (%)	0.53	0.00	2.00	1.04	0.41	1.79	1.45	3.34	0.00	0.34
Portfolio Turnover (%)	63	81	104	94	143	70	95	131	173	24
Total Assets (Millions $)	906	940	1,183	1,395	870	1,030	1,080	941	1,272	1,068

PORTFOLIO (as of 10/31/02)

Portfolio Manager: Penny Dobkin - 2001

Investment Style

Large Cap	Growth
Mid Cap	Value
Small Cap	Grth/Val

Portfolio

2.9%	cash	0.0%	corp bonds
87.6%	stocks	0.0%	gov't bonds
0.0%	preferred	0.0%	muni bonds
0.0%	conv't bds/wrnts	9.6%	other

SHAREHOLDER INFORMATION

Minimum Investment
Initial: $2,500 Subsequent: $250

Minimum IRA Investment
Initial: $500 Subsequent: $250

Maximum Fees
Load: 1.00% redemption 12b-1: none
Other: redemption fee applies for 1 month

Services
✔ IRA
Keogh
✔ Telephone Exchange

Fidelity Overseas (FOSFX)

800-544-8544, 800-522-7297
www.fidelity.com

Foreign Stock

PERFORMANCE

fund inception date: 12/4/84

	3yr Annual	5yr Annual	10yr Annual	Bull	Bear
Return (%)	-19.3	-3.2	5.0	69.2	-49.6
Differ From Category (+/-)	-1.7 blw av	-2.1 blw av	-0.5 av	-8.0 av	-2.4 av

Standard Deviation	Category Risk Index	Beta
18.3%—av	0.99—av	0.80

	2002	2001	2000	1999	1998	1997	1996	1995	1994	1993
Return (%)	-19.4	-20.2	-18.3	42.8	12.8	10.9	13.0	9.0	1.2	40.0
Differ From Category (+/-)	-3.5	0.4	-2.4	-8.9	-0.6	6.0	-2.8	-2.0	2.9	-0.3
Return, Tax-Adjusted (%)	-19.5	-20.2	-20.7	40.8	12.2	9.6	10.9	8.1	0.7	39.1

PER SHARE DATA

	2002	2001	2000	1999	1998	1997	1996	1995	1994	1993
Dividends, Net Income ($)	0.09	0.00	0.86	0.44	0.20	0.34	0.37	0.34	0.00	0.43
Distrib'ns, Cap Gain ($)	0.00	0.00	4.12	2.64	0.51	1.34	1.63	0.35	0.47	0.00
Net Asset Value ($)	22.00	27.42	34.37	48.01	35.98	32.54	30.84	29.07	27.30	27.43
Expense Ratio (%)	1.16	1.12	1.16	1.23	1.24	1.20	1.12	1.08	1.24	1.27
Yield (%)	0.40	0.00	2.23	0.86	0.54	1.00	1.13	1.15	0.00	1.56
Portfolio Turnover (%)	72	95	132	85	69	68	82	47	49	64
Total Assets (Millions $)	2,842	3,481	4,652	5,403	3,846	3,704	3,247	2,409	2,194	1,519

PORTFOLIO (as of 10/31/02)

Portfolio Manager: Richard Mace - 1996

Investment Style

Large Cap	Growth
Mid Cap	Value
Small Cap	Grth/Val

Portfolio

0.0%	cash	0.4%	corp bonds
94.7%	stocks	0.0%	gov't bonds
0.9%	pref/conv't pref	0.0%	muni bonds
0.0%	conv't bds/wrnts	4.0%	other

SHAREHOLDER INFORMATION

Minimum Investment
Initial: $2,500 Subsequent: $250

Minimum IRA Investment
Initial: $500 Subsequent: $250

Maximum Fees
Load: 1.00% redemption 12b-1: none
Other: redemption fee applies for 1 month

Services
✔ IRA
✔ Keogh
✔ Telephone Exchange

Harbor Intl/Inst (HAINX)

800-422-1050, 419-247-2477
www.harborfund.com

Foreign Stock

PERFORMANCE — fund inception date: 12/29/87

	3yr Annual	5yr Annual	10yr Annual	Bull	Bear
Return (%)	-7.9	1.3	10.1	37.3	-28.7
Differ From Category (+/-)	9.7 high	2.4 abv av	4.6 high	-39.9 low	18.5 high

Standard Deviation	Category Risk Index	Beta
18.0%—av	0.98—av	0.75

	2002	2001	2000	1999	1998	1997	1996	1995	1994	1993
Return (%)	-6.3	-12.2	-4.9	23.8	10.3	15.4	20.1	16.0	5.4	45.4
Differ From Category (+/-)	9.6	8.4	11.0	-27.9	-3.1	10.5	4.3	5.0	7.1	5.1
Return, Tax-Adjusted (%)	-7.1	-13.0	-7.4	21.5	8.4	14.4	18.7	15.2	3.9	44.9

PER SHARE DATA

	2002	2001	2000	1999	1998	1997	1996	1995	1994	1993
Dividends, Net Income ($)	0.33	0.26	0.70	0.64	0.57	0.40	0.41	0.40	0.24	0.21
Distrib'ns, Cap Gain ($)	0.53	0.88	3.79	2.86	2.30	0.89	0.79	0.12	0.93	0.00
Net Asset Value ($)	26.86	29.63	35.09	41.86	36.72	35.86	32.20	27.84	24.45	24.32
Expense Ratio (%)	na	0.91	0.92	0.92	0.94	0.97	0.99	1.10	1.10	1.20
Yield (%)	1.20	0.85	1.80	1.43	1.46	1.08	1.24	1.43	0.94	0.86
Portfolio Turnover (%)	na	7	10	1	13	6	9	17	28	15
Total Assets (Millions $)	3,742	3,655	4,828	5,842	5,373	5,276	4,318	3,460	2,953	2,537

PORTFOLIO (as of 9/30/02)

Portfolio Manager: Hakan Castegren - 1987

Investment Style

Large Cap	Growth
Mid Cap	Value
Small Cap	Grth/Val

Portfolio

0.0% cash	0.0% corp bonds
100.0% stocks	0.0% gov't bonds
0.0% preferred	0.0% muni bonds
0.0% conv't bds/wrnts	0.0% other

SHAREHOLDER INFORMATION

Minimum Investment
Initial: $1,000 Subsequent: $100

Minimum IRA Investment
Initial: $500 Subsequent: $100

Maximum Fees
Load: none 12b-1: none
Other: none

Services
✔ IRA
✔ Keogh
✔ Telephone Exchange

Harding Loevner Intl Eqty (HLMIX)

877-435-8105, 800-247-0473
www.hardingloevner.com

Foreign Stock

PERFORMANCE

fund inception date: 5/11/94

	3yr Annual	5yr Annual	10yr Annual	Bull	Bear
Return (%)	-16.3	-0.6	na	69.2	-43.7
Differ From Category (+/-)	1.3 abv av	0.5 abv av	na	-8.0 av	3.5 abv av

Standard Deviation	Category Risk Index	Beta
16.8%—av	0.92—blw av	0.72

	2002	2001	2000	1999	1998	1997	1996	1995	1994	1993
Return (%)	-15.0	-18.1	-15.8	49.7	10.1	-4.2	15.4	11.9	—	—
Differ From Category (+/-)	0.9	2.5	0.1	-2.0	-3.3	-9.1	-0.4	0.9	—	—
Return, Tax-Adjusted (%)	-15.1	-18.2	-17.1	48.2	9.5	-4.7	14.7	11.5	—	—

PER SHARE DATA

	2002	2001	2000	1999	1998	1997	1996	1995	1994	1993
Dividends, Net Income ($)	0.04	0.03	0.00	0.22	0.18	0.10	0.11	0.10	—	—
Distrib'ns, Cap Gain ($)	0.00	0.00	1.14	0.50	0.01	0.06	0.10	0.00	—	—
Net Asset Value ($)	9.65	11.41	13.99	17.98	12.49	11.51	12.20	10.77	—	—
Expense Ratio (%)	na	1.00	0.99	1.00	1.00	1.00	1.00	0.99	—	—
Yield (%)	0.41	0.26	0.00	1.19	1.44	0.86	0.89	0.92	—	—
Portfolio Turnover (%)	na	46	49	35	33	31	17	28	—	—
Total Assets (Millions $)	312	311	339	369	479	402	285	67	—	—

PORTFOLIO (as of 9/30/02)

Portfolio Manager: Simon Hallett - 1994

Investment Style

Large Cap	Growth
Mid Cap	Value
Small Cap	Grth/Val

Portfolio

1.7%	cash	0.0%	corp bonds
98.3%	stocks	0.0%	gov't bonds
0.0%	preferred	0.0%	muni bonds
0.0%	conv't bds/wrnts	0.0%	other

SHAREHOLDER INFORMATION

Minimum Investment
Initial: $100,000 Subsequent: $1

Minimum IRA Investment
Initial: $100,000 Subsequent: $1

Maximum Fees
Load: 2.00% redemption 12b-1: none
Other: redemption fee applies for 3 months

Services
✔ IRA
Keogh
✔ Telephone Exchange

Masters Select Intl (MSILX)

800-656-8864
www.mastersselect.com

Foreign Stock

PERFORMANCE

fund inception date: 12/1/97

	3yr Annual	5yr Annual	10yr Annual	Bull	Bear
Return (%)	-12.5	5.4	na	133.9	-44.0
Differ From Category (+/-)	5.1 high	6.5 high	na	56.7 high	3.2 abv av

Standard Deviation	Category Risk Index	Beta
18.7%—av	1.02—abv av	0.69

	2002	2001	2000	1999	1998	1997	1996	1995	1994	1993
Return (%)	-14.3	-17.9	-5.0	75.0	11.7	—	—	—	—	—
Differ From Category (+/-)	1.6	2.7	10.9	23.3	-1.7	—	—	—	—	—
Return, Tax-Adjusted (%)	-14.4	-18.0	-10.1	73.5	11.3	—	—	—	—	—

PER SHARE DATA

	2002	2001	2000	1999	1998	1997	1996	1995	1994	1993
Dividends, Net Income ($)	0.03	0.03	2.39	0.41	0.08	—	—	—	—	—
Distrib'ns, Cap Gain ($)	0.00	0.00	0.00	0.00	0.00	—	—	—	—	—
Net Asset Value ($)	10.70	12.53	15.31	18.67	10.95	—	—	—	—	—
Expense Ratio (%)	na	1.19	1.18	1.29	1.55	—	—	—	—	—
Yield (%)	0.28	0.23	15.61	2.19	0.73	—	—	—	—	—
Portfolio Turnover (%)	na	174	149	100	73	—	—	—	—	—
Total Assets (Millions $)	344	278	275	218	95	—	—	—	—	—

PORTFOLIO (as of 6/30/02)

Portfolio Manager: Team Managed - 1997

Investment Style

Large Cap	Growth
Mid Cap	Value
Small Cap	Grth/Val

Portfolio

8.5%	cash	0.0%	corp bonds
91.5%	stocks	0.0%	gov't bonds
0.0%	preferred	0.0%	muni bonds
0.0%	conv't bds/wrnts	0.0%	other

SHAREHOLDER INFORMATION

Minimum Investment
Initial: $5,000 Subsequent: $250

Minimum IRA Investment
Initial: $1,000 Subsequent: $250

Maximum Fees
Load: 2.00% redemption 12b-1: none
Other: redemption fee applies for 6 months

Services
✔ IRA
✔ Keogh
✔ Telephone Exchange

Oakmark Intl/I (OAKIX)

800-625-6275, 312-621-0600
www.oakmark.com

Foreign Stock

PERFORMANCE — fund inception date: 9/30/92

	3yr Annual	5yr Annual	10yr Annual	Bull	Bear
Return (%)	-0.7	4.8	9.7	54.9	-10.1
Differ From Category (+/-)	16.9 high	5.9 high	4.2 high	-22.3 blw av	37.1 high

Standard Deviation	Category Risk Index	Beta
20.2%—abv av	1.10—abv av	0.82

	2002	2001	2000	1999	1998	1997	1996	1995	1994	1993
Return (%)	-8.4	-5.1	12.5	39.4	-7.0	3.3	28.0	8.3	-9.0	53.5
Differ From Category (+/-)	7.5	15.5	28.4	-12.3	-20.4	-1.6	12.2	-2.7	-7.3	13.2
Return, Tax-Adjusted (%)	-8.7	-5.5	10.4	37.6	-9.0	-1.8	27.5	5.9	-11.0	52.7

PER SHARE DATA

	2002	2001	2000	1999	1998	1997	1996	1995	1994	1993
Dividends, Net Income ($)	0.12	0.16	0.50	0.48	0.24	0.57	0.16	0.00	0.00	0.08
Distrib'ns, Cap Gain ($)	0.00	0.00	0.50	0.00	0.77	2.86	0.00	1.04	1.05	0.15
Net Asset Value ($)	13.14	14.49	15.46	14.70	10.91	12.83	15.68	12.38	12.41	14.79
Expense Ratio (%)	1.31	1.30	1.30	1.29	1.32	1.26	1.32	1.40	1.37	1.26
Yield (%)	0.91	1.10	3.13	3.26	2.05	3.63	1.02	0.00	0.00	0.53
Portfolio Turnover (%)	24	58	64	54	43	61	42	27	55	21
Total Assets (Millions $)	1,732	964	818	827	740	1,237	1,232	785	1,079	1,108

PORTFOLIO (as of 10/31/02)

Portfolio Manager: David Herro/Michael Welsh - 1992

Investment Style

Large Cap	Growth
Mid Cap	Value
Small Cap	Grth/Val

Portfolio

4.1%	cash	0.0%	corp bonds
95.9%	stocks	0.0%	gov't bonds
0.0%	preferred	0.0%	muni bonds
0.0%	conv't bds/wrnts	0.0%	other

SHAREHOLDER INFORMATION

Minimum Investment
Initial: $1,000 Subsequent: $100

Minimum IRA Investment
Initial: $1,000 Subsequent: $100

Maximum Fees
Load: 2.00% redemption 12b-1: none
Other: redemption fee applies for 3 months

Services
✔ IRA
✔ Keogh
✔ Telephone Exchange

Preferred Intl Value (PFIFX)

800-662-4769
www.preferredgroup.com

Foreign Stock

PERFORMANCE

fund inception date: 7/1/92

	3yr Annual	5yr Annual	10yr Annual	Bull	Bear
Return (%)	-8.4	2.4	8.4	36.1	-22.6
Differ From Category (+/-)	9.2 high	3.5 high	2.9 high	-41.1 low	24.6 high

Standard Deviation	Category Risk Index	Beta
18.0%—av	0.98—av	0.69

	2002	2001	2000	1999	1998	1997	1996	1995	1994	1993
Return (%)	-7.6	-12.7	-4.7	32.8	10.5	6.7	16.0	9.9	3.2	41.5
Differ From Category (+/-)	8.3	7.9	11.2	-18.9	-2.9	1.8	0.2	-1.1	4.9	1.2
Return, Tax-Adjusted (%)	-7.8	-15.0	-8.5	31.3	9.4	5.0	14.7	9.3	1.8	41.0

PER SHARE DATA

	2002	2001	2000	1999	1998	1997	1996	1995	1994	1993
Dividends, Net Income ($)	0.04	0.24	0.34	0.23	0.16	0.24	0.34	0.16	0.12	0.07
Distrib'ns, Cap Gain ($)	0.02	1.24	2.90	0.63	0.47	0.71	0.11	0.01	0.42	0.05
Net Asset Value ($)	10.40	11.33	14.72	18.95	14.95	14.10	14.10	12.55	11.58	11.75
Expense Ratio (%)	1.26	1.20	1.20	1.20	1.22	1.25	1.31	1.32	1.38	1.60
Yield (%)	0.38	1.90	1.92	1.17	1.03	1.62	2.39	1.27	1.00	0.59
Portfolio Turnover (%)	43	29	28	15	17	13	19	29	27	16
Total Assets (Millions $)	214	182	332	376	275	241	209	136	107	65

PORTFOLIO (as of 9/30/02)

Portfolio Manager: Peter Spano - 1992

Investment Style

Large Cap	Growth
Mid Cap	Value
Small Cap	Grth/Val

Portfolio

3.2%	cash	0.0%	corp bonds
96.8%	stocks	0.0%	gov't bonds
0.0%	preferred	0.0%	muni bonds
0.0%	conv't bds/wrnts	0.0%	other

SHAREHOLDER INFORMATION

Minimum Investment
Initial: $1,000 Subsequent: $50

Minimum IRA Investment
Initial: $250 Subsequent: $50

Maximum Fees
Load: none 12b-1: none
Other: none

Services
✔ IRA
✔ Keogh
✔ Telephone Exchange

Schwab Intl Index/I (SWINX)

800-435-4000, 800-266-5623
www.schwab.com

Foreign Stock

PERFORMANCE

fund inception date: 9/9/93

	3yr Annual	5yr Annual	10yr Annual	Bull	Bear
Return (%)	-18.7	-3.6	na	52.3	-49.2
Differ From Category (+/-)	-1.1 av	-2.5 blw av	na	-24.9 blw av	-2.0 av

Standard Deviation	Category Risk Index	Beta
16.5%—av	0.90—blw av	0.76

	2002	2001	2000	1999	1998	1997	1996	1995	1994	1993
Return (%)	-15.6	-22.7	-17.5	33.6	15.8	7.3	9.1	14.2	3.8	—
Differ From Category (+/-)	0.3	-2.1	-1.6	-18.1	2.4	2.4	-6.7	3.2	5.5	—
Return, Tax-Adjusted (%)	-16.3	-23.0	-18.0	33.2	15.4	6.8	8.5	13.7	3.3	—

PER SHARE DATA

	2002	2001	2000	1999	1998	1997	1996	1995	1994	1993
Dividends, Net Income ($)	0.21	0.13	0.24	0.15	0.13	0.15	0.16	0.12	0.11	—
Distrib'ns, Cap Gain ($)	0.00	0.00	0.00	0.00	0.00	0.00	0.00	0.00	0.00	—
Net Asset Value ($)	10.37	12.55	16.43	20.24	15.27	13.30	12.54	11.65	10.31	—
Expense Ratio (%)	na	0.58	0.58	0.41	0.46	0.61	0.69	0.85	0.90	—
Yield (%)	2.02	1.03	1.46	0.74	0.85	1.12	1.27	1.03	1.06	—
Portfolio Turnover (%)	na	18	16	5	6	13	0	0	6	—
Total Assets (Millions $)	438	540	634	543	468	325	259	195	138	—

PORTFOLIO (as of 6/30/02)

Portfolio Manager: Geri Hom/Larry Mano - 1995

Investment Style

Large Cap	Growth
Mid Cap	Value
Small Cap	Grth/Val

Portfolio

0.0%	cash	0.5%	corp bonds
94.3%	stocks	0.0%	gov't bonds
0.0%	preferred	0.0%	muni bonds
1.1%	conv't bds/wrnts	4.1%	other

SHAREHOLDER INFORMATION

Minimum Investment
Initial: $2,500 Subsequent: $500

Minimum IRA Investment
Initial: $500 Subsequent: $100

Maximum Fees
Load: 0.75% redemption 12b-1: none
Other: redemption fee applies for 6 months

Services
✔ IRA
✔ Keogh
✔ Telephone Exchange

Schwab Intl MarketMstrs (SWOIX)

800-435-4000, 800-266-5623
www.schwab.com

Foreign Stock

PERFORMANCE — fund inception date: 10/16/96

	3yr Annual	5yr Annual	10yr Annual	Bull	Bear
Return (%)	-15.6	3.5	na	100.4	-47.0
Differ From Category (+/-)	2.0 abv av	4.6 high	na	23.2 high	0.2 abv av

Standard Deviation	Category Risk Index	Beta
19.0%—abv av	1.04—abv av	0.65

	2002	2001	2000	1999	1998	1997	1996	1995	1994	1993
Return (%)	-18.3	-14.1	-14.4	74.8	13.2	6.8	—	—	—	—
Differ From Category (+/-)	-2.4	6.5	1.5	23.1	-0.2	1.9	—	—	—	—
Return, Tax-Adjusted (%)	-18.3	-15.3	-17.0	69.9	12.7	4.9	—	—	—	—

PER SHARE DATA

	2002	2001	2000	1999	1998	1997	1996	1995	1994	1993
Dividends, Net Income ($)	0.00	0.07	0.76	0.49	0.13	0.33	—	—	—	—
Distrib'ns, Cap Gain ($)	0.00	0.65	0.78	1.83	0.00	0.30	—	—	—	—
Net Asset Value ($)	8.87	10.86	13.50	17.60	11.41	10.19	—	—	—	—
Expense Ratio (%)	na	0.50	0.50	0.50	0.50	0.50	—	—	—	—
Yield (%)	0.00	0.60	5.32	2.52	1.13	3.14	—	—	—	—
Portfolio Turnover (%)	na	51	80	249	236	179	—	—	—	—
Total Assets (Millions $)	210	230	269	155	78	76	—	—	—	—

PORTFOLIO (as of 9/30/02)

Portfolio Manager: Jeffrey Mortimer - 2000

Investment Style

Large Cap	Growth
Mid Cap	Value
Small Cap	Grth/Val

Portfolio

6.5%	cash	0.3%	corp bonds
70.2%	stocks	0.0%	gov't bonds
22.2%	pref/conv't pref	0.0%	muni bonds
0.1%	conv't bds/wrnts	0.8%	other

SHAREHOLDER INFORMATION

Minimum Investment
Initial: $2,500 Subsequent: $500

Minimum IRA Investment
Initial: $1,000 Subsequent: $250

Maximum Fees
Load: 1.50% redemption 12b-1: none
Other: redemption fee applies for 6 months

Services
✔ IRA
✔ Keogh
✔ Telephone Exchange

T Rowe Price Intl Stk (PRITX)

800-638-5660, 410-547-2000
www.troweprice.com

Foreign Stock

PERFORMANCE — fund inception date: 5/9/80

	3yr Annual	5yr Annual	10yr Annual	Bull	Bear
Return (%)	-19.1	-3.7	4.3	56.2	-51.4
Differ From Category (+/-)	-1.5 blw av	-2.6 blw av	-1.2 blw av	-21.0 blw av	-4.2 blw av

Standard Deviation	Category Risk Index	Beta
18.7%—av	1.02—abv av	0.82

	2002	2001	2000	1999	1998	1997	1996	1995	1994	1993
Return (%)	-18.1	-22.0	-17.0	34.6	16.1	2.7	15.9	11.3	-0.7	40.1
Differ From Category (+/-)	-2.2	-1.4	-1.1	-17.1	2.7	-2.2	0.1	0.3	1.0	-0.2
Return, Tax-Adjusted (%)	-18.5	-22.8	-18.4	33.0	14.9	1.3	14.9	10.2	-2.5	39.1

PER SHARE DATA

	2002	2001	2000	1999	1998	1997	1996	1995	1994	1993
Dividends, Net Income ($)	0.11	0.30	0.09	0.13	0.22	0.20	0.18	0.18	0.12	0.09
Distrib'ns, Cap Gain ($)	0.00	0.03	1.18	0.91	0.35	0.55	0.20	0.20	0.62	0.20
Net Asset Value ($)	8.88	10.99	14.52	19.03	14.99	13.42	13.80	12.23	11.32	12.16
Expense Ratio (%)	0.92	0.90	0.84	0.85	0.85	0.85	0.88	0.91	0.97	1.01
Yield (%)	1.23	2.72	0.57	0.65	1.43	1.43	1.28	1.44	1.00	0.72
Portfolio Turnover (%)	22	17	17	17	12	15	11	17	22	29
Total Assets (Millions $)	4,750	6,507	9,729	12,673	10,141	9,720	9,340	6,703	5,786	4,296

PORTFOLIO (as of 9/30/02)

Portfolio Manager: Team Managed - 1980

Investment Style

Large Cap	Growth
Mid Cap	Value
Small Cap	Grth/Val

Portfolio

1.9%	cash	0.0%	corp bonds
98.1%	stocks	0.0%	gov't bonds
0.0%	preferred	0.0%	muni bonds
0.0%	conv't bds/wrnts	0.0%	other

SHAREHOLDER INFORMATION

Minimum Investment
Initial: $2,500 Subsequent: $100

Minimum IRA Investment
Initial: $1,000 Subsequent: $50

Maximum Fees
Load: none 12b-1: none
Other: none

Services
✔ IRA
✔ Keogh
✔ Telephone Exchange

TIAA-CREF Intl Equity (TIINX)

800-223-1200, 212-490-9000
www.tiaa-cref.org

Foreign Stock

PERFORMANCE

fund inception date: 9/2/97

	3yr Annual	5yr Annual	10yr Annual	Bull	Bear
Return (%)	-20.0	-1.0	na	91.0	-54.3
Differ From Category (+/-)	-2.4 blw av	0.1 av	na	13.8 abv av	-7.1 blw av

Standard Deviation	Category Risk Index	Beta
20.1%—abv av	1.10—abv av	0.63

	2002	2001	2000	1999	1998	1997	1996	1995	1994	1993
Return (%)	-15.7	-24.2	-19.9	55.8	19.2	—	—	—	—	—
Differ From Category (+/-)	0.2	-3.6	-4.0	4.1	5.8	—	—	—	—	—
Return, Tax-Adjusted (%)	-16.3	-24.4	-22.6	55.0	18.8	—	—	—	—	—

PER SHARE DATA

	2002	2001	2000	1999	1998	1997	1996	1995	1994	1993
Dividends, Net Income ($)	0.11	0.06	0.08	0.11	0.09	—	—	—	—	—
Distrib'ns, Cap Gain ($)	0.00	0.00	2.00	0.22	0.00	—	—	—	—	—
Net Asset Value ($)	6.68	8.07	10.75	16.08	10.54	—	—	—	—	—
Expense Ratio (%)	na	0.49	0.49	0.49	0.49	—	—	—	—	—
Yield (%)	1.64	0.74	0.62	0.67	0.85	—	—	—	—	—
Portfolio Turnover (%)	na	113	138	74	27	—	—	—	—	—
Total Assets (Millions $)	227	261	275	255	118	—	—	—	—	—

PORTFOLIO (as of 9/30/02)

Portfolio Manager: Team Managed - 1997

Investment Style

Large Cap	Growth
Mid Cap	Value
Small Cap	Grth/Val

Portfolio

0.0%	cash	0.0%	corp bonds
99.2%	stocks	0.0%	gov't bonds
0.0%	preferred	0.0%	muni bonds
0.0%	conv't bds/wrnts	0.9%	other

SHAREHOLDER INFORMATION

Minimum Investment
Initial: $1,500 Subsequent: $50

Minimum IRA Investment
Initial: $500 Subsequent: $50

Maximum Fees
Load: none 12b-1: none
Other: none

Services
✔ IRA
Keogh
✔ Telephone Exchange

USAA Inv:International (USIFX)

800-531-8181, 210-456-7211
www.usaa.com

Foreign Stock

PERFORMANCE

fund inception date: 7/11/88

	3yr Annual	5yr Annual	10yr Annual	Bull	Bear
Return (%)	-12.4	-2.3	6.0	47.4	-38.8
Differ From Category (+/-)	5.2 high	-1.2 av	0.5 abv av	-29.8 low	8.4 high

Standard Deviation	Category Risk Index	Beta
16.2%—av	0.88—low	0.67

	2002	2001	2000	1999	1998	1997	1996	1995	1994	1993
Return (%)	-9.0	-14.5	-13.7	27.5	4.0	8.9	19.1	8.2	2.6	39.8
Differ From Category (+/-)	6.9	6.1	2.2	-24.2	-9.4	4.0	3.3	-2.8	4.3	-0.5
Return, Tax-Adjusted (%)	-9.3	-14.9	-14.2	26.1	3.0	7.0	17.8	7.9	0.9	39.0

PER SHARE DATA

	2002	2001	2000	1999	1998	1997	1996	1995	1994	1993
Dividends, Net Income ($)	0.12	0.18	0.11	0.18	0.19	0.12	0.19	0.06	0.00	0.00
Distrib'ns, Cap Gain ($)	0.00	0.00	0.31	0.95	0.54	1.56	0.50	0.08	0.97	0.35
Net Asset Value ($)	15.13	16.78	19.86	23.45	19.31	19.22	19.15	16.69	15.56	16.10
Expense Ratio (%)	1.32	1.14	1.11	1.12	1.05	1.09	1.19	1.17	1.31	1.50
Yield (%)	0.79	1.07	0.54	0.73	0.95	0.57	0.96	0.35	0.00	0.00
Portfolio Turnover (%)	36	32	39	37	42	46	70	64	44	52
Total Assets (Millions $)	328	368	483	608	531	575	513	351	337	131

PORTFOLIO (as of 9/30/02)

Portfolio Manager: Albert Sebastian - 1996

Investment Style

Large Cap	Growth
Mid Cap	Value
Small Cap	Grth/Val

Portfolio

4.0% cash	0.0% corp bonds
96.0% stocks	0.0% gov't bonds
0.0% preferred	0.0% muni bonds
0.0% conv't bds/wrnts	0.0% other

SHAREHOLDER INFORMATION

Minimum Investment

Initial: $3,000 Subsequent: $50

Minimum IRA Investment

Initial: $250 Subsequent: $50

Maximum Fees

Load: none 12b-1: none

Other: none

Services

✔ IRA

✔ Keogh

✔ Telephone Exchange

Vanguard Intl Gr (VWIGX)

800-662-7447, 610-436-5152
www.vanguard.com

Foreign Stock

PERFORMANCE — fund inception date: 9/30/81

	3yr Annual	5yr Annual	10yr Annual	Bull	Bear
Return (%)	-15.2	-2.0	6.0	55.0	-46.8
Differ From Category (+/-)	2.4 abv av	-0.9 av	0.5 abv av	-22.2 blw av	0.4 abv av

Standard Deviation	Category Risk Index	Beta
17.8%—av	0.97—blw av	0.74

	2002	2001	2000	1999	1998	1997	1996	1995	1994	1993
Return (%)	-17.7	-18.9	-8.6	26.3	16.9	4.1	14.6	14.8	0.7	44.7
Differ From Category (+/-)	-1.8	1.7	7.3	-25.4	3.5	-0.8	-1.2	3.8	2.4	4.4
Return, Tax-Adjusted (%)	-18.2	-19.4	-10.3	24.8	16.2	3.0	13.1	13.8	0.2	44.2

PER SHARE DATA

	2002	2001	2000	1999	1998	1997	1996	1995	1994	1993
Dividends, Net Income ($)	0.18	0.24	0.22	0.26	0.22	0.21	0.19	0.20	0.18	0.11
Distrib'ns, Cap Gain ($)	0.00	0.04	1.42	0.90	0.16	0.52	0.55	0.21	0.00	0.00
Net Asset Value ($)	12.16	15.01	18.87	22.49	18.77	16.39	16.46	15.02	13.43	13.51
Expense Ratio (%)	0.67	0.61	0.53	0.58	0.59	0.57	0.56	0.59	0.46	0.59
Yield (%)	1.48	1.59	1.08	1.11	1.16	1.24	1.11	1.31	1.34	0.81
Portfolio Turnover (%)	40	48	48	37	37	22	22	31	28	51
Total Assets (Millions $)	5,088	6,087	8,899	9,680	7,723	6,808	5,568	3,676	2,927	2,127

PORTFOLIO (as of 9/30/02)

Portfolio Manager: Richard Foulkes - 1981

Investment Style

Large Cap	Growth
Mid Cap	Value
Small Cap	Grth/Val

Portfolio

9.8%	cash	0.0%	corp bonds
90.3%	stocks	0.0%	gov't bonds
0.0%	preferred	0.0%	muni bonds
0.0%	conv't bds/wrnts	0.0%	other

SHAREHOLDER INFORMATION

Minimum Investment
Initial: $3,000 — Subsequent: $100

Minimum IRA Investment
Initial: $1,000 — Subsequent: $100

Maximum Fees
Load: none — 12b-1: none
Other: none

Services
✔ IRA
✔ Keogh
✔ Telephone Exchange

Vanguard Intl Value
(VTRIX)

Foreign Stock

800-662-7447, 610-436-5152
www.vanguard.com

PERFORMANCE — fund inception date: 5/16/83

	3yr Annual	5yr Annual	10yr Annual	Bull	Bear
Return (%)	-11.6	0.0	4.7	37.2	-31.1
Differ From Category (+/-)	6.0 high	1.1 abv av	-0.8 blw av	-40.0 low	16.1 high

Standard Deviation	Category Risk Index	Beta
18.4%—av	1.00—av	0.80

	2002	2001	2000	1999	1998	1997	1996	1995	1994	1993
Return (%)	-13.3	-14.0	-7.4	21.7	19.5	-4.5	10.2	9.6	5.2	30.4
Differ From Category (+/-)	2.6	6.6	8.5	-30.0	6.1	-9.4	-5.6	-1.4	6.9	-9.9
Return, Tax-Adjusted (%)	-13.8	-14.5	-8.5	20.1	16.8	-7.6	4.0	6.4	3.9	29.1

PER SHARE DATA

	2002	2001	2000	1999	1998	1997	1996	1995	1994	1993
Dividends, Net Income ($)	0.29	0.30	0.73	0.66	1.06	0.69	0.82	0.79	0.56	0.81
Distrib'ns, Cap Gain ($)	0.00	0.00	0.19	0.73	0.90	2.95	5.77	2.51	0.63	0.00
Net Asset Value ($)	18.83	22.07	26.03	29.12	25.09	22.64	27.54	31.11	31.48	31.04
Expense Ratio (%)	na	0.64	0.53	0.59	0.52	0.49	0.50	0.38	0.34	0.40
Yield (%)	1.54	1.35	2.78	2.21	4.07	2.69	2.46	2.34	1.74	2.60
Portfolio Turnover (%)	na	37	78	41	39	37	82	43	40	39
Total Assets (Millions $)	1,155	894	835	1,044	806	776	916	988	1,053	982

PORTFOLIO (as of 9/30/02)

Portfolio Manager: Dayal/Holt/Foong - 2000

Investment Style

Large Cap	Growth
Mid Cap	Value
Small Cap	Grth/Val

Portfolio

5.0% cash	0.0% corp bonds
95.0% stocks	0.0% gov't bonds
0.0% preferred	0.0% muni bonds
0.0% conv't bds/wrnts	0.0% other

SHAREHOLDER INFORMATION

Minimum Investment
Initial: $3,000 — Subsequent: $100

Minimum IRA Investment
Initial: $1,000 — Subsequent: $100

Maximum Fees
Load: none — 12b-1: none
Other: none

Services
✔ IRA
✔ Keogh
✔ Telephone Exchange

Vanguard Tot Itl Stk Idx

800-662-7447, 610-436-5152
www.vanguard.com

(VGTSX)

Foreign Stock

PERFORMANCE **fund inception date: 4/29/96**

	3yr Annual	5yr Annual	10yr Annual	Bull	Bear
Return (%)	-16.9	-2.9	na	52.9	-46.3
Differ From Category (+/-)	0.7 abv av	-1.8 blw av	na	-24.3 blw av	0.9 abv av

Standard Deviation	Category Risk Index	Beta
16.9%—av	0.92—blw av	0.75

	2002	2001	2000	1999	1998	1997	1996	1995	1994	1993
Return (%)	-15.0	-20.1	-15.6	29.9	15.6	-0.7	—	—	—	—
Differ From Category (+/-)	0.9	0.5	0.3	-21.8	2.2	-5.6	—	—	—	—
Return, Tax-Adjusted (%)	-15.7	-20.6	-16.2	29.1	14.7	-1.4	—	—	—	—

PER SHARE DATA

	2002	2001	2000	1999	1998	1997	1996	1995	1994	1993
Dividends, Net Income ($)	0.15	0.16	0.20	0.21	0.21	0.17	—	—	—	—
Distrib'ns, Cap Gain ($)	0.00	0.00	0.05	0.01	0.01	0.02	—	—	—	—
Net Asset Value ($)	7.72	9.28	11.83	14.31	11.19	9.87	—	—	—	—
Expense Ratio (%)	na	na	na	na	na	na	—	—	—	—
Yield (%)	1.94	1.72	1.68	1.46	1.87	1.71	—	—	—	—
Portfolio Turnover (%)	na	2	3	1	2	6	—	—	—	—
Total Assets (Millions $)	3,068	2,899	2,919	2,569	1,375	903	—	—	—	—

PORTFOLIO (as of 12/31/02)

Portfolio Manager: Team Managed - 1996

Investment Style

Large Cap	Growth
Mid Cap	Value
Small Cap	Grth/Val

Portfolio

0.0%	cash	0.0%	corp bonds
0.0%	stocks	0.0%	gov't bonds
0.0%	preferred	0.0%	muni bonds
0.0%	conv't bds/wrnts	100.0%	other

SHAREHOLDER INFORMATION

Minimum Investment
Initial: $3,000 Subsequent: $100

Minimum IRA Investment
Initial: $1,000 Subsequent: $100

Maximum Fees
Load: none 12b-1: none
Other: none

Services
✔ IRA
✔ Keogh
Telephone Exchange

Wm Blair:Intl Grth/N

800-635-2886, 312-364-8000
www.wmblair.com

(WBIGX)

Foreign Stock

PERFORMANCE

fund inception date: 10/1/92

	3yr Annual	5yr Annual	10yr Annual	Bull	Bear
Return (%)	-12.3	8.0	9.7	139.2	-39.8
Differ From Category (+/-)	5.3 high	9.1 high	4.2 high	62.0 high	7.4 high

Standard Deviation	Category Risk Index	Beta
17.9%—av	0.98—av	0.65

	2002	2001	2000	1999	1998	1997	1996	1995	1994	1993
Return (%)	-15.1	-13.6	-8.1	96.2	11.4	8.3	10.2	7.2	0.0	35.1
Differ From Category (+/-)	.0.8	7.0	7.8	44.5	-2.0	3.4	-5.6	-3.8	1.7	-5.2
Return, Tax-Adjusted (%)	-15.1	-13.6	-11.5	90.1	11.3	5.4	9.1	6.8	-1.7	33.6

PER SHARE DATA

	2002	2001	2000	1999	1998	1997	1996	1995	1994	1993
Dividends, Net Income ($)	0.00	0.00	0.07	0.00	0.02	0.07	0.06	0.13	0.02	0.13
Distrib'ns, Cap Gain ($)	0.00	0.00	3.97	4.49	0.00	1.86	0.42	0.00	0.78	0.35
Net Asset Value ($)	13.13	15.48	17.93	24.03	14.62	13.14	13.95	13.12	12.36	13.18
Expense Ratio (%)	na	1.60	1.59	1.35	1.36	1.43	1.44	1.50	1.51	1.71
Yield (%)	0.00	0.00	0.31	0.00	0.13	0.46	0.41	0.99	0.15	0.96
Portfolio Turnover (%)	na	112	116	122	98	102	89	72	40	83
Total Assets (Millions $)	396	189	116	38	139	128	105	89	71	40

PORTFOLIO (as of 9/30/02)

Portfolio Manager: George Greig - 1996

Investment Style

Large Cap	Growth
Mid Cap	Value
Small Cap	Grth/Val

Portfolio

2.8% cash	0.0% corp bonds
97.2% stocks	0.0% gov't bonds
0.0% preferred	0.0% muni bonds
0.0% conv't bds/wrnts	0.0% other

SHAREHOLDER INFORMATION

Minimum Investment
Initial: $5,000 Subsequent: $1

Minimum IRA Investment
Initial: $3,000 Subsequent: $1

Maximum Fees
Load: 1.00% redemption 12b-1: 0.25%
Other: redemption fee applies for 2 months

Services
✔ IRA
✔ Keogh
✔ Telephone Exchange

Regional/Country Stock Funds
Category Performance Ranked by 2002 Returns

		Annual Return (%)				Category	Total
Category	Fund (Ticker)	2002	3yr	5yr	10yr	Risk	Risk
IntS-R/C	Matthews Korea (MAKOX)	8.1	-4.4	28.9	na	high	high
IntS-R/C	Fidelity Japan Smaller Co (FJSCX)	0.9	-26.2	12.1	na	abv av	high
IntS-R/C	Fidelity Canada (FICDX)	-4.2	-0.9	3.0	6.5	blw av	abv av
IntS-R/C	Matthews Pacific Tiger (MAPTX)	-6.4	-8.1	6.6	na	abv av	high
IntS-R/C	Fidelity Japan (FJPNX)	-7.3	-26.9	1.6	1.6	av	abv av
IntS-R/C	Strong Asia Pacific (SASPX)	-7.7	-20.1	-0.6	na	av	abv av
IntS-R/C	Fidelity Pacific Basin (FPBFX)	-7.8	-21.8	2.5	3.4	low	av
IntS-R/C	Vanguard Pacific Stk (VPACX)	-9.3	-20.8	-4.4	-1.4	low	av
IntS-R/C	T Rowe Price New Asia (PRASX)	-9.3	-17.3	0.0	0.7	av	high
IntS-R/C	Fidelity Southeast Asia (FSEAX)	-11.3	-15.9	1.3	na	abv av	high
IntS-R/C	Fidelity Europe Cap Appr (FECAX)	-15.0	-11.3	0.9	na	low	av
IntS-R/C	Fidelity China Region (FHKCX)	-15.0	-14.4	1.8	na	av	abv av
IntS-R/C	Vanguard Erpn Stk Idx (VEURX)	-17.9	-15.6	-2.0	8.1	low	av
IntS-R/C	T Rowe Price Latin Amer (PRLAX)	-18.1	-10.1	-5.6	na	high	high
IntS-R/C	T Rowe Price Eurpn Stk (PRESX)	-18.6	-15.5	-1.9	7.9	low	abv av
IntS-R/C	Fidelity Latin America (FLATX)	-20.8	-15.0	-10.1	na	high	high
IntS-R/C	Fidelity Europe (FIEUX)	-25.4	-17.1	-4.0	6.9	av	high
Regional/Country Stock Average		**-12.4**	**-17.4**	**-1.5**	**2.4**	**—**	**high**

Note: AAII members who would like performance figures for no-load and low-load mutual funds they own that do not appear in this Guide can access this information on our Web site at www.aaii.com.

Fidelity Canada
(FICDX)

800-544-8544, 800-522-7297
www.fidelity.com

Regional/Country Stock

PERFORMANCE — fund inception date: 11/17/87

	3yr Annual	5yr Annual	10yr Annual	Bull	Bear
Return (%)	-0.9	3.0	6.5	86.3	-18.3
Differ From Category (+/-)	16.5 high	4.5 high	4.1 high	-42.2 blw av	28.7 high

Standard Deviation	Category Risk Index	Beta
19.7%—abv av	0.83—blw av	0.80

	2002	2001	2000	1999	1998	1997	1996	1995	1994	1993
Return (%)	-4.2	-9.6	12.2	40.5	-14.9	6.1	15.9	19.3	-11.9	25.4
Differ From Category (+/-)	8.2	2.7	36.0	-36.2	-16.5	12.2	2.4	14.6	-7.9	-14.2
Return, Tax-Adjusted (%)	-4.3	-9.7	10.1	40.4	-15.1	3.6	9.3	19.1	-11.9	25.3

PER SHARE DATA

	2002	2001	2000	1999	1998	1997	1996	1995	1994	1993
Dividends, Net Income ($)	0.04	0.03	1.04	0.03	0.07	0.05	0.13	0.08	0.01	0.00
Distrib'ns, Cap Gain ($)	0.00	0.00	0.00	0.00	0.00	2.08	4.29	0.00	0.00	0.04
Net Asset Value ($)	18.12	18.97	21.02	19.63	13.99	16.53	17.62	19.02	16.00	18.19
Expense Ratio (%)	1.46	1.20	1.06	1.06	0.80	0.92	0.98	1.15	1.57	2.00
Yield (%)	0.22	0.15	4.94	0.15	0.50	0.26	0.59	0.42	0.06	0.00
Portfolio Turnover (%)	98	93	1	286	215	139	139	83	59	131
Total Assets (Millions $)	78	85	150	57	47	87	129	174	332	109

PORTFOLIO (as of 10/31/02)

Portfolio Manager: Maxime LeMieux - 2002

Investment Style

Large Cap	Growth
Mid Cap	Value
Small Cap	Grth/Val

Portfolio

0.0%	cash	0.0%	corp bonds
97.3%	stocks	0.0%	gov't bonds
0.0%	preferred	0.0%	muni bonds
0.0%	conv't bds/wrnts	2.7%	other

SHAREHOLDER INFORMATION

Minimum Investment
Initial: $2,500 — Subsequent: $250

Minimum IRA Investment
Initial: $500 — Subsequent: $250

Maximum Fees
Load: 3.00% front — 12b-1: none
Other: 1.5% redemption fee for 3 months

Services
✔ IRA
✔ Keogh
✔ Telephone Exchange

Fidelity China Region (FHKCX)

800-544-8544, 800-522-7297
www.fidelity.com

Regional/Country Stock

PERFORMANCE — fund inception date: 11/1/95

	3yr Annual	5yr Annual	10yr Annual	Bull	Bear
Return (%)	-14.4	1.8	na	166.9	-42.2
Differ From Category (+/-)	3.0 abv av	3.3 abv av	na	38.4 abv av	4.8 abv av

Standard Deviation	Category Risk Index	Beta
21.9%—abv av	0.93—av	0.83

	2002	2001	2000	1999	1998	1997	1996	1995	1994	1993
Return (%)	-15.0	-10.4	-17.5	84.9	-5.3	-22.0	40.9	—	—	—
Differ From Category (+/-)	-2.6	1.9	6.3	8.2	-6.9	-15.9	27.4	—	—	—
Return, Tax-Adjusted (%)	-15.6	-10.8	-18.7	84.2	-6.4	-22.2	40.1	—	—	—

PER SHARE DATA

	2002	2001	2000	1999	1998	1997	1996	1995	1994	1993
Dividends, Net Income ($)	0.19	0.16	0.56	0.17	0.32	0.06	0.14	—	—	—
Distrib'ns, Cap Gain ($)	0.00	0.00	0.00	0.00	0.00	0.00	0.08	—	—	—
Net Asset Value ($)	10.86	13.00	14.70	18.51	10.11	11.02	14.21	—	—	—
Expense Ratio (%)	1.31	1.30	1.21	1.32	1.40	1.31	1.62	—	—	—
Yield (%)	1.74	1.23	3.80	0.91	3.16	0.54	0.97	—	—	—
Portfolio Turnover (%)	53	75	103	84	109	174	118	—	—	—
Total Assets (Millions $)	110	137	175	273	133	180	197	—	—	—

PORTFOLIO (as of 10/31/02)

Portfolio Manager: Joseph Tse - 1995

Investment Style

Large Cap	Growth
Mid Cap	Value
Small Cap	Grth/Val

Portfolio

1.2%	cash	0.0%	corp bonds
94.8%	stocks	0.0%	gov't bonds
0.0%	preferred	0.0%	muni bonds
0.0%	conv't bds/wrnts	4.0%	other

SHAREHOLDER INFORMATION

Minimum Investment
Initial: $2,500 — Subsequent: $250

Minimum IRA Investment
Initial: $500 — Subsequent: $250

Maximum Fees
Load: 3.00% front — 12b-1: none
Other: 1.5% redemption fee for 3 months

Services
✔ IRA
✔ Keogh
✔ Telephone Exchange

Fidelity Europe

800-544-8544, 800-522-7297
www.fidelity.com

(FIEUX)

Regional/Country Stock

PERFORMANCE

fund inception date: 10/1/86

	3yr Annual	5yr Annual	10yr Annual	Bull	Bear
Return (%)	-17.1	-4.0	6.9	46.8	-53.3
Differ From Category (+/-)	0.3 av	-2.5 av	4.5 high	-81.7 low	-6.3 blw av

Standard Deviation	Category Risk Index	Beta
24.2%—high	1.03—av	1.07

	2002	2001	2000	1999	1998	1997	1996	1995	1994	1993
Return (%)	-25.4	-16.0	-9.1	18.6	20.7	22.8	25.6	15.1	6.2	27.1
Differ From Category (+/-)	-13.0	-3.7	14.7	-58.1	19.1	28.9	12.1	10.4	10.2	-12.5
Return, Tax-Adjusted (%)	-25.6	-16.3	-11.4	17.2	18.8	20.5	23.1	14.7	5.6	26.9

PER SHARE DATA

	2002	2001	2000	1999	1998	1997	1996	1995	1994	1993
Dividends, Net Income ($)	0.14	0.24	0.12	0.18	0.28	0.39	0.24	0.12	0.20	0.08
Distrib'ns, Cap Gain ($)	0.00	0.00	4.09	1.94	2.25	2.35	1.73	0.09	0.11	0.00
Net Asset Value ($)	18.32	24.76	29.77	37.47	33.48	29.94	26.61	22.82	20.00	19.12
Expense Ratio (%)	1.13	0.99	1.06	0.89	1.09	1.18	1.27	1.16	1.35	1.25
Yield (%)	0.76	0.96	0.35	0.45	0.78	1.20	0.84	0.52	0.99	0.41
Portfolio Turnover (%)	127	123	144	106	114	57	45	44	49	76
Total Assets (Millions $)	895	1,152	1,406	1,477	1,622	951	773	500	478	494

PORTFOLIO (as of 10/31/02)

Portfolio Manager: Thierry Serero - 1998

Investment Style

Large Cap	Growth
Mid Cap	Value
Small Cap	Grth/Val

Portfolio

0.5%	cash	0.7%	corp bonds
97.5%	stocks	0.0%	gov't bonds
0.0%	preferred	0.0%	muni bonds
0.4%	conv't bds/wrnts	0.9%	other

SHAREHOLDER INFORMATION

Minimum Investment
Initial: $2,500 Subsequent: $250

Minimum IRA Investment
Initial: $500 Subsequent: $250

Maximum Fees
Load: 1.00% redemption 12b-1: none
Other: redemption fee applies for 1 month

Services
✔ IRA
✔ Keogh
✔ Telephone Exchange

Fidelity Europe Cap Appr (FECAX)

800-544-8544, 800-522-7297
www.fidelity.com

Regional/Country Stock

PERFORMANCE — fund inception date: 12/21/93

	3yr Annual	5yr Annual	10yr Annual	Bull	Bear
Return (%)	-11.3	0.9	na	45.9	-35.6
Differ From Category (+/-)	6.1 high	2.4 abv av	na	-82.6 low	11.4 high

Standard Deviation	Category Risk Index	Beta
16.5%—av	0.70—low	0.56

	2002	2001	2000	1999	1998	1997	1996	1995	1994	1993
Return (%)	-15.0	-13.1	-5.7	23.7	21.6	24.9	25.8	14.6	6.8	—
Differ From Category (+/-)	-2.6	-0.8	18.1	-53.0	20.0	31.0	12.3	9.9	10.8	—
Return, Tax-Adjusted (%)	-15.4	-13.4	-6.7	22.9	21.6	21.4	22.0	13.8	6.8	—

PER SHARE DATA

	2002	2001	2000	1999	1998	1997	1996	1995	1994	1993
Dividends, Net Income ($)	0.19	0.17	0.11	0.13	0.00	0.16	0.23	0.23	0.00	—
Distrib'ns, Cap Gain ($)	0.00	0.00	0.87	0.47	0.00	2.09	1.29	0.00	0.00	—
Net Asset Value ($)	13.83	16.50	19.19	21.46	17.86	14.68	13.59	12.06	10.72	—
Expense Ratio (%)	1.32	1.21	1.04	0.97	1.08	1.07	2.00	1.36	1.54	—
Yield (%)	1.37	1.03	0.54	0.59	0.00	0.95	1.54	1.90	0.00	—
Portfolio Turnover (%)	121	67	156	150	179	189	155	138	317	—
Total Assets (Millions $)	397	433	611	710	689	371	189	180	291	—

PORTFOLIO (as of 10/31/02)

Portfolio Manager: Ian Hart - 2000

Investment Style

Large Cap	Growth
Mid Cap	Value
Small Cap	Grth/Val

Portfolio

0.5%	cash	0.9%	corp bonds
91.8%	stocks	0.0%	gov't bonds
0.0%	preferred	0.0%	muni bonds
0.0%	conv't bds/wrnts	6.9%	other

SHAREHOLDER INFORMATION

Minimum Investment
Initial: $2,500 Subsequent: $250

Minimum IRA Investment
Initial: $500 Subsequent: $250

Maximum Fees
Load: 1.00% redemption 12b-1: none
Other: redemption fee applies for 1 month

Services
✔ IRA
✔ Keogh
✔ Telephone Exchange

Fidelity Japan
(FJPNX)

800-544-8544, 800-522-7297
www.fidelity.com

Regional/Country Stock

PERFORMANCE — fund inception date: 9/15/92

	3yr Annual	5yr Annual	10yr Annual	Bull	Bear
Return (%)	-26.9	1.6	1.6	191.8	-58.0
Differ From Category (+/-)	-9.5 low	3.1 abv av	-0.8 av	63.3 high	-11.0 low

Standard Deviation	Category Risk Index	Beta
22.8%—abv av	0.97—av	0.58

	2002	2001	2000	1999	1998	1997	1996	1995	1994	1993
Return (%)	-7.3	-33.8	-36.4	146.0	13.0	-10.7	-11.1	-2.1	16.4	20.4
Differ From Category (+/-)	5.1	-21.5	-12.6	69.3	11.4	-4.6	-24.6	-6.8	20.4	-19.2
Return, Tax-Adjusted (%)	-7.3	-33.8	-39.4	144.4	12.9	-11.3	-11.1	-2.1	15.5	19.3

PER SHARE DATA

	2002	2001	2000	1999	1998	1997	1996	1995	1994	1993
Dividends, Net Income ($)	0.00	0.00	0.00	0.46	0.03	0.18	0.01	0.00	0.00	0.00
Distrib'ns, Cap Gain ($)	0.00	0.00	4.07	0.00	0.00	0.00	0.00	0.00	0.36	0.39
Net Asset Value ($)	8.43	9.10	13.75	27.28	11.30	10.02	11.42	12.87	13.15	11.61
Expense Ratio (%)	1.50	1.40	1.16	1.23	1.48	1.40	1.14	1.15	1.42	1.71
Yield (%)	0.00	0.00	0.00	1.68	0.26	1.79	0.08	0.00	0.00	0.00
Portfolio Turnover (%)	66	75	124	79	62	70	83	86	153	257
Total Assets (Millions $)	287	286	497	1,242	312	215	255	378	389	96

PORTFOLIO (as of 10/31/02)

Portfolio Manager: Yoko Ishibashi - 2000

Investment Style

Large Cap	Growth
Mid Cap	Value
Small Cap	Grth/Val

Portfolio

0.0% cash	0.0% corp bonds
99.0% stocks	0.0% gov't bonds
0.0% preferred	0.0% muni bonds
0.0% conv't bds/wrnts	1.1% other

SHAREHOLDER INFORMATION

Minimum Investment
Initial: $2,500 Subsequent: $250

Minimum IRA Investment
Initial: $500 Subsequent: $250

Maximum Fees
Load: 3.00% front 12b-1: none
Other: 1.5% redemption fee for 3 months

Services
✔ IRA
✔ Keogh
✔ Telephone Exchange

Fidelity Japan Smaller Co (FJSCX)

800-544-8544, 800-522-7297
www.fidelity.com

Regional/Country Stock

PERFORMANCE — fund inception date: 11/1/95

	3yr Annual	5yr Annual	10yr Annual	Bull	Bear
Return (%)	-26.2	12.1	na	323.3	-52.8
Differ From Category (+/-)	-8.8 low	13.6 high	na	194.8 high	-5.8 blw av

Standard Deviation	Category Risk Index	Beta
25.3%—high	1.07—abv av	0.24

	2002	2001	2000	1999	1998	1997	1996	1995	1994	1993
Return (%)	0.9	-20.0	-50.2	237.4	31.1	-30.3	-24.5	—	—	—
Differ From Category (+/-)	13.3	-7.7	-26.4	160.7	29.5	-24.2	-38.0	—	—	—
Return, Tax-Adjusted (%)	0.9	-20.0	-53.9	236.6	31.1	-30.3	-24.6	—	—	—

PER SHARE DATA

	2002	2001	2000	1999	1998	1997	1996	1995	1994	1993
Dividends, Net Income ($)	0.00	0.00	0.00	0.15	0.00	0.01	0.00	—	—	—
Distrib'ns, Cap Gain ($)	0.00	0.00	4.46	0.00	0.00	0.00	0.04	—	—	—
Net Asset Value ($)	6.44	6.38	7.98	24.27	7.24	5.52	7.94	—	—	—
Expense Ratio (%)	1.19	1.19	1.06	1.07	1.23	1.34	1.34	—	—	—
Yield (%)	0.00	0.00	0.00	0.61	0.00	0.18	0.00	—	—	—
Portfolio Turnover (%)	50	52	39	39	39	101	66	—	—	—
Total Assets (Millions $)	360	285	421	2,113	129	76	78	—	—	—

PORTFOLIO (as of 10/31/02)

Portfolio Manager: Kenichi Mizushita - 1996

Investment Style

Large Cap	Growth
Mid Cap	Value
Small Cap	Grth/Val

Portfolio

0.0%	cash	0.0%	corp bonds
96.9%	stocks	0.0%	gov't bonds
0.0%	preferred	0.0%	muni bonds
0.0%	conv't bds/wrnts	3.1%	other

SHAREHOLDER INFORMATION

Minimum Investment
Initial: $2,500 Subsequent: $250

Minimum IRA Investment
Initial: $500 Subsequent: $250

Maximum Fees
Load: 3.00% front 12b-1: none
Other: 1.5% redemption fee for 3 months

Services
✔ IRA
✔ Keogh
✔ Telephone Exchange

Fidelity Latin America (FLATX)

800-544-8544, 800-522-7297
www.fidelity.com

Regional/Country Stock

PERFORMANCE

fund inception date: 4/19/93

	3yr Annual	5yr Annual	10yr Annual	Bull	Bear
Return (%)	-15.0	-10.1	na	91.8	-51.0
Differ From Category (+/-)	2.4 abv av	-8.6 low	na	-36.7 blw av	-4.0 blw av

Standard Deviation	Category Risk Index	Beta
30.6%—high	1.30—high	1.20

	2002	2001	2000	1999	1998	1997	1996	1995	1994	1993
Return (%)	-20.8	-6.0	-17.4	54.9	-38.3	32.8	30.7	-16.4	-23.1	—
Differ From Category (+/-)	-8.4	6.3	6.4	-21.8	-39.9	38.9	17.2	-21.1	-19.1	—
Return, Tax-Adjusted (%)	-21.3	-6.7	-17.6	54.4	-38.9	32.2	29.8	-16.8	-23.1	—

PER SHARE DATA

	2002	2001	2000	1999	1998	1997	1996	1995	1994	1993
Dividends, Net Income ($)	0.17	0.25	0.07	0.14	0.25	0.20	0.23	0.12	0.00	—
Distrib'ns, Cap Gain ($)	0.00	0.00	0.00	0.00	0.00	0.00	0.00	0.00	0.00	—
Net Asset Value ($)	9.33	12.01	13.06	15.91	10.37	17.22	13.11	10.21	12.37	—
Expense Ratio (%)	1.41	1.35	1.23	1.30	1.33	1.29	1.32	1.41	1.48	—
Yield (%)	1.82	2.08	0.53	0.87	2.41	1.16	1.75	1.17	0.00	—
Portfolio Turnover (%)	128	96	51	49	31	64	70	69	77	—
Total Assets (Millions $)	149	209	267	409	306	860	535	473	616	—

PORTFOLIO (as of 10/31/02)

Portfolio Manager: Margaret Reynolds - 2001

Investment Style

Large Cap	Growth
Mid Cap	Value
Small Cap	Grth/Val

Portfolio

0.0%	cash	0.0%	corp bonds
97.3%	stocks	0.0%	gov't bonds
0.0%	preferred	0.0%	muni bonds
0.0%	conv't bds/wrnts	2.7%	other

SHAREHOLDER INFORMATION

Minimum Investment
Initial: $2,500 Subsequent: $250

Minimum IRA Investment
Initial: $500 Subsequent: $250

Maximum Fees
Load: 3.00% front 12b-1: none
Other: 1.5% redemption fee for 3 months

Services
✔ IRA
✔ Keogh
✔ Telephone Exchange

Fidelity Pacific Basin (FPBFX)

800-544-8544, 800-522-7297
www.fidelity.com

Regional/Country Stock

PERFORMANCE — fund inception date: 10/1/86

	3yr Annual	5yr Annual	10yr Annual	Bull	Bear
Return (%)	-21.8	2.5	3.4	162.0	-48.9
Differ From Category (+/-)	-4.4 blw av	4.0 high	1.0 abv av	33.5 abv av	-1.9 av

Standard Deviation	Category Risk Index	Beta
18.6%—av	0.79—low	0.65

	2002	2001	2000	1999	1998	1997	1996	1995	1994	1993
Return (%)	-7.8	-19.8	-35.3	119.6	8.2	-15.0	-2.7	-6.1	-2.8	63.9
Differ From Category (+/-)	4.6	-7.5	-11.5	42.9	6.6	-8.9	-16.2	-10.8	1.2	24.3
Return, Tax-Adjusted (%)	-7.8	-19.8	-37.0	118.8	8.1	-15.7	-2.9	-6.1	-5.9	62.8

PER SHARE DATA

	2002	2001	2000	1999	1998	1997	1996	1995	1994	1993
Dividends, Net Income ($)	0.00	0.00	1.12	0.26	0.02	0.25	0.08	0.00	0.02	0.13
Distrib'ns, Cap Gain ($)	0.00	0.00	0.23	0.00	0.00	0.00	0.00	0.00	2.02	0.27
Net Asset Value ($)	12.76	13.85	17.29	28.74	13.22	12.23	14.70	15.20	16.19	18.80
Expense Ratio (%)	1.50	1.45	1.22	1.36	1.72	1.31	1.24	1.36	1.54	1.59
Yield (%)	0.00	0.00	6.39	0.90	0.15	2.04	0.54	0.00	0.10	0.68
Portfolio Turnover (%)	98	123	144	101	57	42	85	50	88	77
Total Assets (Millions $)	296	330	446	989	227	213	446	469	475	526

PORTFOLIO (as of 10/31/02)

Portfolio Manager: June Kim - 2002

Investment Style

Large Cap	Growth
Mid Cap	Value
Small Cap	Grth/Val

Portfolio

1.0%	cash	0.0%	corp bonds
97.5%	stocks	0.0%	gov't bonds
0.0%	preferred	0.0%	muni bonds
0.0%	conv't bds/wrnts	1.5%	other

SHAREHOLDER INFORMATION

Minimum Investment
Initial: $2,500 — Subsequent: $250

Minimum IRA Investment
Initial: $500 — Subsequent: $250

Maximum Fees
Load: 3.00% front — 12b-1: none
Other: 1.5% redemption fee for 3 months

Services
✔ IRA
✔ Keogh
✔ Telephone Exchange

Fidelity Southeast Asia (FSEAX)

800-544-8544, 800-522-7297
www.fidelity.com

Regional/Country Stock

PERFORMANCE

fund inception date: 4/19/93

	3yr Annual	5yr Annual	10yr Annual	Bull	Bear
Return (%)	-15.9	1.3	na	188.2	-45.3
Differ From Category (+/-)	1.5 av	2.8 abv av	na	59.7 high	1.7 abv av

Standard Deviation	Category Risk Index	Beta
24.9%—high	1.06—abv av	0.95

	2002	2001	2000	1999	1998	1997	1996	1995	1994	1993
Return (%)	-11.3	-3.6	-30.4	91.5	-5.7	-38.8	10.1	12.1	-21.7	—
Differ From Category (+/-)	1.1	8.7	-6.6	14.8	-7.3	-32.7	-3.4	7.4	-17.7	—
Return, Tax-Adjusted (%)	-11.6	-3.7	-30.4	91.4	-5.8	-38.9	8.8	11.4	-21.7	—

PER SHARE DATA

	2002	2001	2000	1999	1998	1997	1996	1995	1994	1993
Dividends, Net Income ($)	0.08	0.03	0.00	0.02	0.02	0.05	0.17	0.23	0.00	—
Distrib'ns, Cap Gain ($)	0.00	0.00	0.00	0.00	0.00	0.00	0.40	0.00	0.00	—
Net Asset Value ($)	9.66	10.98	11.43	16.43	8.59	9.14	15.03	14.17	12.84	—
Expense Ratio (%)	1.50	1.52	1.35	1.43	1.79	1.32	1.12	1.15	1.47	—
Yield (%)	0.82	0.27	0.00	0.12	0.23	0.54	1.10	1.62	0.00	—
Portfolio Turnover (%)	131	91	88	93	95	141	102	90	157	—
Total Assets (Millions $)	238	258	279	502	235	263	762	684	660	—

PORTFOLIO (as of 10/31/02)

Portfolio Manager: Allan Liu - 1993

Investment Style

Large Cap	Growth
Mid Cap	Value
Small Cap	Grth/Val

Portfolio

2.7%	cash	0.2%	corp bonds
92.2%	stocks	0.0%	gov't bonds
0.0%	preferred	0.0%	muni bonds
0.0%	conv't bds/wrnts	4.9%	other

SHAREHOLDER INFORMATION

Minimum Investment
Initial: $2,500 Subsequent: $250

Minimum IRA Investment
Initial: $500 Subsequent: $250

Maximum Fees
Load: 3.00% front 12b-1: none
Other: 1.5% redemption fee for 3 months

Services
✔ IRA
✔ Keogh
✔ Telephone Exchange

Matthews Korea (MAKOX)

800-789-2742
www.matthewsfunds.com

Regional/Country Stock

PERFORMANCE — fund inception date: 1/3/95

	3yr Annual	5yr Annual	10yr Annual	Bull	Bear
Return (%)	-4.4	28.9	na	243.5	6.1
Differ From Category (+/-)	13.0 high	30.4 high	na	115.0 high	53.1 high

Standard Deviation	Category Risk Index	Beta
36.1%—high	1.53—high	1.15

	2002	2001	2000	1999	1998	1997	1996	1995	1994	1993
Return (%)	8.1	71.0	-52.8	108.0	96.1	-64.7	-31.7	—	—	—
Differ From Category (+/-)	20.5	83.3	-29.0	31.3	94.5	-58.6	-45.2	—	—	—
Return, Tax-Adjusted (%)	5.9	69.0	-56.7	103.7	96.1	-64.7	-31.7	—	—	—

PER SHARE DATA

	2002	2001	2000	1999	1998	1997	1996	1995	1994	1993
Dividends, Net Income ($)	0.00	0.00	0.00	0.00	0.00	0.00	0.00	—	—	—
Distrib'ns, Cap Gain ($)	0.38	0.20	1.49	0.87	0.00	0.00	0.00	—	—	—
Net Asset Value ($)	3.52	3.58	2.24	7.63	4.08	2.08	5.90	—	—	—
Expense Ratio (%)	1.75	1.78	1.75	1.77	2.06	2.50	2.23	—	—	—
Yield (%)	0.00	0.00	0.00	0.00	0.00	0.00	0.00	—	—	—
Portfolio Turnover (%)	47	81	47	57	94	112	139	—	—	—
Total Assets (Millions $)	189	181	73	212	131	25	2	—	—	—

PORTFOLIO (as of 11/30/02)

Portfolio Manager: Mark Headley/G Paul Matthews - 1995

Investment Style

Large Cap	Growth
Mid Cap	Value
Small Cap	Grth/Val

Portfolio

0.0%	cash	0.0%	corp bonds
91.4%	stocks	0.0%	gov't bonds
7.0%	pref/conv't pref	0.0%	muni bonds
0.8%	conv't bds/wrnts	0.9%	other

SHAREHOLDER INFORMATION

Minimum Investment
Initial: $2,500 Subsequent: $250

Minimum IRA Investment
Initial: $500 Subsequent: $50

Maximum Fees
Load: 2.00% redemption 12b-1: none
Other: redemption fee applies for 3 months

Services
✔ IRA
Keogh
✔ Telephone Exchange

Matthews Pacific Tiger (MAPTX)

800-789-2742
www.matthewsfunds.com

Regional/Country Stock

PERFORMANCE — fund inception date: 9/12/94

	3yr Annual	5yr Annual	10yr Annual	Bull	Bear
Return (%)	-8.1	6.6	na	242.7	-34.9
Differ From Category (+/-)	9.3 high	8.1 high	na	114.2 high	12.1 high

Standard Deviation	Category Risk Index	Beta
25.7%—high	1.09—abv av	1.02

	2002	2001	2000	1999	1998	1997	1996	1995	1994	1993
Return (%)	-6.4	7.9	-23.2	83.0	-2.8	-40.8	24.1	3.0	—	—
Differ From Category (+/-)	6.0	20.2	0.6	6.3	-4.4	-34.7	10.6	-1.7	—	—
Return, Tax-Adjusted (%)	-6.4	7.8	-26.2	81.9	-3.1	-40.9	24.1	3.0	—	—

PER SHARE DATA

	2002	2001	2000	1999	1998	1997	1996	1995	1994	1993
Dividends, Net Income ($)	0.00	0.01	0.51	0.18	0.01	0.00	0.00	0.00	—	—
Distrib'ns, Cap Gain ($)	0.00	0.02	0.84	0.00	0.06	0.02	0.00	0.00	—	—
Net Asset Value ($)	8.24	8.81	8.20	12.32	6.84	7.15	12.12	9.76	—	—
Expense Ratio (%)	1.79	1.90	1.81	1.90	1.90	1.90	1.90	2.17	—	—
Yield (%)	0.00	0.11	5.64	1.46	0.14	0.00	0.00	0.00	—	—
Portfolio Turnover (%)	57	63	52	98	73	71	125	na	—	—
Total Assets (Millions $)	107	87	71	119	51	37	32	3	—	—

PORTFOLIO (as of 11/30/02)

Portfolio Manager: Mark Headley/G Paul Matthews - 1994

Investment Style

Large Cap	Growth
Mid Cap	Value
Small Cap	Grth/Val

Portfolio

0.0%	cash	0.0%	corp bonds
94.0%	stocks	0.0%	gov't bonds
0.0%	preferred	0.0%	muni bonds
0.0%	conv't bds/wrnts	6.0%	other

SHAREHOLDER INFORMATION

Minimum Investment
Initial: $2,500 Subsequent: $250

Minimum IRA Investment
Initial: $500 Subsequent: $50

Maximum Fees
Load: 2.00% redemption 12b-1: none
Other: redemption fee applies for 3 months

Services
✔ IRA
Keogh
✔ Telephone Exchange

Strong Asia Pacific
(SASPX)

800-368-3863, 414-359-1400
www.strong-funds.com

Regional/Country Stock

PERFORMANCE — fund inception date: 12/31/93

	3yr Annual	5yr Annual	10yr Annual	Bull	Bear
Return (%)	-20.1	-0.6	na	173.1	-49.2
Differ From Category (+/-)	-2.7 blw av	0.9 abv av	na	44.6 abv av	-2.2 av

Standard Deviation	Category Risk Index	Beta
22.9%—abv av	0.97—av	0.62

	2002	2001	2000	1999	1998	1997	1996	1995	1994	1993
Return (%)	-7.7	-12.5	-36.9	96.0	-3.1	-30.9	2.1	5.9	-5.2	—
Differ From Category (+/-)	4.7	-0.2	-13.1	19.3	-4.7	-24.8	-11.4	1.2	-1.2	—
Return, Tax-Adjusted (%)	-7.9	-12.8	-38.1	93.5	-3.4	-31.2	1.0	4.7	-5.6	—

PER SHARE DATA

	2002	2001	2000	1999	1998	1997	1996	1995	1994	1993
Dividends, Net Income ($)	0.03	0.05	0.35	0.40	0.04	0.07	0.17	0.28	0.00	—
Distrib'ns, Cap Gain ($)	0.00	0.00	0.00	0.00	0.00	0.00	0.11	0.00	0.11	—
Net Asset Value ($)	5.66	6.18	7.13	11.88	6.27	6.52	9.54	9.62	9.35	—
Expense Ratio (%)	na	2.00	2.00	1.70	2.00	2.00	2.30	2.00	2.00	—
Yield (%)	0.53	0.80	4.90	3.36	0.63	1.07	1.76	2.91	0.00	—
Portfolio Turnover (%)	na	166	22	206	192	96	91	104	103	—
Total Assets (Millions $)	60	38	56	139	26	24	70	57	57	—

PORTFOLIO (as of 9/30/02)

Portfolio Manager: Anthony Cragg - 1993

Investment Style

Large Cap	Growth
Mid Cap	Value
Small Cap	Grth/Val

Portfolio

5.6% cash	0.0% corp bonds
93.9% stocks	0.0% gov't bonds
0.0% preferred	0.0% muni bonds
0.0% conv't bds/wrnts	0.5% other

SHAREHOLDER INFORMATION

Minimum Investment
Initial: $2,500 Subsequent: $100

Minimum IRA Investment
Initial: $250 Subsequent: $50

Maximum Fees
Load: 1.00% redemption 12b-1: none
Other: redemption fee applies for 1 month

Services
✔ IRA
✔ Keogh
✔ Telephone Exchange

T Rowe Price Eurpn Stk (PRESX)

800-638-5660, 410-547-2000
www.troweprice.com

Regional/Country Stock

PERFORMANCE

fund inception date: 2/28/90

	3yr Annual	5yr Annual	10yr Annual	Bull	Bear
Return (%)	-15.5	-1.9	7.9	35.2	-45.6
Differ From Category (+/-)	1.9 av	-0.4 av	5.5 high	-93.3 low	1.4 abv av

Standard Deviation	Category Risk Index	Beta
18.8%—abv av	0.80—low	0.76

	2002	2001	2000	1999	1998	1997	1996	1995	1994	1993
Return (%)	-18.6	-20.6	-6.6	19.7	25.8	17.0	25.8	21.8	4.0	27.2
Differ From Category (+/-)	-6.2	-8.3	17.2	-57.0	24.2	23.1	12.3	17.1	8.0	-12.4
Return, Tax-Adjusted (%)	-18.9	-21.3	-8.1	17.7	23.0	15.3	24.7	20.5	3.5	27.0

PER SHARE DATA

	2002	2001	2000	1999	1998	1997	1996	1995	1994	1993
Dividends, Net Income ($)	0.14	0.36	0.16	0.14	0.28	0.25	0.26	0.21	0.12	0.04
Distrib'ns, Cap Gain ($)	0.00	0.00	1.42	1.90	2.18	1.01	0.20	0.25	0.05	0.01
Net Asset Value ($)	12.88	16.01	20.64	23.86	21.77	19.36	17.62	14.37	12.17	11.86
Expense Ratio (%)	1.11	1.09	1.02	1.05	1.05	1.06	1.12	1.20	1.25	1.35
Yield (%)	1.08	2.24	0.72	0.54	1.16	1.22	1.45	1.43	0.98	0.33
Portfolio Turnover (%)	16	6	24	15	26	17	14	17	24	21
Total Assets (Millions $)	672	846	1,231	1,587	1,548	1,020	765	531	366	289

PORTFOLIO (as of 9/30/02)

Portfolio Manager: J Ford/R Revel-Chion/J Seddon - 1990

Investment Style

Large Cap	Growth
Mid Cap	Value
Small Cap	Grth/Val

Portfolio

2.1%	cash	0.0%	corp bonds
97.9%	stocks	0.0%	gov't bonds
0.0%	preferred	0.0%	muni bonds
0.0%	conv't bds/wrnts	0.0%	other

SHAREHOLDER INFORMATION

Minimum Investment
Initial: $2,500 Subsequent: $100

Minimum IRA Investment
Initial: $1,000 Subsequent: $50

Maximum Fees
Load: none 12b-1: none
Other: none

Services
✔ IRA
✔ Keogh
✔ Telephone Exchange

T Rowe Price Latin Amer (PRLAX)

800-638-5660, 410-547-2000
www.troweprice.com

Regional/Country Stock

PERFORMANCE — fund inception date: 12/29/93

	3yr Annual	5yr Annual	10yr Annual	Bull	Bear
Return (%)	-10.1	-5.6	na	101.6	-42.0
Differ From Category (+/-)	7.3 high	-4.1 blw av	na	-26.9 av	5.0 abv av

Standard Deviation	Category Risk Index	Beta
29.9%—high	1.27—high	1.14

	2002	2001	2000	1999	1998	1997	1996	1995	1994	1993
Return (%)	-18.1	-0.2	-11.1	59.3	-35.4	31.8	23.3	-18.7	-15.9	—
Differ From Category (+/-)	-5.7	12.1	12.7	-17.4	-37.0	37.9	9.8	-23.4	-11.9	—
Return, Tax-Adjusted (%)	-18.1	-1.2	-11.2	59.1	-35.9	31.2	22.5	-19.0	-15.9	—

PER SHARE DATA

	2002	2001	2000	1999	1998	1997	1996	1995	1994	1993
Dividends, Net Income ($)	0.00	0.15	0.04	0.04	0.14	0.12	0.11	0.06	0.00	—
Distrib'ns, Cap Gain ($)	0.00	0.20	0.00	0.00	0.00	0.00	0.03	0.00	0.00	—
Net Asset Value ($)	7.51	9.17	9.56	10.81	6.81	10.77	8.26	6.81	8.45	—
Expense Ratio (%)	1.53	1.49	1.46	1.62	1.53	1.47	1.66	1.82	1.99	—
Yield (%)	0.00	1.60	0.41	0.37	2.05	1.11	1.32	0.88	0.00	—
Portfolio Turnover (%)	21	30	27	43	19	32	22	18	12	—
Total Assets (Millions $)	128	176	207	268	182	432	211	149	163	—

PORTFOLIO (as of 9/30/02)

Portfolio Manager: J Ford/G Pangaro/ B Thomas - 1993

Investment Style

Large Cap	Growth
Mid Cap	Value
Small Cap	Grth/Val

Portfolio

4.0%	cash	0.0%	corp bonds
84.8%	stocks	0.0%	gov't bonds
0.0%	preferred	0.0%	muni bonds
11.2%	conv't bds/wrnts	0.0%	other

SHAREHOLDER INFORMATION

Minimum Investment
Initial: $2,500 Subsequent: $100

Minimum IRA Investment
Initial: $1,000 Subsequent: $50

Maximum Fees
Load: 2.00% redemption 12b-1: none
Other: redemption fee applies for 12 months

Services
✔ IRA
✔ Keogh
✔ Telephone Exchange

T Rowe Price New Asia (PRASX)

800-638-5660, 410-547-2000
www.troweprice.com

Regional/Country Stock

PERFORMANCE — fund inception date: 9/28/90

	3yr Annual	5yr Annual	10yr Annual	Bull	Bear
Return (%)	-17.3	0.0	0.7	177.8	-49.9
Differ From Category (+/-)	0.1 av	1.5 abv av	-1.7 blw av	49.3 abv av	-2.9 av

Standard Deviation	Category Risk Index	Beta
24.0%—high	1.02—av	0.90

	2002	2001	2000	1999	1998	1997	1996	1995	1994	1993
Return (%)	-9.3	-10.0	-30.7	99.8	-11.1	-37.1	13.5	3.7	-19.1	78.7
Differ From Category (+/-)	3.1	2.3	-6.9	23.1	-12.7	-31.0	0.0	-1.0	-15.1	39.1
Return, Tax-Adjusted (%)	-9.5	-10.0	-30.7	99.5	-11.7	-37.4	13.2	3.3	-20.3	77.6

PER SHARE DATA

	2002	2001	2000	1999	1998	1997	1996	1995	1994	1993
Dividends, Net Income ($)	0.04	0.00	0.00	0.04	0.09	0.08	0.06	0.09	0.07	0.04
Distrib'ns, Cap Gain ($)	0.00	0.00	0.00	0.00	0.00	0.00	0.01	0.00	0.89	0.19
Net Asset Value ($)	5.59	6.21	6.90	9.97	5.01	5.74	9.26	8.22	8.01	11.10
Expense Ratio (%)	1.17	1.22	1.08	1.21	1.29	1.10	1.11	1.15	1.22	1.29
Yield (%)	0.71	0.00	0.00	0.40	1.79	1.39	0.64	1.09	0.78	0.31
Portfolio Turnover (%)	72	49	52	69	68	41	42	63	63	40
Total Assets (Millions $)	597	638	799	1,374	622	782	2,181	1,880	1,987	2,247

PORTFOLIO (as of 9/30/02)

Portfolio Manager: F Dydasco/M Edwards/J Ford - 1990

Investment Style

Large Cap	Growth
Mid Cap	Value
Small Cap	Grth/Val

Portfolio

3.5%	cash	0.0%	corp bonds
95.6%	stocks	0.0%	gov't bonds
0.0%	preferred	0.0%	muni bonds
0.9%	conv't bds/wrnts	0.0%	other

SHAREHOLDER INFORMATION

Minimum Investment
Initial: $2,500 — Subsequent: $100

Minimum IRA Investment
Initial: $1,000 — Subsequent: $50

Maximum Fees
Load: none — 12b-1: none
Other: none

Services
✔ IRA
✔ Keogh
✔ Telephone Exchange

Vanguard Erpn Stk Idx (VEURX)

800-662-7447, 610-436-5152
www.vanguard.com

Regional/Country Stock

PERFORMANCE — fund inception date: 6/18/90

	3yr Annual	5yr Annual	10yr Annual	Bull	Bear
Return (%)	-15.6	-2.0	8.1	32.7	-45.8
Differ From Category (+/-)	1.8 av	-0.5 av	5.7 high	-95.8 low	1.2 av

Standard Deviation	Category Risk Index	Beta
18.5%—av	0.78—low	0.78

	2002	2001	2000	1999	1998	1997	1996	1995	1994	1993
Return (%)	-17.9	-20.3	-8.2	16.6	28.8	24.2	21.2	22.3	1.8	29.1
Differ From Category (+/-)	-5.5	-8.0	15.6	-60.1	27.2	30.3	7.7	17.6	5.8	-10.5
Return, Tax-Adjusted (%)	-18.7	-21.0	-8.8	15.7	27.6	23.2	20.1	21.1	0.7	28.4

PER SHARE DATA

	2002	2001	2000	1999	1998	1997	1996	1995	1994	1993
Dividends, Net Income ($)	0.40	0.45	0.42	0.50	0.52	0.37	0.36	0.32	0.28	0.17
Distrib'ns, Cap Gain ($)	0.00	0.00	0.05	0.15	0.14	0.08	0.06	0.05	0.06	0.00
Net Asset Value ($)	16.21	20.25	25.99	28.83	25.28	20.13	16.57	14.02	11.76	11.88
Expense Ratio (%)	na	0.30	0.29	0.29	0.29	0.31	0.35	0.32	0.32	0.32
Yield (%)	2.46	2.22	1.61	1.72	2.04	1.83	2.16	2.27	2.36	1.43
Portfolio Turnover (%)	na	3	8	7	7	3	4	3	6	4
Total Assets (Millions $)	4,101	4,404	5,610	6,106	4,479	2,432	1,594	1,017	715	600

PORTFOLIO (as of 9/30/02)

Portfolio Manager: Team Managed - 1990

Investment Style

Large Cap	Growth
Mid Cap	Value
Small Cap	Grth/Val

Portfolio

0.0%	cash	0.0%	corp bonds
100.0%	stocks	0.0%	gov't bonds
0.0%	preferred	0.0%	muni bonds
0.0%	conv't bds/wrnts	0.0%	other

SHAREHOLDER INFORMATION

Minimum Investment
Initial: $3,000 — Subsequent: $100

Minimum IRA Investment
Initial: $1,000 — Subsequent: $100

Maximum Fees
Load: none — 12b-1: none
Other: none

Services
✔ IRA
✔ Keogh
✔ Telephone Exchange

Vanguard Pacific Stk (VPACX)

800-662-7447, 610-436-5152
www.vanguard.com

Regional/Country Stock

PERFORMANCE — fund inception date: 6/18/90

	3yr Annual	5yr Annual	10yr Annual	Bull	Bear
Return (%)	-20.8	-4.4	-1.4	98.3	-49.0
Differ From Category (+/-)	-3.4 blw av	-2.9 blw av	-3.8 blw av	-30.2 av	-2.0 av

Standard Deviation	Category Risk Index	Beta
17.7%—av	0.75—low	0.58

	2002	2001	2000	1999	1998	1997	1996	1995	1994	1993
Return (%)	-9.3	-26.3	-25.7	57.0	2.4	-25.6	-7.8	2.8	12.9	35.4
Differ From Category (+/-)	.3.1	-14.0	-1.9	-19.7	0.8	-19.5	-21.3	-1.9	16.9	-4.2
Return, Tax-Adjusted (%)	-9.7	-26.4	-26.1	56.5	2.1	-25.9	-8.1	2.4	12.4	34.9

PER SHARE DATA

	2002	2001	2000	1999	1998	1997	1996	1995	1994	1993
Dividends, Net Income ($)	0.06	0.03	0.12	0.09	0.06	0.09	0.09	0.12	0.08	0.06
Distrib'ns, Cap Gain ($)	0.00	0.00	0.00	0.00	0.00	0.00	0.00	0.00	0.06	0.05
Net Asset Value ($)	5.88	6.56	8.95	12.22	7.84	7.72	10.51	11.50	11.30	10.13
Expense Ratio (%)	na	0.37	0.38	0.37	0.40	0.35	0.35	0.32	0.32	0.32
Yield (%)	1.02	0.45	1.34	0.73	0.76	1.16	0.85	1.04	0.70	0.58
Portfolio Turnover (%)	na	2	6	6	4	8	9	1	4	7
Total Assets (Millions $)	1,445	1,326	1,924	2,526	1,032	827	977	830	697	492

PORTFOLIO (as of 9/30/02)

Portfolio Manager: George Sauter - 2000

Investment Style

Large Cap	Growth
Mid Cap	Value
Small Cap	Grth/Val

Portfolio

0.0%	cash	0.0%	corp bonds
100.0%	stocks	0.0%	gov't bonds
0.0%	preferred	0.0%	muni bonds
0.0%	conv't bds/wrnts	0.0%	other

SHAREHOLDER INFORMATION

Minimum Investment
Initial: $3,000 — Subsequent: $100

Minimum IRA Investment
Initial: $1,000 — Subsequent: $100

Maximum Fees
Load: none — 12b-1: none
Other: none

Services
✔ IRA
✔ Keogh
✔ Telephone Exchange

Emerging Stock Funds
Category Performance Ranked by 2002 Returns

Category	Fund (Ticker)	Annual Return (%) 2002	3yr	5yr	10yr	Category Risk	Total Risk
IntS-E	T Rowe Price Emg Mkt Stk (PRMSX)	-4.9	-12.9	-2.4	na	high	high
IntS-E	USAA Inv:Emerging Mrkts (USEMX)	-5.0	-15.2	-7.2	na	blw av	abv av
IntS-E	SSgA:Emerging Markets (SSEMX)	-5.0	-12.5	-1.5	na	av	abv av
IntS-E	Fidelity Emerging Market (FEMKX)	-6.9	-15.2	-5.2	-3.2	abv av	abv av
IntS-E	Vanguard Em Mkt Stk (VEIEX)	-7.4	-13.3	-2.9	na	abv av	high
Emerging Stock Average		**-6.4**	**-13.7**	**-4.4**	**-2.2**	**—**	**abv av**

Note: AAII members who would like performance figures for no-load and low-load mutual funds they own that do not appear in this Guide can access this information on our Web site at www.aaii.com.

Fidelity Emerging Market (FEMKX)

800-544-8544, 800-522-7297
www.fidelity.com

Emerging Stock

PERFORMANCE — fund inception date: 11/1/90

	3yr Annual	5yr Annual	10yr Annual	Bull	Bear
Return (%)	-15.2	-5.2	-3.2	116.1	-44.7
Differ From Category (+/-)	-1.5 blw av	-0.8 av	-1.0 av	11.6 abv av	-2.8 av

Standard Deviation	Category Risk Index	Beta
23.3%—abv av	1.00—abv av	0.94

	2002	2001	2000	1999	1998	1997	1996	1995	1994	1993
Return (%)	-6.9	-2.4	-32.9	70.4	-26.5	-40.7	9.9	-3.1	-17.9	81.7
Differ From Category (+/-)	-0.5	1.0	-4.0	4.0	-1.5	-30.8	-3.1	0.0	-5.1	11.6
Return, Tax-Adjusted (%)	-7.1	-2.5	-33.0	70.4	-26.5	-41.2	9.3	-3.8	-18.0	81.5

PER SHARE DATA

	2002	2001	2000	1999	1998	1997	1996	1995	1994	1993
Dividends, Net Income ($)	0.05	0.03	0.03	0.00	0.00	0.23	0.25	0.27	0.04	0.05
Distrib'ns, Cap Gain ($)	0.00	0.00	0.00	0.00	0.00	0.00	0.00	0.00	0.00	0.00
Net Asset Value ($)	7.21	7.80	8.03	12.02	7.05	9.60	16.62	15.34	16.13	19.70
Expense Ratio (%)	1.39	1.45	1.35	1.42	1.56	1.35	1.29	1.41	1.52	1.91
Yield (%)	0.69	0.38	0.37	0.00	0.00	2.39	1.50	1.76	0.24	0.25
Portfolio Turnover (%)	120	113	100	94	87	69	77	74	107	57
Total Assets (Millions $)	265	242	269	554	270	446	1,161	1,085	1,508	1,908

PORTFOLIO (as of 10/31/02)

Portfolio Manager: John Carlson - 2001

Investment Style

Large Cap	Growth
Mid Cap	Value
Small Cap	Grth/Val

Portfolio

0.8% cash	0.6% corp bonds
97.9% stocks	0.0% gov't bonds
0.0% preferred	0.0% muni bonds
0.0% conv't bds/wrnts	0.7% other

SHAREHOLDER INFORMATION

Minimum Investment
Initial: $2,500 — Subsequent: $250

Minimum IRA Investment
Initial: $500 — Subsequent: $250

Maximum Fees
Load: 3.00% front — 12b-1: none
Other: 1.50% redemption fee for 3 months

Services
✔ IRA
✔ Keogh
✔ Telephone Exchange

SSgA:Emerging Markets (SSEMX)

800-997-7327, 253-627-7001
www.ssgafunds.com

Emerging Stock

PERFORMANCE — fund inception date: 3/1/94

	3yr Annual	5yr Annual	10yr Annual	Bull	Bear
Return (%)	-12.5	-1.5	na	108.6	-38.7
Differ From Category (+/-)	1.2 high	2.9 high	na	4.1 av	3.2 high

Standard Deviation	Category Risk Index	Beta
23.1%—abv av	1.00—av	0.92

	2002	2001	2000	1999	1998	1997	1996	1995	1994	1993
Return (%)	-5.0	0.4	-29.9	64.8	-15.9	-8.8	14.8	-7.8	—	—
Differ From Category (+/-)	1.4	3.8	-1.0	-1.6	9.1	1.1	1.8	-4.7	—	—
Return, Tax-Adjusted (%)	-5.1	0.4	-30.1	63.6	-17.0	-9.8	14.2	-8.5	—	—

PER SHARE DATA

	2002	2001	2000	1999	1998	1997	1996	1995	1994	1993
Dividends, Net Income ($)	0.03	0.00	0.06	0.23	0.27	0.15	0.10	0.11	—	—
Distrib'ns, Cap Gain ($)	0.00	0.00	0.00	0.00	0.00	0.25	0.05	0.10	—	—
Net Asset Value ($)	8.37	8.85	8.81	12.67	7.86	9.69	10.98	9.70	—	—
Expense Ratio (%)	1.25	1.25	1.25	1.25	1.25	1.25	1.28	1.50	—	—
Yield (%)	0.35	0.00	0.68	1.81	3.43	1.50	0.90	1.12	—	—
Portfolio Turnover (%)	92	49	55	39	38	15	4	20	—	—
Total Assets (Millions $)	394	386	317	414	236	254	148	80	—	—

PORTFOLIO (as of 6/30/02)

Portfolio Manager: Brad Aham - 1997

Investment Style

Large Cap — Growth
Mid Cap — Value
Small Cap — Grth/Val

Portfolio

1.4%	cash	7.5%	corp bonds
86.4%	stocks	0.0%	gov't bonds
0.0%	preferred	0.0%	muni bonds
0.0%	conv't bds/wrnts	4.8%	other

SHAREHOLDER INFORMATION

Minimum Investment
Initial: $1,000 — Subsequent: $100

Minimum IRA Investment
Initial: $250 — Subsequent: $100

Maximum Fees
Load: none — 12b-1: 0.24%
Other: none

Services
✔ IRA
Keogh
✔ Telephone Exchange

T Rowe Price Emg Mkt Stk (PRMSX)

800-638-5660, 410-547-2000
www.troweprice.com

Emerging Stock

PERFORMANCE — fund inception date: 3/31/95

	3yr Annual	5yr Annual	10yr Annual	Bull	Bear
Return (%)	-12.9	-2.4	na	140.5	-44.8
Differ From Category (+/-)	0.8 abv av	2.0 abv av	na	36.0 high	-2.9 av

Standard Deviation	Category Risk Index	Beta
24.5%—high	1.06—high	0.97

	2002	2001	2000	1999	1998	1997	1996	1995	1994	1993
Return (%)	-4.9	-5.6	-26.3	87.4	-28.7	1.2	11.8	—	—	—
Differ From Category (+/-)	1.5	-2.2	2.6	21.0	-3.7	11.1	-1.2	—	—	—
Return, Tax-Adjusted (%)	-5.0	-5.6	-26.3	87.4	-28.8	0.9	10.9	—	—	—

PER SHARE DATA

	2002	2001	2000	1999	1998	1997	1996	1995	1994	1993
Dividends, Net Income ($)	0.02	0.01	0.00	0.00	0.04	0.00	0.04	—	—	—
Distrib'ns, Cap Gain ($)	0.00	0.00	0.00	0.00	0.00	0.15	0.30	—	—	—
Net Asset Value ($)	10.22	10.77	11.43	15.52	8.28	11.68	11.69	—	—	—
Expense Ratio (%)	1.51	1.58	1.50	1.75	1.75	1.75	1.75	—	—	—
Yield (%)	0.19	0.09	0.00	0.00	0.48	0.00	0.33	—	—	—
Portfolio Turnover (%)	71	70	56	59	54	84	41	—	—	—
Total Assets (Millions $)	172	155	152	162	72	123	73	—	—	—

PORTFOLIO (as of 9/30/02)

Portfolio Manager: Team Managed - 1995

Investment Style

Large Cap	Growth
Mid Cap	Value
Small Cap	Grth/Val

Portfolio

2.0%	cash	0.0%	corp bonds
95.7%	stocks	0.0%	gov't bonds
0.0%	preferred	0.0%	muni bonds
2.3%	conv't bds/wrnts	0.0%	other

SHAREHOLDER INFORMATION

Minimum Investment
Initial: $2,500 Subsequent: $100

Minimum IRA Investment
Initial: $1,000 Subsequent: $50

Maximum Fees
Load: 2.00% redemption 12b-1: none
Other: redemption fee applies for 12 months

Services
✔ IRA
✔ Keogh
✔ Telephone Exchange

USAA Inv:Emerging Mrkts (USEMX)

800-531-8181, 210-456-7211
www.usaa.com

Emerging Stock

PERFORMANCE

fund inception date: 11/7/94

	3yr Annual	5yr Annual	10yr Annual	Bull	Bear
Return (%)	-15.2	-7.2	na	98.9	-44.3
Differ From Category (+/-)	-1.5 av	-2.8 av	na	-5.6 blw av	-2.4 abv av

Standard Deviation	Category Risk Index	Beta
22.5%—abv av	0.97—blw av	0.88

	2002	2001	2000	1999	1998	1997	1996	1995	1994	1993
Return (%)	-5.0	-5.7	-31.9	52.4	-26.1	-3.4	16.5	3.6	—	—
Differ From Category (+/-)	1.4	-2.3	-3.0	-14.0	-1.1	6.5	3.5	6.7	—	—
Return, Tax-Adjusted (%)	-5.0	-5.8	-31.9	52.0	-26.4	-3.7	15.0	2.9	—	—

PER SHARE DATA

	2002	2001	2000	1999	1998	1997	1996	1995	1994	1993
Dividends, Net Income ($)	0.00	0.02	0.00	0.07	0.07	0.00	0.00	0.01	—	—
Distrib'ns, Cap Gain ($)	0.00	0.00	0.00	0.00	0.00	0.17	0.50	0.22	—	—
Net Asset Value ($)	6.58	6.93	7.38	10.85	7.17	9.79	10.29	9.26	—	—
Expense Ratio (%)	2.51	1.39	1.28	1.27	1.31	1.81	2.27	2.40	—	—
Yield (%)	0.00	0.28	0.00	0.64	0.97	0.00	0.00	0.10	—	—
Portfolio Turnover (%)	257	196	147	83	41	61	87	46	—	—
Total Assets (Millions $)	47	43	170	323	234	305	55	25	—	—

PORTFOLIO (as of 9/30/02)

Portfolio Manager: Kevin Moore - 1999

Investment Style

Large Cap	Growth
Mid Cap	Value
Small Cap	Grth/Val

Portfolio

2.0%	cash	0.0%	corp bonds
94.0%	stocks	0.0%	gov't bonds
4.0%	pref/conv't pref	0.0%	muni bonds
0.0%	conv't bds/wrnts	0.0%	other

SHAREHOLDER INFORMATION

Minimum Investment
Initial: $3,000 Subsequent: $50

Minimum IRA Investment
Initial: $250 Subsequent: $50

Maximum Fees
Load: none 12b-1: none
Other: none

Services
✔ IRA
✔ Keogh
✔ Telephone Exchange

Vanguard Em Mkt Stk (VEIEX)

800-662-7447, 610-436-5152
www.vanguard.com

Emerging Stock

PERFORMANCE

fund inception date: 5/4/94

	3yr Annual	5yr Annual	10yr Annual	Bull	Bear
Return (%)	-13.3	-2.9	na	105.1	-39.5
Differ From Category (+/-)	0.4 abv av	1.5 abv av	na	0.6 av	2.4 abv av

Standard Deviation	Category Risk Index	Beta
24.0%—high	1.03—abv av	0.98

	2002	2001	2000	1999	1998	1997	1996	1995	1994	1993
Return (%)	-7.4	-2.8	-27.5	61.5	-18.2	-16.7	15.9	0.4	—	—
Differ From Category (+/-)	-1.0	0.6	1.4	-4.9	6.8	-6.8	2.9	3.5	—	—
Return, Tax-Adjusted (%)	-8.0	-3.7	-28.2	60.1	-19.2	-17.4	15.3	-0.3	—	—

PER SHARE DATA

	2002	2001	2000	1999	1998	1997	1996	1995	1994	1993
Dividends, Net Income ($)	0.12	0.21	0.21	0.27	0.26	0.23	0.17	0.18	—	—
Distrib'ns, Cap Gain ($)	0.00	0.00	0.00	0.00	0.00	0.00	0.00	0.00	—	—
Net Asset Value ($)	7.63	8.37	8.84	12.50	7.91	9.99	12.28	10.74	—	—
Expense Ratio (%)	na	0.60	0.59	0.58	0.61	0.57	0.60	0.60	—	—
Yield (%)	1.57	2.50	2.37	2.16	3.28	2.30	1.38	1.67	—	—
Portfolio Turnover (%)	na	23	40	22	22	19	1	6	—	—
Total Assets (Millions $)	915	801	913	1,137	576	660	637	234	—	—

PORTFOLIO (as of 9/30/02)

Portfolio Manager: Team Managed - 1994

Investment Style

Large Cap	Growth
Mid Cap	Value
Small Cap	Grth/Val

Portfolio

10.2%	cash	0.0%	corp bonds
89.8%	stocks	0.0%	gov't bonds
0.0%	preferred	0.0%	muni bonds
0.0%	conv't bds/wrnts	0.0%	other

SHAREHOLDER INFORMATION

Minimum Investment
Initial: $3,000 Subsequent: $100

Minimum IRA Investment
Initial: $1,000 Subsequent: $100

Maximum Fees
Load: 0.50% redemption 12b-1: none
Other: redemption fee applies for 12 months

Services
✔ IRA
✔ Keogh
✔ Telephone Exchange

BALANCED STOCK/BOND FUNDS

Category Performance Ranked by 2002 Returns

Category	Fund (Ticker)	Annual Return (%) 2002	3yr	5yr	10yr	Category Risk	Total Risk
Bal	USAA Mutual:Income (USAIX)	8.6	9.8	6.7	7.2	low	low
Bal	T Rowe Price Spect Inc (RPSIX)	6.8	6.2	5.1	7.3	low	low
Bal	Vanguard Welles Inc/Inv (VWINX)	4.6	9.2	6.7	9.9	low	blw av
Bal	T Rowe Price Cap Apprec (PRWCX)	0.5	10.6	8.9	11.8	av	blw av
Bal	Vanguard Life Income (VASIX)	0.1	4.0	5.5	na	low	blw av
Bal	Fidelity Freedom Income (FFFAX)	-0.2	2.7	5.2	na	low	low
Bal	Fidelity Asset Mgr Income (FASIX)	-0.5	1.4	4.0	6.9	low	blw av
Bal	Fidelity Freedom 2000 (FFFBX)	-1.8	0.6	5.6	na	low	blw av
Bal	Oakmark Eqty & Income/I (OAKBX)	-2.1	11.4	10.9	na	blw av	blw av
Bal	Dodge & Cox Balanced (DODBX)	-2.9	7.1	8.0	11.9	av	blw av
Bal	Vanguard Life Cnsrv Gr (VSCGX)	-5.3	-0.8	4.0	na	low	blw av
Bal	Janus Balanced (JABAX)	-6.5	-4.6	7.0	10.7	blw av	blw av
Bal	Fidelity Freedom 2010 (FFFCX)	-6.8	-3.5	4.9	na	blw av	blw av
Bal	Vanguard Wellington/Inv (VWELX)	-6.8	2.3	4.6	10.3	av	blw av
Bal	Fidelity Puritan (FPURX)	-7.9	-0.6	3.3	9.5	blw av	blw av
Bal	Fidelity Asset Mgr (FASMX)	-8.0	-3.2	3.5	8.3	abv av	blw av
Bal	Fidelity Balanced (FBALX)	-8.4	-0.4	5.2	8.4	av	blw av
Bal	Pax World Balanced (PAXWX)	-8.8	-4.3	5.0	8.7	blw av	blw av
Bal	Vanguard Bal Idx/Inv (VBINX)	-9.5	-4.9	2.8	8.3	av	blw av
Bal	Vanguard STAR (VGSTX)	-9.8	0.1	3.8	9.2	av	blw av
Bal	Vanguard Life Mod Gr (VSMGX)	-10.3	-5.3	2.5	na	abv av	blw av
Bal	Fidelity Freedom 2020 (FFFDX)	-13.7	-8.7	3.0	na	high	blw av
Bal	Fidelity Asset Mgr Growth (FASGX)	-14.0	-8.3	0.6	8.0	high	av
Bal	Vanguard Asset Al/Inv (VAAPX)	-15.4	-5.6	2.0	9.3	high	av
Bal	Vanguard Life Gr (VASGX)	-15.8	-10.1	0.6	na	high	av
Balanced Stock/Bond Average		**-8.7**	**-3.0**	**2.5**	**7.8**	**—**	**blw av**

Note: AAII members who would like performance figures for no-load and low-load mutual funds they own that do not appear in this Guide can access this information on our Web site at www.aaii.com.

Dodge & Cox Balanced (DODBX)

800-621-3979, 415-981-1710
www.dodgeandcox.com

Balanced Stock/Bond

PERFORMANCE

fund inception date: 6/26/31

	3yr Annual	5yr Annual	10yr Annual	Bull	Bear
Return (%)	7.1	8.0	11.9	27.3	14.2
Differ From Category (+/-)	10.1 high	5.5 high	4.1 high	-4.5 av	28.4 high

Standard Deviation	Category Risk Index	Beta
11.1%—blw av	1.02—av	0.45

	2002	2001	2000	1999	1998	1997	1996	1995	1994	1993
Return (%)	-2.9	10.0	15.1	12.0	6.6	21.1	14.7	28.0	1.9	15.9
Differ From Category (+/-)	5.8	12.2	12.9	1.3	-7.1	2.4	0.8	2.6	3.0	1.7
Return, Tax-Adjusted (%)	-4.3	8.0	10.8	9.1	4.2	18.5	12.9	25.5	0.2	13.6

PER SHARE DATA

	2002	2001	2000	1999	1998	1997	1996	1995	1994	1993
Dividends, Net Income ($)	1.88	2.14	2.47	2.22	2.23	2.22	1.99	2.18	1.79	1.67
Distrib'ns, Cap Gain ($)	0.88	2.05	9.22	4.98	3.74	3.27	0.69	0.91	0.33	1.06
Net Asset Value ($)	60.75	65.42	63.42	65.71	65.22	66.78	59.82	54.60	45.21	46.40
Expense Ratio (%)	na	0.53	0.53	0.53	0.54	0.55	0.56	0.58	0.58	0.60
Yield (%)	3.05	3.17	3.40	3.14	3.23	3.16	3.28	3.92	3.93	3.51
Portfolio Turnover (%)	na	21	23	17	26	32	17	20	20	15
Total Assets (Millions $)	7,834	6,040	4,909	5,137	5,700	5,076	3,629	1,800	725	486

PORTFOLIO (as of 9/30/02)

Portfolio Manager: Team Managed - 1931

Investment Style

Large Cap	Growth
Mid Cap	Value
Small Cap	Grth/Val

Portfolio

3.9%	cash	18.2%	corp bonds
60.9%	stocks	15.3%	gov't bonds
1.4%	pref/conv't pref	0.1%	muni bonds
0.0%	conv't bds/wrnts	0.1%	other

SHAREHOLDER INFORMATION

Minimum Investment
Initial: $2,500 Subsequent: $100

Minimum IRA Investment
Initial: $1,000 Subsequent: $100

Maximum Fees
Load: none 12b-1: none
Other: none

Services
✔ IRA
✔ Keogh
✔ Telephone Exchange

Fidelity Asset Mgr
(FASMX)

800-544-8544, 800-522-7297
www.fidelity.com

Balanced Stock/Bond

PERFORMANCE — fund inception date: 12/28/88

	3yr Annual	5yr Annual	10yr Annual	Bull	Bear
Return (%)	-3.2	3.5	8.3	41.1	-19.2
Differ From Category (+/-)	-0.2 abv av	1.0 abv av	0.5 abv av	9.3 abv av	-5.0 av

Standard Deviation	Category Risk Index	Beta
11.4%—blw av	1.05—abv av	0.57

	2002	2001	2000	1999	1998	1997	1996	1995	1994	1993
Return (%)	-8.0	-3.9	2.3	13.5	16.0	22.2	12.7	18.1	-6.6	23.2
Differ From Category (+/-)	0.7	-1.7	0.1	2.8	2.3	3.5	-1.2	-7.3	-5.5	9.0
Return, Tax-Adjusted (%)	-9.2	-5.4	-0.6	11.4	11.3	19.4	9.8	16.8	-7.9	20.6

PER SHARE DATA

	2002	2001	2000	1999	1998	1997	1996	1995	1994	1993
Dividends, Net Income ($)	0.47	0.65	0.65	0.55	0.60	0.61	0.62	0.46	0.40	0.59
Distrib'ns, Cap Gain ($)	0.00	0.00	1.34	0.74	3.15	1.11	0.75	0.00	0.17	0.43
Net Asset Value ($)	13.80	15.50	16.82	18.38	17.39	18.35	16.47	15.85	13.83	15.40
Expense Ratio (%)	0.73	0.71	0.73	0.73	0.74	0.79	0.93	0.97	1.04	1.09
Yield (%)	3.40	4.19	3.57	2.87	2.92	3.13	3.60	2.90	2.85	3.72
Portfolio Turnover (%)	129	133	109	104	136	79	131	137	109	98
Total Assets (Millions $)	10,118	11,923	12,961	13,253	12,879	12,098	10,971	11,165	11,075	9,094

PORTFOLIO (as of 9/30/02)

Portfolio Manager: R Habermann/ J Moore - 2002

Investment Style

Large Cap	Growth
Mid Cap	Value
Small Cap	Grth/Val

Portfolio

0.7%	cash	25.1%	corp bonds
41.5%	stocks	16.0%	gov't bonds
0.1%	pref/conv't pref	0.0%	muni bonds
0.3%	conv't bds/wrnts	16.3%	other

SHAREHOLDER INFORMATION

Minimum Investment
Initial: $2,500 Subsequent: $250

Minimum IRA Investment
Initial: $500 Subsequent: $250

Maximum Fees
Load: none 12b-1: none
Other: none

Services
✔ IRA
✔ Keogh
✔ Telephone Exchange

Fidelity Asset Mgr Growth (FASGX)

800-544-8544, 800-522-7297
www.fidelity.com

Balanced Stock/Bond

PERFORMANCE

fund inception date: 12/30/91

	3yr Annual	5yr Annual	10yr Annual	Bull	Bear
Return (%)	-8.3	0.6	8.0	41.6	-31.0
Differ From Category (+/-)	-5.3 blw av	-1.9 blw av	0.2 av	9.8 abv av	-16.8 low

Standard Deviation	Category Risk Index	Beta
16.0%—av	1.46—high	0.80

	2002	2001	2000	1999	1998	1997	1996	1995	1994	1993
Return (%)	-14.0	-7.2	-3.5	13.9	18.0	26.4	17.5	19.9	-7.3	26.3
Differ From Category (+/-)	-5.3	-5.0	-5.7	3.2	4.3	7.7	3.6	-5.5	-6.2	12.1
Return, Tax-Adjusted (%)	-15.0	-8.2	-7.0	11.8	14.3	23.3	14.4	19.2	-8.2	24.8

PER SHARE DATA

	2002	2001	2000	1999	1998	1997	1996	1995	1994	1993
Dividends, Net Income ($)	0.36	0.42	0.46	0.45	0.35	0.40	0.43	0.23	0.19	0.09
Distrib'ns, Cap Gain ($)	0.00	0.00	2.56	1.10	2.68	1.75	1.07	0.00	0.17	0.51
Net Asset Value ($)	11.97	14.34	15.91	19.67	18.68	18.48	16.35	15.17	12.84	14.25
Expense Ratio (%)	0.81	0.78	0.80	0.80	0.80	0.87	1.01	1.03	1.15	1.19
Yield (%)	3.00	2.92	2.49	2.16	1.63	1.97	2.46	1.51	1.46	0.60
Portfolio Turnover (%)	101	143	197	101	150	70	138	119	104	97
Total Assets (Millions $)	3,341	4,234	4,826	5,490	5,119	4,662	3,377	2,894	2,852	1,795

PORTFOLIO (as of 9/30/02)

Portfolio Manager: R Habermann/J Moore - 2002

Investment Style

Large Cap	Growth
Mid Cap	Value
Small Cap	Grth/Val

Portfolio

0.7%	cash	21.2%	corp bonds
61.3%	stocks	5.9%	gov't bonds
0.1%	pref/conv't pref	0.0%	muni bonds
0.4%	conv't bds/wrnts	10.3%	other

SHAREHOLDER INFORMATION

Minimum Investment
Initial: $2,500 Subsequent: $250

Minimum IRA Investment
Initial: $500 Subsequent: $250

Maximum Fees
Load: none 12b-1: none
Other: none

Services
✔ IRA
✔ Keogh
✔ Telephone Exchange

Fidelity Asset Mgr Income (FASIX)

800-544-8544, 800-522-7297
www.fidelity.com

Balanced Stock/Bond

PERFORMANCE

fund inception date: 10/1/92

	3yr Annual	5yr Annual	10yr Annual	Bull	Bear
Return (%)	1.4	4.0	6.9	15.4	-1.0
Differ From Category (+/-)	4.4 high	1.5 abv av	-0.9 blw av	-16.4 low	13.2 high

Standard Deviation	Category Risk Index	Beta
5.0%—blw av	0.46—low	0.23

	2002	2001	2000	1999	1998	1997	1996	1995	1994	1993
Return (%)	-0.5	1.3	3.6	5.7	10.3	12.4	7.8	16.6	-1.3	15.3
Differ From Category (+/-)	8.2	3.5	1.4	-5.0	-3.4	-6.3	-6.1	-8.8	-0.2	1.1
Return, Tax-Adjusted (%)	-1.9	-0.5	1.1	3.4	7.6	10.0	5.1	14.6	-3.1	13.2

PER SHARE DATA

	2002	2001	2000	1999	1998	1997	1996	1995	1994	1993
Dividends, Net Income ($)	0.41	0.55	0.66	0.61	0.55	0.55	0.61	0.53	0.49	0.49
Distrib'ns, Cap Gain ($)	0.00	0.00	0.22	0.21	0.53	0.29	0.26	0.00	0.00	0.08
Net Asset Value ($)	10.86	11.33	11.73	12.18	12.32	12.18	11.61	11.60	10.42	11.06
Expense Ratio (%)	0.63	0.62	0.65	0.67	0.69	0.77	0.80	0.79	0.71	0.65
Yield (%)	3.77	4.85	5.52	4.92	4.28	4.41	5.13	4.56	4.70	4.39
Portfolio Turnover (%)	164	164	140	121	156	112	148	157	83	47
Total Assets (Millions $)	885	930	1,000	888	940	687	588	600	476	292

PORTFOLIO (as of 9/30/02)

Portfolio Manager: Robert Bertelson - 2002

Investment Style

Large Cap	Growth
Mid Cap	Value
Small Cap	Grth/Val

Portfolio

1.2%	cash	25.2%	corp bonds
15.9%	stocks	21.3%	gov't bonds
0.0%	pref/conv't pref	0.0%	muni bonds
0.1%	conv't bds/wrnts	36.2%	other

SHAREHOLDER INFORMATION

Minimum Investment
Initial: $2,500 Subsequent: $250

Minimum IRA Investment
Initial: $500 Subsequent: $250

Maximum Fees
Load: none 12b-1: none
Other: none

Services
✔ IRA
✔ Keogh
✔ Telephone Exchange

Fidelity Balanced
(FBALX)

800-544-8544, 800-522-7297
www.fidelity.com

Balanced Stock/Bond

PERFORMANCE

fund inception date: 11/6/86

	3yr Annual	5yr Annual	10yr Annual	Bull	Bear
Return (%)	-0.4	5.2	8.4	32.6	-10.0
Differ From Category (+/-)	2.6 abv av	2.7 high	0.6 abv av	0.8 av	4.2 abv av

Standard Deviation	Category Risk Index	Beta
11.2%—blw av	1.03—av	0.56

	2002	2001	2000	1999	1998	1997	1996	1995	1994	1993
Return (%)	-8.4	2.2	5.3	8.8	20.2	23.4	9.3	14.9	-5.3	19.2
Differ From Category (+/-)	0.3	4.4	3.1	-1.9	6.5	4.7	-4.6	-10.5	-4.2	5.0
Return, Tax-Adjusted (%)	-9.3	0.8	3.4	5.3	17.3	19.8	7.4	13.1	-6.5	15.8

PER SHARE DATA

	2002	2001	2000	1999	1998	1997	1996	1995	1994	1993
Dividends, Net Income ($)	0.36	0.45	0.48	0.46	0.46	0.56	0.65	0.57	0.40	0.60
Distrib'ns, Cap Gain ($)	0.00	0.17	0.49	1.98	1.27	1.46	0.00	0.00	0.00	0.64
Net Asset Value ($)	13.29	14.90	15.19	15.36	16.36	15.27	14.08	13.52	12.29	13.39
Expense Ratio (%)	0.66	0.64	0.67	0.65	0.67	0.74	0.79	0.90	1.01	0.93
Yield (%)	2.70	2.98	3.06	2.65	2.60	3.34	4.61	4.21	3.25	4.27
Portfolio Turnover (%)	150	115	139	157	135	70	247	269	157	162
Total Assets (Millions $)	6,549	7,005	6,095	6,122	5,316	4,283	3,919	4,880	4,999	4,684

PORTFOLIO (as of 7/31/02)

Portfolio Manager: Lawrence Rakers - 2002

Investment Style

Large Cap	Growth
Mid Cap	Value
Small Cap	Grth/Val

Portfolio

0.0%	cash	18.2%	corp bonds
58.2%	stocks	17.5%	gov't bonds
0.4%	pref/conv't pref	0.0%	muni bonds
0.2%	conv't bds/wrnts	5.6%	other

SHAREHOLDER INFORMATION

Minimum Investment
Initial: $2,500 Subsequent: $250

Minimum IRA Investment
Initial: $500 Subsequent: $250

Maximum Fees
Load: none 12b-1: none
Other: none

Services
- ✔ IRA
- ✔ Keogh
- ✔ Telephone Exchange

Fidelity Freedom 2000 (FFFBX)

800-544-8544, 801-534-1910
www.fidelity.com

Balanced Stock/Bond

PERFORMANCE — fund inception date: 10/17/96

	3yr Annual	5yr Annual	10yr Annual	Bull	Bear
Return (%)	0.6	5.6	na	31.1	-4.0
Differ From Category (+/-)	3.6 abv av	3.1 high	na	-0.7 av	10.2 abv av

Standard Deviation	Category Risk Index	Beta
5.6%—blw av	0.51—low	0.25

	2002	2001	2000	1999	1998	1997	1996	1995	1994	1993
Return (%)	-1.8	0.0	3.9	12.1	15.2	15.2	—	—	—	—
Differ From Category (+/-)	6.9	2.2	1.7	1.4	1.5	-3.5	—	—	—	—
Return, Tax-Adjusted (%)	-2.8	-0.9	0.2	10.0	13.4	13.7	—	—	—	—

PER SHARE DATA

	2002	2001	2000	1999	1998	1997	1996	1995	1994	1993
Dividends, Net Income ($)	0.30	0.28	0.75	0.52	0.40	0.33	—	—	—	—
Distrib'ns, Cap Gain ($)	0.00	0.00	0.93	0.29	0.21	0.12	—	—	—	—
Net Asset Value ($)	11.01	11.52	11.81	12.99	12.33	11.24	—	—	—	—
Expense Ratio (%)	0.07	0.06	0.08	0.07	0.08	0.08	—	—	—	—
Yield (%)	2.72	2.43	5.88	3.91	3.18	2.90	—	—	—	—
Portfolio Turnover (%)	13	51	37	27	24	19	—	—	—	—
Total Assets (Millions $)	1,194	1,046	648	714	502	81	—	—	—	—

PORTFOLIO (as of 12/31/02)

Portfolio Manager: Ren Cheng - 1996

Investment Style

Large Cap	Growth
Mid Cap	Value
Small Cap	Grth/Val

Portfolio

0.0% cash	0.0% corp bonds
0.0% stocks	0.0% gov't bonds
0.0% preferred	0.0% muni bonds
0.0% conv't bds/wrnts	100.0% other

SHAREHOLDER INFORMATION

Minimum Investment
Initial: $2,500 — Subsequent: $250

Minimum IRA Investment
Initial: $500 — Subsequent: $250

Maximum Fees
Load: none — 12b-1: none
Other: none

Services
✔ IRA
✔ Keogh
✔ Telephone Exchange

Fidelity Freedom 2010 (FFFCX)

800-544-8544, 801-534-1910
www.fidelity.com

Balanced Stock/Bond

PERFORMANCE

fund inception date: 10/17/96

	3yr Annual	5yr Annual	10yr Annual	Bull	Bear
Return (%)	-3.5	4.9	na	47.8	-17.8
Differ From Category (+/-)	-0.5 av	2.4 high	na	16.0 high	-3.6 av

Standard Deviation	Category Risk Index	Beta
9.5%—blw av	0.87—blw av	0.44

	2002	2001	2000	1999	1998	1997	1996	1995	1994	1993
Return (%)	-6.8	-4.3	0.6	19.0	19.3	19.3	—	—	—	—
Differ From Category (+/-)	1.9	-2.1	-1.6	8.3	5.6	0.6	—	—	—	—
Return, Tax-Adjusted (%)	-7.7	-5.7	-1.5	16.9	17.6	17.7	—	—	—	—

PER SHARE DATA

	2002	2001	2000	1999	1998	1997	1996	1995	1994	1993
Dividends, Net Income ($)	0.31	0.37	0.46	0.49	0.35	0.37	—	—	—	—
Distrib'ns, Cap Gain ($)	0.00	0.27	0.67	0.42	0.28	0.09	—	—	—	—
Net Asset Value ($)	11.44	12.61	13.84	14.87	13.30	11.69	—	—	—	—
Expense Ratio (%)	0.07	0.06	0.08	0.07	0.08	0.08	—	—	—	—
Yield (%)	2.70	2.87	3.17	3.20	2.57	3.14	—	—	—	—
Portfolio Turnover (%)	10	42	33	27	20	3	—	—	—	—
Total Assets (Millions $)	4,329	3,490	2,312	1,643	914	123	—	—	—	—

PORTFOLIO (as of 12/31/02)

Portfolio Manager: Ren Cheng - 1996

Investment Style

Large Cap	Growth
Mid Cap	Value
Small Cap	Grth/Val

Portfolio

0.0%	cash	0.0%	corp bonds
0.0%	stocks	0.0%	gov't bonds
0.0%	preferred	0.0%	muni bonds
0.0%	conv't bds/wrnts	100.0%	other

SHAREHOLDER INFORMATION

Minimum Investment
Initial: $2,500 — Subsequent: $250

Minimum IRA Investment
Initial: $500 — Subsequent: $250

Maximum Fees
Load: none — 12b-1: none
Other: none

Services
✔ IRA
✔ Keogh
✔ Telephone Exchange

Fidelity Freedom 2020 (FFFDX)

800-544-8544, 801-534-1910
www.fidelity.com

Balanced Stock/Bond

PERFORMANCE

fund inception date: 10/17/96

	3yr Annual	5yr Annual	10yr Annual	Bull	Bear
Return (%)	-8.7	3.0	na	63.0	-32.0
Differ From Category (+/-)	-5.7 low	0.5 av	na	31.2 high	-17.8 low

Standard Deviation	Category Risk Index	Beta
14.0%—blw av	1.28—high	0.68

	2002	2001	2000	1999	1998	1997	1996	1995	1994	1993
Return (%)	-13.7	-9.0	-3.0	25.3	21.6	21.2	—	—	—	—
Differ From Category (+/-)	-5.0	-6.8	-5.2	14.6	7.9	2.5	—	—	—	—
Return, Tax-Adjusted (%)	-14.4	-10.3	-5.1	23.2	20.2	19.6	—	—	—	—

PER SHARE DATA

	2002	2001	2000	1999	1998	1997	1996	1995	1994	1993
Dividends, Net Income ($)	0.22	0.26	0.39	0.45	0.28	0.34	—	—	—	—
Distrib'ns, Cap Gain ($)	0.00	0.43	0.96	0.57	0.27	0.13	—	—	—	—
Net Asset Value ($)	10.64	12.58	14.56	16.38	13.95	11.93	—	—	—	—
Expense Ratio (%)	0.07	0.06	0.08	0.07	0.08	0.08	—	—	—	—
Yield (%)	2.06	1.99	2.51	2.65	1.96	2.81	—	—	—	—
Portfolio Turnover (%)	10	50	28	18	15	21	—	—	—	—
Total Assets (Millions $)	3,735	2,796	1,893	1,559	859	84	—	—	—	—

PORTFOLIO (as of 12/31/02)

Portfolio Manager: Ren Cheng - 1996

Investment Style

Large Cap	Growth
Mid Cap	Value
Small Cap	Grth/Val

Portfolio

0.0%	cash	0.0%	corp bonds
0.0%	stocks	0.0%	gov't bonds
0.0%	preferred	0.0%	muni bonds
0.0%	conv't bds/wrnts	100.0%	other

SHAREHOLDER INFORMATION

Minimum Investment
Initial: $2,500 Subsequent: $250

Minimum IRA Investment
Initial: $500 Subsequent: $250

Maximum Fees
Load: none 12b-1: none
Other: none

Services
✔ IRA
✔ Keogh
✔ Telephone Exchange

Fidelity Freedom Income (FFFAX)

800-544-8544, 801-534-1910
www.fidelity.com

Balanced Stock/Bond

PERFORMANCE

fund inception date: 10/17/96

	3yr Annual	5yr Annual	10yr Annual	Bull	Bear
Return (%)	2.7	5.2	na	18.5	3.2
Differ From Category (+/-)	5.7 high	2.7 high	na	-13.3 blw av	17.4 high

Standard Deviation	Category Risk Index	Beta
3.6%—low	0.33—low	0.16

	2002	2001	2000	1999	1998	1997	1996	1995	1994	1993
Return (%)	-0.2	2.2	6.2	7.1	11.1	10.9	—	—	—	—
Differ From Category (+/-)	8.5	4.4	4.0	-3.6	-2.6	-7.8	—	—	—	—
Return, Tax-Adjusted (%)	-1.3	0.6	3.7	5.1	9.1	8.9	—	—	—	—

PER SHARE DATA

	2002	2001	2000	1999	1998	1997	1996	1995	1994	1993
Dividends, Net Income ($)	0.30	0.41	0.59	0.51	0.47	0.48	—	—	—	—
Distrib'ns, Cap Gain ($)	0.00	0.07	0.26	0.12	0.12	0.06	—	—	—	—
Net Asset Value ($)	10.60	10.93	11.17	11.33	11.18	10.62	—	—	—	—
Expense Ratio (%)	0.07	0.06	0.08	0.07	0.08	0.08	—	—	—	—
Yield (%)	2.83	3.72	5.16	4.45	4.15	4.49	—	—	—	—
Portfolio Turnover (%)	9	40	37	29	33	32	—	—	—	—
Total Assets (Millions $)	1,096	862	448	292	180	29	—	—	—	—

PORTFOLIO (as of 12/31/02)

Portfolio Manager: Ren Cheng - 1996

Investment Style

Large Cap	Growth
Mid Cap	Value
Small Cap	Grth/Val

Portfolio

0.0%	cash	0.0%	corp bonds
0.0%	stocks	0.0%	gov't bonds
0.0%	preferred	0.0%	muni bonds
0.0%	conv't bds/wrnts	100.0%	other

SHAREHOLDER INFORMATION

Minimum Investment
Initial: $2,500 Subsequent: $250

Minimum IRA Investment
Initial: $500 Subsequent: $250

Maximum Fees
Load: none 12b-1: none
Other: none

Services
✔ IRA
✔ Keogh
✔ Telephone Exchange

Fidelity Puritan

(FPURX)

800-544-8544, 800-522-7297
www.fidelity.com

Balanced Stock/Bond

PERFORMANCE

fund inception date: 4/16/47

	3yr Annual	5yr Annual	10yr Annual	Bull	Bear
Return (%)	-0.6	3.3	9.5	20.1	-8.0
Differ From Category (+/-)	2.4 abv av	0.8 av	1.7 high	-11.7 blw av	6.2 abv av

Standard Deviation	Category Risk Index	Beta
10.2%—blw av	0.93—blw av	0.48

	2002	2001	2000	1999	1998	1997	1996	1995	1994	1993
Return (%)	-7.9	-1.0	7.7	2.8	16.5	22.3	15.1	21.4	1.7	21.4
Differ From Category (+/-)	0.8	1.2	5.5	-7.9	2.8	3.6	1.2	-4.0	2.8	7.2
Return, Tax-Adjusted (%)	-9.0	-2.6	5.4	0.6	13.5	19.6	11.1	19.3	-0.9	16.9

PER SHARE DATA

	2002	2001	2000	1999	1998	1997	1996	1995	1994	1993
Dividends, Net Income ($)	0.50	0.60	0.61	0.64	0.67	0.68	0.62	0.49	0.54	0.72
Distrib'ns, Cap Gain ($)	0.00	0.35	1.01	0.97	1.56	0.96	1.54	0.44	0.71	1.36
Net Asset Value ($)	15.79	17.67	18.83	19.03	20.07	19.38	17.24	17.01	14.81	15.75
Expense Ratio (%)	0.64	0.63	0.64	0.63	0.63	0.66	0.72	0.77	0.79	0.74
Yield (%)	3.16	3.32	3.07	3.20	3.09	3.34	3.30	2.80	3.47	4.20
Portfolio Turnover (%)	79	67	62	80	84	80	139	76	74	76
Total Assets (Millions $)	18,031	20,314	21,368	24,370	25,682	22,821	18,501	15,628	11,769	8,988

PORTFOLIO (as of 7/31/02)

Portfolio Manager: Stephen Petersen - 2000

Investment Style

Large Cap	Growth
Mid Cap	Value
Small Cap	Grth/Val

Portfolio

0.0%	cash	18.1%	corp bonds
57.2%	stocks	18.6%	gov't bonds
1.1%	pref/conv't pref	0.0%	muni bonds
0.2%	conv't bds/wrnts	4.8%	other

SHAREHOLDER INFORMATION

Minimum Investment
Initial: $2,500 Subsequent: $250

Minimum IRA Investment
Initial: $500 Subsequent: $250

Maximum Fees
Load: none 12b-1: none
Other: none

Services
✔ IRA
✔ Keogh
✔ Telephone Exchange

Janus Balanced
(JABAX)

800-525-0020, 303-333-3863
www.janus.com

Balanced Stock/Bond

PERFORMANCE — fund inception date: 9/1/92

	3yr Annual	5yr Annual	10yr Annual	Bull	Bear
Return (%)	-4.6	7.0	10.7	62.4	-18.2
Differ From Category (+/-)	-1.6 av	4.5 high	2.9 high	30.6 high	-4.0 av

Standard Deviation	Category Risk Index	Beta
8.3%—blw av	0.76—blw av	0.37

	2002	2001	2000	1999	1998	1997	1996	1995	1994	1993
Return (%)	-6.5	-5.0	-2.1	23.5	31.1	21.8	15.3	27.3	0.0	10.5
Differ From Category (+/-)	.2.2	-2.8	-4.3	12.8	17.4	3.1	1.4	1.9	1.1	-3.7
Return, Tax-Adjusted (%)	-7.4	-6.0	-4.0	22.3	30.0	18.7	11.6	23.7	-1.8	9.7

PER SHARE DATA

	2002	2001	2000	1999	1998	1997	1996	1995	1994	1993
Dividends, Net Income ($)	0.47	0.53	0.63	0.45	0.35	0.35	0.31	1.06	0.56	0.22
Distrib'ns, Cap Gain ($)	0.00	0.00	1.02	0.31	0.10	1.48	1.34	0.00	0.00	0.00
Net Asset Value ($)	17.88	19.63	21.24	23.39	19.61	15.33	14.14	13.72	11.63	12.19
Expense Ratio (%)	na	0.83	0.85	0.91	1.01	1.10	1.21	1.35	1.42	1.70
Yield (%)	2.62	2.69	2.83	1.89	1.77	2.08	2.00	7.72	4.81	1.80
Portfolio Turnover (%)	na	117	87	64	73	139	151	185	167	131
Total Assets (Millions $)	3,994	4,472	4,739	3,420	1,136	389	219	138	93	77

PORTFOLIO (as of 10/31/02)

Portfolio Manager: Karen Reidy - 1999

Investment Style

Large Cap	Growth
Mid Cap	Value
Small Cap	Grth/Val

Portfolio

12.2%	cash	26.6%	corp bonds
44.3%	stocks	15.6%	gov't bonds
1.3%	pref/conv't pref	0.0%	muni bonds
0.0%	conv't bds/wrnts	0.0%	other

SHAREHOLDER INFORMATION

Minimum Investment
Initial: $2,500 Subsequent: $100

Minimum IRA Investment
Initial: $500 Subsequent: $100

Maximum Fees
Load: none 12b-1: none
Other: none

Services
✔ IRA
✔ Keogh
✔ Telephone Exchange

Oakmark Eqty & Income/I

800-625-6275, 312-621-0600
www.oakmark.com

(OAKBX)

Balanced Stock/Bond

PERFORMANCE — **fund inception date: 11/1/95**

	3yr Annual	5yr Annual	10yr Annual	Bull	Bear
Return (%)	11.4	10.9	na	32.0	25.0
Differ From Category (+/-)	14.4 high	8.4 high	na	0.2 av	39.2 high

Standard Deviation	Category Risk Index	Beta
9.7%—blw av	0.88—blw av	0.37

	2002	2001	2000	1999	1998	1997	1996	1995	1994	1993
Return (%)	-2.1	18.0	19.8	7.8	12.3	26.5	15.2	—	—	—
Differ From Category (+/-)	6.6	20.2	17.6	-2.9	-1.4	7.8	1.3	—	—	—
Return, Tax-Adjusted (%)	-2.6	17.6	17.7	4.8	11.4	24.7	14.4	—	—	—

PER SHARE DATA

	2002	2001	2000	1999	1998	1997	1996	1995	1994	1993
Dividends, Net Income ($)	0.24	0.15	0.24	0.45	0.21	0.23	0.12	—	—	—
Distrib'ns, Cap Gain ($)	0.00	0.04	1.00	1.36	0.20	0.58	0.13	—	—	—
Net Asset Value ($)	17.99	18.63	15.96	14.40	15.03	13.76	11.55	—	—	—
Expense Ratio (%)	0.96	0.98	1.24	1.18	1.31	1.50	2.50	—	—	—
Yield (%)	1.33	0.80	1.41	2.85	1.37	1.60	1.02	—	—	—
Portfolio Turnover (%)	73	124	87	81	46	0	66	—	—	—
Total Assets (Millions $)	2,704	1,099	75	57	66	41	14	—	—	—

PORTFOLIO (as of 10/31/02)

Portfolio Manager: McGregor/ Studzinski - 1995

Investment Style

Large Cap	Growth
Mid Cap	Value
Small Cap	Grth/Val

Portfolio

8.7%	cash	1.7%	corp bonds
52.9%	stocks	36.1%	gov't bonds
0.1%	pref/conv't pref	0.0%	muni bonds
0.5%	conv't bds/wrnts	0.0%	other

SHAREHOLDER INFORMATION

Minimum Investment
Initial: $1,000 — Subsequent: $100

Minimum IRA Investment
Initial: $1,000 — Subsequent: $100

Maximum Fees
Load: none — 12b-1: none
Other: none

Services
✔ IRA
✔ Keogh
✔ Telephone Exchange

Pax World Balanced (PAXWX)

800-767-1729
www.paxfund.com

Balanced Stock/Bond

PERFORMANCE

fund inception date: 8/10/71

	3yr Annual	5yr Annual	10yr Annual	Bull	Bear
Return (%)	-4.3	5.0	8.7	47.6	-21.1
Differ From Category (+/-)	-1.3 av	2.5 high	0.9 abv av	15.8 high	-6.9 av

Standard Deviation	Category Risk Index	Beta
9.2%—blw av	0.84—blw av	0.41

	2002	2001	2000	1999	1998	1997	1996	1995	1994	1993
Return (%)	-8.8	-9.0	5.6	17.2	24.6	25.1	10.3	29.1	2.6	-1.0
Differ From Category (+/-)	-0.1	-6.8	3.4	6.5	10.9	6.4	-3.6	3.7	3.7	-15.2
Return, Tax-Adjusted (%)	-9.4	-9.8	3.2	15.1	22.6	21.9	7.4	26.5	1.1	-2.5

PER SHARE DATA

	2002	2001	2000	1999	1998	1997	1996	1995	1994	1993
Dividends, Net Income ($)	0.32	0.47	0.52	0.45	0.46	0.50	0.55	0.79	0.50	0.50
Distrib'ns, Cap Gain ($)	0.00	0.00	1.75	1.41	0.88	1.65	0.89	0.14	0.00	0.07
Net Asset Value ($)	17.82	19.91	22.41	23.40	21.64	18.52	16.56	16.33	13.39	13.55
Expense Ratio (%)	na	0.94	0.90	0.89	0.95	0.91	0.89	1.00	0.98	0.94
Yield (%)	1.79	2.36	2.15	1.81	2.04	2.47	3.15	4.79	3.73	3.67
Portfolio Turnover (%)	na	38	26	21	28	13	34	28	25	22
Total Assets (Millions $)	1,052	1,161	1,228	1,072	837	628	518	476	388	464

PORTFOLIO (as of 10/31/02)

Portfolio Manager: Christopher Brown - 2001

Investment Style

Large Cap	Growth
Mid Cap	Value
Small Cap	Grth/Val

Portfolio

13.7%	cash	9.7%	corp bonds
57.7%	stocks	17.8%	gov't bonds
1.3%	pref/conv't pref	0.0%	muni bonds
0.0%	conv't bds/wrnts	0.0%	other

SHAREHOLDER INFORMATION

Minimum Investment
Initial: $250 Subsequent: $50

Minimum IRA Investment
Initial: $250 Subsequent: $50

Maximum Fees
Load: none 12b-1: 0.24%
Other: none

Services
✔ IRA
Keogh
✔ Telephone Exchange

T Rowe Price Cap Apprec (PRWCX)

800-638-5660, 410-345-2000
www.troweprice.com

Balanced Stock/Bond

PERFORMANCE — fund inception date: 6/30/86

	3yr Annual	5yr Annual	10yr Annual	Bull	Bear
Return (%)	10.6	8.9	11.8	15.6	26.6
Differ From Category (+/-)	13.6 high	6.4 high	4.0 high	-16.2 low	40.8 high

Standard Deviation	Category Risk Index	Beta
10.8%—blw av	0.99—av	0.38

	2002	2001	2000	1999	1998	1997	1996	1995	1994	1993
Return (%)	0.5	10.2	22.1	7.0	5.7	16.2	16.8	22.5	3.7	15.6
Differ From Category (+/-)	9.2	12.4	19.9	-3.7	-8.0	-2.5	2.9	-2.9	4.8	1.4
Return, Tax-Adjusted (%)	-0.6	8.6	19.4	3.8	1.9	12.6	13.2	19.4	1.1	14.2

PER SHARE DATA

	2002	2001	2000	1999	1998	1997	1996	1995	1994	1993
Dividends, Net Income ($)	0.28	0.38	0.45	0.50	0.50	0.50	0.60	0.44	0.35	0.18
Distrib'ns, Cap Gain ($)	0.23	0.35	0.82	1.13	1.82	1.58	0.90	0.72	0.69	0.33
Net Asset Value ($)	14.21	14.64	13.95	12.51	13.22	14.71	14.47	13.67	12.10	12.66
Expense Ratio (%)	na	0.86	0.87	0.88	0.62	0.64	0.76	1.05	1.10	1.09
Yield (%)	1.93	2.53	3.04	3.66	3.32	3.06	3.90	3.05	2.73	1.38
Portfolio Turnover (%)	na	25	32	28	53	48	44	49	43	39
Total Assets (Millions $)	1,855	1,405	913	855	1,003	1,059	959	864	653	536

PORTFOLIO (as of 9/30/02)

Portfolio Manager: S Boesel/Team
Managed - 2001

Investment Style

Large Cap	Growth
Mid Cap	Value
Small Cap	Grth/Val

Portfolio

11.0%	cash	14.4%	corp bonds
59.1%	stocks	3.0%	gov't bonds
8.1%	pref/conv't pref	0.0%	muni bonds
4.2%	conv't bds/wrnts	0.2%	other

SHAREHOLDER INFORMATION

Minimum Investment
Initial: $2,500 Subsequent: $100

Minimum IRA Investment
Initial: $1,000 Subsequent: $50

Maximum Fees
Load: none 12b-1: none
Other: none

Services
✔ IRA
✔ Keogh
✔ Telephone Exchange

T Rowe Price Spect Inc (RPSIX)

800-638-5660, 410-345-2000
www.troweprice.com

Balanced Stock/Bond

PERFORMANCE

fund inception date: 6/29/90

	3yr Annual	5yr Annual	10yr Annual	Bull	Bear
Return (%)	6.2	5.1	7.3	7.5	13.4
Differ From Category (+/-)	9.2 high	2.6 high	-0.5 av	-24.3 low	27.6 high

Standard Deviation	Category Risk Index	Beta
4.0%—low	0.37—low	0.11

	2002	2001	2000	1999	1998	1997	1996	1995	1994	1993
Return (%)	6.8	4.5	7.3	0.2	6.5	12.1	7.6	19.4	-1.9	12.3
Differ From Category (+/-)	15.5	6.7	5.1	-10.5	-7.2	-6.6	-6.3	-6.0	-0.8	-1.9
Return, Tax-Adjusted (%)	4.8	2.2	4.7	-2.6	3.7	9.3	4.7	16.4	-4.6	9.2

PER SHARE DATA

	2002	2001	2000	1999	1998	1997	1996	1995	1994	1993
Dividends, Net Income ($)	0.54	0.63	0.69	0.79	0.73	0.70	0.71	0.71	0.68	0.69
Distrib'ns, Cap Gain ($)	0.00	0.02	0.00	0.02	0.17	0.15	0.15	0.06	0.10	0.19
Net Asset Value ($)	10.76	10.60	10.77	10.71	11.50	11.66	11.20	11.24	10.11	11.11
Expense Ratio (%)	na	0.80	0.77	na	na	na	na	na	na	na
Yield (%)	5.01	5.93	6.40	7.36	6.25	5.92	6.25	6.28	6.66	6.10
Portfolio Turnover (%)	na	23	19	19	13	14	17	12	23	14
Total Assets (Millions $)	2,659	2,464	2,471	2,548	2,574	2,022	1,355	986	624	587

PORTFOLIO (as of 12/31/02)

Portfolio Manager: E Notzon/Team
Managed - 1998

Investment Style

Large Cap	Growth
Mid Cap	Value
Small Cap	Grth/Val

Portfolio

0.0%	cash	0.0%	corp bonds
0.0%	stocks	0.0%	gov't bonds
0.0%	preferred	0.0%	muni bonds
0.0%	conv't bds/wrnts	100.0%	other

SHAREHOLDER INFORMATION

Minimum Investment
Initial: $2,500 Subsequent: $100

Minimum IRA Investment
Initial: $1,000 Subsequent: $50

Maximum Fees
Load: none 12b-1: none
Other: none

Services
✔ IRA
✔ Keogh
✔ Telephone Exchange

USAA Mutual:Income

800-531-8181, 210-456-7211
www.usaa.com

(USAIX)

Balanced Stock/Bond

PERFORMANCE **fund inception date: 3/4/74**

	3yr Annual	5yr Annual	10yr Annual	Bull	Bear
Return (%)	9.8	6.7	7.2	1.7	26.8
Differ From Category (+/-)	12.8 high	4.2 high	-0.6 blw av	-30.1 low	41.0 high

Standard Deviation	Category Risk Index	Beta
3.8%—low	0.35—low	-0.07

	2002	2001	2000	1999	1998	1997	1996	1995	1994	1993
Return (%)	8.6	7.5	13.3	-3.8	8.7	11.0	1.3	24.4	-5.2	9.9
Differ From Category (+/-)	17.3	9.7	11.1	-14.5	-5.0	-7.7	-12.6	-1.0	-4.1	-4.3
Return, Tax-Adjusted (%)	6.5	4.9	10.5	-6.3	5.4	8.3	-1.2	21.4	-7.9	6.6

PER SHARE DATA

	2002	2001	2000	1999	1998	1997	1996	1995	1994	1993
Dividends, Net Income ($)	0.66	0.79	0.79	0.76	0.84	0.83	0.83	0.84	0.86	0.88
Distrib'ns, Cap Gain ($)	0.00	0.00	0.00	0.02	0.45	0.00	0.00	0.00	0.00	0.25
Net Asset Value ($)	12.40	12.06	11.96	11.30	12.56	12.78	12.31	13.00	11.19	12.71
Expense Ratio (%)	0.55	0.41	0.42	0.38	0.38	0.39	0.40	0.41	0.41	0.41
Yield (%)	5.32	6.55	6.60	6.71	6.45	6.49	6.74	6.46	7.68	6.79
Portfolio Turnover (%)	60	43	24	54	47	57	81	30	25	44
Total Assets (Millions $)	1,698	1,546	1,338	1,319	1,768	1,722	1,738	1,893	1,611	1,945

PORTFOLIO (as of 9/30/02)

Portfolio Manager: Margaret Weinblatt - 2000

Investment Style

Large Cap	Growth
Mid Cap	Value
Small Cap	Grth/Val

Portfolio

5.0%	cash	33.0%	corp bonds
0.0%	stocks	57.0%	gov't bonds
5.0%	pref/conv't pref	0.0%	muni bonds
0.0%	conv't bds/wrnts	0.0%	other

SHAREHOLDER INFORMATION

Minimum Investment
Initial: $3,000 Subsequent: $50

Minimum IRA Investment
Initial: $250 Subsequent: $50

Maximum Fees
Load: none 12b-1: none
Other: none

Services
✔ IRA
✔ Keogh
✔ Telephone Exchange

Vanguard Asset Al/Inv (VAAPX)

800-662-7447, 610-436-5152
www.vanguard.com

Balanced Stock/Bond

PERFORMANCE

fund inception date: 11/3/88

	3yr Annual	5yr Annual	10yr Annual	Bull	Bear
Return (%)	-5.6	2.0	9.3	34.0	-27.3
Differ From Category (+/-)	-2.6 blw av	-0.5 blw av	1.5 high	2.2 av	-13.1 blw av

Standard Deviation	Category Risk Index	Beta
14.3%—av	1.30—high	0.72

	2002	2001	2000	1999	1998	1997	1996	1995	1994	1993
Return (%)	-15.4	-5.3	4.9	5.2	25.3	27.3	15.7	35.4	-2.3	13.4
Differ From Category (+/-)	-6.7	-3.1	2.7	-5.5	11.6	8.6	1.8	10.0	-1.2	-0.8
Return, Tax-Adjusted (%)	-16.1	-6.3	3.0	3.0	22.7	24.5	12.3	32.2	-3.9	10.9

PER SHARE DATA

	2002	2001	2000	1999	1998	1997	1996	1995	1994	1993
Dividends, Net Income ($)	0.39	0.61	1.02	0.88	0.76	0.74	0.72	0.66	0.57	0.48
Distrib'ns, Cap Gain ($)	0.00	0.00	0.27	0.96	1.18	1.01	1.05	0.61	0.00	0.53
Net Asset Value ($)	18.07	21.81	23.67	23.80	24.38	21.05	17.94	17.05	13.54	14.45
Expense Ratio (%)	0.42	0.44	0.44	0.49	0.49	0.49	0.47	0.49	0.50	0.49
Yield (%)	2.15	2.79	4.26	3.55	2.97	3.35	3.79	3.73	4.20	3.20
Portfolio Turnover (%)	54	77	29	11	60	10	47	34	51	31
Total Assets (Millions $)	6,870	7,750	8,889	8,597	6,974	4,099	2,596	1,791	1,125	1,125

PORTFOLIO (as of 9/30/02)

Portfolio Manager: William Fouse/Thomas Loeb - 1988

Investment Style

Large Cap	Growth
Mid Cap	Value
Small Cap	Grth/Val

Portfolio

48.9% cash	0.0% corp bonds
51.1% stocks	0.0% gov't bonds
0.0% preferred	0.0% muni bonds
0.0% conv't bds/wrnts	0.0% other

SHAREHOLDER INFORMATION

Minimum Investment
Initial: $3,000 Subsequent: $100

Minimum IRA Investment
Initial: $1,000 Subsequent: $100

Maximum Fees
Load: none 12b-1: none
Other: none

Services
✔ IRA
✔ Keogh
✔ Telephone Exchange

Vanguard Bal Idx/Inv (VBINX)

800-662-7447, 610-436-5152
www.vanguard.com

Balanced Stock/Bond

PERFORMANCE

fund inception date: 9/28/92

	3yr Annual	5yr Annual	10yr Annual	Bull	Bear
Return (%)	-4.9	2.8	8.3	38.1	-20.8
Differ From Category (+/-)	-1.9 av	0.3 av	0.5 abv av	6.3 abv av	-6.6 av

Standard Deviation	Category Risk Index	Beta
11.0%—blw av	1.00—av	0.55

	2002	2001	2000	1999	1998	1997	1996	1995	1994	1993
Return (%)	-9.5	-3.0	-2.0	13.6	17.8	22.2	13.9	28.6	-1.5	9.9
Differ From Category (+/-)	-0.8	-0.8	-4.2	2.9	4.1	3.5	0.0	3.2	-0.4	-4.3
Return, Tax-Adjusted (%)	-10.6	-4.2	-3.4	12.2	16.3	20.5	12.1	26.7	-3.0	8.3

PER SHARE DATA

	2002	2001	2000	1999	1998	1997	1996	1995	1994	1993
Dividends, Net Income ($)	0.52	0.59	0.64	0.58	0.54	0.53	0.49	0.45	0.40	0.39
Distrib'ns, Cap Gain ($)	0.00	0.02	0.10	0.14	0.14	0.14	0.12	0.05	0.00	0.03
Net Asset Value ($)	15.65	17.86	19.08	20.22	18.48	16.29	13.92	12.77	10.34	10.91
Expense Ratio (%)	na	0.22	0.22	0.20	0.21	0.20	0.20	0.20	0.20	0.20
Yield (%)	3.32	3.29	3.33	2.84	2.90	3.22	3.49	3.51	3.86	3.56
Portfolio Turnover (%)	na	33	28	29	25	18	37	14	16	25
Total Assets (Millions $)	3,060	3,116	3,586	3,128	2,003	1,260	826	590	402	367

PORTFOLIO (as of 9/30/02)

Portfolio Manager: Ken Volpert - 2002

Investment Style

Large Cap	Growth
Mid Cap	Value
Small Cap	Grth/Val

Portfolio

0.5%	cash	19.7%	corp bonds
57.8%	stocks	22.0%	gov't bonds
0.0%	preferred	0.0%	muni bonds
0.0%	conv't bds/wrnts	0.0%	other

SHAREHOLDER INFORMATION

Minimum Investment
Initial: $3,000 Subsequent: $100

Minimum IRA Investment
Initial: $1,000 Subsequent: $100

Maximum Fees
Load: none 12b-1: none
Other: none

Services
✔ IRA
✔ Keogh
Telephone Exchange

Vanguard Life Cnsrv Gr (VSCGX)

800-635-1511, 610-436-5152
www.vanguard.com

Balanced Stock/Bond

PERFORMANCE — fund inception date: 9/30/94

	3yr Annual	5yr Annual	10yr Annual	Bull	Bear
Return (%)	-0.8	4.0	na	25.2	-10.0
Differ From Category (+/-)	2.2 abv av	1.5 abv av	na	-6.6 blw av	4.2 abv av

Standard Deviation	Category Risk Index	Beta
7.7%—blw av	0.71—low	0.39

	2002	2001	2000	1999	1998	1997	1996	1995	1994	1993
Return (%)	-5.3	0.0	3.1	7.8	15.8	16.8	10.3	24.3	—	—
Differ From Category (+/-)	3.4	2.2	0.9	-2.9	2.1	-1.9	-3.6	-1.1	—	—
Return, Tax-Adjusted (%)	-6.6	-1.6	1.1	6.0	13.8	14.7	8.0	22.1	—	—

PER SHARE DATA

	2002	2001	2000	1999	1998	1997	1996	1995	1994	1993
Dividends, Net Income ($)	0.49	0.58	0.70	0.63	0.59	0.56	0.53	0.47	—	—
Distrib'ns, Cap Gain ($)	0.00	0.04	0.16	0.11	0.20	0.19	0.20	0.12	—	—
Net Asset Value ($)	12.82	14.06	14.71	15.10	14.71	13.40	12.14	11.68	—	—
Expense Ratio (%)	na	na	na	na	na	na	na	na	—	—
Yield (%)	3.82	4.11	4.70	4.14	3.95	4.12	4.29	3.98	—	—
Portfolio Turnover (%)	na	14	9	5	3	1	2	0	—	—
Total Assets (Millions $)	2,210	2,026	1,897	1,747	1,415	802	462	219	—	—

PORTFOLIO (as of 12/31/02)

Portfolio Manager: Team Managed - 1994

Investment Style

Large Cap	Growth
Mid Cap	Value
Small Cap	Grth/Val

Portfolio

0.0%	cash	0.0%	corp bonds
0.0%	stocks	0.0%	gov't bonds
0.0%	preferred	0.0%	muni bonds
0.0%	conv't bds/wrnts	100.0%	other

SHAREHOLDER INFORMATION

Minimum Investment
Initial: $3,000 — Subsequent: $100

Minimum IRA Investment
Initial: $1,000 — Subsequent: $100

Maximum Fees
Load: none — 12b-1: none
Other: none

Services
✔ IRA
✔ Keogh
✔ Telephone Exchange

Vanguard Life Gr (VASGX)

800-635-1511, 610-436-5152
www.vanguard.com

Balanced Stock/Bond

PERFORMANCE

fund inception date: 9/30/94

	3yr Annual	5yr Annual	10yr Annual	Bull	Bear
Return (%)	-10.1	0.6	na	49.0	-34.8
Differ From Category (+/-)	-7.1 low	-1.9 blw av	na	17.2 high	-20.6 low

Standard Deviation	Category Risk Index	Beta
15.1%—av	1.38—high	0.77

	2002	2001	2000	1999	1998	1997	1996	1995	1994	1993
Return (%)	-15.8	-8.8	-5.4	17.3	21.4	22.2	15.4	29.2	—	—
Differ From Category (+/-)	-7.1	-6.6	-7.6	6.6	7.7	3.5	1.5	3.8	—	—
Return, Tax-Adjusted (%)	-16.5	-9.6	-6.5	16.2	20.1	20.7	13.8	27.5	—	—

PER SHARE DATA

	2002	2001	2000	1999	1998	1997	1996	1995	1994	1993
Dividends, Net Income ($)	0.32	0.37	0.51	0.45	0.41	0.38	0.35	0.31	—	—
Distrib'ns, Cap Gain ($)	0.00	0.06	0.17	0.16	0.26	0.29	0.23	0.15	—	—
Net Asset Value ($)	14.36	17.43	19.59	21.41	18.79	16.04	13.68	12.36	—	—
Expense Ratio (%)	na	na	na	na	na	na	na	na	—	—
Yield (%)	2.22	2.11	2.58	2.08	2.15	2.32	2.51	2.47	—	—
Portfolio Turnover (%)	na	7	9	1	2	1	0	1	—	—
Total Assets (Millions $)	3,404	3,725	3,738	3,177	1,924	1,183	628	217	—	—

PORTFOLIO (as of 12/31/02)

Portfolio Manager: Team Managed - 1994

Investment Style

Large Cap	Growth
Mid Cap	Value
Small Cap	Grth/Val

Portfolio

0.0%	cash	0.0%	corp bonds
0.0%	stocks	0.0%	gov't bonds
0.0%	preferred	0.0%	muni bonds
0.0%	conv't bds/wrnts	100.0%	other

SHAREHOLDER INFORMATION

Minimum Investment
Initial: $3,000 Subsequent: $100

Minimum IRA Investment
Initial: $1,000 Subsequent: $100

Maximum Fees
Load: none 12b-1: none
Other: none

Services
✔ IRA
✔ Keogh
✔ Telephone Exchange

Vanguard Life Income (VASIX)

800-635-1511, 610-436-5152
www.vanguard.com

Balanced Stock/Bond

PERFORMANCE

fund inception date: 9/30/94

	3yr Annual	5yr Annual	10yr Annual	Bull	Bear
Return (%)	4.0	5.5	na	14.3	5.2
Differ From Category (+/-)	7.0 high	3.0 high	na	-17.5 low	19.4 high

Standard Deviation	Category Risk Index	Beta
4.4%—blw av	0.40—low	0.19

	2002	2001	2000	1999	1998	1997	1996	1995	1994	1993
Return (%)	0.1	4.0	8.0	2.8	13.1	14.2	7.6	22.9	—	—
Differ From Category (+/-)	.8.8	6.2	5.8	-7.9	-0.6	-4.5	-6.3	-2.5	—	—
Return, Tax-Adjusted (%)	-1.6	2.0	5.6	0.6	10.8	11.9	4.9	20.7	—	—

PER SHARE DATA

	2002	2001	2000	1999	1998	1997	1996	1995	1994	1993
Dividends, Net Income ($)	0.55	0.64	0.74	0.69	0.63	0.63	0.64	0.49	—	—
Distrib'ns, Cap Gain ($)	0.00	0.02	0.08	0.07	0.19	0.10	0.21	0.09	—	—
Net Asset Value ($)	12.32	12.86	13.01	12.82	13.22	12.43	11.55	11.54	—	—
Expense Ratio (%)	na	na	na	na	na	na	na	na	—	—
Yield (%)	4.46	4.96	5.65	5.35	4.69	5.02	5.44	4.21	—	—
Portfolio Turnover (%)	na	4	17	11	3	6	22	1	—	—
Total Assets (Millions $)	1,027	809	631	555	448	243	151	120	—	—

PORTFOLIO (as of 12/31/02)

Portfolio Manager: Team Managed - 1994

Investment Style

Large Cap	Growth
Mid Cap	Value
Small Cap	Grth/Val

Portfolio

0.0%	cash	0.0%	corp bonds
0.0%	stocks	0.0%	gov't bonds
0.0%	preferred	0.0%	muni bonds
0.0%	conv't bds/wrnts	100.0%	other

SHAREHOLDER INFORMATION

Minimum Investment
Initial: $3,000 Subsequent: $100

Minimum IRA Investment
Initial: $1,000 Subsequent: $100

Maximum Fees
Load: none 12b-1: none
Other: none

Services
✔ IRA
✔ Keogh
✔ Telephone Exchange

Vanguard Life Mod Gr (VSMGX)

800-635-1511, 610-436-5152
www.vanguard.com

Balanced Stock/Bond

PERFORMANCE — fund inception date: 9/30/94

	3yr Annual	5yr Annual	10yr Annual	Bull	Bear
Return (%)	-5.3	2.5	na	36.3	-22.8
Differ From Category (+/-)	-2.3 av	0.0 av	na	4.5 abv av	-8.6 blw av

Standard Deviation	Category Risk Index	Beta
11.4%—blw av	1.04—abv av	0.58

	2002	2001	2000	1999	1998	1997	1996	1995	1994	1993
Return (%)	-10.3	-4.4	-0.8	12.0	19.0	19.7	12.7	27.9	—	—
Differ From Category (+/-)	-1.6	-2.2	-3.0	1.3	5.3	1.0	-1.2	2.5	—	—
Return, Tax-Adjusted (%)	-11.3	-5.6	-2.3	10.6	17.3	17.9	10.7	26.1	—	—

PER SHARE DATA

	2002	2001	2000	1999	1998	1997	1996	1995	1994	1993
Dividends, Net Income ($)	0.42	0.49	0.64	0.55	0.51	0.49	0.44	0.36	—	—
Distrib'ns, Cap Gain ($)	0.00	0.06	0.14	0.13	0.24	0.21	0.23	0.13	—	—
Net Asset Value ($)	13.87	15.93	17.25	18.18	16.86	14.81	12.97	12.11	—	—
Expense Ratio (%)	na	na	na	na	na	na	na	na	—	—
Yield (%)	3.02	3.06	3.68	3.00	2.98	3.26	3.33	2.94	—	—
Portfolio Turnover (%)	na	16	12	3	5	2	3	1	—	—
Total Assets (Millions $)	4,074	4,243	3,910	3,440	2,201	1,358	825	234	—	—

PORTFOLIO (as of 12/31/02)

Portfolio Manager: Team Managed - 1994

Investment Style

Large Cap	Growth
Mid Cap	Value
Small Cap	Grth/Val

Portfolio

0.0%	cash	0.0%	corp bonds
0.0%	stocks	0.0%	gov't bonds
0.0%	preferred	0.0%	muni bonds
0.0%	conv't bds/wrnts	100.0%	other

SHAREHOLDER INFORMATION

Minimum Investment
Initial: $3,000 — Subsequent: $100

Minimum IRA Investment
Initial: $1,000 — Subsequent: $100

Maximum Fees
Load: none — 12b-1: none
Other: none

Services
- ✔ IRA
- ✔ Keogh
- ✔ Telephone Exchange

Vanguard STAR (VGSTX)

800-662-7447, 610-436-5152
www.vanguard.com

Balanced Stock/Bond

PERFORMANCE — fund inception date: 3/29/85

	3yr Annual	5yr Annual	10yr Annual	Bull	Bear
Return (%)	0.1	3.8	9.2	29.5	-7.7
Differ From Category (+/-)	3.1 abv av	1.3 abv av	1.4 abv av	-2.3 av	6.5 abv av

Standard Deviation	Category Risk Index	Beta
10.7%—blw av	0.98—av	0.52

	2002	2001	2000	1999	1998	1997	1996	1995	1994	1993
Return (%)	-9.8	0.5	10.9	7.1	12.3	21.1	16.1	28.6	-0.2	10.9
Differ From Category (+/-)	-1.1	2.7	8.7	-3.6	-1.4	2.4	2.2	3.2	0.9	-3.3
Return, Tax-Adjusted (%)	-10.9	-1.7	7.7	5.3	9.9	18.1	12.7	25.5	-2.3	8.6

PER SHARE DATA

	2002	2001	2000	1999	1998	1997	1996	1995	1994	1993
Dividends, Net Income ($)	0.48	0.55	0.64	0.61	0.58	0.59	0.59	0.59	0.52	0.47
Distrib'ns, Cap Gain ($)	0.00	0.86	1.65	0.40	0.98	1.20	0.98	0.56	0.25	0.40
Net Asset Value ($)	14.35	16.44	17.81	18.21	17.96	17.38	15.86	15.02	12.60	13.41
Expense Ratio (%)	na	na	na	na	na	na	na	na	na	na
Yield (%)	3.34	3.17	3.28	3.27	3.06	3.17	3.50	3.78	4.04	3.40
Portfolio Turnover (%)	na	6	17	10	16	15	18	8	9	3
Total Assets (Millions $)	7,497	8,242	8,118	8,087	8,082	7,355	5,863	4,841	3,766	3,628

PORTFOLIO (as of 12/31/02)

Portfolio Manager: Team Managed - 1985

Investment Style

Large Cap	Growth
Mid Cap	Value
Small Cap	Grth/Val

Portfolio

0.0%	cash	0.0%	corp bonds
0.0%	stocks	0.0%	gov't bonds
0.0%	preferred	0.0%	muni bonds
0.0%	conv't bds/wrnts	100.0%	other

SHAREHOLDER INFORMATION

Minimum Investment
Initial: $1,000 Subsequent: $100

Minimum IRA Investment
Initial: $1,000 Subsequent: $100

Maximum Fees
Load: none 12b-1: none
Other: none

Services
✔ IRA
✔ Keogh
✔ Telephone Exchange

Vanguard Welles Inc/Inv (VWINX)

800-662-7447, 610-436-5152
www.vanguard.com

Balanced Stock/Bond

PERFORMANCE

fund inception date: 7/1/70

	3yr Annual	5yr Annual	10yr Annual	Bull	Bear
Return (%)	9.2	6.7	9.9	5.8	21.9
Differ From Category (+/-)	12.2 high	4.2 high	2.1 high	-26.0 low	36.1 high

Standard Deviation	Category Risk Index	Beta
5.8%—blw av	0.52—low	0.16

	2002	2001	2000	1999	1998	1997	1996	1995	1994	1993
Return (%)	4.6	7.3	16.1	-4.1	10.9	20.1	9.4	28.9	-4.4	14.6
Differ From Category (+/-)	13.3	9.5	13.9	-14.8	-2.8	1.4	-4.5	3.5	-3.3	0.4
Return, Tax-Adjusted (%)	2.8	4.5	13.4	-7.2	8.0	16.4	6.3	25.8	-7.0	11.5

PER SHARE DATA

	2002	2001	2000	1999	1998	1997	1996	1995	1994	1993
Dividends, Net Income ($)	0.91	1.00	1.06	1.12	1.13	1.20	1.16	1.14	1.11	1.14
Distrib'ns, Cap Gain ($)	0.00	0.86	0.40	1.24	0.96	1.44	0.60	0.28	0.24	0.40
Net Asset Value ($)	19.90	19.91	20.34	18.85	22.12	21.86	20.51	20.44	17.05	19.24
Expense Ratio (%)	na	0.33	0.31	0.30	0.31	0.31	0.31	0.35	0.34	0.33
Yield (%)	4.57	4.81	5.11	5.57	4.89	5.15	5.49	5.50	6.41	5.80
Portfolio Turnover (%)	na	24	28	20	32	36	26	30	31	21
Total Assets (Millions $)	7,402	6,494	6,557	6,976	8,497	7,645	7,012	7,180	5,680	6,011

PORTFOLIO (as of 9/30/02)

Portfolio Manager: John Ryan/Earl McEvoy - 1982

Investment Style

Large Cap	Growth
Mid Cap	Value
Small Cap	Grth/Val

Portfolio

1.7%	cash	58.7%	corp bonds
35.7%	stocks	3.9%	gov't bonds
0.0%	preferred	0.0%	muni bonds
0.0%	conv't bds/wrnts	0.0%	other

SHAREHOLDER INFORMATION

Minimum Investment
Initial: $3,000 Subsequent: $100

Minimum IRA Investment
Initial: $1,000 Subsequent: $100

Maximum Fees
Load: none 12b-1: none
Other: none

Services
✔ IRA
✔ Keogh
✔ Telephone Exchange

Vanguard Wellington/Inv (VWELX)

800-662-7447, 610-436-5152
www.vanguard.com

Balanced Stock/Bond

PERFORMANCE

fund inception date: 7/1/29

	3yr Annual	5yr Annual	10yr Annual	Bull	Bear
Return (%)	2.3	4.6	10.3	16.4	2.3
Differ From Category (+/-)	5.3 high	2.1 abv av	2.5 high	-15.4 blw av	16.5 high

Standard Deviation	Category Risk Index	Beta
10.8%—blw av	0.99—av	0.47

	2002	2001	2000	1999	1998	1997	1996	1995	1994	1993
Return (%)	-6.8	4.1	10.4	4.4	12.0	23.2	16.1	33.3	-0.4	12.0
Differ From Category (+/-)	1.9	6.3	8.2	-6.3	-1.7	4.5	2.2	7.9	0.7	-2.2
Return, Tax-Adjusted (%)	-8.0	2.0	7.8	1.8	8.8	20.3	13.1	30.8	-2.1	9.9

PER SHARE DATA

	2002	2001	2000	1999	1998	1997	1996	1995	1994	1993
Dividends, Net Income ($)	0.84	0.95	1.07	1.14	1.13	1.12	1.06	0.97	0.88	0.92
Distrib'ns, Cap Gain ($)	0.00	1.12	1.48	1.50	2.44	1.57	1.11	0.36	0.03	0.11
Net Asset Value ($)	24.56	27.26	28.21	27.96	29.35	29.45	26.15	24.43	19.39	20.40
Expense Ratio (%)	na	0.36	0.31	0.30	0.31	0.29	0.31	0.37	0.35	0.34
Yield (%)	3.42	3.34	3.60	3.86	3.55	3.61	3.88	3.91	4.53	4.48
Portfolio Turnover (%)	na	33	33	22	29	27	30	30	32	34
Total Assets (Millions $)	20,007	21,724	22,799	25,528	25,760	21,811	16,189	12,656	8,809	8,075

PORTFOLIO (as of 9/30/02)

Portfolio Manager: P Kaplan/E Von Metzsch - 1994

Investment Style

Large Cap	Growth
Mid Cap	Value
Small Cap	Grth/Val

Portfolio

0.0%	cash	24.4%	corp bonds
63.3%	stocks	10.4%	gov't bonds
0.0%	preferred	0.0%	muni bonds
0.0%	conv't bds/wrnts	1.8%	other

SHAREHOLDER INFORMATION

Minimum Investment
Initial: $3,000 Subsequent: $100

Minimum IRA Investment
Initial: $1,000 Subsequent: $100

Maximum Fees
Load: none 12b-1: none
Other: none

Services
✔ IRA
✔ Keogh
✔ Telephone Exchange

TAXABLE BOND FUNDS

Corporate Bond Funds
Category Performance Ranked by 2002 Returns

		Annual Return (%)				Category	Total
Category	**Fund (Ticker)**	**2002**	**3yr**	**5yr**	**10yr**	**Risk**	**Risk**
B-Corp	Vanguard LT Crp (VWESX)	13.2	11.5	7.2	8.4	high	blw av
B-Corp	Vanguard Int Tm Crp (VFICX)	10.2	10.1	7.3	na	abv av	low
B-Corp	Vanguard Sh Tm Crp (VFSTX)	5.1	7.1	6.2	6.2	blw av	low
B-Corp	T Rowe Price Corp Inc (PRPIX)	4.2	7.3	4.6	na	abv av	blw av
B-Corp	Janus Short Term Bond (JASBX)	3.5	6.0	5.5	5.4	low	low
B-Corp	INVESCO Select Income/Inv (FBDSX)	2.7	1.6	2.2	5.6	high	blw av
B-Corp	Strong Corporate Bd/Inv (STCBX)	1.3	5.3	4.5	7.8	high	blw av
B-Corp	Metropolitan West Lw Dr/M (MWLDX)	-0.3	4.7	5.4	na	av	low
Corporate Bond Average		**5.1**	**6.9**	**5.5**	**6.5**	**—**	**low**

Note: AAII members who would like performance figures for no-load and low-load mutual funds they own that do not appear in this Guide can access this information on our Web site at www.aaii.com.

INVESCO Select Income/Inv (FBDSX)

800-525-8085
www.invesco.com

Corporate Bond — *this fund is closed to new investors*

PERFORMANCE AND PER SHARE DATA — **fund inception date: 1/11/77**

	3yr Annual	5yr Annual	10yr Annual	Category Risk Index
Return (%)	1.6	2.2	5.6	1.63—high
Differ From Category (+/-)	-5.3 low	-3.3 low	-0.9 blw av	**Avg Mat** 7.4 yrs

	2002	2001	2000	1999	1998	1997	1996	1995	1994	1993
Return (%)	2.7	-2.8	5.1	-0.7	7.1	11.7	4.8	20.6	-1.2	11.5
Differ From Category (+/-)	-2.4	-9.9	-3.4	-1.7	1.0	2.3	0.4	3.9	0.1	1.5
Return, Tax-Adjusted (%)	0.5	-5.4	2.2	-3.5	4.2	8.5	1.9	17.4	-4.0	7.7
Dividends, Net Income ($)	0.31	0.39	0.43	0.45	0.42	0.45	0.46	0.46	0.45	0.49
Expense Ratio (%)	1.05	1.05	1.06	1.06	1.06	1.03	1.01	1.00	1.11	1.15
Yield (%)	5.96	7.24	7.25	7.41	6.26	6.58	7.00	6.80	7.46	7.25
Total Assets (Millions $)	279	458	572	545	528	331	269	261	136	157

SHAREHOLDER INFORMATION

Minimum Investment
Initial: $1,000 — IRA: $250
Subsequent: $50 — IRA: $50

Maximum Fees
Load: none — 12b-1: 0.25%
Other: none

Janus Short Term Bond (JASBX)

800-525-0020, 303-333-3863
www.janus.com

Corporate Bond

PERFORMANCE AND PER SHARE DATA — **fund inception date: 9/1/92**

	3yr Annual	5yr Annual	10yr Annual	Category Risk Index
Return (%)	6.0	5.5	5.4	0.46—low
Differ From Category (+/-)	-0.9 av	0.0 av	-1.1 blw av	**Avg Mat** 1.4 yrs

	2002	2001	2000	1999	1998	1997	1996	1995	1994	1993
Return (%)	3.5	6.8	7.7	2.9	6.7	6.6	6.1	7.9	0.3	6.1
Differ From Category (+/-)	-1.6	-0.3	-0.8	1.9	0.6	-2.8	1.7	-8.8	1.6	-3.9
Return, Tax-Adjusted (%)	2.1	5.0	5.4	0.7	4.4	4.2	3.9	5.4	-2.1	4.0
Dividends, Net Income ($)	0.10	0.13	0.16	0.16	0.17	0.17	0.16	0.17	0.18	0.14
Expense Ratio (%)	na	0.65	0.65	0.65	0.65	0.65	0.65	0.65	0.65	0.83
Yield (%)	3.40	4.42	5.55	5.65	5.84	5.88	5.55	5.92	6.36	4.65
Total Assets (Millions $)	478	497	172	136	131	69	44	46	45	53

SHAREHOLDER INFORMATION

Minimum Investment
Initial: $2,500 — IRA: $500
Subsequent: $100 — IRA: $100

Maximum Fees
Load: none — 12b-1: none
Other: none

Metropolitan West Lw Dr/M (MWLDX)

800-241-4671, 310-966-8900
www.mws.com

Corporate Bond

PERFORMANCE AND PER SHARE DATA **fund inception date: 3/31/97**

	3yr Annual	5yr Annual	10yr Annual	Category Risk Index
Return (%)	4.7	5.4	na	0.83—av
Differ From Category (+/-)	-2.2 blw av	-0.1 blw av	na	**Avg Mat** 4.8 yrs

	2002	2001	2000	1999	1998	1997	1996	1995	1994	1993
Return (%)	-0.3	7.6	7.3	6.2	6.6	—	—	—	—	—
Differ From Category (+/-)	-5.4	0.5	-1.2	5.2	0.5	—	—	—	—	—
Return, Tax-Adjusted (%)	-2.3	5.0	4.1	3.4	4.0	—	—	—	—	—
Dividends, Net Income ($)	0.52	0.66	0.81	0.70	0.66	—	—	—	—	—
Expense Ratio (%)	0.58	0.58	0.58	0.58	0.58	—	—	—	—	—
Yield (%)	5.52	6.61	8.17	6.95	6.49	—	—	—	—	—
Total Assets (Millions $)	326	333	139	337	210	—	—	—	—	—

SHAREHOLDER INFORMATION

Minimum Investment
Initial: $5,000 IRA: $1,000
Subsequent: $1 IRA: $1

Maximum Fees
Load: none 12b-1: 0.19%
Other: none

Strong Corporate Bd/Inv (STCBX)

800-368-3863, 414-359-1400
www.strong-funds.com

Corporate Bond

PERFORMANCE AND PER SHARE DATA **fund inception date: 12/12/85**

	3yr Annual	5yr Annual	10yr Annual	Category Risk Index
Return (%)	5.3	4.5	7.8	1.63—high
Differ From Category (+/-)	-1.6 blw av	-1.0 blw av	1.3 high	**Avg Mat** 10.3 yrs

	2002	2001	2000	1999	1998	1997	1996	1995	1994	1993
Return (%)	1.3	6.8	7.8	-0.2	7.2	11.8	5.5	25.3	-1.3	16.7
Differ From Category (+/-)	-3.8	-0.3	-0.7	-1.2	1.1	2.4	1.1	8.6	0.0	6.7
Return, Tax-Adjusted (%)	-1.0	4.0	4.9	-2.8	4.6	9.0	2.9	22.1	-4.2	13.8
Dividends, Net Income ($)	0.62	0.74	0.75	0.73	0.74	0.75	0.72	0.76	0.73	0.69
Expense Ratio (%)	1.00	0.90	0.90	0.80	0.90	1.00	1.00	1.10	1.10	1.10
Yield (%)	6.20	7.04	7.12	6.95	6.57	6.69	6.71	6.97	7.79	6.73
Total Assets (Millions $)	655	1,267	954	837	844	560	305	259	123	123

SHAREHOLDER INFORMATION

Minimum Investment
Initial: $2,500 IRA: $250
Subsequent: $100 IRA: $50

Maximum Fees
Load: none 12b-1: none
Other: none

T Rowe Price Corp Inc (PRPIX)

800-638-5660, 410-345-2000
www.troweprice.com

Corporate Bond

PERFORMANCE AND PER SHARE DATA **fund inception date: 10/31/95**

	3yr Annual	5yr Annual	10yr Annual	Category Risk Index
Return (%)	7.3	4.6	na	1.26—abv av
Differ From Category (+/-)	0.4 av	-0.9 blw av	na	**Avg Mat** 11.4 yrs

	2002	2001	2000	1999	1998	1997	1996	1995	1994	1993
Return (%)	4.2	9.7	7.9	-0.8	2.2	12.5	4.6	—	—	—
Differ From Category (+/-)	-0.9	2.6	-0.6	-1.8	-3.9	3.1	0.2	—	—	—
Return, Tax-Adjusted (%)	1.6	6.9	4.9	-3.5	-0.7	9.5	1.8	—	—	—
Dividends, Net Income ($)	0.62	0.65	0.68	0.66	0.73	0.75	0.73	—	—	—
Expense Ratio (%)	0.80	0.80	0.80	0.80	0.80	0.80	0.80	—	—	—
Yield (%)	6.82	6.95	7.45	7.24	7.38	7.21	7.33	—	—	—
Total Assets (Millions $)	82	73	50	51	54	32	15	—	—	—

SHAREHOLDER INFORMATION

Minimum Investment
Initial: $2,500 IRA: $1,000
Subsequent: $100 IRA: $50

Maximum Fees
Load: none 12b-1: none
Other: none

Vanguard Int Tm Crp (VFICX)

800-662-7447, 610-436-5152
www.vanguard.com

Corporate Bond

PERFORMANCE AND PER SHARE DATA **fund inception date: 11/1/93**

	3yr Annual	5yr Annual	10yr Annual	Category Risk Index
Return (%)	10.1	7.3	na	1.23—abv av
Differ From Category (+/-)	3.2 high	1.8 high	na	**Avg Mat** 7.3 yrs

	2002	2001	2000	1999	1998	1997	1996	1995	1994	1993
Return (%)	10.2	9.4	10.7	-1.5	8.3	8.9	2.7	21.3	-4.2	—
Differ From Category (+/-)	5.1	2.3	2.2	-2.5	2.2	-0.5	-1.7	4.6	-2.9	—
Return, Tax-Adjusted (%)	7.9	6.8	7.9	-4.0	5.6	6.3	0.2	18.4	-6.5	—
Dividends, Net Income ($)	0.58	0.63	0.66	0.62	0.62	0.63	0.63	0.65	0.57	—
Expense Ratio (%)	0.21	0.22	0.25	0.27	0.26	0.25	0.28	0.28	0.25	—
Yield (%)	5.73	6.47	6.95	6.70	6.13	6.33	6.45	6.40	6.36	—
Total Assets (Millions $)	2,433	2,015	1,920	1,457	1,181	868	621	361	151	—

SHAREHOLDER INFORMATION

Minimum Investment
Initial: $3,000 IRA: $1,000
Subsequent: $100 IRA: $100

Maximum Fees
Load: none 12b-1: none
Other: none

Vanguard LT Crp (VWESX)

800-662-7447, 610-436-5152
www.vanguard.com

Corporate Bond

PERFORMANCE AND PER SHARE DATA **fund inception date: 6/29/73**

	3yr Annual	5yr Annual	10yr Annual	Category Risk Index
Return (%)	11.5	7.2	8.4	1.97—high
Differ From Category (+/-)	4.6 high	1.7 high	1.9 high	**Avg Mat** 18.7 yrs

	2002	2001	2000	1999	1998	1997	1996	1995	1994	1993
Return (%)	13.2	9.5	11.7	-6.2	9.2	13.7	1.1	26.4	-5.2	14.4
Differ From Category (+/-)	8.1	2.4	3.2	-7.2	3.1	4.3	-3.3	9.7	-3.9	4.4
Return, Tax-Adjusted (%)	10.7	6.9	8.9	-8.7	6.3	10.8	-1.9	23.3	-8.1	10.7
Dividends, Net Income ($)	0.55	0.56	0.57	0.56	0.58	0.61	0.61	0.62	0.61	0.63
Expense Ratio (%)	0.32	0.30	0.30	0.30	0.32	0.28	0.31	0.32	0.30	0.31
Yield (%)	5.95	6.45	6.74	6.86	6.11	6.53	6.82	6.54	7.51	6.65
Total Assets (Millions $)	3,647	3,550	3,703	3,723	4,152	3,637	3,460	3,356	2,552	3,168

SHAREHOLDER INFORMATION

Minimum Investment
Initial: $3,000 IRA: $1,000
Subsequent: $100 IRA: $100

Maximum Fees
Load: none 12b-1: none
Other: none

Vanguard Sh Tm Crp (VFSTX)

800-662-7447, 610-436-5152
www.vanguard.com

Corporate Bond

PERFORMANCE AND PER SHARE DATA **fund inception date: 10/29/82**

	3yr Annual	5yr Annual	10yr Annual	Category Risk Index
Return (%)	7.1	6.2	6.2	0.57—blw av
Differ From Category (+/-)	0.2 av	0.7 abv av	-0.3 av	**Avg Mat** 2.5 yrs

	2002	2001	2000	1999	1998	1997	1996	1995	1994	1993
Return (%)	5.1	8.1	8.1	3.3	6.5	6.9	4.7	12.7	0.0	6.9
Differ From Category (+/-)	0.0	1.0	-0.4	2.3	0.4	-2.5	0.3	-4.0	1.3	-3.1
Return, Tax-Adjusted (%)	3.1	5.6	5.4	0.9	4.1	4.5	2.3	10.1	-2.1	4.4
Dividends, Net Income ($)	0.56	0.67	0.70	0.65	0.66	0.66	0.66	0.66	0.58	0.61
Expense Ratio (%)	0.24	0.24	0.25	0.27	0.28	0.25	0.27	0.28	0.26	0.27
Yield (%)	5.18	6.19	6.57	6.17	6.08	6.10	6.13	6.04	5.63	5.55
Total Assets (Millions $)	8,508	7,382	7,340	6,798	5,427	4,601	4,608	3,743	2,905	3,482

SHAREHOLDER INFORMATION

Minimum Investment
Initial: $3,000 IRA: $1,000
Subsequent: $100 IRA: $100

Maximum Fees
Load: none 12b-1: none
Other: none

Corporate High-Yield Bond Funds
Category Performance Ranked by 2002 Returns

Category	Fund (Ticker)	Annual Return (%) 2002	3yr	5yr	10yr	Category Risk	Total Risk
B-CHY	Buffalo High Yield Fund (BUFHX)	4.0	6.2	3.0	na	low	blw av
B-CHY	Northeast Investors Tr (NTHEX)	3.2	-0.5	0.2	7.4	av	blw av
B-CHY	T Rowe Price High Yld (PRHYX)	3.0	1.8	2.8	6.6	blw av	blw av
B-CHY	Janus High Yield (JAHYX)	2.5	3.2	3.2	na	low	blw av
B-CHY	Fidelity High Income (SPHIX)	2.3	-5.8	-1.4	6.1	abv av	blw av
B-CHY	Payden High Inc/R (PYHRX)	2.1	1.4	2.7	na	blw av	blw av
B-CHY	Vanguard HY Corp/Inv (VWEHX)	1.7	1.2	2.3	6.6	blw av	blw av
B-CHY	Fidelity Capital & Inc (FAGIX)	-0.4	-4.9	0.4	5.6	high	av
Corporate High-Yield Bond Average		**-1.2**	**-2.6**	**-0.1**	**5.2**	**—**	**blw av**

Note: AAII members who would like performance figures for no-load and low-load mutual funds they own that do not appear in this Guide can access this information on our Web site at www.aaii.com.

Buffalo High Yield Fund (BUFHX)

800-492-8332, 800-243-9865
www.babsonfunds.com

Corporate High-Yield Bond

PERFORMANCE AND PER SHARE DATA fund inception date: 5/19/95

	3yr Annual	5yr Annual	10yr Annual	Category Risk Index	
Return (%)	6.2	3.0	na	0.64—low	
Differ From Category (+/-)	8.8 high	3.1 high	na	Avg Mat	na

	2002	2001	2000	1999	1998	1997	1996	1995	1994	1993
Return (%)	4.0	10.5	4.4	1.9	-5.3	15.7	16.6	—	—	—
Differ From Category (+/-)	5.2	9.4	11.5	-3.7	-7.1	1.1	1.1	—	—	—
Return, Tax-Adjusted (%)	1.6	6.9	0.6	-1.5	-7.8	12.6	13.1	—	—	—
Dividends, Net Income ($)	0.62	0.90	1.00	0.95	0.74	0.81	0.81	—	—	—
Expense Ratio (%)	1.04	1.04	1.04	1.05	1.03	na	na	—	—	—
Yield (%)	6.39	9.06	10.19	9.16	6.61	6.32	6.72	—	—	—
Total Assets (Millions $)	111	60	36	49	57	35	16	—	—	—

SHAREHOLDER INFORMATION

Minimum Investment
Initial: $2,500 IRA: $250
Subsequent: $100 IRA: $100

Maximum Fees
Load: 2.00% redemption 12b-1: none
Other: redemption fee applies for 6 months

Fidelity Capital & Inc (FAGIX)

800-544-8544, 800-522-7297
www.fidelity.com

Corporate High-Yield Bond

PERFORMANCE AND PER SHARE DATA fund inception date: 11/1/77

	3yr Annual	5yr Annual	10yr Annual	Category Risk Index	
Return (%)	-4.9	0.4	5.6	1.48—high	
Differ From Category (+/-)	-2.3 av	0.5 av	0.4 av	Avg Mat	5.4 yrs

	2002	2001	2000	1999	1998	1997	1996	1995	1994	1993
Return (%)	-0.4	-4.6	-9.4	13.3	4.7	14.7	8.4	16.7	-4.6	22.5
Differ From Category (+/-)	0.8	-5.7	-2.3	7.7	2.9	0.1	-7.1	-0.7	-2.4	2.6
Return, Tax-Adjusted (%)	-2.9	-7.7	-12.6	9.2	0.4	11.8	6.0	12.7	-7.8	19.5
Dividends, Net Income ($)	0.44	0.61	0.74	0.72	0.94	0.67	0.54	0.87	0.80	0.64
Expense Ratio (%)	0.81	0.78	0.82	0.81	0.82	0.86	0.98	0.96	0.97	0.91
Yield (%)	7.00	8.99	9.57	7.36	9.85	6.69	5.76	9.49	9.26	6.49
Total Assets (Millions $)	2,802	2,874	2,837	2,845	2,195	2,096	2,162	2,322	2,039	2,745

SHAREHOLDER INFORMATION

Minimum Investment
Initial: $2,500 IRA: $500
Subsequent: $250 IRA: $250

Maximum Fees
Load: 1.00% redemption 12b-1: none
Other: redemption fee applies for 9 months

Fidelity High Income (SPHIX)

800-544-8544, 800-522-7297
www.fidelity.com

Corporate High-Yield Bond

PERFORMANCE AND PER SHARE DATA **fund inception date: 8/29/90**

	3yr Annual	5yr Annual	10yr Annual	Category Risk Index	
Return (%)	-5.8	-1.4	6.1	1.24—abv av	
Differ From Category (+/-)	-3.2 blw av	-1.3 blw av	0.9 abv av	**Avg Mat**	7.1 yrs

	2002	2001	2000	1999	1998	1997	1996	1995	1994	1993
Return (%)	2.3	-4.8	-14.2	8.9	2.1	15.9	14.3	17.7	3.2	21.8
Differ From Category (+/-)	3.5	-5.9	-7.1	3.3	0.3	1.3	-1.2	0.3	5.4	1.9
Return, Tax-Adjusted (%)	-1.0	-8.5	-17.2	5.2	-1.2	11.9	10.2	13.6	-0.2	16.1
Dividends, Net Income ($)	0.69	0.89	0.92	1.06	0.92	1.11	1.08	1.08	0.99	1.12
Expense Ratio (%)	0.76	0.74	0.74	0.80	0.80	0.80	0.80	0.80	0.75	0.70
Yield (%)	9.07	10.94	9.73	8.76	7.41	8.32	8.44	8.75	8.57	8.64
Total Assets (Millions $)	1,740	1,551	2,130	3,261	2,861	2,446	1,717	1,080	617	664

SHAREHOLDER INFORMATION

Minimum Investment
Initial: $2,500 IRA: $500
Subsequent: $250 IRA: $250

Maximum Fees
Load: 1.00% redemption 12b-1: none
Other: redemption fee applies for 3 months

Janus High Yield (JAHYX)

800-525-0020, 303-333-3863
www.janus.com

Corporate High-Yield Bond

PERFORMANCE AND PER SHARE DATA **fund inception date: 12/29/95**

	3yr Annual	5yr Annual	10yr Annual	Category Risk Index	
Return (%)	3.2	3.2	na	0.65—low	
Differ From Category (+/-)	5.8 high	3.3 high	na	**Avg Mat**	4.1 yrs

	2002	2001	2000	1999	1998	1997	1996	1995	1994	1993
Return (%)	2.5	4.5	2.4	5.5	0.9	15.4	23.9	—	—	—
Differ From Category (+/-)	3.7	3.4	9.5	-0.1	-0.9	0.8	8.4	—	—	—
Return, Tax-Adjusted (%)	-0.1	1.5	-0.9	2.2	-2.2	11.1	19.7	—	—	—
Dividends, Net Income ($)	0.63	0.75	0.84	0.89	0.90	0.94	0.96	—	—	—
Expense Ratio (%)	na	0.99	1.00	1.00	0.96	1.00	1.00	—	—	—
Yield (%)	7.02	8.00	8.66	8.65	8.48	7.87	8.46	—	—	—
Total Assets (Millions $)	634	433	300	275	295	357	238	—	—	—

SHAREHOLDER INFORMATION

Minimum Investment
Initial: $2,500 IRA: $500
Subsequent: $100 IRA: $100

Maximum Fees
Load: 1.00% redemption 12b-1: none
Other: redemption fee applies for 3 months

Northeast Investors Tr (NTHEX)

800-225-6704, 617-523-3588
www.northeastinvestors.com

Corporate High-Yield Bond

PERFORMANCE AND PER SHARE DATA **fund inception date: 3/1/50**

	3yr Annual	5yr Annual	10yr Annual	Category Risk Index	
Return (%)	-0.5	0.2	7.4	0.86—av	
Differ From Category (+/-)	2.1 abv av	0.3 av	2.2 high	**Avg Mat**	7.0 yrs

	2002	2001	2000	1999	1998	1997	1996	1995	1994	1993
Return (%)	3.2	1.3	-6.0	3.5	-0.2	13.8	20.1	17.2	2.2	23.5
Differ From Category (+/-)	4.4	0.2	1.1	-2.1	-2.0	-0.8	4.6	-0.2	4.4	3.6
Return, Tax-Adjusted (%)	0.0	-2.9	-10.3	-0.5	-3.9	10.4	16.2	13.1	-1.6	19.2
Dividends, Net Income ($)	0.62	0.87	1.06	1.06	1.00	0.96	1.00	0.99	0.98	1.00
Expense Ratio (%)	0.70	0.21	0.61	0.61	0.61	0.64	0.66	0.67	0.70	0.73
Yield (%)	8.79	11.70	12.97	10.84	9.39	8.24	8.99	9.74	10.26	9.71
Total Assets (Millions $)	1,730	1,292	1,208	1,854	2,313	2,161	1,354	805	554	548

SHAREHOLDER INFORMATION

Minimum Investment
Initial: $1,000 IRA: $500
Subsequent: $50 IRA: $50

Maximum Fees
Load: none 12b-1: none
Other: none

Payden High Inc/R (PYHRX)

800-572-9336, 213-625-1900
www.payden.com

Corporate High-Yield Bond

PERFORMANCE AND PER SHARE DATA **fund inception date: 12/30/97**

	3yr Annual	5yr Annual	10yr Annual	Category Risk Index	
Return (%)	1.4	2.7	na	0.85—blw av	
Differ From Category (+/-)	4.0 high	2.8 abv av	na	**Avg Mat**	7.9 yrs

	2002	2001	2000	1999	1998	1997	1996	1995	1994	1993
Return (%)	2.1	4.1	-1.7	3.1	6.3	—	—	—	—	—
Differ From Category (+/-)	3.3	3.0	5.4	-2.5	4.5	—	—	—	—	—
Return, Tax-Adjusted (%)	-1.0	1.2	-5.2	-0.1	3.9	—	—	—	—	—
Dividends, Net Income ($)	0.66	0.62	0.83	0.79	0.60	—	—	—	—	—
Expense Ratio (%)	na	0.57	0.57	0.55	0.54	—	—	—	—	—
Yield (%)	8.53	7.52	9.77	8.33	6.01	—	—	—	—	—
Total Assets (Millions $)	240	231	143	105	92	—	—	—	—	—

SHAREHOLDER INFORMATION

Minimum Investment
Initial: $5,000 IRA: $2,000
Subsequent: $1,000 IRA: $1,000

Maximum Fees
Load: none 12b-1: none
Other: none

T Rowe Price High Yld (PRHYX)

800-638-5660, 410-345-2000
www.troweprice.com

Corporate High-Yield Bond

PERFORMANCE AND PER SHARE DATA **fund inception date: 12/31/84**

	3yr Annual	5yr Annual	10yr Annual	Category Risk Index	
Return (%)	1.8	2.8	6.6	0.81—blw av	
Differ From Category (+/-)	4.4 high	2.9 high	1.4 high	**Avg Mat**	8.8 yrs

	2002	2001	2000	1999	1998	1997	1996	1995	1994	1993
Return (%)	3.0	6.0	-3.2	4.1	4.4	14.4	11.5	15.7	-7.9	21.8
Differ From Category (+/-)	4.2	4.9	3.9	-1.5	2.6	-0.2	-4.0	-1.7	-5.7	1.9
Return, Tax-Adjusted (%)	-0.4	2.1	-7.0	0.5	0.9	10.8	7.9	11.9	-11.1	17.9
Dividends, Net Income ($)	0.59	0.68	0.76	0.75	0.76	0.75	0.75	0.74	0.75	0.81
Expense Ratio (%)	0.83	0.82	0.83	0.82	0.81	0.84	0.85	0.88	0.85	0.89
Yield (%)	9.40	10.19	10.95	9.44	9.09	8.58	8.99	9.03	9.67	8.78
Total Assets (Millions $)	1,891	1,577	1,447	1,681	1,703	1,571	1,325	1,226	1,040	1,631

SHAREHOLDER INFORMATION

Minimum Investment
Initial: $2,500 IRA: $1,000
Subsequent: $100 IRA: $50

Maximum Fees
Load: 1.00% redemption 12b-1: none
Other: redemption fee applies for 12 months

Vanguard HY Corp/Inv (VWEHX)

800-662-7447, 610-436-5152
www.vanguard.com

Corporate High-Yield Bond

PERFORMANCE AND PER SHARE DATA **fund inception date: 12/27/78**

	3yr Annual	5yr Annual	10yr Annual	Category Risk Index	
Return (%)	1.2	2.3	6.6	0.78—blw av	
Differ From Category (+/-)	3.8 abv av	2.4 abv av	1.4 abv av	**Avg Mat**	6.9 yrs

	2002	2001	2000	1999	1998	1997	1996	1995	1994	1993
Return (%)	1.7	2.9	-0.8	2.5	5.6	11.9	9.5	19.1	-1.7	18.2
Differ From Category (+/-)	2.9	1.8	6.3	-3.1	3.8	-2.7	-6.0	1.7	0.5	-1.7
Return, Tax-Adjusted (%)	-1.4	-0.6	-4.2	-0.7	2.3	8.4	6.0	15.4	-5.0	14.5
Dividends, Net Income ($)	0.50	0.59	0.63	0.63	0.66	0.68	0.68	0.67	0.67	0.69
Expense Ratio (%)	0.27	0.27	0.28	0.29	0.28	0.29	0.34	0.34	0.32	0.34
Yield (%)	8.50	9.37	9.41	8.52	8.40	8.41	8.64	8.53	9.30	8.60
Total Assets (Millions $)	5,322	5,160	5,270	5,699	5,380	4,571	3,582	2,899	2,120	2,529

SHAREHOLDER INFORMATION

Minimum Investment
Initial: $3,000 IRA: $1,000
Subsequent: $100 IRA: $100

Maximum Fees
Load: 1.00% redemption 12b-1: none
Other: redemption fee applies for 12 months

Mortgage-Backed Bond Funds

Category Performance Ranked by 2002 Returns

Category	Fund (Ticker)	Annual Return (%) 2002	3yr	5yr	10yr	Category Risk	Total Risk
B-MB	Strong Government Sec/Inv (STVSX)	10.1	10.0	7.3	7.6	high	low
B-MB	Vanguard GNMA (VFIIX)	9.6	9.6	7.2	7.2	abv av	low
B-MB	USAA Inv:GNMA (USGNX)	9.2	9.4	6.4	6.8	high	low
B-MB	T Rowe Price GNMA (PRGMX)	9.0	9.2	6.8	6.8	high	low
B-MB	Fidelity Ginnie Mae (FGMNX)	8.6	8.8	6.8	6.7	blw av	low
B-MB	Amer Cnt Ginnie Mae/Inv (BGNMX)	8.3	8.7	6.6	6.7	blw av	low
B-MB	Scudder GNMA Fund/AARP (AGNMX)	8.3	8.5	6.5	6.1	av	low
B-MB	AMF Adjust Rate Mortgage (ASARX)	3.2	5.4	5.2	5.4	low	low
Mortgage-Backed Bond Average		**7.6**	**8.2**	**6.4**	**6.5**	**—**	**low**

Note: AAII members who would like performance figures for no-load and low-load mutual funds they own that do not appear in this Guide can access this information on our Web site at www.aaii.com.

Amer Cnt Ginnie Mae/Inv (BGNMX)

800-345-2021, 816-531-5575
www.americancentury.com

Mortgage-Backed Bond

PERFORMANCE AND PER SHARE DATA **fund inception date: 9/23/85**

	3yr Annual	5yr Annual	10yr Annual	Category Risk Index	
Return (%)	8.7	6.6	6.7	0.93—blw av	
Differ From Category (+/-)	0.5 av	0.2 abv av	0.2 av	**Avg Mat**	4.0 yrs

	2002	2001	2000	1999	1998	1997	1996	1995	1994	1993
Return (%)	8.3	7.4	10.4	0.9	6.3	8.7	5.2	15.8	-1.6	6.5
Differ From Category (+/-)	0.7	0.1	0.6	-0.1	-0.1	0.3	0.9	1.1	-0.3	-1.0
Return, Tax-Adjusted (%)	6.2	5.0	7.8	-1.5	3.9	6.1	2.5	12.8	-4.1	3.9
Dividends, Net Income ($)	0.58	0.63	0.67	0.65	0.64	0.70	0.71	0.74	0.67	0.70
Expense Ratio (%)	0.59	0.59	0.59	0.59	0.58	0.55	0.58	0.58	0.54	0.56
Yield (%)	5.32	5.93	6.38	6.41	5.98	6.55	6.76	6.92	6.76	6.49
Total Assets (Millions $)	2,056	1,646	1,288	1,297	1,377	1,233	1,130	1,111	952	1,260

SHAREHOLDER INFORMATION

Minimum Investment
Initial: $2,500 IRA: $1,000
Subsequent: $50 IRA: $50

Maximum Fees
Load: none 12b-1: none
Other: none

AMF Adjust Rate Mortgage (ASARX)

800-661-3938, 800-527-3713
www.amffunds.com

Mortgage-Backed Bond

PERFORMANCE AND PER SHARE DATA **fund inception date: 9/18/91**

	3yr Annual	5yr Annual	10yr Annual	Category Risk Index	
Return (%)	5.4	5.2	5.4	0.22—low	
Differ From Category (+/-)	-2.8 low	-1.2 low	-1.1 low	**Avg Mat**	4.0 yrs

	2002	2001	2000	1999	1998	1997	1996	1995	1994	1993
Return (%)	3.2	5.9	7.1	4.6	5.1	6.5	5.9	9.1	1.9	4.7
Differ From Category (+/-)	-4.4	-1.4	-2.7	3.6	-1.3	-1.9	1.6	-5.6	3.2	-2.8
Return, Tax-Adjusted (%)	2.0	3.9	4.6	2.5	2.9	4.1	3.5	6.6	0.1	3.0
Dividends, Net Income ($)	0.30	0.51	0.62	0.53	0.56	0.60	0.59	0.61	0.46	0.42
Expense Ratio (%)	na	0.49	0.48	0.48	0.49	0.50	0.47	0.48	0.47	0.46
Yield (%)	3.01	5.12	6.26	5.38	5.64	6.01	5.92	6.11	4.73	4.20
Total Assets (Millions $)	3,724	2,439	716	799	914	761	749	898	862	1,419

SHAREHOLDER INFORMATION

Minimum Investment
Initial: $10,000 IRA: na
Subsequent: $1 IRA: na

Maximum Fees
Load: none 12b-1: 0.15%
Other: none

Fidelity Ginnie Mae (FGMNX)

800-544-8544, 800-522-7297
www.fidelity.com

Mortgage-Backed Bond

PERFORMANCE AND PER SHARE DATA — fund inception date: 11/8/85

	3yr Annual	5yr Annual	10yr Annual	Category Risk Index
Return (%)	8.8	6.8	6.7	0.93—blw av
Differ From Category (+/-)	0.6 abv av	0.4 abv av	0.2 abv av	Avg Mat 7.8 yrs

	2002	2001	2000	1999	1998	1997	1996	1995	1994	1993
Return (%)	8.6	7.2	10.7	1.2	6.3	8.7	4.8	16.6	-1.9	6.1
Differ From Category (+/-)	1.0	-0.1	0.9	0.2	-0.1	0.3	0.5	1.9	-0.6	-1.4
Return, Tax-Adjusted (%)	6.7	4.9	8.0	-1.2	3.8	6.1	2.3	13.8	-4.3	3.2
Dividends, Net Income ($)	0.53	0.63	0.70	0.66	0.67	0.70	0.69	0.71	0.63	0.62
Expense Ratio (%)	0.60	0.62	0.63	0.64	0.72	0.75	0.75	0.75	0.82	0.80
Yield (%)	4.71	5.80	6.52	6.37	6.15	6.42	6.44	6.51	6.29	5.58
Total Assets (Millions $)	6,807	3,901	1,890	1,757	1,093	862	793	805	704	887

SHAREHOLDER INFORMATION

Minimum Investment
Initial: $2,500 — IRA: $500
Subsequent: $250 — IRA: $250

Maximum Fees
Load: none — 12b-1: none
Other: none

Scudder GNMA Fund/AARP (AGNMX)

800-621-1048
aarp.scudder.com

Mortgage-Backed Bond

PERFORMANCE AND PER SHARE DATA — fund inception date: 1/31/85

	3yr Annual	5yr Annual	10yr Annual	Category Risk Index
Return (%)	8.5	6.5	6.1	0.96—av
Differ From Category (+/-)	0.3 av	0.1 av	-0.4 blw av	Avg Mat 8.6 yrs

	2002	2001	2000	1999	1998	1997	1996	1995	1994	1993
Return (%)	8.3	7.1	10.2	0.5	6.7	7.9	4.4	12.8	-1.6	5.9
Differ From Category (+/-)	0.7	-0.2	0.4	-0.5	0.3	-0.5	0.1	-1.9	-0.3	-1.6
Return, Tax-Adjusted (%)	6.3	4.7	7.7	-1.9	4.1	5.3	1.9	10.0	-4.0	3.2
Dividends, Net Income ($)	0.79	0.89	0.91	0.92	0.98	0.98	0.97	1.01	0.94	1.09
Expense Ratio (%)	0.70	0.73	0.73	0.65	0.61	0.65	0.64	0.67	0.66	0.70
Yield (%)	5.10	5.91	6.10	6.38	6.43	6.43	6.44	6.57	6.45	6.91
Total Assets (Millions $)	3,963	3,816	3,686	4,014	4,535	4,539	4,826	5,257	5,248	6,629

SHAREHOLDER INFORMATION

Minimum Investment
Initial: $1,000 — IRA: $500
Subsequent: $50 — IRA: $50

Maximum Fees
Load: none — 12b-1: none
Other: none

Strong Government Sec/Inv (STVSX)

800-368-3863, 414-359-1400
www.strong-funds.com

Mortgage-Backed Bond

PERFORMANCE AND PER SHARE DATA **fund inception date: 10/29/86**

	3yr Annual	5yr Annual	10yr Annual	Category Risk Index
Return (%)	10.0	7.3	7.6	1.33—high
Differ From Category (+/-)	1.8 high	0.9 high	1.1 high	**Avg Mat** 5.7 yrs

	2002	2001	2000	1999	1998	1997	1996	1995	1994	1993
Return (%)	10.1	8.7	11.3	-1.0	8.1	9.0	2.8	19.9	-3.3	12.7
Differ From Category (+/-)	2.5	1.4	1.5	-2.0	1.7	0.6	-1.5	5.2	-2.0	5.2
Return, Tax-Adjusted (%)	8.0	6.4	9.0	-3.1	5.4	6.6	0.5	17.2	-5.6	9.1
Dividends, Net Income ($)	0.46	0.55	0.59	0.56	0.61	0.64	0.63	0.66	0.62	0.65
Expense Ratio (%)	0.90	0.90	0.90	0.80	0.80	0.80	0.90	0.90	0.90	0.80
Yield (%)	4.03	5.02	5.57	5.55	5.55	5.95	6.01	6.09	6.43	5.89
Total Assets (Millions $)	2,279	1,630	1,336	1,287	1,326	907	659	504	276	221

SHAREHOLDER INFORMATION

Minimum Investment
Initial: $2,500 IRA: $250
Subsequent: $100 IRA: $50

Maximum Fees
Load: none 12b-1: none
Other: none

T Rowe Price GNMA (PRGMX)

800-638-5660, 410-345-2000
www.troweprice.com

Mortgage-Backed Bond

PERFORMANCE AND PER SHARE DATA **fund inception date: 11/26/85**

	3yr Annual	5yr Annual	10yr Annual	Category Risk Index
Return (%)	9.2	6.8	6.8	1.07—high
Differ From Category (+/-)	1.0 high	0.4 abv av	0.3 abv av	**Avg Mat** 8.6 yrs

	2002	2001	2000	1999	1998	1997	1996	1995	1994	1993
Return (%)	9.0	7.6	10.9	0.2	6.5	9.4	3.1	17.8	-1.6	6.1
Differ From Category (+/-)	1.4	0.3	1.1	-0.8	0.1	1.0	-1.2	3.1	-0.3	-1.4
Return, Tax-Adjusted (%)	7.3	5.2	8.3	-2.3	3.9	6.7	0.4	14.8	-4.4	3.3
Dividends, Net Income ($)	0.42	0.56	0.59	0.59	0.62	0.64	0.65	0.67	0.67	0.68
Expense Ratio (%)	0.69	0.70	0.71	0.71	0.70	0.74	0.74	0.76	0.77	0.79
Yield (%)	4.24	5.90	6.31	6.56	6.47	6.68	6.93	6.87	7.54	6.99
Total Assets (Millions $)	1,389	1,138	1,090	1,089	1,146	1,063	927	896	752	918

SHAREHOLDER INFORMATION

Minimum Investment
Initial: $2,500 IRA: $1,000
Subsequent: $100 IRA: $50

Maximum Fees
Load: none 12b-1: none
Other: none

USAA Inv:GNMA (USGNX)

800-531-8181, 210-456-7211
www.usaa.com

Mortgage-Backed Bond

PERFORMANCE AND PER SHARE DATA **fund inception date: 2/1/91**

	3yr Annual	5yr Annual	10yr Annual	Category Risk Index
Return (%)	9.4	6.4	6.8	1.11—high
Differ From Category (+/-)	1.2 high	0.0 av	0.3 abv av	**Avg Mat** 8.1 yrs

	2002	2001	2000	1999	1998	1997	1996	1995	1994	1993
Return (%)	9.2	7.1	12.1	-3.6	8.2	9.5	2.9	16.7	0.0	7.1
Differ From Category (+/-)	1.6	-0.2	2.3	-4.6	1.8	1.1	-1.4	2.0	1.3	-0.4
Return, Tax-Adjusted (%)	7.0	4.7	9.3	-6.0	5.7	6.8	0.3	13.7	-2.7	4.1
Dividends, Net Income ($)	0.57	0.60	0.65	0.63	0.65	0.67	0.69	0.72	0.70	0.78
Expense Ratio (%)	0.41	0.32	0.32	0.31	0.30	0.30	0.32	0.32	0.31	0.32
Yield (%)	5.56	6.04	6.60	6.70	6.25	6.54	6.90	6.92	7.31	7.58
Total Assets (Millions $)	712	532	438	448	452	346	307	297	244	277

SHAREHOLDER INFORMATION

Minimum Investment
Initial: $3,000 IRA: $250
Subsequent: $50 IRA: $50

Maximum Fees
Load: none 12b-1: none
Other: none

Vanguard GNMA (VFIIX)

800-662-7447, 610-436-5152
www.vanguard.com

Mortgage-Backed Bond

PERFORMANCE AND PER SHARE DATA **fund inception date: 6/27/80**

	3yr Annual	5yr Annual	10yr Annual	Category Risk Index
Return (%)	9.6	7.2	7.2	1.04—abv av
Differ From Category (+/-)	1.4 high	0.8 high	0.7 high	**Avg Mat** 8.0 yrs

	2002	2001	2000	1999	1998	1997	1996	1995	1994	1993
Return (%)	9.6	7.9	11.2	0.7	7.1	9.4	5.2	17.0	-0.9	5.8
Differ From Category (+/-)	2.0	0.6	1.4	-0.3	0.7	1.0	0.9	2.3	0.4	-1.7
Return, Tax-Adjusted (%)	7.4	5.4	8.5	-1.8	4.5	6.6	2.4	14.0	-3.5	3.3
Dividends, Net Income ($)	0.58	0.65	0.68	0.66	0.69	0.71	0.72	0.73	0.68	0.65
Expense Ratio (%)	0.27	0.27	0.27	0.30	0.31	0.27	0.29	0.30	0.28	0.29
Yield (%)	5.38	6.26	6.64	6.69	6.59	6.80	7.04	6.99	7.09	6.26
Total Assets (Millions $)	21,386	15,531	13,910	12,548	10,993	8,725	7,441	6,907	5,777	7,073

SHAREHOLDER INFORMATION

Minimum Investment
Initial: $3,000 IRA: $1,000
Subsequent: $100 IRA: $100

Maximum Fees
Load: none 12b-1: none
Other: none

Government: Short-Term Bond Funds
Category Performance Ranked by 2002 Returns

Category	Fund (Ticker)	Annual Return (%) 2002	3yr	5yr	10yr	Category Risk	Total Risk
B-GvST	Payden US Government/R (PYUSX)	8.1	8.5	6.9	na	high	low
B-GvST	Vanguard Sh Tm Trsy (VFISX)	8.0	8.2	6.7	0.2	high	low
B-GvST	Vanguard Sh Tm Fed (VSGBX)	7.6	8.4	6.9	6.3	abv av	low
B-GvST	Excelsior Sh Tm Govt Sec (UMGVX)	6.7	7.3	6.1	5.5	blw av	low
B-GvST	Amer Cnt Sht Tm Govt/Inv (TWUSX)	5.2	6.7	5.5	5.2	av	low
B-GvST	Dreyfus Short Int Govt (DSIGX)	5.2	6.7	5.6	5.7	abv av	low
Gov't: Short-Term Bond Average		**6.3**	**7.3**	**6.0**	**5.6**	**—**	**low**

Note: AAII members who would like performance figures for no-load and low-load mutual funds they own that do not appear in this Guide can access this information on our Web site at www.aaii.com.

Amer Cnt Sht Tm Govt/Inv (TWUSX)

800-345-2021, 816-531-5575
www.americancentury.com

Government: Short-Term Bond

PERFORMANCE AND PER SHARE DATA **fund inception date: 12/15/82**

	3yr Annual	5yr Annual	10yr Annual	Category Risk Index	
Return (%)	6.7	5.5	5.2	1.00—av	
Differ From Category (+/-)	-0.6 blw av	-0.5 blw av	-0.4 low	Avg Mat	2.4 yrs

	2002	2001	2000	1999	1998	1997	1996	1995	1994	1993
Return (%)	5.2	7.1	7.7	1.8	6.0	6.0	4.1	10.4	-0.5	4.6
Differ From Category (+/-)	-1.1	-0.3	-0.4	-0.1	-0.4	-0.1	0.1	-1.2	0.1	-1.4
Return, Tax-Adjusted (%)	3.9	5.1	5.4	-0.2	3.9	3.8	2.0	8.2	-2.3	4.4
Dividends, Net Income ($)	0.31	0.48	0.54	0.49	0.49	0.52	0.51	0.51	0.44	0.37
Expense Ratio (%)	0.59	0.59	0.59	0.59	0.59	0.68	0.70	0.70	0.81	1.00
Yield (%)	3.19	5.03	5.76	5.31	5.13	5.48	5.39	5.32	4.80	3.83
Total Assets (Millions $)	939	823	767	772	824	509	344	390	382	493

SHAREHOLDER INFORMATION

Minimum Investment
Initial: $2,500 IRA: $1,000
Subsequent: $50 IRA: $50

Maximum Fees
Load: none 12b-1: none
Other: none

Dreyfus Short Int Govt (DSIGX)

800-645-6561, 516-794-5452
www.dreyfus.com

Government: Short-Term Bond

PERFORMANCE AND PER SHARE DATA **fund inception date: 4/6/87**

	3yr Annual	5yr Annual	10yr Annual	Category Risk Index	
Return (%)	6.7	5.6	5.7	1.18—abv av	
Differ From Category (+/-)	-0.6 av	-0.4 av	0.1 abv av	Avg Mat	2.4 yrs

	2002	2001	2000	1999	1998	1997	1996	1995	1994	1993
Return (%)	5.2	6.0	8.9	1.8	6.4	6.1	3.9	12.6	-0.7	7.3
Differ From Category (+/-)	-1.1	-1.4	0.8	-0.1	0.0	0.0	-0.1	1.0	-0.1	1.3
Return, Tax-Adjusted (%)	3.8	4.3	6.6	-0.5	3.7	3.6	1.6	9.9	-3.3	4.4
Dividends, Net Income ($)	0.38	0.47	0.60	0.61	0.74	0.67	0.65	0.72	0.75	0.77
Expense Ratio (%)	na	0.73	0.71	0.71	0.70	0.74	0.74	0.62	0.47	0.40
Yield (%)	3.46	4.34	5.63	5.88	6.86	6.18	5.97	6.48	7.12	6.74
Total Assets (Millions $)	474	472	371	421	483	477	561	574	472	541

SHAREHOLDER INFORMATION

Minimum Investment
Initial: $2,500 IRA: $750
Subsequent: $100 IRA: $1

Maximum Fees
Load: none 12b-1: none
Other: none

Excelsior Sh Tm Govt Sec (UMGVX)

800-446-1012, 617-483-7297
www.excelsiorfunds.com

Government: Short-Term Bond

PERFORMANCE AND PER SHARE DATA **fund inception date: 12/31/92**

	3yr Annual	5yr Annual	10yr Annual	Category Risk Index	
Return (%)	7.3	6.1	5.5	1.00—blw av	
Differ From Category (+/-)	0.0 abv av	0.1 abv av	-0.1 abv av	**Avg Mat**	2.3 yrs

	2002	2001	2000	1999	1998	1997	1996	1995	1994	1993
Return (%)	6.7	7.6	7.6	2.4	6.3	5.8	3.9	10.2	1.0	4.0
Differ From Category (+/-)	0.4	0.2	-0.5	0.5	-0.1	-0.3	-0.1	-1.4	1.6	-2.0
Return, Tax-Adjusted (%)	5.1	5.5	5.4	0.4	4.3	3.7	1.8	7.9	-0.7	2.6
Dividends, Net Income ($)	0.27	0.36	0.38	0.34	0.35	0.37	0.38	0.40	0.29	0.22
Expense Ratio (%)	0.51	0.57	0.54	0.58	0.62	0.61	0.61	0.61	0.62	0.62
Yield (%)	3.67	5.02	5.42	4.92	4.94	5.28	5.45	5.64	4.26	3.12
Total Assets (Millions $)	383	148	57	69	50	32	29	22	25	22

SHAREHOLDER INFORMATION

Minimum Investment
Initial: $500 IRA: $250
Subsequent: $50 IRA: $50

Maximum Fees
Load: none 12b-1: none
Other: none

Payden US Government/R (PYUSX)

800-572-9336, 213-625-1900
www.payden.com

Government: Short-Term Bond

PERFORMANCE AND PER SHARE DATA **fund inception date: 12/30/94**

	3yr Annual	5yr Annual	10yr Annual	Category Risk Index	
Return (%)	8.5	6.9	na	1.47—high	
Differ From Category (+/-)	1.2 high	0.9 high	na	**Avg Mat**	2.4 yrs

	2002	2001	2000	1999	1998	1997	1996	1995	1994	1993
Return (%)	8.1	8.5	8.8	1.7	7.5	6.5	2.9	14.7	—	—
Differ From Category (+/-)	1.8	1.1	0.7	-0.2	1.1	0.4	-1.1	3.1	—	—
Return, Tax-Adjusted (%)	6.2	6.5	6.6	-0.5	5.3	4.3	0.8	12.1	—	—
Dividends, Net Income ($)	0.44	0.53	0.58	0.57	0.57	0.57	0.58	0.62	—	—
Expense Ratio (%)	na	0.40	0.40	0.40	0.34	0.45	0.45	0.45	—	—
Yield (%)	3.84	4.81	5.44	5.49	5.28	5.37	5.52	5.74	—	—
Total Assets (Millions $)	67	49	56	68	70	24	25	16	—	—

SHAREHOLDER INFORMATION

Minimum Investment
Initial: $5,000 IRA: $2,000
Subsequent: $1,000 IRA: $1,000

Maximum Fees
Load: none 12b-1: none
Other: none

Vanguard Sh Tm Fed (VSGBX)

800-662-7447, 610-436-5152
www.vanguard.com

Government: Short-Term Bond

PERFORMANCE AND PER SHARE DATA **fund inception date: 12/28/87**

	3yr Annual	5yr Annual	10yr Annual	Category Risk Index
Return (%)	8.4	6.9	6.3	1.24—abv av
Differ From Category (+/-)	1.1 high	0.9 high	0.7 high	**Avg Mat** 2.8 yrs

	2002	2001	2000	1999	1998	1997	1996	1995	1994	1993
Return (%)	7.6	8.6	9.1	2.0	7.2	6.4	4.7	12.3	-0.9	7.0
Differ From Category (+/-)	1.3	1.2	1.0	0.1	0.8	0.3	0.7	0.7	-0.3	1.0
Return, Tax-Adjusted (%)	5.8	6.5	6.7	-0.2	4.9	4.0	2.3	9.8	-3.0	4.7
Dividends, Net Income ($)	0.43	0.54	0.60	0.56	0.58	0.61	0.61	0.61	0.54	0.52
Expense Ratio (%)	0.31	0.28	0.27	0.27	0.27	0.25	0.27	0.28	0.26	0.27
Yield (%)	3.97	5.15	5.89	5.65	5.65	6.02	6.03	5.95	5.56	4.97
Total Assets (Millions $)	2,799	1,783	1,502	1,521	1,634	1,428	1,337	1,403	1,504	1,921

SHAREHOLDER INFORMATION

Minimum Investment
Initial: $3,000 IRA: $1,000
Subsequent: $100 IRA: $100

Maximum Fees
Load: none 12b-1: none
Other: none

Vanguard Sh Tm Trsy (VFISX)

800-662-7447, 610-436-5152
www.vanguard.com

Government: Short-Term Bond

PERFORMANCE AND PER SHARE DATA **fund inception date: 10/28/91**

	3yr Annual	5yr Annual	10yr Annual	Category Risk Index
Return (%)	8.2	6.7	6.2	1.29—high
Differ From Category (+/-)	0.9 abv av	0.7 abv av	0.6 high	**Avg Mat** 2.7 yrs

	2002	2001	2000	1999	1998	1997	1996	1995	1994	1993
Return (%)	8.0	7.7	8.8	1.8	7.3	6.3	4.3	12.1	-0.4	6.3
Differ From Category (+/-)	1.7	0.3	0.7	-0.1	0.9	0.2	0.3	0.5	0.2	0.3
Return, Tax-Adjusted (%)	6.3	5.7	6.4	-0.3	5.1	4.0	2.0	9.6	-2.4	4.2
Dividends, Net Income ($)	0.41	0.52	0.59	0.52	0.55	0.59	0.58	0.62	0.51	0.49
Expense Ratio (%)	0.29	0.27	0.27	0.27	0.27	0.25	0.27	0.28	0.26	0.26
Yield (%)	3.74	4.93	5.74	5.18	5.29	5.77	5.70	6.00	5.19	4.68
Total Assets (Millions $)	2,166	1,393	1,200	1,234	1,184	998	960	869	703	705

SHAREHOLDER INFORMATION

Minimum Investment
Initial: $3,000 IRA: $1,000
Subsequent: $100 IRA: $100

Maximum Fees
Load: none 12b-1: none
Other: none

Government: Intermediate-Term Bond Funds
Category Performance Ranked by 2002 Returns

Category	Fund (Ticker)	Annual Return (%) 2002	3yr	5yr	10yr	Category Risk	Total Risk
B-GvIT	Amer Cnt Target 2010/Inv (BTTNX)	26.7	19.2	11.3	11.7	high	blw av
B-GvIT	Amer Cnt Target 2005/Inv (BTFIX)	14.6	14.2	11.1	10.6	high	blw av
B-GvIT	Vanguard Int Tm Tsy/Inv (VFITX)	14.1	11.8	8.3	7.8	high	blw av
B-GvIT	T Rowe Price Treas Int (PRTIX)	12.0	10.5	7.5	6.9	high	blw av
B-GvIT	Fidelity Spart Govt Inc (SPGVX)	11.5	10.3	7.5	6.9	av	low
B-GvIT	Fidelity Government Inc (FGOVX)	10.9	10.0	7.1	7.0	av	low
B-GvIT	Amer Cnt Govt Bond/Inv (CPTNX)	10.5	9.9	7.2	6.7	abv av	blw av
B-GvIT	Fidelity Intermed Gvt Inc (FSTGX)	10.2	9.4	7.2	6.7	blw av	low
Gov't: Int-Term Bond Average		**11.0**	**10.2**	**7.4**	**7.1**	**—**	**low**

Note: AAII members who would like performance figures for no-load and low-load mutual funds they own that do not appear in this Guide can access this information on our Web site at www.aaii.com.

Amer Cnt Govt Bond/Inv (CPTNX)

800-345-2021, 816-531-5575
www.americancentury.com

Government: Intermediate-Term Bond

PERFORMANCE AND PER SHARE DATA **fund inception date: 5/16/80**

	3yr Annual	5yr Annual	10yr Annual	Category Risk Index
Return (%)	9.9	7.2	6.7	1.05—abv av
Differ From Category (+/-)	-0.3 av	-0.2 av	-0.4 av	**Avg Mat** 5.7 yrs

	2002	2001	2000	1999	1998	1997	1996	1995	1994	1993
Return (%)	10.5	6.7	12.5	-2.0	8.9	8.3	4.0	13.7	-2.3	7.7
Differ From Category (+/-)	-0.5	-0.2	-0.3	-0.3	0.1	-0.6	1.6	-5.1	2.1	-2.9
Return, Tax-Adjusted (%)	8.5	4.8	10.3	-4.0	6.4	6.0	1.8	11.3	-4.2	5.2
Dividends, Net Income ($)	0.37	0.50	0.55	0.50	0.56	0.59	0.57	0.58	0.50	0.47
Expense Ratio (%)	0.51	0.51	0.51	0.51	0.51	0.51	0.53	0.53	0.51	0.53
Yield (%)	3.20	4.63	5.19	5.01	5.13	5.59	5.52	5.53	5.12	4.35
Total Assets (Millions $)	581	440	351	352	444	361	337	307	296	388

SHAREHOLDER INFORMATION

Minimum Investment
Initial: $2,500 IRA: $1,000
Subsequent: $50 IRA: $50

Maximum Fees
Load: none 12b-1: none
Other: none

Amer Cnt Target 2005/Inv (BTFIX)

800-345-2021, 816-531-5575
www.americancentury.com

Government: Intermediate-Term Bond

PERFORMANCE AND PER SHARE DATA **fund inception date: 3/25/85**

	3yr Annual	5yr Annual	10yr Annual	Category Risk Index
Return (%)	14.2	11.1	10.6	1.55—high
Differ From Category (+/-)	4.0 high	3.7 high	3.5 high	**Avg Mat** 3.1 yrs

	2002	2001	2000	1999	1998	1997	1996	1995	1994	1993
Return (%)	14.6	8.3	19.9	1.2	12.5	11.6	-1.2	32.6	-8.9	21.5
Differ From Category (+/-)	3.6	1.4	7.1	2.9	3.7	2.7	-3.6	13.8	-4.5	10.9
Return, Tax-Adjusted (%)	12.9	6.2	17.3	-1.2	10.0	9.0	-3.9	30.2	-11.7	11.5
Dividends, Net Income ($)	3.91	4.26	4.70	3.88	3.60	3.83	3.87	2.40	2.95	4.82
Expense Ratio (%)	0.59	0.59	0.59	0.59	0.59	0.57	0.58	0.70	0.64	0.62
Yield (%)	4.03	4.83	5.79	5.30	4.66	5.66	6.36	3.89	6.29	8.22
Total Assets (Millions $)	420	339	300	453	527	301	242	228	101	128

SHAREHOLDER INFORMATION

Minimum Investment
Initial: $2,500 IRA: $1,000
Subsequent: $50 IRA: $50

Maximum Fees
Load: none 12b-1: none
Other: none

Amer Cnt Target 2010/Inv (BTTNX)

800-345-2021, 816-531-5575
www.americancentury.com

Government: Intermediate-Term Bond

PERFORMANCE AND PER SHARE DATA **fund inception date: 3/25/85**

	3yr Annual	5yr Annual	10yr Annual	Category Risk Index
Return (%)	19.2	11.3	11.7	2.60—high
Differ From Category (+/-)	9.0 high	3.9 high	4.6 high	**Avg Mat** 8.2 yrs

	2002	2001	2000	1999	1998	1997	1996	1995	1994	1993
Return (%)	26.7	3.9	28.8	-12.1	14.5	16.7	-3.5	41.9	-11.5	26.2
Differ From Category (+/-)	15.7	-3.0	16.0	-10.4	5.7	7.8	-5.9	23.1	-7.1	15.6
Return, Tax-Adjusted (%)	24.1	1.4	26.4	-14.3	11.7	14.3	-6.9	39.9	-13.9	18.6
Dividends, Net Income ($)	3.46	3.94	3.27	3.40	2.98	2.60	3.09	1.65	1.82	3.77
Expense Ratio (%)	0.59	0.59	0.59	0.59	0.59	0.62	0.67	0.70	0.68	0.66
Yield (%)	4.16	5.70	4.98	6.34	4.78	4.89	6.64	3.52	5.42	9.42
Total Assets (Millions $)	293	252	269	219	246	157	109	120	55	60

SHAREHOLDER INFORMATION

Minimum Investment
Initial: $2,500 IRA: $1,000
Subsequent: $50 IRA: $50

Maximum Fees
Load: none 12b-1: none
Other: none

Fidelity Government Inc (FGOVX)

800-544-8544, 800-522-7297
www.fidelity.com

Government: Intermediate-Term Bond

PERFORMANCE AND PER SHARE DATA **fund inception date: 4/4/79**

	3yr Annual	5yr Annual	10yr Annual	Category Risk Index
Return (%)	10.0	7.1	7.0	0.98—av
Differ From Category (+/-)	-0.2 abv av	-0.3 av	-0.1 abv av	**Avg Mat** 9.2 yrs

	2002	2001	2000	1999	1998	1997	1996	1995	1994	1993
Return (%)	10.9	6.7	12.6	-2.2	8.5	8.9	2.0	18.0	-5.2	12.3
Differ From Category (+/-)	-0.1	-0.2	-0.2	-0.5	-0.3	0.0	-0.4	-0.8	-0.8	1.7
Return, Tax-Adjusted (%)	9.0	4.5	10.0	-4.4	6.1	6.4	-0.6	15.4	-7.6	8.8
Dividends, Net Income ($)	0.42	0.55	0.61	0.56	0.60	0.61	0.67	0.61	0.61	0.67
Expense Ratio (%)	0.68	0.60	0.66	0.67	0.68	0.73	0.72	0.71	0.69	0.69
Yield (%)	3.95	5.51	6.18	5.98	5.91	6.15	6.91	5.99	6.63	6.29
Total Assets (Millions $)	3,380	2,402	1,699	1,588	1,583	1,164	972	994	611	753

SHAREHOLDER INFORMATION

Minimum Investment
Initial: $2,500 IRA: $500
Subsequent: $250 IRA: $250

Maximum Fees
Load: none 12b-1: none
Other: none

Fidelity Intermed Gvt Inc (FSTGX)

800-544-8544, 800-522-7297
www.fidelity.com

Government: Intermediate-Term Bond

PERFORMANCE AND PER SHARE DATA **fund inception date: 5/2/88**

	3yr Annual	5yr Annual	10yr Annual	Category Risk Index	
Return (%)	9.4	7.2	6.7	0.76—blw av	
Differ From Category (+/-)	-0.8 av	-0.2 abv av	-0.4 av	**Avg Mat**	5.5 yrs

	2002	2001	2000	1999	1998	1997	1996	1995	1994	1993
Return (%)	10.2	7.9	10.3	0.6	7.4	7.6	4.1	13.9	-0.9	6.4
Differ From Category (+/-)	-0.8	1.0	-2.5	2.3	-1.4	-1.3	1.7	-4.9	3.5	-4.2
Return, Tax-Adjusted (%)	8.6	5.6	7.7	-1.8	4.8	4.8	1.5	11.3	-3.1	3.5
Dividends, Net Income ($)	0.41	0.55	0.61	0.59	0.63	0.68	0.65	0.61	0.55	0.58
Expense Ratio (%)	0.59	0.60	0.61	0.53	0.38	0.54	0.62	0.65	0.65	0.65
Yield (%)	3.94	5.60	6.34	6.33	6.39	6.95	6.67	6.10	5.88	5.66
Total Assets (Millions $)	1,367	918	765	820	759	758	712	829	830	1,356

SHAREHOLDER INFORMATION

Minimum Investment
Initial: $2,500 IRA: $500
Subsequent: $250 IRA: $250

Maximum Fees
Load: none 12b-1: none
Other: none

Fidelity Spart Govt Inc (SPGVX)

800-544-8544, 801-534-1910
www.fidelity.com

Government: Intermediate-Term Bond

PERFORMANCE AND PER SHARE DATA **fund inception date: 12/20/88**

	3yr Annual	5yr Annual	10yr Annual	Category Risk Index	
Return (%)	10.3	7.5	6.9	1.00—av	
Differ From Category (+/-)	0.1 abv av	0.1 abv av	-0.2 abv av	**Avg Mat**	9.6 yrs

	2002	2001	2000	1999	1998	1997	1996	1995	1994	1993
Return (%)	11.5	6.9	12.7	-2.0	9.0	9.2	2.6	18.1	-4.1	7.3
Differ From Category (+/-)	0.5	0.0	-0.1	-0.3	0.2	0.3	0.2	-0.7	0.3	-3.3
Return, Tax-Adjusted (%)	9.6	4.7	10.1	-4.3	6.6	6.7	0.1	15.4	-6.5	4.4
Dividends, Net Income ($)	0.49	0.58	0.65	0.62	0.62	0.64	0.67	0.66	0.65	0.61
Expense Ratio (%)	0.50	0.49	0.50	0.51	0.60	0.60	0.65	0.65	0.65	0.65
Yield (%)	4.33	5.46	6.20	6.25	5.76	6.11	6.56	6.21	6.77	5.57
Total Assets (Millions $)	1,211	874	719	468	642	279	276	249	231	376

SHAREHOLDER INFORMATION

Minimum Investment
Initial: $25,000 IRA: $25,000
Subsequent: $1,000 IRA: $1,000

Maximum Fees
Load: none 12b-1: none
Other: none

T Rowe Price Treas Int (PRTIX)

800-638-5660, 410-345-2000
www.troweprice.com

Government: Intermediate-Term Bond

PERFORMANCE AND PER SHARE DATA **fund inception date: 9/28/89**

	3yr Annual	5yr Annual	10yr Annual	Category Risk Index	
Return (%)	10.5	7.5	6.9	1.14—high	
Differ From Category (+/-)	0.3 high	0.1 high	-0.2 av	**Avg Mat**	5.8 yrs

	2002	2001	2000	1999	1998	1997	1996	1995	1994	1993
Return (%)	12.0	7.5	12.1	-3.2	10.1	8.1	2.3	15.8	-2.2	8.0
Differ From Category (+/-)	1.0	0.6	-0.7	-1.5	1.3	-0.8	-0.1	-3.0	2.2	-2.6
Return, Tax-Adjusted (%)	10.1	5.6	9.8	-5.3	7.7	5.7	0.0	13.2	-4.5	5.7
Dividends, Net Income ($)	0.23	0.25	0.28	0.26	0.28	0.30	0.31	0.32	0.30	0.28
Expense Ratio (%)	0.64	0.65	0.64	0.62	0.61	0.64	0.65	0.69	0.79	0.80
Yield (%)	3.97	4.63	5.32	5.18	5.07	5.68	5.98	5.94	6.04	5.18
Total Assets (Millions $)	382	280	225	244	262	199	193	183	163	171

SHAREHOLDER INFORMATION

Minimum Investment
Initial: $2,500 IRA: $1,000
Subsequent: $100 IRA: $50

Maximum Fees
Load: none 12b-1: none
Other: none

Vanguard Int Tm Tsy/Inv (VFITX)

800-662-7447, 610-436-5152
www.vanguard.com

Government: Intermediate-Term Bond

PERFORMANCE AND PER SHARE DATA **fund inception date: 10/28/91**

	3yr Annual	5yr Annual	10yr Annual	Category Risk Index	
Return (%)	11.8	8.3	7.8	1.17—high	
Differ From Category (+/-)	1.6 high	0.9 high	0.7 high	**Avg Mat**	7.5 yrs

	2002	2001	2000	1999	1998	1997	1996	1995	1994	1993
Return (%)	14.1	7.5	14.0	-3.5	10.6	8.9	1.9	20.4	-4.3	11.4
Differ From Category (+/-)	3.1	0.6	1.2	-1.8	1.8	0.0	-0.5	1.6	0.1	0.8
Return, Tax-Adjusted (%)	11.7	5.3	11.5	-5.7	8.3	6.4	-0.5	17.7	-6.6	8.0
Dividends, Net Income ($)	0.57	0.62	0.64	0.62	0.63	0.64	0.64	0.66	0.59	0.62
Expense Ratio (%)	0.29	0.28	0.27	0.27	0.27	0.25	0.28	0.28	0.26	0.26
Yield (%)	4.76	5.62	5.89	6.12	5.65	5.99	6.14	6.06	6.11	5.57
Total Assets (Millions $)	2,627	1,971	1,761	1,704	1,863	1,505	1,274	1,195	844	984

SHAREHOLDER INFORMATION

Minimum Investment
Initial: $3,000 IRA: $1,000
Subsequent: $100 IRA: $100

Maximum Fees
Load: none 12b-1: none
Other: none

Government: Long-Term Bond Funds
Category Performance Ranked by 2002 Returns

		Annual Return (%)				Category	Total
Category	Fund (Ticker)	2002	3yr	5yr	10yr	Risk	Risk
B-GvLT	Amer Cnt Target 2020/Inv (BTTTX)	36.6	21.5	9.7	12.9	high	abv av
B-GvLT	Amer Cnt Target 2025/Inv (BTTRX)	35.0	22.8	12.2	na	high	abv av
B-GvLT	Amer Cnt Target 2015/Inv (BTFTX)	27.0	19.3	10.6	12.5	high	blw av
B-GvLT	Wasatch-Hoisington:US Trs (WHOSX)	16.8	13.6	8.0	8.0	abv av	blw av
B-GvLT	Vanguard LT Treas/Inv (VUSTX)	16.6	13.3	8.5	9.1	abv av	blw av
B-GvLT	T Rowe Price Treas Long (PRULX)	15.1	12.3	7.8	8.3	av	blw av
B-GvLT	Dreyfus US Treasury Long (DRGBX)	11.4	10.3	6.4	7.3	av	blw av
B-GvLT	INVESCO US Govt Secur/Inv (FBDGX)	9.7	9.8	6.7	7.4	blw av	blw av
Gov't: Long-Term Bond Average		**15.8**	**12.5**	**7.5**	**8.0**	—	**blw av**

Note: AAII members who would like performance figures for no-load and low-load mutual funds they own that do not appear in this Guide can access this information on our Web site at www.aaii.com.

Amer Cnt Target 2015/Inv (BTFTX)

800-345-2021, 816-531-5575
www.americancentury.com

Government: Long-Term Bond

PERFORMANCE AND PER SHARE DATA **fund inception date: 9/1/86**

	3yr Annual	5yr Annual	10yr Annual	Category Risk Index
Return (%)	19.3	10.6	12.5	1.67—high
Differ From Category (+/-)	6.8 high	3.1 high	4.5 high	**Avg Mat** 15.4 yrs

	2002	2001	2000	1999	1998	1997	1996	1995	1994	1993
Return (%)	27.0	0.2	33.5	-14.9	14.4	22.9	-6.0	51.7	-14.0	30.5
Differ From Category (+/-)	11.2	-1.9	12.4	-5.8	2.5	7.9	-5.6	25.0	-8.8	16.1
Return, Tax-Adjusted (%)	24.9	-2.2	30.8	-17.0	12.3	19.4	-8.6	47.0	-15.0	12.6
Dividends, Net Income ($)	2.84	3.22	2.80	2.60	2.19	2.29	2.19	2.48	0.74	5.41
Expense Ratio (%)	0.59	0.59	0.59	0.59	0.59	0.61	0.65	0.70	0.68	0.63
Yield (%)	4.40	6.06	5.31	6.24	4.48	5.19	6.26	6.63	3.06	15.85
Total Assets (Millions $)	156	130	159	200	178	133	117	140	123	74

SHAREHOLDER INFORMATION

Minimum Investment
Initial: $2,500 IRA: $1,000
Subsequent: $50 IRA: $50

Maximum Fees
Load: none 12b-1: none
Other: none

Amer Cnt Target 2020/Inv (BTTTX)

800-345-2021, 816-531-5575
www.americancentury.com

Government: Long-Term Bond

PERFORMANCE AND PER SHARE DATA **fund inception date: 12/29/89**

	3yr Annual	5yr Annual	10yr Annual	Category Risk Index
Return (%)	21.5	9.7	12.9	2.69—high
Differ From Category (+/-)	9.0 high	2.2 high	4.9 high	**Avg Mat** 20.2 yrs

	2002	2001	2000	1999	1998	1997	1996	1995	1994	1993
Return (%)	36.6	-11.2	48.0	-20.7	12.0	28.6	-8.4	61.2	-17.6	35.6
Differ From Category (+/-)	20.8	-13.3	26.9	-11.6	0.1	13.6	-8.0	34.5	-12.4	21.2
Return, Tax-Adjusted (%)	32.6	-15.2	43.4	-25.3	4.5	21.9	-10.7	59.8	-18.2	25.7
Dividends, Net Income ($)	2.13	2.98	1.79	2.21	2.57	2.76	1.54	0.57	0.27	2.33
Expense Ratio (%)	0.59	0.59	0.59	0.59	0.59	0.53	0.61	0.70	0.70	0.70
Yield (%)	4.31	7.51	4.30	6.62	6.04	8.24	6.40	2.17	1.65	10.79
Total Assets (Millions $)	189	192	304	270	423	599	889	726	125	48

SHAREHOLDER INFORMATION

Minimum Investment
Initial: $2,500 IRA: $1,000
Subsequent: $50 IRA: $50

Maximum Fees
Load: none 12b-1: none
Other: none

Amer Cnt Target 2025/Inv (BTTRX)

800-345-2021, 816-531-5575
www.americancentury.com

Government: Long-Term Bond

PERFORMANCE AND PER SHARE DATA **fund inception date: 2/15/96**

	3yr Annual	5yr Annual	10yr Annual	Category Risk Index
Return (%)	22.8	12.2	na	2.60—high
Differ From Category (+/-)	10.3 high	4.7 high	na	**Avg Mat** 25.0 yrs

	2002	2001	2000	1999	1998	1997	1996	1995	1994	1993
Return (%)	35.0	-3.7	42.6	-20.8	21.6	29.9	—	—	—	—
Differ From Category (+/-)	19.2	-5.8	21.5	-11.7	9.7	14.9	—	—	—	—
Return, Tax-Adjusted (%)	31.0	-7.1	39.1	-22.3	19.3	28.4	—	—	—	—
Dividends, Net Income ($)	2.06	2.50	1.99	1.16	1.34	0.72	—	—	—	—
Expense Ratio (%)	0.59	0.59	0.59	0.59	0.59	0.62	—	—	—	—
Yield (%)	5.05	7.68	6.00	4.70	4.26	2.81	—	—	—	—
Total Assets (Millions $)	185	244	592	696	303	193	—	—	—	—

SHAREHOLDER INFORMATION

Minimum Investment
Initial: $2,500 IRA: $1,000
Subsequent: $50 IRA: $50

Maximum Fees
Load: none 12b-1: none
Other: none

Dreyfus US Treasury Long (DRGBX)

800-645-6561, 516-794-5452
www.dreyfus.com

Government: Long-Term Bond

PERFORMANCE AND PER SHARE DATA **fund inception date: 3/27/87**

	3yr Annual	5yr Annual	10yr Annual	Category Risk Index
Return (%)	10.3	6.4	7.3	0.90—av
Differ From Category (+/-)	-2.2 av	-1.1 blw av	-0.7 av	**Avg Mat** 19.3 yrs

	2002	2001	2000	1999	1998	1997	1996	1995	1994	1993
Return (%)	11.4	2.5	17.7	-8.2	10.8	11.6	0.8	24.9	-9.1	16.5
Differ From Category (+/-)	-4.4	0.4	-3.4	0.9	-1.1	-3.4	1.2	-1.8	-3.9	2.1
Return, Tax-Adjusted (%)	9.6	0.5	15.4	-10.2	8.7	9.1	-1.7	22.0	-11.6	13.7
Dividends, Net Income ($)	0.71	0.78	0.81	0.81	0.79	0.93	0.98	0.96	1.00	1.02
Expense Ratio (%)	na	0.80	0.80	0.80	0.80	0.80	0.80	0.93	0.98	0.78
Yield (%)	4.38	5.13	5.19	5.78	4.90	6.07	6.70	6.19	7.54	6.50
Total Assets (Millions $)	98	108	116	121	142	133	136	145	124	215

SHAREHOLDER INFORMATION

Minimum Investment
Initial: $2,500 IRA: na
Subsequent: $100 IRA: na

Maximum Fees
Load: none 12b-1: none
Other: none

INVESCO US Govt Secur/Inv (FBDGX)

800-525-8085
www.invesco.com

Government: Long-Term Bond ***this fund is closed to new investors***

PERFORMANCE AND PER SHARE DATA **fund inception date: 1/2/86**

	3yr Annual	5yr Annual	10yr Annual	Category Risk Index
Return (%)	9.8	6.7	7.4	0.56—blw av
Differ From Category (+/-)	-2.7 blw av	-0.8 av	-0.6 av	**Avg Mat** 21.4 yrs

	2002	2001	2000	1999	1998	1997	1996	1995	1994	1993
Return (%)	9.7	5.4	14.6	-5.3	10.1	12.2	0.4	22.1	-2.2	10.3
Differ From Category (+/-)	-6.1	3.3	-6.5	3.8	-1.8	-2.8	0.8	-4.6	3.0	-4.1
Return, Tax-Adjusted (%)	7.9	3.6	12.4	-7.5	6.5	9.5	-1.8	19.5	-6.2	7.5
Dividends, Net Income ($)	0.26	0.33	0.36	0.41	0.38	0.43	0.42	0.44	0.79	0.42
Expense Ratio (%)	1.00	1.00	1.02	1.01	1.01	1.01	1.02	1.00	1.32	1.40
Yield (%)	3.35	4.50	4.95	6.13	4.70	5.47	5.66	5.61	11.60	5.28
Total Assets (Millions $)	162	127	96	76	71	53	57	45	31	34

SHAREHOLDER INFORMATION

Minimum Investment
Initial: $1,000 IRA: $250
Subsequent: $50 IRA: $50

Maximum Fees
Load: none 12b-1: 0.25%
Other: none

T Rowe Price Treas Long (PRULX)

800-638-5660, 410-345-2000
www.troweprice.com

Government: Long-Term Bond

PERFORMANCE AND PER SHARE DATA **fund inception date: 9/28/89**

	3yr Annual	5yr Annual	10yr Annual	Category Risk Index
Return (%)	12.3	7.8	8.3	1.00—av
Differ From Category (+/-)	-0.2 av	0.3 abv av	0.3 abv av	**Avg Mat** 15.6 yrs

	2002	2001	2000	1999	1998	1997	1996	1995	1994	1993
Return (%)	15.1	3.4	19.1	-8.7	12.8	14.7	-2.3	28.5	-5.7	12.9
Differ From Category (+/-)	-0.7	1.3	-2.0	0.4	0.9	-0.3	-1.9	1.8	-0.5	-1.5
Return, Tax-Adjusted (%)	13.0	1.4	16.7	-10.9	10.5	12.3	-4.5	25.7	-8.2	9.5
Dividends, Net Income ($)	0.57	0.59	0.61	0.62	0.62	0.63	0.63	0.65	0.68	0.67
Expense Ratio (%)	0.66	0.63	0.64	0.66	0.67	0.80	0.80	0.80	0.80	0.80
Yield (%)	4.60	5.22	5.30	6.00	5.14	5.59	6.04	5.72	7.21	6.09
Total Assets (Millions $)	290	306	314	324	309	206	73	71	58	57

SHAREHOLDER INFORMATION

Minimum Investment
Initial: $2,500 IRA: $1,000
Subsequent: $100 IRA: $50

Maximum Fees
Load: none 12b-1: none
Other: none

Vanguard LT Treas/Inv (VUSTX)

800-662-7447, 610-436-5152
www.vanguard.com

Government: Long-Term Bond

PERFORMANCE AND PER SHARE DATA **fund inception date: 5/19/86**

	3yr Annual	5yr Annual	10yr Annual	Category Risk Index
Return (%)	13.3	8.5	9.1	1.05—abv av
Differ From Category (+/-)	0.8 abv av	1.0 abv av	1.1 high	**Avg Mat** 18.5 yrs

	2002	2001	2000	1999	1998	1997	1996	1995	1994	1993
Return (%)	16.6	4.3	19.7	-8.6	13.0	13.9	-1.2	30.0	-7.0	16.7
Differ From Category (+/-)	0.8	2.2	-1.4	0.5	1.1	-1.1	-0.8	3.3	-1.8	2.3
Return, Tax-Adjusted (%)	14.2	2.1	17.1	-10.9	10.6	11.3	-3.6	26.4	-9.8	13.4
Dividends, Net Income ($)	0.58	0.60	0.62	0.61	0.63	0.64	0.65	0.67	0.66	0.68
Expense Ratio (%)	0.29	0.29	0.28	0.27	0.27	0.25	0.27	0.28	0.26	0.27
Yield (%)	4.86	5.57	5.68	6.23	5.54	6.01	6.51	6.08	7.20	6.33
Total Assets (Millions $)	1,607	1,372	1,357	1,223	1,415	1,035	918	917	644	823

SHAREHOLDER INFORMATION

Minimum Investment
Initial: $3,000 IRA: $1,000
Subsequent: $100 IRA: $100

Maximum Fees
Load: none 12b-1: none
Other: none

Wasatch-Hoisington:US Trs (WHOSX)

800-551-1700, 801-533-0777
www.wasatchfunds.com

Government: Long-Term Bond

PERFORMANCE AND PER SHARE DATA **fund inception date: 12/19/86**

	3yr Annual	5yr Annual	10yr Annual	Category Risk Index
Return (%)	13.6	8.0	8.0	1.41—abv av
Differ From Category (+/-)	1.1 abv av	0.5 abv av	0.0 abv av	**Avg Mat** 25.1 yrs

	2002	2001	2000	1999	1998	1997	1996	1995	1994	1993
Return (%)	16.8	2.8	21.9	-12.3	14.6	15.7	7.8	11.4	1.5	3.9
Differ From Category (+/-)	1.0	0.7	0.8	-3.2	2.7	0.7	8.2	-15.3	6.7	-10.5
Return, Tax-Adjusted (%)	14.8	0.4	19.8	-14.5	13.5	13.6	5.8	9.5	-0.8	2.0
Dividends, Net Income ($)	0.63	0.77	0.55	0.72	0.28	0.56	0.51	0.45	0.58	0.46
Expense Ratio (%)	0.75	0.75	0.75	0.75	0.75	0.75	0.93	1.00	1.00	1.00
Yield (%)	4.72	6.44	4.44	6.79	2.15	4.83	4.86	4.40	6.06	4.59
Total Assets (Millions $)	74	58	63	65	88	13	9	4	2	3

SHAREHOLDER INFORMATION

Minimum Investment
Initial: $2,000 IRA: $1,000
Subsequent: $1 IRA: $1

Maximum Fees
Load: 2.00% redemption 12b-1: none
Other: redemption fee applies for 2 months

General Bond Funds

Category Performance Ranked by 2002 Returns

		Annual Return (%)				Category	Total
Category	Fund (Ticker)	2002	3yr	5yr	10yr	Risk	Risk
B-Gen	Vanguard LT Bd Idx (VBLTX)	14.3	12.8	8.2	na	high	blw av
B-Gen	Vanguard Int Tm Bd (VBIIX)	10.8	10.9	7.8	na	high	blw av
B-Gen	Dodge & Cox Income (DODIX)	10.7	10.5	7.7	7.9	blw av	low
B-Gen	Harbor Bond/Inst (HABDX)	10.6	10.3	7.9	8.0	abv av	low
B-Gen	Fidelity Spart Inv Grade (FSIBX)	9.5	9.7	7.3	7.6	av	low
B-Gen	Fremont:Bond (FBDFX)	9.4	10.3	7.8	na	high	low
B-Gen	Fidelity Invest Grade Bd (FBNDX)	9.3	9.5	7.0	7.2	av	low
B-Gen	Fidelity Intermed Bond (FTHRX)	9.1	9.2	7.1	6.9	blw av	low
B-Gen	Schwab Inv Tot Bd Mkt (SWLBX)	8.7	9.3	7.0	na	abv av	low
B-Gen	Vanguard Tot Bd Mkt (VBMFX)	8.2	9.3	7.1	7.2	av	low
B-Gen	T Rowe Price New Inc (PRCIX)	7.4	8.9	5.9	6.5	av	low
B-Gen	Fidelity Short Tm Bond (FSHBX)	6.7	7.3	6.3	5.6	low	low
B-Gen	Schwab Inv Sh Tm Bd Mkt (SWBDX)	6.5	7.6	6.2	5.7	blw av	low
B-Gen	Vanguard Sh Tm Bd Idx (VBISX)	6.1	7.9	6.6	na	blw av	low
B-Gen	T Rowe Price Sht Tm Bond (PRWBX)	5.3	7.4	6.1	5.3	low	low
B-Gen	Strong Ul Sh Trm Inc/Inv (STADX)	0.5	3.8	4.2	5.3	low	low
General Bond Average		**7.2**	**8.0**	**6.2**	**6.4**	**—**	**low**

Note: AAII members who would like performance figures for no-load and low-load mutual funds they own that do not appear in this Guide can access this information on our Web site at www.aaii.com.

Dodge & Cox Income (DODIX)

800-621-3979, 415-981-1710
www.dodgeandcox.com

General Bond

PERFORMANCE AND PER SHARE DATA — **fund inception date: 1/2/89**

	3yr Annual	5yr Annual	10yr Annual	Category Risk Index
Return (%)	10.5	7.7	7.9	0.94—blw av
Differ From Category (+/-)	2.5 high	1.5 high	1.5 high	**Avg Mat** 11.1 yrs

	2002	2001	2000	1999	1998	1997	1996	1995	1994	1993
Return (%)	10.7	10.3	10.7	-0.8	8.0	10.0	3.6	20.2	-2.8	11.3
Differ From Category (+/-)	3.5	2.9	1.2	-1.1	0.9	1.8	-0.3	4.2	-0.3	1.2
Return, Tax-Adjusted (%)	8.5	7.8	8.0	-3.2	5.5	7.5	1.2	17.1	-5.4	8.2
Dividends, Net Income ($)	0.66	0.74	0.78	0.71	0.72	0.73	0.74	0.81	0.76	0.78
Expense Ratio (%)	na	0.45	0.46	0.46	0.47	0.49	0.50	0.54	0.54	0.60
Yield (%)	5.14	6.04	6.61	6.20	5.84	6.04	6.33	6.72	7.04	6.46
Total Assets (Millions $)	3,141	1,512	1,020	973	952	705	532	303	195	180

SHAREHOLDER INFORMATION

Minimum Investment
Initial: $2,500 IRA: $1,000
Subsequent: $100 IRA: $100

Maximum Fees
Load: none 12b-1: none
Other: none

Fidelity Intermed Bond (FTHRX)

800-544-8544, 800-522-7297
www.fidelity.com

General Bond

PERFORMANCE AND PER SHARE DATA — **fund inception date: 5/23/75**

	3yr Annual	5yr Annual	10yr Annual	Category Risk Index
Return (%)	9.2	7.1	6.9	0.88—blw av
Differ From Category (+/-)	1.2 abv av	0.9 high	0.5 abv av	**Avg Mat** 6.1 yrs

	2002	2001	2000	1999	1998	1997	1996	1995	1994	1993
Return (%)	9.1	8.8	9.7	0.9	7.3	7.5	3.7	12.8	-1.9	12.2
Differ From Category (+/-)	1.9	1.4	0.2	0.6	0.2	-0.7	-0.2	-3.2	0.6	2.1
Return, Tax-Adjusted (%)	7.2	6.5	7.1	-1.4	4.9	5.0	1.1	10.2	-4.5	9.0
Dividends, Net Income ($)	0.50	0.58	0.63	0.60	0.62	0.64	0.67	0.64	0.64	0.78
Expense Ratio (%)	0.63	0.63	0.66	0.65	0.65	0.71	0.71	0.68	0.64	0.61
Yield (%)	4.65	5.62	6.27	6.14	6.03	6.29	6.62	6.14	6.45	7.17
Total Assets (Millions $)	6,247	4,807	3,469	3,253	3,443	3,193	3,079	2,821	2,127	1,840

SHAREHOLDER INFORMATION

Minimum Investment
Initial: $2,500 IRA: $500
Subsequent: $250 IRA: $250

Maximum Fees
Load: none 12b-1: none
Other: none

Fidelity Invest Grade Bd (FBNDX)

800-544-8544, 800-522-7297
www.fidelity.com

General Bond

PERFORMANCE AND PER SHARE DATA **fund inception date: 8/6/71**

	3yr Annual	5yr Annual	10yr Annual	Category Risk Index
Return (%)	9.5	7.0	7.2	1.03—av
Differ From Category (+/-)	1.5 high	0.8 high	0.8 high	**Avg Mat** 9.7 yrs

	2002	2001	2000	1999	1998	1997	1996	1995	1994	1993
Return (%)	9.3	8.5	10.8	-1.0	7.9	8.9	3.0	15.5	-5.2	16.2
Differ From Category (+/-)	2.1	1.1	1.3	-1.3	0.8	0.7	-0.9	-0.5	-2.7	6.1
Return, Tax-Adjusted (%)	7.3	6.2	8.2	-3.3	5.5	6.4	0.5	12.7	-8.2	13.1
Dividends, Net Income ($)	0.31	0.40	0.44	0.42	0.42	0.45	0.46	0.47	0.50	0.56
Expense Ratio (%)	0.66	0.64	0.69	0.70	0.72	0.76	0.76	0.75	0.74	0.68
Yield (%)	4.03	5.44	6.14	6.09	5.66	6.18	6.46	6.34	7.17	7.09
Total Assets (Millions $)	4,766	3,701	2,497	2,079	2,191	1,649	1,455	1,245	995	1,042

SHAREHOLDER INFORMATION

Minimum Investment
Initial: $2,500 IRA: $500
Subsequent: $250 IRA: $250

Maximum Fees
Load: none 12b-1: none
Other: none

Fidelity Short Tm Bond (FSHBX)

800-544-8544, 800-522-7297
www.fidelity.com

General Bond

PERFORMANCE AND PER SHARE DATA **fund inception date: 9/15/86**

	3yr Annual	5yr Annual	10yr Annual	Category Risk Index
Return (%)	7.3	6.3	5.6	0.52—low
Differ From Category (+/-)	-0.7 blw av	0.1 av	-0.8 blw av	**Avg Mat** 2.4 yrs

	2002	2001	2000	1999	1998	1997	1996	1995	1994	1993
Return (%)	6.7	7.6	7.8	3.2	6.1	6.2	4.7	9.8	-4.0	9.1
Differ From Category (+/-)	-0.5	0.2	-1.7	2.9	-1.0	-2.0	0.8	-6.2	-1.5	-1.0
Return, Tax-Adjusted (%)	5.0	5.5	5.4	1.0	3.8	3.7	2.2	7.3	-6.4	6.3
Dividends, Net Income ($)	0.38	0.46	0.52	0.48	0.51	0.54	0.56	0.54	0.57	0.66
Expense Ratio (%)	0.58	0.58	0.63	0.65	0.70	0.70	0.68	0.69	0.80	0.77
Yield (%)	4.22	5.22	6.03	5.64	5.85	6.20	6.42	6.08	6.62	6.91
Total Assets (Millions $)	5,194	3,338	1,773	1,333	841	875	995	1,196	1,514	2,469

SHAREHOLDER INFORMATION

Minimum Investment
Initial: $2,500 IRA: $500
Subsequent: $250 IRA: $250

Maximum Fees
Load: none 12b-1: none
Other: none

Fidelity Spart Inv Grade (FSIBX)

800-544-8544, 801-534-1910
www.fidelity.com

General Bond

PERFORMANCE AND PER SHARE DATA **fund inception date: 9/30/92**

	3yr Annual	5yr Annual	10yr Annual	Category Risk Index
Return (%)	9.7	7.3	7.6	1.03—av
Differ From Category (+/-)	1.7 high	1.1 high	1.2 high	**Avg Mat** 9.7 yrs

	2002	2001	2000	1999	1998	1997	1996	1995	1994	1993
Return (%)	9.5	8.7	11.0	-0.7	8.7	9.2	3.1	18.6	-5.1	15.7
Differ From Category (+/-)	2.3	1.3	1.5	-1.0	1.6	1.0	-0.8	2.6	-2.6	5.6
Return, Tax-Adjusted (%)	7.3	6.3	8.4	-3.0	6.1	6.7	0.7	15.8	-7.8	12.6
Dividends, Net Income ($)	0.49	0.59	0.65	0.62	0.63	0.64	0.63	0.65	0.70	0.78
Expense Ratio (%)	0.50	0.50	0.50	0.47	0.38	0.48	0.65	0.65	0.65	0.65
Yield (%)	4.48	5.61	6.35	6.30	5.93	6.17	6.23	6.22	7.42	7.29
Total Assets (Millions $)	2,652	2,680	1,892	1,553	1,261	658	359	161	118	120

SHAREHOLDER INFORMATION

Minimum Investment
Initial: $25,000 IRA: $1
Subsequent: $1,000 IRA: $1

Maximum Fees
Load: none 12b-1: none
Other: none

Fremont:Bond (FBDFX)

800-548-4539, 800-565-0254
www.fremontfunds.com

General Bond

PERFORMANCE AND PER SHARE DATA **fund inception date: 4/30/93**

	3yr Annual	5yr Annual	10yr Annual	Category Risk Index
Return (%)	10.3	7.8	na	1.15—high
Differ From Category (+/-)	2.3 high	1.6 high	na	**Avg Mat** 7.3 yrs

	2002	2001	2000	1999	1998	1997	1996	1995	1994	1993
Return (%)	9.4	9.7	11.7	-1.2	9.9	9.7	5.0	21.2	-4.0	—
Differ From Category (+/-)	2.2	2.3	2.2	-1.5	2.8	1.5	1.1	5.2	-1.5	—
Return, Tax-Adjusted (%)	7.5	7.0	9.1	-3.5	6.9	6.9	2.4	17.6	-6.2	—
Dividends, Net Income ($)	0.35	0.57	0.62	0.58	0.61	0.64	0.66	0.67	0.55	—
Expense Ratio (%)	na	0.57	0.60	0.60	0.60	0.61	0.68	0.60	0.66	—
Yield (%)	3.28	5.51	6.21	6.09	5.81	6.25	6.63	6.46	6.01	—
Total Assets (Millions $)	1,163	783	297	174	215	109	72	93	59	—

SHAREHOLDER INFORMATION

Minimum Investment
Initial: $2,000 IRA: $1,000
Subsequent: $100 IRA: $100

Maximum Fees
Load: none 12b-1: none
Other: none

Harbor Bond/Inst (HABDX)

800-422-1050, 419-247-2477
www.harborfund.com

General Bond

PERFORMANCE AND PER SHARE DATA **fund inception date: 12/29/87**

	3yr Annual	5yr Annual	10yr Annual	Category Risk Index	
Return (%)	10.3	7.9	8.0	1.09—abv av	
Differ From Category (+/-)	2.3 high	1.7 high	1.6 high	**Avg Mat**	8.9 yrs

	2002	2001	2000	1999	1998	1997	1996	1995	1994	1993
Return (%)	10.6	9.0	11.3	-0.3	9.5	9.3	4.9	19.1	-3.7	12.4
Differ From Category (+/-)	3.4	1.6	1.8	-0.6	2.4	1.1	1.0	3.1	-1.2	2.3
Return, Tax-Adjusted (%)	7.9	6.7	9.1	-2.3	6.4	6.5	2.5	16.1	-5.8	8.8
Dividends, Net Income ($)	0.65	0.53	0.55	0.56	0.63	0.66	0.70	0.78	0.60	0.64
Expense Ratio (%)	na	0.56	0.60	0.61	0.65	0.67	0.70	0.76	0.77	0.72
Yield (%)	5.43	4.53	4.86	5.24	5.34	5.68	6.22	6.83	5.83	5.41
Total Assets (Millions $)	1,377	1,005	787	618	494	384	288	233	167	171

SHAREHOLDER INFORMATION

Minimum Investment
Initial: $1,000 IRA: $500
Subsequent: $100 IRA: $100

Maximum Fees
Load: none 12b-1: none
Other: none

Schwab Inv Sh Tm Bd Mkt (SWBDX)

800-435-4000, 800-266-5623
www.schwab.com

General Bond

PERFORMANCE AND PER SHARE DATA **fund inception date: 11/5/91**

	3yr Annual	5yr Annual	10yr Annual	Category Risk Index	
Return (%)	7.6	6.2	5.7	0.67—blw av	
Differ From Category (+/-)	-0.4 blw av	0.0 av	-0.7 blw av	**Avg Mat**	3.3 yrs

	2002	2001	2000	1999	1998	1997	1996	1995	1994	1993
Return (%)	6.5	7.3	9.1	1.5	6.9	6.8	4.0	10.9	-2.7	7.8
Differ From Category (+/-)	-0.7	-0.1	-0.4	1.2	-0.2	-1.4	0.1	-5.1	-0.2	-2.3
Return, Tax-Adjusted (%)	4.8	5.1	6.6	-0.5	4.7	4.4	1.6	8.4	-4.8	5.3
Dividends, Net Income ($)	0.45	0.55	0.59	0.50	0.53	0.58	0.59	0.60	0.54	0.55
Expense Ratio (%)	0.35	0.35	0.35	0.35	0.46	0.49	0.49	0.58	0.60	0.60
Yield (%)	4.42	5.50	5.99	5.21	5.32	5.90	6.05	6.02	5.65	5.23
Total Assets (Millions $)	563	388	256	215	173	138	131	156	159	271

SHAREHOLDER INFORMATION

Minimum Investment
Initial: $2,500 IRA: $500
Subsequent: $500 IRA: $100

Maximum Fees
Load: none 12b-1: none
Other: none

Schwab Inv Tot Bd Mkt (SWLBX)

800-435-4000, 800-266-5623
www.schwab.com

General Bond

PERFORMANCE AND PER SHARE DATA **fund inception date: 3/5/93**

	3yr Annual	5yr Annual	10yr Annual	Category Risk Index
Return (%)	9.3	7.0	na	1.06—abv av
Differ From Category (+/-)	1.3 abv av	0.8 abv av	na	**Avg Mat** 11.3 yrs

	2002	2001	2000	1999	1998	1997	1996	1995	1994	1993
Return (%)	8.7	8.2	11.0	-1.0	8.4	9.9	1.0	22.4	-5.7	—
Differ From Category (+/-)	1.5	0.8	1.5	-1.3	1.3	1.7	-2.9	6.4	-3.2	—
Return, Tax-Adjusted (%)	6.8	5.7	8.4	-3.2	6.0	7.3	-1.5	19.4	-8.2	—
Dividends, Net Income ($)	0.43	0.56	0.62	0.55	0.58	0.63	0.65	0.67	0.63	—
Expense Ratio (%)	0.35	0.35	0.35	0.35	0.31	0.20	0.00	0.00	0.10	—
Yield (%)	4.13	5.52	6.25	5.77	5.66	6.29	6.69	6.51	7.00	—
Total Assets (Millions $)	1,047	963	743	551	341	94	21	15	8	—

SHAREHOLDER INFORMATION

Minimum Investment
Initial: $2,500 IRA: $500
Subsequent: $500 IRA: $100

Maximum Fees
Load: none 12b-1: none
Other: none

Strong Ul Sh Trm Inc/Inv (STADX)

800-368-3863, 414-359-1400
www.strong-funds.com

General Bond

PERFORMANCE AND PER SHARE DATA **fund inception date: 11/25/88**

	3yr Annual	5yr Annual	10yr Annual	Category Risk Index
Return (%)	3.8	4.2	5.3	0.42—low
Differ From Category (+/-)	-4.2 low	-2.0 low	-1.1 low	**Avg Mat** na

	2002	2001	2000	1999	1998	1997	1996	1995	1994	1993
Return (%)	0.5	4.2	6.7	5.2	4.7	6.5	6.6	7.5	3.5	7.8
Differ From Category (+/-)	-6.7	-3.2	-2.8	4.9	-2.4	-1.7	2.7	-8.5	6.0	-2.3
Return, Tax-Adjusted (%)	-1.0	2.0	4.1	2.9	2.4	4.0	4.2	4.9	1.3	5.5
Dividends, Net Income ($)	0.38	0.55	0.63	0.58	0.59	0.62	0.61	0.66	0.54	0.59
Expense Ratio (%)	0.80	0.80	0.80	0.70	0.80	0.80	0.80	0.80	0.80	0.90
Yield (%)	4.03	5.64	6.37	5.87	5.92	6.15	6.05	6.57	5.40	5.78
Total Assets (Millions $)	2,037	3,002	2,115	2,266	2,631	2,040	1,417	989	910	415

SHAREHOLDER INFORMATION

Minimum Investment
Initial: $2,500 IRA: $250
Subsequent: $100 IRA: $50

Maximum Fees
Load: none 12b-1: none
Other: none

T Rowe Price New Inc (PRCIX)

800-638-5660, 410-345-2000
www.troweprice.com

General Bond

PERFORMANCE AND PER SHARE DATA **fund inception date: 10/15/73**

	3yr Annual	5yr Annual	10yr Annual	Category Risk Index
Return (%)	8.9	5.9	6.5	1.03—av
Differ From Category (+/-)	0.9 abv av	-0.3 blw av	0.1 abv av	**Avg Mat** 9.9 yrs

	2002	2001	2000	1999	1998	1997	1996	1995	1994	1993
Return (%)	7.4	8.1	11.1	-1.5	5.0	8.9	2.3	18.3	-2.1	9.5
Differ From Category (+/-)	0.2	0.7	1.6	-1.8	-2.1	0.7	-1.6	2.3	0.4	-0.6
Return, Tax-Adjusted (%)	5.5	5.8	8.5	-3.8	1.9	6.3	-0.2	15.4	-4.9	6.8
Dividends, Net Income ($)	0.42	0.49	0.53	0.51	0.70	0.58	0.59	0.60	0.64	0.60
Expense Ratio (%)	0.72	0.73	0.73	0.72	0.71	0.74	0.75	0.78	0.82	0.84
Yield (%)	4.72	5.64	6.23	6.25	7.94	6.39	6.63	6.46	7.62	6.49
Total Assets (Millions $)	1,968	1,802	1,715	1,795	2,103	1,945	1,688	1,668	1,367	1,562

SHAREHOLDER INFORMATION

Minimum Investment
Initial: $2,500 IRA: $100
Subsequent: $100 IRA: $50

Maximum Fees
Load: none 12b-1: none
Other: none

T Rowe Price Sht Tm Bond (PRWBX)

800-638-5660, 410-345-2000
www.troweprice.com

General Bond

PERFORMANCE AND PER SHARE DATA **fund inception date: 3/2/84**

	3yr Annual	5yr Annual	10yr Annual	Category Risk Index
Return (%)	7.4	6.1	5.3	0.52—low
Differ From Category (+/-)	-0.6 blw av	-0.1 av	-1.1 low	**Avg Mat** 2.2 yrs

	2002	2001	2000	1999	1998	1997	1996	1995	1994	1993
Return (%)	5.3	8.4	8.4	2.2	6.1	6.2	3.9	9.7	-2.9	6.5
Differ From Category (+/-)	-1.9	1.0	-1.1	1.9	-1.0	-2.0	0.0	-6.3	-0.4	-3.6
Return, Tax-Adjusted (%)	3.5	6.2	6.0	0.1	3.9	3.9	1.6	7.2	-5.1	4.0
Dividends, Net Income ($)	0.21	0.26	0.27	0.25	0.26	0.27	0.27	0.29	0.27	0.31
Expense Ratio (%)	0.55	0.59	0.72	0.73	0.72	0.74	0.72	0.79	0.74	0.76
Yield (%)	4.37	5.45	5.80	5.49	5.53	5.76	5.78	6.07	5.83	6.13
Total Assets (Millions $)	874	598	466	304	346	344	446	464	474	681

SHAREHOLDER INFORMATION

Minimum Investment
Initial: $2,500 IRA: $1,000
Subsequent: $100 IRA: $50

Maximum Fees
Load: none 12b-1: none
Other: none

Vanguard Int Tm Bd
(VBIIX)

800-662-7447, 610-436-5152
www.vanguard.com

General Bond

PERFORMANCE AND PER SHARE DATA **fund inception date: 3/1/94**

	3yr Annual	5yr Annual	10yr Annual	Category Risk Index
Return (%)	10.9	7.8	na	1.39—high
Differ From Category (+/-)	2.9 high	1.6 high	na	**Avg Mat** 7.8 yrs

	2002	2001	2000	1999	1998	1997	1996	1995	1994	1993
Return (%)	10.8	9.2	12.7	-3.0	10.0	9.4	2.5	21.0	—	—
Differ From Category (+/-)	3.6	1.8	3.2	-3.3	2.9	1.2	-1.4	5.0	—	—
Return, Tax-Adjusted (%)	8.5	6.7	10.0	-5.4	7.3	6.8	0.0	18.1	—	—
Dividends, Net Income ($)	0.59	0.65	0.65	0.62	0.64	0.66	0.64	0.66	—	—
Expense Ratio (%)	na	0.21	0.21	0.20	0.20	0.20	0.20	0.20	—	—
Yield (%)	5.48	6.32	6.48	6.49	6.06	6.47	6.42	6.35	—	—
Total Assets (Millions $)	2,350	2,096	1,641	1,448	1,102	686	460	345	—	—

SHAREHOLDER INFORMATION

Minimum Investment
Initial: $3,000 IRA: $1,000
Subsequent: $100 IRA: $100

Maximum Fees
Load: none 12b-1: none
Other: none

Vanguard LT Bd Idx
(VBLTX)

800-662-7447, 610-436-5152
www.vanguard.com

General Bond

PERFORMANCE AND PER SHARE DATA **fund inception date: 3/1/94**

	3yr Annual	5yr Annual	10yr Annual	Category Risk Index
Return (%)	12.8	8.2	na	2.15—high
Differ From Category (+/-)	4.8 high	2.0 high	na	**Avg Mat** 22.9 yrs

	2002	2001	2000	1999	1998	1997	1996	1995	1994	1993
Return (%)	14.3	8.0	16.4	-7.8	11.9	14.2	-0.2	29.7	—	—
Differ From Category (+/-)	7.1	0.6	6.9	-8.1	4.8	6.0	-4.1	13.7	—	—
Return, Tax-Adjusted (%)	12.0	5.5	13.7	-10.1	9.4	11.5	-2.7	26.6	—	—
Dividends, Net Income ($)	0.65	0.67	0.66	0.66	0.66	0.67	0.67	0.69	—	—
Expense Ratio (%)	na	0.21	0.21	0.20	0.20	0.20	0.20	0.18	—	—
Yield (%)	5.56	6.18	6.19	6.74	5.80	6.21	6.64	6.36	—	—
Total Assets (Millions $)	749	542	416	313	210	87	44	24	—	—

SHAREHOLDER INFORMATION

Minimum Investment
Initial: $3,000 IRA: $1,000
Subsequent: $100 IRA: $100

Maximum Fees
Load: none 12b-1: none
Other: none

Vanguard Sh Tm Bd Idx (VBISX)

800-662-7447, 610-436-5152
www.vanguard.com

General Bond

PERFORMANCE AND PER SHARE DATA **fund inception date: 3/1/94**

	3yr Annual	5yr Annual	10yr Annual	Category Risk Index	
Return (%)	7.9	6.6	na	0.64—blw av	
Differ From Category (+/-)	-0.1 av	0.4 abv av	na	Avg Mat	2.8 yrs

	2002	2001	2000	1999	1998	1997	1996	1995	1994	1993
Return (%)	6.1	8.7	8.9	2.0	7.6	7.0	4.5	12.8	—	—
Differ From Category (+/-)	-1.1	1.3	-0.6	1.7	0.5	-1.2	0.6	-3.2	—	—
Return, Tax-Adjusted (%)	4.3	6.3	6.5	-0.2	5.2	4.6	2.2	10.2	—	—
Dividends, Net Income ($)	0.45	0.56	0.60	0.53	0.57	0.59	0.58	0.62	—	—
Expense Ratio (%)	na	0.21	0.21	0.20	0.20	0.20	0.20	0.20	—	—
Yield (%)	4.35	5.46	6.01	5.43	5.61	5.90	5.84	6.15	—	—
Total Assets (Millions $)	2,380	1,679	1,286	1,155	708	446	328	207	—	—

SHAREHOLDER INFORMATION

Minimum Investment
Initial: $3,000 IRA: $1,000
Subsequent: $100 IRA: $100

Maximum Fees
Load: none 12b-1: none
Other: none

Vanguard Tot Bd Mkt (VBMFX)

800-662-7447, 610-436-5152
www.vanguard.com

General Bond

PERFORMANCE AND PER SHARE DATA **fund inception date: 12/11/86**

	3yr Annual	5yr Annual	10yr Annual	Category Risk Index	
Return (%)	9.3	7.1	7.2	1.00—av	
Differ From Category (+/-)	1.3 abv av	0.9 high	0.8 high	Avg Mat	9.0 yrs

	2002	2001	2000	1999	1998	1997	1996	1995	1994	1993
Return (%)	8.2	8.4	11.3	-0.7	8.5	9.4	3.5	18.1	-2.6	9.6
Differ From Category (+/-)	1.0	1.0	1.8	-1.0	1.4	1.2	-0.4	2.1	-0.1	-0.5
Return, Tax-Adjusted (%)	6.0	5.9	8.6	-3.1	6.0	6.8	1.0	15.3	-5.1	6.7
Dividends, Net Income ($)	0.57	0.63	0.64	0.61	0.62	0.64	0.64	0.64	0.62	0.63
Expense Ratio (%)	na	0.22	0.22	0.20	0.20	0.20	0.20	0.20	0.18	0.18
Yield (%)	5.48	6.20	6.42	6.37	6.01	6.34	6.50	6.31	6.76	6.19
Total Assets (Millions $)	16,200	14,115	11,180	9,477	7,764	5,129	2,961	2,405	1,730	1,540

SHAREHOLDER INFORMATION

Minimum Investment
Initial: $3,000 IRA: $1,000
Subsequent: $100 IRA: $100

Maximum Fees
Load: none 12b-1: none
Other: none

MUNICIPAL BOND FUNDS

National Muni: Short-Term Bond Funds
Category Performance Ranked by 2002 Returns

Category	Fund (Ticker)	Annual Return (%) 2002	3yr	5yr	10yr	Category Risk	Total Risk
B-MNST	Vanguard Ltd Tm TE (VMLTX)	6.3	6.0	4.9	4.8	high	low
B-MNST	USAA Tax Ex:Short Term (USSTX)	5.0	5.3	4.5	4.6	av	low
B-MNST	Strong Sht Tm Mu Bond/Inv (STSMX)	5.0	5.1	4.3	4.4	abv av	low
B-MNST	Vanguard Sh Tm TE (VWSTX)	3.4	4.3	4.0	3.9	av	low
Nat'l Muni: Short-Term Bond Average		**4.1**	**4.6**	**4.1**	**4.2**	—	**low**

Note: AAII members who would like performance figures for no-load and low-load mutual funds they own that do not appear in this Guide can access this information on our Web site at www.aaii.com.

Strong Sht Tm Mu Bond/Inv (STSMX)

800-368-3863, 414-359-1400
www.strong-funds.com

National Muni: Short-Term Bond

PERFORMANCE AND PER SHARE DATA **fund inception date: 12/31/91**

	3yr Annual	5yr Annual	10yr Annual	Category Risk Index
Return (%)	5.1	4.3	4.4	1.00—abv av
Differ From Category (+/-)	0.5 abv av	0.2 abv av	0.2 abv av	**Avg Mat** 2.3 yrs

	2002	2001	2000	1999	1998	1997	1996	1995	1994	1993
Return (%)	5.0	5.1	5.0	1.1	5.5	6.9	4.8	5.3	-1.6	6.7
Differ From Category (+/-)	0.9	0.5	0.0	-0.9	0.9	1.8	0.7	-1.4	-2.0	1.3
Return, Tax-Adjusted (%)	5.0	5.1	5.0	1.1	5.5	6.9	4.8	5.3	-1.6	6.5
Dividends, Net Income ($)	0.39	0.42	0.46	0.45	0.48	0.47	0.49	0.47	0.45	0.44
Expense Ratio (%)	0.60	0.60	0.60	0.60	0.60	0.70	0.70	0.80	0.70	0.60
Yield (%)	3.98	4.32	4.77	4.67	4.81	4.73	5.03	4.81	4.62	4.21
Total Assets (Millions $)	592	511	311	281	263	180	145	132	161	216

SHAREHOLDER INFORMATION

Minimum Investment
Initial: $2,500 IRA: na
Subsequent: $100 IRA: na

Maximum Fees
Load: none 12b-1: none
Other: none

USAA Tax Ex:Short Term (USSTX)

800-531-8181, 210-456-7211
www.usaa.com

National Muni: Short-Term Bond

PERFORMANCE AND PER SHARE DATA **fund inception date: 3/19/82**

	3yr Annual	5yr Annual	10yr Annual	Category Risk Index
Return (%)	5.3	4.5	4.6	1.00—av
Differ From Category (+/-)	0.7 high	0.4 high	0.4 high	**Avg Mat** 2.7 yrs

	2002	2001	2000	1999	1998	1997	1996	1995	1994	1993
Return (%)	5.0	5.0	6.0	1.6	4.9	5.8	4.0	8.1	0.8	5.5
Differ From Category (+/-)	0.9	0.4	1.0	-0.4	0.3	0.7	-0.1	1.4	0.4	0.1
Return, Tax-Adjusted (%)	5.0	5.0	6.0	1.6	4.9	5.8	4.0	8.1	0.8	5.5
Dividends, Net Income ($)	0.36	0.44	0.49	0.47	0.49	0.48	0.45	0.50	0.45	0.46
Expense Ratio (%)	0.48	0.38	0.38	0.38	0.39	0.41	0.42	0.42	0.43	0.43
Yield (%)	3.31	4.11	4.62	4.48	4.54	4.46	4.23	4.69	4.35	4.29
Total Assets (Millions $)	1,223	1,122	1,003	987	1,005	936	785	776	810	954

SHAREHOLDER INFORMATION

Minimum Investment
Initial: $3,000 IRA: na
Subsequent: $50 IRA: na

Maximum Fees
Load: none 12b-1: none
Other: none

Vanguard Ltd Tm TE (VMLTX)

800-662-7447, 610-436-5152
www.vanguard.com

National Muni: Short-Term Bond

PERFORMANCE AND PER SHARE DATA **fund inception date: 8/31/87**

	3yr Annual	5yr Annual	10yr Annual	Category Risk Index	
Return (%)	6.0	4.9	4.8	1.40—high	
Differ From Category (+/-)	1.4 high	0.8 high	0.6 high	**Avg Mat**	3.0 yrs

	2002	2001	2000	1999	1998	1997	1996	1995	1994	1993
Return (%)	6.3	5.5	6.3	1.4	5.1	5.1	4.0	8.5	0.0	6.3
Differ From Category (+/-)	2.2	0.9	1.3	-0.6	0.5	0.0	-0.1	1.8	-0.4	0.9
Return, Tax-Adjusted (%)	6.3	5.5	6.3	1.4	5.1	5.1	4.0	8.5	0.0	6.2
Dividends, Net Income ($)	0.41	0.47	0.47	0.45	0.45	0.47	0.47	0.48	0.45	0.46
Expense Ratio (%)	na	0.19	0.18	0.18	0.21	0.19	0.21	0.22	0.20	0.20
Yield (%)	3.69	4.33	4.38	4.26	4.14	4.36	4.38	4.46	4.33	4.24
Total Assets (Millions $)	2,700	2,103	2,932	2,568	2,391	2,022	1,792	1,683	1,629	1,817

SHAREHOLDER INFORMATION

Minimum Investment
Initial: $3,000 IRA: na
Subsequent: $100 IRA: na

Maximum Fees
Load: none 12b-1: none
Other: none

Vanguard Sh Tm TE (VWSTX)

800-662-7447, 610-436-5152
www.vanguard.com

National Muni: Short-Term Bond

PERFORMANCE AND PER SHARE DATA **fund inception date: 9/1/77**

	3yr Annual	5yr Annual	10yr Annual	Category Risk Index	
Return (%)	4.3	4.0	3.9	0.60—av	
Differ From Category (+/-)	-0.3 av	-0.1 av	-0.3 blw av	**Avg Mat**	4.5

	2002	2001	2000	1999	1998	1997	1996	1995	1994	1993
Return (%)	3.4	4.7	4.9	2.5	4.3	4.0	3.6	5.9	1.6	3.8
Differ From Category (+/-)	-0.7	0.1	-0.1	0.5	-0.3	-1.1	-0.5	-0.8	1.2	-1.6
Return, Tax-Adjusted (%)	3.4	4.7	4.9	2.5	4.3	4.0	3.6	5.9	1.6	3.8
Dividends, Net Income ($)	0.41	0.60	0.63	0.57	0.60	0.61	0.60	0.61	0.54	0.57
Expense Ratio (%)	na	0.19	0.18	0.18	0.20	0.19	0.20	0.22	0.20	0.20
Yield (%)	2.59	3.82	4.04	3.68	3.83	3.91	3.85	3.90	3.52	3.64
Total Assets (Millions $)	1,983	1,358	2,116	1,916	1,656	1,491	1,455	1,410	1,463	1,464

SHAREHOLDER INFORMATION

Minimum Investment
Initial: $3,000 IRA: na
Subsequent: $100 IRA: na

Maximum Fees
Load: none 12b-1: none
Other: none

National Muni: Intermediate-Term Bond Funds
Category Performance Ranked by 2002 Returns

Category	Fund (Ticker)	Annual Return (%) 2002	3yr	5yr	10yr	Category Risk	Total Risk
B-MNIT	Northern Intm Tax Ex (NOITX)	9.1	8.3	6.3	na	high	low
B-MNIT	Fidelity Spart Int Muni (FLTMX)	9.0	7.9	5.5	6.1	av	low
B-MNIT	T Rowe Price TF Int Bd (PTIBX)	8.7	7.7	5.4	6.1	av	low
B-MNIT	T Rowe Price Sum Mu Int (PRSMX)	8.6	7.6	5.4	na	blw av	low
B-MNIT	Vanguard Int Tm TE (VWITX)	7.9	7.3	5.4	6.0	av	low
B-MNIT	Schwab Inv Sh/Int TF Bd (SWITX)	7.6	6.2	4.7	na	low	low
B-MNIT	USAA Tax Ex:Intmed Term (USATX)	7.6	7.6	5.2	6.1	blw av	low
B-MNIT	Fidelity Spart Sh Int Mun (FSTFX)	6.5	6.1	4.9	4.9	low	low
Nat'l Muni: Int-Term Bond Average		**8.3**	**7.3**	**5.2**	**5.7**	**—**	**low**

Note: AAII members who would like performance figures for no-load and low-load mutual funds they own that do not appear in this Guide can access this information on our Web site at www.aaii.com.

Fidelity Spart Int Muni (FLTMX)

800-544-8544, 801-534-1910
www.fidelity.com

National Muni: Intermediate-Term Bond

PERFORMANCE AND PER SHARE DATA **fund inception date: 4/15/77**

	3yr Annual	5yr Annual	10yr Annual	Category Risk Index	
Return (%)	7.9	5.5	6.1	0.97—av	
Differ From Category (+/-)	0.6 high	0.3 high	0.4 high	**Avg Mat**	8.2 yrs

	2002	2001	2000	1999	1998	1997	1996	1995	1994	1993
Return (%)	9.0	5.4	9.2	-1.0	5.4	8.2	4.4	14.8	-4.7	12.2
Differ From Category (+/-)	0.7	0.5	0.4	0.1	-0.3	1.1	0.6	1.9	-1.6	1.4
Return, Tax-Adjusted (%)	8.9	5.4	9.2	-1.0	5.3	8.1	4.3	14.8	-4.8	11.5
Dividends, Net Income ($)	0.43	0.45	0.47	0.46	0.43	0.48	0.48	0.49	0.51	0.51
Expense Ratio (%)	na	0.39	0.49	0.48	0.50	0.55	0.56	0.58	0.56	0.57
Yield (%)	4.17	4.56	4.80	4.88	4.28	4.80	4.93	5.00	5.66	4.98
Total Assets (Millions $)	1,752	1,487	1,209	1,061	1,145	911	901	941	881	1,195

SHAREHOLDER INFORMATION

Minimum Investment
Initial: $10,000 IRA: na
Subsequent: $1,000 IRA: na

Maximum Fees
Load: 0.50% redemption 12b-1: none
Other: redemption fee applies for 1 month

Fidelity Spart Sh Int Mun (FSTFX)

800-544-8544, 801-534-1910
www.fidelity.com

National Muni: Intermediate-Term Bond

PERFORMANCE AND PER SHARE DATA **fund inception date: 12/24/86**

	3yr Annual	5yr Annual	10yr Annual	Category Risk Index	
Return (%)	6.1	4.9	4.9	0.61—low	
Differ From Category (+/-)	-1.2 low	-0.3 blw av	-0.8 low	**Avg Mat**	3.3 yrs

	2002	2001	2000	1999	1998	1997	1996	1995	1994	1993
Return (%)	6.5	5.6	6.2	1.8	4.6	5.4	3.8	8.4	0.0	7.2
Differ From Category (+/-)	-1.8	0.7	-2.6	2.9	-1.1	-1.7	0.0	-4.5	3.1	-3.6
Return, Tax-Adjusted (%)	6.4	5.6	6.2	1.8	4.6	5.4	3.8	8.4	0.0	7.2
Dividends, Net Income ($)	0.33	0.39	0.41	0.41	0.41	0.42	0.42	0.42	0.43	0.46
Expense Ratio (%)	na	0.41	0.45	0.55	0.55	0.55	0.54	0.55	0.47	0.55
Yield (%)	3.11	3.79	4.05	4.12	4.03	4.15	4.19	4.18	4.45	4.54
Total Assets (Millions $)	1,680	1,188	958	765	639	699	737	904	913	1,188

SHAREHOLDER INFORMATION

Minimum Investment
Initial: $10,000 IRA: na
Subsequent: $1,000 IRA: na

Maximum Fees
Load: 0.50% redemption 12b-1: none
Other: redemption fee applies for 1 month

Northern Intm Tax Ex (NOITX)

800-595-9111
www.northernfunds.com

National Muni: Intermediate-Term Bond

PERFORMANCE AND PER SHARE DATA **fund inception date: 4/4/94**

	3yr Annual	5yr Annual	10yr Annual	Category Risk Index	
Return (%)	8.3	6.3	na	1.14—high	
Differ From Category (+/-)	1.0 high	1.1 high	na	**Avg Mat**	7.3 yrs

	2002	2001	2000	1999	1998	1997	1996	1995	1994	1993
Return (%)	9.1	7.8	8.0	-1.0	8.2	5.8	3.3	11.9	—	—
Differ From Category (+/-)	0.8	2.9	-0.8	0.1	2.5	-1.3	-0.5	-1.0	—	—
Return, Tax-Adjusted (%)	8.7	7.6	8.0	-1.0	8.0	5.8	3.0	11.7	—	—
Dividends, Net Income ($)	0.37	0.69	0.41	0.38	0.69	0.39	0.40	0.40	—	—
Expense Ratio (%)	0.85	0.85	0.85	0.85	0.85	0.85	0.85	0.85	—	—
Yield (%)	3.41	6.66	3.99	3.83	6.57	3.76	3.89	3.83	—	—
Total Assets (Millions $)	676	690	664	682	330	290	254	238	—	—

SHAREHOLDER INFORMATION

Minimum Investment
Initial: $2,500 IRA: na
Subsequent: $50 IRA: na

Maximum Fees
Load: none 12b-1: none
Other: none

Schwab Inv Sh/Int TF Bd (SWITX)

800-435-4000, 800-266-5623
www.schwab.com

National Muni: Intermediate-Term Bond

PERFORMANCE AND PER SHARE DATA **fund inception date: 4/21/93**

	3yr Annual	5yr Annual	10yr Annual	Category Risk Index	
Return (%)	6.2	4.7	na	0.72—low	
Differ From Category (+/-)	-1.1 low	-0.5 low	na	**Avg Mat**	4.1 yrs

	2002	2001	2000	1999	1998	1997	1996	1995	1994	1993
Return (%)	7.6	4.4	6.6	0.5	4.7	5.1	3.5	9.2	-1.1	—
Differ From Category (+/-)	-0.7	-0.5	-2.2	1.6	-1.0	-2.0	-0.3	-3.7	2.0	—
Return, Tax-Adjusted (%)	7.6	4.4	6.6	0.5	4.7	5.1	3.5	9.2	-1.1	—
Dividends, Net Income ($)	0.33	0.37	0.40	0.40	0.40	0.41	0.41	0.40	0.37	—
Expense Ratio (%)	0.49	0.49	0.49	0.49	0.49	0.49	0.49	0.49	0.48	—
Yield (%)	3.08	3.60	3.92	4.02	3.88	4.00	4.04	3.92	3.81	—
Total Assets (Millions $)	158	114	83	84	74	54	51	52	55	—

SHAREHOLDER INFORMATION

Minimum Investment
Initial: $2,500 IRA: na
Subsequent: $500 IRA: na

Maximum Fees
Load: none 12b-1: none
Other: none

T Rowe Price Sum Mu Int (PRSMX)

800-638-5660, 410-345-2000
www.troweprice.com

National Muni: Intermediate-Term Bond

PERFORMANCE AND PER SHARE DATA **fund inception date: 10/29/93**

	3yr Annual	5yr Annual	10yr Annual	Category Risk Index	
Return (%)	7.6	5.4	na	0.92—blw av	
Differ From Category (+/-)	0.3 abv av	0.2 abv av	na	**Avg Mat**	7.0 yrs

	2002	2001	2000	1999	1998	1997	1996	1995	1994	1993
Return (%)	8.6	5.6	8.7	-1.2	5.7	8.4	4.6	13.6	-1.6	—
Differ From Category (+/-)	0.3	0.7	-0.1	-0.1	0.0	1.3	0.8	0.7	1.5	—
Return, Tax-Adjusted (%)	8.6	5.6	8.7	-1.2	5.7	8.3	4.6	13.6	-1.6	—
Dividends, Net Income ($)	0.45	0.47	0.48	0.46	0.47	0.48	0.48	0.47	0.44	—
Expense Ratio (%)	0.50	0.50	0.50	0.50	0.50	0.50	0.50	0.50	0.50	—
Yield (%)	4.08	4.44	4.58	4.55	4.39	4.51	4.67	4.57	4.63	—
Total Assets (Millions $)	108	93	82	79	81	53	30	22	16	—

SHAREHOLDER INFORMATION

Minimum Investment
Initial: $25,000 IRA: na
Subsequent: $1,000 IRA: na

Maximum Fees
Load: none 12b-1: none
Other: none

T Rowe Price TF Int Bd (PTIBX)

800-638-5660, 410-345-2000
www.troweprice.com

National Muni: Intermediate-Term Bond

PERFORMANCE AND PER SHARE DATA **fund inception date: 11/30/92**

	3yr Annual	5yr Annual	10yr Annual	Category Risk Index	
Return (%)	7.7	5.4	6.1	1.00—av	
Differ From Category (+/-)	0.4 abv av	0.2 abv av	0.4 abv av	**Avg Mat**	7.9 yrs

	2002	2001	2000	1999	1998	1997	1996	1995	1994	1993
Return (%)	8.7	5.2	9.4	-1.2	5.7	7.2	4.1	13.0	-2.6	12.6
Differ From Category (+/-)	0.4	0.3	0.6	-0.1	0.0	0.1	0.3	0.1	0.5	1.8
Return, Tax-Adjusted (%)	8.7	5.2	9.4	-1.3	5.6	7.1	4.1	13.0	-2.7	12.4
Dividends, Net Income ($)	0.45	0.48	0.54	0.47	0.48	0.48	0.47	0.48	0.45	0.48
Expense Ratio (%)	0.60	0.60	0.63	0.65	0.65	0.65	0.65	0.65	0.33	0.00
Yield (%)	3.92	4.36	4.94	4.46	4.29	4.33	4.35	4.43	4.47	4.41
Total Assets (Millions $)	159	131	116	115	119	105	96	91	79	97

SHAREHOLDER INFORMATION

Minimum Investment
Initial: $2,500 IRA: na
Subsequent: $100 IRA: na

Maximum Fees
Load: none 12b-1: none
Other: none

USAA Tax Ex:Intmed Term (USATX)

800-531-8181, 210-456-7211
www.usaa.com

National Muni: Intermediate-Term Bond

PERFORMANCE AND PER SHARE DATA **fund inception date: 3/19/82**

	3yr Annual	5yr Annual	10yr Annual	Category Risk Index
Return (%)	7.6	5.2	6.1	0.92—blw av
Differ From Category (+/-)	0.3 av	0.0 av	0.4 high	**Avg Mat** 8.6 yrs

	2002	2001	2000	1999	1998	1997	1996	1995	1994	1993
Return (%)	7.6	5.5	9.8	-2.6	6.3	9.3	4.4	15.0	-4.0	11.4
Differ From Category (+/-)	-0.7	0.6	1.0	-1.5	0.6	2.2	0.6	2.1	-0.9	0.6
Return, Tax-Adjusted (%)	7.6	5.5	9.8	-2.6	6.3	9.3	4.4	15.0	-4.1	11.1
Dividends, Net Income ($)	0.64	0.67	0.68	0.69	0.70	0.71	0.72	0.71	0.68	0.70
Expense Ratio (%)	0.46	0.36	0.36	0.36	0.37	0.37	0.38	0.40	0.40	0.42
Yield (%)	4.80	5.15	5.24	5.53	5.18	5.30	5.57	5.42	5.64	5.22
Total Assets (Millions $)	2,523	2,397	2,230	2,146	2,251	1,936	1,711	1,673	1,416	1,660

SHAREHOLDER INFORMATION

Minimum Investment
Initial: $3,000 IRA: na
Subsequent: $50 IRA: na

Maximum Fees
Load: none 12b-1: none
Other: none

Vanguard Int Tm TE (VWITX)

800-662-7447, 610-436-5152
www.vanguard.com

National Muni: Intermediate-Term Bond

PERFORMANCE AND PER SHARE DATA **fund inception date: 9/1/77**

	3yr Annual	5yr Annual	10yr Annual	Category Risk Index
Return (%)	7.3	5.4	6.0	1.00—av
Differ From Category (+/-)	0.0 blw av	0.2 abv av	0.3 abv av	**Avg Mat** 6.7 yrs

	2002	2001	2000	1999	1998	1997	1996	1995	1994	1993
Return (%)	7.9	5.0	9.2	-0.5	5.7	7.0	4.1	13.6	-2.1	11.5
Differ From Category (+/-)	-0.4	0.1	0.4	0.6	0.0	-0.1	0.3	0.7	1.0	0.7
Return, Tax-Adjusted (%)	7.8	5.0	9.2	-0.5	5.6	6.9	4.1	13.6	-2.4	11.3
Dividends, Net Income ($)	0.60	0.63	0.64	0.64	0.65	0.66	0.66	0.67	0.68	0.69
Expense Ratio (%)	na	0.19	0.18	0.18	0.21	0.19	0.20	0.22	0.20	0.20
Yield (%)	4.38	4.73	4.82	5.01	4.81	4.89	4.98	5.01	5.42	5.07
Total Assets (Millions $)	7,186	6,652	8,925	7,919	7,895	6,891	6,139	5,770	4,696	5,238

SHAREHOLDER INFORMATION

Minimum Investment
Initial: $3,000 IRA: na
Subsequent: $100 IRA: na

Maximum Fees
Load: none 12b-1: none
Other: none

National Muni: Long-Term Bond Funds
Category Performance Ranked by 2002 Returns

Category	Fund (Ticker)	Annual Return (%) 2002	3yr	5yr	10yr	Category Risk	Total Risk
B-MNLT	Fidelity Spart Muni Inc (FHIGX)	10.3	9.1	6.1	6.4	blw av	blw av
B-MNLT	SAFECO Muni Bond/Inv (SFCOX)	10.3	9.7	5.7	6.5	high	blw av
B-MNLT	Vanguard LT TE (VWLTX)	10.1	9.3	5.9	6.8	high	blw av
B-MNLT	Vanguard Ins LT TE (VILPX)	10.0	9.2	6.0	6.7	abv av	blw av
B-MNLT	Northern Tax Ex (NOTEX)	9.8	8.9	5.5	na	blw av	blw av
B-MNLT	USAA Tax Ex:Long Term (USTEX)	9.7	8.6	5.2	6.6	av	blw av
B-MNLT	T Rowe Price TF Inc (PRTAX)	9.2	8.5	5.4	6.3	blw av	low
B-MNLT	Dreyfus Muni Bond (DRTAX)	7.1	7.2	4.1	5.2	abv av	blw av
Nat'l Muni: Long-Term Bond Average		**8.9**	**8.2**	**5.0**	**5.9**	**—**	**blw av**

Note: AAII members who would like performance figures for no-load and low-load mutual funds they own that do not appear in this Guide can access this information on our Web site at www.aaii.com.

Dreyfus Muni Bond (DRTAX)

800-645-6561, 516-794-5452
www.dreyfus.com

National Muni: Long-Term Bond

PERFORMANCE AND PER SHARE DATA **fund inception date: 10/4/76**

	3yr Annual	5yr Annual	10yr Annual	Category Risk Index
Return (%)	7.2	4.1	5.2	1.02—abv av
Differ From Category (+/-)	-1.0 blw av	-0.9 low	-0.7 low	**Avg Mat** 22.3 yrs

	2002	2001	2000	1999	1998	1997	1996	1995	1994	1993
Return (%)	7.1	2.7	11.9	-5.9	5.6	7.9	3.8	15.6	-6.9	12.7
Differ From Category (+/-)	-1.8	-1.3	0.1	-1.5	-0.1	-1.3	-0.1	-1.1	-0.8	0.3
Return, Tax-Adjusted (%)	7.1	2.7	11.9	-5.9	5.2	7.8	3.8	15.6	-7.0	12.0
Dividends, Net Income ($)	0.59	0.61	0.59	0.61	0.63	0.66	0.68	0.70	0.73	0.77
Expense Ratio (%)	0.71	0.72	0.76	0.73	0.73	0.71	0.71	0.69	0.68	0.69
Yield (%)	4.97	5.24	4.94	5.43	4.92	5.16	5.44	5.50	6.23	5.62
Total Assets (Millions $)	2,356	2,489	2,610	2,605	3,249	3,414	3,603	3,938	3,625	4,571

SHAREHOLDER INFORMATION

Minimum Investment
Initial: $2,500 IRA: na
Subsequent: $100 IRA: na

Maximum Fees
Load: 0.10% redemption 12b-1: none
Other: redemption fee applies for 1 month

Fidelity Spart Muni Inc (FHIGX)

800-544-8544, 801-534-1910
www.fidelity.com

National Muni: Long-Term Bond

PERFORMANCE AND PER SHARE DATA **fund inception date: 11/30/77**

	3yr Annual	5yr Annual	10yr Annual	Category Risk Index
Return (%)	9.1	6.1	6.4	0.94—blw av
Differ From Category (+/-)	0.9 high	1.1 high	0.5 abv av	**Avg Mat** 16.1 yrs

	2002	2001	2000	1999	1998	1997	1996	1995	1994	1993
Return (%)	10.3	5.0	12.2	-2.4	6.0	9.2	4.9	16.1	-7.4	12.5
Differ From Category (+/-)	1.4	1.0	0.4	2.0	0.3	0.0	1.0	-0.6	-1.3	0.1
Return, Tax-Adjusted (%)	10.0	4.9	12.2	-2.4	6.0	9.1	4.8	16.1	-7.4	11.4
Dividends, Net Income ($)	0.60	0.61	0.62	0.59	0.60	0.61	0.64	0.66	0.75	0.69
Expense Ratio (%)	na	0.43	0.48	0.49	0.53	0.55	0.56	0.57	0.56	0.56
Yield (%)	4.48	4.79	4.88	4.95	4.68	4.78	5.20	5.33	6.66	5.13
Total Assets (Millions $)	4,788	4,513	4,452	4,062	4,638	2,347	1,796	1,794	1,671	2,108

SHAREHOLDER INFORMATION

Minimum Investment
Initial: $10,000 IRA: na
Subsequent: $1,000 IRA: na

Maximum Fees
Load: 0.50% redemption 12b-1: none
Other: redemption fee applies for 1 month

Northern Tax Ex (NOTEX)

800-595-9111
www.northernfunds.com

National Muni: Long-Term Bond

PERFORMANCE AND PER SHARE DATA **fund inception date: 4/4/94**

	3yr Annual	5yr Annual	10yr Annual	Category Risk Index
Return (%)	8.9	5.5	na	0.94—blw av
Differ From Category (+/-)	0.7 abv av	0.5 abv av	na	**Avg Mat** 15.3 yrs

	2002	2001	2000	1999	1998	1997	1996	1995	1994	1993
Return (%)	9.8	4.7	12.4	-4.2	5.8	8.7	2.8	17.3	—	—
Differ From Category (+/-)	0.9	0.7	0.6	0.2	0.1	-0.5	-1.1	0.6	—	—
Return, Tax-Adjusted (%)	9.5	4.7	12.4	-4.2	5.4	8.5	2.7	17.2	—	—
Dividends, Net Income ($)	0.46	0.46	0.48	0.43	0.45	0.48	0.50	0.47	—	—
Expense Ratio (%)	0.85	0.85	0.85	0.85	0.85	0.85	0.85	0.85	—	—
Yield (%)	4.16	4.37	4.57	4.38	4.12	4.43	4.77	4.38	—	—
Total Assets (Millions $)	556	537	535	514	199	154	132	125	—	—

SHAREHOLDER INFORMATION

Minimum Investment
Initial: $2,500 IRA: na
Subsequent: $50 IRA: na

Maximum Fees
Load: none 12b-1: none
Other: none

SAFECO Muni Bond/Inv (SFCOX)

800-624-5711, 206-545-7319
www.safecofunds.com

National Muni: Long-Term Bond

PERFORMANCE AND PER SHARE DATA **fund inception date: 11/18/81**

	3yr Annual	5yr Annual	10yr Annual	Category Risk Index
Return (%)	9.7	5.7	6.5	1.15—high
Differ From Category (+/-)	1.5 high	0.7 high	0.6 abv av	**Avg Mat** 24.1 yrs

	2002	2001	2000	1999	1998	1997	1996	1995	1994	1993
Return (%)	10.3	5.0	14.1	-6.1	6.3	10.6	3.1	21.4	-8.2	12.6
Differ From Category (+/-)	1.4	1.0	2.3	-1.7	0.6	1.4	-0.8	4.7	-2.1	0.2
Return, Tax-Adjusted (%)	10.0	5.0	14.1	-6.1	6.0	10.4	3.1	21.4	-8.3	12.0
Dividends, Net Income ($)	0.68	0.69	0.69	0.69	0.73	0.74	0.75	0.76	0.76	0.78
Expense Ratio (%)	na	0.62	0.62	0.60	0.51	0.53	0.53	0.56	0.52	0.53
Yield (%)	4.63	4.93	4.94	5.35	4.96	5.04	5.36	5.31	6.08	5.29
Total Assets (Millions $)	548	532	498	469	539	498	480	521	434	572

SHAREHOLDER INFORMATION

Minimum Investment
Initial: $2,500 IRA: na
Subsequent: $100 IRA: na

Maximum Fees
Load: none 12b-1: none
Other: none

T Rowe Price TF Inc (PRTAX)

800-638-5660, 410-345-2000
www.troweprice.com

National Muni: Long-Term Bond

PERFORMANCE AND PER SHARE DATA **fund inception date: 10/26/76**

	3yr Annual	5yr Annual	10yr Annual	Category Risk Index
Return (%)	8.5	5.4	6.3	0.90—blw av
Differ From Category (+/-)	0.3 av	0.4 abv av	0.4 abv av	**Avg Mat** 15.7 yrs

	2002	2001	2000	1999	1998	1997	1996	1995	1994	1993
Return (%)	9.2	4.3	12.2	-3.9	5.9	9.3	3.2	17.6	-5.4	12.7
Differ From Category (+/-)	0.3	0.3	0.4	0.5	0.2	0.1	-0.7	0.9	0.7	0.3
Return, Tax-Adjusted (%)	9.2	4.3	12.2	-3.9	5.8	9.3	3.2	17.6	-5.5	12.2
Dividends, Net Income ($)	0.46	0.47	0.49	0.49	0.51	0.51	0.51	0.52	0.52	0.53
Expense Ratio (%)	0.54	0.54	0.55	0.55	0.55	0.57	0.58	0.59	0.59	0.61
Yield (%)	4.59	4.88	5.06	5.38	5.09	5.13	5.31	5.30	5.88	5.25
Total Assets (Millions $)	1,470	1,415	1,395	1,327	1,481	1,384	1,344	1,358	1,253	1,504

SHAREHOLDER INFORMATION

Minimum Investment
Initial: $2,500 IRA: na
Subsequent: $100 IRA: na

Maximum Fees
Load: none 12b-1: none
Other: none

USAA Tax Ex:Long Term (USTEX)

800-531-8181, 210-456-7211
www.usaa.com

National Muni: Long-Term Bond

PERFORMANCE AND PER SHARE DATA **fund inception date: 3/19/82**

	3yr Annual	5yr Annual	10yr Annual	Category Risk Index
Return (%)	8.6	5.2	6.6	0.98—av
Differ From Category (+/-)	0.4 abv av	0.2 av	0.7 high	**Avg Mat** 20.1 yrs

	2002	2001	2000	1999	1998	1997	1996	1995	1994	1993
Return (%)	9.7	4.3	12.1	-5.0	5.9	10.3	9.0	18.5	-7.9	12.5
Differ From Category (+/-)	0.8	0.3	0.3	-0.6	0.2	1.1	5.1	1.8	-1.8	0.1
Return, Tax-Adjusted (%)	9.7	4.3	12.1	-5.0	5.9	10.3	9.0	18.5	-8.1	11.4
Dividends, Net Income ($)	0.66	0.71	0.74	0.75	0.76	0.77	1.37	0.80	0.77	0.84
Expense Ratio (%)	0.46	0.36	0.36	0.36	0.36	0.37	0.37	0.38	0.38	0.39
Yield (%)	4.79	5.38	5.55	5.95	5.41	5.50	10.20	5.86	6.26	5.70
Total Assets (Millions $)	2,185	2,074	2,070	1,910	2,172	2,002	1,872	1,910	1,661	2,013

SHAREHOLDER INFORMATION

Minimum Investment
Initial: $3,000 IRA: na
Subsequent: $50 IRA: na

Maximum Fees
Load: none 12b-1: none
Other: none

Vanguard Ins LT TE (VILPX)

800-662-7447, 610-436-5152
www.vanguard.com

National Muni: Long-Term Bond

PERFORMANCE AND PER SHARE DATA **fund inception date: 10/1/84**

	3yr Annual	5yr Annual	10yr Annual	Category Risk Index
Return (%)	9.2	6.0	6.7	1.02—abv av
Differ From Category (+/-)	1.0 high	1.0 high	0.8 high	**Avg Mat** 11.7 yrs

	2002	2001	2000	1999	1998	1997	1996	1995	1994	1993
Return (%)	10.0	4.2	13.6	-2.9	6.1	8.6	4.0	18.5	-5.5	13.0
Differ From Category (+/-)	1.1	0.2	1.8	1.5	0.4	-0.6	0.1	1.8	0.6	0.6
Return, Tax-Adjusted (%)	9.9	4.1	13.6	-2.9	6.0	8.5	3.8	18.5	-5.9	12.6
Dividends, Net Income ($)	0.59	0.62	0.64	0.64	0.65	0.67	0.67	0.67	0.70	0.70
Expense Ratio (%)	na	0.19	0.19	0.19	0.21	0.19	0.20	0.22	0.20	0.20
Yield (%)	4.54	4.98	5.10	5.49	5.11	5.27	5.39	5.31	6.14	5.39
Total Assets (Millions $)	1,919	1,847	2,438	2,152	2,268	2,090	1,964	2,017	1,737	2,161

SHAREHOLDER INFORMATION

Minimum Investment
Initial: $3,000 IRA: na
Subsequent: $100 IRA: na

Maximum Fees
Load: none 12b-1: none
Other: none

Vanguard LT TE (VWLTX)

800-662-7447, 610-436-5152
www.vanguard.com

National Muni: Long-Term Bond

PERFORMANCE AND PER SHARE DATA **fund inception date: 9/1/77**

	3yr Annual	5yr Annual	10yr Annual	Category Risk Index
Return (%)	9.3	5.9	6.8	1.06—high
Differ From Category (+/-)	1.1 high	0.9 high	0.9 high	**Avg Mat** 12.4 yrs

	2002	2001	2000	1999	1998	1997	1996	1995	1994	1993
Return (%)	10.1	4.6	13.4	-3.5	6.0	9.2	4.4	18.7	-5.7	13.4
Differ From Category (+/-)	1.2	0.6	1.6	0.9	0.3	0.0	0.5	2.0	0.4	1.0
Return, Tax-Adjusted (%)	10.0	4.5	13.4	-3.5	5.8	9.1	4.3	18.7	-6.1	12.9
Dividends, Net Income ($)	0.53	0.56	0.58	0.56	0.57	0.58	0.58	0.59	0.61	0.62
Expense Ratio (%)	na	0.19	0.19	0.18	0.21	0.19	0.20	0.23	0.20	0.20
Yield (%)	4.59	5.08	5.23	5.43	5.01	5.11	5.28	5.32	6.08	5.39
Total Assets (Millions $)	1,226	1,186	1,745	1,486	1,536	1,291	1,147	1,114	920	1,103

SHAREHOLDER INFORMATION

Minimum Investment
Initial: $3,000 IRA: na
Subsequent: $100 IRA: na

Maximum Fees
Load: none 12b-1: none
Other: none

STATE-SPECIFIC BOND FUNDS

Category Performance Ranked by 2002 Returns

Category	Fund (Ticker)	Annual Return (%) 2002	3yr	5yr	10yr	Category Risk	Total Risk
B-MS-NY	Fidelity Spart NY Muni In (FTFMX)	10.9	9.3	6.0	6.7	av	blw av
B-MS-FL	Vanguard FL Lg Term TE/Iv (VFLTX)	10.8	9.4	6.3	6.9	high	blw av
B-MS-NY	Vanguard NY Lg Term TE/Iv (VNYTX)	10.7	9.4	6.1	6.7	high	blw av
B-MS-OH	Vanguard OH Lg Tm TE (VOHIX)	10.7	9.3	6.1	6.6	high	blw av
B-MS-CT	Fidelity Spart CT Muni (FICNX)	10.0	8.7	5.8	6.5	high	low
B-MS-PA	Vanguard PA Lg Term TE/Iv (VPAIX)	10.0	9.1	6.0	6.6	high	blw av
B-MS-NJ	Vanguard NJ Lg Term TE/Iv (VNJTX)	9.9	8.9	6.0	6.6	high	blw av
B-MS-MA	Fidelity Spart MA Muni (FDMMX)	9.7	8.6	5.7	6.5	high	blw av
B-MS-MI	Fidelity Spart MI Muni (FMHTX)	9.7	8.5	5.5	6.0	high	low
B-MS-NJ	Fidelity Spart NJ Muni (FNJHX)	9.7	8.2	5.8	6.3	abv av	low
B-MS-VA	T Rowe Price TF VA TF Bd (PRVAX)	9.7	8.8	5.7	6.4	abv av	low
B-MS-NY	T Rowe Price TF NY TF Bd (PRNYX)	9.6	8.8	5.4	6.3	abv av	blw av
B-MS-OH	Fidelity Spart OH Muni (FOHFX)	9.6	8.6	5.6	6.3	av	low
B-MS-NY	USAA Tax Ex:New York Bond (USNYX)	9.5	9.5	5.8	6.4	high	blw av
B-MS-CA	Vanguard CA Lg Term TE/Iv (VCITX)	9.4	9.2	6.0	6.8	abv av	blw av
B-MS-MD	T Rowe Price TF MD TF Bd (MDXBX)	9.4	8.5	5.6	6.3	high	low
B-MS-FL	Amer Cnt FL Muni Bond/Inv (ACBFX)	9.3	7.9	5.8	na	av	low
B-MS-FL	Fidelity Spart FL Income (FFLIX)	9.2	8.2	5.5	6.5	abv av	low
B-MS-NY	Dreyfus Gen NY Muni Bond (GNYMX)	9.2	8.3	5.2	6.0	av	blw av
B-MS-VA	USAA Tax Ex:Virginia Bond (USVAX)	9.2	8.8	5.4	6.3	high	blw av
B-MS-CA	Vanguard CA Int TE/Iv (VCAIX)	9.1	8.1	5.9	na	blw av	blw av
B-MS-PA	Fidelity Spart PA Muni (FPXTX)	9.1	8.2	5.5	6.4	abv av	low
B-MS-AZ	Amer Cnt AZ Muni Bond/Inv (BEAMX)	9.0	8.0	5.7	na	high	low
B-MS-CA	Amer Cnt CA Hi Yield (BCHYX)	9.0	8.8	5.8	7.0	av	blw av
B-MS-NY	Dreyfus NY Tax Ex Bond (DRNYX)	9.0	8.2	5.3	5.8	blw av	low
B-MS-GA	T Rowe Price TF GA TF Bd (GTFBX)	8.8	8.3	5.4	na	high	blw av
B-MS-CA	Amer Cnt CA Intm TF/Inv (BCITX)	8.7	7.7	5.4	5.8	blw av	low
B-MS-FL	USAA State TF:FL TF Inc (UFLTX)	8.7	8.8	5.1	na	high	blw av
B-MS-CA	Amer Cnt CA Long Tm/Inv (BCLTX)	8.6	9.1	5.5	6.6	abv av	blw av
B-MS-MD	Fidelity Spart MD Income (SMDMX)	8.6	8.1	5.5	na	abv av	low
B-MS-MN	Fidelity Spart MN Muni (FIMIX)	8.5	7.9	5.2	6.0	high	low
B-MS-CA	Fidelity Spart CA Muni (FCTFX)	8.4	8.5	5.7	6.4	av	blw av
B-MS-MA	Dreyfus MA Tax Exempt Bd (DMEBX)	8.4	8.2	5.1	5.9	abv av	low
B-MS-CA	T Rowe Price CA TF Bd (PRXCX)	8.1	8.2	5.3	6.2	av	blw av
B-MS-CA	Schwab Inv CA Lg Tm TFBd (SWCAX)	8.1	9.3	5.4	6.3	abv av	blw av
B-MS-CT	Dreyfus CT Intmed Muni Bd (DCTIX)	8.1	6.8	4.9	5.7	blw av	low
B-MS-HI	Hawaii Municipal Fund (SURFX)	8.1	6.9	4.7	5.3	high	low
B-MS-KY	Dupree:KY Tx Fr Income (KYTFX)	7.1	6.7	4.8	5.9	high	low
B-MS-KY	Dupree:KY Tx Fr Short-Med (KYSMX)	6.5	5.8	4.4	4.4	av	low
B-MS-CA	Amer Cnt CA Ltd TF/Inv (BCSTX)	6.3	6.1	4.8	4.6	low	low
B-MS-CA	Schwab Inv CA Sh Int TFBd (SWCSX)	6.1	6.0	4.7	na	low	low

Note: AAII members who would like performance figures for no-load and low-load mutual funds they own that do not appear in this Guide can access this information on our Web site at www.aaii.com.

Amer Cnt AZ Muni Bond/Inv (BEAMX)

800-345-2021, 816-531-5575
www.americancentury.com

Muni: Arizona Bond

PERFORMANCE AND PER SHARE DATA **fund inception date: 4/11/94**

	3yr Annual	5yr Annual	10yr Annual	Category Risk Index
Return (%)	8.0	5.7	na	1.00—high
Differ From Category (+/-)	0.0 high	0.0 high	na	**Avg Mat** 9.7 yrs

	2002	2001	2000	1999	1998	1997	1996	1995	1994	1993
Return (%)	9.0	5.3	9.6	-0.9	5.8	6.8	3.7	13.1	—	—
Differ From Category (+/-)	0.0	0.0	0.0	0.0	0.0	0.0	0.0	0.0	—	—
Return, Tax-Adjusted (%)	8.9	5.2	9.6	-1.0	5.7	6.7	3.7	13.1	—	—
Dividends, Net Income ($)	0.41	0.46	0.49	0.47	0.46	0.45	0.47	0.52	—	—
Expense Ratio (%)	0.51	0.51	0.51	0.51	0.54	0.79	0.14	0.00	—	—
Yield (%)	3.65	4.28	4.60	4.60	4.24	4.19	4.48	4.91	—	—
Total Assets (Millions $)	70	58	46	39	44	37	27	23	—	—

SHAREHOLDER INFORMATION

Minimum Investment
Initial: $5,000 IRA: na
Subsequent: $50 IRA: na

Maximum Fees
Load: none 12b-1: none
Other: none

Amer Cnt CA Hi Yield (BCHYX)

800-345-2021, 816-531-5575
www.americancentury.com

Muni: California Bond

PERFORMANCE AND PER SHARE DATA **fund inception date: 12/30/86**

	3yr Annual	5yr Annual	10yr Annual	Category Risk Index
Return (%)	8.8	5.8	7.0	0.96—av
Differ From Category (+/-)	0.8 abv av	0.6 high	0.9 high	**Avg Mat** 19.3 yrs

	2002	2001	2000	1999	1998	1997	1996	1995	1994	1993
Return (%)	9.0	5.0	12.6	-3.3	6.6	10.5	5.8	18.2	-5.3	12.9
Differ From Category (+/-)	1.0	0.9	0.4	-0.3	0.7	2.1	1.7	1.4	0.8	0.7
Return, Tax-Adjusted (%)	9.0	5.0	12.6	-3.3	6.4	10.3	5.8	18.2	-5.3	12.5
Dividends, Net Income ($)	0.51	0.52	0.51	0.49	0.50	0.53	0.55	0.56	0.55	0.54
Expense Ratio (%)	0.54	0.54	0.54	0.54	0.54	0.50	0.51	0.51	0.51	0.55
Yield (%)	5.16	5.44	5.31	5.43	5.04	5.35	5.80	5.89	6.44	5.55
Total Assets (Millions $)	356	321	327	302	323	219	158	130	96	116

SHAREHOLDER INFORMATION

Minimum Investment
Initial: $5,000 IRA: na
Subsequent: $1 IRA: na

Maximum Fees
Load: none 12b-1: none
Other: none

Amer Cnt CA Intm TF/Inv (BCITX)

800-345-2021, 816-531-5575
www.americancentury.com

Muni: California Bond

PERFORMANCE AND PER SHARE DATA **fund inception date: 11/9/83**

	3yr Annual	5yr Annual	10yr Annual	Category Risk Index
Return (%)	7.7	5.4	5.8	0.85—blw av
Differ From Category (+/-)	-0.3 blw av	0.2 abv av	-0.3 blw av	**Avg Mat** 8.4 yrs

	2002	2001	2000	1999	1998	1997	1996	1995	1994	1993
Return (%)	8.7	4.3	10.1	-1.0	5.5	7.4	4.2	13.5	-3.7	10.4
Differ From Category (+/-)	0.7	0.2	-2.1	2.0	-0.4	-1.0	0.1	-3.3	2.4	-1.8
Return, Tax-Adjusted (%)	8.6	4.2	10.1	-1.0	5.3	7.1	4.1	13.5	-3.7	10.2
Dividends, Net Income ($)	0.45	0.49	0.50	0.49	0.51	0.53	0.54	0.54	0.53	0.52
Expense Ratio (%)	0.51	0.51	0.51	0.51	0.51	0.48	0.48	0.48	0.48	0.50
Yield (%)	3.86	4.37	4.45	4.59	4.47	4.63	4.82	4.79	5.08	4.53
Total Assets (Millions $)	469	440	444	439	480	436	439	426	393	468

SHAREHOLDER INFORMATION

Minimum Investment
Initial: $5,000 IRA: na
Subsequent: $1 IRA: na

Maximum Fees
Load: none 12b-1: none
Other: none

Amer Cnt CA Long Tm/Inv (BCLTX)

800-345-2021, 816-531-5575
www.americancentury.com

Muni: California Bond

PERFORMANCE AND PER SHARE DATA **fund inception date: 11/9/83**

	3yr Annual	5yr Annual	10yr Annual	Category Risk Index
Return (%)	9.1	5.5	6.6	1.15—abv av
Differ From Category (+/-)	1.1 abv av	0.3 abv av	0.5 high	**Avg Mat** 17.0 yrs

	2002	2001	2000	1999	1998	1997	1996	1995	1994	1993
Return (%)	8.6	4.2	14.8	-5.2	6.2	9.7	3.5	19.8	-6.5	13.7
Differ From Category (+/-)	0.6	0.1	2.6	-2.2	0.3	1.3	-0.6	3.0	-0.4	1.5
Return, Tax-Adjusted (%)	8.6	4.2	14.8	-5.2	6.0	9.3	3.5	19.8	-6.6	12.6
Dividends, Net Income ($)	0.52	0.54	0.55	0.56	0.57	0.60	0.61	0.61	0.61	0.65
Expense Ratio (%)	0.51	0.51	0.51	0.51	0.51	0.48	0.48	0.49	0.48	0.49
Yield (%)	4.40	4.75	4.81	5.34	4.86	5.09	5.38	5.27	5.94	5.38
Total Assets (Millions $)	533	310	319	299	340	311	296	295	249	323

SHAREHOLDER INFORMATION

Minimum Investment
Initial: $5,000 IRA: na
Subsequent: $1 IRA: na

Maximum Fees
Load: none 12b-1: none
Other: none

Amer Cnt CA Ltd TF/Inv (BCSTX)

800-345-2021, 816-531-5575
www.americancentury.com

Muni: California Bond

PERFORMANCE AND PER SHARE DATA **fund inception date: 6/1/92**

	3yr Annual	5yr Annual	10yr Annual	Category Risk Index	
Return (%)	6.1	4.8	4.6	0.54—low	
Differ From Category (+/-)	-1.9 low	-0.4 blw av	-1.5 low	**Avg Mat**	3.5 yrs

	2002	2001	2000	1999	1998	1997	1996	1995	1994	1993
Return (%)	6.3	4.9	7.0	1.1	4.9	5.3	3.9	8.3	-0.6	5.7
Differ From Category (+/-)	-1.7	0.8	-5.2	4.1	-1.0	-3.1	-0.2	-8.5	5.5	-6.5
Return, Tax-Adjusted (%)	6.3	4.8	7.0	1.1	4.9	5.3	3.9	8.3	-0.6	5.6
Dividends, Net Income ($)	0.32	0.40	0.41	0.39	0.40	0.42	0.43	0.42	0.38	0.36
Expense Ratio (%)	0.51	0.51	0.51	0.51	0.52	0.49	0.49	0.51	0.51	0.36
Yield (%)	2.94	3.79	3.92	3.83	3.82	4.05	4.19	4.08	3.83	3.46
Total Assets (Millions $)	214	165	144	144	151	130	108	100	106	125

SHAREHOLDER INFORMATION

Minimum Investment
Initial: $5,000 IRA: na
Subsequent: $1 IRA: na

Maximum Fees
Load: none 12b-1: none
Other: none

Fidelity Spart CA Muni (FCTFX)

800-544-8544, 801-534-1910
www.fidelity.com

Muni: California Bond

PERFORMANCE AND PER SHARE DATA **fund inception date: 7/3/84**

	3yr Annual	5yr Annual	10yr Annual	Category Risk Index	
Return (%)	8.5	5.7	6.4	1.00—av	
Differ From Category (+/-)	0.5 av	0.5 abv av	0.3 abv av	**Avg Mat**	14.6 yrs

	2002	2001	2000	1999	1998	1997	1996	1995	1994	1993
Return (%)	8.4	4.6	12.5	-2.7	6.5	9.8	4.7	19.1	-8.8	13.4
Differ From Category (+/-)	0.4	0.5	0.3	0.3	0.6	1.4	0.6	2.3	-2.7	1.2
Return, Tax-Adjusted (%)	8.3	4.6	12.5	-2.8	6.3	9.8	4.7	19.1	-9.1	12.8
Dividends, Net Income ($)	0.54	0.55	0.57	0.55	0.57	0.59	0.60	0.62	0.69	0.72
Expense Ratio (%)	0.43	0.42	0.49	0.52	0.53	0.59	0.58	0.56	0.57	0.60
Yield (%)	4.22	4.46	4.63	4.77	4.55	4.79	5.09	5.23	6.47	5.67
Total Assets (Millions $)	1,686	1,603	1,429	1,223	1,318	1,209	481	507	443	591

SHAREHOLDER INFORMATION

Minimum Investment
Initial: $10,000 IRA: na
Subsequent: $1,000 IRA: na

Maximum Fees
Load: 0.50% redemption 12b-1: none
Other: redemption fee applies for 1 month

Schwab Inv CA Lg Tm TF Bond (SWCAX)

800-435-4000, 800-266-5623
www.schwab.com

Muni: California Bond

PERFORMANCE AND PER SHARE DATA **fund inception date: 2/24/92**

	3yr Annual	5yr Annual	10yr Annual	Category Risk Index
Return (%)	9.3	5.4	6.3	1.10—abv av
Differ From Category (+/-)	1.3 high	0.2 abv av	0.2 abv av	**Avg Mat** 20.8 yrs

	2002	2001	2000	1999	1998	1997	1996	1995	1994	1993
Return (%)	8.1	4.9	15.2	-6.1	6.4	10.0	4.3	19.6	-8.7	12.8
Differ From Category (+/-)	0.1	0.8	3.0	-3.1	0.5	1.6	0.2	2.8	-2.6	0.6
Return, Tax-Adjusted (%)	8.1	4.9	15.2	-6.1	6.4	10.0	4.3	19.6	-8.7	12.5
Dividends, Net Income ($)	0.51	0.53	0.55	0.54	0.53	0.56	0.56	0.56	0.55	0.56
Expense Ratio (%)	0.49	0.49	0.49	0.49	0.49	0.49	0.49	0.58	0.60	0.60
Yield (%)	4.34	4.67	4.85	5.21	4.57	4.91	5.13	5.08	5.66	4.93
Total Assets (Millions $)	233	215	190	166	198	137	108	97	87	131

SHAREHOLDER INFORMATION

Minimum Investment
Initial: $2,500 IRA: na
Subsequent: $500 IRA: na

Maximum Fees
Load: none 12b-1: none
Other: none

Schwab Inv CA Sh Int TF Bond (SWCSX)

800-435-4000, 800-266-5623
www.schwab.com

Muni: California Bond

PERFORMANCE AND PER SHARE DATA **fund inception date: 4/20/93**

	3yr Annual	5yr Annual	10yr Annual	Category Risk Index
Return (%)	6.0	4.7	na	0.56—low
Differ From Category (+/-)	-2.0 low	-0.5 low	na	**Avg Mat** 4.3 yrs

	2002	2001	2000	1999	1998	1997	1996	1995	1994	1993
Return (%)	6.1	4.8	7.2	0.6	4.8	5.1	3.9	10.4	-2.0	—
Differ From Category (+/-)	-1.9	0.7	-5.0	3.6	-1.1	-3.3	-0.2	-6.4	4.1	—
Return, Tax-Adjusted (%)	6.1	4.8	7.2	0.6	4.8	5.1	3.9	10.4	-2.0	—
Dividends, Net Income ($)	0.33	0.37	0.39	0.38	0.40	0.42	0.42	0.42	0.38	—
Expense Ratio (%)	0.49	0.49	0.49	0.49	0.49	0.49	0.49	0.50	0.48	—
Yield (%)	3.08	3.55	3.79	3.81	3.88	4.11	4.15	4.13	3.95	—
Total Assets (Millions $)	184	145	138	118	107	61	48	42	40	—

SHAREHOLDER INFORMATION

Minimum Investment
Initial: $2,500 IRA: na
Subsequent: $500 IRA: na

Maximum Fees
Load: none 12b-1: none
Other: none

T Rowe Price CA TF Bd (PRXCX)

800-638-5660, 410-345-2000
www.troweprice.com

Muni: California Bond

PERFORMANCE AND PER SHARE DATA **fund inception date: 9/15/86**

	3yr Annual	5yr Annual	10yr Annual	Category Risk Index
Return (%)	8.2	5.3	6.2	1.00—av
Differ From Category (+/-)	0.2 av	0.1 av	0.1 av	**Avg Mat** 17.2 yrs

	2002	2001	2000	1999	1998	1997	1996	1995	1994	1993
Return (%)	8.1	3.8	12.8	-3.3	6.0	9.0	4.5	17.3	-5.7	12.3
Differ From Category (+/-)	0.1	-0.3	0.6	-0.3	0.1	0.6	0.4	0.5	0.4	0.1
Return, Tax-Adjusted (%)	8.1	3.8	12.8	-3.3	5.9	9.0	4.5	17.3	-5.8	11.7
Dividends, Net Income ($)	0.45	0.51	0.52	0.51	0.48	0.54	0.54	0.55	0.54	0.54
Expense Ratio (%)	0.54	0.54	0.56	0.58	0.58	0.62	0.63	0.60	0.60	0.60
Yield (%)	4.04	4.75	4.80	5.04	4.35	4.97	5.15	5.20	5.66	4.94
Total Assets (Millions $)	267	248	235	214	219	188	156	146	122	154

SHAREHOLDER INFORMATION

Minimum Investment
Initial: $2,500 IRA: na
Subsequent: $100 IRA: na

Maximum Fees
Load: none 12b-1: none
Other: none

Vanguard CA Int TE/Iv (VCAIX)

800-662-7447, 610-436-5152
www.vanguard.com

Muni: California Bond

PERFORMANCE AND PER SHARE DATA **fund inception date: 3/4/94**

	3yr Annual	5yr Annual	10yr Annual	Category Risk Index
Return (%)	8.1	5.9	na	0.94—blw av
Differ From Category (+/-)	0.1 av	0.7 high	na	**Avg Mat** 7.5 yrs

	2002	2001	2000	1999	1998	1997	1996	1995	1994	1993
Return (%)	9.1	4.4	10.9	-0.5	6.0	7.6	5.4	13.1	—	—
Differ From Category (+/-)	1.1	0.3	-1.3	2.5	0.1	-0.8	1.3	-3.7	—	—
Return, Tax-Adjusted (%)	9.0	4.4	10.9	-0.5	6.0	7.6	5.3	13.1	—	—
Dividends, Net Income ($)	0.46	0.49	0.49	0.48	0.48	0.50	0.50	0.51	—	—
Expense Ratio (%)	na	0.17	0.17	0.17	0.19	0.18	0.19	0.21	—	—
Yield (%)	4.00	4.46	4.45	4.62	4.39	4.64	4.75	4.87	—	—
Total Assets (Millions $)	1,630	1,498	1,783	1,262	1,033	626	353	213	—	—

SHAREHOLDER INFORMATION

Minimum Investment
Initial: $3,000 IRA: na
Subsequent: $100 IRA: na

Maximum Fees
Load: none 12b-1: none
Other: none

Vanguard CA Lg Term TE/Iv (VCITX)

800-662-7447, 610-436-5152
www.vanguard.com

Muni: California Bond

PERFORMANCE AND PER SHARE DATA **fund inception date: 4/7/86**

	3yr Annual	5yr Annual	10yr Annual	Category Risk Index
Return (%)	9.2	6.0	6.8	1.15—abv av
Differ From Category (+/-)	1.2 high	0.8 high	0.7 high	**Avg Mat** 13.2 yrs

	2002	2001	2000	1999	1998	1997	1996	1995	1994	1993
Return (%)	9.4	3.3	15.1	-3.1	6.2	9.1	4.9	18.5	-5.6	12.8
Differ From Category (+/-)	1.4	-0.8	2.9	-0.1	0.3	0.7	0.8	1.7	0.5	0.6
Return, Tax-Adjusted (%)	9.4	3.3	15.1	-3.1	6.1	8.9	4.7	18.5	-5.6	12.4
Dividends, Net Income ($)	0.55	0.56	0.57	0.56	0.57	0.59	0.59	0.60	0.60	0.60
Expense Ratio (%)	na	0.18	0.18	0.18	0.19	0.16	0.19	0.21	0.19	0.19
Yield (%)	4.57	4.86	4.88	5.24	4.89	5.07	5.21	5.27	5.92	5.20
Total Assets (Millions $)	1,449	1,479	1,808	1,492	1,502	1,234	1,060	985	830	1,089

SHAREHOLDER INFORMATION

Minimum Investment
Initial: $3,000 IRA: na
Subsequent: $100 IRA: na

Maximum Fees
Load: none 12b-1: none
Other: none

Dreyfus CT Intmed Muni Bd (DCTIX)

800-645-6561, 516-794-5452
www.dreyfus.com

Muni: Connecticut Bond

PERFORMANCE AND PER SHARE DATA **fund inception date: 6/26/92**

	3yr Annual	5yr Annual	10yr Annual	Category Risk Index
Return (%)	6.8	4.9	5.7	0.77—blw av
Differ From Category (+/-)	-0.9 blw av	-0.4 blw av	-0.4 av	**Avg Mat** 6.3 yrs

	2002	2001	2000	1999	1998	1997	1996	1995	1994	1993
Return (%)	8.1	4.9	7.5	-1.1	5.4	7.5	3.7	14.2	-4.6	12.7
Differ From Category (+/-)	-0.7	0.1	-2.0	0.8	-0.5	-0.8	-0.1	-1.1	1.2	-1.0
Return, Tax-Adjusted (%)	8.1	4.9	7.5	-1.1	5.4	7.5	3.7	14.2	-4.6	12.7
Dividends, Net Income ($)	0.57	0.61	0.59	0.57	0.58	0.59	0.59	0.60	0.66	0.68
Expense Ratio (%)	0.77	0.79	0.79	0.80	0.78	0.78	0.72	0.34	0.01	0.00
Yield (%)	3.98	4.42	4.30	4.27	4.12	4.24	4.36	4.40	5.29	4.93
Total Assets (Millions $)	154	140	130	131	138	130	129	134	124	139

SHAREHOLDER INFORMATION

Minimum Investment
Initial: $2,500 IRA: na
Subsequent: $100 IRA: na

Maximum Fees
Load: 1.00% redemption 12b-1: none
Other: redemption fee applies for 1 month

Fidelity Spart CT Muni (FICNX)

800-544-8544, 801-534-1910
www.fidelity.com

Muni: Connecticut Bond

PERFORMANCE AND PER SHARE DATA **fund inception date: 10/27/87**

	3yr Annual	5yr Annual	10yr Annual	Category Risk Index
Return (%)	8.7	5.8	6.5	1.08—high
Differ From Category (+/-)	1.0 high	0.5 high	0.4 high	**Avg Mat** 14.0 yrs

	2002	2001	2000	1999	1998	1997	1996	1995	1994	1993
Return (%)	10.0	5.2	10.9	-2.0	5.8	9.1	4.2	17.1	-7.0	14.7
Differ From Category (+/-)	1.2	0.4	1.4	-0.1	-0.1	0.8	0.4	1.8	-1.2	1.0
Return, Tax-Adjusted (%)	9.9	5.1	10.9	-2.0	5.7	8.9	4.2	17.1	-7.3	13.4
Dividends, Net Income ($)	0.49	0.56	0.55	0.52	0.53	0.55	0.56	0.61	0.63	0.67
Expense Ratio (%)	na	0.41	0.42	0.49	0.54	0.55	0.52	0.55	0.55	0.55
Yield (%)	4.11	4.92	4.85	4.83	4.58	4.75	5.03	5.42	6.14	5.48
Total Assets (Millions $)	468	410	356	330	372	344	330	357	312	448

SHAREHOLDER INFORMATION

Minimum Investment
Initial: $10,000 IRA: na
Subsequent: $1,000 IRA: na

Maximum Fees
Load: 0.50% redemption 12b-1: none
Other: redemption fee applies for 1 month

Amer Cnt FL Muni Bond/Inv (ACBFX)

800-345-2021, 816-531-5575
www.americancentury.com

Muni: Florida Bond

PERFORMANCE AND PER SHARE DATA **fund inception date: 4/11/94**

	3yr Annual	5yr Annual	10yr Annual	Category Risk Index
Return (%)	7.9	5.8	na	1.00—av
Differ From Category (+/-)	0.0 av	0.5 high	na	**Avg Mat** 9.8 yrs

	2002	2001	2000	1999	1998	1997	1996	1995	1994	1993
Return (%)	9.3	4.7	9.8	-0.5	6.4	8.2	3.6	13.4	—	—
Differ From Category (+/-)	0.3	0.0	-0.3	1.9	0.4	-0.1	-0.2	-2.5	—	—
Return, Tax-Adjusted (%)	9.2	4.5	9.8	-0.5	6.2	7.9	3.5	13.3	—	—
Dividends, Net Income ($)	0.41	0.45	0.47	0.44	0.44	0.45	0.48	0.53	—	—
Expense Ratio (%)	0.51	0.51	0.51	0.51	0.54	0.54	0.13	0.00	—	—
Yield (%)	3.69	4.21	4.42	4.34	4.09	4.21	4.63	5.04	—	—
Total Assets (Millions $)	63	51	56	57	41	22	14	11	—	—

SHAREHOLDER INFORMATION

Minimum Investment
Initial: $5,000 IRA: na
Subsequent: $50 IRA: na

Maximum Fees
Load: none 12b-1: none
Other: none

Fidelity Spart FL Income (FFLIX)

800-544-8544, 801-534-1910
www.fidelity.com

Muni: Florida Bond

PERFORMANCE AND PER SHARE DATA **fund inception date: 3/16/92**

	3yr Annual	5yr Annual	10yr Annual	Category Risk Index
Return (%)	8.2	5.5	6.5	1.08—abv av
Differ From Category (+/-)	0.3 abv av	0.2 abv av	0.3 abv av	**Avg Mat** 14.3 yrs

	2002	2001	2000	1999	1998	1997	1996	1995	1994	1993
Return (%)	9.2	5.2	10.3	-2.7	6.2	8.7	3.9	18.6	-6.7	14.8
Differ From Category (+/-)	0.2	0.5	0.2	-0.3	0.2	0.4	0.1	2.7	-1.0	1.2
Return, Tax-Adjusted (%)	9.1	5.2	10.3	-2.7	6.0	8.6	3.9	18.6	-6.7	14.3
Dividends, Net Income ($)	0.50	0.52	0.49	0.51	0.52	0.53	0.54	0.56	0.58	0.61
Expense Ratio (%)	na	0.40	0.49	0.55	0.55	0.55	0.55	0.55	0.54	0.25
Yield (%)	4.20	4.57	4.33	4.74	4.45	4.59	4.85	4.98	5.80	5.29
Total Assets (Millions $)	614	519	438	412	455	419	392	403	339	450

SHAREHOLDER INFORMATION

Minimum Investment
Initial: $10,000 IRA: na
Subsequent: $1,000 IRA: na

Maximum Fees
Load: 0.50% redemption 12b-1: none
Other: redemption fee applies for 1 month

USAA State TF:FL TF Inc (UFLTX)

800-531-8181, 210-456-7211
www.usaa.com

Muni: Florida Bond

PERFORMANCE AND PER SHARE DATA **fund inception date: 10/1/93**

	3yr Annual	5yr Annual	10yr Annual	Category Risk Index
Return (%)	8.8	5.1	na	1.30—high
Differ From Category (+/-)	0.9 high	-0.2 av	na	**Avg Mat** 20.0 yrs

	2002	2001	2000	1999	1998	1997	1996	1995	1994	1993
Return (%)	8.7	4.9	12.8	-6.3	6.3	11.1	4.3	18.9	-10.0	—
Differ From Category (+/-)	-0.3	0.2	2.7	-3.9	0.3	2.8	0.5	3.0	-4.3	—
Return, Tax-Adjusted (%)	8.7	4.9	12.8	-6.3	6.3	11.1	4.3	18.9	-10.0	—
Dividends, Net Income ($)	0.45	0.48	0.48	0.49	0.49	0.51	0.51	0.51	0.48	—
Expense Ratio (%)	0.56	0.49	0.48	0.47	0.50	0.50	0.50	0.50	0.50	—
Yield (%)	4.51	5.00	5.00	5.46	4.86	5.12	5.39	5.32	5.64	—
Total Assets (Millions $)	219	202	187	169	180	137	95	68	37	—

SHAREHOLDER INFORMATION

Minimum Investment
Initial: $3,000 IRA: na
Subsequent: $50 IRA: na

Maximum Fees
Load: none 12b-1: none
Other: none

Vanguard FL Lg Term TE/Iv (VFLTX)

800-662-7447, 610-436-5152
www.vanguard.com

Muni: Florida Bond

PERFORMANCE AND PER SHARE DATA **fund inception date: 8/31/92**

	3yr Annual	5yr Annual	10yr Annual	Category Risk Index
Return (%)	9.4	6.3	6.9	1.35—high
Differ From Category (+/-)	1.5 high	1.0 high	0.7 high	**Avg Mat** 12.4 yrs

	2002	2001	2000	1999	1998	1997	1996	1995	1994	1993
Return (%)	10.8	4.5	13.2	-2.7	6.6	8.9	4.1	17.7	-4.7	13.4
Differ From Category (+/-)	1.8	-0.2	3.1	-0.3	0.6	0.6	0.3	1.8	1.0	-0.2
Return, Tax-Adjusted (%)	10.6	4.4	13.2	-2.7	6.4	8.9	4.1	17.7	-4.7	13.2
Dividends, Net Income ($)	0.52	0.54	0.55	0.54	0.54	0.56	0.55	0.55	0.55	0.53
Expense Ratio (%)	na	0.15	0.15	0.18	0.20	0.19	0.19	0.20	0.22	0.21
Yield (%)	4.33	4.75	4.82	5.09	4.67	4.93	5.01	4.96	5.54	4.80
Total Assets (Millions $)	752	804	994	885	892	694	549	483	328	311

SHAREHOLDER INFORMATION

Minimum Investment
Initial: $3,000 IRA: na
Subsequent: $100 IRA: na

Maximum Fees
Load: none 12b-1: none
Other: none

T Rowe Price TF GA TF Bd (GTFBX)

800-638-5660, 410-345-2000
www.troweprice.com

Muni: Georgia Bond

PERFORMANCE AND PER SHARE DATA **fund inception date: 3/31/93**

	3yr Annual	5yr Annual	10yr Annual	Category Risk Index
Return (%)	8.3	5.4	na	1.00—high
Differ From Category (+/-)	0.0 high	0.0 high	na	**Avg Mat** 17.7 yrs

	2002	2001	2000	1999	1998	1997	1996	1995	1994	1993
Return (%)	8.8	4.7	11.6	-3.6	6.1	9.6	3.9	17.8	-5.9	—
Differ From Category (+/-)	0.0	0.0	0.0	0.0	0.0	0.0	0.0	0.0	0.0	—
Return, Tax-Adjusted (%)	8.8	4.7	11.6	-3.6	6.1	9.6	3.9	17.8	-6.0	—
Dividends, Net Income ($)	0.48	0.50	0.51	0.49	0.50	0.51	0.51	0.52	0.50	—
Expense Ratio (%)	0.65	0.65	0.65	0.65	0.65	0.65	0.65	0.65	0.65	—
Yield (%)	4.27	4.63	4.72	4.82	4.52	4.67	4.88	4.92	5.27	—
Total Assets (Millions $)	85	74	66	58	58	46	37	31	20	—

SHAREHOLDER INFORMATION

Minimum Investment
Initial: $2,500 IRA: na
Subsequent: $100 IRA: na

Maximum Fees
Load: none 12b-1: none
Other: none

Hawaii Municipal Fund (SURFX)

808-988-8088

Muni: Hawaii Bond

PERFORMANCE AND PER SHARE DATA **fund inception date: 11/30/88**

	3yr Annual	5yr Annual	10yr Annual	Category Risk Index
Return (%)	6.9	4.7	5.3	1.00—high
Differ From Category (+/-)	0.0 high	0.0 high	0.0 high	**Avg Mat** 18.7 yrs

	2002	2001	2000	1999	1998	1997	1996	1995	1994	1993
Return (%)	8.1	4.2	8.5	-1.9	4.8	7.0	4.1	14.3	-4.9	10.5
Differ From Category (+/-)	0.0	0.0	0.0	0.0	0.0	0.0	0.0	0.0	0.0	0.0
Return, Tax-Adjusted (%)	8.1	4.2	8.5	-1.9	4.8	7.0	4.1	14.3	-5.1	10.3
Dividends, Net Income ($)	0.46	0.49	0.51	0.53	0.54	0.54	0.54	0.54	0.54	0.57
Expense Ratio (%)	1.02	1.03	0.98	0.94	0.89	0.98	0.98	0.97	0.95	0.95
Yield (%)	4.13	4.56	4.73	5.08	4.83	4.83	4.92	4.87	5.26	4.98
Total Assets (Millions $)	132	123	115	112	115	108	55	53	46	57

SHAREHOLDER INFORMATION

Minimum Investment
Initial: $1,000 IRA: na
Subsequent: $100 IRA: na

Maximum Fees
Load: none 12b-1: 0.15%
Other: none

Dupree:KY Tx Fr Income (KYTFX)

800-866-0614, 859-254-7741
www.dupree-funds.com

Muni: Kentucky Bond

PERFORMANCE AND PER SHARE DATA **fund inception date: 7/2/79**

	3yr Annual	5yr Annual	10yr Annual	Category Risk Index
Return (%)	6.7	4.8	5.9	1.19—high
Differ From Category (+/-)	0.5 high	0.2 high	0.8 high	**Avg Mat** 16.5 yrs

	2002	2001	2000	1999	1998	1997	1996	1995	1994	1993
Return (%)	7.1	5.0	8.0	-1.4	5.6	8.0	3.6	14.8	-2.9	12.6
Differ From Category (+/-)	0.3	-0.2	1.3	-0.8	0.5	1.5	-0.1	4.3	-2.0	3.5
Return, Tax-Adjusted (%)	7.1	5.0	8.0	-1.4	5.6	8.0	3.6	14.6	-2.9	12.4
Dividends, Net Income ($)	0.35	0.36	0.37	0.37	0.38	0.39	0.39	0.44	0.40	0.41
Expense Ratio (%)	0.59	0.60	0.61	0.61	0.62	0.63	0.62	0.63	0.69	0.67
Yield (%)	4.60	4.84	4.97	5.11	4.92	5.07	5.20	5.74	5.64	5.28
Total Assets (Millions $)	569	498	442	413	412	349	312	293	246	271

SHAREHOLDER INFORMATION

Minimum Investment
Initial: $100 IRA: na
Subsequent: $100 IRA: na

Maximum Fees
Load: none 12b-1: none
Other: none

Dupree:KY Tx Fr Short-Med (KYSMX)

800-866-0614, 859-254-7741
www.dupree-funds.com

Muni: Kentucky Bond

PERFORMANCE AND PER SHARE DATA **fund inception date: 9/15/87**

	3yr Annual	5yr Annual	10yr Annual	Category Risk Index
Return (%)	5.8	4.4	4.4	0.81—av
Differ From Category (+/-)	-0.4 av	-0.2 av	-0.7 av	**Avg Mat** 5.5 yrs

	2002	2001	2000	1999	1998	1997	1996	1995	1994	1993
Return (%)	6.5	5.4	5.4	0.2	4.6	5.1	3.9	6.2	1.0	5.6
Differ From Category (+/-)	-0.3	0.2	-1.3	0.8	-0.5	-1.4	0.2	-4.3	1.9	-3.5
Return, Tax-Adjusted (%)	6.5	5.4	5.4	0.2	4.6	5.1	3.9	6.2	1.0	5.6
Dividends, Net Income ($)	0.19	0.21	0.22	0.20	0.21	0.21	0.21	0.20	0.20	0.21
Expense Ratio (%)	0.69	0.70	0.69	0.72	0.74	0.72	0.75	0.72	0.72	0.76
Yield (%)	3.53	4.00	4.24	3.89	3.94	3.96	4.00	3.80	3.88	3.96
Total Assets (Millions $)	89	77	50	57	60	53	56	55	61	70

SHAREHOLDER INFORMATION

Minimum Investment
Initial: $100 IRA: na
Subsequent: $100 IRA: na

Maximum Fees
Load: none 12b-1: none
Other: none

Dreyfus MA Tax Exempt Bd (DMEBX)

800-645-6561, 516-794-5452
www.dreyfus.com

Muni: Massachusetts Bond

PERFORMANCE AND PER SHARE DATA **fund inception date: 6/11/85**

	3yr Annual	5yr Annual	10yr Annual	Category Risk Index
Return (%)	8.2	5.1	5.9	1.00—abv av
Differ From Category (+/-)	0.2 abv av	-0.2 av	-0.2 av	**Avg Mat** 21.5 yrs

	2002	2001	2000	1999	1998	1997	1996	1995	1994	1993
Return (%)	8.4	4.5	11.8	-4.5	6.0	9.0	4.0	15.5	-6.0	12.4
Differ From Category (+/-)	-0.7	0.1	1.2	-2.1	0.2	0.4	0.4	-0.4	-0.1	-0.6
Return, Tax-Adjusted (%)	8.4	4.5	11.8	-4.5	5.9	9.0	4.0	15.5	-6.0	11.6
Dividends, Net Income ($)	0.68	0.78	0.82	0.81	0.82	0.84	0.86	0.89	0.90	0.93
Expense Ratio (%)	0.80	0.81	0.85	0.82	0.81	0.79	0.79	0.80	0.80	0.81
Yield (%)	3.99	4.77	5.00	5.23	4.77	4.94	5.24	5.35	5.91	5.29
Total Assets (Millions $)	148	144	146	142	161	156	156	158	146	192

SHAREHOLDER INFORMATION

Minimum Investment
Initial: $2,500 IRA: na
Subsequent: $100 IRA: na

Maximum Fees
Load: 1.00% redemption 12b-1: none
Other: redemption fee applies for 1 month

Fidelity Spart MA Muni (FDMMX)

800-544-8544, 801-534-1910
www.fidelity.com

Muni: Massachusetts Bond

PERFORMANCE AND PER SHARE DATA **fund inception date: 11/10/83**

	3yr Annual	5yr Annual	10yr Annual	Category Risk Index
Return (%)	8.6	5.7	6.5	1.02—high
Differ From Category (+/-)	0.6 high	0.4 high	0.4 abv av	**Avg Mat** 17.0 yrs

	2002	2001	2000	1999	1998	1997	1996	1995	1994	1993
Return (%)	9.7	4.4	11.8	-2.1	5.6	9.3	3.5	18.0	-6.0	12.9
Differ From Category (+/-)	0.6	0.0	1.2	0.3	-0.2	0.7	-0.1	2.1	-0.1	-0.1
Return, Tax-Adjusted (%)	9.6	4.4	11.8	-2.1	5.5	9.3	3.5	18.0	-6.5	12.3
Dividends, Net Income ($)	0.53	0.55	0.56	0.55	0.57	0.59	0.60	0.65	0.70	0.71
Expense Ratio (%)	0.42	0.42	0.49	0.49	0.53	0.56	0.54	0.55	0.54	0.55
Yield (%)	4.28	4.66	4.73	4.93	4.75	4.95	5.23	5.56	6.53	5.73
Total Assets (Millions $)	1,998	1,885	1,613	1,278	1,366	1,210	1,138	1,179	993	1,375

SHAREHOLDER INFORMATION

Minimum Investment
Initial: $10,000 IRA: na
Subsequent: $1,000 IRA: na

Maximum Fees
Load: 0.50% redemption 12b-1: none
Other: redemption fee applies for 1 month

Fidelity Spart MD Income (SMDMX)

800-544-8544, 801-534-1910
www.fidelity.com

Muni: Maryland Bond

PERFORMANCE AND PER SHARE DATA **fund inception date: 4/22/93**

	3yr Annual	5yr Annual	10yr Annual	Category Risk Index
Return (%)	8.1	5.5	na	1.08—abv av
Differ From Category (+/-)	1.0 abv av	0.5 abv av	na	**Avg Mat** 14.1 yrs

	2002	2001	2000	1999	1998	1997	1996	1995	1994	1993
Return (%)	8.6	4.7	11.0	-2.1	5.9	8.8	3.8	17.7	-7.5	—
Differ From Category (+/-)	1.2	-0.2	1.9	-0.8	0.3	1.5	0.3	3.8	-3.3	—
Return, Tax-Adjusted (%)	8.6	4.7	11.0	-2.1	5.9	8.8	3.8	17.7	-7.5	—
Dividends, Net Income ($)	0.44	0.46	0.48	0.45	0.45	0.46	0.47	0.52	0.55	—
Expense Ratio (%)	0.47	0.40	0.55	0.55	0.55	0.55	0.39	0.15	0.03	—
Yield (%)	4.01	4.37	4.58	4.54	4.25	4.41	4.68	5.13	6.06	—
Total Assets (Millions $)	100	80	60	46	46	39	45	46	35	—

SHAREHOLDER INFORMATION

Minimum Investment
Initial: $10,000 IRA: na
Subsequent: $1,000 IRA: na

Maximum Fees
Load: 0.50% redemption 12b-1: none
Other: redemption fee applies for 1 month

T Rowe Price TF MD TF Bd (MDXBX)

800-638-5660, 410-345-2000
www.troweprice.com

Muni: Maryland Bond

PERFORMANCE AND PER SHARE DATA **fund inception date: 3/31/87**

	3yr Annual	5yr Annual	10yr Annual	Category Risk Index
Return (%)	8.5	5.6	6.3	1.14—high
Differ From Category (+/-)	1.4 high	0.6 high	0.4 high	**Avg Mat** 18.9 yrs

	2002	2001	2000	1999	1998	1997	1996	1995	1994	1993
Return (%)	9.4	4.9	11.4	-3.1	6.1	8.6	3.7	16.4	-5.0	12.7
Differ From Category (+/-)	2.0	0.0	2.3	-1.8	0.5	1.3	0.2	2.5	-0.8	0.4
Return, Tax-Adjusted (%)	9.4	4.9	11.4	-3.1	6.1	8.6	3.7	16.4	-5.1	12.4
Dividends, Net Income ($)	0.49	0.51	0.53	0.53	0.55	0.55	0.55	0.56	0.55	0.56
Expense Ratio (%)	0.49	0.49	0.51	0.51	0.51	0.54	0.54	0.57	0.57	0.61
Yield (%)	4.49	4.88	5.07	5.35	5.11	5.15	5.31	5.31	5.74	5.19
Total Assets (Millions $)	1,315	1,186	1,082	989	1,038	908	807	799	675	825

SHAREHOLDER INFORMATION

Minimum Investment
Initial: $2,500 IRA: na
Subsequent: $100 IRA: na

Maximum Fees
Load: none 12b-1: none
Other: none

Fidelity Spart MI Muni (FMHTX)

800-544-8544, 801-534-1910
www.fidelity.com

Muni: Michigan Bond

PERFORMANCE AND PER SHARE DATA **fund inception date: 11/12/85**

	3yr Annual	5yr Annual	10yr Annual	Category Risk Index
Return (%)	8.5	5.5	6.0	1.00—high
Differ From Category (+/-)	0.0 high	0.0 high	0.0 high	**Avg Mat** 13.7 yrs

	2002	2001	2000	1999	1998	1997	1996	1995	1994	1993
Return (%)	9.7	4.7	11.1	-2.6	5.2	9.0	3.3	15.4	-7.5	13.8
Differ From Category (+/-)	0.0	0.0	0.0	0.0	0.0	0.0	0.0	0.0	0.0	0.0
Return, Tax-Adjusted (%)	9.7	4.7	11.1	-2.6	5.2	8.8	3.3	15.4	-7.9	13.2
Dividends, Net Income ($)	0.53	0.55	0.56	0.55	0.51	0.57	0.63	0.61	0.68	0.70
Expense Ratio (%)	na	0.44	0.45	0.52	0.55	0.56	0.59	0.60	0.57	0.59
Yield (%)	4.40	4.79	4.87	5.05	4.35	4.86	5.57	5.27	6.32	5.56
Total Assets (Millions $)	571	504	457	424	478	456	452	491	434	561

SHAREHOLDER INFORMATION

Minimum Investment
Initial: $10,000 IRA: na
Subsequent: $1,000 IRA: na

Maximum Fees
Load: 0.50% redemption 12b-1: none
Other: redemption fee applies for 1 month

Fidelity Spart MN Muni (FIMIX)

800-544-8544, 801-534-1910
www.fidelity.com

Muni: Minnesota Bond

PERFORMANCE AND PER SHARE DATA — fund inception date: 11/21/85

	3yr Annual	5yr Annual	10yr Annual	Category Risk Index
Return (%)	7.9	5.2	6.0	1.23—high
Differ From Category (+/-)	0.5 high	0.4 high	0.0 high	**Avg Mat** 14.4 yrs

	2002	2001	2000	1999	1998	1997	1996	1995	1994	1993
Return (%)	8.5	4.6	10.6	-2.4	5.5	8.8	3.7	15.8	-5.9	12.4
Differ From Category (+/-)	0.8	-0.6	1.3	0.7	-0.3	0.4	-1.0	2.0	-3.3	0.0
Return, Tax-Adjusted (%)	8.5	4.6	10.6	-2.4	5.5	8.8	3.7	15.8	-6.1	12.4
Dividends, Net Income ($)	0.50	0.52	0.52	0.51	0.53	0.55	0.56	0.61	0.63	0.64
Expense Ratio (%)	na	0.46	0.46	0.51	0.55	0.56	0.60	0.55	0.59	0.61
Yield (%)	4.30	4.64	4.64	4.79	4.64	4.85	5.11	5.49	6.16	5.55
Total Assets (Millions $)	343	314	292	284	310	295	293	314	277	341

SHAREHOLDER INFORMATION

Minimum Investment
Initial: $10,000 — IRA: na
Subsequent: $1,000 — IRA: na

Maximum Fees
Load: 0.50% redemption — 12b-1: none
Other: redemption fee applies for 1 month

Fidelity Spart NJ Muni (FNJHX)

800-544-8544, 801-534-1910
www.fidelity.com

Muni: New Jersey Bond

PERFORMANCE AND PER SHARE DATA — fund inception date: 12/31/87

	3yr Annual	5yr Annual	10yr Annual	Category Risk Index
Return (%)	8.2	5.8	6.3	1.00—abv av
Differ From Category (+/-)	0.1 abv av	0.4 high	0.3 high	**Avg Mat** 16.8 yrs

	2002	2001	2000	1999	1998	1997	1996	1995	1994	1993
Return (%)	9.7	4.2	10.9	-1.4	6.1	8.3	4.1	15.3	-5.7	13.3
Differ From Category (+/-)	0.4	-0.2	0.3	1.1	0.2	0.0	0.7	-0.4	-0.1	0.2
Return, Tax-Adjusted (%)	9.6	4.1	10.9	-1.4	6.0	8.2	3.7	15.3	-5.7	12.9
Dividends, Net Income ($)	0.49	0.52	0.51	0.52	0.59	0.56	0.59	0.61	0.63	0.66
Expense Ratio (%)	na	0.41	0.45	0.55	0.55	0.55	0.52	0.55	0.55	0.55
Yield (%)	4.12	4.57	4.46	4.81	5.11	4.86	5.21	5.31	5.99	5.51
Total Assets (Millions $)	580	495	400	366	390	363	350	366	325	429

SHAREHOLDER INFORMATION

Minimum Investment
Initial: $10,000 — IRA: na
Subsequent: $1,000 — IRA: na

Maximum Fees
Load: 0.50% redemption — 12b-1: none
Other: redemption fee applies for 1 month

Vanguard NJ Lg Term TE/Iv (VNJTX)

800-662-7447, 610-436-5152
www.vanguard.com

Muni: New Jersey Bond

PERFORMANCE AND PER SHARE DATA **fund inception date: 2/3/88**

	3yr Annual	5yr Annual	10yr Annual	Category Risk Index
Return (%)	8.9	6.0	6.6	1.07—high
Differ From Category (+/-)	0.8 high	0.6 high	0.6 high	**Avg Mat** 11.1 yrs

	2002	2001	2000	1999	1998	1997	1996	1995	1994	1993
Return (%)	9.9	4.5	12.4	-2.3	6.3	8.5	3.1	17.3	-5.2	13.3
Differ From Category (+/-)	0.6	0.1	1.8	0.2	0.4	0.2	-0.3	1.6	0.4	0.2
Return, Tax-Adjusted (%)	9.8	4.5	12.4	-2.3	6.2	8.5	3.0	17.1	-5.2	13.1
Dividends, Net Income ($)	0.57	0.58	0.59	0.58	0.59	0.60	0.61	0.62	0.62	0.63
Expense Ratio (%)	na	0.20	0.19	0.19	0.20	0.18	0.20	0.22	0.21	0.20
Yield (%)	4.63	4.93	4.99	5.23	4.92	5.05	5.28	5.23	5.81	5.26
Total Assets (Millions $)	957	930	1,283	1,118	1,123	971	843	803	653	766

SHAREHOLDER INFORMATION

Minimum Investment
Initial: $3,000 IRA: na
Subsequent: $100 IRA: na

Maximum Fees
Load: none 12b-1: none
Other: none

Dreyfus Gen NY Muni Bond (GNYMX)

800-645-6561, 516-794-5452
www.dreyfus.com

Muni: New York Bond

PERFORMANCE AND PER SHARE DATA **fund inception date: 11/19/84**

	3yr Annual	5yr Annual	10yr Annual	Category Risk Index
Return (%)	8.3	5.2	6.0	0.96—av
Differ From Category (+/-)	-0.1 av	-0.2 blw av	0.0 abv av	**Avg Mat** 18.5 yrs

	2002	2001	2000	1999	1998	1997	1996	1995	1994	1993
Return (%)	9.2	3.9	11.9	-4.6	6.3	9.5	3.0	16.5	-7.1	14.1
Differ From Category (+/-)	-0.1	-0.1	-0.1	-1.1	0.3	0.9	-0.5	0.7	-1.3	1.6
Return, Tax-Adjusted (%)	9.0	3.9	11.9	-4.6	6.0	9.3	2.8	16.3	-7.3	13.7
Dividends, Net Income ($)	0.90	0.92	0.92	0.93	0.95	0.97	1.00	1.04	1.12	1.16
Expense Ratio (%)	na	0.89	0.91	0.92	0.90	0.91	0.91	0.81	0.76	0.69
Yield (%)	4.40	4.70	4.67	5.02	4.60	4.73	5.05	5.11	6.05	5.41
Total Assets (Millions $)	325	329	340	338	293	317	312	335	293	401

SHAREHOLDER INFORMATION

Minimum Investment
Initial: $2,500 IRA: na
Subsequent: $100 IRA: na

Maximum Fees
Load: 0.10% redemption 12b-1: 0.20%
Other: redemption fee applies for 1 month

Dreyfus NY Tax Ex Bond (DRNYX)

800-645-6561, 516-794-5452
www.dreyfus.com

Muni: New York Bond

PERFORMANCE AND PER SHARE DATA **fund inception date: 7/26/83**

	3yr Annual	5yr Annual	10yr Annual	Category Risk Index
Return (%)	8.2	5.3	5.8	0.93—blw av
Differ From Category (+/-)	-0.2 av	-0.1 abv av	-0.2 av	**Avg Mat** 17.1 yrs

	2002	2001	2000	1999	1998	1997	1996	1995	1994	1993
Return (%)	9.0	4.5	11.1	-3.8	6.6	9.1	2.4	16.2	-6.9	12.6
Differ From Category (+/-)	-0.3	0.5	-0.9	-0.3	0.6	0.5	-1.1	0.4	-1.1	0.1
Return, Tax-Adjusted (%)	8.8	4.4	11.1	-4.0	6.4	8.9	2.3	16.1	-7.1	11.9
Dividends, Net Income ($)	0.71	0.73	0.71	0.73	0.74	0.75	0.77	0.80	0.85	0.90
Expense Ratio (%)	0.70	0.73	0.75	0.75	0.73	0.74	0.71	0.72	0.71	0.70
Yield (%)	4.60	4.90	4.75	5.12	4.71	4.82	5.11	5.15	5.99	5.44
Total Assets (Millions $)	1,436	1,430	1,455	1,440	1,660	1,681	1,761	1,879	1,699	2,134

SHAREHOLDER INFORMATION

Minimum Investment
Initial: $2,500 IRA: na
Subsequent: $100 IRA: na

Maximum Fees
Load: 0.10% redemption 12b-1: none
Other: redemption fee applies for 1 month

Fidelity Spart NY Muni In (FTFMX)

800-544-8544, 801-534-1910
www.fidelity.com

Muni: New York Bond

PERFORMANCE AND PER SHARE DATA **fund inception date: 7/10/84**

	3yr Annual	5yr Annual	10yr Annual	Category Risk Index
Return (%)	9.3	6.0	6.7	0.98—av
Differ From Category (+/-)	0.9 high	0.6 high	0.7 high	**Avg Mat** 15.8 yrs

	2002	2001	2000	1999	1998	1997	1996	1995	1994	1993
Return (%)	10.9	4.3	12.8	-3.2	6.3	9.7	3.7	19.5	-8.0	14.5
Differ From Category (+/-)	1.6	0.3	0.8	0.3	0.3	1.1	0.2	3.7	-2.2	2.0
Return, Tax-Adjusted (%)	10.6	4.3	12.8	-3.2	6.1	9.7	3.7	19.5	-8.5	13.0
Dividends, Net Income ($)	0.57	0.58	0.60	0.58	0.60	0.62	0.63	0.63	0.67	0.72
Expense Ratio (%)	0.44	0.42	0.49	0.53	0.55	0.59	0.58	0.58	0.58	0.61
Yield (%)	4.22	4.56	4.70	4.88	4.60	4.81	5.10	5.03	5.93	5.28
Total Assets (Millions $)	1,493	1,315	1,150	1,041	1,171	444	411	434	380	484

SHAREHOLDER INFORMATION

Minimum Investment
Initial: $10,000 IRA: na
Subsequent: $1,000 IRA: na

Maximum Fees
Load: 0.50% redemption 12b-1: none
Other: redemption fee applies for 1 month

T Rowe Price TF NY TF Bd (PRNYX)

800-638-5660, 410-345-2000
www.troweprice.com

Muni: New York Bond

PERFORMANCE AND PER SHARE DATA **fund inception date: 8/28/86**

	3yr Annual	5yr Annual	10yr Annual	Category Risk Index
Return (%)	8.8	5.4	6.3	1.02—abv av
Differ From Category (+/-)	0.4 abv av	0.0 abv av	0.3 abv av	**Avg Mat** 19.0 yrs

	2002	2001	2000	1999	1998	1997	1996	1995	1994	1993
Return (%)	9.6	4.1	12.8	-4.7	6.4	9.5	3.7	17.2	-5.8	13.3
Differ From Category (+/-)	0.3	0.1	0.8	-1.2	0.4	0.9	0.2	1.4	0.0	0.8
Return, Tax-Adjusted (%)	9.6	4.1	12.8	-4.7	6.1	9.5	3.7	17.2	-6.0	12.9
Dividends, Net Income ($)	0.49	0.51	0.53	0.52	0.54	0.56	0.57	0.57	0.58	0.59
Expense Ratio (%)	0.56	0.56	0.58	0.59	0.61	0.65	0.65	0.60	0.60	0.60
Yield (%)	4.30	4.69	4.84	5.09	4.73	4.98	5.27	5.18	5.81	5.18
Total Assets (Millions $)	232	207	201	187	209	171	141	134	110	135

SHAREHOLDER INFORMATION

Minimum Investment
Initial: $2,500 IRA: na
Subsequent: $100 IRA: na

Maximum Fees
Load: none 12b-1: none
Other: none

USAA Tax Ex:New York Bond (USNYX)

800-531-8181, 210-456-7211
www.usaa.com

Muni: New York Bond

PERFORMANCE AND PER SHARE DATA **fund inception date: 10/15/90**

	3yr Annual	5yr Annual	10yr Annual	Category Risk Index
Return (%)	9.5	5.8	6.4	1.09—high
Differ From Category (+/-)	1.1 high	0.4 high	0.4 high	**Avg Mat** 17.8 yrs

	2002	2001	2000	1999	1998	1997	1996	1995	1994	1993
Return (%)	9.5	4.3	14.8	-5.0	6.6	10.6	3.7	18.0	-8.9	13.4
Differ From Category (+/-)	0.2	0.3	2.8	-1.5	0.6	2.0	0.2	2.2	-3.1	0.9
Return, Tax-Adjusted (%)	9.5	4.3	14.8	-5.0	6.6	10.6	3.7	18.0	-8.9	12.7
Dividends, Net Income ($)	0.54	0.57	0.59	0.60	0.61	0.63	0.63	0.63	0.61	0.62
Expense Ratio (%)	0.61	0.50	0.50	0.50	0.50	0.50	0.50	0.50	0.50	0.50
Yield (%)	4.53	5.00	5.13	5.68	5.19	5.43	5.68	5.56	5.99	5.11
Total Assets (Millions $)	123	113	96	84	81	66	56	54	45	61

SHAREHOLDER INFORMATION

Minimum Investment
Initial: $3,000 IRA: na
Subsequent: $50 IRA: na

Maximum Fees
Load: none 12b-1: none
Other: none

Vanguard NY Lg Term TE/Iv (VNYTX)

800-662-7447, 610-436-5152
www.vanguard.com

Muni: New York Bond

PERFORMANCE AND PER SHARE DATA — fund inception date: 4/7/86

	3yr Annual	5yr Annual	10yr Annual	Category Risk Index
Return (%)	9.4	6.1	6.7	1.09—high
Differ From Category (+/-)	1.0 high	0.7 high	0.7 high	**Avg Mat** 12.8 yrs

	2002	2001	2000	1999	1998	1997	1996	1995	1994	1993
Return (%)	10.7	4.1	13.7	-3.3	6.2	8.7	4.0	17.7	-5.6	13.0
Differ From Category (+/-)	1.4	0.1	1.7	0.2	0.2	0.1	0.5	1.9	0.2	0.5
Return, Tax-Adjusted (%)	10.5	4.0	13.7	-3.3	6.0	8.7	3.9	17.5	-5.6	13.0
Dividends, Net Income ($)	0.50	0.52	0.55	0.54	0.56	0.57	0.56	0.57	0.59	0.59
Expense Ratio (%)	na	0.20	0.20	0.20	0.21	0.20	0.20	0.23	0.22	0.19
Yield (%)	4.29	4.71	4.95	5.24	4.96	5.09	5.14	5.14	5.93	5.28
Total Assets (Millions $)	1,339	1,296	1,725	1,426	1,421	1,166	950	870	698	826

SHAREHOLDER INFORMATION

Minimum Investment
Initial: $3,000 IRA: na
Subsequent: $100 IRA: na

Maximum Fees
Load: none 12b-1: none
Other: none

Fidelity Spart OH Muni (FOHFX)

800-544-8544, 801-534-1910
www.fidelity.com

Muni: Ohio Bond

PERFORMANCE AND PER SHARE DATA — fund inception date: 11/15/85

	3yr Annual	5yr Annual	10yr Annual	Category Risk Index
Return (%)	8.6	5.6	6.3	0.93—av
Differ From Category (+/-)	-0.3 av	-0.2 av	-0.1 av	**Avg Mat** 15.2 yrs

	2002	2001	2000	1999	1998	1997	1996	1995	1994	1993
Return (%)	9.6	4.7	11.6	-2.8	5.3	8.7	4.2	16.3	-5.5	12.5
Differ From Category (+/-)	-0.5	0.1	-0.6	0.0	-0.4	0.2	0.0	-0.2	-0.2	-0.1
Return, Tax-Adjusted (%)	9.5	4.7	11.6	-2.8	5.1	8.5	4.0	16.3	-5.9	11.9
Dividends, Net Income ($)	0.52	0.53	0.55	0.53	0.49	0.55	0.56	0.61	0.65	0.69
Expense Ratio (%)	na	0.46	0.46	0.51	0.55	0.56	0.59	0.58	0.57	0.57
Yield (%)	4.29	4.59	4.76	4.87	4.13	4.64	4.86	5.26	6.06	5.62
Total Assets (Millions $)	434	397	378	352	392	387	381	403	349	456

SHAREHOLDER INFORMATION

Minimum Investment
Initial: $10,000 IRA: na
Subsequent: $1,000 IRA: na

Maximum Fees
Load: 0.50% redemption 12b-1: none
Other: redemption fee applies for 1 month

Vanguard OH Lg Tm TE (VOHIX)

800-662-7447, 610-436-5152
www.vanguard.com

Muni: Ohio Bond

PERFORMANCE AND PER SHARE DATA **fund inception date: 6/18/90**

	3yr Annual	5yr Annual	10yr Annual	Category Risk Index
Return (%)	9.3	6.1	6.6	1.07—high
Differ From Category (+/-)	0.4 high	0.3 high	0.2 high	**Avg Mat** 11.8 yrs

	2002	2001	2000	1999	1998	1997	1996	1995	1994	1993
Return (%)	10.7	4.6	12.8	-2.9	6.2	8.4	4.2	16.8	-5.1	12.7
Differ From Category (+/-)	0.6	0.0	0.6	-0.1	0.5	-0.1	0.0	0.3	0.2	0.1
Return, Tax-Adjusted (%)	10.6	4.5	12.8	-2.9	6.2	8.4	4.1	16.8	-5.1	12.6
Dividends, Net Income ($)	0.56	0.57	0.59	0.58	0.59	0.59	0.60	0.60	0.60	0.60
Expense Ratio (%)	na	0.17	0.19	0.19	0.20	0.17	0.20	0.21	0.23	0.21
Yield (%)	4.50	4.83	4.98	5.24	4.91	4.97	5.18	5.12	5.67	5.08
Total Assets (Millions $)	526	478	418	366	326	259	216	198	147	172

SHAREHOLDER INFORMATION

Minimum Investment
Initial: $3,000 IRA: na
Subsequent: $100 IRA: na

Maximum Fees
Load: none 12b-1: none
Other: none

Fidelity Spart PA Muni (FPXTX)

800-544-8544, 801-534-1910
www.fidelity.com

Muni: Pennsylvania Bond

PERFORMANCE AND PER SHARE DATA **fund inception date: 8/6/86**

	3yr Annual	5yr Annual	10yr Annual	Category Risk Index
Return (%)	8.2	5.5	6.4	1.00—abv av
Differ From Category (+/-)	-0.3 blw av	-0.1 blw av	-0.1 av	**Avg Mat** 13.3 yrs

	2002	2001	2000	1999	1998	1997	1996	1995	1994	1993
Return (%)	9.1	4.6	10.9	-2.0	5.4	8.3	4.0	17.4	-4.6	13.4
Differ From Category (+/-)	0.1	-0.3	-0.6	0.2	-0.2	0.1	-0.1	1.1	-1.1	0.4
Return, Tax-Adjusted (%)	9.0	4.5	10.9	-2.1	5.2	8.2	3.8	17.4	-5.4	13.0
Dividends, Net Income ($)	0.48	0.45	0.49	0.48	0.44	0.50	0.52	0.59	0.68	0.70
Expense Ratio (%)	na	0.45	0.44	0.50	0.55	0.55	0.53	0.55	0.55	0.55
Yield (%)	4.32	4.21	4.60	4.74	4.02	4.61	4.92	5.52	6.84	6.21
Total Assets (Millions $)	299	268	242	241	267	263	270	287	241	305

SHAREHOLDER INFORMATION

Minimum Investment
Initial: $10,000 IRA: na
Subsequent: $1,000 IRA: na

Maximum Fees
Load: 0.50% redemption 12b-1: none
Other: redemption fee applies for 1 month

Vanguard PA Lg Term TE/Iv (VPAIX)

800-662-7447, 610-436-5152
www.vanguard.com

Muni: Pennsylvania Bond

PERFORMANCE AND PER SHARE DATA **fund inception date: 4/7/86**

	3yr Annual	5yr Annual	10yr Annual	Category Risk Index
Return (%)	9.1	6.0	6.6	1.15—high
Differ From Category (+/-)	0.6 high	0.4 high	0.1 high	**Avg Mat** 11.6 yrs

	2002	2001	2000	1999	1998	1997	1996	1995	1994	1993
Return (%)	10.0	4.7	12.7	-2.6	6.1	8.2	4.3	16.4	-4.5	12.7
Differ From Category (+/-)	1.0	-0.2	1.2	-0.4	0.5	0.0	0.2	0.1	-1.0	-0.3
Return, Tax-Adjusted (%)	9.9	4.6	12.7	-2.6	5.9	8.2	4.1	16.3	-4.5	12.5
Dividends, Net Income ($)	0.54	0.56	0.58	0.57	0.59	0.59	0.60	0.61	0.62	0.62
Expense Ratio (%)	na	0.20	0.19	0.19	0.20	0.18	0.19	0.22	0.20	0.20
Yield (%)	4.60	5.00	5.15	5.41	5.13	5.17	5.37	5.37	6.01	5.38
Total Assets (Millions $)	1,598	1,513	2,007	1,793	1,940	1,778	1,640	1,582	1,299	1,525

SHAREHOLDER INFORMATION

Minimum Investment
Initial: $3,000 IRA: na
Subsequent: $100 IRA: na

Maximum Fees
Load: none 12b-1: none
Other: none

T Rowe Price TF VA TF Bd (PRVAX)

800-638-5660, 410-345-2000
www.troweprice.com

Muni: Virginia Bond

PERFORMANCE AND PER SHARE DATA **fund inception date: 4/30/91**

	3yr Annual	5yr Annual	10yr Annual	Category Risk Index
Return (%)	8.8	5.7	6.4	1.02—abv av
Differ From Category (+/-)	0.5 abv av	0.5 high	0.5 high	**Avg Mat** 15.4 yrs

	2002	2001	2000	1999	1998	1997	1996	1995	1994	1993
Return (%)	9.7	4.8	11.9	-3.4	6.1	8.9	4.1	16.8	-5.0	12.5
Differ From Category (+/-)	0.6	0.7	0.1	0.5	0.5	0.1	0.4	0.6	1.1	0.2
Return, Tax-Adjusted (%)	9.7	4.8	11.9	-3.4	5.9	8.9	4.1	16.8	-5.0	12.1
Dividends, Net Income ($)	0.51	0.53	0.55	0.53	0.56	0.57	0.57	0.57	0.56	0.56
Expense Ratio (%)	0.53	0.54	0.55	0.57	0.58	0.65	0.65	0.65	0.65	0.65
Yield (%)	4.33	4.72	4.90	5.02	4.83	4.97	5.15	5.09	5.53	4.91
Total Assets (Millions $)	393	351	307	265	269	226	189	177	143	164

SHAREHOLDER INFORMATION

Minimum Investment
Initial: $2,500 IRA: na
Subsequent: $100 IRA: na

Maximum Fees
Load: none 12b-1: none
Other: none

USAA Tax Ex:Virginia Bond (USVAX)

800-531-8181, 210-456-7211
www.usaa.com

Muni: Virginia Bond

PERFORMANCE AND PER SHARE DATA — fund inception date: 10/15/90

	3yr Annual	5yr Annual	10yr Annual	Category Risk Index
Return (%)	8.8	5.4	6.3	1.07—high
Differ From Category (+/-)	0.5 high	0.2 abv av	0.4 abv av	**Avg Mat** 19.2 yrs

	2002	2001	2000	1999	1998	1997	1996	1995	1994	1993
Return (%)	9.2	4.2	13.1	-4.6	6.0	9.4	5.0	17.0	-6.3	12.6
Differ From Category (+/-)	0.1	0.1	1.3	-0.7	0.4	0.6	1.3	0.8	-0.2	0.3
Return, Tax-Adjusted (%)	9.2	4.2	13.1	-4.6	6.0	9.4	5.0	17.0	-6.3	12.2
Dividends, Net Income ($)	0.52	0.56	0.58	0.59	0.60	0.62	0.63	0.63	0.61	0.62
Expense Ratio (%)	0.52	0.43	0.43	0.43	0.44	0.46	0.48	0.50	0.49	0.50
Yield (%)	4.47	5.03	5.16	5.63	5.18	5.38	5.67	5.62	6.01	5.34
Total Assets (Millions $)	492	461	417	371	385	330	284	263	215	253

SHAREHOLDER INFORMATION

Minimum Investment
Initial: $3,000 IRA: na
Subsequent: $50 IRA: na

Maximum Fees
Load: none 12b-1: none
Other: none

INTERNATIONAL BOND FUNDS

Category Performance Ranked by 2002 Returns

		Annual Return (%)				Category	Total
Category	Fund (Ticker)	2002	3yr	5yr	10yr	Risk	Risk
IntB	Amer Cnt Intl Bond/Inv (BEGBX)	23.5	6.2	4.8	6.1	abv av	blw av
IntB	T Rowe Price Intl Bd (RPIBX)	21.8	4.4	3.8	5.8	abv av	blw av
IntB	Fidelity New Markets Inc (FNMIX)	13.8	12.0	8.3	na	high	blw av
IntB	Cr Suisse Gl Fx Inc/Cmn (CGFIX)	10.2	6.8	5.8	6.9	low	low
IntB	T Rowe Price Emg Mkt Bd (PREMX)	9.5	11.3	5.4	na	high	blw av
IntB	Payden Glbl Fixed Inc/R (PYGFX)	7.8	8.9	7.4	7.9	blw av	low
International Bond Average		**13.3**	**7.6**	**5.5**	**6.3**	—	**blw av**

Note: AAII members who would like performance figures for no-load and low-load mutual funds they own that do not appear in this Guide can access this information on our Web site at www.aaii.com.

Amer Cnt Intl Bond/Inv (BEGBX)

800-345-2021, 816-531-5575
www.americancentury.com

International Bond

PERFORMANCE AND PER SHARE DATA **fund inception date: 1/7/92**

	3yr Annual	5yr Annual	10yr Annual	Category Risk Index
Return (%)	6.2	4.8	6.1	1.40—abv av
Differ From Category (+/-)	-1.4 blw av	-0.7 av	-0.2 av	**Avg Mat** na

	2002	2001	2000	1999	1998	1997	1996	1995	1994	1993
Return (%)	23.5	-1.6	-1.1	-10.3	17.8	-4.6	6.3	24.4	-0.9	14.3
Differ From Category (+/-)	10.2	-6.3	-6.6	-15.3	15.4	-9.4	-9.7	5.9	5.6	-0.3
Return, Tax-Adjusted (%)	22.5	-1.6	-1.6	-12.0	16.7	-5.4	3.5	21.0	-2.2	12.1
Dividends, Net Income ($)	0.25	0.00	0.10	0.42	0.17	0.17	0.72	0.90	0.35	0.37
Expense Ratio (%)	na	0.86	0.87	0.85	0.84	0.84	0.83	0.72	0.86	0.85
Yield (%)	2.05	0.00	0.96	3.90	1.34	1.53	6.03	7.53	3.37	3.33
Total Assets (Millions $)	245	115	110	113	158	169	252	252	193	356

SHAREHOLDER INFORMATION

Minimum Investment
Initial: $2,500 IRA: $1,000
Subsequent: $100 IRA: $100

Maximum Fees
Load: none 12b-1: none
Other: none

Cr Suisse Gl Fx Inc/Cmn (CGFIX)

800-927-2874, 212-878-0600
www.creditsuissefunds.com

International Bond

PERFORMANCE AND PER SHARE DATA **fund inception date: 11/1/90**

	3yr Annual	5yr Annual	10yr Annual	Category Risk Index
Return (%)	6.8	5.8	6.9	0.53—low
Differ From Category (+/-)	-0.8 av	0.3 av	0.6 abv av	**Avg Mat** 11.3 yrs

	2002	2001	2000	1999	1998	1997	1996	1995	1994	1993
Return (%)	10.2	3.1	7.2	0.3	8.4	2.1	9.9	16.0	-5.4	19.6
Differ From Category (+/-)	-3.1	-1.6	1.7	-4.7	6.0	-2.7	-6.1	-2.5	1.1	5.0
Return, Tax-Adjusted (%)	7.3	1.4	3.4	-2.2	6.0	-1.1	6.5	12.7	-6.7	16.2
Dividends, Net Income ($)	0.71	0.42	0.94	0.66	0.62	0.88	0.93	0.85	0.36	0.78
Expense Ratio (%)	na	0.95	0.97	0.96	0.95	0.96	0.95	0.95	0.95	0.49
Yield (%)	7.21	4.37	9.68	6.61	5.84	8.48	8.44	7.79	3.54	6.95
Total Assets (Millions $)	109	107	122	128	155	174	142	80	84	69

SHAREHOLDER INFORMATION

Minimum Investment
Initial: $2,500 IRA: $500
Subsequent: $100 IRA: $50

Maximum Fees
Load: none 12b-1: none
Other: none

Fidelity New Markets Inc (FNMIX)

800-544-8544, 800-522-7297
www.fidelity.com

International Bond

PERFORMANCE AND PER SHARE DATA **fund inception date: 5/4/93**

	3yr Annual	5yr Annual	10yr Annual	Category Risk Index
Return (%)	12.0	8.3	na	1.68—high
Differ From Category (+/-)	4.4 high	2.8 high	na	**Avg Mat** na

	2002	2001	2000	1999	1998	1997	1996	1995	1994	1993
Return (%)	13.8	7.9	14.3	36.7	-22.3	16.4	41.3	7.1	-16.5	—
Differ From Category (+/-)	0.5	3.2	8.8	31.7	-24.7	11.6	25.3	-11.4	-10.0	—
Return, Tax-Adjusted (%)	10.2	3.3	9.7	32.3	-26.0	11.4	37.6	3.8	-18.6	—
Dividends, Net Income ($)	1.01	1.34	1.29	1.01	1.21	1.19	0.93	0.84	0.55	—
Expense Ratio (%)	na	0.99	0.99	1.07	1.13	1.08	1.09	1.20	1.28	—
Yield (%)	8.91	12.28	11.32	9.07	13.45	8.59	7.17	8.44	5.28	—
Total Assets (Millions $)	418	293	257	214	206	371	305	173	179	—

SHAREHOLDER INFORMATION

Minimum Investment
Initial: $2,500 IRA: $500
Subsequent: $250 IRA: $1

Maximum Fees
Load: 1.00% redemption 12b-1: none
Other: redemption fee applies for 6 months

Payden Glbl Fixed Inc/R (PYGFX)

800-572-9336, 213-625-1900
www.payden.com

International Bond

PERFORMANCE AND PER SHARE DATA **fund inception date: 9/1/92**

	3yr Annual	5yr Annual	10yr Annual	Category Risk Index
Return (%)	8.9	7.4	7.9	0.54—blw av
Differ From Category (+/-)	1.3 abv av	1.9 high	1.6 high	**Avg Mat** 8.4 yrs

	2002	2001	2000	1999	1998	1997	1996	1995	1994	1993
Return (%)	7.8	5.5	13.5	-0.5	11.6	9.0	5.7	17.9	-3.0	13.1
Differ From Category (+/-)	-5.5	0.8	8.0	-5.5	9.2	4.2	-10.3	-0.6	3.5	-1.5
Return, Tax-Adjusted (%)	6.1	2.3	10.3	-2.8	8.3	5.3	2.8	14.3	-4.5	10.4
Dividends, Net Income ($)	0.40	0.83	0.78	0.58	0.67	0.95	0.76	0.88	0.38	0.50
Expense Ratio (%)	na	0.53	0.51	0.49	0.49	0.49	0.53	0.50	0.55	0.70
Yield (%)	3.89	8.35	7.63	5.94	6.24	9.27	7.37	8.38	3.91	4.69
Total Assets (Millions $)	250	351	426	504	526	493	658	583	421	285

SHAREHOLDER INFORMATION

Minimum Investment
Initial: $5,000 IRA: $2,000
Subsequent: $1,000 IRA: $1,000

Maximum Fees
Load: none 12b-1: none
Other: none

T Rowe Price Emg Mkt Bd (PREMX)

800-638-5660, 410-547-2000
www.troweprice.com

International Bond

PERFORMANCE AND PER SHARE DATA **fund inception date: 12/30/94**

	3yr Annual	5yr Annual	10yr Annual	Category Risk Index
Return (%)	11.3	5.4	na	1.56—high
Differ From Category (+/-)	3.7 high	-0.1 av	na	**Avg Mat** 14.1 yrs

	2002	2001	2000	1999	1998	1997	1996	1995	1994	1993
Return (%)	9.5	9.3	15.1	22.9	-23.0	16.8	36.7	25.8	—	—
Differ From Category (+/-)	-3.8	4.6	9.6	17.9	-25.4	12.0	20.7	7.3	—	—
Return, Tax-Adjusted (%)	6.3	5.0	11.0	18.3	-27.1	12.9	31.8	19.7	—	—
Dividends, Net Income ($)	0.84	1.15	1.04	1.08	1.31	1.14	1.03	1.02	—	—
Expense Ratio (%)	na	1.16	1.21	1.25	1.25	1.25	1.25	1.25	—	—
Yield (%)	8.06	11.14	9.86	10.68	13.90	8.17	7.70	8.95	—	—
Total Assets (Millions $)	200	155	163	173	148	113	39	9	—	—

SHAREHOLDER INFORMATION

Minimum Investment
Initial: $2,500 IRA: $1,000
Subsequent: $100 IRA: $50

Maximum Fees
Load: none 12b-1: none
Other: none

T Rowe Price Intl Bd (RPIBX)

800-638-5660, 410-547-2000
www.troweprice.com

International Bond

PERFORMANCE AND PER SHARE DATA **fund inception date: 9/10/86**

	3yr Annual	5yr Annual	10yr Annual	Category Risk Index
Return (%)	4.4	3.8	5.8	1.28—abv av
Differ From Category (+/-)	-3.2 low	-1.7 blw av	-0.5 av	**Avg Mat** 7.8 yrs

	2002	2001	2000	1999	1998	1997	1996	1995	1994	1993
Return (%)	21.8	-3.4	-3.1	-7.9	15.0	-3.1	7.1	20.3	-1.8	19.8
Differ From Category (+/-)	8.5	-8.1	-8.6	-12.9	12.6	-7.9	-8.9	1.8	4.7	5.2
Return, Tax-Adjusted (%)	20.6	-4.9	-4.8	-9.7	12.9	-5.2	4.4	17.3	-4.7	15.7
Dividends, Net Income ($)	0.25	0.32	0.39	0.48	0.51	0.54	0.71	0.62	0.59	0.70
Expense Ratio (%)	na	0.95	1.15	0.90	0.88	0.86	0.87	0.92	0.98	0.99
Yield (%)	2.69	4.07	4.60	5.24	4.87	5.63	6.78	5.86	6.17	6.50
Total Assets (Millions $)	975	761	752	778	926	825	969	1,015	738	745

SHAREHOLDER INFORMATION

Minimum Investment
Initial: $2,500 IRA: $1,000
Subsequent: $100 IRA: $50

Maximum Fees
Load: none 12b-1: none
Other: none

Appendix: Index Funds

STOCK INDEXES

S&P 500:
Fidelity Spart 500 Index (Stk-LC: FSMKX)
Vanguard 500 Idx/Inv (Stk-LC: VFINX)

S&P 500/BARRA Growth:
Vanguard Gr Idx/Inv (Stk-LC: VIGRX)

S&P 500/BARRA Value:
Vanguard Value Idx/Inv (Stk-LC: VIVAX)

S&P MidCap 400:
CA Inv: S&P MidCap Index (Stk-MC: SPMIX)
Dreyfus Index: Midcap Idx (Stk-MC: PESPX)

Wilshire 4500:
Vanguard Ext Mkt Idx/Inv (Stk-SC: VEXMX)

Wilshire 5000:
Fidelity Spart Total Mkt (Stk-LC: FSTMX)
Vanguard Tot Stk Idx/Inv (Stk-LC: VTSMX)

Wilshire 5000 (60%)/Lehman Aggregate Bond (40%):
Vanguard Bal Idx/Inv (Bal: VBINX)

Russell 2000:
Vanguard Small Cap Idx/Inv (Stk-SC: NAESX)

Schwab 1000:
Schwab Inv 1000 Fd/I (Stk-LC: SNXFX)

Schwab Small Cap 1000:
Schwab Cap Tr Sm Cp Ix/I (Stk-SC: SWSMX)

Nasdaq 100:
Rydex:OTC/Inv (Stk-LC: RYOCX)

FTSE Gold Mines:
Amer Cnt Global Gold/Inv (Sec-G: BGEIX)

Morgan Stanley REIT:
Vanguard REIT Idx (Sec-R: VGSIX)

BOND INDEXES

Lehman Brothers Aggregate Bond:
Schwab Inv Tot Bd Mkt (B-Gen: SWLBX)
Vanguard Tot Bd Mkt (B-Gen: VBMFX)

Lehman Brothers Short (1-5) Government/Corporate:
Schwab Inv Sh Tm Bd Mkt (B-Gen: SWBDX)
Vanguard Sh Tm Bd Idx (B-Gen: VBISX)

Lehman Brothers Intermediate (5-10) Government/Corporate:
Vanguard Int Tm Bd (B-Gen: VBIIX)

Lehman Brothers Long (10+) Government/Corporate:
Vanguard LT Bd Idx (B-Gen: VBLTX)

FOREIGN INDEXES

MSCI Europe:
Vanguard Erpn Stk Idx (IntS-R/C: VEURX)

MSCI Pacific:
Vanguard Pacific Stk (IntS-R/C: VPACX)

MSCI Emerging Markets Free:
Vanguard Em Mkt Stk (IntS-E: VEIEX)

MSCI EAFA + MSCI Emerging Markets Free:
Vanguard Tot Itl Stk Idx (IntS-F: VGTSX)

Schwab International:
Schwab Intl Index/I (IntS-F: SWINX)

Index

A

B

C

D

I

J

K

L

M

N

O

P

R

S

T

U

V

W

Y